Beginning MySQL®

Robert Sheldon and Geoff Moes

Wiley Publishing, Inc.

Beginning MySQL®

Published by
Wiley Publishing, Inc.
10475 Crosspoint Boulevard
Indianapolis, IN 46256
www.wiley.com

Copyright © 2005 by Wiley Publishing, Inc., Indianapolis, Indiana

Published simultaneously in Canada

ISBN: 0-7645-7950-9

Manufactured in the United States of America

10 9 8 7 6 5 4 3 2

1B/RW/QT/QV/IN

For general information on our other products and services or to obtain technical support, please contact our Customer Care Department within the U.S. at (800) 762-2974, outside the U.S. at (317) 572-3993 or fax (317) 572-4002.

Wiley also publishes its books in a variety of electronic formats. Some content that appears in print may not be available in electronic books.

Library of Congress Cataloging-in-Publication Data

Sheldon, Robert, 1955-

 Beginning MySQL / Robert Sheldon and Geoff Moes.

     p. cm.

 Includes bibliographical references and indexes.

 ISBN 0-7645-7950-9 (paper/website : alk. paper)

 1. SQL (Computer program language) 2. MySQL (Electronic resource) I. Moes, Geoff, 1963- II. Title.

QA76.3.S67S54 2005

005.75'65--dc22

                    2004031058

About the Authors

Robert Sheldon

Robert Sheldon's MySQL programming is rooted in ten years of experience working with SQL, as it is implemented not only in a MySQL environment, but also within SQL Server, Microsoft Access, and Oracle environments. He has programmed with SQL directly through database interfaces and script files and indirectly through PHP, JSP, ASP, and ASP.NET applications that connected to various databases and issued SQL statements. Robert has also managed the maintenance and development of Web sites and online tools, which has included performing project analysis, developing functional specifications, and managing database and Web development. He has designed and implemented various Microsoft Access, SQL Server, and MySQL databases, as well as developed and implemented a variety of Web-based solutions. In all these roles, he has had to perform numerous types of ad hoc queries and modifications, build databases, create and modify database objects, create and review embedded statements, and troubleshoot system- and data-related problems.

In addition to having a technical and SQL background, Robert has written or co-written nine books on various network and server technologies, including two that have focused on SQL Server design and implementation, one on SQL programming (based on the SQL:1999 standard), and one on Microsoft Office Access 2003. The books that Robert has written contain training material that is designed to teach users specific skills and to test their knowledge of the material covered. Having contracted as the senior developmental editor for the Microsoft certification team, he brought to these books his experience developing exam items that helped to focus readers on the skills necessary to perform specific tasks. Robert has also written and edited a variety of other documentation related to SQL databases and other computer technologies. He works as an independent technical consultant and writer in the Seattle area.

Geoff Moes

Geoff Moes is a software architect and developer who has designed and implemented databases in MySQL as well as having designed and implemented software systems in PHP, Java/J2EE, and ASP.NET that have utilized MySQL databases through various database connectivity interfaces. Geoff received his bachelor's degree in Computer Science from Virginia Tech and has worked in the software industry for 18 years. He specializes in software and database architecture and development as it relates to Web-based systems. He has worked with several database products in addition to MySQL, including SQL Server, DB2, and Oracle. He has also developed a variety of software applications that have connected to various databases using several different languages and platforms including Java J2EE/JDBC/EJB, C++/ODBC, and ASP.NET/ODBC/OLEDB.

Geoff's publishing credits include "Passing Arrays Between Jscript and C++" (September 7, 2000, ASPToday.com, under WROX) and three articles published in *Windows & .NET Magazine* (online): "Common Internet Hacker Attacks" (December 1, 1998), "Remote Web Administration, Part 2" (November 1, 1998), and "Remote Web Administration, Part 1" (October 1, 1998). Geoff works as an independent software consultant in the Washington D.C. metro area. When he is not in front of the keyboard, he enjoys photography, mountain biking, hiking, and international travel.

Credits

Acquisitions Editor
Debra Williams Cauley

Development Editor
Brian Herrmann

Technical Editor
David Mercer

Copy Editor
Nancy Hannigan

Editorial Manager
Mary Beth Wakefield

Vice President & Executive Group Publisher
Richard Swadley

Vice President and Publisher
Joseph B. Wikert

Project Coordinator
Erin Smith

Quality Control Technician
Brian H. Walls

Text Design and Composition
Wiley Composition Services

Proofreading and Indexing
TECHBOOKS Production Services

Acknowledgments

As with any publication, too many people were involved in the development of *Beginning MySQL* to name them all, but we would like to acknowledge those who we worked with the closest in order to complete this project in a timely manner (and with our sanity still somewhat intact). Our special thanks goes to Debra Williams-Cauley, the acquisitions editor at John Wiley & Sons, Inc., who pulled this project together in such a professional and responsive manner. And we particularly want to thank Brian Herrmann, the development editor on this book who patiently and efficiently (and pleasantly, we might add) kept this project moving forward, while always paying attention to details and answering our never-ending stream of questions. We also want to acknowledge David Mercer, the technical editor, for his grasp of the subject matter and his invaluable input into the book. In addition, we want to acknowledge all the editors, proofreaders, indexers, designers, illustrators, and other participants whose efforts made this book possible. Finally, we want to thank our agent, Margot Maley Hutchison, at Waterside Productions, Inc., for her help in moving forward on this project and for tending to all the details.

Contents

Contents

Contents

Contents

Contents

Contents

Contents

Contents

Contents

Introduction

Welcome to *Beginning MySQL*, the definitive resource for anyone new to the MySQL database management system. As the most popular open source database system in the world, MySQL has gained not only recognition among its peers but a place of prominence in the worldwide technical industry, ensuring an ever-growing need for information and training on how to implement a MySQL database and access and manage data in that database.

Because of its ease of implementation, low overhead, reliability, and lower Total Cost of Ownership (TCO), MySQL has made remarkable inroads in the database management system market. As a result, the number of programmers who must connect to a MySQL database and embed SQL statements in their applications is growing steadily. There are now over five million MySQL installations worldwide, and that number is increasing rapidly. In addition, MySQL supports connectivity to numerous application languages and environments, including C, C++, PHP, ASP, ASP.NET, Java, Perl, C#, and Python, and it can be implemented on a number of platforms, including Windows, Linux, Unix, Solaris, FreeBSD, Mac OS, and HP-UX.

Corporate implementations continue to grow and include such companies as Yahoo!, Cox Communications, Google, Cisco, Texas Instruments, UPS, Sabre Holdings, HP, and the Associated Press. Even NASA and the U.S. Census Bureau have implemented MySQL solutions. MySQL has been proven to work in large deployments, while reducing system downtimes and administrative overhead and lowering hardware expenditures and licensing costs.

As organizations continue to seek ways to cut their TCO, MySQL will continue to gain in popularity—and its user-base will continue to grow. As a result, MySQL will gain further ground in becoming a prominent force in the industry. To meet this demand, *Beginning MySQL* provides you with a valuable resource and step-by-step learning tool that supplies you with the background information, examples, and hands-on exercises that you need to implement MySQL and manage data in its databases. Concepts are introduced in a logical manner, with each chapter building on the previous chapters. By the end of this book, you'll have a complete foundation in MySQL, its implementation, and the methods necessary to connect to databases and manipulate data.

Who This Book Is For

Before beginning any book that covers a computer technology such as MySQL, it's always useful to know who the book is intended for, what assumptions are made about your level of knowledge, and what system setup—if any—is required to perform the exercises in the book. *Beginning MySQL* is no exception. So before you delve into the book too deeply, take a closer look at each of these issues.

Because MySQL is such a robust, flexible, and easy-to-implement application, a beginner's book about the product will benefit a wide audience, both at home and at the office. The primary audience for *Beginning MySQL* can be any of the following readers:

❑ Experienced PHP, Java, or ASP.NET programmers who are developing applications that access backend databases and who are new to MySQL

Introduction

- ❏ Experienced application programmers in any language who are new to MySQL and who want to better understand how to implement a MySQL database and use SQL as it is implemented in MySQL

- ❏ Experienced SQL programmers new to MySQL

- ❏ Experienced database designers, administrators, or implementers who are migrating to MySQL

- ❏ First-time SQL programmers who have no database experience

- ❏ First-time database designers, administrators, or implementers new to MySQL

- ❏ Users new to application programming and databases

In addition to the primary audiences, *Beginning MySQL* can be useful to the following readers:

- ❏ The home user who wants to create simple databases for such information stores as address books, CD collections, or recipes

- ❏ The home business owner who wants to create database applications for such tasks as managing customers and contacts, tracking inventories, or recording orders

- ❏ Managers and owners of small businesses who need database solutions that are both easy and inexpensive to implement

- ❏ Group managers in larger companies who need database solutions that meet immediate needs in their groups

- ❏ Directors, staff, or volunteers at nonprofit organizations who require database solutions that are simple and inexpensive to implement

- ❏ Any other individual who wants to learn how to create and manage a MySQL database that can support various data-driven applications

Nearly anyone new to MySQL will be able to benefit from *Beginning MySQL*. In addition, users who have had experience with earlier versions of MySQL or with other database products will be able to use the book to refresh and expand their skills.

To benefit from *Beginning MySQL,* you do not have to have a strong background in databases or any other computer technology. You should, however, have at least a basic understanding of the following:

- ❏ You should know to negotiate your way around your operating system environment. The book focuses on implementing MySQL on Linux and Windows, so whichever one you choose, you should know how to use that system to copy and access files, add programs, change system settings, or whatever tasks are common to your particular environment. If you're using a Unix-like system other than Linux, you should find that much of the Linux-related information will apply to your system.

- ❏ You will need to know how to use your Web browser to access the Internet and download files and view information.

- ❏ You should know how to use a text editor to create and edit text files.

These requirements are all you really need to use *Beginning MySQL* successfully and learn about how to implement MySQL databases and manage data in those databases. For Chapters 17, 18, or 19, you should have at least basic knowledge of Web development techniques. These three chapters focus on developing a Web application that accesses data in a MySQL database. Chapter 17 covers PHP, Chapter 18 covers

JSP/Java, and Chapter 19 covers ASP.NET/C#. Each chapter assumes that you have a basic knowledge of developing an application in that language and of Web development in general. If you're new to these technologies and you want to build an application in one of these languages, it's recommended that you first review documentation specific to that language and to Web development in general.

What This Book Covers

The book uses a task-oriented structure that allows you to work through the steps necessary to install MySQL 4.1 on Linux and Windows platforms, create and manage MySQL databases, query and manipulate data stored in those databases, administer the MySQL database management system, and connect to MySQL databases from your PHP, JSP/Java, and ASP.NET/C# applications.

The next section, which describes the book's structure, provides additional details about the specifics of what the book covers.

How This Book Is Structured

Beginning MySQL provides you with an instructional tool that gives you a complete look at MySQL, how it is implemented, and how it is accessed from various programming languages. The book takes a task-oriented, step-by-step approach to explain concepts and demonstrate how those concepts are used in real-world situations.

The structure of *Beginning MySQL* supports the complete beginner (those new to databases and SQL) as well as those who are experienced with programming and other database products, but new to MySQL. The book provides the conceptual and background information necessary for all readers to understand individual topics, but each chapter is modular to support those readers who simply dip into different parts of the book to use it as a reference. For example, someone completely new to databases might read the book from cover to cover, applying information learned in one chapter to the material in the next chapter. On the other hand, an experienced PHP programmer might want to reference only the chapters related to SQL statements and PHP connectivity, without having to review chapters on database design or administration.

Beginning MySQL describes and demonstrates each step necessary to create a MySQL database and access and manage data in that database. Each chapter correlates with one of the primary tasks necessary to implement MySQL and to access data, either directly or through an application programming language. The goal of the book is to provide you with a complete learning experience.

In Chapters 1 through 4, you are introduced to MySQL and relational databases. You are shown the steps necessary to install MySQL on Windows and Linux, set up the initial MySQL configuration, and access the MySQL server. You are also shown where to find MySQL components on your system and what tools are available to access and manipulate data. Finally, you learn how to design a database that conforms to the relational model. From this information, you will be ready to build a database in which you can store and manage data.

Chapters 5 through 12 build on the concepts introduced to you in the first four chapters. These chapters describe how to create databases that store data and help to enforce the integrity of that data. You then learn how to insert data into those databases, update that data, and then delete the data. You also learn a variety of methods to retrieve data from the database so that you can display exactly the data you need and perform operations on that data. You are also shown the steps necessary to copy, import, and export data.

Introduction

In Chapters 13 through 16, you learn how to perform tasks related to administering MySQL. The chapters include the steps necessary to perform such tasks as verify system settings and perform server-related operations, set up logging, manage security, optimize performance, back up and restore your system, and set up replication.

Chapters 17 through 19 are a little different from the other chapters. Each chapter describes how to access a MySQL database from a specific programming language, including PHP, JSP/Java, and ASP.NET/C#. You learn how to establish a connection to a database and issue SQL statements against the database. In each chapter, you will build a data-driven application that allows you to display data that you retrieve from a MySQL database.

In addition to the 19 chapters in this book, *Beginning MySQL* includes several appendices that provide additional information about MySQL and the book. Appendix A provides the answers to the exercises presented in each chapter. (The exercises are described in the text that follows.) Appendix B includes a brief description of each application programming interface (API) supported by MySQL, and Appendix C gives you an overview of features that you can expect to see in the next release of MySQL.

By the end of the book, you will have installed MySQL, configured it, created a database and its tables, added data to the database and manipulated that data, performed administrative tasks, and created applications that access the data in the database. To support this process, the chapters contain a number of elements, including examples that demonstrate how to perform various tasks, Try It Out sections that provide you with hands-on experience in using MySQL, and exercises that help you better understand the concepts explained in each chapter.

Exercises and Examples

To provide the various examples and exercises throughout the chapters, *Beginning MySQL* is based on MySQL 4.1. This means that the statement and command structures, various procedures, and expected results all conform to that version of the product. Specifically, most of what you find in the book applies to the MySQL 4.1.7 release or later. If you use another release of MySQL, however, you might find that some procedures and their results are different from what are described here.

As you work your way through the you'll find that MySQL sometimes supports more than one way that an SQL statement can be written to achieve the same results. As MySQL has evolved, so too have the statements—to improve performance, simplify the statement, or conform to industry standards. The original version of the statements, however, continues to be maintained to support legacy MySQL systems or to provide portability from one database system to the next. In these situations, you should use whatever approach is best suited to your particular situation. This sometimes means trying different versions of a statement to determine which one performs the best. Often, you'll find that using the simplest version not only is the easiest approach but will meet most of your needs.

Some of the code that you'll run in the examples and Try It Out sections is available for download. Be sure to visit the Wrox Web site at www.wrox.com to determine whether code is available. Generally, anything that is more than a few lines (anything that you cannot easily type yourself) is available for download.

Each chapter in *Beginning MySQL* includes a number of elements that demonstrate how to perform specific tasks related to implementing MySQL databases and managing data in those databases. In addition to providing a thorough explanation of each concept, the chapters include examples, Try It Out sections, and exercises.

Examples

For each concept presented in the book, one or more examples are provided to demonstrate that concept. When appropriate, statement or command syntax precedes the examples. Syntax refers to the basic form that the statement or command should take. The syntax shows which elements must be included, which elements are optional, how parameters should be included, and in what order the elements should be placed. In other words, the syntax provides a blueprint for how a statement or command should be constructed. (Chapter 1 provides you with more information about syntax and supplies an example of how it is used.)

After the syntax has been provided, the chapter includes examples that demonstrate how real-life statements and commands are created. The examples are meant only as a way to demonstrate the actual code. You are not expected to try out the examples in an actual database environment. With the correct setup, the statements and commands do indeed work.

If you decide to try out an example, you can use the test database installed by default when you install MySQL, or you can create your own database for testing purposes. Keep in mind, however, that you have to pay particular attention to how the database is set up to try out the examples. You cannot assume that a table named Books used in the examples in one chapter is defined the same as a table named Books in another chapter. In addition, you cannot assume that, as examples progress through a chapter, they necessarily build on each other, although this is sometimes the case.

Whenever appropriate, a chapter will provide you with details about how the system is set up to demonstrate the examples. For instance, you're often provided with the details about how a table is defined and what data it includes before the examples are provided. You can then use this table setup information to create your own table in order to try out an example. One example, however, can affect a table in such a way as to change its original structure or data, so you must be aware of this from one example to the next.

Again, the examples are meant only to demonstrate how a statement or command works. You're not expected to try out each example, so if you do, pay close attention to your setup. The book also includes a number of Try It Out sections, which provide you with a more controlled environment to try out statements and commands.

Try It Out Sections

Most chapters include one or more Try It Out sections that provide the details necessary for you to try out the concepts explained in the chapter. Each Try It Out section contains steps that you should follow to perform specific tasks correctly. Each step explains what action you should take and, when applicable, provides the code that you should execute. At the end of each Try It Out section, you will find a How It Works section that explains in detail the steps that you took in the Try It Out section.

Many of the Try It Out sections build on each other as you progress through the book. For example, in Chapter 4 you design a database, in Chapter 5 you create a database based on that design, and in Chapter 6 you add data to the database. The same database is then used in most of the Try It Out sections that follow Chapter 6. In fact, you will use the same database to support the data-driven application that you create in Chapter 17, 18, or 19.

As you work your way through the book, you'll also find that concepts introduced in earlier chapters and demonstrated in the related Try It Out sections are not explained in detail in later Try It Out sections. The assumption in the later Try It Out sections is that you performed the earlier exercises and now know the material.

In general, you'll find that the most effective way to use the Try It Out sections is to perform them in sequential order and make certain that you thoroughly understand them before moving on to the next set of Try It Out sections. By performing the exercises sequentially, you will have, by the end of the chapter, designed and created a database, added data to and manipulated data in that database, administered the MySQL server and the database, and built a PHP, JSP/Java, or ASP.NET/C# application that accesses data in the database.

Exercises

In addition to the examples and the Try It Out sections, each chapter ends with a set of exercises that allow you to further build on and test the knowledge that you acquired in that chapter. The answers to these exercises can be found in Appendix A. Keep in mind, however, that the answers provided for the exercises sometimes represent only one possible solution. As a result, you might come up with an answer that is also correct but different from what is shown in Appendix A. If this is the case, you can refer to the actual chapter content to confirm your answer. The answers shown in the appendix normally represent the most straightforward solution to the exercise, based on the information in the chapter.

Overall, you'll find the exercises to be a useful tool to help better comprehend the concepts presented in the chapter. The exercises, along with the examples and Try it Out sections, provide you with a cohesive presentation of the material so that you can understand each concept completely. By taking advantage of each of these elements, you will have a thorough foundation of MySQL and will understand the steps necessary to install and implement MySQL and manipulate data in a MySQL database.

What You Need to Use This Book

Beginning MySQL contains numerous examples and exercises. If you plan to try out these exercises, you need a system on which to implement MySQL. Specifically, your system should meet the following requirements:

❑ You should be working on a computer that has a Windows or Linux operating system installed. You can usually substitute another Unix-like system for Linux, although some of the exercises might work a little differently from those that focus on Linux.

❑ Eventually, you will need to install the MySQL database management system on your computer. Chapter 2 explains how to install MySQL.

❑ If you plan to download MySQL or any other files from the Web, you will need high-speed Internet access.

❑ You will need a text editor such as Vim (for Linux) and Notepad (for Windows).

❑ For Chapters 17, 18, and 19, you will need the appropriate environment in which to implement your application. For example, PHP requires a Web server such as Apache. JSP/Java requires a Web server or application server such as JBoss. Depending on your JSP/Java Web server or application server, you might also need a special compiler. ASP.NET/C# requires a Web server such as Internet Information Services. In addition, regardless of the type of application you create, your system must be set up with the MySQL driver necessary to allow your application to connect to the MySQL server.

Once you have your system set up the way you need it, you're ready to begin working your way through *Beginning MySQL*.

Conventions

To help you get the most from the text and keep track of what's happening, a number of conventions are used throughout the book.

Try It Out

The *Try It Out* is an exercise you should work through, following the text in the book.

1. They usually consist of a set of steps.
2. Each step has a number.
3. Follow through the steps with your copy of the database.

How It Works

After each *Try It Out*, the code you've typed will be explained in detail.

Tips, hints, tricks, and asides to the current discussion are offset and placed in italics like this.

As for styles in the text:

- New terms and important words are *italicized* when they are introduced.
- Keyboard strokes are shown like this: Ctrl+A.
- File names, URLs, and code in the text are shown like so: `persistence.properties`.
- Code is presented in two different ways:

```
In code examples we highlight new and important code with a gray background.
```

```
The gray highlighting is not used for code that is less important in the present
context or has been shown before.
```

Source Code

As you work through the examples in this book, you may choose either to type all the code manually or to use the source code files that accompany the book. Much of the source code used in this book is available for download at `http://www.wrox.com`. (Generally, if the code in an example or in a step in a Try It Out section is only a few lines, that code is not included.) Once at the site, simply locate the book's title (either by using the Search box or by using one of the title lists) and click the Download Code link on the book's detail page to obtain all the source code for the book.

Because many books have similar titles, you may find it easiest to search by ISBN; for this book the ISBN is 0-764-57950-9.

Once you download the code, just decompress it with your favorite compression tool. Alternately, you can go to the main Wrox code download page at `http://www.wrox.com/dynamic/books/download.aspx` to see the code available for this book and all other Wrox books.

Errata

We make every effort to ensure that there are no errors in the text or in the code. No one is perfect, though, and mistakes do occur. If you find an error in one of our books, such as a spelling mistake or faulty piece of code, we would be very grateful for your feedback. By sending in errata, you may save another reader hours of frustration, and at the same time you will be helping us provide even higher-quality information.

To find the errata page for this book, go to http://www.wrox.com and locate the title using the Search box or one of the title lists. Then, on the book details page, click the Book Errata link. On this page you can view all errata submitted for this book and posted by Wrox editors. A complete book list including links to each's book's errata is also available at www.wrox.com/misc-pages/booklist.shtml.

If you don't spot "your" error on the Book Errata page, go to www.wrox.com/contact/techsupport.shtml and complete the form there to send us the error you have found. We'll check the information and, if appropriate, post a message to the book's errata page and fix the problem in subsequent editions of the book.

p2p.wrox.com

For author and peer discussion, join the P2P forums at p2p.wrox.com. The forums are a Web-based system for you to post messages relating to Wrox books and related technologies and interact with other readers and technology users. The forums offer a subscription feature to e-mail you topics of interest of your choosing when new posts are made to the forums. Wrox authors, editors, other industry experts, and your fellow readers are present on these forums.

At http://p2p.wrox.com you will find a number of different forums that will help you not only as you read this book, but also as you develop your own applications. To join the forums, just follow these steps:

1. Go to p2p.wrox.com and click the Register link.
2. Read the terms of use and click Agree.
3. Complete the required information to join as well as any optional information you wish to provide and click Submit.
4. You will receive an e-mail with information describing how to verify your account and complete the joining process.

You can read messages in the forums without joining P2P, but in order to post your own messages, you must join.

Once you join, you can post new messages and respond to messages other users post. You can read messages at any time on the Web. If you would like to have new messages from a particular forum e-mailed to you, click the Subscribe to this Forum icon by the forum name in the forum listing.

For more information about how to use the Wrox P2P, be sure to read the P2P FAQs for answers to questions about how the forum software works as well as many common questions specific to P2P and Wrox books. To read the FAQs, click the FAQ link on any P2P page.

Introducing the MySQL Relational Database Management System

In the world of online auction houses, instant mortgages, worldwide reservations, global communication, and overnight deliveries, it's not surprising that even the least technically savvy individuals in our culture are, to some degree, familiar with the concept of a database. As anyone who works with data knows, databases form the backbone for this age of information, and access to those databases can determine one's ability to perform critical tasks effectively and efficiently. To meet the ever-increasing demands for information, programmers are continuously building bigger and better applications that can access and modify data stored in various database systems. Yet in order to create these applications, programmers must have some knowledge of the systems that contain the needed data.

Over the years, as the demands for information have grown, so too have the database systems that have attempted to meet these demands. However, along with this evolution, we have seen an increase in the costs associated with storing data as well as an increase in the demand for products that can run on multiple platforms and can be optimized based on the needs of specific types of organizations. In response to this changing climate, MySQL has emerged as the most popular open-source database management system (DBMS) in the world. Consequently, organizations everywhere are jumping on the MySQL bandwagon, increasing the demand for those who know how to use MySQL to manage data and those who know how to create applications that can access data in MySQL databases.

In learning to use MySQL, whether to work directly in the MySQL environment or create data-driven applications, an individual should have a thorough understanding of how MySQL, as a relational database management system (RDBMS), allows you to manage data and support applications that rely on access to MySQL data. To this end, this chapter introduces you to MySQL and provides you with an overview of databases, RDBMSs, SQL, and data-driven applications. By the end of the chapter, you will understand the following concepts:

❑   What a relational database is, how it differs from other types of databases, and how it relates to a database management system.

❑   The programming language SQL, how to interpret SQL syntax, how to create SQL statements, and how SQL is implemented in MySQL.

❑   How applications can use a host programming language, a MySQL application programming interface (API), and SQL statements to access information in a MySQL database.

Databases and Database Management Systems

Databases and database management systems have become the backbone of most Web-related applications as well as an assortment of other types of applications and systems that rely on data stores to support dynamic information needs. Without the availability of flexible, scalable data sources, many organizations would come to a standstill, their ability to provide services, sell goods, rent movies, process orders, issue forms, lend books, plan events, admit patients, and book reservations undermined by the inability to access the data essential to conducting business. As a result, few lives are unaffected by the use of databases in one form or another, and their ubiquitous application in your everyday existence can only be expected to grow.

What Is a Database?

Over the years, the term *database* has been used to describe an assortment of products and systems that have included anything from a collection of files to a complex structure made up of user interfaces, data storage and access mechanisms, and client/server technologies. For example, a small company might store payroll records in individual files, while a regional electric company uses an integrated system to maintain records on all its customers; generate electric bills to those customers; and create reports that define power usage patterns, profit and loss statements, or changes in customer demographics. In both cases, the organizations might refer to each of their systems as databases.

Despite how a database is used, the amount of data that it stores, or the complexity of the data, a number of common elements define what a database is. At its simplest, a database is a collection of data that is usually related in some fashion. For instance, a database that a bookstore uses might contain information about authors, book titles, and publishers. Yet a database is more than simply a collection of related data. The data must be organized and classified in a structured format that is described by *metadata*, which is data that describes the data being stored. In other words, the metadata defines how the data is stored within the database. Together, the data and the metadata provide an environment that logically organizes the data in a way that can be efficiently maintained and accessed.

One way to better understand what constitutes a database is to use the analogy of a telephone book. A phone book contains the names, addresses, and phone numbers of most of the telephone customers in a particular town or region. If you think of that phone book as a database, you find a set of related data (the names, addresses, and phone numbers of the telephone customers) and you find a structured format (the metadata) that is defined by the way that the pages are bound and by how the information is organized. The phone book provides a system that allows you easy and efficient access to the data contained in its pages. Without the structure of the phone book, it would be next to impossible to locate specific customer data.

In the same way that a phone book provides structure to the customer information, the metadata of a database defines a structure that organizes data logically within that structure. However, not all database structures are the same, and through the years, a number of different data models have emerged. Of these various models, the three most commonly implemented are the hierarchical, network, and relational models.

The Hierarchical Model

In the early days of database design, one of the first data models to emerge was the *hierarchical* model. This model provides a simple structure in which individual records are organized in a parent-child relationship to form an inverted tree. The tree creates a hierarchical structure in which data is decomposed into logical categories and subcategories that use records to represent the logical units of data.

Take a look at an example to help illustrate how to structure a hierarchical database. Suppose you're working with a database that stores parts information for a company that manufactures wind generators. Each model of wind generator is associated with a parent record. The parts that make up that model are then divided into categories that become child records of the model's parent record, as shown in Figure 1-1. In this case, the parent record — Wind Generator Number 101 — is linked to three child records: Tower assemblies, Power assemblies, and Rotor assemblies. The child records are then divided into subcategories that are assigned their own child records. As a result, the original child records now act as parent records as well. For example, the Tower assemblies record is a parent of the Towers record but a child of the Wind Generator Number 101 record.

As you can see in the figure, a parent record can be associated with multiple child records, but a child record can be associated with only one parent record. This structure is similar to what you might see in a directory structure viewed through a graphical user interface (GUI) file management application, such as Windows Explorer. At the top of the directory structure would be Wind Generator Number 101. Beneath this, would be Tower assemblies, Power assemblies, and Rotor assemblies, each with their own set of subdirectories.

After its introduction, the hierarchical data model achieved a great deal of success. One of the most popular implementations of this model is found in IBM's Information Management System (IMS), which was introduced in the 1960s and is still widely used on IBM mainframe computers.

However, despite the popularity of the hierarchical model, it is unsuitable for many of today's applications. Inherent in the simplicity of the parent-child organization is a rigid structure that results in a cumbersome navigation process that requires application developers to programmatically navigate through the connected records to find the necessary information. Records must be accessed one at a time by moving up and down through the hierarchical levels, which often made modifications to the database and application a complicated, time-consuming process. In addition, the hierarchical structure cannot support complex relationships between records. For example, if you return to the wind generator database example, you discover that Figure 1-1 doesn't show a record for the belts used to connect the generators to the shafts. If you were to create a child record for belts, should it be added under the Generators record or the Shaft assemblies record? The hierarchical design makes it difficult to fully represent the relationship that exists between the belts and the generators and shafts. Indeed, a child record can be associated with only one parent record.

Chapter 1

Even with the limitations of the hierarchical model, a large amount of data is still being stored in hierarchical databases, and many management systems have found ways to work around some of these limitations. In addition, this is the type of system used primarily for file management systems associated with operating systems because it allows users to go directly where they need to go to find a file, rather than having to iterate through a lot of nodes. As a result, the hierarchical database probably isn't going anywhere anytime soon.

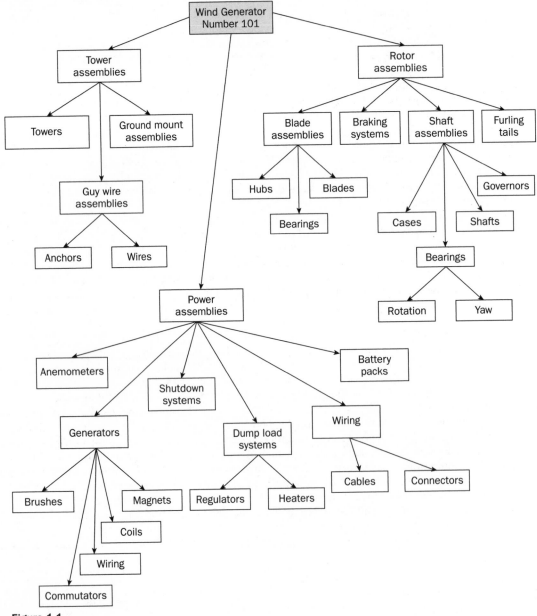

Figure 1-1

The Network Model

To work around the limitations of hierarchical databases, a new model of database design, built upon the hierarchical model, emerged in the 1970s. The *network* model enhanced the hierarchical model by allowing records to participate in multiple parent-child relationships. For example, suppose the wind generator database must also store data about employees, customers, and orders. A hierarchical database might contain four parent records: Orders, Employees, Customers, and Wind generators. Each of these records would then contain the necessary child records to support this structure, as shown in Figure 1-2.

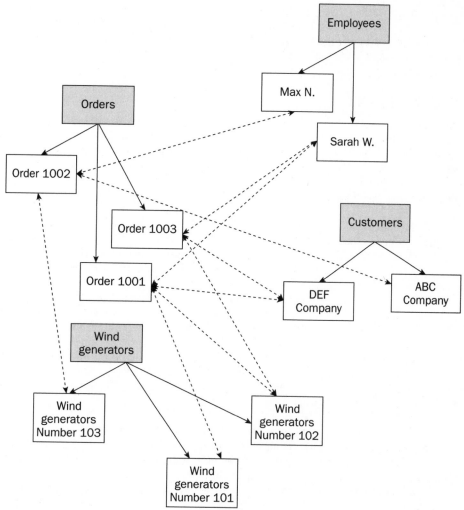

Figure 1-2

If each of these categories operated without interaction with each other, then the need for the network model would be minimal. However, if you consider the fact that each order is related to the employee who took the order, the customer who bought the order, and the wind generator model that was purchased, you can see that the hierarchical model is inadequate to support the complex relationships that exist between records. For example, Sarah W. took Order 1001 for the DEF Company. The company bought two wind generators: models 101 and 102. As a result, the Order 1001 record is related to the Sarah W. record, the DEF Company record, the Wind Generator Number 101 record, and the Wind Generator Number 102 record.

The network model still has many of the disadvantages of the hierarchical model, but it provides far more flexibility in allowing programmers to navigate through records. Despite the flexibility, developers must still program record navigation within the application. In addition, any changes to the database or application can result in complicated updates. A database must be well planned in advance, taking into account record navigation at the application level.

The Relational Model

Because of the limitations of the hierarchical and network models, a new model began gaining momentum in the late 1970s, and by the end of the 1980s, emerged as the standard for the next generation of databases. The *relational* data model represents a radical departure from the rigid structures of the hierarchical and network models. Applications accessing a hierarchical database rely on a defined implementation of that database, and the database structure must be hard-coded into the application's programming language. If the database changes, the application must change.

However, a relational database is independent of the application. It's possible to modify the database design without affecting the application because the relational model replaces the parent-child framework with a structure based on rows and columns that form tables of related data. As a result, you can define complex relationships between the tables, without the restrictions of earlier models.

For example, suppose you want to change the original wind generator database that you saw in Figure 1-1 to a relational database. The database might include a table for the individual parts and a table of the individual categories of parts, as shown in Figure 1-3. As you can see from the illustration, the Parts table includes a list of parts from different areas of the wind generator. The table could contain every part for the entire wind generator, with each row in the table representing a specific part, just as a record in the hierarchical database represents a specific part. For example, the guy wire assembly (in the first row of the Parts table) is a component of the tower assembly, and the generator (in the fifth row) is a component of the power assembly.

Each row in the Parts table represents one part. The part is assigned a unique part ID, a name, and a reference to the category to which it belongs. The Categories table lists each category. Note that the last column in the Parts table references the first column in the Categories table. A relationship exists between these two tables. For instance, the brushes product has been assigned a PartID value of 1004. If you look in the CatID column for this product, you see that it contains a value of 504. If you now look at the Categories table, you find that 504 refers to the Generator category, which is itself a part. Because of this structure, programmers are less restricted when moving through data, resulting in applications that can be more flexible when retrieving information and databases that can better accommodate change after the applications have been written.

> *Don't be concerned if you do not fully grasp the concepts of tables, rows, and columns or the relation-ships between the tables. Chapter 4 discusses the relational model in greater detail.*

Parts

PartID	PartName	CatID
1001	Guy wire assembly	503
1002	Magnet	504
1003	Regulator	505
1004	Brushes	504
1005	Generator	506
1006	Dump load system	506
1007	Power assembly	501
1008	Tower assembly	501
1009	Rotor assembly	501

Categories

CatID	CatName	Parent
501	Wind Generator 101	NULL
502	Rotor assembly	501
503	Tower assembly	501
504	Generator	506
505	Dump load system	506
506	Power assembly	501

Figure 1-3

As the popularity of the relational model has grown, so too has the number of database products that use this model to store and manage data. Included in the family of relational products are DB2, Oracle, SQL Server, and of course, MySQL. However, a relational database alone is not enough to provide the type of data management, storage, connectivity, security, analysis, and manipulation that is required of a dynamic information store. For this, you need a complete management system that works in conjunction with the relational database to provide the full spectrum of database services.

Database Management Systems

Most databases rely on a database management system to manage the data stored within the system's databases and to make the data available to users who need access to specific types of information. A DBMS is made up of a comprehensive set of server and client tools that support various administrative and data-related tasks. For example, most DBMSs provide some type of client tool that allows you to interact directly with the data stored in a database.

At the very least, a DBMS must store data and allow data to be retrieved and modified in a way that protects the data against operations that could corrupt or insert inconsistencies into the data. However, most systems provide many more capabilities. In general, nearly any comprehensive DBMS supports the following types of functionality:

- ❑ Managing storage
- ❑ Maintaining security
- ❑ Maintaining metadata
- ❑ Managing transactions
- ❑ Supporting connectivity
- ❑ Optimizing performance
- ❑ Providing back-up and recovery mechanisms
- ❑ Processing requests for data retrieval and modification

The extent to which a DBMS supports a particular functionality and the exact nature in which that functionality is implemented is specific to the DBMS. For any one system, you must refer to the product documentation to determine what and how specific functionality is implemented.

The MySQL RDBMS

As database models evolved, so too did the DBMS products that supported the various types of databases. It's not surprising, then, that if there are DBMSs, there are RDBMSs. MySQL is such as system, as are Oracle, DB2, SQL Server, and PostgreSQL. These products, like any DBMS, allow you to access and manipulate data within their databases, protect the data from corruption and inconsistencies, and maintain the metadata necessary to define the data being stored. The primary difference, then, between a DBMS and a RDBMS is that the latter is specific to relational databases. It supports not only the storage of data in table-like structures, but also the relationships between those tables.

Emerging as a major player in the RDBMS market is MySQL. As with other RDBMS products, MySQL provides you with a rich set of features that support a secure environment for storing, maintaining, and accessing data. MySQL is a fast, reliable, scalable alternative to many of the commercial RDBMSs available today. The following list provides an overview of the important features found in MySQL:

❑ **Scalability:** MySQL can handle large databases, which has been demonstrated by its implementation in organizations such as Yahoo!, Cox Communications, Google, Cisco, Texas Instruments, UPS, Sabre Holdings, HP, and the Associated Press. Even NASA and the US Census Bureau have implemented MySQL solutions. According to the MySQL product documentation, some of the databases used by MySQL AB, the company that created MySQL, contain 50 million records, and some MySQL users report that their databases contain 60,000 tables and 5 billion rows.

❑ **Portability:** MySQL runs on an assortment of operating systems, including Unix, Linux, Windows, QS/2, Solaris, and MacOS. MySQL can also run on different architectures, ranging from low-end PCs to high-end mainframes.

❑ **Connectivity:** MySQL is fully networked and supports TCP/IP sockets, Unix sockets, and named pipes. In addition, MySQL can be accessed from anywhere on the Internet, and multiple users can access a MySQL database simultaneously. MySQL also provides an assortment of application programming interfaces (APIs) to support connectivity from applications written in such languages as C, C++, Perl, PHP, Java, and Python.

❑ **Security:** MySQL includes a powerful system to control access to data. The system uses a host- and user-based structure that controls who can access specific information and the level of access to that information. MySQL also supports the Secure Sockets Layer (SSL) protocol in order to allow encrypted connections.

❑ **Speed:** MySQL was developed with speed in mind. The amount of time it takes a MySQL database to respond to a request for data is as fast as or faster than many commercial RDBMSs. The MySQL Web site (www.mysql.com) provides the results of numerous benchmark tests that demonstrate the fast results you receive with a MySQL implementation.

❑ **Ease of use:** MySQL is simple to install and implement. A user can have a MySQL installation up and running within minutes after downloading the files. Even at an administrative level, MySQL is relatively easy to optimize, especially compared to other RDBMS products.

❑ **Open-source code:** MySQL AB makes the MySQL source code available to everyone to download and use. The open-source philosophy allows a global audience to participate in the review, testing, and development of code. (See the Open-Source Movement section below for information about open-source technology.)

As you can see, MySQL can provide you with a fast, reliable solution to your database needs. Not only is it easy to use and implement, it offers the advantages and flexibility of an open-source technology. You can download the MySQL distribution files directly from the MySQL Web site, and start using the product immediately.

The Open-Source Movement

One of the most distinctive features of MySQL compared to RDBMSs such as Oracle and DB2 is that MySQL is an open-source application. As a result, the MySQL source code is available for anyone to use and modify, within the constraints of the GNU General Public License (GPL), an open-source licensing structure that supports the distribution of free software. (GNU, pronounced *Guh-New,* is an acronym for "GNU's Not Unix." GNU is an operating system based on the Linux kernel.)

> *For specific information about the most current MySQL licensing structure, visit the MySQL site at* www.mysql.com. *For information about the GNU GPL, visit the GNU licensing site at* www.gnu.org/licenses.

The open-source nature of MySQL is part of a worldwide movement that promotes the free access of application source code. As a result, users are allowed to download and use open-source applications for free. One of the most well known examples of this technology is the Linux operating system, which has been instrumental in unifying the open-source community and promoting a wider base of users and developers who test and contribute to the operating system's development. The same is true of MySQL, which is reported to be the most popular open-source RDBMS in the world. As an open-source application, developers everywhere contribute to the development process, and millions of users test new versions of the application as it is being developed.

As applications such as MySQL and Linux continue to see a steady growth in their global user base, so too does the acceptance of the open-source philosophy, evidenced by the increasing number of other types of applications and technologies that now participate in the open-source movement, providing a richer user experience, a more robust developer environment, and a wider spectrum of options for everyone.

The SQL Framework

Soon after the relational data model appeared on the database scene, research began on the development of relational databases. From this research came the realization that traditional programming languages, such as COBOL or Fortran, were not suited to implementing these types of databases and that a special language was needed. Out of these beginnings came SQL, a database-specific language that has become the definitive language of relational databases and that, as a result, has seen widespread implementation and usage, regardless of products, platforms, or operating system environments.

> *There is some debate about what SQL stands for and how to pronounce it. In some sources, you see SQL defined as an acronym that means Structured Query Language, yet other sources treat SQL as simply the three letters that stand for the language. The American National Standards Institute (ANSI), which published the SQL:2003 standard, makes no mention of "structured query language" and treats SQL simply as the three letters. As a result, no definite resource says that SQL stands for Structured Query Language, despite the fact that many publications define it this way.*

Another area of debate that surrounds SQL is whether to pronounce it one letter at a time, as in "S-Q-L,"
or to pronounce it as a word, as in "sequel." This is why some publications, when preceding SQL with
an article, use the word an ("an SQL database") and some use the word a ("a SQL database"). With
regard to this particular issue, the SQL:2003 standard prefers "S-Q-L," so that is the convention used
in this book.

What is SQL?

SQL is, above all else, a computer language used to manage and interact with data in a relational
database. SQL is the most universally implemented database language in use, and it has become the
standard language for database management. SQL works in conjunction with a RDBMS to define
the structure of the database, store data in that database, manipulate the data, retrieve the data, control
access to the data, and ensure the integrity of the data. Although other languages have been developed
to implement the relational model, SQL has emerged as the clear winner.

Nearly all RDBMSs implement some form of SQL in order to manage their relational database. This is
true not only for MySQL, but also for SQL Server, DB2, Oracle, PostgreSQL, and all the major players in
the world of RDBMSs. However, do not confuse SQL with the programming languages used to develop
the RDBMS. For example, MySQL is built with C and C++. The functions that such an application performs
in order to support connectivity, provide APIs, enable network access, or interact with client tools are
carried out at the C and C++ programming level. The primary purpose of SQL is to allow the RDBMS to
interact with the data. The C and C++ environment provides the structure that houses the SQL environment, which itself allows you to define and interact with the data. In other words, the RDBMS facilitates
the ability of SQL to manage data.

Figure 1-4 illustrates how SQL interacts with the MySQL RDBMS. In this figure, MySQL is running as a
server on a specific platform such as Linux or Unix. The database, stored either internally or externally,
depending on your storage configuration, hosts the actual database files. Although the RDBMS facilitates (through the C/C++ applications) the creation and maintenance of the database and the data
within the database, SQL actually creates and maintains the database and data.

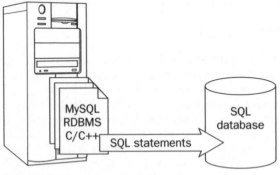

Figure 1-4

SQL, then, is a standardized language, not a stand-alone product, such as MySQL. SQL relies on the interaction with a RDBMS in order to manage data. You cannot develop an SQL-based application, although you can build an application that connects to a database managed by a RDBMS and then sends SQL statements to the database in order to request and modify data. (You learn more about how SQL fits into application development later in the chapter, in the section Data-Driven Applications.) However, despite the inability of SQL to stand on its own, it remains the foundation of most relational databases; therefore, anyone who creates applications that interact with an SQL database should have a basic understanding of SQL.

A Brief History of SQL

After the relational model was introduced to the database development community in the early 1970s, IBM began researching ways to implement that model. IBM's research, referred to as the System/R project, resulted in a prototype of the first RDBMS. As part of the System/R project, IBM produced the first incarnation of a relational database language, which was known Structured English Query Language (SEQUEL). Over the next few years, IBM updated the prototype and released SEQUEL/2, which was later renamed to SQL.

In the late 1970s, IBM released System R to a number of its customers for evaluation. The development and release of System R brought with it increased attention to relational databases, RDBMSs, and SQL, and reconfirmed to the public IBM's commitment to the relational model. Soon a group of engineers formed Relational Software, Inc., a company whose primary goal was to develop a RDBMS system based on SQL. Before long, the company released its own product — Oracle — the first commercial RDBMS to hit the market. It wasn't until 1981 that IBM released their first commercial RDBMS — SQL/DS.

The ANSI Standard

By the mid-1980s, relational databases and SQL had become an industry standard. During this time, the performance of RDBMSs had improved dramatically, and other companies were investing into the relational technologies, either releasing or preparing to release their own SQL-based RDBMSs. However, as SQL became more widely implemented, so too did the need to standardize the language across various products. In an attempt to achieve this goal, ANSI released the first published SQL standard (SQL-86) in 1986, giving SQL official status in the software development industry.

ANSI updated the standard in 1989 (SQL-89) and again in 1992 (SQL-92). SQL-92 represented a major revision to the language and included expanded and improved features, some of which exceeded the capabilities of existing RDBMSs. In fact, SQL-92 was substantially longer than SQL-89 in an attempt to address many of the weaknesses of the earlier standard.

Because of the significant expansion of the standard, SQL-92 defined three levels of conformance:

❑ **Entry:** This level represented the most basic stage of conformance, and was based primarily on the SQL-89 standard, with only a few improvements.

❑ **Intermediate:** Although this level represented significant advancements to the product, it was believed that most products could achieve compliance.

❑ **Full:** A RDBMS had to be in complete compliance with the standard.

To be in conformance to the SQL-92 standard, a RDBMS had to comply with at least the Entry level, which has been achieved by most RDBMSs on the market. However, no known product achieved an Intermediate level of conformance, let alone Full. Part of the problem is that some of the features specified in the Intermediate level met with little interest from users. As a result, RDBMS vendors saw little reason to implement these features.

In 1999, ANSI, along with the International Organization for Standardization (ISO) published SQL:1999, the first complete update to the SQL standard since 1992. However, during those seven years, interim standards were published to incorporate features that RDBMS vendors were already being implementing. These interim publications were then incorporated in the SQL:1999 standard, which represented another significant expansion of the standard.

Because most products reached only an Entry level of conformance to SQL-92, the SQL:1999 standard took a different approach to conformance levels. To be in conformance to the new standard, a RDBMS had to be in compliance with Core SQL. Core SQL contained all the features of Entry level SQL-92, many of the features of Intermediate level, and some of the features of Full level, plus some features new to SQL:1999. In addition to claiming Core SQL conformance, a RDBMS could claim conformance to one of the supported packages. A *package* is a set of features that a vendor could implement in a RDBMS. The SQL:1999 standard supported the following packages:

- ❑ **PKG001:** Enhanced date/time facilities
- ❑ **PKG002:** Enhanced integrity management
- ❑ **PKG003:** OLAP (online analytical processing) facilities
- ❑ **PKG004:** PSM (persistent stored module)
- ❑ **PKG005:** CLI (call-level interface)
- ❑ **PKG006:** Basic object support
- ❑ **PKG007:** Enhanced object support
- ❑ **PKG008:** Active database
- ❑ **PKG009:** SQL/MM (multimedia) support

Most RDBMSs, including MySQL, conform to the Entry level of SQL-92 and achiev some conformance to Core SQL in SQL:1999. However, ANSI and ISO have released yet another version of the standard — SQL:2003. In many ways, the new standard merely reorganizes and makes corrections to SQL:1999. However, the latest standard does include additional features that were not part of SQL:1999, particularly in the area of Extensible Markup Language (XML). As a result, compliance with SQL:1999 does not necessarily imply compliance to SQL:2003.

With the advent of SQL:2003, future releases of RDBMS products will inevitably change, and some vendors are already working on achieving compliance with the new standard. However, as of today, no product claims compliance to SQL:2003.

> You can purchase the ANSI/ISO SQL:2003 standard online at the ANSI eStandards Store (`http://webstore.ansi.org`). The standard is divided into 14 parts, which you must purchase individually.

Object-Relational Model

As explained earlier, SQL was developed as a way to implement the relational model. To this end, the language has been quite successful, attested to by its widespread implementation and the commitment of companies such as Microsoft, IBM, Oracle, and MySQL AB to relational databases and SQL. However, most RDBMS vendors have extended the SQL-based capabilities of their products to include features that go beyond the pure relational nature of SQL. Many of these new features are similar to some of the characteristics found in *object-oriented programming,* a type of programming based on self-contained collections of routines and data structures that each perform a specific task. As SQL, as well as various RDBMS products, has become more advanced, it has taken a turn toward object-oriented programming (although, strictly speaking, SQL is far from being an object-oriented language).

> *Java and C# are both examples of object-oriented programming languages. In these languages, objects interact with one another in a way that addresses complex programming issues that cannot be easily addressed with traditional procedural languages.*

A good example of the object-oriented nature of some of the extended features in RDBMSs is the stored procedure. A *stored procedure* is a collection of SQL statements that are grouped together to perform a specific operation. The SQL statements are saved as a single object stored in the database and that users can evoke as needed.

By the mid-1990s, most RDBMS products had implemented some form of the stored procedure. To address this trend, ANSI released in 1996 an interim publication referred to as SQL/PSM, or PSM-96. (PSM refers to *persistent stored module.)* A PSM is a type of procedure or function stored as an object in the database. A *procedure* is a set of one or more SQL statements stored as a unit, and a *function* is a type of operation that performs a specific task and then returns a value.

The SQL/PSM standard defined how to implement PSMs in SQL. Specifically, SQL/PSM included the language necessary to support stored procedures (which were referred to as *SQL-invoked procedures* in the standard). SQL/PSM was later incorporated into the SQL:1999 standard.

The problem that ANSI ran into when trying to standardize the SQL language related to stored procedures is that the way in which stored procedures were implemented from product to product varied widely. As a result, the manner in which stored procedures are called and retrieved can be very different not only between products and the SQL:1999 standard, but also among the products themselves. As a result, the implementation of stored procedures remains very proprietary, with few products conforming to the actual standard.

> *MySQL currently does not support stored procedures, although SQL AB is including this functionality in version 5.0. The stored procedure functionality is based on the SQL:2003 standard.*

The differences among the products extend beyond only stored procedures. Other features have experienced the same fate as stored procedures because so many of these features had been implemented prior to the standardization of related SQL statements. Still, many of SQL's advanced features, with their object-oriented characteristics, are here to stay, as can be seen in both the SQL:1999 and SQL:2003 standards and in the RDBMS products, making SQL an *object-relational* database language and the RDBMS products *object-relational database management systems.*

The Nonprocedural Nature of SQL

Despite the influence of object-oriented programming on SQL, SQL is still very different from other programming languages. Traditional procedural programming languages such as COBOL, Fortran, and C were designed for very specific purposes, none of which were for accessing data. For this reason, SQL was intended for use in conjunction with these languages in order to build applications that could easily access data. For this reason, SQL is not intended for use as a standalone language, which is why it is sometimes referred to as a *sublanguage.* Insufficient for writing complete applications, SQL was designed with the idea that there would always be a *host language* for application building.

Traditional programming languages, which range from Fortran to C, are considered to be *procedural languages;* that is, they define how to carry out an application's operations and the order in which to carry them out. SQL, on the other hand, is nonprocedural in nature. It is concerned primarily with the results of an operation. The host language determines how to process the operation. Of course, this doesn't mean that SQL doesn't include procedural elements. For example, stored procedures are such an element, and certainly RDBMS vendors recognize the need for at least some procedural functionality.

Yet these procedural elements do not make SQL a procedural language. SQL doesn't have many of the basic programming capabilities of the other languages. As a result, you cannot build an application with SQL alone. You must use a procedural language that works in conjunction with SQL to manipulate data stored in a RDBMS.

SQL Statements

SQL is made up of a set of statements that define the structure of a database, store and manage data within that structure, and control access to the data. At the heart of each SQL statement is a syntactical structure that specifies how to create the statement can be created. The syntax acts as blueprint for building statements that the RDBMS interprets. Most RDBMS products provide little leeway for statements that don't adhere strictly to the syntactical foundations. As a result, you should know how to read and interpret statement syntax if you plan to use SQL in your applications or access data in an SQL database.

Working with Statement Syntax

When you create an SQL statement, you must often rely on the statement syntax defined in a product's documentation. The syntax provides the guidelines you need to create a statement that RDBMS can interpret. For each statement, the syntax — through the use of keywords and symbols — defines the statement's structure, the elements required within the statement, and options you can include to help refine the statement.

When you first look at the complete syntax for any statement, it might seem overwhelming, depending on the statement. For some statements, there are relatively few elements, so interpretation is easy. However, other syntax can be pages long. Despite the complexities of a particular statement, the basic syntax elements are the same, and if you learn how to interpret those elements, you can, with practice, understand any syntax presented to you.

The elements comprising a syntactic structure can vary from reference to reference and from product to product, although in many cases, the symbols used are the same. This book follows ANSI's SQL:2003 standards. You may encounter partial syntax throughout this book. In some cases, there are simply too many syntactic elements, and many of those elements are rarely implemented. Whenever you want to be certain that you're seeing a statement's syntax in its entirety, be certain to check the MySQL documentation.

Below is an example of a statement's syntax so that you can get a better feel for how to compose an SQL statement. The example below is based on the MySQL CREATE TABLE statement. The statement varies somewhat from the statement as it's defined in the SQL:2003 standard; however, the basic elements are the same. The following syntax demonstrates all the elements that comprise any SQL statement, in terms of the structure and symbols used:

```
<table definition>::=
CREATE [TEMPORARY] TABLE [IF NOT EXISTS] <table name>
(<table element> [{, <table element>}...])
[ENGINE = {BDB | MEMORY | ISAM | INNODB | MERGE | MRG_MYISAM | MYISAM}]

<table element>::=
{<column name> <type> [NOT NULL | NULL] [DEFAULT <value>] [AUTO_INCREMENT]}
| {PRIMARY KEY (<column name> [{, <column name>}...])}
| {INDEX [<index name>] (<column name> [{, <column name>}...])}
```

The syntax shown here does not represent the CREATE TABLE statement in its entirety, but it does include the fundamental components. Chapter 5 examines the table definition syntax in far more detail, but for now, the primary concern is that you learn how to interpret SQL statement syntax.

The syntax method employed here is referred to as BNF (Backus Naur Form) notation. Most resources that discuss syntax for SQL statements use BNF notation or something similar to this.

Before examining the syntax example in detail, review the symbols used as part of syntax notation. The following conventions define how to create a statement, based on the meaning of the symbols within the context of the syntax:

❑ **Vertical bar (|):** The vertical bar can be interpreted to mean "or." Whenever you can choose from two or more options, those options are separated with a vertical bar. For example, in the sixth line, you can choose either NOT NULL *or* NULL.

❑ **Square brackets ([ ]):** A set of square brackets indicates that the syntax enclosed in those brackets is optional.

❑ **Angle brackets (< >):** A set of angle brackets indicates that the syntax enclosed is a placeholder, in which case, you must insert a specific value in place of the angle brackets and the text within those brackets. If the meaning of the placeholder is not self-evident, a later section within the syntax usually defines it.

❑ **Curly brackets ({ }):** A set of curly brackets indicates that the syntax enclosed in those brackets should be treated as a unit. As a result, if one element within the brackets is used, all elements are used, unless a vertical bar separates options within the brackets.

❑ **Three periods (...):** A set of three periods means that the clause that immediately precedes the periods can be repeated as often as necessary.

❑ **Two colons/equal sign (::=):** The colon/equal sign construction defines placeholders. Literally, it is the equivalent to an equal sign. The syntax to the right of the symbols defines the specified placeholder to the left.

Once you understand how to use these six symbols, you should be able to interpret most syntax. However, one other syntactic element that you should be aware of is the use and placement of keywords. A *keyword* is a reserved word or set of reserved words that are part of the SQL lexicon. The keywords define a statement's action and how that action is carried out. For example, the CREATE TABLE keywords indicate that this statement does what you would expect it to do — create a table.

Normally, keywords are represented in all uppercase to distinguish them from placeholders, but SQL is a case-insensitive language, so the use of uppercase is meant only as a way to write more readable code. You could also write Create Table, create table, or CREate taBLE, and MySQL would interpret the code in the same way.

> *Not only is SQL indifferent to capitalization, it also isn't concerned with tabs, extra spaces, or line breaks. In theory, you could write your entire SQL statement on one line, or you could place each word on separate lines. However, it's recommended that you construct your statements in such a way that they are easy to read and understand, so breaking a statement into several lines is a common approach to take.*

Returning to the example syntax and reviewing it line by line, the syntax begins by identifying the type of statement that is being defined:

```
<table definition>::=
```

Literally, the syntax means that the <table definition> placeholder is equivalent to the syntax that follows. SQL-related documentation often omits this introductory line, and it is seldom necessary at the beginning of the syntax. Usually, the syntax itself clearly defines the statement's purpose. However, it's included here so that you recognize it should you run into it in SQL documentation. To review the second line of the syntax:

```
CREATE [TEMPORARY] TABLE [IF NOT EXISTS] <table name>
```

This line represents the actual first part of a CREATE TABLE statement. Notice that the keyword TEMPORARY separates the CREATE TABLE keywords. Because square brackets enclose this keyword, the keyword is optional. You would include it only if you plan to create a temporary table. (Temporary tables are discussed in Chapter 5.) Because of the optional keyword, a table definition can begin with CREATE TABLE or CREATE TEMPORARY TABLE.

The next part in this line of syntax is the keywords IF NOT EXISTS. Again, these keywords are optional and would be included only if you want to check for the existence of a table with the same name. Note, however, that when a set of brackets encloses multiple words in this manner, all the keywords are included or none are included. You would not use IF, NOT, or EXISTS alone within this context of this part of the statement. In other words, you would never create a statement that begins with the following:

```
CREATE TABLE EXISTS <table name>
```

Notice that the final element in this line of syntax is the <table name> placeholder. This is the position within the statement in which you provide a name for the table that you're creating. When the table is added to the database, it is assigned the name that you provide here, and this is the name that you use whenever referring to the table. Now look at the next line of syntax:

```
(<table element> [{, <table element>}...])
```

The first thing you might notice is that parentheses enclose all the elements. Whenever you include parentheses in this way (and the parentheses are not enclosed by square brackets), the parentheses are required. As a result, the required elements of this line are (<table element>). Because the <table element> placeholder represents a more complex syntax than merely the name of an object, the placeholder is defined later in the code.

The important point to remember is that at least one `<table element>` is required, but you can include as many as necessary. However, this is when the syntax gets a little trickier. Notice that several elements are enclosed in square brackets — [{, <table element>}...] — telling you that this part of the syntax is optional. However, curly brackets group together parts of the syntax within the square brackets — {, <table element>} — and they are followed by three periods. The curly brackets mean that the elements within those brackets must be kept together, and the periods mean that the group of elements can be repeated as often as necessary. As a result, whenever you include an additional `<table element>` in your statement, you must precede it with a comma, but you can do this as many times as necessary. For example, if the statement includes four table elements, your syntax would be as follows:

```
(<table element>, <table element>, <table element>, <table element>)
```

As you can see, when you include more than one `<table element>`, you must follow each one with a comma, except for the last one. And keep in mind that parentheses must enclose them all. Moving on to the next line of syntax:

```
[ENGINE = {BDB | MEMORY | ISAM | INNODB | MERGE | MRG_MYISAM | MYISAM}]
```

One of the first things that you notice is that square brackets enclose the entire line, which means that the entire line is optional. The line defines the type of table that you plan to create. If you do include this line in your CREATE TABLE statement, then you must include ENGINE = plus one of the table type options. You can tell that you're allowed to select only one option because a vertical bar separates each option. You could read this as BDB *or* MEMORY *or* ISAM *or* INNOBD, and so on. For example, if you want to define the table as an INNODB table, you would include the following line in your syntax:

```
ENGINE = INNODB
```

You should now have a basic understanding of how to create a CREATE TABLE statement. However, as you may recall, the <table element> placeholder could not be easily defined by its placement or usage. As a result, the syntax goes on to define the components that can make up a <table element>. You can tell that the syntax defines the <table element> placeholder because it precedes the definition with the actual placeholder, as shown in the first line in the next section of syntax:

```
<table element>::=
```

From this, you know that whatever follows is part of the syntax that defines the <table element> placeholder. Before you look too closely at the first line in the <table element> definition, take a look at all three lines that make up that definition:

```
{<column name> <type> [NOT NULL | NULL] [DEFAULT <value>] [AUTO_INCREMENT]}
| {PRIMARY KEY (<column name> [{, <column name>}...])}
| {INDEX [<index name>] (<column name> [{, <column name>}...])}
```

What you might have noticed is that a vertical bar precedes the last two lines and that curly brackets enclose all three lines. This means that each line represents one of the options you can use to define a `<table element>` placeholder. In other words, for each `<table element>` that you include in your CREATE TABLE statement, you can define a column, a primary key, or an index.

> *A primary key is a constraint placed on one or more columns within a table to indicate that the columns act as the primary identifier for each row in that table. Values within a primary key's columns must be unique when taken as a whole. You learn about primary keys in Chapter 5, which discusses how to create a table.*

Take a look at the first line of the `<table element>` definition:

```
{<column name> <type> [NOT NULL | NULL] [DEFAULT <value>] [AUTO_INCREMENT]}
```

This line defines a column within the table. Each column definition must include a name (`<column name>`) and a data type (`<type>`). A *data type* determines the type of data that can be stored in a table. The line also includes three optional elements. The first of these is `[NOT NULL | NULL]`, which means that you can set a column as NOT NULL or NULL. A *null* value indicates that a value is undefined or unknown. It is not the same as zero or blank. Instead it means that a value is absent. When you include NOT NULL in your column definition, you're saying that the column does not permit null values. On the other hand, the NULL option permits null values.

The next optional element in the column definition is `[DEFAULT <value>]`. This option allows you to define a value that is automatically inserted into a column if a value isn't inserted into the column when you create a row. When you include the DEFAULT keyword in your column definition, you must include a value in place of the `<value>` placeholder.

The final optional element of the column definition is `[AUTO INCREMENT]`. You include this option in your definition if you want MySQL to automatically generate sequential numbers for this column whenever a new row is added to the table.

With regard to the three options available in the `<table element>` definition, the column definition is the one you use most often. However, as stated above, you can choose any of three options, so take a look at the second line:

```
| {PRIMARY KEY (<column name> [{, <column name>}...])}
```

The purpose of this line is to define a primary key for the table. If you choose this option, you must include the PRIMARY KEY keywords and at least one column name, enclosed in parentheses. The elements contained in the square brackets—`[{, <column name>}...]`—indicate that you can include one or more additional columns and that a comma must precede each additional column. For example, if you base your primary key on three columns, your syntax is as follows:

```
PRIMARY KEY (<column name>, <column name>, <column name>)
```

> *Don't worry if you don't understand how primary keys are created or how they can be made up of multiple columns. Primary keys are discussed in detail in Chapter 5.*

Now examine the last optional element in the `<table element>` definition:

```
| {INDEX [<index name>] (<column name> [{, <column name>}...])}
```

This line creates an index. If you use this option, you must include the INDEX keyword and at least one column name, enclosed in parentheses. As was the case when creating a primary key, you can also include additional columns, as long as a comma precedes each additional column. However, unlike a primary key, the index name is optional. It's up to you whether you want to name the index, although naming all objects in a database is generally considered a good practice.

You should now have a fairly good sense of how to interpret a statement's syntax. As you have seen from the table definition example, the syntax for an SQL statement can contain many elements. However, once you're comfortable with syntax structure and how symbols define this structure, you should be able to interpret the syntax for nearly any SQL statement (albeit some statements might present a far greater challenge than other statements). The next section discusses how to use this syntax to create an SQL statement.

Creating an SQL Statement

An SQL statement can range from very simple — only a few words — to very complicated. If at any point in the statement-creation process you're uncertain how to proceed, you can refer to the syntax for direction. Even experienced SQL programmers must often refer back to the syntax in order to understand the subtleties of a particular statement, but once you have that syntax as a frame of reference, you're ready to build your statement.

Below is an example of a statement based on the table definition syntax. The following CREATE TABLE statement creates a table named Parts:

```
/* Creates the Parts table */
CREATE TABLE Parts
(
    PartID INT NOT NULL,
    PartName VARCHAR(40) NOT NULL,
    CatID INT NOT NULL,
    PRIMARY KEY (PartID)
)
ENGINE=MYISAM;
```

The first thing to note is that the CREATE TABLE example is a single SQL statement. Notice that it ends with a semi-colon, which is sometimes referred to as a *terminator*. When you access a MySQL database directly (for example, by using the mysql client utility), you must terminate each SQL statement with a semi-colon.

As mentioned earlier, SQL is indifferent to extra spaces, tabs, and line breaks. However, the statement is written in such a way as to facilitate readability and to make it easier to explain each element. For example, the table elements are indented and the opening and closing parentheses are placed on their own lines.

The first line of code reads:

```
/* Creates the Parts table */
```

The code is merely a comment and is not processed by MySQL. (In fact, you normally wouldn't use comments when working with MySQL interactively, but the comment is included here to demonstrate how they work.) It is there only to provide information to anyone who might be viewing the code. Adding comments to your code to explain the purpose of each part or to provide any special information is always a good idea. Comments are particularly useful when updating code you had created in the past or when someone else is working on code that you created. Comments are also very useful if you're trying to debug your code.

> *You can also create a comment by preceding the text with double dashes (--). However, the comment cannot include any line breaks.*

As you can see from the line of code, a comment begins with /* and ends with */. Everything between the two symbols, including line breaks, is considered part of the comment and therefore ignored by MySQL when processing the SQL statements.

The next line of code is the first line of the actual CREATE TABLE statement:

```
CREATE TABLE Parts
```

As you can see, the line includes the CREATE TABLE keywords and the name of the new table—Parts. If you refer to the related line of syntax, you can see how to form the CREATE TABLE clause :

```
CREATE [TEMPORARY] TABLE [IF NOT EXISTS] <table name>
```

Notice that the optional keyword TEMPORARY and the optional keywords IF NOT EXISTS are not included in the clause, only the required elements. Now take a look at the <table element> definitions:

```
(
    PartID INT NOT NULL,
    PartName VARCHAR(40) NOT NULL,
    CatID INT NOT NULL,
    PRIMARY KEY (PartID)
)
```

This part of the CREATE TABLE statement includes four <table element> components. The first three represent column definitions and the last represents a primary key definition. The elements are enclosed in parentheses and separated by commas. If you compare this to the syntax, you can see how the <table element> placeholders represent each component:

```
(<table element>, <table element>, <table element>, <table element>)
```

However, as you may recall, this is only a part of the story because the syntax further defines the `<table element>` placeholder to include three options: a column definition, a primary key definition, and an index definition. Take a look at one of the column definitions in the sample CREATE TABLE statement to illustrate how it compares to the syntax:

```
PartID INT NOT NULL,
```

In this case, the column's name is PartID, it is configured with INT data type (to permit up to four numerals), and null values are not permitted. If you compare this to the syntax, you can see why the column definition is structured as it is:

```
<column name> <type> [NOT NULL | NULL] [DEFAULT <value>] [AUTO_INCREMENT]
```

As you can see, `PartID` is the value used for the `<column name>` placeholder, `INT` is the value used for the `<type>` placeholder, and the only optional element used is `NOT NULL`. The `<type>` placeholder refers to the column's data type, which in this case is `INT`. Notice also that this `<table element>` definition ends with a comma because another `<table element>` definition follows. Now look at the primary key definition:

```
PRIMARY KEY (PartID)
```

This line only includes the PRIMARY KEY keywords and one column name. As a result, a comma is not required after the column name. However, parentheses must still enclose the column name. Also, because this is the last `<table element>` definition, you don't need to use a comma after the primary key definition. Compare this to the syntax:

```
PRIMARY KEY (<column name> [{, <column name>}...])
```

As you can see, you use none of the optional elements, only what is essential for a primary key definition. Moving on to the final line of the CREATE TABLE statement:

```
ENGINE=MYISAM;
```

This part of the statement defines the type of table that is being created. If you compare this to the syntax, you see that you've chosen one of the available options:

```
[ENGINE = {BDB | MEMORY | ISAM | INNODB | MERGE | MRG_MYISAM | MYISAM}]
```

As the syntax indicates, this entire line of code is optional. However, if you're going to include it, you must include `ENGINE=` and exactly one of the options.

As you can see from this example, creating an SQL statement is a matter of conforming to the structure as it is defined in the statement syntax. Running the CREATE TABLE statement in the example above adds a table to your database. From there, you could add data to the table, access that data, and modify it as necessary. Figure 1-5 shows what the table might look like in a MySQL database once you've executed the CREATE TABLE statement and then added data to the table.

Parts table

PartID	PartName	CatID
1001	Guy wire assembly	503
1002	Magnet	504
1003	Regulator	505
1004	Brushes	504
1005	Generator	506
1006	Dump load system	506
1007	Power assembly	501
1008	Tower assembly	501
1009	Rotor assembly	501
1010	Hub	611
1011	Shaft assembly	612
1012	Governor	619
1013	Furling tail	612

Figure 1-5

As displayed in the figure, the Parts table includes the three columns — PartID, PartName, and CatID — as well as the sample data. You could have created a table with as many columns as necessary, depending on the design of your database and your requirements for storing data, and you could have added many more rows of data.

MySQL provides a client utility named mysql, which allows you to interact directly with MySQL databases. The mysql client utility is similar to a command prompt as you would see in an operating system command window. If you were use the client utility to view the contents of the table, you would see the data displayed in a manner similar the following:

```
+--------+--------------------+-------+
| PartID | PartName           | CatID |
+--------+--------------------+-------+
|   1001 | Guy wire assembly  |   503 |
|   1002 | Magnet             |   504 |
|   1003 | Regulator          |   505 |
|   1004 | Brushes            |   504 |
|   1005 | Generator          |   506 |
|   1006 | Dump load system   |   506 |
|   1007 | Power assembly     |   501 |
|   1008 | Tower assembly     |   501 |
|   1009 | Rotor assembly     |   501 |
|   1010 | Hub                |   611 |
|   1011 | Shaft assembly     |   612 |
|   1012 | Governor           |   619 |
|   1013 | Furling tail       |   612 |
+--------+--------------------+-------+
13 rows in set (0.03 sec)
```

These results aren't quite as elegant as the table in Figure 1-5, but they display the same information. In addition, this option represents the way you're likely to see data displayed if you're working with MySQL directly.

MySQL, the RDBMS, is very different from mysql the command-line utility. The mysql utility is a client tool that provides an interactive environment in which you can work directly with MySQL databases. In most documentation, including the MySQL product documentation, the utility is shown in all lowercase. You learn more about using the mysql client tool in Chapter 3.

Now that you have an overview of how to use statement syntax to create SQL statements, you can learn about the different types of statements that SQL supports.

Types of SQL Statements

As you work your way through this book, you find that SQL supports many different types of statements and that most of these statements include a number of options. SQL is generally broken down into three categories of statements: data definition language (DDL), data manipulation language (DML), and data control language (DCL). The following three sections discuss each of these statement types and provide you with examples. These examples use the table in Figure 1-5. However, keep in mind that these examples are meant only to introduce you to SQL statements. Each statement is covered in much greater detail later in the book, but the examples help to provide you with an overview of how to create SQL statements.

Using DDL Statements

In MySQL, DDL statements create, alter, and delete data structures within the database. DDL statements define the structure of a MySQL database and determine the type of data that can be stored in the database and how to store that data. Specifically, DDL statements allow you to do the following:

❑   Create and remove databases (the CREATE DATABASE and DROP DATABASE statements)

❑   Create, alter, rename, and remove tables (the CREATE TABLE, ALTER TABLE, RENAME TABLE, and DROP TABLE statements)

❑   Create and remove indexes (the CREATE INDEX and DROP INDEX statements)

As you move through the book, you learn more about databases, tables, and indexes and are provided with details on how to create statements that allow you to work with those objects. In the meantime, here's a brief description of each of these objects so you have a better idea of the nature of DDL statements:

❑   **Database:** As you learned at the beginning of the chapter, a database is a collection of related data organized in a structural format that is described by metadata.

❑   **Table:** A table is a grid-like structure that consists of a set of columns and rows that represent a single entity within the database. Each row is a unique record that stores a set of specific data.

❑   **Index:** An index is a list of values taken from a specified column. Indexes are used to speed up searches and reduce the time it takes to execute an SQL query.

Earlier in the chapter, you saw an example of a DDL statement — the CREATE TABLE statement — which you used to create a table named Parts. Another example of a DDL statement, the following DROP TABLE statement removes the Parts table from the database:

```
/* Removes the Parts table from the database */
DROP TABLE Parts;
```

As this example demonstrates, some DDL statements (as well as some DML and DCL statements) can be quite simple. In this case, you need only to specify the table's name along with the keywords DROP TABLE to remove its contents from the database. (As you may recall, the first line in this code is merely a comment that provides information about the statement to come.)

In Chapter 5, you learn how to create, alter, rename, and drop tables, as well as how to create and drop databases and indexes. The next section outlines DML statements.

Using DML Statements

Unlike DDL statements, DML statements are more concerned with the data stored in the database than the database structure itself. For example, you can use DDL statements to request information from the database as well as insert, update, and delete data; however, you would not use a DML statement to create or modify the tables that hold the data. Specifically, DML statements allow you to do the following:

- ❑ Query a database for specific types of information from one or more tables (the SELECT statement)

- ❑ Insert data into a table (the INSERT, REPLACE, and LOAD DATA INFILE statements)

- ❑ Update existing data in a table (the INSERT and REPLACE statements)

- ❑ Delete data from a table (the DELETE FROM and TRUNCATE TABLE statements)

The SELECT statement is perhaps the statement that you use more than any other. The SELECT statement allows you to retrieve data from one or more tables in a database. Whenever you query a database, you use the SELECT statement to initiate that query. The statement can be relatively simple or very complex, depending on the type of information you're trying to retrieve and the degree to which you want to refine your search.

The following SELECT statement provides you with an example of how you can retrieve data from the Parts table:

```
/* Retrieves data for parts with CatID less than 600 */
SELECT PartName, PartID, CatID
FROM Parts
WHERE CatID < 600
ORDER BY PartName;
```

Again, a comment that describes the code's purpose introduces the statement. The actual statement begins on the second line and is divided into four clauses, each written on its own line. A clause is simply a section of a statement. The clause is usually referred to by the keyword that starts the clause. For example, the first clause is the SELECT statement is the SELECT clause. The first clause in any

SELECT statement is always the SELECT clause, which indicates which columns to include in the query. In this case, the SELECT clause retrieves data from the PartName, PartID, and CatID columns. (You can refer back to Figure 1-5 to view the table and its contents.) The FROM clause is next, and it provides the name of the table or tables to include in the query. The WHERE clause refines the query based on the conditions specified in the clause. In this case, only rows with a CatID value less than 600 are included in the query results. This is indicated by the name of the column (CatID), the less than operator (<), and the number 600. The final clause, ORDER BY, determines the order in which the query results list data. This SELECT statement lists the query results in alphabetical order based on the values in the PartName column.

> *The intent of providing you an example SELECT statement is merely to provide you with a high overview of one type of DML statement. You don't need to worry about all the components of a SELECT statement at or any other DML statement at this time. The SELECT statement is a complex statement that can contain a considerable number of options and can be structured in many different ways. Chapter 7 provides you with a detailed explanation of the statement's syntax and the various ways that you can construct a statement.*

Using the mysql command-line utility to execute the SELECT statement above provides the following results:

```
+--------------------+--------+-------+
| PartName           | PartID | CatID |
+--------------------+--------+-------+
| Brushes            |   1004 |   504 |
| Dump load system   |   1006 |   506 |
| Generator          |   1005 |   506 |
| Guy wire assembly  |   1001 |   503 |
| Magnet             |   1002 |   504 |
| Power assembly     |   1007 |   501 |
| Regulator          |   1003 |   505 |
| Rotor assembly     |   1009 |   501 |
| Tower assembly     |   1008 |   501 |
+--------------------+--------+-------+
9 rows in set (0.03 sec)
```

Notice that the columns appear in the order specified in the SELECT clause. Also notice that the query results include only those rows whose CatID value is less than 600 and that the rows are ordered according to the values in the PartName column.

The SELECT statement shown in the example is only one type of DML statement. MySQL also allows you to use DML statements to insert, update, and delete data, which you discover as you progress through the book. The following section examines DCL statements.

Using DCL Statements

As you learned above, DDL statements allow you to define the structure of a MySQL database, and DML statements allow you to access and manipulate data within the database. DCL statements represent yet another function supported by SQL statements: controlling access to a database. Specifically, DCL statements allow you to do the following:

- ❑ Grant access privileges to users (the GRANT statement)
- ❑ Revoke access privileges to users (the REVOKE statement)

When you grant access to a database, you can grant access to specific tables and you can assign specific privileges. As a result, you can specify the exact level of access that each user or groups of users should have to specific data. For example, the following GRANT statement grants privileges to a user account named ethan.

```
/* grant privileges to ethan */
GRANT SELECT, INSERT
ON test.parts
TO ethan@localhost
IDENTIFIED BY 'pw1';
```

The statement is divided into four clauses. The GRANT clause grants the user SELECT and INSERT privileges. As a result, the user can execute SELECT and INSERT statements against the specified database. However, the user does not have any other privileges. After the GRANT clause, the ON clause grants the user privileges to the Parts table in the test database.

The test database is a sample database that is installed by default when you install MySQL. You can use the database to test the installation and practice using the product. Chapter 2 explains how to install MySQL.

The next clause is the TO clause, which identifies the user account to whom privileges are being granted. In this case, the user account ethan is granted privileges from the local computer. This means that the ethan user account can access the Parts table from the local computer. Access is granted to this account from any other computer. In addition, if the ethan user account doesn't already exist, the account is created.

The final clause in the GRANT statement is the IDENTIFIED BY clause. This clause assigns a password to the user account, which, in this case, is *pw1*.

Indeed, DCL statements provide a very different function from DDL and DML statements. In Chapter 14 you learn more about database security and about using DCL languages to manage access to your MySQL databases. However, the next thing this chapter covers is the different ways in which you can execute an SQL statement.

Types of Execution

The SQL:2003 standard defines four methods for executing an SQL statement: direct invocation, module binding, embedded SQL, and call-level interface (CLI). However, not all RDBMS products support all four types of execution. Nearly all RDBMSs support some form of direct invocation, many support embedded SQL statements, few support module binding, and nearly all support the use of CLIs. The primary methods used to execute SQL statements in a MySQL database are direct invocation and CLIs, although limited support exists for embedded SQL. This section provides an overview of all four methods to ensure that you have the full picture of data access and to make sure that you understand how methods for executing SQL statements can differ, regardless of the RDBMS product.

Direct Invocation

Most RDBMS products provide some sort of client application to work interactively with their databases. As a result, you can create ad hoc SQL statements that you can execute at will and receive your results immediately — or as immediately as your hardware, software, and network environments permit. This process — known as *direct invocation* — is often the most expeditious way to create and modify the database structure; control access to data; and view, insert, update, or delete data.

The nature in which SQL statements are executed and the results displayed depends on the client tool supported for a RDBMS. In MySQL, the primary tool available for directly invoking SQL statements is the mysql command-line utility, which you run from the command prompt of the operating system where MySQL is installed. For example, if you run MySQL on Windows Server 2003, you can open a Command Prompt window, change to the \mysql\bin directory, and run the mysql utility, as shown in Figure 1-6. As you can see, mysql has been used to execute a SELECT statement against the Parts table in the Test database. The query results display directly beneath where you enter your statement.

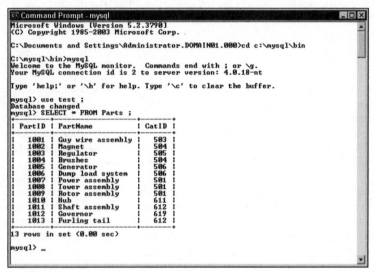

Figure 1-6

You can also run the mysql utility from a command prompt on a remote computer. The client program must be installed on the remote computer and you must provide the necessary parameters when you launch the utility. The mysql tool is discussed in detail in Chapter 3.

The mysql tool is not limited to SELECT statements. You can execute DDL statements such as the CREATE DATABASE statement, DMS statements such as the UPDATE statement, and DCL statements such as the REVOKE statement. However, unlike a SELECT statement, which normally returns rows of data, the other statements return only a message that reports the success of the statement executed.

The statement below demonstrates how the mysql utility works. Suppose you want to create a table named Categories. (You can refer back to Figure 1-3 to view this table.) You can use the mysql utility to execute the following statement:

```
/* Creates the Categories table */
CREATE TABLE Categories
(
    CatID INT NOT NULL,
    CatName VARCHAR(40) NOT NULL,
    Parent INT NOT NULL,
    PRIMARY KEY (CatID)
)
ENGINE=MYISAM;
```

As you can see, the statement creates a table that contains three columns: CatID, CatName, and Parent. The statement also defines a primary key on the CatID column and defines the table as type MYISAM. When you execute the statement, the table is added to the database, and mysql returns the following message:

```
Query OK, 0 rows affected (0.06 sec)
```

From this message, you can see that the statement processed with no problem and that the statement affected no rows, which is expected if you're creating a table. If you were to run a statement such as the INSERT statement, the message would reflect the number of rows inserted into the table or the number of rows affected in some other way, depending on the type of statement. In addition to information about whether the query ran without error and the number of rows affected, the message tells you how long it took to process your query, which in this case is .06 seconds.

The greatest advantage, then, of using the mysql utility is that it allows you to execute and receive immediate responses to your SQL statements. However, directly invoking SQL statements through a client tool such as mysql has another advantage — it avoids a condition known as *impedance mismatch*, which occurs when a data type used in a programming language is not compatible with a data type used in a MySQL database.

Whenever you pass data between an application programming language and a MySQL database, you must ensure that the data type used to define the data in the database is compatible with the data type used to define that same data in the application language. If they are not compatible, an impedance mismatch can occur, resulting in an error in your application or in the loss of data.

> *As you might recall from earlier in the chapter, a data type determines the type of data that can be stored in a table's column. Data types are discussed in greater detail in Chapter 5.*

Accessing a MySQL database interactively avoids the issue of impedance mismatch and provides immediate results to your SQL statements. However, only specific types of users, such as database administrators or programmers, generally use this method. The majority of users access data in a MySQL database through the applications in which they're working. Still, for the purposes of this book, you use the mysql utility to learn how to create database objects and manipulate data. Once you have a better understanding of how MySQL implements SQL, you can create applications that pass SQL statements to MySQL databases.

Module Binding

Few RDBMS vendors have implemented module binding in their products, and MySQL is *not* one of them. As a result, this chapter covers the topic only briefly. The only reason it's covered at all is because it is part of the SQL:2003 standard, and you should have as complete a picture of SQL as possible.

Module binding is a type of statement execution in which modules made up of SQL statements are called from within a host programming language. A module includes properties that define the module itself as well as one or more SQL statements that are invoked when the programming language calls the module. The module is stored as an object separate from the host programming language, so the host language contains calls to the module that invoke the SQL statements within the module.

Embedded SQL

At one time, embedded SQL was one of the most common methods used to access data in a database from within a programming language. As the name suggests, *embedded SQL* refers to SQL statements that are embedded directly within the programming language to allow that language to access and modify data within an SQL database. The SQL:2003 standard defines how SQL statements are to be embedded into a language and recommends which languages a RDBMS should support. According to the standard, the supported languages should include C, COBOL, Fortran, and several others.

Despite the SQL:2003 standard's recommendations, few RDBMSs support all the suggested programming languages. Some products support a few of the languages, while others support languages other than the ones listed in the SQL:2003 standard. Regardless of how extensively a RDBMS supports embedded SQL, most systems support at least a couple of languages, and MySQL AB is no exception. MaxDB, an enterprise-level RDBMS, includes a precompiler that allows you to embed SQL in your C and C++ applications. The precompiler removes the SQL statements from the code and places them in a file separate from the original application file. The precompiler then replaces the statements in the original file with calls to the SQL statements.

In order to embed an SQL statement into a C or C++ application, you must precede each statement with the keywords EXEC SQL and end the statement with a semi-colon. For example, the following embedded SQL statement inserts data into a table named Parts:

```
/* Embed an INSERT INTO statement in the application */
EXEC SQL INSERT INTO Parts
(PartID, PartName, CatID)
VALUES (1014, 'Heater', 505);
```

Notice that you can include comments with your SQL statement. A comment must begin with / and end with */.*

There are, of course, more elements to embedded SQL than those shown here, not only with regard to how you embed the actual statements, but also in terms of the various options that you can use when running the precompiler. However, a more thorough discussion of embedded SQL is beyond the scope of this book. This is due primarily to the fact that embedded SQL is used on a limited basis when developing applications that connect to a MySQL database. The method used most commonly for establishing that connection and executing SQL statements is through one of the APIs that MySQL supports.

Call-Level Interface

When the SQL:2003 standard defines the methods available for accessing data in a database, it includes the call-level interface. A *call-level interface* is essentially an API that allows a programming language to communicate directly with an SQL database. A call-level interface, or API, includes a set of routines that the programming language can call in order to facilitate data access from within that language. The routines access the data as defined within the programming language and return that data to the program, where the host programming language can process it.

MySQL supports a number of APIs that allow applications written in various types of programming languages to communicate with MySQL databases. The following descriptions provide an overview of several of these APIs.

- ❑ **C:** The C API, which is distributed with MySQL, is the main programming interface that allows applications to connect to MySQL. Most of the client applications included in the MySQL distribution are written in C and rely on this API. In addition, the other APIs, except those used for Java applications, are based on the C client library, which defines the C API.

- ❑ **ODBC:** MySQL supports Open Database Connectivity (ODBC) through the MySQL AB product MySQL Connector/ODBC. ODBC is a database connectivity standard that allows different types of applications to connect to different types of databases. ODBC-compliant applications can use MySQL Connector/ODBC to connect to MySQL databases.

- ❑ **JDBC:** MySQL supports Java Database Connectivity (JDBC) through the MySQL AB product MySQL Connector/JDBC. JDBC is a database connectivity standard that allows Java applications to connect to different types of databases. JDBC-compliant applications can use MySQL Connector/ODBC to connect to MySQL databases.

- ❑ **PHP:** The PHP API, which is now included with the PHP preprocessor, allows a PHP script on a Web page to communicate directly with a MySQL database. Database connections and requests for data (through SQL statements) are coded directly in the PHP script.

MySQL supports many more APIs than are listed here. However, these are the four that this book is most concerned with because, by the end of the book, you learn how to connect to a MySQL database from within a PHP application, a JDBC-compliant application, and an ODBC-compliant application. (The ODBC and PHP APIs interface with the C client library, which is why the C API is also included here.) For more information about each of these APIs and the other APIs supported by MySQL, see Appendix B.

As already mentioned, the MySQL APIs are the most common method used for accessing data in MySQL databases. An API allows your application to establish a connection to MySQL and its databases, send SQL statements to the databases, and process the results that the statements return. For this reason, this book includes considerable coverage of database connectivity within PHP, JDBC, and ODBC applications. (See chapters 18, 19, and 20, respectively.) In addition, you are introduced to data-driven applications in more detail later in this chapter, where you see an example of how an application uses an API to access data within a MySQL database.

Implementation-Specific SQL

By now, you should have a good overview of SQL and how to create SQL statements. As you have seen, there are several types of SQL statements (DDL, DML, and DCL). For example, the CREATE TABLE statement is a type of DDL statement. However, not all CREATE TABLE statements are created equally, or any other type of statement for that matter. What this means is that each RDBMS product implements SQL in its own way. Although most of them try to reach at least some conformance to the ANSI standard, many of a statement's details are unique to the product. In other words, a CREATE TABLE statement in MySQL is not quite the same as a CREATE TABLE statement in Oracle. And the CREATE TABLE statements in both products are implemented a little differently from how the SQL:2003 standard defines the statement.

Still, generally a number of similarities exist between statements as they appear in the products and in the SQL standard. The following example takes a close look at the CREATE TABLE statement to help illustrate the differences. Earlier in the chapter you learned the basic table definition syntax. The first three lines of the syntax for the actual statement are as follows:

```
CREATE [TEMPORARY] TABLE [IF NOT EXISTS] <table name>
(<table element> [{, <table element>}...])
[ENGINE = {BDB | MEMORY | ISAM | INNODB | MERGE | MRG_MYISAM | MYISAM}]
```

The opening line (`<table definition>::=`) of the table definition is omitted because it's not important to the discussion here.

The statement syntax provided previously was for the CREATE TABLE statement as it is used in a MySQL database. When creating a table in MySQL, you can create a basic table or a temporary table, and you can create the table whose creation is dependant on whether a table by that name already exists. In addition, you can select the type of table that you want to create, for example, an INNODB table.

The first few lines of the table definition syntax as it appears in the SQL:2003 standard appear below:

```
CREATE [{GLOBAL | LOCAL} TEMPORARY] TABLE <table name>
(<table element> [{, <table element>}...])
[ON COMMIT {PRESERVE|DELETE} ROWS]
```

The basic syntax is the same; however, there are a number of differences in the optional syntax elements. For example, according to the SQL standard, if you create a temporary table, you define it as GLOBAL or LOCAL. In addition, the SQL standard includes no facility for checking whether a table already exists. (There is no set of IF NOT EXISTS keywords.) The options in the third row are also very different between the SQL standard and the statement its use in MySQL. MySQL gives you the ability to define the type of table that you want to create; the SQL standard does not.

Another difference between MySQL and the SQL standard is the ON COMMIT option that the standard supports. In actuality, MySQL supports a similar option, but it isn't covered in this chapter. However, MySQL implements this functionality in a manner different from the standard. For more information about all the options of the CREATE TABLE statement, as MySQL implements is, see Chapter 5.

Now that you've seen how the CREATE TABLE statement can differ between MySQL and the SQL:2003 standard, take a look at yet another version of the statement. The following CREATE TABLE syntax shows the first few lines of the CREATE TABLE syntax as SQL Server 2000 defines it:

```
CREATE TABLE <table name>
(<table element> [{, <table element>}...])
[ON {<filegroup> | DEFAULT}]
```

The first two lines of the statement contain elements that are basically the same as in MySQL and the SQL:2003 standard. However, the third line, which is optional, contains elements that you won't see in MySQL or in the SQL:2003 standard.

In addition, if you were to compare the <table element> definitions for these three syntax examples, you would find a number of differences at this level as well. The point here is that each product implements SQL differently from one another. This can be important if you're writing applications that could be used to access databases in different RDBMS products. In other words, if you're writing an application that uses SQL to access data, you must be sure that you're familiar with how that product implements SQL, which is why SQL statements are covered, as they're implemented in MySQL, in considerable detail.

Data-Driven Applications

The goal for many of you in reading this book is to learn about MySQL so that you can create data-driven applications that can access MySQL databases. For some of you, this may mean installing MySQL, designing and creating databases, populating the databases with data, and administering the MySQL environment. However, many of you may be concerned primarily with how to build applications in a specific programming language that can connect to those databases.

In order to build an effective data-driven application, it's helpful to have a high-level understanding of how these types of applications operate. You've already been introduced to MySQL, relational databases, and SQL, and have been provided an overview of how these components fit together. As you may recall, the MySQL RDBMS provides the structure necessary to support and interact with SQL databases. However, MySQL is only part of the equation in any data-driven application. The application itself must reside within some sort of framework in order to operate and communicate with the database.

A good example of how this structure works is the Web-based application. The application must be called from within the context of a Web server (for example, Apache or Internet Information Services) and must reside in an environment that supports the application's functionality. The next section gives you an example to better illustrate these concepts.

The Application Server

Web-based applications are one of the most widely implemented types of data-driven applications in use today. Nearly every time you access a Web site, you're using an application that in some way interacts with a database. Whether you're shopping online, searching for information, or managing your bank account, you're working with a data-driven application.

Web-based applications based on PHP and MySQL are becoming increasingly popular. PHP is a server-side scripting language that is embedded directly in a Web page. The PHP preprocessor, which includes the MySQL API, processes the PHP script on a Web page on the server and provides Hypertext Markup Language (HTML) output that is then sent to the client computer along with the other HTML elements on the page.

This section outlines an example of a server that is set up to support PHP applications. Figure 1-7 shows how to use PHP, Apache, and Linux together to support a PHP application. At the first layer on any system you're setting up is the operating system, which in this case is Linux; however, this could be any operating system that would support the necessary PHP environment. At the next layer is Apache, a Web server that runs in the Linux environment. Apache supports a variety of Web-based applications, including PHP. The PHP preprocessor runs in conjunction with Apache and includes the PHP MySQL API.

Together, Linux, Apache, and the PHP preprocessor provide the necessary environment to support a PHP application. The application (.php) files are located within the Linux file structure, are hosted within the Apache environment, and are processed through the PHP preprocessor. However, you need one more ingredient to allow the PHP application to communicate with a MySQL database — the PHP MySQL API. The API facilitates the communication with MySQL and its databases, allowing the application to access data within the databases.

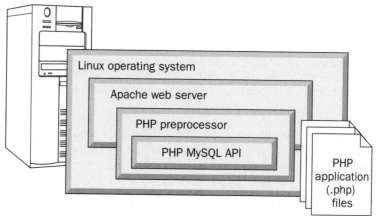

Figure 1-7

Connecting to a MySQL Database

In order to communicate with MySQL, a PHP application must include within its script the elements necessary to establish and maintain a connection with MySQL. You achieve the connection by leveraging the MySQL API, which is based on the C client library in MySQL. When a client computer requests data from a PHP application, the PHP preprocessor executes the PHP code and replaces it with whatever output is produced by executing that code. If code execution includes retrieval from a MySQL database, the data is retrieved and the output is incorporated into the output that the preprocessor produces. The output is rendered as HTML and returned to the client computer requesting the information. If you refer to Figure 1-8, you can get a better idea of how this process works.

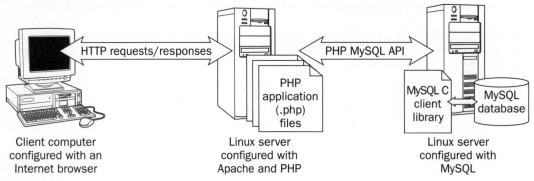

Client computer
configured with an
Internet browser

Linux server
configured with
Apache and PHP

Linux server
configured with
MySQL

Figure 1-8

As the figure indicates, a number of steps are necessary in order to support a PHP data-driven application. The following list takes a closer look at each step so you can better understand how a PHP application retrieves data:

1. A client computer, running a browser such as Netscape, issues a Hypertext Transfer Protocol (HTTP) request to the PHP application on the Apache Web server. (This would be the same thing as entering a URL in the address box of your browser.) When Apache receives the request, it begins to process the requested page.

2. If a requested page has a .php file extension, the PHP preprocessor kicks in and reads the file. The preprocessor treats everything that is not marked as PHP script as literal text. This would include all your HTML tags that are outside the enclosed PHP script.

3. The PHP preprocessor begins executing the PHP script.

4. If data is requested from a MySQL database, PHP uses the MySQL API to connect to MySQL and request data. The API is based the MySQL C client library, which is part of the MySQL installation.

5. MySQL returns the requested data.

6. The PHP preprocessor incorporates the data retrieved from the MySQL database into the script-execution process and outputs all processed scripts into HTML.

7. The Apache Web server responds to the client computer with an HTML page that includes the information that the PHP preprocessor generates.

Of course, other application programming languages and applications environments work a little differently than what is shown here, but this at least provides you with an overview of a data-driven application. However, note that, although the application server and database server are shown as separate computers, this does not necessarily have to be the case. You can install Apache, PHP, and MySQL on the same computers (which is a typical configuration for developers). In fact, you could also install the browser on the same computer.

Creating a Data-Driven Application

Now that you have an overview of how a data-driven application works, take a look at a sample PHP application that connects to a MySQL database. The following application connects to the Parts table in the MySQL Test database and using a SELECT statement to retrieve data from that table.

```
<html>
<head>
<title>The Parts Table</title>
</head>

<body bgcolor="white">

<?php

// Define the variables necessary to access MySQL.
$host="localhost";
$user="ethan";
$pw="pw1";

$db="test";

// Establish a connection to MySQL.
$connection=mysql_connect($host,$user,$pw) or die ("Connection failed!");

// Select the MySQL database.
mysql_select_db($db) or die ("Unable to connect to database.");

// Create an SQL query.
$query="SELECT PartName, PartID FROM Parts ORDER BY PartName";

// Execute the query and store the query results in memory.
$result=mysql_query($query) or die ("Query failed!");

// Process the query results.
if (mysql_num_rows($result) > 0)
{
    echo "<h2>Data from the Parts table<br>in the MySQL Test database<h2>";
    echo "<br>";
    echo "<table cellpadding=10 border=1>";
    echo "<tr bgcolor='#FFCCCC'>
            <td><b>Part Name</b></td>
            <td><b>Part Number</b></td>
        </tr>";
    while($row=mysql_fetch_row($result))
    {
        echo "<tr>";
        echo "<td>" . $row[0] . "</td>";
        echo "<td>" . $row[1] . "</td>";
        echo "</tr>";
    }
    echo "</table>";
}
```

```
else
{
    echo "The Parts table is empty.";
}

// Free the memory used for the query results.
mysql_free_result($result);

// Close the connection to MySQL.
mysql_close($connection);

?>

</body>

</html>
```

You can write the application in any text editor, as long as you save the file to the appropriate directory and with a .php extension. The directory to which you save the file depends on your Web server's configuration.

The PHP application above is a data-driven application at its simplest and is not meant to be anything more than that. It appears here only as way to provide you with a basic understanding of how an application connects to a MySQL database and with a more thorough overview of how a data-driven application works. Chapter 18 discusses PHP in greater detail.

As you can see from the application code above, PHP includes a number of elements that allow the application to connect to the database and retrieve data. Examine the code so you can see how to establish the database connection. The file begins with many of the elements typical of an HTML Web page:

```
<html>
<head>
<title>The Parts Table</title>
</head>

<body bgcolor="white">

<?php
```

As you can see, the <html> tag identifies the page, which is followed by a <head></head> section. Next comes the opening <body> tag, which identifies the page's background color. After these tags come the opening <?php tag, which tells the PHP preprocessor should process the following text, up to the closing PHP tag (?>), as PHP script.

If you're not familiar with HTML, you should spend a little time learning about it before you tackle PHP. There are numerous books on the subject and knowledge of HTML can help you better understand how PHP is implemented on an HTML page.

After the opening PHP tag, you can begin to define the PHP elements of your application. In many cases, you want to use variables within your application. A *variable* is a type of placeholder that holds a value in memory during the execution of the script. Variables are particularly useful for information that's repeated or that's likely to change. They're also a useful way to group similar information together, as shown in the following code:

```
// Define the variables necessary to access MySQL.
$host="localhost";
$user="ethan";
$pw="pw1";
$db="test";
```

This code defines four variables:

❑ **$host:** Identifies the server on which MySQL is installed. If you use "localhost," then it refers to the same server where the PHP application resides.

❑ **$user:** Identifies the MySQL user account. In this case, the user account is ethan. This account must already be set up in MySQL before you can use the application.

❑ **$pw:** Identifies the password for the user account named ethan. In this case, the password is pw1.

❑ **$db:** Identifies the database that contains the information that the application must access. In this case, the database is test (a sample database installed by default when you install MySQL).

Once you define your variables, you can use them in functions that establish a connection to MySQL. A *function* is a set of predefined code that performs a specific task. In addition to defining the variables, the code also includes a comment, which is indicated by the double forward slashes that precede the comments. As with SQL statements, comments are a useful way to explain your code and provide information to other developers or reminders to yourself.

Moving on to the next line of code, which uses the `mysql_connect()` function to assign a value to the `$connection` variable:

```
// Establish a connection to MySQL.
$connection=mysql_connect($host,$user,$pw) or die ("Connection failed!");
```

The `mysql_connect()` function uses three of the variables that you defined in the previous section as its arguments. An *argument* is a value that is passed to a function in order for that function to complete its assigned task. The function uses those variables to carry out the task of connecting to the database. The `$connection` variable can then refer to this connection.

The idea of establishing a connection is important to any data-driven application. Most application languages provide some mechanism for opening a connection to a database server. As you can see in the sample PHP application above, the mechanism used in this case is the `mysql_connect` function, which establishes a connection to MySQL, passes the connection parameters to MySQL, and maintains that connection until it is specifically closed.

Notice that the code also includes an or die condition. This is added in case the requested operation fails. In other words, if the mysql_connect() function fails to establish a connection to MySQL, PHP returns the phrase "Connection failed!" You can use the or die option anywhere an operation should be carried out but could fail. (Using the or die method to handle errors is only one method available for checking for errors in PHP.)

The next line of code uses the mysql_select_db() function to select the database that contains the targeted data:

```
// Select the MySQL database.
mysql_select_db($db) or die ("Unable to connect to database.");
```

The $db variable serves as an argument in the mysql_select_db() function to connect to the Test database. Once you select the database, you can define a query, as shown in the following code:

```
// Create an SQL query.
$query="SELECT PartName, PartID FROM Parts ORDER BY PartName";
```

As you can see, you assign the query to the $query variable. By assigning the query to a variable, you can call that query in your code whenever necessary. The query in this case is a SELECT statement that retrieves data from the Parts table. (The Parts table must include data in order for this statement to return any information.) Once you define the query, you can use the mysql_query() function to execute that query:

```
// Execute the query and store the query results in memory.
$result=mysql_query($query) or die ("Query failed!");
```

The result set (the data returned by the query) that the executed query generates is assigned to the $result variable, which processes the query results, as you can see in the following code:

```
// Process the query results.
if (mysql_num_rows($result) > 0)
{
    echo "<h2>Data from the Parts table<br>in the MySQL Test database<h2>";
    echo "<br>";
    echo "<table cellpadding=10 border=1>";
    echo "<tr bgcolor='#FFCCCC'>
            <td><b>Part Name</b></td>
            <td><b>Part Number</b></td>
        </tr>";
    while($row=mysql_fetch_row($result))
    {
        echo "<tr>";
        echo "<td>" . $row[0] . "</td>";
        echo "<td>" . $row[1] . "</td>";
        echo "</tr>";
    }
    echo "</table>";
}

else
{
    echo "The Parts table is empty.";
}
```

The code uses a loop and the `mysql_fetch_row()` function to process the result set. The results are placed into a table that includes a row for each row in the result set. The loop is based on an if . . . else construction: *if* the results contain rows, a table is created and the data is displayed, or *else* the user receives a message saying that the Parts table is empty.

> *This chapter doesn't go into too much detail about creating a loop in order to process a result set. Chapter 18 explains loops and other elements of PHP in greater detail.*

Once you process the result set, you can use the `mysql_free_result()` function to free up the memory used for the query results:

```
// Free the memory used for the query results.
mysql_free_result($result);
```

Notice that you again use the `$result` variable as an argument in the `mysql_free_result()` function. This allows you to easily clear the memory used for the result set (which could grow quite large in some cases). Once you clear the memory, you can use the `mysql_close()` function and the `$connection` variable to close the connection to MySQL:

```
// Close the connection to MySQL.
mysql_close($connection);
```

The final pieces of the application are the closing tags for PHP (`?>`), the body section (`</body>`), which encloses all the PHP script, and the HTML page (`</html>`):

```
?>

</body>

</html>
```

This completes your PHP application. Despite its simplicity, it demonstrates how you would connect to a MySQL database from within a PHP application. If you create applications in other languages, you find similar constructions for establishing a connection and accessing data. Basically, an application, in order to use an API to connect to a MySQL database, must be able to do the following:

- ❏ Establish a connection to MySQL.
- ❏ Select a database.
- ❏ Define an SQL query.
- ❏ Execute the query and, if necessary, make the results accessible for processing.
- ❏ Process the query results.
- ❏ Free up memory and, when appropriate, close connections.

Now that you've seen the code that makes up a PHP application, take a look at the results you can expect if you implement that application. Figure 1-9 shows how this Web page might look if you access it through a browser. (This example uses Internet Explorer.) As you can see from the figure, the query results display in a table. Because the table contains more rows than can be displayed in the viewable part of the table, you must scroll down to see the rest of the data.

Based on the example provided here, you should now have a better idea of how a data-driven application accesses a MySQL database. At this point, it might be helpful to refer once again to Figure 1-8 and take a look at how the Apache/PHP server implements the PHP application that you just created and how the application uses PHP MySQL API to connect to the MySQL database. As Figure 1-8 illustrates, a number of components make up a data-driven application, including the application files, the preprocessor, the Web server, and the RDBMS, which relies on SQL to provide data access and management. Once you have a good overview on how the pieces fit together, you are better equipped to build applications that can connect to your MySQL database.

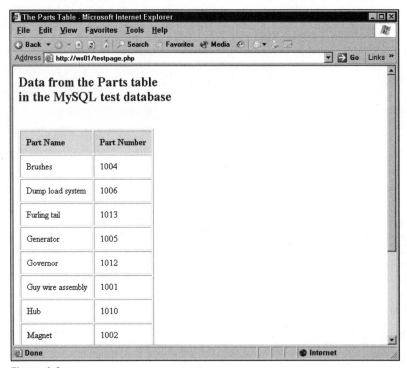

Figure 1-9

Summary

One of this book's main objectives is to provide you with the examples and hands-on experience you need to work with MySQL and create applications that connect to MySQL databases. And certainly in the chapters that follow, you perform a number of exercises that demonstrate the various concepts that the chapters introduce. However, this chapter is a bit of a departure from that approach. Although it provided multiple examples to help illustrate various concepts, this chapter contained no hands-on exercises that allowed you try out these concepts. Instead, this chapter focused primarily on the background information you need in order to move through the subsequent chapters.

The reasoning behind this approach is twofold. First, in order to properly understand MySQL, work with MySQL databases, and build data-driven application, you need the background information necessary to provide a solid foundation for performing actual tasks, whether working directly with MySQL or creating applications that access MySQL databases. Without the necessary foundation, you may not thoroughly understand many concepts, making it more difficult to apply what you learn here to other situations

Another reason that this chapter focused on providing you with the background information, rather the delving immediately into hands-on exercises, is because perhaps the most effective way to learn about a technology is to be presented with information in a logical order. For example, it would be counterintuitive to provide you with an in-depth discussion about modifying data without first discussing how to create the tables that hold the data. Likewise, discussing how to create tables before walking you through the installation process and getting you started using MySQL is illogical. (The CREATE TABLE statement that you saw in this chapter was provided only as a method to explain how to work with SQL syntax.) For these reasons, this chapter provided you with a solid introduction to the essentials of relational databases, SQL, and data-driven applications, which includes the following concepts:

❑   A comprehensive overview of databases, relational databases, and RDBMSs, including the MySQL RDBMS

❑   An understanding of the differences between hierarchical, network, and relational databases

❑   A foundation in SQL, including its history and characteristics, and in how SQL is implemented in MySQL

❑   An overview of how to work with SQL statement syntax and how to create an SQL statement based on that syntax

❑   An understanding of the different types of SQL statements (DDL, DML, and DCL) and the different methods used to execute those statements

❑   An overview of the components that make up a data-driven application

❑   A basic knowledge of how a PHP application connects to a MySQL database to retrieve and process data

With a strong background in each of these areas, you are ready to move on to the rest of the book. In the next chapter, you learn how to install MySQL, and from there, you learn how to use the tools that MySQL provides. Once you install MySQL and understand how to work within the MySQL environment, you can create databases, manage data, and access data from your applications.

Exercises

The following exercises help you build on the information you learned in this chapter. Although this chapter only introduced you to how to create SQL statements and PHP applications, you should still have enough information to respond to the exercises. To view the answers, see Appendix A.

1. Explain the differences between hierarchical, network, and relational databases.

2. Create a two-column table named Employees. Title the first column EmpID, base it on the INT data type, and do not permit null values. Title the second column EmpName, base it on the VARCHAR(40) data type, and also do not permit null values. The table includes a primary key based on the EmpID column, and the table type is MYISAM. How should you define your SQL statement to create the table?

3. Creating a PHP application in which you define the following parameters:

```
$host="localhost";
$user="linda";
$pw="password1";
```

You plan to use the mysql_connect() function to establish a connection to MySQL. You also plan to use the mysql_connect() function to assign a value to the $connection variable. In addition, you want to ensure that if the connection fails users receive a message that reads, "Connection failed!" How should you write the PHP code?

Installing MySQL

Regardless of how you plan to use MySQL — whether to access data from within a data-driven application or to build databases that support data-driven applications — there will no doubt come a time when you want to install MySQL yourself. You might choose to do this in order to develop and test your own applications, or you might be the one in your organization responsible for implementing MySQL in a production environment. And it certainly wouldn't be unheard of if you found yourself having to do both.

Fortunately for everyone, MySQL is a relatively easy application to install, and it can be installed on a number of platforms. For example, you can install MySQL on a computer running FreeBSD or on an Apple computer running Mac OS X. The possibilities are numerous. This chapter, though, focuses only on how to install MySQL on computers running Linux or Windows, although much of what you learn can translate to other operating systems.

It should take you little preparation to install MySQL on Linux or Windows. To do so, you must make several preliminary decisions on exactly what you want to install, and then you must download the necessary files. From there, you can install MySQL on your selected platform, which is explained later in this chapter. Specifically, this chapter covers the following topics:

❑   What steps you must take before installing MySQL. This includes making preliminary decisions about the MySQL version, platform, distribution type, and edition.

❑   Step-by-step instructions on how to install MySQL on Linux and Windows. The instructions also include details about how to start the MySQL server in both environments.

❑   How to test your Linux and Windows installations and verify that the mysql administrative database has been properly initialized.

Getting Started

Two of the features that make MySQL such a valuable relational database management system (RDBMS) are its ability to be implemented on multiple platforms and its different versions, editions, and distribution types. Before you can actually install MySQL, you must make several preliminary decisions about the installation, and then, based on these decisions, you must download the appropriate distribution files.

Making the Preliminary Decisions

From its inception, MySQL AB has aimed to provide an RDBMS that users can implement in different ways and on different platforms. As a result, whenever you're preparing to install MySQL, you must first decide which version to install, on which platform to install it, which distribution type to select, and which edition to use.

Selecting a Version of MySQL

MySQL is a constantly evolving RDBMS. You can download the latest stable release of the product, or you can download a version that is in some stage of development. As a result, your choice of versions depends, in part, on weighing the need for stability against the need for features that might be available only in a version currently in development.

Each version of MySQL available for download is released in one of the following stages:

❑ **Alpha:** A version of MySQL in this stage has not been fully tested. In addition, major code changes could still occur, and major new features could be added.

❑ **Beta:** This is the next stage after alpha. At the beta stage, all code has been tested and no major new features will be added. A version of MySQL in the beta stage is considered fairly stable.

❑ **Gamma:** Once a version of MySQL has been in the beta stage for a while and the product appears to be stable and operating without significant problems, it is promoted to the gamma stage. At this point, only minor fixes are applied to the product.

❑ **Production:** This version of the product is considered very stable. It has been running at different sites with no significant problems. At this stage, only critical bug fixes are applied.

All releases, regardless of which stage they are in, are thoroughly tested to ensure that they're safe to use. Unless there are features that you specifically need to implement that are available only in a nonproduction release, your best bet is to go with the latest production release available to ensure that you have the most stable product.

Selecting a Platform to Run MySQL

Once you determine which version of MySQL that you want to install, you must then decide on the platform on which to run MySQL. For many of you, the platform is decided by default (it's the only type of computer that you have to work on), and you're simply looking for the appropriate copy of MySQL to run on your existing computer. Some of you, however, can select the platform; in that case, you have a number of options from which to choose.

You can install MySQL on a variety of operating systems and computer architectures. The following list provides you with some of the options available for running MySQL:

❑ **Linux:** You can run MySQL on different versions of Linux running on multiple types of computer architectures, including x86, S/390, IA64, Alpha, PPC, and AMD64.

❑ **Windows:** You can run MySQL on different versions of Windows (including Windows 95, Windows 98, Windows ME, Windows NT, Windows 2000, Windows XP, and Windows 2003) on x86 computers.

❑ **Solaris:** You can run MySQL on Solaris 8 and 9 on multiple types of computer architectures, including 32-bit SPARC, 64-bit SPARC, and 32-bit x86.

❑ **FreeBSD:** You can run MySQL on FreeBSD on multiple types of computer architectures, including x86 and LinuxThreads.

❑ **Mac OS X:** You can run MySQL on Mac OS X 10.2 and 10.3.

The platforms listed here do not represent a complete list but merely provide an overview of the options available to you. Keep in mind, however, that the exact platforms supported (in terms of operating systems and computer architectures) can vary from version to version of MySQL, so be sure to review the MySQL Web site (www.mysql.com) for platform-specific information about the specific version of MySQL that you want to install.

You should note, however, that although supported platforms change, the core platforms remain the same.

In general, you can install MySQL on most Unix-like operating systems. MySQL tends to run more efficiently on some operating systems than others. According to the MySQL product documentation (which you can view on the Web site), MySQL is developed primary on the SuSE and Red Hat versions of Linux, FreeBSD, and Sun Solaris 8 and 9, and not surprisingly, these platforms have proven to be some of the best platforms on which to run Linux.

In the end, your choice of platforms might be somewhat limited because of the environment in which you work or because you simply do not want to mess with upgrading and changing platforms until you spend time working with MySQL. For the purposes of simply learning how to use MySQL and how to develop MySQL applications that connect to MySQL databases, the choice of platforms is not as critical at this time, although it could become a critical factor in the future. In any case, be sure always to check the most current platform-related information available on the MySQL Web site whenever you're preparing to implement MySQL.

Selecting a MySQL Distribution Type

Once you determine which version of MySQL to install and on which platform to install it, you must select the distribution type to use for your installation. The *distribution type* refers to the format in which MySQL is available for download and installation. MySQL supports two distribution types:

❑ **Binaries:** Binaries are installation packages comprising precompiled files that allow you to install MySQL without having to work with or manipulate the source code. Binaries are provided for a number of operating systems (such as Linux, Solaris, and FreeBSD) and are packaged in compressed tar archive files. A *tar* file is a type of archive that stores files. For some platforms, the binary files are available in native format. For example, MySQL AB supplies RPM Package Manager (RPM) files for Linux installations, .dmg package installers for Mac OS X installations, and zipped files for Windows installations.

❑ **Source code:** As the name suggests, the source code distribution type refers to those files that contain the source code for MySQL. The code has not been compiled, so it is up to you to compile it prior to installation. The files that hold the source code come in three formats: compressed archive files for Unix-like machines, RPM files for Linux, and zipped files for Windows.

MySQL AB recommends that you use binary files for your installation, if they exist for your platform. They're generally easier to use than working directly with the source code, and they're an excellent way for beginning MySQL users to get acquainted with MySQL and the installation process. If an RPM binary file and a tar binary file are available for a Linux installation, you're usually better off using the RPM file because it makes MySQL installation much easier.

Some circumstances may arise in which you prefer using the source code. For example, you might want to configure MySQL with extra features or remove features that are inherent in MySQL. Or perhaps a MySQL binary isn't available for the platform you're using. Or maybe you simply prefer the control that compiling your own code provides. Whatever your reason, using a source code distribution is a viable alternative, but if using the source code isn't necessary, you should, at least at first, use binary files for your installation.

A discussion of using source code to install MySQL is beyond the scope of this book. If you want to learn more about working directly with the source code, be sure to visit the MySQL Web site at www.mysql.com.

Selecting an Edition of MySQL

In addition to determining the distribution type, you must determine which edition of MySQL you plan to install. MySQL AB provides binary files for the following editions of MySQL:

❑ **Standard:** This is the basic edition of MySQL and the edition that you're most likely to install. It includes all the fully tested functionality available in MySQL.

❑ **Max:** The Max edition includes all the features available in the Standard edition plus features that most users do not require or that have not been fully tested. In addition, the Max edition includes the Berkeley DB storage engine.

❑ **Debug:** The Debug binaries are compiled with additional debug data, which means that they can affect performance. These binaries are not intended for use in a production environment.

Binary files for the Debug edition for Linux are not available as RPM files or zipped Windows files. In addition, if you use RPM files to install MySQL-Max on Linux, you must first install the Standard RPM and then install the Max RPM. Also, the zipped Windows file includes all editions in one file. After you install MySQL, you determine which edition to use.

For most users, including beginning MySQL users, the Standard edition provides you with all the features that you need to learn about MySQL and to create applications that connect to MySQL.

Downloading Distribution Files

Once you determine which version of MySQL to install, on which platform to install it, which distribution type to select, and which edition to use, you're ready to download the necessary files. To download the files, follow these steps:

1. Go to http://dev.mysql.com/downloads.

2. Click the link to the version of the MySQL database server and clients that you want to install.

3. From the list of files, locate the applicable platform, distribution type, and edition.

4. Click the Pick a mirror link for the file you want to download, and then select a mirror. (A *mirror* is a Web site that hosts the files that are available for download. MySQL downloads are normally available at numerous mirror sites.)

5. Download the file.

For most distribution types, you need to download only one file. For Linux RPM files, you must download a file for each component of MySQL that you want to install. At the very least, you should download the server RPM file and the client program's RPM file. Later in this chapter you learn more about installing MySQL from RPM files.

When you're downloading files from the MySQL Web site, notice that the files follow a specific naming convention. For the basic binary files, the files use the following format:

```
mysql-<edition>-<version>-<platform>.tar.gz
```

For example, the following filename identifies the distribution file for the Max edition of MySQL version 4.1.5-gamma:

```
mysql-max-4.1.5-gamma-pc-linux-i686.tar.gz
```

In this case, the platform is Linux running on an x86 computer. If you were going to download the RPM file for the same platform (as well as edition and version), the filename would be as follows:

```
MySQL-Max-4.1.5-0.i386.rpm
```

Although the RPM file indicates that this is the Max edition, because it is an RPM file, Max refers only to the Max upgrade for the server component of MySQL. If this were for the Standard version of the server, the name of the file would be as follows:

```
MySQL-server-4.1.5-0.i386.rpm
```

Windows installation files follow a slightly different convention than Linux installation files. If you want to use the Microsoft Windows Installer to install the full MySQL program, you would use a file similar to the following:

```
mysql-4.1.5-gamma-win.zip
```

The necessary setup file is compressed in a zip file and installs MySQL 4.1.5-gamma. If you want to install a more basic MySQL package, you can use the following file:

```
mysql-4.1.5-gamma-essential-win.zip
```

Notice that this is a Windows Installer (.msi) file and that it includes the word "essential" in the filename, indicating that this is the file to use to install the MySQL Essential package, a package that is similar to the regular version, except that it includes fewer features. In most cases, though, the Essential package provides all the necessary functionality you need to get started using MySQL, and it is the package that MySQL recommends for your basic installation. The examples shown in this book are based on the Essential package.

From the filenames, you should be able to determine all the information you need about which file you downloaded. This is handy in case you download multiple versions, editions, or distribution types and need to be able to easily distinguish among them. Once you've downloaded the files that you need, you're ready to install MySQL.

MySQL recommends that, when you download a file, you verify the integrity of that file. They suggest that you use the MD5 checksums and GnuPG signatures to verify file integrity. For more information about how to verify files, go to www.mysql.com.

Installing MySQL

As explained, you can install MySQL on a variety of platforms; however, it isn't possible to discuss the installation process for every one of these platforms. As a result, this section focuses on the following three scenarios:

❑ Using RPM files to install MySQL on Linux

❑ Using a tar file to install MySQL on Linux

❑ Using a zipped file to install MySQL on Windows

You have several reasons for choosing Linux and Windows. First, Linux, like MySQL, is an open-source application, which means that you can implement MySQL in a completely open-source environment and take advantage of the flexibility and cost savings that this provides. In addition, MySQL was developed primarily on Linux, which means that the Linux version of MySQL is the most tested and widely implemented version. In addition, Linux is similar to other Unix-like operating systems, so installation and configuration are similar among products.

To round out the choice of Linux, this section also describes how to install MySQL on Windows. The advantage of installing MySQL on Windows is that Windows has a wide user base, which has translated to an increasing number of users implementing MySQL on Windows. Knowing how to install MySQL on Windows is steadily becoming a more important consideration when implementing databases and data-driven applications.

For both Linux and Windows, you're running the Standard edition of MySQL on an x86 computer. Consequently, if you plan to follow the installation steps in this chapter, you must download the appropriate file or files for your specific platform. For example, if you're using RPM files to install MySQL on Linux, you should download the following two files, along with any additional files you want to include:

```
MySQL-server-<version>.i386.rpm
MySQL-client-<version>.i386.rpm
```

The `<version>` placeholder refers to the version number and, if applicable, the release cycle, such as alpha, beta, or gamma. If you plan to use a tar file to install MySQL on Linux, you must download the following file:

```
mysql-standard-<version>-pc-linux-i686.tar.gz
```

Finally, for those of you who want to install MySQL on Windows, you must download the following file:

```
mysql-<version>-win.zip
```

Notice that, although the platforms (Linux and Windows on an x86 computer), the edition (Standard), and the distribution types (RPM, tar, and zipped files) are selected, only placeholders designate the version. This is because you should download the most current production version of MySQL. The installation process for various versions of 4.0 and 4.1 is consistent across versions.

> *The exercises and examples in this book employ the latest version of MySQL 4.1. You may find that most of the code samples work in version 4.0 as well.*

If you're unable to implement MySQL on one of the two platforms described here, you can try to install MySQL from one of the binary files provided for other platforms. You should find the installation process on any Unix-like system to be similar to using tar files to install MySQL on Linux.

Once you download the necessary installation file or files, you can go to the appropriate section in this chapter for details about installing MySQL on Linux or Windows.

Using RPM Files to Install MySQL on Linux

Of all the methods available for installing MySQL, using RPM files is by far the easiest. Basically, you need to copy the files to a directory on your computer and then unpack the files. The following steps explain how to copy and unpack the files:

1. Log on to Linux as the root user. If you're logged on as another user, type the following command at the command prompt and press Enter to execute the command:

```
su - root
```

The su command, which stands for *substitute user,* allows you to run Linux commands as the specified user.

2. The next step is to copy the RPM files to the /tmp directory or whichever directory you want to use. For the purposes of explaining the installation process, this chapter assumes that you're using the /tmp directory. If you're using another directory, simply replace /tmp with that directory path whenever the instructions reference /tmp. Before you actually copy the files, you might have to mount the drive where they are located, as could be the case with a CD-ROM drive. For example, if you plan to copy the files from a CD, insert the CD into the drive, type the following command, and then press Enter:

```
mount /mnt/cdrom
```

The mount command mounts the CD-ROM drive. You can then access the drive in the same way you would a directory.

3. Now you can copy the RPM file for MySQL server to the /tmp directory. For example, if the file is located in the Linux folder on the CD that you just mounted, you would use the following command:

```
cp /mnt/cdrom/linux/mysql-server-<version>.i386.rpm /tmp
```

The cp command allows you to copy files from one directory to another. Executing the command shown here copies the specified file to the /tmp directory.

When you use this method to copy a file from a CD to a Linux directory, the file is saved exactly as the cp command specifies. For example, if the filename on the CD uses uppercase, as in MySQL, the capitalization is lost if the filename in the cp command is all lowercase. This is important when working in a Linux environment because Linux is case sensitive; you must use the exact case when working with Linux directories and files. As a result, you should stay aware of how you save files to a Linux directory. This book uses all lowercase here to make it easier to work with the files later.

4. Your next step is to copy the RPM file for the MySQL client utilities to the /tmp directory:

```
cp /mnt/cdrom/linux/mysql-client-<version>.i386.rpm /tmp
```

As you can see, the only difference between this command and the previous command is that server replaces client.

5. After you copy the files to the /tmp directory, you might have to unmount your drive. Again, using the example of the CD-ROM drive, you would unmount the drive by using the following command:

```
umount /mnt/cdrom
```

Once you unmount the drive, you can remove the CD.

6. Now that you have copied the necessary RPM files to the /tmp directory, you're ready to install MySQL. The next step, then, is to change to the /tmp directory (or to the directory where you copied the files):

```
cd /tmp
```

The cd command, which stands for *change directory*, moves you to the directory that you specify, and your command prompt should reflect your directory change.

7. Before you actually run the installation, it's a good idea to make sure that the RPM files were copied to the directory correctly by entering the following command:

```
ls
```

The ls command allows you to view the contents of the active directory. When you run this command, you should see the two RPM files that you copied over.

8. Once you confirm the presence of the RPM files, you're ready to install the server and client utilities. Begin with the server. Enter the following command at the command prompt and press Enter:

```
rpm -i mysql-server-<version>.i386.rpm
```

The rpm utility allows you to work with RPM package files. The -i switch indicates that you want to install the specified package. When you execute this command, a number of events occur:

❑ The mysql user account and mysql group account are created in Linux.

❑ The MySQL files are extracted from the RPM package and copied to their appropriate directories.

❑ The mysql administrative database initializes.

❑ Ownership of MySQL-related directories and files is altered.

❑ The MySQL server starts.

❑ The MySQL server is set up to start automatically when you start up Linux.

You can get a glimpse of what's happening with the RPM extraction process in the command window as it is printing out. Figure 2-1 gives you an idea of what you might expect to see as you are installing MySQL. After the installation is complete, you're returned to the command prompt.

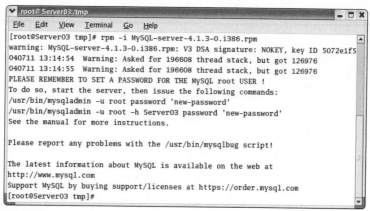

Figure 2-1

9.   Once the server is installed, you're ready to install the client utilities:

```
rpm -i mysql-client-<version>.i386.rpm
```

The command installs the client utilities on your system.

At this point, the MySQL server and client utilities are installed. You're ready to test your installation. (See the "Testing Your MySQL Installation" section later in the chapter.)

Using a Tar File to Install MySQL on Linux

As you did with RPM files, you can use a tar file to install MySQL on Linux. The process, though, is not nearly as simple as it is with the RPM approach. Still, you might find that you're working on a version of Linux that doesn't support RPM installations or that you want to have more control over the installation process.

To use a tar file to install MySQL, you need to follow five specific steps:

1.   Create a logon account and a group account.
2.   Copy the tar files to your computer.
3.   Unpack the distribution file.
4.   Initialize the installation.
5.   Start the MySQL server.

Each of these steps is described in detail in the text that follows. They're broken down into subsections so you're clear on the purpose of each task.

Creating the User and Group Accounts

The first step that you need to take in preparing for a tar-based installation is to create the necessary Linux user and group accounts. For the purposes of this book, create a user account named mysql and a group account named mysql. You could use different names for the account; however, because the RPM installation creates accounts with these names, this book uses the same names as well, just to be consistent and to avoid confusion later in the book. To create the two Linux accounts, follow these steps:

1. Log on to Linux as the root user. If you're logged on as another user, type the following command at the command prompt and press Enter to execute the command:

```
su - root
```

The su command, which stands for *substitute user,* allows you to run Linux commands as a substitute user, which in this case is the root user.

2. The next step is to create the group account:

```
groupadd mysql
```

The groupadd utility creates a group account that uses the specified name, which in this case is mysql.

3. Next, you must create the user account:

```
useradd -g mysql mysql
```

The useradd utility creates a user named mysql in a group named mysql. The -g switch indicates that the new user account should be added to the group account that follows the switch.

That's all there is to creating the necessary accounts. You can now move on to the next phase of the installation process.

Copying the Tar File

The next step in the MySQL installation process is to copy the tar file to the /usr/local directory or whichever directory you want to use. If you downloaded the file from the MySQL Web site into a directory on your computer, you can copy the file from the location where you copied it to the target directory. For the purposes of explaining the installation process, this book assumes that you're using the /usr/local directory. If you're using another directory, simply replace /usr/local with that directory path whenever instructions reference /usr/local.

The following steps explain how to copy the tar file:

1. Before you actually copy the file, you might have to mount the drive where the file is located, as could be the case with a CD-ROM drive. For example, if you plan to copy the files from a CD, insert the CD into the drive, type the following command, and then press Enter:

```
mount /mnt/cdrom
```

The mount command mounts the CD-ROM drive. You can then access the drive in the same way you would a directory.

2. Now you can copy the tar file to the /usr/local directory. For example, if the file is located in the Linux folder on the CD that you just mounted, you would use the following command:

```
cp /mnt/cdrom/linux/mysql-standard-<version>-pc-linux-i686.tar.gz /usr/local
```

The cp command allows you to copy files from one directory to another. When you execute the command shown here, the specified file is copied to the /usr/local directory.

When you use this method to copy a file from a CD to a Linux directory, the file is saved exactly as it is specified in the cp command. For example, if the filename on the CD uses uppercase, as in MySQL, the capitalization is lost if the filename in the cp command is all lowercase. This is important when working in a Linux environment because Linux is case sensitive; you must use the exact case when working with Linux directories and files. As a result, you should stay aware of how you save files to a Linux directory. These instructions use all lowercase here to make it easier to work with the files later.

3. After copying the file to the /usr/local directory, you might have to unmount your drive. Again, using the example of the CD-ROM drive, you would unmount the drive by using the following command:

```
umount /mnt/cdrom
```

Once you've unmounted the drive, you can remove the CD.

Once the file has been copied, you're ready to unpack the tar file.

Unpacking the Distribution File

Now that the necessary tar file is copied to the /usr/local directory, you're about ready to install MySQL. To do that, you must unpack the tar archive file. Before you unpack the file, you should change to the directory where the file is located and view the contents of that directory to be sure that the file was properly copied. Then you can extract the MySQL files, as shown in the following steps:

1. Execute the following command:

```
cd /usr/local
```

The cd command, which stands for *change directory*, moves you to the directory that you specify. Your command prompt should now reflect your directory change.

2. Before you actually run the installation, it's a good idea make sure that the file was copied over by entering the following command:

```
ls
```

The ls command allows you to view the contents of the active directory. When you run this command, you should see the tar file that you copied over.

3. Once you confirm the presence of the tar file, you're ready to install MySQL. Type the following command in the command prompt and press Enter:

```
tar xzvf mysql-standard-<version>-pc-linux-i686.tar.gz
```

The tar utility is an archiving program that allows you to store and extract files. The x switch indicates that files should be extracted from an archive. The z switch indicates the archive should be filtered through gzip, which is a file compression utility. The v switch indicates that files should be listed as they're being extracted, and the f switch specifies the use of an archive file. The name of the archive file is then specified. Figure 2-2 gives you an idea of what you might expect to see when you run the tar utility against this file.

After the extraction process completes, you're returned to the command prompt.

```
root@Server03:/usr/local                                          _ □ ✕
File   Edit   View   Terminal   Go   Help
mysql-standard-4.1.3-beta-pc-linux-i686/man/man1/mysql_fix_privilege_tables.1  ▲
mysql-standard-4.1.3-beta-pc-linux-i686/man/man1/mysql_zap.1
mysql-standard-4.1.3-beta-pc-linux-i686/man/man1/mysqlaccess.1
mysql-standard-4.1.3-beta-pc-linux-i686/man/man1/mysqladmin.1
mysql-standard-4.1.3-beta-pc-linux-i686/man/man1/mysqld.1
mysql-standard-4.1.3-beta-pc-linux-i686/man/man1/mysqld_multi.1
mysql-standard-4.1.3-beta-pc-linux-i686/man/man1/mysqld_safe.1
mysql-standard-4.1.3-beta-pc-linux-i686/man/man1/mysqldump.1
mysql-standard-4.1.3-beta-pc-linux-i686/man/man1/mysqlshow.1
mysql-standard-4.1.3-beta-pc-linux-i686/man/man1/perror.1
mysql-standard-4.1.3-beta-pc-linux-i686/man/man1/replace.1
mysql-standard-4.1.3-beta-pc-linux-i686/data/
mysql-standard-4.1.3-beta-pc-linux-i686/data/mysql/
mysql-standard-4.1.3-beta-pc-linux-i686/data/test/
mysql-standard-4.1.3-beta-pc-linux-i686/COPYING
mysql-standard-4.1.3-beta-pc-linux-i686/README
mysql-standard-4.1.3-beta-pc-linux-i686/INSTALL-BINARY
mysql-standard-4.1.3-beta-pc-linux-i686/configure
[root@Server03 local]#                                                         ▼
```

Figure 2-2

4. When you use the tar utility to extract a file, a directory is created in the current directory where you're located. The directory shares the same name as the version of the product that you're installing. For example, a directory named /usr/local/mysql-standard-<version>-pc-linux-i686 should have been created when you ran the tar utility in the previous step. As you can see, referring to this directory by name can translate to a lot of typing (and most likely a lot of errors). The way around this is to assign an alias to that directory, as shown in the following step:

```
ln -s mysql-standard-<version>-pc-linux-i686 mysql
```

The ln command-line utility creates a link to the specified directory. The -s switch specifies that this is a symbolic link rather than a hard link. You specify the name of the link (mysql) after the actual directory name. Once you run this command, you can refer to the directory as /usr/local/mysql.

5. As one final check in this process, you can view the contents of the /usr/local/ directory to see for yourself the directory that has been created.

```
ls -al
```

The -al switch indicates that the ls utility should list all directory content in a long format. You should see a directory named mysql-standard-<version>-pc-linux-i686 and one named mysql. The mysql directory should contain a pointer (->) to the mysql-standard-<version>-pc-linux-i686 directory.

Once you verify the contents of the /usr/local directory, you're ready to move on to the next step.

Initializing the Installation

After extracting the files from the tar package, you must initialize the mysql database that is created as part of the installation process. The MySQL files that you just extracted include a script named mysql_install_db, which is included in the /usr/local/mysql/scripts directory. After you run the script, you must change ownership of a couple of directories to complete the MySQL installation.

The following steps allow you to initiate your MySQL installation:

1. First, change into the new directory that you created (/usr/local/mysql) using the following command:

```
cd mysql
```

Your command prompt should reflect that you're in the mysql directory

2. Next, you must run the mysql_install_db script by executing the following command:

```
scripts/mysql_install_db --user=mysql
```

The script works behind the scenes, and you don't need to do anything but wait. Once it completes, you're returned to the command prompt.

3. The next step is to change ownership of the current directory and its subdirectories to the root user:

```
chown -R root .
```

The chown utility allows you to change the ownership of a particular file or directory. The -R switch specifies a *recursive* change, which means that it affects any subdirectories and files in that directory. The period indicates that the change applies to the current directory (mysql).

4. Next, you must change the ownership of the data directory to the mysql user account that you created earlier:

```
chown -R mysql data
```

This time, the chown command references a specific directory rather than using a period. As a result, the change applies only to the data directory and the files and directories that it contains. (The data directory contains the actual database files.)

5. Finally, you must change the group ownership of the mysql directory to the mysql group:

```
chgrp -R mysql .
```

The chgrp utility, like the chown utility, changes the ownership of a file or directory, except that it applies to a group, not a user. In this case, it grants the mysql group ownership on the current directory (mysql).

This completes the MySQL installation process. Before you can start working with the MySQL server, however, you must start the server.

Starting the MySQL Server

MySQL supports two methods for starting the MySQL server: starting the server manually and starting the server automatically. In either case, you must launch the mysqld program (or some version of that program) from a command prompt or through a script. The mysqld program is the MySQL server that that supports data storage and management and allows you to access the databases and their data.

Starting the Server Manually

When you first install MySQL, you probably want to try it out. Before you can do that, you must start the server, which is actually a very straightforward process. To start MySQL server, take the following steps:

1. The following command launches the `mysqld` program in safe mode. If you're already in the `/usr/local/mysql` directory, you do not need to enter that part of the path. Type the following command and press Enter:

```
/usr/local/mysql/bin/mysqld_safe --user=mysql &
```

Starting `mysqld` in safe mode adds safety features such as logging errors and restarting the server if necessary. Normally, using safe mode is the recommended way to start the MySQL server. The `--user=mysql` option instructs MySQL to run under the mysql user account. The ampersand (&) at the end of the command is specific to Linux and indicates that the `mysqld_safe` script should run as a process in the background to support the script's monitoring capabilities.

2. If, after you execute the `mysqld_safe` command, you're not returned to the command prompt right away, press Enter to display the prompt.

That's all there is to starting the server. There might be times when you want to stop the server after you've started it. To stop the MySQL server, execute the following command:

```
/usr/local/mysql/bin/mysqladmin shutdown
```

This command uses the `mysqladmin` utility, along with the `shutdown` option, to stop the server. Once the server is stopped, you can simply use the `mysqld_safe` command to start it back up again.

Starting the Server Automatically

Although it's useful to know how to start and stop the MySQL server manually, you may find that, in most cases, you want the server to start automatically when you start up Linux. To do this, you must copy the `mysql.server` script to the proper directory, which, in this case, is `/etc/init.d`. The `mysql.server` script, located in `/usr/local/mysql/support-files`, provides the necessary commands to start MySQL automatically.

To set up the MySQL server to start automatically, you must take the following steps:

1. First, copy the `mysql.server` script to the appropriate directory. As you're copying the script, assign it the name mysql, as shown in the following command:

```
cp /usr/local/mysql/support-files/mysql.server /etc/init.d/mysql
```

The command uses the `cp` utility to copy the `mysql-server` script to the `/etc/init.d` directory. At the same time, the name `mysql` is assigned to the script.

2. Change the permissions for the `mysql` script:

```
chmod +x /etc/init.d/mysql
```

The command uses the `chmod` utility to change the permissions of the specified file. The `+x` switch indicates that execute permission will be added to the file.

3. You must next activate the script. In Linux, to activate a script, use the following command:

```
chkconfig --add mysql
```

The chkconfig utility allows you to maintain configuration information. By using the utility with the --add mysql option, you're ensuring that the mysql service has a start entry in every run level. (For more information about startup scripts and the chkconfig utility, see the Linux documentation.)

Once you set up the mysql service to run automatically and start the MySQL server, you're ready to test your installation. (See the "Testing Your MySQL Installation" section later in the chapter.)

Installing MySQL on Windows

The process for installing MySQL on Windows is relatively simple. Basically, you run the installation program and then run the MySQL Server Instance Configuration Wizard. You should find that, for the most part, the MySQL installation process is the same from one Windows operating system to the next. In addition, MySQL should operate in a fairly similar manner on the different systems. If you're running MySQL on Windows NT, Windows 2000, Windows XP, or Windows Server 2003, you can run the MySQL server as a service. These four operating systems also support named pipe and TCP/IP connections. In contrast to this, Windows 95, Windows 98, and Windows Me do not allow you to run MySQL as a service, and they do not support named pipe connections, only TCP/IP connections.

The process for installing MySQL on Windows XP and Windows Server 2003 is the same for both operating systems. Basic installation should be consistent on most Windows operating systems, although you might discover minor differences. Be sure to check out the MySQL product documentation for more information about installing MySQL on different versions of Windows.

Running the Installation Program

The installation process is essentially the same whether you install MySQL from a .zip file or a .msi file. The only difference is in how you begin the installation process. Once you start that process, the steps are the same. For the purposes of this book, the .msi file is used to install an Essential MySQL package. The steps that follow also apply to installing MySQL from a .zip file. The following steps describe how to install MySQL on Windows:

1. Log on to the Windows computer with an account that has administrative privileges.

2. Open Windows Explorer, and locate the .zip file or .msi file that you downloaded from the MySQL Web site. To open Windows Explorer, right-click the Start button, and click Explore.

   If you're installing MySQL from a .zip file, you must extract the Setup.exe file from the .zip file. In Windows Server 2003 and Windows XP, you can extract the Setup.exe file simply by double-clicking the .zip file. A Windows Explorer window then opens and displays the Setup.exe file. From there, double-click the Setup.exe file to start the MySQL installation process. When the installation process begins, a MySQL Setup message book temporarily appears, indicating that the installation files are being extracted. Then a Windows Installer message box appears temporarily, indicating that your system is preparing to install MySQL.

   If you have an extraction utility such as WinZip installed on your system, you can use that to extract the files. If you're uncertain how to use the utility, check the utility's product documentation for details.

   If you're installing MySQL from a .msi file, double-click the file to start the MySQL installation process. When the installation process begins, a Windows Installer message box appears temporarily, indicating that your system is preparing to install MySQL.

Once any messages boxes have cleared, the first screen of the Setup Wizard appears, as shown in Figure 2-3.

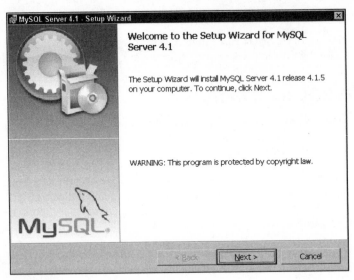

Figure 2-3

3. Click Next. The Setup Type screen appears (shown in Figure 2-4) and provides you with several options that describe the types of setups that you can perform.

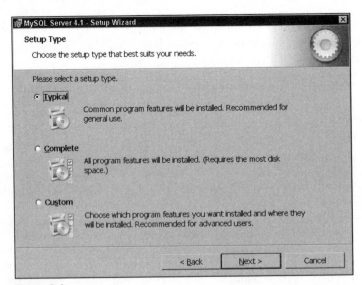

Figure 2-4

In most cases, you should choose the Typical installation. This normally provides you with all the functionality that you need at this time. As you become more familiar with MySQL, or if you're simply the type who likes to know exactly what you're installing, select the Custom option and choose which components to install. The examples and exercises in this book use a Typical installation.

4. Click Next. The Ready to Install the Program screen appears (shown in Figure 2-5) and provides the details of your installation.

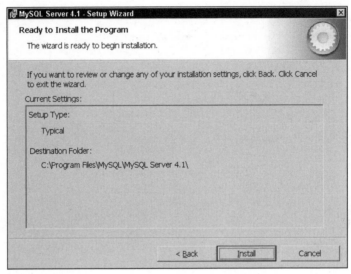

Figure 2-5

Be sure to review the information on the screen. If you want to change any of the settings, click the Back button to return to the appropriate screen.

5. Click Install to begin the actual installation. The Installing MySQL Server screen appears and provides you with the progress of your installation, as shown in Figure 2-6.

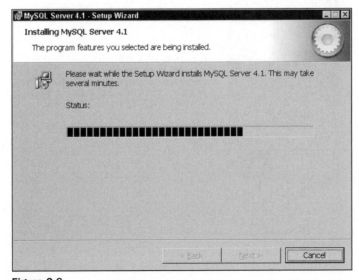

Figure 2-6

After the main part of the installation process is complete, the MySQL.com Sign-Up screen appears, as shown in Figure 2-7, providing options for creating a MySQL.com account.

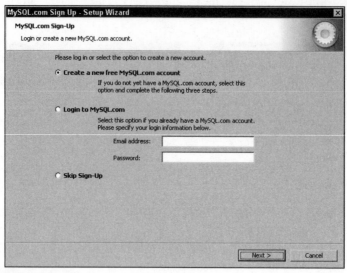

Figure 2-7

For now, skip the sign-up process and continue with the installation; however, you can create an account at a later time.

6. Select the Skip Sign-Up option, and click Next. The Wizard Completed screen appears, as shown in Figure 2-8.

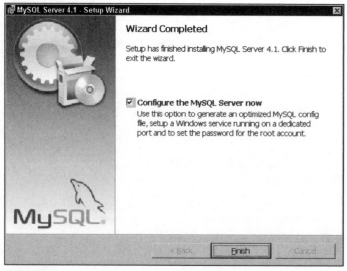

Figure 2-8

The Wizard Completed screen includes the option Configure the MySQL Server now. This option is selected by default. As a result, when you close the Setup Wizard, the MySQL Server Instance Configuration Wizard is launched automatically, allowing you to set up your system's initial MySQL configuration.

7. Ensure that the Configure the MySQL Server now option is selected, and click Finish.

The MySQL installation is now complete, and the first screen of the MySQL Server Instance Configuration screen appears.

Configuring the MySQL Server

Once you complete the MySQL installation, you can run the MySQL Server Instance Configuration Wizard to set up your system. The wizard allows you to specify the type of configuration, install MySQL as a service, and set up initial security settings. If you selected the Configure the MySQL Server now option in the last screen of the MySQL Setup Wizard, the MySQL Server Configuration Wizard launches automatically. You can also launch the wizard from the Windows Start menu (as part of the MySQL program group).

Once you launch the MySQL Server Instance Configuration Wizard, you can follow these steps to set up the MySQL server:

1. Verify that the MySQL Server Instance Configuration Wizard has been launched. The first screen of the wizard is shown in Figure 2-9.

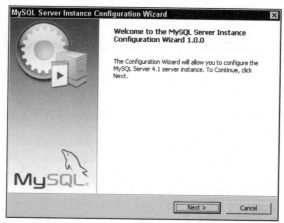

Figure 2-9

2. Click Next. The next screen of the wizard appears (shown in Figure 2-10), allowing you to choose a configuration type.

The MySQL Server Instance Configuration Wizard allows you to select the Detailed Configuration option or the Standard Configuration option. Detailed Configuration steps you through a process for identifying configuration settings that are specific to your environment. For example, you can specify whether you're working on a developer computer, a server computer, or a dedicated MySQL computer. You can also specify such configuration settings as the primary types of databases that will be supported, the number of concurrent users, and the port setting. If you select the Standard Configuration option, the MySQL server is set up with a general-purpose configuration. For the purposes of this book, you use the standard configuration.

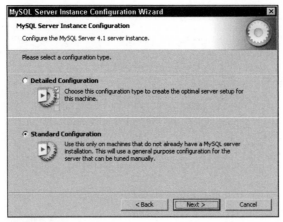

Figure 2-10

3.   Ensure that the Standard Configuration option is selected; then click Next. The next screen of the wizard appears, as shown in Figure 2-11.

Figure 2-11

The screen allows you to specify whether to set up MySQL as a service. If you're running MySQL on Windows NT, Windows 2000, Windows XP, or Windows Server 2003, you can run the MySQL server as a service, which is the recommended method to use. By default, the Install As Windows Service option is selected, MySQL is selected in the Service Name drop-down list, and the Launch the MySQL Server automatically option is selected. By accepting the default options, MySQL runs automatically whenever you start your computer.

4. Ensure that the default settings are selected; then click Next. The next screen of the MySQL Server Instance Configuration Wizard appears (shown in Figure 2-12), allowing you to modify the initial security settings.

Figure 2-12

In this screen, you can modify the initial security settings by assigning a password to the root user account, the primary administrative user account automatically created in MySQL. If you select the Modify Security Settings option, you can also select the Root may only connect from localhost option, which is used to specify that the root user cannot connect to the MySQL server remotely. In addition, if you select the Modify Security Settings option, you can also select the Create An Anonymous Account option, which allows you to create an anonymous account on the MySQL server.

5. Ensure that the Modify Security Settings option is selected, and then enter a password in the New root password text box and in the Confirm text box. Also, ensure that the Root may only connect from the localhost option and that the Create An Anonymous Account option are *not* selected. Then click Next. The next screen of the wizard appears, as shown in Figure 2-13.

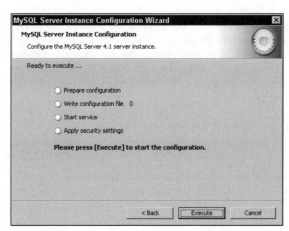

Figure 2-13

6. Click Execute. The screen shown in Figure 2-13 provides you with a status report (by checking the option) as each task is completed. When the configuration process has been completed, all tasks should be checked. The screen should then appear as it does in Figure 2-14.

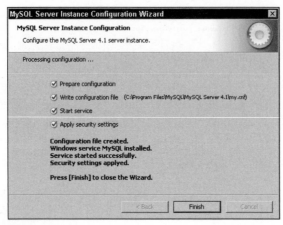

Figure 2-14

As you can see, the screen now indicates that a configuration file has been created, MySQL has been installed as a service, the service has been started, and the security settings have been applied.

7. Click Finish. The wizard closes, and MySQL is ready to use.

Editions of the MySQL Server

When you use the MySQL Server Instance Configuration Wizard to set up the initial configuration of the MySQL server, one of the tasks that it performs is to set up the MySQL server as a service. When the service is started, it accesses the mysqld-nt server file to run MySQL. The mysqld-nt file, however, is not the only file that you can use to run MySQL on Windows.

Earlier in the chapter, you learned that MySQL supports a Standard edition and a Max edition. (The Debug edition is rarely a consideration.) As you probably noticed when you downloaded the Windows distribution file, you were not given the option to select an edition. Windows distribution files, unlike other operating systems, include all editions in one file, so you do not have to make a decision about editions until after you install MySQL. Initially, that choice is made for you by running the MySQL Server Instance Configuration Wizard. There might come a time, though, when you want to choose a different edition of the server.

The Windows distribution of MySQL includes five editions of the MySQL server. These editions can be divided into the broader categories that you saw earlier—Standard and Max. The following table describes the five server editions available in a MySQL Windows installation.

Server edition	Description
mysqld	This is the basic compiled edition of the MySQL server. It supports all the basic features found in a production release of MySQL. This edition also contains full debugging support, which means that it might run more slowly and use more memory than other editions of the MySQL server.
mysqld-debug	The binaries are compiled with additional debug data and are not intended for use in a production environment.
mysqld-nt	This edition of the MySQL server is optimized to run on Windows NT, Windows 2000, Windows XP, and Windows Server 2003. In addition, the mysqld-nt server supports named pipes.
mysqld-max	The mysqld-max server is the Max edition of the MySQL server. As a result, it includes all features found in the mysqld server, plus additional features.
mysqld-max-nt	Like the mysqld-nt server, the mysqld-max-nt server is optimized to run on Windows NT, Windows 2000, Windows XP, and Windows Server 2003, and it supports named pipes. In addition, because the mysqld-max-nt server is the Max edition of the MySQL server, it includes all features found in the mysqld-nt server, plus additional features.

If you're running MySQL on Windows NT, Windows 2000, Windows XP, or Windows Server 2003, it's advisable that you run the mysqld-nt server, which is the edition used in the book (and the edition installed by default). If at some point you decide that you want the additional features available in the Max edition, you can switch over at that time.

Testing Your MySQL Installation

Now that you have installed MySQL and have started it, you're ready to test your installation. This is a simple process that is intended to verify that the MySQL server is running and that the mysql administrative database has been properly initialized. For those of you who installed MySQL on Linux, see the "Verifying Your Linux Installation" section that follows. For those of you who installed MySQL on Windows, see the "Verifying Your Windows Installation" section later in the chapter.

> *It's unfortunate that MySQL AB uses the same name for so many objects associated with MySQL. When you do a default installation, the term mysql describes the client utility, one of the default databases, the installation directory, the default user and group, and the name assigned to the startup script used to start MySQL automatically in Linux. Despite this, the text attempts to minimize any confusion surrounding its usage.*

Verifying Your Linux Installation

After you install MySQL, you should verify that it has been properly installed. To do this, launch two of the MySQL client utilities. (You should still be logged on to Linux as the root user.) Follow these steps to verify that the MySQL server is working properly and that the administrative tables in the mysql database have been initialized:

1. Verify which version of MySQL is running. Do this simply to verify that MySQL was properly installed. If you used RPM packages to install MySQL, type the following command at the command prompt, then press Enter:

```
/usr/bin/mysqladmin version
```

If you used a tar file to install MySQL, type the following command at the command prompt; then press Enter:

```
/usr/local/mysql/bin/mysqladmin version
```

Information about the MySQL installation displays, including information about the version number and the edition of the MySQL server.

2. Next, verify whether the MySQL databases have been properly installed and configured. You achieve this by running the mysql command-line utility to access the databases. If you're using an RPM installation of MySQL, enter the following command:

```
/usr/bin/mysql
```

If you're using a tar installation of MySQL, enter the following command:

```
/usr/local/mysql/bin/mysql
```

You receive a message that welcomes you to the MySQL monitor and provides information about command termination, the MySQL connection, and getting help. In addition, the command prompt displays as follows:

```
mysql>
```

At the command prompt, simply type SQL commands as you would type commands in any Linux or Windows shell. When sending commands to MySQL, though, you must terminate your commands with a semi-colon.

3. Try out a couple of commands to verify that the databases have been set up properly. Enter the following command:

```
SHOW DATABASES;
```

You should receive the following results:

```
+----------+
| Database |
+----------+
| mysql    |
| test     |
+----------+
2 rows in set (0.00 sec)
```

As you can see, two databases have been installed: mysql and test.

4. Next take a look at the tables contained in the mysql database. To do that, you must first switch to the database:

```
use mysql
```

After executing the command, you receive a message saying that the database has been changed. You can now run queries against the mysql database.

5. Enter the following command to display the tables in the mysql database:

```
SHOW TABLES;
```

You should receive results similar to the following:

```
+---------------------------+
| Tables_in_mysql           |
+---------------------------+
| columns_priv              |
| db                        |
| func                      |
| help_category             |
| help_keyword              |
| help_relation             |
| help_topic                |
| host                      |
| tables_priv               |
| time_zone_                |
| time_zone_leap_second     |
| time_zone_name            |
| time_zone_transition      |
| time_zone_transition_type |
| user                      |
+---------------------------+
15 rows in set (0.00 sec)
```

Depending on the version of MySQL that you're running, you may not see exactly these tables, but you should still see many of the same ones. You will learn more about these tables as the book progresses. For now, it's enough to know that the tables have been properly created.

6. The next step is to verify that the user table contains the proper host and user rows. Execute the following command:

```
SELECT host, user FROM user;
```

A SELECT statement retrieves data from the user table. Specifically, you want to retrieve information from the host column and the user column. You should receive results similar to the following:

```
+-----------+------+
| host      | user |
+-----------+------+
| <host>    |      |
| <host>    | root |
| localhost |      |
| localhost | root |
+-----------+------+
4 rows in set (0.00 sec)
```

The <host> placeholder refers to the name of the computer on which MySQL is installed. In other words, you see the name of your computer in place of <host>. The localhost entry also refers to the current computer. Notice that for one of the <host> rows and one of the localhost rows, the user is defined as root. In MySQL, the root user is the primary MySQL user account. When you first begin to use MySQL, you're using it under the root account. Later in the book, you learn how to modify the mysql tables, create users, assign passwords, and log into MySQL under a different account name.

7. Now you can exit the `mysql` utility. To do so, type and enter the following command:

```
exit
```

You can also use the following method to exit mysql:

```
quit
```

After you execute one of the commands, you're returned to the Linux command prompt.

If you were able to complete the preceding steps, you can assume that MySQL has been successfully installed and is operating properly. If you ran into any problems, such as not being able to launch any of the utilities or not being able to access the database, make sure that you typed in each command correctly and that you launched each utility from the correct directory. In addition, make certain that you completed the entire installation process before trying to test the installation, particularly if you performed a tar installation. However, once you have successfully verified the MySQL installation, you're ready to go. You can now start creating databases, adding data, and building applications that access the data.

Verifying Your Windows Installation

To verify that you correctly installed MySQL in your Windows environment, you must open a Command Prompt window and enter commands at the command prompt. Follow these steps to verify that the MySQL server is working properly and that the administrative tables in the mysql database have been initialized:

1. Change to the directory where the MySQL utilities are located:

```
cd c:\program files\mysql\mysql server <version>\bin
```

The `<version>` placeholder refers to the version of MySQL that you just installed on your computer. The command prompt should indicate that you're in the `C:\Program Files\MySQL\ MySQL Server <version>\bin` directory.

2. The first step to take is to check which version of MySQL is running. Do this simply to verify that MySQL was properly installed. Type the following command at the command prompt, and then press Enter:

```
mysqladmin -u root -p version
```

After you press Enter, you are prompted for a password. Type the password that you entered in the MySQL Server Instance Configuration Wizard when you configured your MySQL installation, and then press Enter. Information about the MySQL installation displays, including information about the version number and the edition of the MySQL server.

3. Next, verify whether the MySQL databases have been properly installed and configured. Achieve this by running the `mysql` command-line utility to access the databases. Enter the following command:

```
mysql -u root -p
```

You are again prompted for a password. Enter the password and press Enter. You receive a message that welcomes you to the MySQL monitor and that provides information about command termination, the MySQL connection, and getting help. In addition, the command prompt displays as follows:

```
mysql>
```

Whenever you use the mysql client utility, the command prompt displays in this manner, unless you configure it to display other prompts. At the command prompt, you simply type in SQL commands as you would type in commands at the Windows command shell. When sending commands to MySQL, though, you must terminate your commands with a semi-colon.

4. Try out a couple of commands to verify that the databases have been set up properly. Enter the following command:

```
SHOW DATABASES;
```

You should receive the following results:

```
+----------+
| Database |
+----------+
| mysql    |
| test     |
+----------+
2 rows in set (0.31 sec)
```

5. Next, take a look at the tables contained in the mysql database. To do that, you must first switch to the database:

```
use mysql
```

You receive a message saying that the database has been changed. You can now run queries against the mysql database.

6. Enter the following command to display the tables in the mysql database:

```
SHOW TABLES;
```

You should receive results similar to the following:

```
+---------------------------+
| Tables_in_mysql           |
+---------------------------+
| columns_priv              |
| db                        |
| func                      |
| help_category             |
| help_keyword              |
| help_relation             |
| help_topic                |
| host                      |
| tables_priv               |
| time_zone_                |
| time_zone_leap_second     |
| time_zone_name            |
| time_zone_transition      |
| time_zone_transition_type |
| user                      |
+---------------------------+
15 rows in set (0.01 sec)
```

Depending on the version of MySQL that you're running, you may not see exactly these tables, but you should still see many of the same ones. You will learn more about these tables as the book progresses. For now, it's enough to know that you created the tables properly.

7.   The next step is to verify that the user table contains the proper host and user rows. Execute the following command:

```
SELECT host, user FROM user;
```

A SELECT statement retrieves data from the user table. Specifically, you want to retrieve information from the host column and the user column. You should receive results similar to the following:

```
+-----------+------+
| host      | user |
+-----------+------+
| %         | root |
| localhost | root |
+-----------+------+
4 rows in set (0.00 sec)
```

The % wildcard indicates that any host has access to MySQL. The localhost entry refers to the current computer. Notice that the % rows and the localhost row each define the user as root. In MySQL, the root user is the primary MySQL user account. When you first begin to use MySQL, you're using it under the root account. Later in the book, you learn how to modify the mysql tables, create users, assign passwords, and log in to MySQL under a different account name.

8.   Now you can exit the mysql utility. To do so, type and enter the following command:

```
exit
```

You can also use the following method to exit mysql:

```
quit
```

After you execute one of these commands, you're returned to the Linux command prompt.

If you were able to complete the preceding steps, you can assume that MySQL has been successfully installed and is operating properly. If you ran into any problems, such as not being able to launch any of the utilities or not being able to access the database, be sure that you typed each command correctly and that you launched each utility from the correct directory. In addition, make certain that MySQL has been installed as a service and is started. (You can use the Services utility in Windows to verify if MySQL is running properly.) Once you have successfully verified the MySQL installation, you can start creating databases, adding data, and building applications that access the data.

Summary

As you have seen in this chapter, installing MySQL is a very straightforward process. It is, of course, easier to install MySQL using RPM files on Linux or a zipped file on Windows than it is to use a tar file to install the product. But once you know how to use a tar file to install MySQL on Linux, you should be able to install it on any Unix-like operating system. This chapter, then, has provided you with the background information and steps necessary to perform the following tasks:

- ❑   Select which version of MySQL to install

- ❑   Choose a platform on which to run MySQL

- ❑   Choose a distribution type

- ❑   Select an edition of MySQL

- ❑   Download the appropriate distribution files

- ❑   Install MySQL on Linux (using RPM and tar files) or install MySQL on Windows (using a zipped file)

- ❑   Start the MySQL server and, if installing on Windows, set up the server as a service

- ❑   Test your MySQL installation on Linux or Windows

Once you've installed MySQL and tested the installation, you can create databases and tables; insert, modify, and retrieve data; modify the configuration settings; and create data-driven applications that connect to the databases. As you progress through the book, you will learn how to do each of these tasks. Before you learn how to perform any of them, you should have a strong foundation in MySQL itself—how it is set up on your computer, what client tools are provided, and how to use those tools, which are the subjects of Chapter 3.

Exercises

The following exercises provide you with the opportunity to test yourself on some of what you learned in this chapter. To view the answers to these questions, see Appendix A.

1.   You are preparing to install the Max edition of MySQL 4.0.20 on an x86 computer that is running Linux. You plan to install mysql from a tar archive file. What file or files should you download from the MySQL Web site?

2.   You are installing the Standard edition of MySQL on an x86 computer that is running Linux. You plan to use RPM files to install the server and client tools for MySQL 5.0.0-0. You copy the necessary files to the /tmp directory on your computer and then change to that directory. Which command should you use to install the MySQL server on your computer?

3.   You used a tar file to install the Standard edition of MySQL on an x86 computer that is running Linux. You performed the installation in the /usr/local directory. You now want to start the server in safe mode in the context of the mysql user. Which command should you use?

4.   You installed MySQL on a Windows XP computer. You now want to set up the mysqld-nt server as a service on your system. You then want to start the service. In addition, you want to create a configuration file and assign a password to the MySQL root user account. What is the easiest way to accomplish these tasks?

Working with MySQL

After installing and initializing MySQL, you can begin working with the server and client tools that are included in that installation. Before you begin creating databases and tables, inserting and manipulating data, or modifying server and client configurations, you should have a basic understanding of how to use MySQL. This includes not only finding your way through the MySQL directory structure, but also knowing what server-related and client programs are included in the MySQL installation and what steps you can take to control how those programs run. In addition, you must know how to protect your installation so that only those users that you want to have access to MySQL are permitted access.

To prepare you to start using MySQL, this chapter covers many of the topics that can give you the foundation necessary to work with MySQL. The chapter contains details about the directory structure set up when you install MySQL, the programs available as part of that installation, and the methods used to configure the options available to those programs. In addition, the chapter includes information about how to secure MySQL so that you can prevent access by unauthorized users. Specifically, the chapter covers the following topics:

❑   The MySQL directory structure that is used in Linux RPM and tar installations and in Windows installations. In addition, you'll learn about the data directory and the grant tables, as they're implemented in Linux and in Windows.

❑   Information about MySQL server-related and client programs. You'll learn how to specify program options at the command prompt and in a configuration file, and you will be instructed on how to use the mysql client utility.

❑   How to assign passwords to MySQL user accounts.

Understanding the MySQL Directory Structure

When you install MySQL, a directory structure is set up to support the various database-related functions. The directories contain the files necessary to initialize the database, start the MySQL server, and set up the server to run automatically. In addition, the directories include the server-related and client programs included with MySQL, as well as script, log, and document files related to the MySQL operation. This section discusses the details of the directory structure and then focuses specifically on the data directory, which houses the actual database files.

MySQL File Storage

The way in which the MySQL directories are structured can vary depending on the operating system on which MySQL is installed and the distribution type used to perform that installation. Because Chapter 2 explained how to install MySQL on Linux (using RPM and tar files) and on Windows, these are the three directory structures that are reviewed here. For each installation type, you are given a table that outlines how the MySQL files are stored. In addition to reviewing the appropriate table, be sure to view the contents in each directory so that you can become familiar with where the files are located. As you work your way through the book, you can refer back to the table to determine where a file is located.

File Storage for a Linux RPM Installation

As you'll recall from Chapter 2, when you execute the RPM installation files on your Linux computer, the MySQL files are extracted to your hard disk, the databases are initialized, and the server is set up to start automatically. When many of the files are extracted to your hard disk, they are distributed among directories that already exist in the Linux structure. In addition, several directories specific to MySQL are created, although most of the distributed files, as shown in the following table, are extracted to existing directories.

Directory	Contents
/usr/bin	Contains many of the binary program files and script files that you need to set up and interact with MySQL, including mysql, mysqladmin, mysqld_safe, and mysql_install_db. The /usr/bin directory is usually the first place you should look if you're trying to locate a MySQL program. Note that this directory also contains numerous programs and scripts that are unrelated to MySQL.
/usr/lib/mysql	Contains a symbol file named mysqld.sym that is used to troubleshoot MySQL in case it fails.
/usr/sbin	Contains the mysqld program file for the MySQL server.
/usr/share/ doc/packages/ MySQL-server	Contains the MySQL users' manual in .html and .txt file formats. The directory also contains the five sample configuration files: my-huge.cnf, my-innodb-heavy-4G.cnf, my-large.cnf, my-medium.cnf, and my-small.cnf.
/usr/share/info	Contains the MySQL manual in a compressed format (mysql.info.gz). A .gz file is a file that has been compressed with the Gzip utility.
/usr/share/man/ man1	Contains manual pages that provide information about individual MySQL programs, such as mysql, mysqladmin, and mysqld.
/usr/share/mysql	Contains error messages for the different languages supported by MySQL. For each of these languages, an errmsg.sys and errmsg.txt file are provided. The directory also contains miscellaneous script and support files.
/var/lib/mysql	Contains log files as well as directories and files related to MySQL databases.

As you can see, an RPM installation spreads the files out into a number of directories. Unlike other distribution types, which tend to consolidate the MySQL files into a central location, the RPM distribution uses a less intuitive approach to file organization, so it can sometimes take a while to locate a specific file. The location that you're likely to be the most concerned with as you're learning about MySQL is the `/usr/bin` directory, which contains the majority of the program files used to run, access, and configure MySQL. Although you need to access other directories when using MySQL, you launch most of your MySQL programs from the `/usr/bin` directory.

Keep in mind that an RPM installation is based on individual RPM files. The preceding table reflects only the server and client installations. If you install additional RPM packages, your directory structure will reflect those installations.

File Storage for a Linux Tar Installation

A tar installation, although more complicated to implement than an RPM installation, organizes the MySQL files in a far simpler structure, which often makes locating files easier and quicker. As the following table demonstrates, you can access all the MySQL files through the `/usr/local/mysql` directory.

Directory	Contents
/usr/local/mysql/bin	Contains binary program files such as mysql, mysqld, and mysqld_safe. The /usr/local/mysql/bin directory is usually the first place you should look if you're trying to locate a MySQL program.
/usr/local/mysql/data	Contains log files as well as directories and files related to MySQL databases.
/usr/local/mysql/docs	Contains the MySQL users' manual in .html and .txt file formats. The directory also contains the manual saved as a mysql.info file.
/usr/local/mysql/include	Contains MySQL include files, such as config.h, hash.h, and my_dir.h.
/usr/local/mysql/lib	Contains compiled library files, such as libdbug.a and libmysqld.a.
/usr/local/mysql/man	Contains manual pages that provide information about individual MySQL programs, such as mysql, mysqladmin, and mysqld.
/usr/local/mysql/mysql-test	Contains the MySQL Test Suite, which allows you to perform regression tests on the MySQL code.
/usr/local/mysql/scripts	Contains the mysql_install_db initialization script.
/usr/local/mysql/share	Contains error messages for the different languages supported by MySQL. For each of these languages, an errmsg.sys file and an errmsg.txt file are provided.
/usr/local/mysql/sql-bench	Contains the files necessary to perform benchmark tests.

Table continued on following page

Directory	Contents
/usr/local/mysql/support-files	Contains the five sample configuration files: my-huge.cnf, my-innodb-heavy-4G.cnf, my-large.cnf, my-medium.cnf, and my-small.cnf. The directory also contains scripts, including mysql.server.

As you can see from the table, the directory structure is far simpler than that found in an RPM installation. In fact, for this reason alone you might consider a tar installation rather than an RPM installation. As you found with the RPM installation, the tar directory structure also includes a single directory that contains most of the MySQL programs. This directory — /usr/local/mysql/bin — is the one that you access the most as you're learning about MySQL, although you'll have to access other directories for files such as script files and sample configuration files.

File Storage for a Windows Installation

The directory structure in a Windows installation is similar to what you find in a tar installation on Linux. The MySQL files are all organized in a common directory structure under the C:\Program Files\MySQL\MySQL Server <version> directory, as shown in the following table.

Directory	Contents
C:\Program Files\MySQL\ MySQL Server <version>\	Contains the six sample configuration files: my-huge.ini, my-innodb-heavy-4G.ini, my-large.ini, my-medium.ini, my-small.ini, and my-template.ini. In addition, the initial configuration file (my.ini) created by the MySQL Server Instance Configuration Wizard is placed in this directory. The directory also contains files that provide licensing information.
C:\Program Files\MySQL\ MySQL Server <version>\bin	Contains binary program files such as mysql.exe, mysqld-nt.exe, and mysqladmin.exe. This is usually the first place you should look if you're trying to locate a MySQL program.
C:\Program Files\MySQL\ MySQL Server <version>\data	Contains log files as well as directories and files related to MySQL databases.
C:\Program Files\MySQL\ MySQL Server <version>	Contains the MySQL users' manual in .html and .txt file formats. This directory is included only for a .zip file installation, not a .msi file installation.
C:\Program Files\MySQL\ MySQL Server <version>\share	Contains error messages for the different languages supported by MySQL. For each of these languages, an errmsg.sys file and an errmsg.txt file are provided.

In Windows, the MySQL program files are located in the C:\Program Files\MySQL\MySQL Server <version>\bin directory. Although you have to access files from other directories, the C:\Program Files\MySQL\MySQL Server <version> \bin directory is the one that you access the most often as you're learning to use MySQL.

The Data Directory

Now that you have an overview of the directory structures for the three installation types discussed so far, you can take a closer look at the data directory, which contains the database files used to support the MySQL databases. The data directory also contains log files related to those databases.

As you saw earlier in the chapter, the location of your data folder depends on your computer's operating system and on the distribution method you used to install MySQL. For the three platforms and installation types discussed, the data directories are located as follows:

- ❑ For an RPM installation on Linux: `/var/lib/mysql`
- ❑ For a tar file installation on Linux: `/usr/local/mysql/data`
- ❑ For a Windows installation: `C:\Program Files\MySQL\MySQL Server <version>\data`
  `C:\mysql\data`

In addition to log files, the data directory contains a subdirectory for each database that exists in MySQL. The database subdirectories share the same names as the databases themselves. For example, suppose you add a database named TestDB to your MySQL installation. In Windows, the directory associated with the TestDB database is `C:\Program Files\MySQL\MySQL Server <version> \data\TestDB`. In an RPM installation of Linux, the directory associated with the TestDB database is `/var/lib/mysql/TestDB`. In a tar installation, the directory is `/usr/local/mysql/data/TestDB`.

When you first install MySQL and initialize that installation, the following two databases are created by default:

- ❑ **mysql:** An administrative database that contains the system tables necessary to control user access, provide help-related information, and support time-zone-related functionality.
- ❑ **test:** A sample database that you can use to test MySQL functionality. The database contains no tables, although you can add tables as necessary.

As a result of there being two default databases included in your MySQL installation, there are two default subdirectories: `mysql` and `test`. Each database subdirectory contains files that map to any tables that exist in that database. Because the test database contains no tables, there are no files associated with that database. If you were to add tables, the necessary files would be added to the test subdirectory. Because the mysql database contains tables, the `mysql` subdirectory contains numerous files.

Whenever you add a table to a database, one or more of the following types of files are created in the database subdirectory:

- ❑ **.frm:** The primary table-related file that is used to define the table's format. All table types have an associated .frm file.
- ❑ **.MYD:** The file that stores the data contained in several table types.
- ❑ **.MYI:** An index file used by several table types.
- ❑ **.MRG:** A special type of file that is used to list the names of merged tables.

Which files are created for a table depends on the table's type. The following table provides a brief description of each table type supported by MySQL and lists the files that are created when you add a table to a database.

Table type	Description	Files used
BDB	A transaction-safe table that the Berkeley DB handler manages. For the most part, InnoDB tables have replaced BDB tables.	.frm, .MYD, .MYI
MEMORY	A table whose contents are stored in memory. The data stored in the tables is available only as long as the MySQL server is available. If the server crashes or is shut down, the data disappears.	.frm
InnoDB	A transaction-safe table that the InnoDB handler manages. As a result, data is not stored in a .MYD file, but instead is managed in the InnoDB tablespace.	.frm
ISAM	A deprecated table type that was once the default table type in MySQL. The MyISAM table type has replaced it, although it is still supported for backward compatibility.	.frm, .MYD, .MYI
MERGE	A virtual table that is made up of multiple MyISAM tables. Data is not stored in the MERGE table, but rather in the underlying MyISAM tables.	.frm, .MRG
MyISAM	The default table type in MySQL. MyISAM tables, which have replaced ISAM tables, support extensive indexing and are optimized for compressions and speed.	.frm, .MYD, .MYI

You define the table type when you create a table. If you specify no table type , a MyISAM table is created by default. For more information about table types and how they apply to table definitions, see Chapter 5.

The files created for a table that is added to a MySQL database share the same name as that table. For example, the mysql database includes a table named user. Because the user table is a MyISAM table type, three files exist for that table — user.frm, user.MYD, and user.MYI — and the files are stored in the mysql subdirectory. For instance, in Windows, the user.frm file is located at `C:\Program Files\ MySQL\MySQL Server <version>\data\mysql\user.frm`; in an RPM installation on Linux, the file is located at `/var/lib/mysql/mysql/user.frm`; and in a tar installation on Linux, the file is located at `/usr/local/mysql/data/mysql/user.frm`.

The mysql Database

The mysql database is an administrative database that contains tables related to securing the MySQL installation, storing user-defined functions, and providing data related to the MySQL help system and to time-zone functionality. The mysql database must be initialized before you can start using MySQL. When you use RPM files to install MySQL on Linux or you install MySQL on Windows, the mysql database is initialized by default. If you use a tar file to initialize MySQL, you must run the `mysql_install_db` script. (See Chapter 2 for details about running the `mysql_install_db` script.)

By default, the mysql database includes 15 tables. The following table provides a brief description of the data included in each table.

Table	Contents
columns_priv	Contains access-control data for individual columns within a specified table.
db	Contains access-control data that defines the type of privileges a user is granted on a specified database.
func	Contains data about user-defined functions that have been added to MySQL.
help_category, help_keyword, help_relation, help_topic	Contains data related to the MySQL help system. There are four help-related tables in all.
host	Contains access-control data that defines the type of privileges a host is granted on a specified database.
tables_priv	Contains access-control data for individual tables in a specified database.
time_zone, time_zone_leap_second, time_zone_name, time_zone_transition, time_zone_transition_type	Contains data related to time-zone functionality in MySQL. There are five tables related to time-zone functionality.
user	Contains access-control data that defines which users can connect to the MySQL server, from which computers those users can access MySQL, and the type of global privileges that the users have in order to access MySQL and its databases.

When you first begin using MySQL, you're most concerned with the tables that determine the privileges available to anyone who connects to MySQL. These tables, referred to as grant tables, are discussed in the following section.

The Grant Tables

A *grant table* is any one of the tables in the mysql database that are used to control access to MySQL and the MySQL databases. By default, MySQL creates the following five grant tables:

- ❏ columns_priv
- ❏ db
- ❏ host
- ❏ tables_priv
- ❏ user

The grant tables define which users can access MySQL, from which computers that access is supported, what actions those users can perform, and on which objects those actions can be performed. For example, the grant tables allow you to specify which users can view data in a particular database and which users can actually update that data.

The actions that users are permitted to take and the data that they are permitted to access are controlled through a set of privileges. The following table lists each of the privileges available in MySQL and the actions that they permit a user to take.

Privilege	Allows user to:
Select_priv	Query data in a database.
Insert_priv	Insert data into a database.
Update_priv	Update data in a database.
Delete_priv	Delete data from a database.
Create_priv	Create a table in a database.
Drop_priv	Remove a table from a database.
Reload_priv	Reload the data in the grant tables into MySQL.
Shutdown_priv	Shut down the MySQL server.
Process_priv	View a list of MySQL processes.
File_priv	Export data from a database into a file.
Grant_priv	Grant privileges on database objects.
References_priv	Functionality not yet supported, but the intention of this privilege appears to be to allow a user to configure foreign key constraints.
Index_priv	Create and delete indexes in a database.
Alter_priv	Alter database objects.
Show_db_priv	View all databases.
Super_priv	Perform advanced administrative tasks.
Create_tmp_table_priv	Create temporary tables.
Lock_tables_priv	Place locks on tables.
Execute_priv	Run a stored procedure. Functionality will not be supported until MySQL version 5.0.
Repl_slave_priv	Read binary logs for a replication master.
Repl_client_priv	Request information about slave and master servers used for replication.
Table_priv	Access a specified table in a database.
Column_priv	Access a specified column in a table in a database.

When you first install MySQL, a number of privileges are configured by default. The privileges are configured in the grant tables, as they exist in the mysql database. By default, no privileges are assigned in the columns_priv, tables_priv, and host tables. In fact, these three tables are empty; however, the user table and db table contain users that have been granted privileges. For that reason, the following sections describe the user and db tables in more detail.

Chapter 14 discusses the grant tables and user privileges in much more detail. The information is presented here only as a way to give you an understanding of the mysql database, how users access MySQL, and what you can do to prevent unauthorized access.

The user Table

The user table is the primary grant table in the mysql database. The table controls who can connect to MySQL, from which hosts they can connect, and what superuser privileges they have. A *superuser* privilege applies globally to MySQL. A user assigned a superuser privilege can perform the task defined by that privilege on any database in the system. Every MySQL user is listed in the user table, whether or not they are assigned privileges in that table. The user table provides the widest scope in a MySQL implementation, followed by the db and host tables. If a user is not listed in the user table, that user cannot connect to MySQL.

The user table is configured differently for a Linux installation than it is for a Windows installation. Consequently, this section looks at the table as it appears in each implementation.

Linux Implementation

When you install and initialize MySQL on Linux, entries are added to the user table for the root user and for anonymous users. The root user in MySQL is not the same as the root user in Linux. The root user in MySQL is specific to MySQL. By default, the user table contains two records for the MySQL root user and two records for anonymous users, as shown in Figure 3-1.

host	user	password	privileges
localhost	root		all privileges
<local computer name>	root		all privileges
<local computer name>			no privileges
localhost			no privileges

Figure 3-1

The figure represents how the user table is configured in MySQL. The privileges column is actually a consolidation of all the privilege-related columns in that table. For example, in the first record, the root user has been granted all privileges from the localhost, and in the second record, the same user has been granted all privileges from the local computer (represented by the <local computer name> placeholder) where MySQL is installed. Essentially, the first two records are the same. However, by creating one record for localhost and one record for the actual computer name, you can use either name as a program option.

The table also includes two records for anonymous users. Anonymous users are shown in the user table by a blank value in the user column. Unlike the root user, the anonymous users have not been granted any privileges. Like the root user, however, anonymous users do not have to provide a password. As a result, the default configuration of the user table provides the following access to the users specified in the table:

❑ The root user has superuser access that allows that account to perform all administrative tasks. This access, however, is from the local computer only.

❑ No password is assigned to the root user, so anyone can sign in as the root user from the local computer and have full administrative access to MySQL.

❑ Anonymous users can connect to MySQL from the local computer, although they are denied superuser access.

As you can see, this is not a secure installation. It is up to you to determine whether this default configuration is adequate or whether you need to restrict access. It's generally not a good idea, though, to leave access as open-ended as it is here.

Windows Implementation

Like the Linux installation, entries have been added to the user table for the root user, as shown in Figure 3-2. The user table, though, is configured slightly differently in a Windows environment. (Again, the privileges column is merely a consolidation of all the privilege-related columns in the user table.) Notice that, in Windows, the root user can connect to MySQL from any host, as the percentage (%) placeholder represents. In Linux, the root user can connect only from the local computer.

host	user	password	privileges
localhost	root	*AA25B3745CB38F87F8BB4C12F28200463FC2D2E3	all privileges
%	root	*AA25B3745CB38F87F8BB4C12F28200463FC2D2E3	all privileges

Figure 3-2

Another difference between the Windows installation and the Linux installation is that, in Windows, each instance of the root user is assigned a password, shown as an encrypted value in the table. This is the password that you assigned to the root user when you ran the MySQL Server Instance Configuration Wizard. As with the Linux root user, the Windows root user is assigned all privileges. As a result, the root user has superuser access that allows root to perform all administrative tasks—from any computer.

As the user table shows, a Windows installation is, initially, more secure than a Linux installation. Later in the chapter, you will learn how to secure your Linux installation so that access is more restrictive than it is by default.

The db table

The db table is configured initially to allow access to anonymous users. The db table defines which users can connect to which databases from which hosts. The db table is configured the same in Linux and Windows installations, as shown in Figure 3-3.

host	db	user	privileges
%	test		all privileges except those that allow the user to grant privileges
%	test_%		all privileges except those that allow the user to grant privileges

Figure 3-3

The db table includes two rows, both for anonymous users, and both rows allow the users to connect from any host. As a result, any user can access the test database from any host. In addition, any user can access any database that begins with test_ from any host. (The backslash [\] that precedes the underscore indicates that the underscore should be used as a literal character. The percentage sign [%] indicates that any value can follow the underscore.) For users to be granted the access that is configured in the db table, they must exist as users in the user table.

Using the MySQL Programs

Now that you have an overview of how directories are structured in MySQL, take a look at the programs included in a MySQL installation. MySQL includes programs that are related to running the MySQL server or that are client tools used to interact with the server. For all the MySQL programs, you can specify a variety of options that affect how that program runs and the context in which it operates.

Specifying Program Options

Most MySQL programs support numerous options that you can specify when you invoke the program. The number of options that you might choose to include with one program might become a bit unwieldy, especially if you have to retype those options over and over again. As a result, MySQL supports a variety of ways to specify options available to your programs:

- ❑ **Command prompt entries:** You can specify options and, when applicable, their values when you type the command at a command prompt.

- ❑ **Configuration files:** You can add options to a configuration file that are specific to a program or available to all client programs. For example, you can specify the user and password to use for a specific program.

- ❑ **Aliases:** If your operating system supports the creation of aliases, you can create an alias whose definition includes specific options that you want to set.

- ❑ **Scripts:** You can create a shell script that defines the program and its options, and then you can call that script from within your shell.

- ❑ **Environment variables:** You can set environment variables that affect MySQL program operations. For example, you can use the MYSQL_HOST environment variable to define the name of a host to connect to when connecting to a MySQL server.

Of the methods available for specifying program options, using command prompt entries and using configuration files are the most common. For that reason, these are the two methods focused on in this chapter. For more information about creating scripts and aliases, see your operating system's documentation. For more information about environment variables, see the MySQL product documentation.

Specifying Options at a Command Prompt

The first step in specifying options for any program is to know what options are available for that program. The easiest way to determine what options are available is to use the help option. To use the help option, simply type the name of the program at your shell's command prompt and add --help, as shown in the following command:

```
mysqlaccess --help
```

When you execute this statement, information about the mysqlaccess program displays. This information, which includes details about which options are available and what those options are used for, displays in your shell. You can also access help by using a shorter version of the command:

```
mysqlaccess -?
```

This command returns the same results as `--help`.

Most programs include a long and a short name for each option. In addition, for many of the options, you must specify values. For example, suppose you want to operate the mysql client utility in the context of the root user. You would type the following command:

```
mysql --user=root
```

When mysql launches, it runs under the context of the specified user. You could have also specified the option by using the short name for that option, as in the following command:

```
mysql -u root
```

Notice that, when specifying the short name, you need to use only a single dash, rather than two, and you do not use the equal sign (=). This is typical for most MySQL programs. In addition, if you use the short name for the option, you do not have to separate the option name from the values. For example, you can use the `-u` option in the following manner:

```
mysql -uroot
```

As you can see, there is no space between the `-u` and the word root. For most options, you can specify the argument with or without a space. For the short name of the password option (`-p`), though, you can never add a space. The password, when specified, must always follow immediately after the `-p`. But this is generally not a concern because you normally use the password option without specifying the actual password until after you press Enter. As a result, your command would look like the following:

```
mysql -u root -p
```

When you press Enter, you're prompted for the password. At the prompt, you enter the password and then press Enter again.

Not all options require the use of an option name to precede its value. For example, if you want to specify a database when you start the mysql utility, you simply type the database name, after the name of the program, as in the following command:

```
mysql test -u root -p
```

When mysql launches, it prompts you for a password and then opens in the context of the root user account and the test database.

You will find, as you're working with various MySQL programs, that a number of options are common to those programs. You already saw examples of some of them, such as `--help` (`-?`), `--host` (`-h`), `--user` (`-u`), and `--password` (`-p`). In addition to these common options, each program includes options specific to the program. In some cases, the options that are available to a specific program can depend on the operating system being used and the edition of MySQL.

You might discover when you're entering commands at a command prompt that you're repeating the same commands over and over, which can become tedious very quickly. One way around this repetition is to use the functionality available at your particular command prompt that allows you to repeat commands. For example, you might be able to use the Up arrow to repeat a previous command. Be sure to check the documentation for your shell window to determine how to repeat commands.

You also might want to consider modifying the PATH *environment variable for your operating system so you don't have to type in a complete path every time you want to start a MySQL program. For example, you could modify the* root/.bash_profile *file on a Linux tar installation by adding* :/usr/local/mysql/bin *to the* PATH *environment variable. (The colon separates the path from the previous entry.) Because the RPM MySQL installation on Linux installs many of the MySQL programs in* /usr/bin*, you might not need to modify the* PATH *environment variable because* /usr/bin *is already a supported path for some versions of Linux.*

Modifying environment variables in Windows is a little different from Linux. For Windows, you can use the System utility in Control Panel to modify the environment variable. To change the variable, open the System utility, click the Environment Variables button on the Advanced tab, and then edit the PATH variable by adding ;C:\Program Files\MySQL\MySQL Server <version> \bin *to the path list. (The semi-colon separates the path from the previous entry.) You can also use the set command from a Command Prompt window to set the PATH environment variable.*

If you modify an environment variable, be sure to close the command shell and then reopen it to make sure that the new path specification takes effect.

Specifying Options in a Configuration File

A *configuration file* (or *option file*) is referenced by a number of MySQL programs when those programs are launched. The configuration files contain settings that are comparable to the options that you can specify at a command line when you run the program. Any options available at a command line are available to use in a configuration file. You can use only the long-name version of the option, and you don't use the dashes. For example, suppose you want to include the user option in a configuration file. If you were going to specify that option at a command prompt, you would enter it as follows:

```
mysqladmin --user=root
```

If you were going to include this option in a configuration file, you would type the following:

```
user=root
```

The option is added beneath the program heading, which in this case is [mysqladmin]. You could then add more options on the lines beneath the one you just entered. Unlike using options on a command line, place the options in a configuration file on separate lines, as in the following:

```
[mysqladmin]
host=server12
user=root
user=pw1
```

Any option placed under the [mysqladmin] heading is used when you run the mysqladmin program. You can override these options by specifying the option at a command prompt when you run the program.

Both Linux and Windows (as well as other operating systems) support configuration files. On Linux, the name of the configuration file is my.cnf, and you can place it in any of the following locations, depending on the intended scope of the file:

❑ **Global options:** /etc/my.cnf

❑ **Server-specific options:** <data directory>/my.cnf

❑ **User-specific options:** ~/.my.cnf

On Windows, the name of the configuration file is my.ini. When you run the MySQL Server Instance Configuration Wizard (right after you install MySQL), the wizard creates a my.ini file and places it in the C:\Program Files\MySQL\MySQL Server <version> directory. By default, this is the location that the MySQL service looks for the my.ini file when it starts the MySQL server. The MySQL client tools, however, look for the my.ini file in the C:\WINDOWS directory. As a result, you must maintain two separate configuration files or re-create the MySQL service so that it points to the C:\WINDOWS directory. Regardless of the location of the option file, the options specified are global.

> To re-create the MySQL service, you must stop the service, remove the service, create a new service, and then start that service. The new service should point to the mysqld-nt.exe program file in the C:\Program Files\MySQL\MySQL Server <version>\bin directory and the my.ini configuration file in the C:\WINDOWS directory. In Chapter 13 you will learn how to re-create the service when you implement logging. For details about Windows services, see the Windows product documentation.

In any configuration file, the options are grouped according to a program or type of program. Each grouping is preceded by a program heading, which is the name of the program in brackets, as you saw previously with [mysqladmin]. You can create a configuration file from scratch or copy one of the sample configuration files. If you're working in Windows, you can also copy the my.ini file from the C:\Program Files\MySQL\MySQL Server <version> directory to the C:\WINDOWS directory.

In Linux, MySQL includes five sample configuration files: my-huge.cnf, my-innodb-heavy-4G.cnf, my-large.cnf, my-medium.cnf, and my-small.cnf. Windows includes the same five (but with an .ini extension rather than .cnf), plus an additional template file named my-template.ini. The differences among these files have mostly to do with the sizes of the cache and buffer settings. To determine which configuration file might be best for your use, take a look at the contents of each file and decide, based on your system's configuration, which one is best for you.

Each sample configuration file provides program headers for a number of the programs available in MySQL. Much of the content in these files are comments, which are indicated by the number sign (#) at the beginning of a line. The program ignores comments. For example, the following code is from the my-small.ini configuration file available in a Windows installation:

```
# Example MySQL config file for small systems.
#
# This is for a system with little memory (<= 64M) where MySQL is only used
# from time to time and it's important that the mysqld daemon
# doesn't use much resources.
#
# You can copy this file to
# /etc/my.cnf to set global options,
# mysql-data-dir/my.cnf to set server-specific options (in this
# installation this directory is /usr/local/mysql/var) or
# ~/.my.cnf to set user-specific options.
#
# In this file, you can use all long options that a program supports.
# If you want to know which options a program supports, run the program
# with the "--help" option.

# The following options will be passed to all MySQL clients
[client]
#password       = your_password
port            = 3306
socket          = /tmp/mysql.sock
```

```
    # Here follows entries for some specific programs

    # The MySQL server
    [mysqld]
    port            = 3306
    socket          = /tmp/mysql.sock
    skip-locking
    key_buffer = 16K
    max_allowed_packet = 1M
    table_cache = 4
    sort_buffer_size = 64K
    read_buffer_size = 256K
    read_rnd_buffer_size = 256K
    net_buffer_length = 2K
    thread_stack = 64K

    # Don't listen on a TCP/IP port at all. This can be a security enhancement,
    # if all processes that need to connect to mysqld run on the same host.
    # All interaction with mysqld must be made via Unix sockets or named pipes.
    # Note that using this option without enabling named pipes on Windows
    # (using the "enable-named-pipe" option) will render mysqld useless!
    #
    #skip-networking
    server-id       = 1

    # Uncomment the following if you want to log updates
    #log-bin

    # Uncomment the following if you are NOT using BDB tables
    #skip-bdb

    # Uncomment the following if you are using InnoDB tables
    #innodb_data_home_dir = /usr/local/mysql/var/
    #innodb_data_file_path = ibdata1:10M:autoextend
    #innodb_log_group_home_dir = /usr/local/mysql/var/
    #innodb_log_arch_dir = /usr/local/mysql/var/
    # You can set .._buffer_pool_size up to 50 - 80 %
    # of RAM but beware of setting memory usage too high
    #innodb_buffer_pool_size = 16M
    #innodb_additional_mem_pool_size = 2M
    # Set .._log_file_size to 25 % of buffer pool size
    #innodb_log_file_size = 5M
    #innodb_log_buffer_size = 8M
    #innodb_flush_log_at_trx_commit = 1
    #innodb_lock_wait_timeout = 50

    [mysqldump]
    quick
    max_allowed_packet = 16M

    [mysql]
    no-auto-rehash
    # Remove the next comment character if you are not familiar with SQL
    #safe-updates
```

```
[isamchk]
key_buffer = 8M
sort_buffer_size = 8M

[myisamchk]
key_buffer = 8M
sort_buffer_size = 8M

[mysqlhotcopy]
interactive-timeout
```

Notice that most of the lines in this file are comments, which means that the program disregards these lines when it is launched. The comments serve as guidelines. You can use the settings suggested in the comments or define the options as best fit your needs.

One section of the configuration file that you should be aware of is the one that uses the [client] heading. Any options specified in this section apply to all MySQL client programs. Whenever you start one of the client programs, it checks the section specific to the program and also checks the [client] section.

As you can see, the configuration files are a handy way to specify your program's options. This is especially useful for those programs that require multiple options or that you invoke over and over again. With a configuration file, all you need to specify is the name of the program at a command prompt; the options are applied automatically.

Server-Related Programs, Scripts, and Library Files

MySQL includes a number of programs, scripts, and library files related to the operation of the server. The following table provides a description of each of these. To learn which options are available for each one, type the filename, along with the --help option, at a command prompt, and then press Enter.

Server-related file	Description
libmysqld	Library file that is used to embed the MySQL server into other applications. The libmysqld file is not actually a program, but it can be used with other stand-alone programs so that they can include a MySQL server.
mysql.server	Script file that you can use on Unix-like systems to start and stop the MySQL server automatically. The script invokes the mysqld_safe startup program file. If you use an RPM file to install the MySQL server on a Linux computer, the mysql.server script is implemented automatically.
mysql_install_db	Script file that creates and populates the initial databases (mysql and test) after MySQL has been installed. If you perform a tar-based installation of MySQL, you must run the mysql_install_db script manually to initialize the databases.
mysqld	MySQL server program file. The mysqld program must be running to support client connections because access to the data is through the server. Windows installations include versions of this program that are optimized for Windows.

Server-related file	Description
mysqld-max	MySQL server program file that includes features in addition to what's found in the standard mysqld program file. The mysqld-max program must be running to support client connections because access to the data is through the server. Windows installations include versions of this program that are optimized for Windows.
mysqld_multi	Script file that you can use to manage multiple mysqld processes. The script can start and stop the servers as well as report their current status.
mysqld_safe	Script file that starts the MySQL server automatically, restarts it if necessary, and monitors it. Using the mysqld_safe script is the recommended way to start MySQL.

Client Programs

The MySQL client programs allow you to interact with the MySQL server and the data stored in MySQL. The following table describes many of the client programs available in MySQL.

Client program	Description
myisamchk	Checks and repairs MyISAM tables. The MyISAM format is the default table type in MySQL and provides the basic functionality you would expect from a table in a database. The myisamchk utility is an updated version of the isamchk utility, which is used for ISAM tables. You should not use the myisamchk utility when the server is running.
myisampack	Compresses MyISAM tables into read-only tables in order to reduce storage requirements. The myisampack utility is an updated version of the pack_isam utility.
mysql	Supports access to the data in a MySQL database. You can use the utility in interactive mode or batch mode. Interactive mode allows you to access the data directly and perform ad hoc queries against the database. Batch mode allows you to execute queries stored in a script file and save the results of those queries to a file.
mysqlaccess	Checks access privileges as they're configured in the grant tables of the mysql database.
mysqladmin	Provides an administrative interface for the MySQL installation. You can perform a variety of administrative tasks, such as obtaining information about the MySQL configuration, setting passwords, stopping the server, creating and dropping databases, and reloading privileges.
mysqlbinlog	Displays the binary update log file in a text format.
mysqlbug	Generates bug reports on Unix-like systems that you can then post to a MySQL mailing list.

Table continued on following page

Client program	Description
mysqlcheck	Checks and repairs MyISAM tables. You must use the mysqlcheck utility when the MySQL server is running, which is different from myisamchk, which you should not use when the server is running.
mysqldump	Copies the data in database tables into text files. This can be useful if you want to back up the data, create a test database, or move a database to another server.
mysqlhotcopy	Makes a quick backup of a database. It can run only on Unix-like systems and NetWare systems and must run on the same machine where the data directory is located.
mysqlimport	Copies data from a text file into tables in a MySQL database.
mysqlshow	Displays a list of the databases that currently exist in MySQL, a list of tables in a database, or information about a specific table.
perror	Displays a description of a system error code or of a table handler error code for MyISAM, ISAM, and DBD tables.

The programs listed in the table are not a complete list of all the client programs available in MySQL, although this list represents some of the more common ones. Be sure to check the MySQL product documentation for a complete list of programs, the options available for each program, and the platforms that support the programs. In addition, you can execute the program name and the `--help` option at a command prompt to learn more about that program.

The mysql Utility

One of the most useful programs included with MySQL is the mysql client utility that you use at a command prompt. The mysql utility allows you to perform a number of administrative tasks and to interact directly with the data stored in MySQL. You can use the mysql utility in interactive mode and in batch mode.

Using mysql in Interactive Mode

When you use the mysql utility in interactive mode, you launch the tool from a command prompt. For example, you can open the mysql utility in the context of the test database located on server1 as the root user. To do so, you would specify the following command:

```
mysql mysql -h server1 -u root -p
```

If you include these options in a configuration file, then you don't need to specify them here, unless you want to override the options as they're defined in the configuration file. If you don't need to override the options, then you can simply specify the program name, and the utility launches. When mysql opens, the command prompt changes to the mysql command prompt, as shown in the following:

```
mysql>
```

Once at the mysql command prompt you can execute SQL statements as well as commands specific to the mysql utility. For example, to execute a SELECT statement, you would simply type in a statement such as the following and then press Enter:

```
SELECT host, user FROM user;
```

The SELECT statement retrieves data from the host and user columns of the user table. When you execute the statement, you receive results similar to the following:

```
+-----------+-------+
| host      | user  |
+-----------+-------+
| %         | root  |
| localhost | admin |
| localhost | root  |
+-----------+-------+
3 rows in set (0.00 sec)
```

In this previous example, the SELECT statement is written on one line; however, a statement can span multiple lines. For example, you can enter the SELECT clause (the section of the statement that is introduced by the SELECT keyword) on one line, press Enter, type the FROM clause and the semi-colon, and then press Enter again. The statement is not processed until mysql sees the semi-colon.

The mysql client utility also allows you to execute commands that are specific to the mysql client utility. These commands are useful for performing such tasks as clearing your entry from the command prompt, exiting the mysql utility, and switching databases.

All mysql commands include a long form and a short form. For example, you can also write the prompt command as the \R command. You should note, however, that the short form is case sensitive. For instance, the \R command is the short form of the prompt command, but the \r command is the short form of the connect command.

To view a list of the mysql commands, type help at the mysql command prompt. You'll find that you'll need to use a number of these commands regularly. For these reasons, each command is examined individually. This section covers only the most commonly used mysql commands; for information about all the commands, see the MySQL product documentation.

When you execute a mysql command, you do not need to terminate the command with a semi-colon. Using a semi-colon, though, presents no problem.

The clear Command

The clear (\c) command is quite useful if you decide part way through a statement that you want to discontinue the statement. For example, suppose you start a SELECT statement on one line and then press Enter, before you complete or terminate the statement. You will receive the following prompt:

```
->
```

The prompt indicates that mysql is waiting for you to complete the statement. To end the statement, you can enter \c and then press Enter, as shown in the following example.

```
SELECT host, user
\c
```

When you type the \c command and then press Enter, mysql clears the statement and then returns you to the mysql prompt, and no statements are executed.

With the clear command, you can use only the short form of the command to clear an SQL statement. All other mysql commands permit you to use the long form or the short form.

The exit and quit Commands

You should use the exit or quit (\q) command whenever you want to quit the mysql client utility. Simply type one of the commands at the mysql command prompt; then press Enter. For example, to quit mysql, type and enter the following command:

```
exit
```

You can also use the short form:

```
\q
```

When you execute the exit or quit command, the system returns you to your shell's command prompt, and your connection to the MySQL server is terminated.

The help Command

The help (\? or ?) command displays a list of commands specific to the mysql utility. To use the help command, type it at the mysql command prompt, then press Enter. The commands then display.

The prompt Command

The prompt (\R) command allows you to change how the mysql prompt displays. For example, if you want the mysql prompt to display the name of the current database, you could type the following command:

```
prompt db:\d>
```

When you execute the command, the prompt changes to the following:

```
db:mysql>
```

The new prompt displays until you end the mysql session. If you want to use this prompt every time you use the mysql client utility, you should define the prompt option in the configuration file.

The prompt command supports a number of options that allow you to display the mysql prompt in various ways. The following table describes each of the options available to the prompt command. Note that these options are case sensitive and must be typed exactly as shown here.

Option	Description
\	Space (A space follows the backslash.)
_	Space
\\	Backslash
\c	A counter that increments by one for each statement that you execute (This option is not the same as the mysql clear (\c) command. The \c option shown here is specifically used as a switch for the prompt command.)
\d	Current database
\D	Current date
\h	Server host
\m	Minutes from current time
\n	New line (no prompt)
\o	Current month (numeric format)
\O	Current month (three-letter format)
\p	Current socket name, port number, or named pipe
\P	a.m./p.m.
\r	Current time (12-hour clock)
\R	Current time (24-hour clock)
\s	Seconds of the current time
\t	Tab
\u	Username
\U	Username and hostname
\v	Version of server
\w	Current day of the week (three-letter format)
\y	Current year (two-digit format)
\Y	Current year (three-digit format)

Any letter not used as a command, when preceded by a backward slash, is used literally. For example, \Big would be displayed as Big, but \Out would be displayed as <current month>ut, as in Decut.

If you execute the prompt command without any options, the default mysql command prompt displays.

The source Command

The source (\.) command executes a query that is in a specified file. For example, suppose you have a file named user_info.sql that contains a SELECT statement. You can execute the statement by using the source command to call the file, as in the following example:

```
\. c:\program files\mysql server <version>\user_info.sql
```

The source command accesses the user_info.sql file, which is stored in the C:\Program Files\MySQL\ MySQL Server <version> directory, and executes the SQL statements in the file.

The status Command

The status (\s) command returns information about the current MySQL session, including the current user, database, connection ID, and server version. To use this command, type the command at the mysql command prompt and press Enter. The information then displays at the mysql command prompt.

The tee and notee Commands

The tee (\T) command is very useful if you want to keep a record of the commands that you type and the data that is returned by executing those commands. Using this command does not affect how data displays when you're viewing it interactively. It simply saves the input and output to a text file. For example, you can start logging your session by executing a command similar to the following:

```
tee c:\program files\mysql server <version>\shell.txt
```

A file named shell.txt is created if necessary and stored in the C:\Program Files\MySQL\MySQL Server <version> directory. You can stop logging to the file by simply executing the notee (\t) command. If you want to start logging your session again, simply reexecute the tee command. The new data is then appended to the existing text file.

The use Command

The use (\u) command allows you to change the current database. Whichever database you specify becomes the active database, assuming that you have the privileges necessary to access that database. For example, if you want to change the current database to the test database, you would use the following command:

```
use test
```

When you execute the command, the test database becomes the current database, and you can begin executing SQL statements against that database.

As you can see, mysql is a flexible tool that enables you to interact with MySQL data directly. You can perform ad hoc queries that allow you to administer MySQL and manage the data stored in the MySQL databases. The following Try It Out illustrates the mysql utility's flexibility.

Try It Out   Using the mysql Client Interactively

To use the mysql client utility interactively, take the following steps:

1. If necessary, open a shell for your operating system:

If you're using a graphical user interface (GUI) such as GNOME or KDW in a Linux environment, use a Terminal window.

If you're using Linux without a GUI, use the shell's command prompt.

If you're working in a Windows environment, use a Command Prompt window.

2. Next, launch the mysql client utility in interactive mode. If you're using a Linux RPM installation of MySQL, enter the following command:

```
/usr/bin/mysql mysql -u root
```

If you're using a Linux tar installation of MySQL, enter the following command:

```
/usr/local/mysql/bin/mysql mysql -u root
```

If you're using a Windows installation of MySQL, enter the following command:

```
c:\program files\mysql\mysql server <version>\bin\mysql mysql -u root
```

You receive a message that welcomes you to the MySQL monitor and provides information about command termination, the MySQL connection, and getting help. In addition, the command prompt displays as follows:

```
mysql>
```

At the command prompt, you simply type SQL commands as you would type in commands in any Linux or Windows shell. When sending commands to MySQL, you must terminate your commands with a semi-colon, unless those commands are specific to the mysql utility, such as the exit or quit command.

3. Now, try out a couple of mysql-specific commands. In the first one, you list the commands that are specific to the mysql client. Execute the following command:

```
help
```

When you execute the help command, mysql returns a list of available commands, as shown in the following results:

```
For the complete MySQL Manual online visit:
    http://www.mysql.com/documentation

For info on technical support from MySQL developers visit:
    http://www.mysql.com/support

For info on MySQL books, utilities, consultants, etc. visit:
    http://www.mysql.com/portal

List of all MySQL commands:
Note that all text commands must be first on line and end with ';'
?         (\?) Synonym for `help'.
clear     (\c) Clear command.
connect   (\r) Reconnect to the server. Optional arguments are db and host.
delimiter (\d) Set query delimiter.
ego       (\G) Send command to mysql server, display result vertically.
exit      (\q) Exit mysql. Same as quit.
go        (\g) Send command to mysql server.
help      (\h) Display this help.
notee     (\t) Don't write into outfile.
print     (\p) Print current command.
prompt    (\R) Change your mysql prompt.
quit      (\q) Quit mysql.
rehash    (\#) Rebuild completion hash.
source    (\.) Execute a SQL script file. Takes a file name as an argument.
```

```
status      (\s) Get status information from the server.
tee         (\T) Set outfile [to_outfile]. Append everything into given outfile.
use         (\u) Use another database. Takes database name as argument.

For server side help, type 'help all'
```

The list of commands available to mysql can vary depending on version and operating system. Be sure to review the list that appears on your system.

4. Next, type in a SELECT statement, but don't include the terminator (semi-colon). Type the following at the command prompt and then press Enter:

```
SELECT host, user FROM user
```

Because you didn't include the terminator, mysql interprets this to mean that you have not completed the statement. As a result, the command prompt changes to the following:

```
->
```

At this point, you can complete the statement, add a semi-colon, or clear it to start over.

5. If you decide that you don't want to complete this statement, use the following command to clear it:

```
\c
```

The clear command tells mysql to disregard the statement and return you to the command prompt.

6. Another mysql command that you use quite often is the use command, which specifies the name of the database in which you'll be working. For example, you would change to the test database by using the use command:

```
use test
```

After you execute this command, you receive a message telling you that the database has been changed, and you're returned to the command prompt.

7. Finally, to exit the mysql utility, you can simply execute the following command:

```
quit
```

You could have also used the exit command or the \q command to exit mysql. Once you execute one of these commands, you're returned to your shell's command prompt.

How It Works

Once you're in your operating system's shell, you can launch the mysql client utility along with the options necessary to operate the utility. In the preceding exercise, you included two options, as shown in the following code:

```
/usr/bin/mysql mysql -u root
```

The first mysql refers to the client utility. If you want, you can launch the utility without specifying any options; however, if you do specify options, they follow the name of the utility. For example, the second mysql is an option that provides the name of a specific database, which in this case is the mysql administrative database that is installed by default as part of your MySQL installation. You can specify any database that currently exists in your MySQL environment. By specifying the mysql database, you're telling mysql to operate in the context of that database. Once in the mysql shell, you can specify another database if you desire.

The second option used in the command is the user option: `-u root`. The option specifies that the mysql utility should interact with MySQL in the context of the root user account. Whatever privileges are granted to the specified user account are available during that mysql client session.

> *Because you haven't yet created any user accounts or modified the existing accounts, it isn't necessary to specify the root user. We used it here simply to demonstrate how that option is specified. Once you've created additional user accounts and assigned privileges to those accounts, you can log into the mysql client in the context of one of those accounts.*

After you logged into the mysql client utility, you were able to execute mysql commands, such as `help`, `\c`, `use`, and `quit`. These commands are specific to the mysql utility and, as a result, do not require that you terminate them with a semi-colon, as would be the case with an SQL statement. You can use a terminator, however, and the commands will run as they would without it. In addition, if you are executing several commands consecutively, as would be the case when creating a batch file, you must use the terminator so MySQL recognizes the end of one statement and the beginning of the next.

Using mysql in Batch Mode

Using the mysql client utility in batch mode provides you with a way to execute statements in a file from your shell's command prompt, without having to go into the mysql utility. To use the mysql client utility in batch mode, you must type the mysql command followed by the name of the source file, as shown in the following command:

```
mysql < <source file>
```

The source file can be any text file that contains SQL statements and mysql commands. If you execute this command, the results returned by the query are displayed at the command prompt. You can save those results to another file by adding that file to your command:

```
mysql < <source file> > <target file>
```

As you can see, you must define both a source file and a target file. Whenever you specify a file in this way, you must specify the appropriate path for each file.

As you have learned, the mysql utility is available not only in interactive mode, but in batch mode as well. The following Try It Out shows you how to use mysql in batch mode.

Try It Out   Using mysql in Batch Mode

To use the mysql client utility in batch mode, take the following steps:

1. Before you actually use mysql in batch mode, you need to create a file that contains an SQL statement. For this you need to use a text editor in order to create the file that includes the necessary commands. The new text file should contain the following statements:

```
use mysql;
SELECT host, user, select_priv FROM user;
```

Save the file as user_info.sql in a directory on your system.

2. If necessary, open a shell for your operating system:

    If you're using a graphical user interface (GUI) such as GNOME or KDW in a Linux environment, use a Terminal window.

    If you're using Linux without a GUI, use the shell's command prompt.

    If you're working in a Windows environment, use a Command Prompt window.

3. Next, launch the mysql client utility in batch mode. If you're using a Linux RPM installation of MySQL, enter the following command:

```
/usr/bin/mysql < <path>/user_info.sql
```

The `<path>` placeholder refers to the path where you stored the user_info.sql file that you created in Step 1. If you're using a Linux tar installation of MySQL, enter the following command:

```
/usr/local/mysql/bin/mysql < <path>\user_info.sql
```

If you're using a Windows installation of MySQL, enter the following command:

```
c:\program files\mysql\mysql server <version>\bin\mysql < <path>\user_info.sql
```

When you execute on these commands, you receive the results of your SELECT statement without having to be in the mysql shell. These results are displayed in a manner similar to the following:

```
host      user     select_priv
localhost          root      Y
%         root     Y
```

Of course, your exact results depend on whether you're working on a Linux or a Windows computer. The results displayed here are from a Windows computer.

This step provided the full directory path necessary to launch the mysql client program. The rest of this exercise assumes that you know how to launch the program from its correct path, so it provides only the command itself.

4. As you can see from these query results, they're much more difficult to read than if you were working directly in the mysql shell. You can improve the display by adding the -t option to you command:

```
mysql -t < <path>\user_info.sql
```

The -t option, which you can also write as --table, returns the query in a tabular format, similar to what you would expect to see in the mysql shell, as shown by the following query results:

```
+-----------+-------+-------------+
| host      | user  | select_priv |
+-----------+-------+-------------+
| localhost | root  | Y           |
| %         | root  | Y           |
+-----------+-------+-------------+
```

As you can see, this approach is far easier to read.

5. There might be times in which you don't want to view the results of your query, but instead want to save the results to a file. You can do this by modifying the command as follows:

```
mysql -t < <path>\user_info.sql > <path>\user_results.txt
```

When you execute this command, a file named user_results.txt is created in the specified directory. The new file contains the results of your query.

How It Works

Using mysql in batch mode allows you to execute SQL script files without having to interact directly with MySQL. As a result, before you can use mysql in batch mode, the source files have to exist. For this reason, you had to create the user_info.sql file to contain the following statements:

```
use mysql;
SELECT host, user, select_priv FROM user;
```

The first line in this statement instructs mysql to use the mysql database. The use command is a mysql command that allows you to specify a working database. The next line is a SELECT statement that retrieves information from the user table. Specifically, the statement returns data from the host, user, and select_priv columns in the user table.

Once you created the file, you were able to use the mysql utility to process the contents of the file, as shown in the following command:

```
mysql < <path>\user_info.sql
```

The command specifies the mysql client utility, followed by a left angle bracket, and the path and filename. The left angle bracket indicates to the mysql utility that it should be run in batch mode and that the file that follows the bracket contains the statements to be executed.

The statements contained in the file are executed, and the results are displayed at the command prompt. Whatever results you would normally expect to see when working with mysql interactively are displayed at the shell's command prompt. As a result, you did not have to launch mysql, type in the SQL statements, execute those statements, and then exit mysql. Instead, you were able to perform everything in one step, and you can rerun the query as often as you like, without having to retype it each time.

You then further refined the command by adding the -t option, which allowed the results to be displayed in the same format as you would see them if you executed the query while working in mysql interactively. You then refined your command even further by sending the query results to a separate file (user_results.txt), rather than displaying them at the command prompt, as shown in the following command:

```
mysql -t < <path>\user_info.sql > <path>\user_results.txt
```

The command specifies the mysql client utility, followed by a left angle bracket, and the path and filename. This is then followed by a right angle bracket and the path and filename of the target file. The right angle bracket indicates to the mysql utility that it should take the results returned by executing the statements in the first file and insert them into the second file.

By taking this approach, the query results are saved to a file, and you can view them or use the data as necessary, without having to run your query additional times. This is especially handy when working with large result sets or when you need to generate the same query numerous times on data that changes little or not at all.

Assigning Account Passwords

When you installed MySQL on Windows, you ran the MySQL Server Instance Configuration Wizard, which assigned a password to the MySQL root user account. When you installed Linux, though, you did not assign a password to the root account. As a result, anyone can sign into MySQL as the root user, without having to supply a password. As a result, one of your first steps in protecting MySQL should be to assign a password to root.

MySQL supports a couple ways to assign a password to a user account. The first method is to use the `mysqladmin` utility at your shell's command prompt. For example, suppose you want to assign a password to the myadmin account. You would use the following command:

```
mysqladmin -u myadmin password pw1
```

The command assigns the password pw1 to the account. From here on in, whenever that user connects to MySQL, the user must use the new password. If the account already has been assigned a password, you must know the current password when executing the command; in that case, your command might look like the following:

```
mysqladmin -u myadmin -p password pw1
```

When you execute this command, you are prompted for the current password, and then the account is assigned the new password. You can also assign a password from within the mysql client utility, in which case you would use a SET PASSWORD statement, as shown in the following example:

```
SET PASSWORD FOR 'myadmin'@'localhost' = PASSWORD('pw1');
```

Notice that you must also define the user and the host when assigning the password. The user must exist in order to use the SET statement to assign a password. If you're setting the password for an account that has multiple records in the user table, as is the case with the root account, you should use the SET PASSWORD statement, rather than the `mysqladmin` utility, and you should execute a SET PASSWORD statement for each record for that user, being certain to specify the correct computer in each case.

> *Whether you use the `mysqladmin` utility or a SET PASSWORD statement to assign a password to a user account, the password is saved to the user table in an encrypted format, and the user must supply the password when connecting to mysql.*

Once you set a password, you should reload the grant tables. Generally, it's a good idea to reload your grant tables into memory whenever you modify the tables in any way. Although it is not always necessary to reload the tables, it is not always clear under what circumstances they must be reloaded, so it's a good habit to foster. To reload the grant tables, run the following command at the mysql command prompt:

```
FLUSH PRIVILEGES;
```

Alternatively, you can run the `mysqladmin` utility at your shell's command prompt, as shown in the following command:

```
mysqladmin flush-privileges
```

Once the grant tables have been reloaded, the user must use a password to connect to MySQL.

As you have learned, one of the first steps that you should take before starting to use MySQL is to assign a password to the root user and to remove anonymous users. If you installed MySQL on Windows, you already assigned a password to the root user. If you installed MySQL on Linux, though, you still need to assign a password to the root user. The following Try It Out walks you through this process. If you're a Windows user, you can still work through this exercise.

Try It Out   Securing MySQL Data

The following steps demonstrate how to assign a password to the MySQL root user account:

1. You create the necessary passwords from within the mysql utility. As usual, launch the utility from your shell's command prompt. This exercise assumes that you'll be launching the utility from the correct directory. Now open a shell window, and execute the following command at the command prompt:

```
mysql mysql
```

The mysql utility launches, and the mysql database is the active database.

2. Next, you use the SET PASSWORD statement to assign a password to the root account. You need to replace the *<password>* placeholder in the following statement with a password of your choice. If you're a Windows user, you can use the same password that already exists, or you can assign a new password to the root account.

    At the mysql command prompt, execute the following command:

```
SET PASSWORD FOR 'root'@'localhost' = PASSWORD('<password>');
```

The SET PASSWORD statement uses the PASSWORD( ) function to assign the password to the root user at the local computer.

3. Next, you must execute the SET PASSWORD statement a second time. For Linux installations, replace the *<computer>* placeholder with the name of your computer. For Windows installations, replace the *<computer>* placeholder with the percentage (%) wildcard. Now execute the following command:

```
SET PASSWORD FOR 'root'@'<computer>' = PASSWORD('<password>');
```

The SET PASSWORD statement assigns the password to the second root record in the user table.

4. Next, you should reload the grant tables to ensure that MySQL is using the most current information. Execute the following command:

```
FLUSH PRIVILEGES;
```

The FLUSH PRIVILEGES command reloads the changes that you just made. You might not always need to execute this command when updating the user table, but it's generally a good

idea in order to ensure that the system remains secure and that it behaves in the manner you would expect.

5. Now take a look at the changes that you just made to the user table. Execute the following command:

```
SELECT host, user, password FROM user;
```

On Linux, you should see results similar to the following:

```
+-----------+------+-------------------------------------------+
| host      | user | password                                  |
+-----------+------+-------------------------------------------+
| localhost | root | *2B602296A79E0A8784ACC5C88D92E46588CCA3C3 |
| <name>    | root | *2B602296A79E0A8784ACC5C88D92E46588CCA3C3 |
| localhost |      |                                           |
| <name>    |      |                                           |
+-----------+------+-------------------------------------------+
4 rows in set (0.00 sec)
```

Instead of the <name> placeholder, you will see the name of your computer. If you decided to try out this exercise on a Windows installation, your results should be similar to the following:

```
+-----------+------+-------------------------------------------+
| host      | user | password                                  |
+-----------+------+-------------------------------------------+
| localhost | root | *2B602296A79E0A8784ACC5C88D92E46588CCA3C3 |
| %         | root | *2B602296A79E0A8784ACC5C88D92E46588CCA3C3 |
+-----------+------+-------------------------------------------+
2 rows in set (0.06 sec)
```

6. Next, exit the mysql utility. Execute the following command:

```
exit
```

You're returned to your shell's command prompt.

7. The next step is to start the mysql utility again. Only this time, you specify the user option, username, and password option, as shown in the following code:

```
mysql mysql -u root -p
```

When you execute this command, you'll be prompted for a password. Enter the password that you created earlier in this exercise, and then press Enter. You're then connected to MySQL as the root user.

8. Now that you've tested the new password, you can exit the mysql client utility and return to your operating system's command prompt.

How It Works

In this exercise, you used the mysql client utility to configure a password for the root user account, as shown in the following command:

```
SET PASSWORD FOR 'root'@'localhost' = PASSWORD('<password>');
```

As you can see, the command sets a password for root@localhost. As you'll recall, the user table contains two records for the root user. The first record is assigned to the localhost computer, and the second record is assigned to a host with the same name as your computer (on Linux) or assigned to all hosts (on Windows). As a result, you must execute the SET PASSWORD statement a second time:

```
SET PASSWORD FOR 'root'@'<computer>' = PASSWORD('<password>');
```

Although setting these passwords ensures that no one can log in as the root user without supplying the correct password, these changes don't prevent anonymous users from having at least some level of access to MySQL on Linux. In Chapter 14, you learn how to revoke permissions to users as well as remove users from the MySQL grant tables.

Setting Up a Configuration File

Once you assign a password to the root user account in MySQL and delete the anonymous accounts, you must include your username, password, and any other desired options whenever you connect to MySQL. This can result in a lot of retyping if you access the mysql client utility often. As you learned earlier in the chapter, though, you can place these options in a configuration file in the appropriate directory. That way, any time you connect as the root user, the options are called automatically from the configuration file.

If you're running MySQL on Linux, you need to create a configuration (option) file. The configuration file can be based on one of the four sample configuration files included with MySQL, or you can create your own. If you're running MySQL on Windows, you can copy the configuration file that was created when you first ran the MySQL Server Instance Configuration Wizard. After you copy the file, you can update it as necessary. To configure a configuration file for your MySQL installation, refer to one of the following two Try It Out sections. The first section covers Linux, and the second one covers Windows.

Try It Out   Setting Up a Configuration File in Linux

The following steps allow you to create a my.cnf configuration file and add the options necessary to connect to MySQL through the mysql utility:

1. Open a Terminal window (if you're working in a GUI environment) or use the shell's command prompt. In either case, you should be at the root directory.

2. You must copy the my-small.cnf configuration file to the root directory and rename it .my.cnf. For an RPM installation, execute the following command:

```
cp /usr/share/doc/packages/MySQL-server/my-small.cnf .my.cnf
```

For a tar installation, execute the following command:

```
cp /usr/local/mysql/support-files/my-small.cnf .my.cnf
```

The cp command copies the my-small.cnf file to the root directory and renames the file .my.cnf.

3. Once the file has been copied over, you can configure it as necessary for your MySQL programs. To edit the file, execute the following command:

```
vi .my.cnf
```

The vi command opens the Vim text editor in Linux, which allows you to edit text files.

4. In order to edit the files, you must change the Vim utility to insert mode by typing the following letter:

```
i
```

As soon as you type this command, you are placed in insert mode.

5. Scroll down to the section that begins with [mysql], and add a blank line beneath the [mysql] heading.

6. Add the following code beneath the [mysql] heading:

```
user=root
password=pw1
database=mysql
```

Be certain that you type the options correctly, or you will not be able to connect to MySQL. Notice the inclusion of the mysql database as the last option. As a result, whenever you start mysql, it opens in the mysql database. Later, as you're creating other databases, you might want to change this option or delete it entirely.

7. Press the Escape key to get out of Insert mode.

8. To indicate to the Vim utility that you have completed your edit, you must type the following command:

```
:
```

When you type this command, a colon is inserted at the bottom of the screen and your cursor is moved to the position after the colon.

9. At the colon, type the following command and press Enter:

```
wq
```

The w option tells the Vim utility to save the edits upon exiting, and the q option tells Vim to exit the program. When you execute this command, you're returned to the command prompt (at the root).

10. Next, open the mysql utility to ensure that you can connect to mysql without entering the required options. At the appropriate directory, execute the following command:

```
mysql
```

You should be connected to MySQL, and the mysql prompt should be displayed.

11. Now type the following command to exit from mysql:

```
exit
```

You're returned to your shell's command prompt.

How It Works

Setting up a configuration file on a Linux computer is a fairly straightforward process. You can use one of the sample files to create your configuration file, or you can create one from scratch. In this exercise, you copied the my-small.cnf sample file to your root directory and renamed it. From there, you edited the file so that it included the following options for the mysql client utility:

```
user=root
password=pw1
database=mysql
```

These options are the same options that you would enter into at the command prompt when you invoked the mysql utility; however, there are a few differences. For example, in the configuration file, you do not have to precede the `user` option or `password` option with hyphens. In addition, when you specify a database in the configuration file, you must precede the name of the database with the option name and an equal sign. When you specify the database option at a command prompt, you need only to specify the name of the database, and nothing else, as shown in the following command:

```
mysql mysql
```

Once you modify and save the configuration file, the options are used whenever you start mysql. As a result, you do not need to include any of the options that you defined in the configuration file, unless you want to override the options in the file. This next Try It Out covers how to set up a configuration file in a Windows environment.

Try It Out   Setting Up a Configuration File in Windows

The following steps allow you to set up the my.ini configuration file to include the options necessary to connect to MySQL:

1. Copy the `my.ini` file in `C:\Program Files\MySQL\MySQL Server <version>` to `C:\WINDOWS`.

2. Open the new file in Notepad or any text editor.

3. Scroll down to after the `[client]` section and before the `[mysqld]` section, and add the following `[mysql]` section:

```
[mysql]
user=root
password=<password>
database=mysql
```

Be sure to replace the *<password>* placeholder with the password that you created for the root user account.

Notice the inclusion of the mysql database as the last option. As a result, whenever you start mysql, it opens in the mysql database. Later, as you're creating other databases, you might want to change this option or delete it entirely.

4. Save and close the `my.ini` file.

5. Open a Command Prompt window, and change to the `C:\Program Files\MySQL\MySQL Server <version>\bin` directory. Execute the following command:

```
mysql
```

Your username, password, and the mysql database are automatically used with this command. You can then use the mysql client utility from within the mysql database, or you can switch to another database.

6. Now type the following command to exit from mysql:

```
exit
```

You're returned to your shell's command prompt.

How It Works

In this exercise, you copied the `my.ini` file that was created when you ran the MySQL Server Instance Configuration Wizard. You then modified the file to include the following code:

```
[mysql]
user=root
password=pw1
database=mysql
```

The `[mysql]` heading indicates that the code following that heading applies specifically to the mysql utility. In this case, the options specify a user, password, and database. These options are the same options that you would use at the command prompt when invoking the mysql utility; however, there are a few differences. For example, in the configuration file, you do not have to precede the `user` option or `password` option with hyphens. In addition, when you specify a database in the configuration file, you must precede the name of the database with the option name and an equal sign. When you specify the database option at a command prompt, you need to specify only the name of the database, nothing else.

After you have modified and saved the configuration file, the options specified in the file will be used whenever you launch mysql. As a result, you will not need to specify any of the options that you defined in the configuration file, unless you want to override those options with new values.

Summary

This chapter provided a lot of detail about how to set up MySQL on your computer and find the programs that you use to interact with MySQL. The chapter also explained how to use the mysql client utility to work with data in a database. As a result, you are able to use this information to create databases and tables, add data to the tables, query and manipulate that data, and perform administrative tasks. You also learned how to secure your MySQL installation in order to avoid unauthorized users accessing your system. By the end of the chapter, you were provided with the background information and examples necessary to perform the following tasks:

❑   Work with the MySQL files as they are stored in your system's directories

❑   Work with the data directory and database files

❑   Work with the mysql administrative database

❑   Use the programs, scripts, and library files that are included with your MySQL installation

❑   Use the mysql client utility in interactive mode and in batch mode

❑   Assign passwords to MySQL user accounts

❑   Setting up your configuration file

Now that you are familiar with how to use MySQL and you have secured your installation, you're ready to add data and manipulate that data. Before you can store data in MySQL, though, the tables must exist that hold the data, and before the tables can exist, you must create the appropriate database to support those tables. Before you create a database, you should plan the structure of that database to ensure that it meets your needs as you begin adding data. As a result, the next step in working with MySQL is to learn how to design a relational database that you can implement in MySQL, which is what Chapter 4 covers.

Exercises

The following questions are provided as a way for you to better acquaint yourself with the material covered in this chapter. Be sure to work through each exercise carefully. To view the answers to these questions, see Appendix A.

1. You have used RPM files to install MySQL on Linux. You now want to launch the mysql client utility. In which directory will you find that utility?

2. You plan to use the mysql client utility to connect to MySQL. You will connect at a command prompt with the myadmin user account. You want to be prompted for your password when you launch the mysql utility. What command should you use to connect to MySQL?

3. You are modifying the configuration file on your system. You want the file to include options for the mysqladmin client utility. The file should specify that you're connecting to a host named system3 as a user named myadmin. The file should also specify the password as pw1. What code should you add to your configuration file?

4. You are working with a MySQL installation in Windows. You plan to use the mysql client utility in batch mode to run a query that has been saved to a file in the C:\mysql_files directory. The name of the file is users.sql, and it includes a command to use the mysql database, which the query targets. You want to save the results of the query to a file named users.txt, which should also be saved to the C:\mysql_files directory. What command should you use to execute the query?

5. You are using the mysql client utility to assign a password to the myadmin user account, which can access MySQL from any computer on your network. You want to assign the password pw1 to the user account. Which SQL statement should you use to assign the password?

Designing a Relational Database

Chapter 1 introduced you to databases and databases management systems. As you'll recall from that discussion, a database is a collection of related data organized and classified in a structured format that is defined by metadata. Not all databases are structured the same, though, as can be attested to by the different data models that have emerged over the years. Yet many of these models — and subsequently the systems that were built on them — lacked the flexibility necessary to support increasingly sophisticated software applications. One data model emerged that addressed the limitations of its predecessors and provided the flexibility necessary to meet the demands of today's application technologies. This model — the relational model — has become the standard on which most database management systems are now built.

MySQL is one of the database management systems based on the relational model. As a result, to design effective databases, you should have a good understanding of that model and how it applies to database design. To that end, this chapter provides you with a conceptual overview of the relational model and explains the components that make up a relational database. The chapter also discusses how data is organized in the relational model and how tables of data are related to one another. Specifically, the chapter covers the following topics:

❑ You are introduced to the relational model and the components that make up that model.

❑ You learn how data in a relational structure is organized according to normal forms, which are prescriptive methods for organizing data in a relational database.

❑ You are provided with the information necessary to identify the relationships between tables in a relational database, including one-to-one, one-to-many, and many-to-many relationships.

❑ You learn how to create a data model. The process includes identifying entities, normalizing data, identifying relationships, and refining the data model.

The Relational Model

The relational model first entered the database scene in 1970, when Dr. E. F. Codd published his seminal work, "A Relational Model of Data for Large Shared Data Banks" in the journal *Communication of the ACM*, Volume 13, Number 6 (June 1970). In this paper, Codd introduced a relational data structure that was based on the mathematical principles of set theory and predicate logic. The data structure allowed data to be manipulated in a manner that was predictable and resistant to error. To this end, the relational model would enforce data accuracy and consistency, support easy data manipulation and retrieval, and provide a structure independent of the applications accessing the data.

At the heart of the relational model—and of any relational database—is the *table*, which is made up of a set of related data organized in a column/row structure, similar to what you might see in a spreadsheet program such as Microsoft Excel. The data represents the physical implementation of some type of object that is made up of a related set of data, such entities as people, places, things, or even processes. For example, the table in Figure 4-1 contains data about authors. Notice that all the values in the table are in some way related to the central theme of authors.

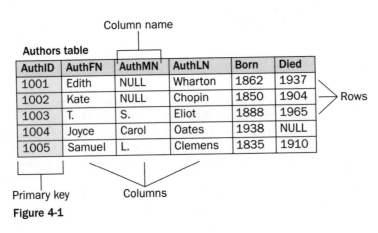

Figure 4-1

Each table in a relational database is made up of one or more columns. A *column* is a structure in a table that stores the same type of data. For example, the table in Figure 4-1 includes a column named AuthMN. The column is intended to hold a value for each author that is equal to the author's middle name, if one is known. The column can hold only data that conforms to the restrictions placed on that column.

Along with the columns, each table contains zero or more rows. A *row* is a structure in a table made up of a set of related data. A row can be thought of as a record that represents one instance of the object defined by the table. For example, in Figure 4-1 the last row contains data about the author Samuel L. Clemens, who was born in 1835 and died in 1910. The author is identified by an AuthID value of 1005. Together, this set of data makes up one row.

One other item that is important to note in a table is the primary key. A *primary key* is one or more columns in a table that uniquely identify each row so that no two rows are identical. In Figure 4-1, a primary key is defined on the AuthID column. Because this column is the primary key, no values can be repeated in the column. As a result, even if two authors share the same name, same year of birth, and same year of death, the values in the primary key column would provide a unique identifier for each row.

Although the table serves as the foundation for every relational database, the relational model includes other important characteristics, including the normalization of data and the relationships that exist between tables. The following section discusses how data is normalized in a relational database and, after that, reviews the types of relationships that can exist between tables.

Data Normalization

One of the concepts most important to a relational database is that of normalized data. *Normalized data* is organized into a structure that preserves the integrity of the data while minimizing redundant data. The goal of all normalized data is to prevent lost data and inconsistent data, while minimizing redundant data.

A normalized database is one whose tables are structured according to the rules of normalization. These rules — referred to as *normal forms* — specify how to organize data so that it is considered normalized. When Codd first introduced the relational model, he included three normal forms. Since then, more normal forms have been introduced, but the first three still remain the most critical to the relational model.

The degree to which a database is considered normalized depends on which normal forms can be applied. For example, some database designs aim for only the second normal form; however, some databases strive to achieve conformance to the fourth or fifth normal form. There is often a trade-off between strict adherence to the normal forms and system performance. Often, the more normalized the data, the more taxing it can be on a system. As a result, a database design must strike a balance between a fully normalized database and system performance. In most situations, the first three normal forms provide that balance.

First Normal Form

Of all the normal forms, the first is the most important. It provides the foundation on which all other normal forms are built and represents the core characteristics of any table. To be in compliance with the first normal form, a table must meet the following requirements:

❑ Each column in a row must be atomic. In other words, the column can contain only one value for any given row.

❑ Each row in a table must contain the same number of columns. Given that each column can contain only one value, this means that each row must contain the same number of values.

❑ All rows in a table must be different. Although rows might include the same values, each row, when taken as a whole, must be unique in the table.

Take a look at an example to help illustrate these requirements. Figure 4-2 contains a table that violates the first normal form. For example, the fifth row contains two values in the BookTitle column: *Postcards* and *The Shipping News*. Although a value can consist of more than one word, as in *The Shipping News*, only one value can exist in a column. As a result, the BookTitle column for that row is not atomic because it contains two values. In addition, the row as a whole contains more values than the other rows in the table, which also violates the first normal form.

AuthorBook

AuthFN	AuthMN	AuthLN	BookTitle
Hunter	S.	Thompson	Hell's Angels
Rainer	Maria	Rilke	Letters to a Young Poet
Rainer	Maria	Rilke	Letters to a Young Poet
John	Kennedy	Toole	A Confederacy of Dunces
Annie	NULL	Proulx	Postcards, The Shipping News
Nelson	NULL	Algren	Nonconformity

Figure 4-2

Another way in which the table violates the first normal form is found in the second and third rows, which are identical. Duplicate rows can exist for a number of reasons, and without the necessary data to distinguish them, you cannot tell whether this is an error in data entry or whether there are supposed to be two records for this one book. For example, the rows might be duplicated because they refer to different editions of the book, or perhaps the book has been translated into different languages. The point is, each row in a table must be unique.

In order to conform to the first normal form, you must eliminate the duplicate values in the BookTitle column, ensure that each row contains the same number of values, and avoid duplicated rows. One way to achieve the necessary normalization is to place the data in separate tables, based on the objects represented by the data. In this case, the obvious place to start is with authors and books. All data related to authors is placed in one table, and all data related to books is placed in another table, as shown in Figure 4-3. Notice that a row has been created for each book and that a translation-related column has been added for that table. This eliminates the duplicated rows, as long as two books with the same name are not translated into the same language.

Authors

AuthID	AuthFN	AuthMN	AuthLN
1006	Hunter	S.	Thompson
1007	Rainer	Maria	Rilke
1008	John	Kennedy	Toole
1009	Annie	NULL	Proulx
1010	Nelson	NULL	Algren

AuthorBook

AuthID	BookID
1006	14356
1007	12786
1007	14555
1008	17695
1009	19264
1009	19354
1010	16284

Books

BookID	BookTitle	Trans
14356	Hell's Angels	English
12786	Letters to a Young Poet	English
14555	Letters to a Young Poet	French
17695	A Confederacy of Dunces	English
19264	Postcards	English
19354	The Shipping News	English
16284	Nonconformity	English

Figure 4-3

To get around the possibility of two rows containing data about books with the same name and language, an identifying column (BookID) is added to the table and configured as the primary key (shown in gray). Because the column is the primary key, each value in the column must be unique. As a result, even the rows that contain duplicated book titles and languages remain unique from one another (when taken as a whole). The same is true of the Authors table. Because the AuthID column is defined a primary key (shown in gray), authors can share the same name and each row will still be unique.

By creating tables for both authors and books, adding a primary key column to each table, and placing only one value in each column, you are ensuring that the data conforms to the first normal form. As you can see in Figure 4-3, a third table (AuthorBook) is also being used. This table allows you to match the

IDs for authors and books in a way that supports books written by multiple authors, authors who have written multiple books, and multiple authors who have written multiple books. Had you tried to match the authors to their books in one of the two tables, the table would potentially fill with enormous amounts of redundant data, which would defeat one of the purposes of the relational database.

Another thing to notice is that a primary key has been defined on the AuthorBook table. The primary key is made up of two columns. (Both columns are shown in gray.) As a result, each set of values in the two columns must be unique. In other words, no two rows can contain the same AuthID *and* BookID values, although values can be repeated in individual columns. For example, the AuthID value of 1009 is repeated, but each instance of that value is associated with a different BookID value. Because of the primary key, no AuthID value can be associated with a BookID value more than once.

A primary key made up of more than one column is referred to as a composite primary key.

Creating this table might appear as though all you've done is to create a lot more data than you initially had to start. The example here, however, represents only a small amount of data. The advantages of normalizing data are best seen when working with large quantities of data.

Second Normal Form

The second normal form builds on and expands the first normal form. To be in compliance with the second normal form, a table must meet the following requirements:

❑   The table must be in first normal form.

❑   All nonprimary key columns in the table must be dependent on the entire primary key.

Given that the first of these two rules is fairly obvious, take a look at the second one. As you'll recall from earlier in the chapter, a primary key is one or more columns in a table that uniquely identify each row so that no two rows, when taken as a whole, are identical. To illustrate how the second normal form works, first take a look at an example of a table that violates the second normal form. In the AuthorBook table in Figure 4-4, a primary key is defined on the AuthLN and BookTitle columns. Together, the values in these two columns must uniquely identify each row in the table.

AuthorBook

AuthFN	AuthMN	AuthLN	BookTitle	Copyright
Hunter	S.	Thompson	Hell's Angels	1966
Rainer	Maria	Rilke	Letters to a Young Poet	1934
John	Kennedy	Toole	A Confederacy of Dunces	1980
Annie	NULL	Proulx	Postcards	1992
Annie	NULL	Proulx	The Shipping News	1993
Nelson	NULL	Algren	Nonconformity	1996

Primary key

Figure 4-4

You can see how the primary key works in the fourth and fifth rows, which are related to the author Annie Proulx. Although both rows are concerned with the same author, they refer to different books. As a result, the values Proulx and Postcards identify one row, and the values Proulx and The Shipping News identify the second row. Although the values in either one of the individual primary key columns can be duplicated (in that column), the values in both columns, when taken as a whole, must be unique. This is another example of a composite primary key.

Now examine how this table applies to the second normal form. As previously stated, all nonprimary key columns in the table must be dependent on the entire primary key, which, in this case, is made up of the author's last name and the book title. Based on the way that the table is currently defined, the AuthFN and AuthMN columns are dependent on the AuthLN column, and the Copyright column is dependent on the BookTitle column. The AuthFN and AuthMN columns are not dependent on the BookTitle column, though, and the Copyright column is not dependent on the AuthLN column. As a result, the table violates the second normal form.

Another problem with the table is the columns used for the primary key. By defining the primary key in this way, you're assuming that two authors with the same last name won't write a book with the same title and that no one author will write two books with the same title. This assumption, though, might not necessarily be true. If two authors with the same last name write books with the same title, the primary key would prevent you from adding the second book to the table.

The most effective way to normalize the data in the AuthorBook table is to use the solution that you saw for the first normal form: Create a table for the authors and one for the books, add a primary key column to each table, and create a third table that matches up the identifiers for authors and books, as shown in Figure 4-5. For the Authors table, the primary key is the AuthID column, and for the Books, table, the primary key is the BookID column. Now the columns in each table are dependent on their respective primary keys, and no columns exist that are not dependent on the primary key.

Authors

AuthID	AuthFN	AuthMN	AuthLN
1006	Hunter	S.	Thompson
1007	Rainer	Maria	Rilke
1008	John	Kennedy	Toole
1009	Annie	NULL	Proulx
1010	Nelson	NULL	Algren

AuthorBook

AuthID	BookID
1006	14356
1007	12786
1008	17695
1009	19264
1009	19354
1010	16284

Books

BookID	BookTitle	Copyright
14356	Hell's Angels	1966
12786	Letters to a Young Poet	1934
17695	A Confederacy of Dunces	1980
19264	Postcards	1992
19354	The Shipping News	1993
16284	Nonconformity	1996

Figure 4-5

In addition, a primary key has been defined on the AuthID and BookID columns of the AuthorBook table. As a result, any of the primary key columns in a row, when taken as a whole, must be unique from all other rows. Because there are no other columns in this table, the issue of dependent columns is not a concern, so you can assume that this table also conforms to the second normal form.

Third Normal Form

As with the second normal form, the third normal form builds on and expands the previous normal form. To be in compliance with the third normal form, a table must meet the following requirements:

❑ The table must be in second normal form.

❑ All nonprimary key columns in the table must be dependent on the primary key and must be independent of each other.

If you take a look at Figure 4-6, you see an example of a table that violates the third normal form. Notice that a primary key is defined on the BookID column. For each book, there is a unique ID that identifies that book. No other book can have that ID; therefore, all characteristics related to that book are dependent on that ID. For example, the BookTitle and Copyright columns are clearly dependent on the primary key. For each book ID, there is a title and a copyright date.

To illustrate this better, take a look at the first row in the table. As you can see, the book is assigned a BookID value of 14356. The title for this ID is Hell's Angels, and the copyright is 1966. Once that ID is assigned to that title and copyright, that title and copyright become dependent on that ID. It identifies that title and copyright as part of a unique row. Despite their dependence on the primary key, the BookTitle and Copyright columns are independent from each other. In other words, you can include the BookTitle and the Copyright columns, but you don't necessarily need to include both because one isn't dependent on the other for their meaning. The ChineseSign column is very different from the BookTitle and Copyright columns. It provides the Chinese astrological year sign for the year that the book was copyrighted. The ChineseSign value has nothing to do with the BookID and is not related to the book itself. Instead, the ChineseSign column is totally dependent on the Copyright column. Without the Copyright column, the ChineseSign column would have no meaning. As a result, the ChineseSign column violates the third normal form.

Books

BookID	BookTitle	Copyright	ChineseSign
14356	Hell's Angels	1966	Horse
12786	Letters to a Young Poet	1934	Dog
17695	A Confederacy of Dunces	1980	Monkey
19264	Postcards	1992	Monkey
19354	The Shipping News	1993	Rooster
16284	Nonconformity	1996	Rat

Figure 4-6

To ensure that the data conforms to the third normal form, you should separate the data into two tables, one for books and one for Chinese astrological year, as shown in Figure 4-7. From there, you should assign a primary key to the Year column of the ChineseYears table. Because each year must be unique, it is a good candidate for a primary key column. You don't necessarily have to add a column to a table to use as a primary key if an existing column or columns will work.

By separating the data into two tables, each column is now dependent on its respective primary key, and no columns are dependent on nonkey columns.

Books

BookID	BookTitle	Copyright
14356	Hell's Angels	1966
12786	Letters to a Young Poet	1934
17695	A Confederacy of Dunces	1980
19264	Postcards	1992
19354	The Shipping News	1993
16284	Nonconformity	1996

ChineseYears

Year	Sign
1989	Snake
1990	Horse
1991	Goat
1992	Monkey
1993	Rooster
1994	Dog
1995	Pig
1996	Rat
1997	Ox
1998	Tiger
1999	Cat
2000	Dragon

Figure 4-7

By making certain that the data conforms to the third normal form, you're ensuring that it has been normalized according to all three normal forms. And although there are even more normal forms that you can conform to, for the most part, the first three normal forms meet most of your database design needs. If you plan to focus heavily on database design or plan to design complex databases, you're encouraged to research other references for more details about all normal forms and the relational model.

In the meantime, you can go a long way to achieving a normalized database by thinking in terms of separating data into *entities*, discrete categories of information. For example, books represent one entity; publishers represent another. If you keep in mind that, whenever designing a database, you want each table to represent a distinct entity, you go a long way in designing a database that achieves the third normal form.

Relationships

One of the defining characteristics of a relational database is the fact that various types of relationships exist between tables. These relationships allow the data in the tables to be associated with each other in meaningful ways that help ensure the integrity of normalized data. Because of these relationships, actions in one table cannot adversely affect data in another table.

For any relational database, there are three fundamental types of relationships that can exist between tables: one-to-one relationships, one-to-many relationships, and many-to-many relationships. This section takes a look at each of these relationships.

One-to-One Relationships

A one-to-one relationship can exist between any two tables in which a row in the first table can be related to only one row in the second table and a row in the second table can be related to only one row in the first table. The following example demonstrates how this works. In Figure 4-8, a one-to-one relationship exists between the Authors table and the AuthorsBios table. (The line that connects the tables represents the one-to-one relationship that exists between the tables.)

Several different systems are used to represent the relationships between tables, all of which connect the tables with lines that have special notations at the ends of those lines. The examples in this book use a very basic system to represent the relationships.

Authors

AuthID	AuthFN	AuthMN	AuthLN
1001	Edith	NULL	Wharton
1002	Kate	NULL	Chopin
1003	T.	S.	Eliot
1004	Joyce	Carol	Oates
1005	Samuel	L.	Clemens

AuthorsBios

AuthID	Born	Died
1001	1862	1937
1002	1850	1904
1003	1888	1965
1004	1938	NULL
1005	1835	1910

Figure 4-8

Each table includes a primary key that is defined on the AuthID column. For any one row in the Authors table, there can be only one associated row in the AuthorsBios table, and for any one row in the AuthorsBios table, there can be only one associated row in the Authors table. For example, the Authors table includes a row for the author record that has an AuthID value of 1001 (Edith Wharton). As a result, the AuthorsBios table can contain only one row associated with author 1001. In other words, there can be only one biography for each author.

If you refer again to Figure 4-8, you'll see that the AuthorsBios table includes a row that contains an AuthID value of 1004. Because a one-to-one relationship exists between the two tables, only one record can exist in the Authors table for author 1004. As a result, only one author can be associated with that author biography.

Generally, one-to-one relationships are the least likely type of relationships to be implemented in a relational database; however, there are sometimes reasons to use them. For example, you might want to separate tables simply because one table would contain too much data, or perhaps you would want to separate data into different tables so you could set up one table with a higher level of security. Even so, most databases contain relatively few, if any, one-to-one relationships. The most common type of relationship you're likely to find is the one-to-many.

One-to-Many Relationships

As with one-to-one relationships, a one-to-many relationship can exist between any two tables in your database. A one-to-many relationship differs from a one-to-one relationship in that a row in the first table can be related to one or more rows in the second table, but a row in the second table can be related to only one row in the first table. Figure 4-9 illustrates how the one-to-many relationship works.

Authors

AuthID	AuthFN	AuthMN	AuthLN
1006	Hunter	S.	Thompson
1007	Rainer	Maria	Rilke
1008	John	Kennedy	Toole
1009	Annie	NULL	Proulx
1010	Nelson	NULL	Algren

AuthorBook

AuthID	BookID
1006	14356
1007	12786
1008	17695
1009	19264
1009	19354
1010	16284

Books

BookID	BookTitle	Copyright
14356	Hell's Angels	1966
12786	Letters to a Young Poet	1934
17695	A Confederacy of Dunces	1980
19264	Postcards	1992
19354	The Shipping News	1993
16284	Nonconformity	1996

Figure 4-9

As you can see in the figure, there are three tables: Authors, AuthorBook, and Books. Notice that the lines connecting the Authors table and the Books table to the AuthorBook table have three prongs on the AuthorBook side. This is sometimes referred to as a *crow's foot*. The three prongs represent the *many* side of the relationship. What this means is that, for every row in the Authors table, there can be one or more associated rows in the AuthorBook table, and for every row in the Books table, there can be one or more associated rows in the AuthorBook table. For every row in the AuthorBook table, however, there can be only one associated row in the Authors table or the Books table.

Notice that each table includes an identifying column designated as the primary key. In the Authors table, the primary key is the AuthID column, and in the Books table, the primary key is the BookID column. For the AuthorBook table, the primary key is defined on both columns. This is another example of a composite primary key.

If you take a look at the AuthorBook table, notice that the first column is AuthID. The column contains AuthID values from the Authors table. This is how the one-to-many relationship is implemented, by referencing the primary key of the *one* side of the relationship in a column on the *many* side. The same thing is true for the Books table. The BookID column in the AuthorBook table contains the BookID values from the Books table. For example, the first row in the AuthorBook table contains an AuthID value of 1006 and a BookID value of 14356. This indicates that author 1006 wrote book 14356. If you now refer to the Authors table, notice that author 1006 is Hunter S. Thompson. If you refer to the Books table, you'll see that book 14356 is *Hell's Angels*. If an author has written more than one book, the AuthorBook table contains more than one row for that author. If a book is written by more than one author, the AuthorBook table contains more than one row for that book.

A one-to-many relationship is probably the most common type of relationship you'll see in your databases. (This would also include the many-to-one relationship, which is simply a reversing of the order in which the tables are physically represented.) The next section deals with the many-to-many relationship.

Many-to-Many Relationships

A many-to-many relationship can exist between any two tables in which a row in the first table can be related to one or more rows in the second table, but a row in the second table can be related to one or more rows in the first table. Take a look at an example to help illustrate how this relationship works. In Figure 4-10, you can see three tables: Authors, AuthorBook, and Books. Authors and Books are connected by a dotted line that represents the many-to-many relationship. There are three prongs on each end. For any one author in the Authors table, there can be one or more associated books. For any one book in the Books table, there can be one or more authors. For example, author 1009 — Annie Proulx — is the author of books 19264 and 19354 — Postcards and The Shipping News, respectively — and authors 1011 and 1012 — Black Elk and John G. Neihardt, respectively — are the authors of Black Elk Speaks.

Authors

AuthID	AuthFN	AuthMN	AuthLN
1006	Hunter	S.	Thompson
1007	Rainer	Maria	Rilke
1008	John	Kennedy	Toole
1009	Annie	NULL	Proulx
1010	Nelson	NULL	Algren

AuthorBook

AuthID	BookID
1006	14356
1007	12786
1008	17695
1009	19264
1009	19354
1010	16284

Books

BookID	BookTitle	Copyright
14356	Hell's Angels	1966
12786	Letters to a Young Poet	1934
17695	A Confederacy of Dunces	1980
19264	Postcards	1992
19354	The Shipping News	1993
16284	Nonconformity	1996

Figure 4-10

Also notice in the Authors and Books tables that there is no reference in the Authors table to the books that the authors have written, and there is no reference in the Books table to the authors that have written the books. When a many-to-many relationship exists, it is implemented by adding a third table between these two tables that matches the primary key values of one table to the primary key values of the second table. You saw examples of this during the discussion of normalizing data earlier in this chapter. The many-to-many relationship is logical and is not physically implemented, which is why a dotted line represents the relationship in Figure 4-10. In the next section, "Creating a Data Model," you learn how identifying many-to-many relationships is part of the database design process.

Creating a Data Model

As you have seen in this chapter, the relational model is based on tables that contain normalized data and on the meaningful relationships between those tables. Specifically, a table is made up of columns and rows that form a table-like structure. The rows are identified through the use of primary keys, and the data is normalized based on the rules of the normal forms. From these concepts, you should be able to design a database that adheres to the standards of the relational model.

An important part of the database design process is the development of a data model. A *data model* is a physical representation of the components that make up the database as well as the relationships between those components. A data model for a relational database should show all of the following information:

❑ The tables that make up the database

❑ The columns that make up each table

❑ The data type that defines each column

❑ The primary key that identifies each row

❑ The relationships that exist between tables

Ultimately, a data model should be concerned with how the represented database is implemented in a particular RDBMS. For this reason, some database designers will develop a logical data model and, from that, design a physical data model. A logical data model is concerned with data storage in its purest sense, adhering strictly to the rules of normalization and the relational model, while a physical data model provides a representation of how that database will actually be implemented in a particular RDBMS. The logical model is indifferent to *how* the database will be implemented. The physical model is specific to a particular implementation.

For the purposes of this book, you need to be concerned with only one data model. Because the goal is to design a database specific to MySQL, it is not necessary to create two models.

As part of the data modeling process, you must identify the data type for each column. Because you do not learn about data types until Chapter 5, the types are provided for you. In addition to identifying data types, you need to identify the foreign keys. A *foreign key* is one or more columns in a table whose values match the values in one or more columns in another table. The values in the foreign key of the first table usually come from the primary key in the second table. Use a foreign key when a relationship exists between two tables. The foreign key allows you to associate data between tables. As you get deeper into the topic of data modeling, you get a better sense of how foreign keys work.

Now take a look at an example to help illustrate how to use a data model to design a database. Figure 4-11 shows a model that contains five tables: Authors, AuthorBook, Publishers, BookPublisher, and Books. Each table is represented by a rectangle, with the name of the table on top. In each rectangle there is a list of columns — along with their data types — included in that particular table.

Now take a closer look at one of the tables. The Books table includes four columns: BookID, BookTitle, Copyright, and PubID. Each column is listed with the data type that defines the type of data that is permitted in the column. For example, the BookTitle column is defined with the VARCHAR(60) data type. Data types are assigned to columns based on the business rules defined for that database and the restrictions of data types in MySQL. Chapter 5 discusses data types in far greater detail. For now, all you need to know is that a particular data type has been assigned to a specific column. Once you're more familiar with data types, you can assign them yourself.

Returning to the Books table in Figure 4-11, another aspect to notice is that a line separates the BookID column from the other columns. In a data model such as this one, any column listed above the line participates in the primary key. As a result, the primary key in the Books table is made up of the BookID column and no other columns.

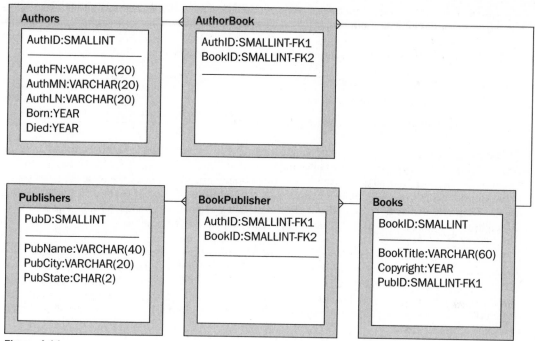

Authors

AuthID:SMALLINT
_____
AuthFN:VARCHAR(20)
AuthMN:VARCHAR(20)
AuthLN:VARCHAR(20)
Born:YEAR
Died:YEAR

AuthorBook

AuthID:SMALLINT-FK1
BookID:SMALLINT-FK2
_____

Publishers

PubD:SMALLINT
_____
PubName:VARCHAR(40)
PubCity:VARCHAR(20)
PubState:CHAR(2)

BookPublisher

AuthID:SMALLINT-FK1
BookID:SMALLINT-FK2
_____

Books

BookID:SMALLINT
_____
BookTitle:VARCHAR(60)
Copyright:YEAR
PubID:SMALLINT-FK1

Figure 4-11

One other aspect to notice in the Books table is the PubID column, which is followed by FK1. *FK* is an acronym for foreign key. As a foreign key, the PubID column contains values from the associated data in the PubID column in the Publishers table. The foreign key exists because a relationship exists between the two tables. The relationship is designated by the line that connects the two tables and the three prongs at one end, indicating that the tables are participating in a one-to-many relationship. As a result, a publisher listed in the Publishers table can publish one or more books, but only one publisher can publish a book, and that publisher is identified by the value in the foreign key column (PubID).

Also notice in Figure 4-11 that a number that follows the FK designates each foreign key table. For example, the AuthorBook table includes an FK1 and an FK2 because there are two foreign keys. The numbers are used because some tables might include multiple foreign keys in which one or more of those keys are made up of more than one column. If this were to occur, it could become confusing as to which columns participate in which foreign keys. By numbering the foreign keys, you can avoid this confusion.

The foreign keys in the AuthorBook table participate in one-to-many relationships with the Authors table and the Books table. All relationships in a data model are indicated by the connecting lines, with three prongs used on the many end. In the case of this data model, three one-to-many relationships exist in all.

As you can see, a data model includes a number of elements that you can use to build your database. The model acts as a blueprint from which you can create tables, define columns, and establish relationships. The modeling method used here is only one type of method available to database designers, and each method uses its own approach for identifying elements in the database. The basic objects, as they're represented here, are fairly similar among the various methods, and ultimately, the goal of any data model should be to represent the final database design clearly and concisely, as it will be implemented in your RDBMS.

Regardless of which data modeling system you use, there are generally four steps that you should follow when developing a data model:

❑ Identifying the potential entities that will exist in the database

❑ Normalizing the data design to support data storage in the identified entities

❑ Identifying the relationships that exist between tables

❑ Refining the data model to ensure full normalization

Whenever you're developing a data model, you're generally following the business rules that have been defined for a particular project. Return once more to Figure 4-11 for an example of how a business rule might work. Suppose that, as part of the project development process, one of the business rules states that an author can write one or more books, a book can be written by one or more authors, and one or more authors can write one or more books. To ensure that you meet this business rule, your database design must correctly reflect the relationship between authors and books.

Although the process of developing business rules is beyond the scope of this book, you should still be aware that, at the root of any database design, there are requirements that specify the storage data needs that the database should support. For that reason, whenever you're designing a database, you should take into account the requirements defined by your business rules and be certain that your database design correctly incorporates these requirements. Now take a closer look at each step involved in the data modeling process.

Identifying Entities

Early in the design process, you want to identify the entities and attributes that ultimately create your data model. An *entity* is an object that represents a set of related data. For example, authors and books are each considered an entity. You can think of identifying entities as the first step in identifying the tables that will be created in your database. Each entity is associated with a set of attributes. An *attribute* is an object that describes the entity. An attribute can be thought of as a property of the entity. For example, an author's first name is an attribute of the author's entity. You can think of identifying attributes as the first step in identifying the columns that make up your tables.

The first step in developing a data model is to identify the objects (entities and attributes) that represent the type of data stored in your database. The purpose of this step is to name any types of information, categories, or actions that require the storage of data in the database. Initially, you don't need to be concerned with tables or columns or how to group data together. You want only to identify the type of data that you need to store.

Take a look at an example in order to illustrate how this works. Suppose that you're developing a database for a bookstore. You need to design that database based on the following business rules:

❑ The database must store information about the authors of the books sold by the bookstore. The information should include each author's first, middle, and last names, the author's year of birth, and if applicable, the author's year of death.

❑ The database must store information about the books sold by the bookstore. The information should include the title for each book, the year the book was copyrighted, the publisher who published the book, and the city and state in which the publisher is located.

❑   One author can write one or more books, one or more authors can write one book, and one or more authors can write one or more books.

❑   One publisher can publish one or more books, and one or more publishers can publish one book.

From this information, you should be able to create a list of objects that require data storage. For example, the author's first name is an example of one of the objects that exists in this scenario. The first step in creating a data model is to record each object as it appears in the business rules. Figure 4-12 provides an example of how you might list the objects described in these sample business rules.

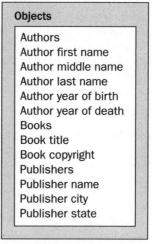

Objects

Authors
Author first name
Author middle name
Author last name
Author year of birth
Author year of death
Books
Book title
Book copyright
Publishers
Publisher name
Publisher city
Publisher state

Figure 4-12

As you can see, any object included in the business rules is listed here. From this information, you can begin to identify the entities and attributes and group them together into logical categories. For example, from the list of objects shown here, you might determine that there are three primary categories of information (entities): data related to authors, data related to books, and data related to publishers, as shown in Figure 4-13.

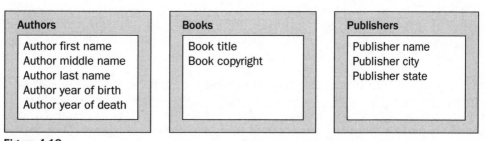

Authors

Author first name
Author middle name
Author last name
Author year of birth
Author year of death

Books

Book title
Book copyright

Publishers

Publisher name
Publisher city
Publisher state

Figure 4-13

By separating the object into logical categories, you provide yourself with a foundation from which you can begin to identify the tables in your database. At this point, the data model is far from complete, and you need to continue to modify it as you progress through the data modeling process. Categorizing the entities in this way provides you with a foundation to begin normalizing the data structure, which is the next step in the data modeling process.

Normalizing Data

Once you define and categorize the primary entities and attributes in your data model, you can begin normalizing that structure, which results in the initial tables that make up your database. As you apply the rules of normalization to the structure, you identify tables, define the columns in those tables, assign data types to the columns, and establish a primary key.

Returning to Figure 4-13, you can see that there are three distinct entities: Authors, Books, and Publishers. The next step is to begin applying the rules of normalization to the entities. You've already started the process by organizing the objects into entities and their related attributes. As a result, you have a good start in identifying at least some of the tables needed in your database. Initially, your database includes the Authors, Books, and Publishers tables. From here, you can identify primary keys for each table, keeping in mind that all non-primary key columns must be dependent on the primary key columns and independent of each other.

For each table, you must determine whether to use existing columns for your primary key or to add one or more columns. For example, in the Authors table, you might consider using the author's first, middle, and last names as a composite primary key. The problem with this is that names can be duplicated, so they are seldom good candidates to use as primary keys. In addition, because you often refer to a primary key through a foreign key, you want to keep your primary keys as short as possible to minimize data redundancy and reduce storage needs. As a result, you're usually better off adding a column to the table that identifies each row and can be configured as the primary key, as shown in Figure 4-14.

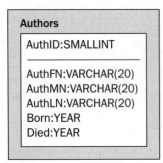
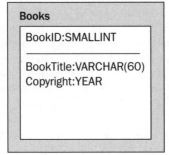

Figure 4-14

As you can see, the Authors table now has a primary key — AuthID — which is assigned the SMALLINT data type. (You learn about data types in greater detail in Chapter 5.) The other columns have been given names to represent the attributes, and they have also been assigned data types. When you begin assigning names to columns, you want to ensure that you use a system that is consistent throughout your database. For example, if you use mixed case to name your database objects, as is the case here, you should use that convention throughout. An alternative would be to use underscores to separate elements in a name, as in author_fname. Again, whichever method you use, you should remain consistent. In addition, regardless of the method you use, you must adhere to the following requirements to create objects in MySQL:

- ❑ Names can contain any alphanumeric characters that are included in the default character set.

- ❑ Names can include underscores (_) and dollar signs ($).

- ❑ Names can start with any acceptable character, including digits.

- ❑ Names *cannot* be made up entirely of digits.

- ❑ Names *cannot* include a period (.).

- ❑ Names *cannot* include an operating system's pathname separator, such as a backslash (\) or forward slash (/).

You should keep your naming conventions as simple as possible. In addition, object names should clearly reflect the meaning of that object. For example, you wouldn't want to assign arbitrary names and numbers to columns (such as Col1, Col2, Col3, etc.) because they provide no indication of what content that column might contain. Basically, you want to make sure that you use a logical naming structure when assigning names to the objects in your database so developers and administrators can easily identify their meaning.

Return to the bookstore database example to continue the normalization process. If you refer back to Figure 4-13, you can see that the second entity is Books, which contains book-related attributes. In this case, neither column would make a good candidate as a primary key. Even taken together they cannot ensure uniqueness. As a result, the best solution for a primary key is to add a column that uniquely identifies each row. The same is true for the Publishers table, which requires an additional column for a primary key. The additional column provides not only an easy way to ensure uniqueness in the table, but also an efficient way to reference a row in the table from another table, without having to repeat a lot of data.

If you return to Figure 4-14, notice that all three tables now have primary keys and column names with data types. In addition, all columns are dependent on their respective primary keys, and no columns are dependent on nonprimary key columns.

Identifying Relationships

The next step in creating a data model is to identify the relationships that exist between the tables. This step is usually a straightforward process of looking at each set of two tables, determining whether a relationship exists, and determining the type of relationship. Figure 4-15 demonstrates how this works.

Figure 4-15

Because your data model contains three tables, three possible relationships can exist among them:

❑ Authors/Books

❑ Authors/Publishers

❑ Books/Publishers

First take a look at the Authors/Books table set. As you'll recall from the business rules outlined for this example, one author can write one or more books, one or more authors can write one book, and one or more authors can write one or more books. Not only does this imply that a relationship exists between authors and their books; it is a many-to-many relationship. As a result, you must add the appropriate line (with a three-pronged end) between the Authors and Books tables.

Moving on to the Authors/Publishers book set, you can find no relationship between these two tables. Nothing in the business rules implies a relationship between the two tables, and no entities suggest such a relationship. (And certainly in the real world, the question of any sort of relationship existing between authors and their publishers is one that is constantly open to debate.) If the business rules had included information that suggested a relationship between authors and publishers, it would have to be included in the data model.

The business rules, though, do imply a relationship between the Books and Publishers tables. According to the rules, one publisher can publish one or more books, and one or more publishers can publish a book. This clearly indicates that a many-to-many relationship exists between the Books table and the Publishers table, as shown in Figure 4-15. As a result, you must add the appropriate relationship line to your data model.

Refining the Data Model

Once you identify the relationships that exist between the tables, you can refine your data model as necessary. You might discover at this point that an entity isn't properly represented or that the data hasn't been fully normalized. This is a good time to review your business rules to ensure that your data model complies with all the specifications.

One way in which you're likely to need to refine your data model is to address any many-to-many relationships that you identified in the last stage of the data modeling process. In MySQL, and in most RDBMSs for that matter, a many-to-many relationship is implemented by adding a third table between the two tables in the relationship. The third table, referred to as a *junction table,* acts as a bridge between the two tables to support the many-to-many relationship. If you refer to Figure 4-11, you can see how the addition of the AuthorBook table to the model bridges the Authors and Books tables and how the addition of the BookPublisher table bridges the Books and Publishers tables. When you add a junction table, the many-to-many relationship is implemented as two one-to-many relationships. For example, a one-to-many relationship now exists between the Authors and AuthorBook table and the Books and AuthorBook table.

Junction tables of this nature usually include, at the very least, the primary key values from their respective tables. As a result, the AuthorBook table includes two foreign keys: one on the AuthID column and one on the BookID column. In addition, together these two columns form a primary key, which enforces the uniqueness of each row in that table. Through these two columns, one author can be associated with multiple books, multiple authors can be associated with one book, and multiple authors can be associated with multiple books. The BookPublisher table works the same way as the AuthorBook table. The BookPublisher table includes two foreign keys: one on the PubID column and one on the BookID column. Together these two columns form the primary key. Once you add the junction table and indicate which columns are foreign keys, you must properly show the two one-to-many relationships that result from adding the table. Be sure to add the correct relationship lines to your data model between the Authors and AuthorBook table and the Books and AuthorBook table. Once again, refer to Figure 4-11, which shows the final data model.

After adding any necessary junction tables and relationship lines, you should review the data model once more to ensure that your changes didn't affect any of the other tables adversely or that more changes aren't necessary. Once you're satisfied that this stage is complete, your data model is ready for you to use to begin creating your database.

Designing the DVDRentals Database

Now that you have an idea of how to create a data model, it's time to try it out for yourself. The following four Try It Out sections walk you through the steps necessary to create your own data model. The model that you design in these exercises is used in Chapter 5 to create the DVDRentals database. All subsequent exercises through the rest of the book are based on that database, including the applications that you develop in Chapters 17–20.

The data model that you design here is created for a fictional store that rents DVDs to its customers. The database tracks the inventory of DVDs, provides information about the DVDs, records rental transactions, and stores the names of the store's customers and employees. To create the data model, you need to use the following business rules:

❑ The database stores information about the DVDs available for rent. For each DVD, the information includes the DVD name, the number of disks included with the set, the year the DVD was released, the movie type (for example, Action), the studio that owns the movie rights (such as Columbia Pictures), the movie's rating (PG and so forth), the DVD format (Widescreen, for example), and the availability status (Checked Out). Multiple copies of the same DVD are treated as individual products.

❑ The database should store the names of actors, directors, producers, executive producers, co-producers, assistant producers, screenwriters, and composers who participated in making the movies available to rent. The information includes the participants' full names and the role or roles that they played in making the movie.

❑ The database should include the full names of the customers who rent DVDs and the employees who work at the store. Customer records should be distinguishable from employee records.

❑ The database should include information about each DVD rental transaction. The information includes the customer who rented the DVD, the employee who ran the transaction, the DVD that was rented, the date of the rental, the date that the DVD is due back, and the date that the DVD is actually returned. Each DVD rental should be recorded as an individual transaction. Every transaction is part of exactly one order. One or more transactions are treated as a single order under the following conditions: (1) the transaction or transactions are for a single customer checking out one or more DVDs at the same time and (2) the transaction or transactions are being run by a single employee.

The business rules provided here are not meant to be an exhaustive listing of all the specifications that would be required to create a database, particularly if those specifications were to include a front-end application that would be interfacing with the database. The business rules shown here, however, are enough to get you started in creating your data model. Later in the book, as you add other elements to your database, the necessary business rules are provided.

To perform the exercises in the Try It Out sections, you need only a paper and pencil. If you have a draw program or a data modeling program, feel free to use that, although it isn't necessary.

Try It Out   Identifying Entities

As you learned earlier in the chapter, the first step in creating a data model is to identify the possible objects (entities and attributes) to include in that model. Refer to the preceding business rules to perform the following steps:

1. Identify the possible objects listed in the first business rule. On a piece of paper, draw a rectangle for this business rule. Label the rectangle as "DVDs for rent." In the rectangle, list the potential objects found in that business rule.

2. Repeat the process for the second business rule. Label the rectangle "Movie participants," and include any objects that you identify in that business rule. This one might be trickier because it covers the roles in the movie (such as producer or actor) and the participants' full names. Remember, though, that the actors, directors, producers, and so forth, are the participants.

3. Create two rectangles for the third business rule, label one "Customers" and the other "Employees," and add the necessary objects.

4. For the fourth business rule, create a rectangle and label it "Transactions/orders." Include in the rectangle each object that makes up a transaction. You should now have five rectangles with objects in each one. Your diagram should look similar to Figure 4-16.

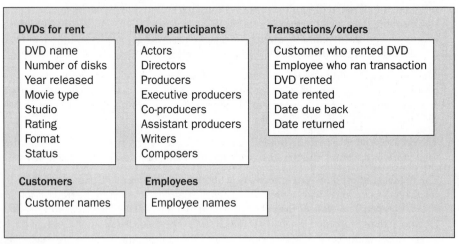

Figure 4-16

5. The next step is to organize the objects into entities. You've already done some of the work simply by listing the objects. For example, the DVDs for rent group of objects can be left together as you have them, although you can simplify the category name to "DVDs." The Transactions/orders group of entities also provides you with a natural category. You probably want to separate the customers and employees into separate categories and specify that an attribute be created for each part of the name. You should separate employees and customers into two entities so that you can easily distinguish between the two. In addition, this approach allows you to treat each category as a separate entity, which could be a factor in securing the database.

Another reason for separating employees from customers is that, if this were actually a database that would be implemented in a production environment, there would probably be more attributes for each entity. For example, you would probably want to know the customers' home addresses and phone numbers, or you might want to include your employees' social security numbers. For the purposes of demonstrating how to model a database, the information you've included here should be enough.

6. The last objects you should categorize are those in the Movie participants group. This group is a little different from the others because you're working with a list of participant types, and for each of those types, you must include the full names of the participants. One way to approach this would be to create an entity for each participant type. Because different people can participate in different ways in one or more movies, though, you could be creating a situation in which your database includes a great deal of redundant data. Another approach would be to create one entity that includes the different parts of each participant's name and to include an attribute that identifies the role that the participant plays. Figure 4-17 demonstrates how this would work.

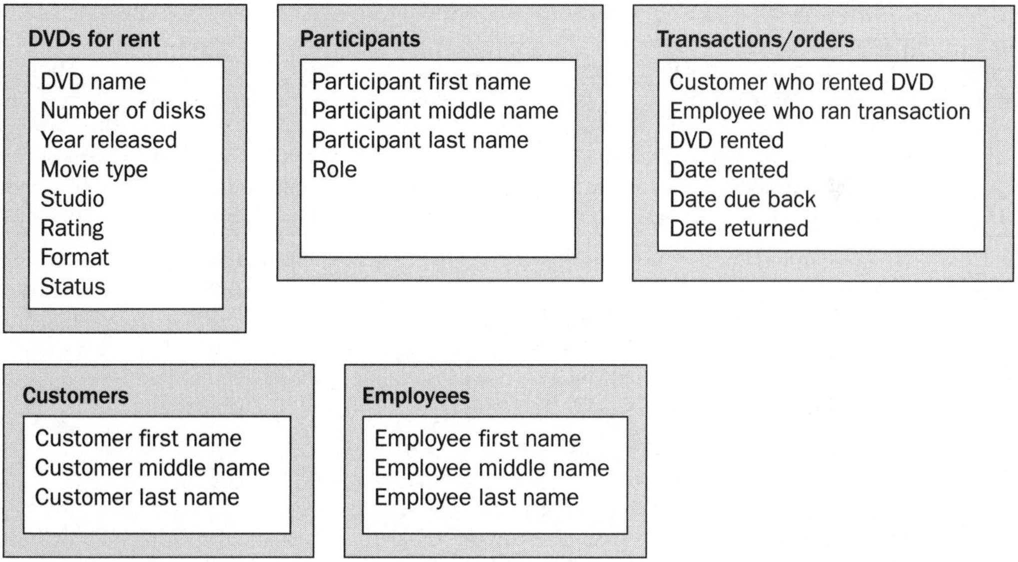

DVDs for rent

DVD name
Number of disks
Year released
Movie type
Studio
Rating
Format
Status

Participants

Participant first name
Participant middle name
Participant last name
Role

Transactions/orders

Customer who rented DVD
Employee who ran transaction
DVD rented
Date rented
Date due back
Date returned

Customers

Customer first name
Customer middle name
Customer last name

Employees

Employee first name
Employee middle name
Employee last name

Figure 4-17

Notice that only one entity exists for participants and that it includes the name attributes and a role attribute. Now a participant's name needs to be listed only once in the database.

How It Works

In this exercise, you identified the potential entities and attributes that help form the foundation for your data model. First, you organized your objects according to the business rules in which they appeared. From there, you separated the objects into logical categories that grouped together entities and attributes in a meaningful way. At the same time, you divided the name attributes into first, middle, and last names, and you organized the participant data into a consolidated format that will help reduce data redundancy. From this organization, you can begin to normalize the data, which is the subject of the following Try It Out.

Try It Out   **Normalizing Data**

Once you identify and categorize the entities and attributes for your database, you can begin to normalize the data structure and define the tables and columns. Usually, the best way to do this is to work with one entity at a time. The following steps help you normalize the data structure that you created in the previous exercise:

1. Start with the DVDs entity. This entity already provides a solid foundation for a table because it clearly groups together similar attributes. The first step should be to define a primary key for the table. Because there can be multiple copies of the same DVD, and because different DVDs can share the same name, there is no column or columns that you can easily use as a primary key. As a result, the easiest solution is to add a column that uniquely identifies each row in the table. That way, each DVD has a unique ID.

2. At this point, you could leave the table as is and simply assign names and data types to the columns. (Note that, for the purposes of this exercise, the data types are provided for you.) When you have repeating values, such as status and format, an effective way to control the values that are permitted in a column is to create a table specifically for the values. That way you can add and modify permitted values without affecting the column definitions themselves. These types of tables are often referred to as *lookup tables*. Using lookup tables tends to decrease the amount of redundant data because the repeated value is often smaller than the actual value. For example, suppose you use an ID of s1 to identify the status value of Checked Out. Instead of repeating Checked Out for every row that this status applies to, the repeated value is s1, which requires less storage space and is easier to process.

   In the case of the DVDs s, you would probably want to create lookup tables for the movie type, studio, rating, format, and status attributes. Each of these tables would contain a primary key column and a column that describes the option available to the DVDs table. You would then add a column to the DVDs table that references the primary key in the lookup table. Also, be sure to name all your columns. This exercise uses a mixed case convention to name data objects. For example, a column named DVDName represents the DVD name attribute.

3. Next, take a look at the Participants entity. Notice that it includes an entry for the participant's role. This is another good candidate for a lookup table. Again, you should include a column that acts as the primary key and one that lists the role's name. Once you create a Roles table, you can add a column for the role ID to the Participants table. In addition, that table should include a primary key column that uniquely identifies each participant. Also, be sure to assign column names to the entities.

4. For both the Employees entity and the Customers entity, add a primary key column and assign a column name to the other attributes.

5. The next step is to separate the Transactions/orders entity into two tables because transactions are subsets of orders. For every order, there can be one or more transactions. In addition, each order must have one customer and one employee. As a result, you should create an Orders table.

The table should include a column that references the customer ID and a column that references the employee ID. The table should also include a primary key column.

Because you're tracking the customer and the employee at the order level, you do not need to include them at the transaction level. As a result, your Transactions table does not need to reference the employee or customer, but it does need to reference the order. In addition, it must reference the DVD that is being rented. Finally, you need to add a column to the Transactions table that acts as the primary key. Your data model should now be similar to the one found in Figure 4-18.

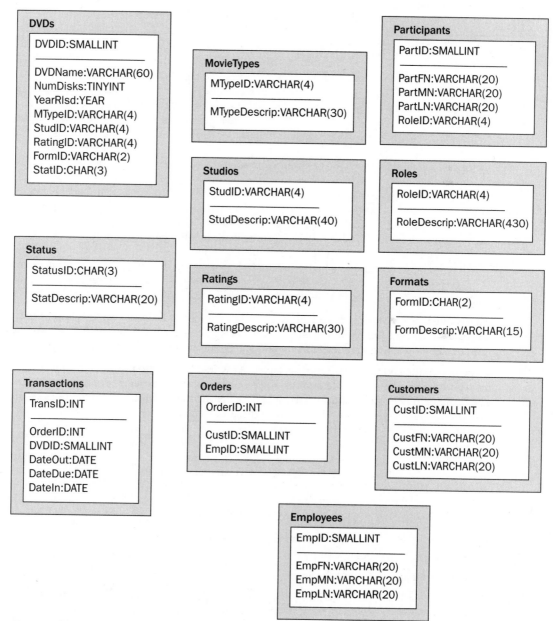

Figure 4-18

How It Works

As part of the data modeling process, you identified the tables included in the database and you listed the columns in each table. Normally, you would also assign data types to the columns, but for now, these were assigned for you. In determining how to set up the tables in your data model, you had to apply the rules of normalization to the entities and their attributes. For example, by adding a primary key to each table, you provided a way to uniquely identify each row so that the tables would conform to the normal forms. You also took steps to minimize redundant data by creating lookup tables that placed repeated values in separate tables. By the time you finished this exercise, the data structure should have been fairly normalized, and you're now ready to define the relationships between the tables.

Try It Out   Identifying Relationships

Now that you've identified the tables and their columns, you can begin defining the relationships between the tables. In most cases, it should be fairly obvious from the business rules and table structures where relationships exist and the type of relationships those are, although it's always a good idea to review each pair of tables to verify whether a relationship exists between those tables. For the purposes of brevity, this exercise focuses only on those sets of tables between which a relationship exists.

To identify the relationships between the tables in your data model, take the following steps:

1. Start with the DVDs table again, and compare it to other tables. You know from the previous exercise that lookup tables were created for several of the entities in this table. These include the MovieTypes, Studios, Ratings, Formats, and Status tables. Because of the nature of these tables and their origin with the DVDs table, you can assume that a one-to-many relationship exists between the DVDs table and the other five tables, with the DVDs table being the *many* side of the relationship. For example, the Studios table includes a list of the studios that own the rights to the movies. A studio can be associated with one or more movies; however, a movie can be associated with only one studio. As a result, a one-to-many relationship exists between those two tables.

   To indicate these relationships on your data model, use a line to connect each lookup table to the DVDs table, using the three-prong end on the DVDs side. In addition, add an FK followed by a number for each column in the DVDs table that references one of the lookup tables.

2. Now look at the DVDs and Participants tables. As would be expected with an inventory of movies, each movie can include one or more participants, each participant can participate in one or more movies, and multiple participants can participate in multiple movies. As a result, a many-to-many relationship exists between those two tables.

   Draw the relationship on your data model. Be sure to use the three-prong end on both sides.

3. Another table paired with the DVDs table is the Transactions table. Because each transaction must list the DVD that's being rented, you can assume that a relationship exists between these two tables. For every DVD there can be one or more transactions. For every transaction, there can be only one DVD. As a result, a one-to-many relationship exists between these tables, with the Transactions table on the *many* side of the relationship.

   Draw the relationship on your data model. Remember to add the FK reference to the referencing column in the Transactions table.

4. The next pair of tables to examine are the Participants and Roles tables. As you recall, each participant can play multiple roles, each role can be played by multiple participants, and multiple participants can play multiple roles, so a many-to-many relationship exists between these two tables.

Draw the relationship on your data model. Use the three-prong end on both sides.

5. Next look at the Transactions and Orders tables. Every order can contain one or more transactions, but each transaction can be part of only one order, so a one-to-many relationship exists between these two tables, with the Transactions table being the *many* side of the relationship.

Draw the relationship on your data model.

6. If you return to the Orders table, notice that it references the customer ID and employee ID, which means that a relationship exists between the Orders table and the Customers table as well as the Orders table and the Employees table. For every order, there can be only one employee and one customer, although each customer and employee can participate in multiple orders. As a result, the Orders table is on the *many* side of a one-to-many relationship with each of these other two tables.

For each of the relationships, you draw the correct relationship line on your data model, including the three-prong ends, where appropriate. Be sure to include the FK reference next to the referencing columns. Your data model should now be similar to the one shown in Figure 4-19.

How It Works

Once you normalized your data structure, you were able to determine the relationships that exist between the tables. As you discovered, there are a number of one-to-many relationships and two many-to-many relationships. In the model, every table participates in some type of relationship. The relationships provide a way to minimize data errors and data redundancy. As you may have noticed, no one-to-one relationships exist. These types of relationships are used more infrequently than the others, although they do have their benefits.

The final step in creating your data model is to refine your design. This includes not only making final adjustments to the model, but also addressing any many-to-many relationships.

Try It Out   Refining the Data Model

To finalize your data model, take the following steps:

1. Review the data model for inconsistencies or data that is not fully normalized. Once satisfied with the model, you can move on to the next step.

2. The next step is to address the many-to-many relationships. As you recall, these relationships are implemented through the use of a junction table to create one-to-many relationships. The Participants table is part of two different many-to-many relationships, which presents you with a unique situation.

To address these relationships, the best place to start is to define the situation: For each movie, there can be one or more participants who are playing one or more roles. In addition, each participant can play more than one role in one or more movies. As a result, movies are associated with participants, and participants are associated with roles. To address this situation, you can create one junction table that is related to all three tables: Roles, Participants, and DVDs. In each case, the junction table participates in a one-to-many relationship with the other tables, with the junction table on the *many* side of each relationship.

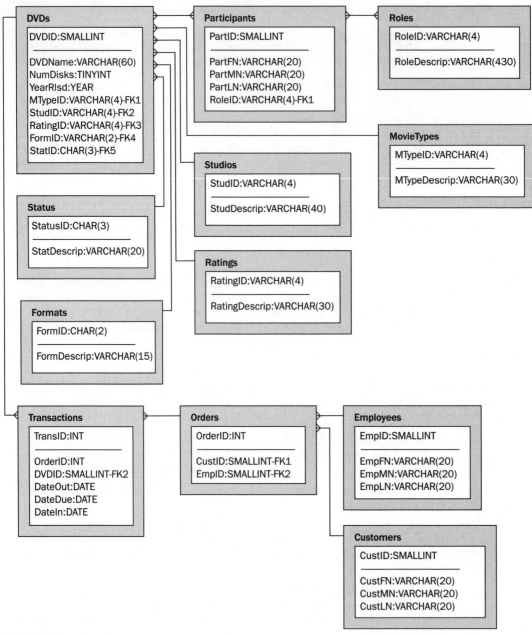

Figure 4-19

On your data model, add a junction table named DVDParticipant. Include a column that references the DVDs table, a column that references the Participants table, and a column that references the Roles table. Mark each column with an FK reference, followed by a number. Define the primary key on all three columns. Also, be sure to mark the one-to-many relationship on your model, and remove the RoleID column from the Participants table. The column is no longer needed in the Participants table, because it is included in the DVDParticipant table.

Your data model should now look like the model illustrated in Figure 4-20.

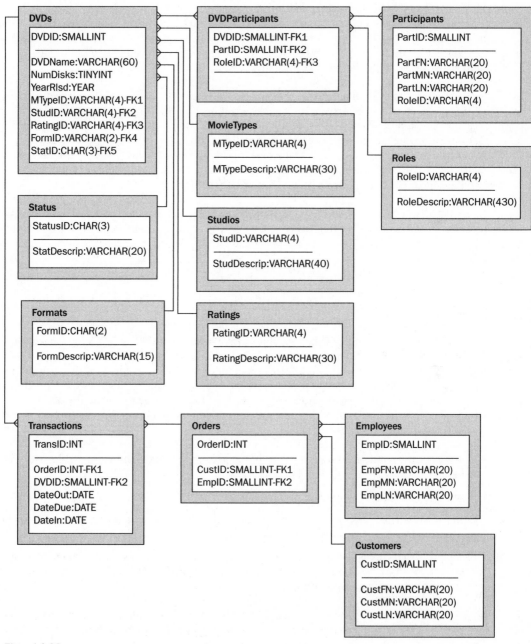

Figure 4-20

How It Works

In this exercise, you took the final step in completing your data model by adding a junction table that bridged the many-to-many relationship between the DVDs and Participants table and the many-to-many relationship between the Participants and the Roles tables. The junction table—DVDParticipant—allows you to associate a DVD with a participant and a role. For example, one row in the junction table could show that Sydney Pollack was the producer of the movie *Out of Africa*, and another row in that table could show that Sydney Pollack was the director of that movie. By using the junction table, multiple participants are able to participate in multiple movies and do so in multiple roles. At the same time, the movies are listed only once (in the DVDs table), the participants are listed only once (in the Participants table), and roles are listed only once (in the Roles table).

When you have a table like DVDParticipant, which is on the many side of three different one-to-many relationships, you have what is referred to as a *ternary* relationship. Although ternary relationships are commonly implemented in a database, it's generally a good idea to work around them if possible. This sometimes means adding tables and creating more junction tables so that those junction tables are involved in no more than two one-to-many relationships. In cases like the DVDParticipant table, where there are no easy ways to work around the ternary relationship, this is a fairly efficient solution, particularly when the junction table is made up only of foreign key values.

Once you create the junction table, add the necessary FK references, draw the one-to-many relationships, and remove the RoleID column from the Participants table, you're ready to start building the DVDRentals database. Remember to hang on to your data model because you'll need to refer to it as you're developing your database.

Summary

As you worked your way through this chapter, you learned how to structure a relational database to support your data storage needs. The process of defining tables and their columns, ensuring that the data structure adheres to the rules of normalization, and identifying the relationships between tables allows you to create a data model that helps to ensure the integrity of the data being stored. In addition, a properly designed database helps to reduce redundant data and improve the reliability of that data. To allow you to create an effective data model, you were provided with the background information and skills necessary to perform the following tasks:

- ❑ Understand the relational model and the components of the model, including tables, columns, rows, and primary keys.

- ❑ Normalize data according to the first three normal forms.

- ❑ Define the relationships between tables, including one-to-one, one-to-many, and many-to-many relationships.

- ❑ Perform the steps necessary to create a data model, including identifying the potential entities to include in a database, normalizing the data design, identifying the relationships between tables, and refining your data model.

By creating a data model, you provided yourself with a blueprint for developing your database. From the model, you can create the necessary tables, include the appropriate column definitions in those tables, assign data types, define primary keys, and establish relationships between tables. From there, you can create additional constraints in the database that meet any additional specifications outlined in your business requirements. Once you've created your database, you can add, retrieve, and manipulate data. Chapter 5 shows you how to assign data types and how to create and manage databases, tables, and indexes.

Exercises

The following questions are provided as a way for you to better acquaint yourself with the material covered in this chapter. Be sure to work through each exercise carefully. To view the answers to these questions, see Appendix A.

1. What are the components that make up a table in the relational model?

2. What requirements must a relation meet to be in compliance to the first normal form?

3. How does a one-to-many relationship differ from a many-to-many relationship?

4. You are creating a data model for a MySQL database. You identify the entities that you found in the business rules. You then group those entities into categories of related data. What step should you take next?

5. How are many-to-many relationships implemented in MySQL?

Managing Databases, Tables, and Indexes

In the first four chapters of the book, you were provided with the information necessary to install and use MySQL and design relational databases that could be implemented in MySQL. You were also provided with a foundation in the principles of SQL and the relational model. From all this information, you should now have the background you need to begin creating databases and adding the objects that those databases should contain.

The first step in setting up a MySQL database is to create the actual database object, which serves as a container for the tables in that database. The database acts as a central point of administration for the tables in the database. The actual data is stored in the tables, which provide a structured organization for the data and maintain the integrity of that data. Associated with each table is a set of indexes that facilitate access to the data in the tables.

In this chapter, you learn how to create and manage the database object, the tables in the database, and the indexes associated with the tables. To provide you with the information necessary to perform all these tasks, the chapter covers the following topics:

❏   How to create a database and specify a character set and collation name for that database. You also learn how to modify database properties and remove a database from your system.

❏   The information necessary to create a table, define columns in that table, add constraints to the table, create indexes on the table, and specify the type of table to be created.

❏   Information about the various types of indexes that you can add to a table, how to add indexes to a table, and how to remove an index from a table.

❏   How to retrieve information about databases and tables so that you can see what databases and tables exist and how those databases and tables are configured.

Managing Databases

Once you install MySQL and are comfortable using the tools in MySQL—particularly the mysql client utility—you can begin creating databases in the MySQL environment. Recall from Chapter 4 that when you add a database to MySQL, a corresponding subdirectory is automatically added to the data directory. Any tables added to the database appear as files in the subdirectory. If you then remove a database, the corresponding subdirectory and files are also deleted.

As you can see, the first step in setting up a database in MySQL is to create the database object and, subsequently, the corresponding subdirectories. From there, you can modify the database definition or delete the database. This section discusses each of these tasks.

Creating Databases

Creating a database in MySQL is one of the easier tasks that you're likely to perform. At its most basic, a database definition statement requires only the keywords CREATE DATABASE, followed by the name of the new database, as shown in the following syntax:

```
<database definition>::=
CREATE DATABASE [IF NOT EXISTS] <database name>
[[DEFAULT] CHARACTER SET <character set name>]
[[DEFAULT] COLLATE <collation name>]
```

As the syntax shows, very few components of the CREATE DATABASE statement are actually required. The statement does include several optional elements. The first of these—IF NOT EXISTS—determines how MySQL responds to a CREATE DATABASE statement if a database with the same name already exists. If a database already exists and the IF NOT EXISTS clause is not used, MySQL returns an error. If the clause is used, MySQL returns a warning, without returning any errors. Regardless of whether the clause is included in the statement, the effect on the database is the same: If a database with the same name exists, no new database is created.

The next optional components of the CREATE DATABASE statement are the CHARACTER SET clause and the COLLATE clause. You can specify either one of the two clauses or both. (The DEFAULT keyword is optional in either case and has no effect on the outcome.) The CHARACTER SET clause specifies the default character set to use for a new database, and the COLLATE clause specifies which default collation to use. A *character set* is a collection of letters, numbers, and symbols that create the values in a database. For example, A, B, C, a, b, c, 1, 2, 3, >, +, and * are all part of a character set. A *collation* is a named sorting order used for a specified character set. Collations define the way in which values made up of a particular character set are compared, sorted, and grouped together. Most character sets have one or more collations associated with them. For example, some of the collations associated with the default character set, latin1, include latin1_bin, latin1_general_ci, and latin1_swedish_ci, which is the default collation. If you do not specify the CHARACTER SET or COLLATION clause, the database uses the default MySQL character set or collation.

You can view the character sets and collations available in your system by executing the SHOW CHARACTER SET and SHOW COLLATION statements in the mysql client utility. Also note that character sets and collations affect only string data (letters, numbers, and symbols), as opposed to all numerical data or data related to dates and times.

Now that you have an understanding of the syntax used to create a database, take a look at a couple examples. The first example is a basic CREATE DATABASE statement that includes no optional components:

```
CREATE DATABASE BookSales;
```

When you execute the statement, a database named BookSales is added to your system. The database uses the default character set and collation because you specified neither.

When you create databases and tables in Windows, all names are converted to lowercase. Because Windows filenames and directory names are case insensitive, it follows that case is not a factor when specifying database and table names. In Linux and other Unix-like operating systems, the case is preserved. Because filenames and directory names are case sensitive, you must specify the correct case when referencing database and table names.

In the next example, the CREATE DATABASE statement specifies the character set and collation:

```
CREATE DATABASE BookSales
DEFAULT CHARACTER SET latin1
DEFAULT COLLATE latin1_bin;
```

In this example, the CHARACTER SET clause specifies the latin1 character set, and the COLLATE clause specifies the latin1_bin collation. In both cases, you use the DEFAULT keyword, but it isn't required. Executing the statement creates a database named BookSales, which uses the specified character set and collation.

In the Try It Out sections in Chapter 4, you created a data model for the DVDRentals database. In the Try It Out examples in this chapter, however, you create the database based on that model. Later in the chapter, you create the tables in the DVDRentals database.

Try It Out   Creating the DVDRentals Database

To create the database, follow these steps:

1. Open the mysql client utility, type the following command, and press Enter:

```
CREATE DATABASE DVDRentals;
```

You should receive a message indicating that your statement executed successfully.

2. In order to create tables or execute any statements in the context of the new database, you should switch over to that new database by using the following command:

```
use DVDRentals
```

You should receive a message indicating the database change.

How It Works

In this exercise, you used a CREATE DATABASE statement to create the DVDRentals database. This is the database for which you created a data model in Chapter 4. Because you didn't specify any character set or collation, the database uses the default values, which for a standard MySQL installation are the character set latin1 and the collation latin1_swedish_ci. Once you create the DVDRentals database, you can begin adding the necessary tables.

Modifying Databases

There might be times when you want to change the character set or collation used for your database. To do this, you can use an ALTER DATABASE statement to specify the new settings. As you can see from the following syntax, the ALTER DATABASE statement is similar to the CREATE DATABASE statement:

```
ALTER DATABASE <database name>
[[DEFAULT] CHARACTER SET <character set name>]
[[DEFAULT] COLLATE <collation name>]
```

In this statement, you must specify the ALTER DATABASE keywords and the name of the database, along with the CHARACTER SET clause, the COLLATE clause, or both. For either clause, simply specify the name of the character set and collation. For example, to change the character set to latin1 for the BookSales database, use the following ALTER DATABASE statement:

```
ALTER DATABASE BookSales
CHARACTER SET latin1;
```

As you can see, the statement specifies only a CHARACTER SET clause, which means the current collation remains the same.

> *Use caution when changing the character set for a database. In some cases, changing the character set can result in the database no longer supporting all the characters stored as data in the database.*

Deleting Databases

Deleting a database from your system is merely a matter of executing a DROP DATABASE statement. The following syntax shows the components that make up the statement:

```
DROP DATABASE [IF EXISTS] <database name>
```

The statement requires only the DROP DATABASE keywords and the name of the database. In addition, you can specify the IF EXISTS clause. If you specify this clause and a database with that name doesn't exist, you receive a warning message rather than an error. Now take a look at an example of the DROP DATABASE statement:

```
DROP DATABASE BookSales;
```

This example removes the BookSales database from the system. When you remove a database, you also remove the tables in that database and any data contained in the table. As a result, you want to be extremely cautious whenever you execute the DROP DATABASE command.

Managing Tables

The next step in setting up a database, after creating the actual database object, is to add the necessary tables to that database. The tables provide a structure for storing and securing the data. All data exists within the structure of the tables, and all tables exist within the structure of the database. In addition to creating tables, you can also modify the table definitions or delete the tables from the database. This section explains how to perform each of these tasks.

Creating Tables

To create a table in MySQL, you must use the CREATE TABLE statement to define the columns in the table and configure the appropriate constraints on the table. The CREATE TABLE statement is one of the most complex SQL statements in MySQL. It contains numerous components and provides many options for defining the exact nature of a particular table. The following syntax represents the elements that make up a CREATE TABLE statement:

```
<table definition>::=
CREATE [TEMPORARY] TABLE [IF NOT EXISTS] <table name>
(<table element> [{, <table element>}...])
[<table option> [<table option>...]]

<table element>::=
<column definition>
| {[CONSTRAINT <constraint name>] PRIMARY KEY
    (<column name> [{, <column name>}...])}
| {[CONSTRAINT <constraint name>] FOREIGN KEY [<index name>]
    (<column name> [{, <column name>}...]) <reference definition>}
| {[CONSTRAINT <constraint name>] UNIQUE [INDEX] [<index name>]
    (<column name> [{, <column name>}...])}
| {{INDEX | KEY} [<index name>] (<column name> [{, <column name>}...])}
| {FULLTEXT [INDEX] [<index name>] (<column name> [{, <column name>}...])}

<column definition>::=
<column name> <type> [NOT NULL | NULL] [DEFAULT <value>] [AUTO_INCREMENT]
[PRIMARY KEY] [COMMENT '<string>'] [<reference definition>]

<type>::=
<numeric data type>
| <string data type>
| <data/time data type>

<reference definition>::=
REFERENCES <table name> [(<column name> [{, <column name>}...])]
[ON DELETE {RESTRICT | CASCADE | SET NULL | NO ACTION | SET DEFAULT }]
[ON UPDATE {RESTRICT | CASCADE | SET NULL | NO ACTION | SET DEFAULT }]
[MATCH FULL | MATCH PARTIAL]

<table option>::=
{ENGINE = {BDB | MEMORY | ISAM | INNODB | MERGE | MYISAM}}
| <additional table options>
```

As you can see, many elements make up a CREATE TABLE statement. In fact, the syntax shown here is not the CREATE TABLE statement in its entirety. As you move through the chapter, other elements are introduced and some elements, which are beyond the scope of this book, are not discussed at all. Still, this chapter covers all the essential components, so by the end of the chapter, you should have a fairly comprehensive foundation on how to create a table definition.

Now take a closer look at the CREATE TABLE syntax. The best place to begin is at the first section:

```
<table definition>::=
CREATE [TEMPORARY] TABLE [IF NOT EXISTS] <table name>
(<table element> [{, <table element>}...])
[<table option> [<table option>...]]
```

This section represents the entire CREATE TABLE statement, with individual components being explained later in the syntax. The first line of the actual statement requires only the keywords CREATE TABLE, followed by the name of the new table. This line also contains two optional components. The first — TEMPORARY — indicates that this is a temporary table used only during the current session by the current user. A temporary table exists only as long as the session is open or the table is explicitly dropped. The second optional element is the IF NOT EXISTS clause. You've seen this clause before in the CREATE DATABASE statement. When you include it in your CREATE TABLE statement, a warning is generated, rather than an error, if a table by the same name already exists when you execute this statement.

The next line of syntax allows you to define the individual table elements, as represented by the <table element> placeholder. A table element is an individual object that is defined on a table, such as a column or PRIMARY KEY constraint. Each CREATE TABLE statement includes one or more table elements. If more than one table element exists, they are separated by commas. Regardless of how many table elements exist, they are all enclosed in a set of parentheses.

The last line in the first section of syntax allows you to define individual table options. Table options are options that apply to the table as a whole. For example, you can define the type of table that you want to create. All table options are optional; however, you can define as many as are necessary.

As you can see from the first section of syntax, a CREATE TABLE statement can be as simple or as complicated as you need to make it. The only required elements are the CREATE TABLE clause and at least one table element enclosed in parentheses, as shown in the following syntax:

```
CREATE TABLE <table name> (<table element>)
```

Because a table element is a required component, take a look at the next section of syntax:

```
<table element>::=
<column definition>
| {[CONSTRAINT <constraint name>] PRIMARY KEY
      (<column name> [{, <column name>}...])}
| {[CONSTRAINT <constraint name>] FOREIGN KEY [<index name>]
      (<column name> [{, <column name>}...]) <reference definition>}
| {[CONSTRAINT <constraint name>] UNIQUE [INDEX] [<index name>]
      (<column name> [{, <column name>}...])}
| {{INDEX | KEY} [<index name>] (<column name> [{, <column name>}...])}
| {FULLTEXT [INDEX] [<index name>] (<column name> [{, <column name>}...])}
```

A table element can represent one of many different options. The most commonly used option is the one represented by the <column definition> placeholder, which, as the name suggests, allows you to define a column to include in your table definition. You are likely, though, to use the other options with regularity. For this reason, the following sections examine each of these options individually.

Creating Column Definitions

A column definition is one type of table element that you can define in a table definition. You must create a column definition for each column that you want to include in your table. The following syntax provides you with the structure that you should use when creating a column definition:

```
<column definition>::=
<column name> <type> [NOT NULL | NULL] [DEFAULT <value>] [AUTO_INCREMENT]
[PRIMARY KEY] [COMMENT '<string>'] [<reference definition>]
```

As you can see, only two elements are required in a column definition: the column name (represented by the `<column name>` placeholder) and the data type (represented by the `<type>` placeholder). The name can be any acceptable identifier in MySQL, and the database can be any of the supported data types. Each additional element of the column definition is optional and, along with data types, they are discussed individually in the following sections.

Defining Data Types

As you recall from earlier chapters, a data type is a constraint placed on a particular column to limit the type of values that you can store in that column. MySQL supports three categories of data types, as represented by the following syntax:

```
<type>::=
<numeric data type>
| <string data type>
| <data/time data type>
```

Whenever you add a column to your table, you must define the column with a data type that is in one of these three categories. Each category of types has its own specific characteristics, and each places restrictions on the type of data that you can include in a particular column. Take a closer look at each category to better understand the characteristics of each.

Numeric Data Types

As the name suggests, *numeric* data types are concerned with numbers. If you have a column that will contain nothing but numbers, chances are that you want to configure that column with a numeric data type.

You can divide numeric data types into two categories, as the following syntax suggests:

```
<numeric data type>::=
<integer data type> [(<length>)] [UNSIGNED] [ZEROFILL]
| <fractional data type> [(<length>, <decimals>)] [UNSIGNED] [ZEROFILL]
```

Each of the two categories of integer data types supports several options. The first of these is represented by the `<length>` placeholder, which indicates the maximum number of displayed characters for a particular column. You can specify that the length be anywhere from 1 to 255. The fractional data types also include the `<decimals>` placeholder. This value indicates the number of decimal places to be displayed for a value in the column. You can specify that the number of decimal places be anywhere from 0 to 30; however, `<decimals>` must always be at least two less than `<length>`.

The next option available for the numeric data types is UNSIGNED. When this option follows a numeric data type, no negative values are permitted in the column. If you specify ZEROFILL, zeros are added to the beginning of a value so that the value is displayed with the number of characters represented by the `<length>` placeholder. For example, if you define `<length>` as 4 and you specify ZEROFILL, the number 53 displays as 0053. ZEROFILL is most useful when used in conjunction with a specified length. In addition, UNSIGNED is assumed when you specify ZEROFILL, even if UNSIGNED isn't explicitly specified. In other words, you can't use ZEROFILL for negative numbers.

Now take a look at the two categories of numeric data types. The first of these is the *integer* data type. Integer data types allow you to store only whole numbers in your column (no fractions or decimals). MySQL supports the integer data types shown in the following syntax:

```
<integer data type>::=
TINYINT | SMALLINT | MEDIUMINT | INT | INTEGER | BIGINT
```

Each of these data types specifies not only that whole numbers must be stored in the column, but also that the numbers stored must fall within a specific range of values, as shown in the following table.

Data type	Acceptable values	Storage requirements
TINYINT	Signed: −128 to 127 Unsigned: 0 to 255	1 byte
SMALLINT	Signed: −32768 to 32767 Unsigned: 0 to 65535	2 bytes
MEDIUMINT	Signed: −8388608 to 8388607 Unsigned: 0 to 16777215	3 bytes
INT	Signed: −2147483648 to 2147483647 Unsigned: 0 to 4294967295	4 bytes
INTEGER	Same values as the INT data type. (INTEGER is a synonym for INT.)	4 bytes
BIGINT	Signed: −9223372036854775808 to 9223372036854775807 Unsigned: 0 to 18446744073709551615	8 bytes

The range of acceptable values for each integer data type has nothing to do with the <length> place-holder. Whether you were to specify a length of 2 or 20, the stored value would be the same, as would be the value limitations. As the table demonstrates, signed values are different from unsigned values. If a column doesn't require negative values, using the UNSIGNED option increases the upper end of the range of stored values, although the storage requirements remain the same. For example, a value in a TINYINT column requires 1 byte of storage whether the column is signed or unsigned.

Now take a look at an example of a CREATE TABLE statement that includes two column definitions, one that uses the SMALLINT data type and one that uses the INT data type. The following statement creates a table named Inventory:

```
CREATE TABLE Inventory
(
    ProductID SMALLINT(4) UNSIGNED ZEROFILL,
    Quantity INT UNSIGNED
);
```

As you can see, the table includes a column named ProductID and a column named Quantity. The ProductID column is configured with a SMALLINT data type that specifies 4 as its maximum display length. Because a SMALLINT value can have a range of 0 to 65535, the display of 4 might not apply to all values. You would specify a display size smaller than the capacity only if you're certain that all digits will fall into that range. If your value does require the full five digits, they will all be displayed, despite the <length> value of 4. As a result, the only time including the length is useful is when you're also including the ZEROFILL option, which is the case in this column definition. As a result, no negative values are allowed and zeros are added to all values less than four characters wide.

The next column defined in this statement is the Quantity column. This column is defined with an `INT` data type, and it is also unsigned. As a result, negative numbers are not allowed in this column, which means that acceptable values can fall in the range of 0 to 4294967295.

Another thing to notice about this `CREATE TABLE` statement is that the column definitions are enclosed in parentheses and separated by a comma. All table elements, including column definitions, are treated in this manner.

Now take a look at the fractional data types, which are shown in the following syntax:

```
<fractional data type>::=
FLOAT | DOUBLE | DOUBLE PRECISION | REAL | DECIMAL | DEC | NUMERIC |FIXED
```

The *fractional* data types, unlike the integer data types, support the use of decimals. In fact, that is the key characteristic of these data types, which are described in the following table:

Data type	Description
FLOAT	An approximate numeric data type that uses 4 bytes of storage. The data type supports the following values: –3.402823466E+38 to –1.175494351E–38 0 1.175494351E–38 to 3.402823466E+38
DOUBLE	An approximate numeric data type that uses 8 bytes of storage. The data type supports the following values: –1.7976931348623157E+308 to –2.2250738585072014E–308 0 2.2250738585072014E–308 to 1.7976931348623157E+308
DOUBLE PRECISION	Synonym for the DOUBLE data type
REAL	Synonym for the DOUBLE data type
DECIMAL	An exact numeric data type whose range storage requirements depend on the <length> and <decimals> values specified in the column definition
DEC	Synonym for the DECIMAL data type
NUMERIC	Synonym for the DECIMAL data type
FIXED	Synonym for the DECIMAL data type

As described in the table, there are only three basic fractional data types: `FLOAT`, `DOUBLE`, and `DECIMAL`. The rest are synonyms for the `DOUBLE` and `DECIMAL` data types.

The `DOUBLE` data type supports a greater degree of precision than does the `FLOAT` data type. In other words, `DOUBLE` supports more decimal places than `FLOAT`. If you need the greater precision, you would use `DOUBLE`, although you should be aware that this doubles your storage requirements. In both cases, values are stored as numeric data and are subject to errors caused by numbers being rounded, which is why they're referred to as *approximate* numeric types. Generally numbers are rounded according to the column <length> and <decimals> specifications, which can sometimes result in imprecise results.

The DECIMAL data type, which is referred to as an *exact* numeric data type, gets around the issue of round-off errors by storing the values as strings, with the <length> and <decimals> specifications determining storage requirements and range. You should use the DECIMAL data type when you require values to be completely accurate, such as when you're storing information about money. The drawback to using the DECIMAL data type is that there are trade-offs in performance compared to the approximate numeric types. For this reason, if you plan to store values that don't require the accuracy of the DECIMAL type, use FLOAT or DOUBLE.

Now take a look at a table definition that uses the DECIMAL and FLOAT data types. The following CREATE TABLE statement creates a table named Catalog:

```
CREATE TABLE Catalog
(
    ProductID SMALLINT,
    Price DECIMAL(7,2),
    Weight FLOAT(8,4)
);
```

As you can see, the table includes a DECIMAL column (named Price) and a FLOAT column (named Weight). The Price column contains a <length> value of 7 and a <decimals> value of 2. As a result, the values display with up to 7 characters and 2 decimal places, such as 46264.45 and 242.90.

> *Because of the storage requirements for DECIMAL values, positive DECIMAL values (as opposed to negative values) receive one extra character to display values. For example, a DECIMAL column that has a <length> value of 7 and a <decimals> value of 2 can actually have up to eight numeric characters — plus one character for the decimal point — for positive numbers, but only seven characters — plus one character for the negative sign and one for the decimal point — for negative numbers. FLOAT and DOUBLE values do not operate in the same way.*

The second column in the preceding example is configured with the FLOAT data type. In this case, the total display can be eight characters long, with four characters to the right of the decimal point. The implication in this case is that the Weight value does not have to be as exact as the Price value, so you don't have to worry about errors caused by values that have been rounded.

String Data Types

The string data types provide a great deal of flexibility for storing various types of data from individual bits to large files. String data types are normally used to store names and titles and any value that can include letters and numbers. MySQL supports four categories of string data types, as shown in the following syntax:

```
<string data type>::=
<character data type>
| <binary data type>
| <text data type>
| <list data type>
```

The character data types are the ones that you probably use the most often. As the following syntax shows, there are two types of character data types:

```
<character data type>::=
CHAR (<length>) [BINARY | ASCII | UNICODE]
VARCHAR (<length>) [BINARY]
```

The CHAR data type is a fixed-length character data type that can store up to 255 characters. The <length> placeholder specifies the number of characters stored. Although the actual value can be made up of fewer characters than the amount specified, the actual storage space is fixed at the specified amount. Take a look at an example to demonstrate how this works. The following table definition includes a column definition for the Category column:

```
CREATE TABLE Catalog
(
    ProductID SMALLINT,
    Description VARCHAR(40),
    Category CHAR(3),
    Price DECIMAL(7,2)
);
```

The Category column is defined with the CHAR(3) data type. As a result, the column can store zero to three characters per value, but the storage amount allotted to that value is always three bytes, one for each character.

The CHAR data type is an appropriate data type to use when you know how many characters most values in a column will consist of and when the values are made up of alphanumeric characters, as opposed to all numerals. If you don't know how many characters each value will be, you should use a VARCHAR data type. The VARCHAR data type also allows you to specify a maximum length; however, storage requirements are based on the actual number of characters, rather than on the <length> value.

Return to the preceding example. Notice that the Description column is configured with the VARCHAR(40) data type. This means that the values can be of varying length, up to 40 characters long. As a result, the amount of actual storage ranges between zero bytes and 40 bytes, depending on the actual value. For example, a value of "Bookcase" requires fewer bytes than a value of "Three-piece living room set."

The VARCHAR data type, like the CHAR data type, can store up to 255 characters. Along with the flexibility offered by VARCHAR, compared to CHAR, comes a performance cost. CHAR columns are processed more efficiently than VARCHAR columns, yet CHAR columns can result in wasted storage. Generally, for columns with values that vary widely in length, the VARCHAR data type might often be your best choice.

If you return again to the <character data type> syntax, you'll see that the CHAR data type allows you to specify the BINARY, ASCII, or UNICODE attribute, and the VARCHAR data type allows you to specify the BINARY attribute. The three attributes result in the following effects:

- ❑ **BINARY:** Makes sorting and comparisons case sensitive.
- ❑ **ASCII:** Assigns the latin1 character set to the column.
- ❑ **UNICODE:** Assigns the ucs2 character set to the column.

In addition to string data types, MySQL supports four types of binary data types, as shown in the following syntax:

```
<binary data type>::=
TINYBLOB | BLOB | MEDIUMBLOB | LONGBLOB
```

Binary data types support the storage of large amounts of data, such as image and sound files. These types are useful when you expect values to grow large or to vary widely. The four binary data types are identical except for the maximum amount of data that each one supports. The following table shows the maximum size of values permitted in a column configured with one of these data types.

Data type	Maximum size
TINYBLOB/TINYTEXT	255 characters (355 bytes)
BLOB/TEXT	65,535 characters (64 KB)
MEDIUMBLOB/MEDIUMTEXT	16,777,215 characters (16 MB)
LONGBLOB/LONGTEXT	4,294,967,295 characters (4 GB)

The text data types are also included in the table because they are similar to the binary data types and because the maximum size limitations are the same. The text data types are discussed later in this section.

The binary data types do not take any arguments. As with data in a VARCHAR column, the storage used for binary data varies according to the size of the value, but you do not specify a maximum length. When defining a column with a binary data type, you simply type the name of the data type in the column definition. For example, the following table definition includes a BLOB column named Photo:

```
CREATE TABLE Inventory
(
    ProductID SMALLINT UNSIGNED,
    Name VARCHAR(40),
    Photo BLOB,
    Quantity INT UNSIGNED
);
```

The Photo column can store binary data up to 64 KB in size. The assumption in this case is that a photo can be taken of the product and saved in a small enough file to fit into this column. If you anticipate that the photos might be larger, you should step this up to MEDIUMBLOB.

The text data types are very similar to the binary data types and, as the following syntax shows, have a direct counterpart to each of the four binary data types:

```
<text data type>::=
TINYTEXT | TEXT | MEDIUMTEXT | LONGTEXT
```

The text data types also have the same size limitations and storage requirements as the binary data types. If you refer to the previous table, you can see how the sizes correspond between the binary data types and the text data types. The main difference between the two types is that the text data types are associated with a specific character set. Binary columns are treated as strings, and sorting is case sensitive. Text columns are treated according to their character sets, and sorting is based on the collation for that character set.

The following CREATE TABLE statement provides an example of a TEXT column named DescriptionDoc:

```
CREATE TABLE Catalog
(
    ProductID SMALLINT UNSIGNED,
    Name VARCHAR(40),
    DescriptionDoc TEXT CHARACTER SET latin1 COLLATE latin1_bin
);
```

As you can see, the DescriptionDoc column includes a CHARACTER SET and COLLATE clause. The latin1 character set and the latin1_bin collation are specific to the values in the DescriptionDoc column. The advantage of this is that you can use a character set and collation that differ from that of the table, database, or server.

Now take a look at the list data types, which are the last set of string data types. As the following syntax shows, the list data types include ENUM and SET:

```
<list data type>::=
{ENUM | SET} (<value> [{, <value>}...])
```

The ENUM data type allows you to specify a list of values that you can use in a column configured with that type. When you insert a row in the table, you can also insert one of the values defined for the data type in the column. The column can contain only one value, and it must be one of the listed values. A SET data type also specifies a list of values to be inserted in the column. Unlike the ENUM data type, in which you can specify only one value, the SET data type allows you to specify multiple values from the list.

The following table definition illustrates how you can configure an ENUM column and a SET column:

```
CREATE TABLE Orders
(
    OrderID SMALLINT UNSIGNED,
    BikeModel VARCHAR(40),
    BikeColor ENUM('red', 'blue', 'green', 'yellow'),
    BikeOptions SET('rack', 'light', 'helmet', 'lock')
);
```

Notice that the list of values follows the data type. The values are enclosed in single quotes and separated by commas, and all values are enclosed in parentheses. For an ENUM data type, you can specify up to 65,535 values. For a SET data type, you can specify up to 64 values.

Date/Time Data Types

The final category of data types is the date/time data types, which are shown in the following syntax:

```
<date/time data type>::=
DATE | TIME | DATETIME | YEAR | TIMESTAMP
```

The date/time data types allow you to specify columns that contain data specific to dates and times. The date/time data types support the ranges and formats shown in the following table:

Data type	Format	Range
DATE	YYYY-MM-DD	1000-01-01 through 9999
TIME	HH:MM:SS	–838:59:59 to 838:59:59
DATETIME	YYYY-MM-DD HH:MM:SS	1000-01-01 00:00:00 through 9999
YEAR	YYYY	1901 to 2155 (and 0000)
TIMESTAMP	YYYY-MM-DD HH:MM:SS	1970-01-01 00:00:00 to partway through 2037

The date/time data types are handy if you want to store specific types of date information. For example, if you want to record only the date and not the year, you would use the DATE data type. The values that you entered in this column would have to conform to the format defined by that data type. However, of particular interest is the TIMESTAMP data type, which is slightly different from the other data types. When you configure a column with this data type, a row, when inserted or updated, is automatically provided a value for the TIMESTAMP column that is based on the current time and date. This provides a handy way to record each transaction that occurs in a particular table.

Now take a look at a table that uses time/date data types. The following table definition includes a YEAR column and a TIMESTAMP:

```
CREATE TABLE BookOrders
(
    OrderID SMALLINT UNSIGNED,
    BookID SMALLINT UNSIGNED,
    Copyright YEAR,
    OrderDate TIMESTAMP
);
```

The Copyright column allows you to add a value to the column that falls in the range of 1901 to 2155; however, you're restricted from adding any other types of values. The OrderDate column automatically records the current data and time when a particular row is inserted or updated, so you don't have to insert any values in this column.

Defining a Column's Nullability

Up to this point, the focus has been on identifying only the required elements of a CREATE TABLE statement and the column definitions. As a result, the column definitions have included only the column names and the data types assigned to those columns. The next component of the column definition examined in this chapter is the column's nullability, which is specified through the NULL and NOT NULL keywords.

A column's nullability refers to a column's ability to accept null values. Recall from Chapter 1 that a null value indicates that a value is undefined or unknown. It is not the same as zero or blank, but instead means that the value is absent. When you include NOT NULL in your column definition, you're saying that the column does not permit null values. In other words, a specific value must always be provided for that column. On the other hand, the NULL option permits null values. If neither option is specified, NULL is assumed, and null values are permitted in the column.

Now take a look at a table definition that specifies the nullability of its columns. The following example creates the Catalog table and includes two NOT NULL columns:

```
CREATE TABLE Catalog
(
    ProductID SMALLINT UNSIGNED NOT NULL,
    Name VARCHAR(40) NOT NULL
);
```

You must provide a value for both the ProductID column and the Name column. Whenever you insert rows in the table or update rows in this table, you cannot use NULL as a value for either of those columns. In general, whenever you configure a column as NOT NULL, you must supply a value other than NULL to the column when inserting and modifying rows. There are, however, two exceptions to this rule. If you configure a column with the TIMESTAMP data type or if you use the AUTO_INCREMENT option, then inserting NULL automatically sets the value of the column to the correct TIMESTAMP value or the AUTO_INCREMENT value. (The AUTO_INCREMENT option is discussed later in the chapter.) But other than these two exceptions, a NOT NULL column cannot accept a null value.

Defining Default Values

Situations might arise in which you want a column to use a default value when inserting or updating a row, if no value is provided for a column. This is useful when a value is often repeated in a column or it is the value most likely to be used in that column. MySQL allows you to assign default values through the use of a DEFAULT clause. For example, the following table definition includes a column defined with a default value of Unknown:

```
CREATE TABLE AuthorBios
(
    AuthID SMALLINT UNSIGNED NOT NULL,
    YearBorn YEAR NOT NULL,
    CityBorn VARCHAR(40) NOT NULL DEFAULT 'Unknown'
);
```

In this CREATE TABLE statement, the CityBorn column is configured with the VARCHAR data type and the NOT NULL option. In addition, the column definition includes a DEFAULT clause. In that clause, the keyword DEFAULT is specified, followed by the actual default value, which in this case is Unknown. If you insert a row in the table and do not specify a value for the CityBorn column, the value Unknown is automatically inserted in that column.

You can also specify a default value in a column configured with a numeric data type. In the following table definition, the NumBooks column is configured with the SMALLINT data type and a default value of 1:

```
CREATE TABLE AuthorBios
(
    AuthID SMALLINT UNSIGNED NOT NULL,
    YearBorn YEAR NOT NULL,
    NumBooks SMALLINT NOT NULL DEFAULT 1
);
```

Notice that you do not need to enclose the default value in single quotes. The quote marks are used only for defaults that are string values.

You can also specify NULL *as a default value. The column, though, must permit null values in order to specify it as a default.*

If you do not assign a default value to a column, MySQL automatically assigns a default to the column. If a column accepts null values, the default is NULL. If a column does not accept null values, the default depends on how the column is defined:

❑ For columns configured with the TIMESTAMP data type, the default value for the first TIMESTAMP column is the current date and time. The default values for any other TIMESTAMP columns in the table are zero values in place of the date and time.

❑ For columns configured with a date/time data type other than TIMESTAMP, the default values are zero values in place of the date and time.

❑ For columns configured with the AUTO_INCREMENT option, the default value is the next number in the incremented sequence of numbers. (The AUTO_INCREMENT option is discussed later in the chapter.)

❑ For numeric columns that are not configured with the AUTO_INCREMENT option, the default value is 0.

❑ For columns configured with the ENUM data type, the default value is the first value specified in the column definition.

❑ For columns configured with a string data type other than the ENUM type, the default value is an empty string.

As you can see, the rules for defaults in NOT NULL columns are more complex than for columns that permit null values. As a result, you might consider defining defaults on any columns whose default value you want to control.

Most relational database management systems (RDBMSs) do not automatically assign default values to all columns. For these systems, trying to insert a value in a column for which you defined no default and null values are not permitted results in an error. As you can see with MySQL, all columns are assigned a default value.

Defining Primary Keys

In Chapter 4, when you were learning how to create a data model, you were introduced to the concept of primary keys and how they ensure the uniqueness of each row in a table. A primary key is one or more columns in a table that uniquely identify each row in that table. For nearly any table you create, you should define a primary key for that table.

The easiest way to define a single-column primary key is to specify the PRIMARY KEY option in the column definition, as shown in the following example:

```
CREATE TABLE Orders
(
    OrderID SMALLINT UNSIGNED NOT NULL PRIMARY KEY,
    ModelID SMALLINT UNSIGNED NOT NULL,
    ModelDescrip VARCHAR(40)
);
```

In this table definition, the primary key for the Orders table is defined on the OrderID column. You only need to add the PRIMARY KEY clause to the column definition. In order to define a column as a primary key, the column must be configured as NOT NULL. If you do not explicitly specify the NOT NULL option, NOT NULL is assumed. In addition, a table can have only one primary key, which you can define in the column definition or as a separate constraint, as shown in the following syntax:

```
[CONSTRAINT <constraint name>] PRIMARY KEY (<column name> [{, <column name>}...])
```

When you define a primary key as a separate constraint, you're including it as a table element in your table definition, as you would other table elements, such as column definitions. For example, you can define the same primary key that is shown in the preceding example as a table element. The following table definition for the Orders table removes the PRIMARY KEY clause from the OrderID column definition and uses a PRIMARY KEY constraint:

```
CREATE TABLE Orders
(
    OrderID SMALLINT UNSIGNED NOT NULL,
    ModelID SMALLINT UNSIGNED NOT NULL,
    ModelDescrip VARCHAR(40),
    PRIMARY KEY (OrderID)
);
```

As you can see, the PRIMARY KEY constraint is added as another table element, just like the three columns. The table element needs to include only the keywords PRIMARY KEY and the name of the primary key column, enclosed in parentheses. If you were creating a primary key on more than one column, you would include both of those column names in the parentheses, as shown in the following table definition:

```
CREATE TABLE Orders
(
    OrderID SMALLINT UNSIGNED NOT NULL,
    ModelID SMALLINT UNSIGNED NOT NULL,
    ModelDescrip VARCHAR(40),
    PRIMARY KEY (OrderID, ModelID)
);
```

Notice that the PRIMARY KEY constraint now specifies the OrderID column and the ModelID column. As a result, the primary key for the Orders table will be created on these two columns, which means that no two value pairs can be alike, although values can be repeated in individual columns. Any time that you plan to define a primary key on two or more columns, you must use the table-level constraint. You cannot define a primary key on multiple columns at the column level, as you can when you include only one column in the primary key.

Defining Auto-Increment Columns

In some cases, you may want to generate the numbers in your primary key automatically. For example, each time you add an order to a new table, you want to assign a new number to identify that order. The more rows that the table contains, the more order numbers there will be. For this reason, MySQL allows you to define a primary key column with the AUTO_INCREMENT option. The AUTO_INCREMENT option allows you to specify that numbers be generated automatically for your foreign key column. For example, the primary key column in the following example is configured with the AUTO_INCREMENT option:

```
CREATE TABLE Catalog
(
    ProductID SMALLINT UNSIGNED NOT NULL AUTO_INCREMENT,
    Name VARCHAR(40) NOT NULL,
    PRIMARY KEY (ProductID)
);
```

In this example, the ProductID column is configured with the SMALLINT data type and is configured as the primary key (through the use of a PRIMARY KEY constraint). The column definition also includes the NOT NULL option and the AUTO_INCREMENT option. As a result, whenever you add a new row to the Catalog table, a new number is automatically assigned to the ProductID column. The number is incremented by 1, based on the highest value existing in that column. For example, if a row exists with a ProductID value of 1347, and this is the highest ProductID value in the table, the next row inserted in the table is assigned a ProductID value of 1348.

You can use the AUTO_INCEREMENT option only on a column configured with an integer data type and the NOT NULL option. In addition, the table must be set up as a primary key or with a unique index, and there can be only one AUTO_INCREMENT column per table. (Unique indexes are discussed later in the chapter.) Also, the AUTO_INCREMENET column cannot be defined with a default value.

Defining Foreign Keys

In Chapter 4, you learned how tables in a relational database form relationships with each other in order to associate data in a meaningful way and to help ensure data integrity. When you created your data model, you showed these relationships by connecting related tables with lines that indicated the type of relationship. In your final data model, you found that the most common type of relationship was the one-to-many, which was represented by a line that had three prongs on the *many* side of the relationship.

In order to implement these relationships in MySQL, you must define foreign keys on the referencing tables. You define the foreign key on the column or columns in the table that references the column or columns in the referenced table. The referencing table, the table that contains the foreign key, is often referred to as the *child* table, and the referenced table is often referred to as the *parent* table.

The foreign key maintains the consistency of the data between the child table the parent table. In order to insert a row in the child table or to update a row in that table, the value in the foreign key column must exist in the referenced column in the parent table.

For example, suppose you have a table that tracks sales for a bookstore. One of the columns in the table stores the IDs for the books that have sold. Data about the books themselves is actually stored in a separate table, and each book is identified in that table by its ID. As a result, the book ID column in the sales table references the book ID column in the books table. To associate the data in these two columns, the book ID column in the sales table is configured as a foreign key. Because of the foreign key, no book ID can be added to the sales table that doesn't exist in the books table. The sales table, then, is the child table, and the books table is the parent table.

To add a foreign key to a table, you can define it in the column definition or as a constraint in a separate table element. To add the foreign key to a column definition, you must add a reference definition, which is shown in the following syntax:

```
<reference definition>::=
REFERENCES <table name> [(<column name> [{, <column name>}...])]
[ON DELETE {RESTRICT | CASCADE | SET NULL | NO ACTION | SET DEFAULT }]
[ON UPDATE {RESTRICT | CASCADE | SET NULL | NO ACTION | SET DEFAULT }]
```

As you can see from the syntax, the clause includes several required elements: the REFERENCES keyword, the name of the referenced (parent) table, and at least one column in that table, enclosed in parentheses. The syntax also includes an optional ON DELETE clause and an optional ON UPDATE clause. The ON DELETE clause specifies how MySQL treats related data in the child table when a row in the parent table is deleted. The ON UPDATE clause specifies how MySQL treats related data in the child table when a row in the parent table is updated. For each clause, five options are available. You can specify only one option for each clause. These options are described in the following table:

Option	Description
RESTRICT	If the child table contains values in the referencing columns that match values in the referenced columns in the parent table, rows in the parent table cannot be deleted, and values in the referenced columns cannot be updated. This is the default option if an ON DELETE or ON UPDATE clause is not specified.
CASCADE	Rows in the child table that contain values that also exist in the referenced columns of the parent table are deleted when the associated rows are deleted from the parent table. Rows in the child table that contain values that also exist in the referenced columns of the parent table are updated when the associated values are updated in the parent table.
SET NULL	Values in the referencing columns of the child table are set to NULL when rows with referenced data in the parent table are deleted from the parent table or when the referenced data in the parent table is updated. To use this option, all referencing columns in the child table must permit null values.
NO ACTION	No action is taken in the child table when rows are deleted from the parent table or values in the referenced columns in the parent table are updated.
SET DEFAULT	Values in the referencing columns of the child table are set to their default values when rows are deleted from the parent table or the referenced columns of the parent table are updated.

When you define a foreign key, you can include an ON DELETE clause, an ON UPDATE clause, or both. If you include both, you can configure them with the same option or with different options. If you exclude one or both, the RESTRICT option is assumed in either case, which means that updates and deletes are limited to rows with nonreferenced values. In addition, when defining a foreign key, the referencing columns must have data types compatible with the referenced columns. For integer data types, the size and signed/unsigned status must be the same. The length of a string data type, however, doesn't have to be the same. It's generally a good idea to configure the referencing and referenced columns with the same data type and type-related options.

Now that you have an overview of how to use a reference definition to add a foreign key to a column definition, take a look at an example to help demonstrate how this works. In the following CREATE TABLE statement, a reference definition has been added to the ModelID column:

```
CREATE TABLE Orders
(
    OrderID SMALLINT UNSIGNED NOT NULL PRIMARY KEY,
    ModelID SMALLINT UNSIGNED NOT NULL REFERENCES Models (ModelID),
    ModelDescrip VARCHAR(40)
);
```

In this example, the ModelID column is configured with a SMALLINT data type (unsigned), a NOT NULL option, and a REFERENCES clause, which specifies the name of the parent table (Models) and the name of the referenced column (ModelID) in the parent table. As a result, the ModelID column of the Orders table can include only values that are listed in the ModelID column of the Models table.

You can also define this foreign key as a separate table element by adding a FOREIGN KEY constraint to your table definition. The following syntax shows how to define a FOREIGN KEY constraint:

```
[CONSTRAINT <constraint name>] FOREIGN KEY [<index name>]
    (<column name> [{, <column name>}...]) <reference definition>
```

As the syntax indicates, you must include the keywords FOREIGN KEY, the name of the referencing columns in the child table, enclosed in parentheses, and a reference definition. The reference definition is the same definition used in a column definition to add a foreign key. To illustrate this, rewrite the last example table definition, but this time use a FOREIGN KEY constraint to define the foreign key:

```
CREATE TABLE Orders
(
    OrderID SMALLINT UNSIGNED NOT NULL PRIMARY KEY,
    ModelID SMALLINT UNSIGNED NOT NULL,
    ModelDescrip VARCHAR(40),
    FOREIGN KEY (ModelID) REFERENCES Models (ModelID)
        ON DELETE CASCADE ON UPDATE CASCADE
);
```

In this example, the FOREIGN KEY constraint is added as a table element, along with the column definitions. The same column (ModelID) is being configured as a foreign key that references the ModelID column of the Models table. The only difference between this example and the last example is that the reference definition in the last example includes an ON DELETE clause and an ON UPDATE clause, both of which are configured with the CASCADE option. As a result, the child table reflects changes to the parent table.

If you want to define a foreign key on more than one column, you must use a FOREIGN KEY constraint, rather than adding a referencing definition to the column definition. In addition, you must separate the column names by commas and enclose all the column names in parentheses.

Defining Table Types

When you were first introduced to the table definition syntax earlier in the chapter, one of the last elements in that syntax was the <table option> placeholder. For each table definition, you can include one or more table options.

For the most part, these options are beyond the scope of this book. If you want to learn more about them, you are encouraged to review the MySQL product documentation.

One of the table options that is especially important when learning about MySQL is the one that allows you to define the type of table that you create in your table definition. Recall from Chapter 3 that MySQL allows you to create six different types of tables, which are shown in the following syntax:

```
ENGINE = {BDB | MEMORY | ISAM | INNODB | MERGE | MYISAM}
```

To define a table type, you must include an ENGINE clause at the end of your table definition, after the parentheses that enclose your table elements. For example, the following table definition specifies the InnoDB table type:

```
CREATE TABLE AuthorBios
(
    AuthID SMALLINT UNSIGNED NOT NULL,
    YearBorn YEAR NOT NULL,
    CityBorn VARCHAR(40) NOT NULL DEFAULT 'Unknown'
)
ENGINE=INNODB;
```

In this definition, an ENGINE clause is added after the last column definition and closing parentheses. Notice that you simply specify the ENGINE keyword, the equal sign, and one of the seven table types. Each table type in MySQL supports a specific set of functionality and serves specific purposes. In addition, each type is associated with a related storage engine (handler) that processes the data in that table. For example, the MyISAM engine processes data in MyISAM tables. The following table discusses each of the six types of tables.

Table type	Description
BDB	A transaction-safe table that is managed by the Berkeley DB (BDB) handler. The BDB handler also supports automatic recovery and page-level locking. The BDB handler does not work on all the operating systems on which MySQL can operate. For the most part, InnoDB tables have replaced BDB tables.
MEMORY	A table whose contents are stored in memory. The data stored in the tables is available only as long as the MySQL server is available. If the server crashes or is shut down, the data disappears. Because these types of tables are stored in memory, they are very fast and are good candidates for temporary tables. MEMORY tables can also be referred to as HEAP tables, although MEMORY is now the preferable keyword.
InnoDB	A transaction-safe table that is managed by the InnoDB handler. As a result, data is not stored in a .MYD file, but instead is managed in the InnoDB tablespace. InnoDB tables also support full foreign key functionality in MySQL, unlike other tables. In addition, the InnoDB handler supports automatic recovery and row-level locking. InnoDB tables do not perform as well as MyISAM tables.
ISAM	A deprecated table type that was once the default table type in MySQL. The MyISAM table type has replaced it, although it is still supported for backward compatibility. Eventually, ISAM tables will no longer be supported.

Table continued on following page

MERGE	A virtual table that is made up of identical MyISAM tables. Data is not stored in the MERGE table, but in the underlying MyISAM tables. Changes made to the MERGE table definition do not affect the underlying MyISAM tables. MERGE tables can also be referred to as MRG_MyISAM tables
MyISAM	The default table type in MySQL. MyISAM tables, which are based on and have replaced ISAM tables, support extensive indexing and are optimized for compression and speed. Unlike other table types, BLOB and TEXT columns can be indexed and null values are allowed in indexed columns. MyISAM tables are not transaction safe, and they do not support full foreign key functionality.

You can use the TYPE keyword to specify the table type, rather than the ENGINE keyword. However, TYPE has been deprecated in MySQL, which means that it will eventually be phased out. If you use TYPE, you receive a warning about its deprecated state, but the table is still created.

Creating Tables in the DVDRentals Database

Now that you have learned how to create a table in MySQL, it's time to try it out for yourself. The following three Try It Out sections walk you through the steps necessary to create the tables in the DVDRentals database. The tables are based on the final database design that you developed in Chapter 4. The tables are divided into three categories that correspond to the following Try It Out sections. The first group of tables acts as lookup tables in the database. They must be developed before you create tables that reference the lookup table. The second category of tables holds data about the people who will participate somehow in the database system. These include the movie participants, the employees, and the customers. The last group includes the tables that contain foreign keys. You must create this group of tables last because they contain columns that reference other tables. In addition, you must create these tables in a specific order because of how they reference each other.

In this Try It Out, you create the six lookup tables that are part of the DVDRentals database, which you created in the Try It Out section earlier in the chapter. These tables include the Roles, MovieTypes, Studios, Ratings, Formats, and Status tables. As you work your way through this exercise, you should reference the data model that you created in Chapter 4. From there, you can compare the SQL statement that you use here to that model.

Try It Out   Creating the Lookup Tables

Follow these steps to create the six lookup tables:

1. Open the mysql client utility, type the following command, and press Enter:

```
use DVDRentals
```

You should receive a message indicating that you switched to the DVDRentals database.

2. To create the Roles table, type the following CREATE TABLE statement at the mysql command prompt, and then press Enter:

```
CREATE TABLE Roles
   (
   RoleID VARCHAR(4) NOT NULL,
   RoleDescrip VARCHAR(30) NOT NULL,
   PRIMARY KEY (RoleID)
   )
ENGINE=INNODB;
```

You should receive a message indicating that the statement executed successfully.

3. To create the MovieTypes table, type the following CREATE TABLE statement at the mysql command prompt, and then press Enter:

```
CREATE TABLE MovieTypes
   (
   MTypeID VARCHAR(4) NOT NULL,
   MTypeDescrip VARCHAR(30) NOT NULL,
   PRIMARY KEY (MTypeID)
   )
ENGINE=INNODB;
```

You should receive a message indicating that the statement executed successfully.

4. To create the Studios table, type the following CREATE TABLE statement at the mysql command prompt, and then press Enter:

```
CREATE TABLE Studios
   (
   StudID VARCHAR(4) NOT NULL,
   StudDescrip VARCHAR(40) NOT NULL,
   PRIMARY KEY (StudID)
   )
ENGINE=INNODB;
```

You should receive a message indicating that the statement executed successfully.

5. To create the Ratings table, type the following CREATE TABLE statement at the mysql command prompt, and then press Enter:

```
CREATE TABLE Ratings
   (
   RatingID VARCHAR(4) NOT NULL,
   RatingDescrip VARCHAR(30) NOT NULL,
   PRIMARY KEY (RatingID)
   )
ENGINE=INNODB;
```

You should receive a message indicating that the statement executed successfully.

6. To create the Formats table, type the following CREATE TABLE statement at the mysql command prompt, and then press Enter:

```
CREATE TABLE Formats
   (
   FormID CHAR(2) NOT NULL,
   FormDescrip VARCHAR(15) NOT NULL,
   PRIMARY KEY (FormID)
   )
ENGINE=INNODB;
```

You should receive a message indicating that the statement executed successfully.

7. To create the Status table, type the following CREATE TABLE statement at the mysql command prompt, and then press Enter:

```
CREATE TABLE Status
    (
    StatID CHAR(3) NOT NULL,
    StatDescrip VARCHAR(20) NOT NULL,
    PRIMARY KEY (StatID)
    )
ENGINE=INNODB;
```

You should receive a message indicating that the statement executed successfully.

How It Works

In this exercise, you created the six lookup tables in the DVDRentals database. The table definitions should be consistent with the final data model that you created in Chapter 4 for the DVDRentals database. In addition, the six tables are very similar. Take a look at one of them, and review the code that you used to create the table. You used the following CREATE TABLE statement to create the Roles table:

```
CREATE TABLE Roles
    (
    RoleID VARCHAR(4) NOT NULL,
    RoleDescrip VARCHAR(30) NOT NULL,
    PRIMARY KEY (RoleID)
    )
ENGINE=INNODB;
```

The statement begins with the CREATE TABLE statement, which identifies the name of the new table (Roles). The table definition then includes three table elements, which are separated by commas and enclosed in parentheses. The first two table elements are column definitions. The RoleID column definition creates a column that is configured with a VARCHAR data type. The data type permits up to four characters. In addition, the column does not permit null values. You use a VARCHAR data type for the RoleID column, rather than a CHAR data type because MySQL converts CHAR data types to VARCHAR data types whenever more than three characters are specified for the value length *and* there are other varying-length columns in the table (which is the case for the RoleDescrip column). Otherwise, you would use CHAR(4) because the values in the column have a fixed length of four characters.

The second column defined in the Roles table definition is the RoleDescrip column, which is configured with a VARCHAR data type and a maximum length of 30 characters. This column also does not permit null values. The last table element in the CREATE TABLE statement is the PRIMARY KEY constraint, which defines a primary key on the RoleID column. As a result, this column uniquely identifies each role in the table.

The last component of the Roles table definition is the ENGINE table option, which species that the table type is InnoDB. You specify this table type because InnoDB is the only type that supports transactions and foreign keys, both of which are important to the DVDRentals database.

The other five tables that you created in the exercise are nearly identical to the Roles table, except for the names of the tables and columns. The only other difference is that string columns with a length less than four are configured with CHAR data types rather than VARCHAR.

Once you create the six lookup tables, you can create the three tables that contain the people (explained in the following Try It Out). Because these tables do not contain foreign keys that reference other tables, you could have created these three tables first. In fact, you could have created the nine tables in any order, as long as all referenced (parent) tables are created before the referencing (child) tables. You grouped the tables together in the manner you did just to keep similar types of tables together in order to make explanations simpler.

Try It Out   **Creating the People Tables**

The following steps describe how to create the three tables that contain people:

1. To create the Participants table, type the following CREATE TABLE statement at the mysql command prompt, and then press Enter:

```
CREATE TABLE Participants
    (
    PartID SMALLINT NOT NULL AUTO_INCREMENT PRIMARY KEY,
    PartFN VARCHAR(20) NOT NULL,
    PartMN VARCHAR(20) NULL,
    PartLN VARCHAR(20) NULL
    )
ENGINE=INNODB;
```

You should receive a message indicating that the statement executed successfully.

2. To create the Employees table, type the following CREATE TABLE statement at the mysql command prompt, and then press Enter:

```
CREATE TABLE Employees
    (
    EmpID SMALLINT NOT NULL AUTO_INCREMENT PRIMARY KEY,
    EmpFN VARCHAR(20) NOT NULL,
    EmpMN VARCHAR(20) NULL,
    EmpLN VARCHAR(20) NOT NULL
    )
ENGINE=INNODB;
```

You should receive a message indicating that the statement executed successfully.

3. To create the Customers table, type the following CREATE TABLE statement at the mysql command prompt, and then press Enter:

```
CREATE TABLE Customers
    (
    CustID SMALLINT NOT NULL AUTO_INCREMENT PRIMARY KEY,
    CustFN VARCHAR(20) NOT NULL,
    CustMN VARCHAR(20) NULL,
    CustLN VARCHAR(20) NOT NULL
    )
ENGINE=INNODB;
```

You should receive a message indicating that the statement executed successfully.

How It Works

As with the previous exercise, this exercise adds several tables to the DVDRentals database. Except for the names of the tables and columns, the table definitions are nearly identical. As a result, this explanation covers only one of these definitions to understand how the statements work. The following CREATE TABLE statement is the one you used to create the Participants table:

```
CREATE TABLE Participants
    (
    PartID SMALLINT NOT NULL AUTO_INCREMENT PRIMARY KEY,
    PartFN VARCHAR(20) NOT NULL,
    PartMN VARCHAR(20) NULL,
    PartLN VARCHAR(20) NULL
    )
ENGINE=INNODB;
```

The Participants table definition includes four table elements, separated by commas and enclosed in parentheses. All four table elements are column definitions. The first column definition defines the PartID column, which is configured with the SMALLINT data type, the NOT NULL option, and the AUTO_INCREMENT option. The column is also defined as the primary key. As a result, values in the column uniquely identify each row in the table, null values are not allowed, and the values inserted in the column are generated automatically.

The remaining three columns are configured with the VARCHAR data type and are assigned a length of 20 characters. Null values are not allowed in the PartFN column, but they are allowed in the PartMN columns and the PartLN columns. The columns are set up this way to allow for actors and other movie participants who are known by only one name. (Cher comes to mind as one example.) The other two tables—Employees and Customers—are different in this respect because a last name is required. This, of course, is a business decision, and the business rules collected for this project would dictate which names are actually required. In the case of these three tables, a middle name is not required for any of them.

As with the six lookup table that you created in the previous exercise, all three of the tables in this exercise have been created as InnoDB tables. To support foreign key functionality, all tables participating in relationships must be configured as InnoDB tables.

Now that you've created all the referenced tables in the DVDRentals database, you're ready to create the referencing tables, which are each configured with one or more foreign keys. The order in which you create these remaining four tables is important because dependencies exist among these four tables. For example, you must create the DVDs table before you create the DVDParticipant and Transactions tables because both these tables reference the DVDs table. In addition, you must create the Orders table before you create the Transactions table because the Transactions table references the Orders table. The following Try It Out shows you how to create all the necessary foreign key tables.

Try It Out   Creating the Foreign Key Tables

The following steps describe how to create the four referencing tables:

1. To create the DVDs table, type the following CREATE TABLE statement at the mysql command prompt, and then press Enter:

```
CREATE TABLE DVDs
   (
   DVDID SMALLINT NOT NULL AUTO_INCREMENT PRIMARY KEY,
   DVDName VARCHAR(60) NOT NULL,
   NumDisks TINYINT NOT NULL DEFAULT 1,
   YearRlsd YEAR NOT NULL,
   MTypeID VARCHAR(4) NOT NULL,
   StudID VARCHAR(4) NOT NULL,
   RatingID VARCHAR(4) NOT NULL,
   FormID CHAR(2) NOT NULL,
   StatID CHAR(3) NOT NULL,
   FOREIGN KEY (MTypeID) REFERENCES MovieTypes (MTypeID),
   FOREIGN KEY (StudID) REFERENCES Studios (StudID),
   FOREIGN KEY (RatingID) REFERENCES Ratings (RatingID),
   FOREIGN KEY (FormID) REFERENCES Formats (FormID),
   FOREIGN KEY (StatID) REFERENCES Status (StatID)
   )
ENGINE=INNODB;
```

You should receive a message indicating that the statement executed successfully.

This table definition is based on MySQL version 4.1 or later. This statement will not work for versions earlier than 4.1.

2. To create the DVDParticipant table, type the following CREATE TABLE statement at the mysql command prompt, and then press Enter:

```
CREATE TABLE DVDParticipant
   (
   DVDID SMALLINT NOT NULL,
   PartID SMALLINT NOT NULL,
   RoleID VARCHAR(4) NOT NULL,
   PRIMARY KEY (DVDID, PartID, RoleID),
   FOREIGN KEY (DVDID) REFERENCES DVDs (DVDID),
   FOREIGN KEY (PartID) REFERENCES Participants (PartID),
   FOREIGN KEY (RoleID) REFERENCES Roles (RoleID)
   )
ENGINE=INNODB;
```

You should receive a message indicating that the statement executed successfully.

3. To create the Orders table, type the following CREATE TABLE statement at the mysql command prompt, and then press Enter:

```
CREATE TABLE Orders
   (
   OrderID INT NOT NULL AUTO_INCREMENT PRIMARY KEY,
   CustID SMALLINT NOT NULL,
   EmpID SMALLINT NOT NULL,
   FOREIGN KEY (CustID) REFERENCES Customers (CustID),
   FOREIGN KEY (EmpID) REFERENCES Employees (EmpID)
   )
ENGINE=INNODB;
```

You should receive a message indicating that the statement executed successfully.

4. To create the Transactions table, type the following CREATE TABLE statement at the mysql command prompt, and then press Enter:

```
CREATE TABLE Transactions
  (
  TransID INT NOT NULL AUTO_INCREMENT PRIMARY KEY,
  OrderID INT NOT NULL,
  DVDID SMALLINT NOT NULL,
  DateOut DATE NOT NULL,
  DateDue DATE NOT NULL,
  DateIn DATE NOT NULL,
  FOREIGN KEY (OrderID) REFERENCES Orders (OrderID),
  FOREIGN KEY (DVDID) REFERENCES DVDs (DVDID)
  )
ENGINE=INNODB;
```

You should receive a message indicating that the statement executed successfully.

How It Works

Because you created the DVDs table first, that is the first table reviewed. The following CREATE TABLE statement creates a table definition that includes 14 table elements:

```
CREATE TABLE DVDs
  (
  DVDID SMALLINT NOT NULL AUTO_INCREMENT PRIMARY KEY,
  DVDName VARCHAR(60) NOT NULL,
  NumDisks TINYINT NOT NULL DEFAULT 1,
  YearRlsd YEAR NOT NULL,
  MTypeID VARCHAR(4) NOT NULL,
  StudID VARCHAR(4) NOT NULL,
  RatingID VARCHAR(4) NOT NULL,
  FormID CHAR(2) NOT NULL,
  StatID CHAR(3) NOT NULL,
  FOREIGN KEY (MTypeID) REFERENCES MovieTypes (MTypeID),
  FOREIGN KEY (StudID) REFERENCES Studios (StudID),
  FOREIGN KEY (RatingID) REFERENCES Ratings (RatingID),
  FOREIGN KEY (FormID) REFERENCES Formats (FormID),
  FOREIGN KEY (StatID) REFERENCES Status (StatID)
  )
ENGINE=INNODB;
```

As you can see, the DVDs table definition includes nine columns. Each column is configured with a data type appropriate to that column. Any column defined as a foreign key is configured with a data type identical to the referenced column. In addition, every column is configured with the NOT NULL option, which means that null values are not permitted. The first column, DVDID, is defined as the primary key and includes the AUTO_INCREMENT option, so unique values are automatically assigned to that column.

Of particular interest in this table definition is the NumDisks column definition, which includes a DEFAULT clause (with a default value of 1). As a result, whenever a row is inserted in the table, the value for the NumDisks column is set to 1, unless otherwise specified. This was done because most DVDs come with one disk, although some include more.

The table definition also includes five FOREIGN KEY constraints, one for each referencing column. In each case, the constraint specifies the referencing column, the referenced table, and the referenced column. For example, the first FOREIGN KEY constraint specifies the MTypeID column as the referencing column, the MovieTypes table as the referenced table, and the MTypeID column in the MovieTypes table as the referenced column.

The other three tables that you defined in this exercise include column and foreign key definitions similar to what you've seen in the DVD table definition and the table definitions in the previous two exercises. In addition, all four tables are defined as InnoDB tables to support transactions and foreign key functionality. The DVDParticipant table definition includes an element that you have not seen, so that definition is worth a closer look:

```
CREATE TABLE DVDParticipant
    (
    DVDID SMALLINT NOT NULL,
    PartID SMALLINT NOT NULL,
    RoleID VARCHAR(4) NOT NULL,
    PRIMARY KEY (DVDID, PartID, RoleID),
    FOREIGN KEY (DVDID) REFERENCES DVDs (DVDID),
    FOREIGN KEY (PartID) REFERENCES Participants (PartID),
    FOREIGN KEY (RoleID) REFERENCES Roles (RoleID)
    )
ENGINE=INNODB;
```

In this table definition, a composite primary key is defined on the DVDID, PartID, and RoleID columns, all of which are configured as individual foreign keys. As this table demonstrates, primary keys can consist of multiple columns, and those columns can also be configured as foreign keys. Because the three columns, when taken as a whole, uniquely identify each row in the table, you do not have to create an additional column in order to create a primary key. The table, as it exists here, is complete.

Once you create the four remaining tables in the DVDRentals database, you can begin adding the data necessary to populate the tables. As you learned earlier in this chapter, the data must exist in the referenced columns before you can insert it in the referencing columns. What this means is that the lookup tables and the tables that contain people's names must be populated before the other tables. Chapter 6 provides more detail on how you insert data in your tables, but for now, the focus switches to modifying table definitions.

Modifying Tables

It is not uncommon to find that, after creating a table, you want to modify the table definition. Fortunately, MySQL allows you to change a number of table elements after creating a table. For example, you can add columns, alter existing columns, add PRIMARY KEY and FOREIGN KEY constraints, or remove columns and constraints.

To modify an existing table definition, you must use the ALTER TABLE statement. The following syntax shows how to create an ALTER TABLE statement and the options available to that statement:

```
ALTER TABLE <table name>
<alter option> [{, <alter option>}...]

<alter option>::=
{ADD [COLUMN] <column definition> [FIRST | AFTER <column name>]}
| {ADD [COLUMN] (<table element> [{, <table element>}...])}
| {ADD [CONSTRAINT <constraint name>] PRIMARY KEY
      (<column name> [{, <column name>}...])}
| {ADD [CONSTRAINT <constraint name>] FOREIGN KEY [<index name>]
      (<column name> [{, <column name>}...]) <reference definition>}
| {ADD [CONSTRAINT <constraint name>] UNIQUE [<index name>]
      (<column name> [{, <column name>}...])}
| {ADD INDEX [<index name>] (<column name> [{, <column name>}...])}
| {ADD FULLTEXT [<index name>] (<column name> [{, <column name>}...])}
| {ALTER [COLUMN] <column name> {SET DEFAULT <value> | DROP DEFAULT}}
| {CHANGE [COLUMN] <column name> <column definition> [FIRST | AFTER <column name>]}
| {MODIFY [COLUMN] <column definition> [FIRST | AFTER <column name>]}
| {DROP [COLUMN] <column name>}
| {DROP PRIMARY KEY}
| {DROP INDEX <index name>}
| {DROP FOREIGN KEY <constraint name>}
| {RENAME [TO] <new table name>}
| {ORDER BY <column name> [{, <column name>}...]}
| {<table option> [<table option>...]}
```

The basic elements of the ALTER TABLE statement are the ALTER TABLE keywords, the name of the table that you want to modify, and one or more alter options. If you chose more than one option, you must separate the options with a comma. Each of the alter options maps directly to a table definition option, except that you must also include an action keyword such as ADD, ALTER, or DROP. In addition, several of the alter options include additional elements that help to define the option. Take a look at an example to help illustrate this concept. Suppose that you create the following table:

```
CREATE TABLE Books
(
    BookID SMALLINT NOT NULL,
    BookName VARCHAR(40) NOT NULL,
    PubID SMALLINT NOT NULL DEFAULT 'Unknown'
)
ENGINE=INNODB;
```

As you can see, the table definition creates a table named Books, the table contains three columns, and the PubID column contains a default value of Unknown. Now suppose that you want to modify the table to include a primary key, foreign key, and an additional column. The following ALTER TABLE statement modifies the table accordingly:

```
ALTER TABLE Books
ADD PRIMARY KEY (BookID),
ADD CONSTRAINT fk_1 FOREIGN KEY (PubID) REFERENCES Publishers (PubID),
ADD COLUMN Format ENUM('paperback', 'hardcover') NOT NULL AFTER BookName;
```

The statement begins with the ALTER TABLE statement, which identifies the name of the table being modified, which in this case is Books. The next line adds a primary key to the table. The primary key is based on the BookID column. The third line in the ALTER TABLE statement adds a FOREIGN KEY constraint to the table. The name of the constraint is fk_1, the foreign key is defined on the PubID column, and the foreign key references the PubID column in the Publishers table.

The final line of the ALTER TABLE statement adds a column to the table. As you can see, a column definition follows the ADD COLUMN keywords. The name of the column is Format. The column is configured with an ENUM data type that is defined with two values: paperback and hardcover. The column is also configured with the NOT NULL option. The AFTER clause, which is unique to the ALTER TABLE statement, specifies that the new column should be added after the column named BookName.

As you can see, the options available to the ALTER TABLE statement are very consistent to their CREATE TABLE statement counterparts, at least in terms of adding and modifying columns. If you plan to remove a component of a table, the options are much simpler, as shown in the following example:

```
ALTER TABLE Books
DROP PRIMARY KEY,
DROP FOREIGN KEY fk_1,
DROP COLUMN Format;
```

In this ALTER TABLE statement, the primary key, the fk_1 FOREIGN KEY constraint, and the Format column are all removed form the table. As these examples demonstrate, the ALTER TABLE syntax contains few elements that you haven't seen, except for the action keywords and the few options specific to the ALTER TABLE statement. In addition, these examples also demonstrate that you can modify most of the components that you define in a CREATE TABLE statement with an ALTER TABLE statement.

Deleting Tables

Deleting a table from the database is simply a matter of executing a DROP TABLE statement. As the following syntax shows, the only elements required in a DROP TABLE statement are the DROP TABLE keywords and the name of the table:

```
DROP [TEMPORARY] TABLE [IF EXISTS] <table name> [{, <table name>}...]
```

The DROP TABLE statement also includes the optional TEMPORARY keyword, which you use if you want to ensure that you drop only a temporary table and do not inadvertently drop a permanent table. The other optional element in the DROP TABLE statement is the IF EXISTS clause. If you specify the clause, you receive a warning message, rather than an error, if you try to drop a table that doesn't exist. The one other aspect of the DROP TABLE syntax to consider is the ability to add optional table names. You can use this statement to drop multiple tables, as long as you separate them by a comma.

Now that you've seen the syntax, look at an example of a DROP TABLE statement to demonstrate how one works. The following example removes a table named Books from your database:

```
DROP TABLE IF EXISTS Books;
```

As you can see, the statement includes the DROP TABLE keywords, along with the name of the table. In addition, the statement includes the IF EXISTS clause, which means that, if the table doesn't exist, you receive a warning rather than an error when trying to drop a table.

You cannot drop a parent table referenced in a foreign key. You must first remove the foreign key in the child table and then drop the parent table.

In the following exercise, you create a table named InStock, alter the table definition, and then delete the table from your database.

Try It Out   Altering and Dropping Tables

To perform the tasks mentioned here, follow these steps:

1. Open the mysql client utility, type the following command, and press Enter:

```
use test
```

You should receive a message indicating that you switched to the test database.

2. To create the InStock table, type the following CREATE TABLE statement at the mysql command prompt, and then press Enter:

```
CREATE TABLE InStock
(
    ProductID SMALLINT
);
```

You should receive a message indicating that the statement executed successfully.

3. Next, add a column, modify the ProductID column, and add a primary key. To make these changes, type the following ALTER TABLE statement at the mysql command prompt, and then press Enter:

```
ALTER TABLE InStock
ADD COLUMN Quantity SMALLINT UNSIGNED NOT NULL,
MODIFY ProductID SMALLINT UNSIGNED NOT NULL,
ADD PRIMARY KEY (ProductID);
```

You should receive a message indicating that the statement executed successfully.

4. Next, drop the column and the primary key that you added in the previous step. To make these changes, type the following ALTER TABLE statement at the mysql command prompt, and then press Enter:

```
ALTER TABLE InStock
DROP COLUMN Quantity,
DROP PRIMARY KEY;
```

You should receive a message indicating that the statement executed successfully.

5. Finally, remove the InStock table from the test database. To remove the table, type the following DROP TABLE statement at the mysql command prompt, and then press Enter:

```
DROP TABLE InStock;
```

You should receive a message indicating that the statement executed successfully.

How It Works

In this exercise, you used a CREATE TABLE statement to create the InStock table in the test database. Once you created the table, you used the following ALTER TABLE statement to modify the InStock table definition:

```
ALTER TABLE InStock
ADD COLUMN Quantity SMALLINT UNSIGNED NOT NULL,
MODIFY ProductID SMALLINT UNSIGNED NOT NULL,
ADD PRIMARY KEY (ProductID);
```

The ALTER TABLE statement includes three alter options. The first one adds a column named Quantity to the InStock table. The column is configured with the SMALLINT data type (unsigned) and the NOT NULL option. The next alter option modifies the ProductID column by configuring the SMALLINT data type to be unsigned and by adding the NOT NULL option. The final alter option adds a primary key to the table. The primary key is based on the ProductID column.

The next step used the following statement to again modify the table:

```
ALTER TABLE InStock
DROP COLUMN Quantity,
DROP PRIMARY KEY;
```

This statement removes the Quantity column from the InStock table and then drops the primary key. After altering the table, you used a DROP TABLE statement to remove the InStock table from the database.

Managing Indexes

Earlier in the chapter, when you were introduced to the CREATE TABLE statement, you no doubt noticed that some of the table elements were related to indexes. An *index* is a device that MySQL uses to speed up searches and reduce the time it takes to execute complex queries. An index works under the same principles as an index you would find at the end of a book. The index provides an organized list of pointers to the actual data. As a result, when MySQL is executing a query, it does not have to scan each table in its entirety to locate the correct data, but it can instead scan the index, thus resulting in quicker and more efficient access.

Indexes, however, do have their trade-offs. First, they can affect the performance of operations that involve the modification of data in a table because the index must be updated whenever the table has been updated. In addition, indexes require additional disk space, which, for large tables, can translate to a substantial amount of storage. Despite these drawbacks, indexes play a critical role in data access, and few tables in a MySQL database are not indexed in some way.

Index Types

MySQL supports five types of indexes that can be created on a table. As you have worked your way through this chapter, you have already created two types of indexes: primary keys and foreign keys. Whenever you create a primary key or a foreign key, you are automatically creating an index on the columns specified in those keys. In fact, when you create a FOREIGN KEY constraint, you have the option to provide a name for the index that is being created. If you don't provide a name, MySQL assigns a name based on the first referencing column. In addition, MySQL assigns the name PRIMARY to all primary key indexes.

> *When you are setting up a foreign key on columns in an InnoDB table, the referencing foreign key columns and the referenced columns in the parent table must both be indexed.*

In addition to primary key and foreign key indexes, MySQL also supports unique indexes, regular (non-unique) indexes, and full-text indexes. The following table provides an overview of each of the five types of indexes.

Index type	Description
Primary key	Requires that each value or set of values be unique in the columns on which the primary key is defined. In addition, null values are not allowed. Also, a table can include only one primary key.
Foreign key	Enforces the relationship between the referencing columns in the child table where the foreign key is defined and the referenced columns in the parent table.
Regular	A basic index that permits duplicate values and null values in the columns on which the index is defined.
Unique	Requires that each value or set of values be unique in the columns on which the index is defined. Unlike primary key indexes, null values are allowed.
Full-text	Supports full-text searches of the values in the columns on which the index is defined. A full-text index permits duplicate values and null values in those columns. A full-text index can be defined only on MyISAM tables and only on CHAR, VARCHAR, and TEXT columns.

When creating a table definition that includes indexes, you should place the primary key columns first, followed by the unique index columns, and then followed by any nonunique index columns. This process helps to optimize index performance. Later in the book, in Chapter 15, you learn more about how to use indexes to optimize query performance, but for now, take a look at how you actually create indexes on columns in a table.

Creating Indexes

MySQL supports several methods for adding indexes to a table. You can include the indexes in your column definition, you can use an ALTER TABLE statement to add an index to a table, or you can use the CREATE INDEX statement to add an index to a table.

Defining Indexes When Creating Tables

When using the CREATE TABLE statement to create a table, you can include a number of table elements in your statement. For example, you can include column definitions, a PRIMARY KEY constraint, or FOREIGN KEY constraints. In addition, you can define a primary key and foreign keys in your column definitions. Regardless of the method that you use to create a primary key or a foreign key, whenever you create such a key, you're automatically creating an index on the columns participating in a particular key.

It is worth noting here that, in MySQL, the keyword KEY and the keyword INDEX are often used synonymously.

Because you're already familiar with how to create primary key and foreign key indexes in a CREATE TABLE statement, take a look at creating unique, regular, and full-text indexes.

Creating Unique Indexes

To create a unique index, you should use a UNIQUE constraint, which is one of the table element options included in the CREATE TABLE statement. The following syntax shows you how to create a UNIQUE constraint:

```
[CONSTRAINT <constraint name>] UNIQUE [INDEX] [<index name>]
    (<column name> [{, <column name>}...])
```

When adding a unique index to a table definition, you need to include only the keyword UNIQUE and the name of the indexed column, enclosed in parentheses. If you're creating the index on more than one column, then you must separate the column names with a comma. In addition, you can include the CONSTRAINT keyword along with the name of the constraint, the INDEX keyword, or an index name. If you don't include a constraint name or an index name, MySQL provides names automatically. Whether or not you include these optional elements, the basic index is the same.

A unique index is also considered a constraint because it ensures that each value in a column is unique, in addition to indexing these values.

Now take a look at an example to demonstrate how to include a unique index in the table definition. The following CREATE TABLE statement defines a unique index on the OrderID and ModelID columns:

```
CREATE TABLE Orders
(
    OrderID SMALLINT UNSIGNED NOT NULL,
    ModelID SMALLINT UNSIGNED NOT NULL,
    ModelDescrip VARCHAR(40),
    PRIMARY KEY (OrderID),
    UNIQUE (OrderID, ModelID)
);
```

The CREATE TABLE statement actually creates two indexes: one primary key and one unique. Notice that the OrderID column participates in two indexes and that the unique index is defined on two columns. As a result, the OrderID column can contain only unique values, and the OrderID and ModelID values, when taken together, can include only unique value pairs. The ModelID column, however, can include duplicate values.

Creating Regular (Nonunique) Indexes

There might be times when you want to index a column but you don't want to require that the values in the column be unique. For those situations you can use a regular index. As with unique indexes, you can include a regular index in a table definition by adding it as a table element, as shown in the following syntax:

```
{INDEX | KEY} [<index name>] (<column name> [{, <column name>}...])
```

When you define a regular index, you must specify the INDEX or KEY keyword and the name of the indexed column, enclosed in parentheses. If you want to index more than one column, you must separate the columns by a comma. For example, suppose that your database includes a table that lists the first name and the last name of a company's customers. You might want to create a composite index (an index on more than one column) on the column that contains the first name and the column that contains the last name so that the entire name can be easily searched.

In addition to specifying the indexed columns, you can provide a name for your index. If you don't provide a name, MySQL names the index automatically.

The following CREATE TABLE statement demonstrates how to include a regular index in a table definition:

```
CREATE TABLE Orders
(
    OrderID SMALLINT UNSIGNED NOT NULL,
    ModelID SMALLINT UNSIGNED NOT NULL,
    PRIMARY KEY (OrderID),
    INDEX (ModelID)
);
```

This statement creates a regular index on the ModelID column. You do not need to specify any other elements to add the index. MySQL provides a name for the index automatically.

Creating Full-Text Indexes

Now take a look at how to add a full-text index to a MyISAM table. As you recall, you can add this type of index only to the CHAR, VARCHAR, or TEXT columns. The following syntax shows how you add a full-text index to a table definition:

```
FULLTEXT [INDEX] [<index name>] (<column name> [{, <column name>}...])
```

Adding a full-text index is almost identical to adding a regular index, except that you have to specify the keyword FULLTEXT. The following CREATE TABLE statement demonstrates how this works:

```
CREATE TABLE Orders
(
    OrderID SMALLINT UNSIGNED NOT NULL,
    ModelID SMALLINT UNSIGNED NOT NULL,
    ModelName VARCHAR(40),
    PRIMARY KEY (OrderID),
    FULLTEXT (ModelName)
);
```

This example defines a full-text index on the ModelName column, which is configured with a VARCHAR data type. In addition, because you specify no table type option in this table definition, MySQL uses the default table type, which is MyISAM.

Now that you have an overview of how to add an index in a CREATE TABLE statement, you can try it out. In this exercise, you create a table named CDs. The table definition includes a regular index on the CDName column.

| Try It Out | Creating a Table with an Index |

Follow these steps to complete this exercise:

1. Open the mysql client utility, type the following command, and press Enter:

```
use test
```

You should receive a message indicating that you switched to the test database.

2. Next create the CDs table, which includes an index on the CDName column. To create the CDs table, type the following CREATE TABLE statement at the mysql command prompt, and then press Enter:

```
CREATE TABLE CDs
(
    CDID SMALLINT UNSIGNED NOT NULL,
    CDName VARCHAR(40) NOT NULL,
    INDEX (CDName)
);
```

You should receive a message indicating that the statement executed successfully.

3. Next, remove the CDs table from the test database. To remove the table, type the following DROP TABLE statement at the mysql command prompt, and then press Enter:

```
DROP TABLE CDs;
```

You should receive a message indicating that the statement executed successfully.

How It Works

In this exercise, you created the CDs table in the test database. To create this table, you used the following CREATE TABLE statement:

```
CREATE TABLE CDs
(
    CDID SMALLINT UNSIGNED NOT NULL,
    CDName VARCHAR(40) NOT NULL,
    INDEX (CDName)
);
```

The statement created a MyISAM table that includes two columns. The last table element in the table definition defines a regular index on the CDName column. After you created the table, you removed it from the database with a DROP TABLE statement.

This chapter covers only how to add an index to your table definition. In Chapter 15, you learn more about indexing and how indexes can be used to optimize performance.

Adding Indexes to Existing Tables

In addition to including indexes in a table definition, you can add an index to an existing table. You can use two methods to add an index: the ALTER TABLE statement and the CREATE INDEX statement.

Using the ALTER TABLE Statement

The ALTER TABLE statement allows you to add primary key, foreign key, unique, regular, and full-text indexes to a table. You already saw examples of this earlier in the chapter when you used the ALTER TABLE statement to add primary keys and foreign keys to a table. Now look at another example. Suppose that you used the following table definition to create a table named Orders:

```
CREATE TABLE Orders
(
    OrderID SMALLINT UNSIGNED NOT NULL PRIMARY KEY,
    ModelID SMALLINT UNSIGNED NOT NULL
);
```

As you can see, the table includes a primary key on the OrderID column, which means that this column has an index defined on it. Now suppose that you want to add a unique index to the table that is placed on both the OrderID column and the ModelID column. To do this, you would use the following ALTER TABLE statement:

```
ALTER TABLE Orders
ADD UNIQUE (OrderID, ModelID);
```

By adding the unique index, values in the two columns, when taken together, must be unique, although the ModelID column can still contain duplicate values.

In the following Try It Out you create a table named CDs, use an ALTER TABLE statement to add a full-text index, and then drop the table from the database.

Try It Out   Creating an Index with the ALTER TABLE Statement

To complete these tasks, follow these steps:

1. Open the mysql client utility, type the following command, and press Enter:

```
use test
```

You should receive a message indicating that you switched to the test database.

2. Next create the CDs table. To create the table, type the following CREATE TABLE statement at the mysql command prompt, and then press Enter:

```
CREATE TABLE CDs
(
    CDID SMALLINT UNSIGNED NOT NULL PRIMARY KEY,
    CDName VARCHAR(40) NOT NULL
);
```

You should receive a message indicating that the statement executed successfully.

3. Now you use an ALTER TABLE statement to add a FULLTEXT index to the CDs table. Type the following ALTER TABLE statement at the mysql command prompt, and then press Enter:

```
ALTER TABLE CDs
ADD FULLTEXT (CDName);
```

You should receive a message indicating that the statement executed successfully.

4. Finally, remove the CDs table from the test database. To remove the table, type the following DROP TABLE statement at the mysql command prompt, and then press Enter:

```
DROP TABLE CDs;
```

You should receive a message indicating that the statement executed successfully.

How It Works

After creating the CDs table in the test database, you used the following ALTER TABLE statement to add a full-text index to the table:

```
ALTER TABLE CDs
ADD FULLTEXT (CDName);
```

As you can see from the statement, you placed the full-text index on the CDName column. Because this column is configured with a VARCHAR data type, a full-text index could be supported. In addition, the table is set up as a MyISAM table because it is the default table type and you specified no other table type. MyISAM tables are the only tables that support full-text indexing. After adding the index to the table, you removed the table from the test database.

Using the CREATE INDEX Statement

The CREATE INDEX statement allows you to add unique, regular, and full-text indexes to a table, but not primary key or foreign key indexes. The following syntax shows you how to define a CREATE INDEX statement:

```
CREATE [UNIQUE | FULLTEXT] INDEX <index name>
ON <table name> (<column name> [{, <column name>}...])
```

To create a regular index, you need to include only the CREATE INDEX keyword, a name for the index, and an ON clause that specifies the name of the table and the columns to be indexed. If you want to create a unique index, you must also include the UNIQUE keyword, and if you want to create a full-text index, you must include the FULLTEXT keyword. In either case, you must place UNIQUE or FULLTEXT between the CREATE INDEX keywords, as in CREATE UNIQUE INDEX or CREATE FULLTEXT INDEX.

To demonstrate how to use a CREATE INDEX statement, take a look at an example based on the following table definition:

```
CREATE TABLE Orders
(
    OrderID SMALLINT UNSIGNED NOT NULL PRIMARY KEY,
    ModelID SMALLINT UNSIGNED NOT NULL
);
```

The CREATE TABLE statement shown here creates a table named Orders that contains the OrderID column and the ModelID column. The OrderID column is configured with a primary key. To add a regular index to the ModelID column, you can use the following CREATE INDEX statement:

```
CREATE INDEX index_1 ON Orders (ModelID);
```

Executing this statement creates a regular index named `index_1` on the ModelID column of the Orders table.

In the following exercise, you create a table named CDs, add a regular index to the table, and then drop the table from the database.

Try It Out   **Creating an Index with the CREATE INDEX Statement**

To complete these tasks, follow these steps:

1. Open the mysql client utility, type the following command, and press Enter:

```
use test
```

You should receive a message indicating that you switched to the test database.

2. Next create the CDs table. To create the table, type the following CREATE TABLE statement at the mysql command prompt, and then press Enter:

```
CREATE TABLE CDs
(
    CDID SMALLINT UNSIGNED NOT NULL PRIMARY KEY,
    CDName VARCHAR(40) NOT NULL
);
```

You should receive a message indicating that the statement executed successfully.

3. Now use a CREATE INDEX statement to add an index to the CDs table. Type the following CREATE INDEX statement at the mysql command prompt, and then press Enter:

```
CREATE INDEX index_1 ON CDs (CDName);
```

You should receive a message indicating that the statement executed successfully.

4. Finally, remove the CDs table from the test database. To remove the table, type the following DROP TABLE statement at the mysql command prompt, and then press Enter:

```
DROP TABLE CDs;
```

You should receive a message indicating that the statement executed successfully.

How It Works

After you switched to the test database, you created a table named CDs. The table includes the CDID and the CDName columns, with a primary key defined on the CDID column. You then used the following CREATE INDEX statement to add a regular index to the table:

```
CREATE INDEX index_1 ON CDs (CDName);
```

The statement creates a regular index named `index_1` (specified in the CREATE INDEX statement) on the CDName column of the CDs table (specified in the ON clause). After adding the index, you dropped the table from the test database, which also dropped the index.

Removing Indexes

MySQL provides a couple of methods for removing an index from a table. The first of these is the ALTER TABLE statement, and the other is the DROP INDEX statement. To demonstrate how each of these statements works, take a look at the following CREATE TABLE statement:

```
CREATE TABLE Orders
(
    OrderID SMALLINT UNSIGNED NOT NULL PRIMARY KEY,
    ModelID SMALLINT UNSIGNED NOT NULL,
    UNIQUE unique_1 (OrderID, ModelID)
);
```

The statement defines a table named Orders. The table contains two columns: OrderID and ModelID. The table is defined with a primary key on the OrderID column and a unique index on the OrderID and ModelID columns. Now suppose that you want to drop the unique index. You could use the following ALTER TABLE statement:

```
ALTER TABLE Orders
DROP INDEX unique_1;
```

In this statement, a DROP INDEX clause drops the index named unique_1. As you can see, you merely need to specify the DROP INDEX keywords and the name of the index (in addition to the ALTER TABLE statement). You can also use a DROP INDEX statement to remove an index, as shown in the following syntax:

```
DROP INDEX <index name> ON <table name>
```

To use this statement, you must specify the DROP INDEX keywords, the name of the index, and the name of the table in the ON clause, as shown in the following example:

```
DROP INDEX unique_1 ON Orders;
```

This DROP INDEX statement removes the unique_1 index from the Orders table, just as the ALTER TABLE statement does previously.

Retrieving Information About Database Objects

Up till this point in the chapter, you've been creating, modifying, and deleting objects in MySQL. MySQL, however, also provides methods that allow you to view information about those objects. In this section, you learn about a number of statements that display information about databases and their tables. The statements can be divided into two broad categories: SHOW statements and DESCRIBE statements.

Using SHOW Statements

The SHOW statements in MySQL display a variety of information about databases and their tables. The database-related SHOW statements include the SHOW CREATE DATABASE and SHOW DATABASES statement. The table-related SHOW statements include SHOW COLUMNS, SHOW CREATE TABLE, SHOW INDEX, and SHOW TABLES. When using the table-related statements, you should be working in the context of the database, unless you specify the database name as part of the SHOW statement.

Using Database-Related SHOW Statements

The SHOW CREATE DATABASE statement allows you to view the database definition for a specific database. The following syntax shows how to create a SHOW CREATE DATABASE statement:

```
SHOW CREATE DATABASE <database name>
```

As you can see, you need to specify only the SHOW CREATE DATABASE keywords and the name of the database, as shown in the following example:

```
SHOW CREATE DATABASE mysql;
```

In this case, the statement retrieves information about the mysql database definition. When you execute the statement, you should receive results similar to the following:

```
+----------+------------------------------------------------------------------+
| Database | Create Database                                                  |
+----------+------------------------------------------------------------------+
| mysql    | CREATE DATABASE `mysql` /*!40100 DEFAULT CHARACTER SET latin1 */  |
+----------+------------------------------------------------------------------+
1 row in set (0.00 sec)
```

The entire results cannot be displayed here, because the row is too long. The actual results that you see depend on your system, but the basic information is the same.

The next statement to examine is the SHOW DATABASE statement. The statement lists the MySQL databases that exist in your system. The following syntax illustrates the SHOW DATABASE statement:

```
SHOW DATABASES [LIKE '<value>']
```

Notice that the statement includes an optional LIKE clause. The clause lets you specify a value for database names. MySQL returns only names of databases that match that value. You usually use the LIKE clause in conjunction with a wildcard to return names that are similar to the specified value. (In SQL, the percent [%] character serves as a wildcard in much the same way as the asterisk [*] character serves as a wildcard in other applications.) For example, the following SHOW DATABASE returns only those databases whose name begins with "my:"

```
SHOW DATABASES LIKE 'my%';
```

When you execute this statement, you should receive results similar to the following:

```
+----------------+
| Database (my%) |
+----------------+
| mysql          |
+----------------+
1 row in set (0.00 sec)
```

As you can see, only databases that begin with "my" are returned. In this case, only the mysql database is displayed.

Using Table-Related SHOW Statements

The SHOW COLUMNS statement lists the columns in a table, along with information about the columns. The following syntax illustrates the SHOW COLUMNS statement:

```
SHOW [FULL] COLUMNS FROM <table name> [FROM <database name>] [LIKE '<value>']
```

To use this statement, you must specify the SHOW COLUMNS FROM keywords, the name of the table, and optionally the name of the database, if you're not working in the context of that database. To show more complete information about each column, you should also use the FULL keyword. In addition, you can use the LIKE clause to limit the values returned, as shown in the following example:

```
SHOW COLUMNS FROM user FROM mysql LIKE '%priv';
```

This SHOW COLUMNS statement returns column information from the user table in the mysql database. The LIKE clause limits the columns returned to those ending with "priv." (The % wildcard indicates that the value can begin with any characters.) The SHOW COLUMNS statement shown here should produce results similar to the following:

```
+----------------------+---------------+------+-----+---------+-------+
| Field                | Type          | Null | Key | Default | Extra |
+----------------------+---------------+------+-----+---------+-------+
| Select_priv          | enum('N','Y') |      |     | N       |       |
| Insert_priv          | enum('N','Y') |      |     | N       |       |
| Update_priv          | enum('N','Y') |      |     | N       |       |
| Delete_priv          | enum('N','Y') |      |     | N       |       |
| Create_priv          | enum('N','Y') |      |     | N       |       |
| Drop_priv            | enum('N','Y') |      |     | N       |       |
| Reload_priv          | enum('N','Y') |      |     | N       |       |
| Shutdown_priv        | enum('N','Y') |      |     | N       |       |
| Process_priv         | enum('N','Y') |      |     | N       |       |
| File_priv            | enum('N','Y') |      |     | N       |       |
| Grant_priv           | enum('N','Y') |      |     | N       |       |
| References_priv      | enum('N','Y') |      |     | N       |       |
| Index_priv           | enum('N','Y') |      |     | N       |       |
| Alter_priv           | enum('N','Y') |      |     | N       |       |
| Show_db_priv         | enum('N','Y') |      |     | N       |       |
| Super_priv           | enum('N','Y') |      |     | N       |       |
| Create_tmp_table_priv| enum('N','Y') |      |     | N       |       |
| Lock_tables_priv     | enum('N','Y') |      |     | N       |       |
| Execute_priv         | enum('N','Y') |      |     | N       |       |
| Repl_slave_priv      | enum('N','Y') |      |     | N       |       |
| Repl_client_priv     | enum('N','Y') |      |     | N       |       |
+----------------------+---------------+------+-----+---------+-------+
21 rows in set (0.00 sec)
```

Notice that each column name ends in "priv." Also notice that the results include details about each column. You can also retrieve information about a table by using a SHOW CREATE TABLE statement, which displays the table definition. The following syntax shows how to create a SHOW CREATE TABLE statement:

```
SHOW CREATE TABLE <table name>
```

In this statement, you need to specify the SHOW CREATE TABLE keywords, along with the name of the table, as shown in the following example:

```
SHOW CREATE TABLE func;
```

This SHOW CREATE TABLE statement returns the table definition for the func table. When you execute this statement, you should receive results similar to the following:

```
+-------+-----------------------------------------------------------------------
| Table | Create Table
+-------+-----------------------------------------------------------------------
| func  | CREATE TABLE `func` (`name` char(64) character set latin1 collate latin1_
+-------+-----------------------------------------------------------------------
1 row in set (0.02 sec)
```

The entire results could not fit on the screen because the row is too long. The data that you see depends on your system.

The next statement displays a list of indexes in a table. The SHOW INDEX statement is shown in the following syntax:

```
SHOW INDEX FROM <table name> [FROM <database name>]
```

The only required elements of this statement are the SHOW INDEX FROM keywords and the name of the table. You can also use the FROM clause to specify the name of the database, which you would do if you're not working in the context of that database. For example, the following SHOW INDEX statement displays information about the indexes in the user table in the mysql database:

```
SHOW INDEX FROM user FROM mysql;
```

When you execute this statement, you should receive results similar to the following:

```
+-------+------------+----------+--------------+-------------+-----------+---------
| Table | Non_unique | Key_name | Seq_in_index | Column_name | Collation | Cardinal
+-------+------------+----------+--------------+-------------+-----------+---------
| user  |          0 | PRIMARY  |            1 | Host        | A         |        N
| user  |          0 | PRIMARY  |            2 | User        | A         |
+-------+------------+----------+--------------+-------------+-----------+---------
2 rows in set (0.00 sec)
```

Once again, the entire results are not displayed here because the rows are too long. The exact results that you see on your system vary; however, the basic information should be the same.

The next statement is the SHOW TABLES statement, which displays a list of tables in the current database or a specified database. The syntax for the statement is as follows:

```
SHOW TABLES [FROM <database name>] [LIKE '<value>']
```

As you can see, the only elements that you need to specify are the SHOW TABLES keywords. You can also specify the database in the FROM clause, and you can specify a value in the LIKE clause, as shown in the following example:

```
SHOW TABLES FROM mysql LIKE 'help%';
```

In this SHOW TABLES statement, you display all tables in the mysql database that begin with "help," as shown in following results:

```
+------------------------+
| Tables_in_mysql (help%) |
+------------------------+
| help_category          |
| help_keyword           |
| help_relation          |
| help_topic             |
+------------------------+
4 rows in set (0.00 sec)
```

As you can see, the list includes only tables that begin with "help."

Using DESCRIBE Statements

Another statement useful for viewing information about tables is the DESCRIBE statement. The following syntax describes how to define a DESCRIBE statement:

```
DESCRIBE <table name> [<column name> | '<value>']
```

The only required elements of the DESCRIBE statement are the DESCRIBE keyword and the name of the table. You can also specify a column name or a value used to return columns with names similar to the value, in which case you would use a wildcard. The following example shows a DESCRIBE statement that returns information about all columns in the user table that end with "priv":

```
DESCRIBE user '%priv';
```

If you execute this statement, you should receive results similar to the following:

```
+----------------------+-----------------+------+-----+---------+-------+
| Field                | Type            | Null | Key | Default | Extra |
+----------------------+-----------------+------+-----+---------+-------+
| Select_priv          | enum('N','Y')   |      |     | N       |       |
| Insert_priv          | enum('N','Y')   |      |     | N       |       |
| Update_priv          | enum('N','Y')   |      |     | N       |       |
| Delete_priv          | enum('N','Y')   |      |     | N       |       |
| Create_priv          | enum('N','Y')   |      |     | N       |       |
| Drop_priv            | enum('N','Y')   |      |     | N       |       |
| Reload_priv          | enum('N','Y')   |      |     | N       |       |
| Shutdown_priv        | enum('N','Y')   |      |     | N       |       |
| Process_priv         | enum('N','Y')   |      |     | N       |       |
| File_priv            | enum('N','Y')   |      |     | N       |       |
| Grant_priv           | enum('N','Y')   |      |     | N       |       |
```

```
|  References_priv     |  enum('N','Y')  |     |  N  |     |     |
|  Index_priv          |  enum('N','Y')  |     |  N  |     |     |
|  Alter_priv          |  enum('N','Y')  |     |  N  |     |     |
|  Show_db_priv        |  enum('N','Y')  |     |  N  |     |     |
|  Super_priv          |  enum('N','Y')  |     |  N  |     |     |
|  Create_tmp_table_priv |  enum('N','Y')  |     |  N  |     |     |
|  Lock_tables_priv    |  enum('N','Y')  |     |  N  |     |     |
|  Execute_priv        |  enum('N','Y')  |     |  N  |     |     |
|  Repl_slave_priv     |  enum('N','Y')  |     |  N  |     |     |
|  Repl_client_priv    |  enum('N','Y')  |     |  N  |     |     |
+----------------------+-----------------+-----+-----+---------+-------+
21 rows in set (0.00 sec)
```

Notice that only columns that end in "priv" are displayed. The DESCRIBE statement is a handy way to view the information that you need quickly.

In this exercise, you try out some of the SHOW and DESCRIBE statements that you learned about in this section of the chapter.

Try It Out   Displaying Database Information

The following steps lead you through a series of statements:

1. Open the mysql client utility, type the following command, and press Enter:

```
SHOW DATABASES;
```

You should receive results similar to the following:

```
+------------+
| Database   |
+------------+
| dvdrentals |
| mysql      |
| test       |
+------------+
3 rows in set (0.00 sec)
```

At the very least, you should see the two databases that are installed by default — mysql and test — and the DVDRentals database, which you created earlier in the chapter.

2. Next, you view the CREATE DATABASE statement for the DVDRentals database. To view the database definition, type the following SHOW CREATE DATABASE statement at the mysql command prompt, and then press Enter:

```
SHOW CREATE DATABASE DVDRentals;
```

You should receive results similar to the following:

```
+------------+-----------------------------------------------------------------
| Database   | Create Database
+------------+-----------------------------------------------------------------
| dvdrentals | CREATE DATABASE `dvdrentals` /*!40100 DEFAULT CHARACTER SET latin1 *
+------------+-----------------------------------------------------------------
1 row in set (0.01 sec)
```

Because the row is so long, only a part of the results are displayed here. The amount of data that is displayed on your system and the way that it is displayed vary from system to system. As a result, you might have to scroll to the right or up and down to view all the results.

3. Now you will switch to the DVDRentals database. Type the following command at the mysql command prompt, and press Enter:

```
use DVDRentals
```

You should receive a message indicating that you switched to the DVDRentals database.

4. To display a list of the tables in the DVDRentals database, type the following command at the mysql command prompt, and then press Enter:

```
SHOW TABLES;
```

You should see results similar to the following:

```
+---------------------+
| Tables_in_dvdrentals |
+---------------------+
| customers           |
| dvdparticipant      |
| dvds                |
| employees           |
| formats             |
| movietypes          |
| orders              |
| participants        |
| ratings             |
| roles               |
| status              |
| studios             |
| transactions        |
+---------------------+
13 rows in set (0.00 sec)
```

All the tables that you created earlier in the chapter should be displayed. As you can see, there are 13 tables in all.

5. Next, view the table definition for the Orders table. Type the following SHOW CREATE TABLE statement at the mysql command prompt, and then press Enter:

```
SHOW CREATE TABLE Orders;
```

You should receive results similar to the following:

```
+--------+---------------------------------------------------------------------
| Table  | Create Table
+--------+---------------------------------------------------------------------
| Orders | CREATE TABLE `orders` (`OrderID` int(11) NOT NULL auto_increment, `CustI
+--------+---------------------------------------------------------------------
1 row in set (0.01 sec)
```

As before, only part of the results can be displayed here. The amount of data displayed and the way it will be displayed vary from system to system.

6. Next, display the columns that are in the Transactions table. Type the following command at the mysql command prompt, and then press Enter:

```
SHOW COLUMNS FROM Transactions;
```

You should receive results similar to the following:

```
+----------+-------------+------+-----+------------+----------------+
| Field    | Type        | Null | Key | Default    | Extra          |
+----------+-------------+------+-----+------------+----------------+
| TransID  | int(11)     |      | PRI | NULL       | auto_increment |
| OrderID  | int(11)     |      | MUL | 0          |                |
| DVDID    | smallint(6) |      | MUL | 0          |                |
| DateOut  | date        |      |     | 0000-00-00 |                |
| DateDue  | date        |      |     | 0000-00-00 |                |
| DateIn   | date        |      |     | 0000-00-00 |                |
+----------+-------------+------+-----+------------+----------------+
6 rows in set (0.00 sec)
```

Notice that each column is listed, along with the data type, the column's nullability, and additional column settings.

7. Another way to view information about a table is to use a DESCRIBE statement. Type the following command at a mysql command prompt, and then press Enter:

```
DESCRIBE DVDParticipant;
```

You should receive results similar to the following:

```
+--------+-------------+------+-----+---------+-------+
| Field  | Type        | Null | Key | Default | Extra |
+--------+-------------+------+-----+---------+-------+
| DVDID  | smallint(6) |      | PRI | 0       |       |
| PartID | smallint(6) |      | PRI | 0       |       |
| RoleID | varchar(4)  |      | PRI |         |       |
+--------+-------------+------+-----+---------+-------+
3 rows in set (0.00 sec)
```

As with the SHOW COLUMNS statement, you see a list of columns, along with information about each column.

8. The final step is to view the indexes that have been created on a table. Type the following SHOW INDEX statement at the mysql command prompt, and then press Enter:

```
SHOW INDEX FROM DVDs;
```

You should see results similar to the following:

```
+-------+------------+----------+--------------+-------------+-----------+----------
| Table | Non_unique | Key_name | Seq_in_index | Column_name | Collation | Cardinal
+-------+------------+----------+--------------+-------------+-----------+----------
| DVDs  |          0 | PRIMARY  |            1 | DVDID       | A         |
| DVDs  |          1 | MTypeID  |            1 | MTypeID     | A         |
| DVDs  |          1 | StudID   |            1 | StudID      | A         |
| DVDs  |          1 | RatingID |            1 | RatingID    | A         |
| DVDs  |          1 | FormID   |            1 | FormID      | A         |
| DVDs  |          1 | StatID   |            1 | StatID      | A         |
+-------+------------+----------+--------------+-------------+-----------+----------
6 rows in set (0.00 sec)
```

Notice that the primary key and foreign keys are listed as indexes. As you learned earlier in the chapter, there are a number of different types of indexes, including primary keys and foreign keys.

How It Works

In this exercise, you executed a number of SHOW statements and one DESCRIBE statement to view information about the databases that exist in your server, to view the DVDRentals database definition, and to view information about different tables in the DVDRentals database. As you have seen, these statements can be very useful when trying to find information about an existing database and the tables in that database.

As you work your way through this book, you might find that you use these statements often. In that case, you should refer to this chapter as necessary to reference these commands.

Summary

In this chapter, you learned how to create, modify, and remove databases, tables, and indexes from your system. The chapter provided the syntax of the various statements necessary to perform these tasks, explained how to use the syntax to create SQL statements, and provided examples that demonstrated how to implement the various statements. In addition, you created the tables necessary to support the DVDRentals database. The tables were based on the data model that you created in Chapter 4. The chapter also explained how to use SHOW and DESCRIBE statements to view information about your database. Specifically, the chapter provided you with the information you need to perform the following tasks:

- ❑ Create a database definition that specifies the character set and collation for that database.
- ❑ Modify the character set and collation associated with a database.
- ❑ Delete a database.
- ❑ Create a table definition that includes column definitions, primary keys, foreign keys, and indexes.
- ❑ Alter table definitions, including adding, modifying, and removing columns, primary keys, foreign keys, and indexes.
- ❑ Remove tables from a database.
- ❑ Generate SQL statements that retrieve information about the databases and tables in your system.

Once you know how to create a database, add tables to the database, and configure the elements in the tables, you can create the tables that you need to support your databases. In these tables you can insert, modify, and delete data. In the next chapter, you learn how to manage data in your MySQL database. From there, you learn how to retrieve data, import and export data, and manage transactions. You can even create applications that can access the data from within the application languages.

Exercises

The following exercises help you build on the information you learned in this chapter. To view the answers, see Appendix A.

1. You are creating a database named NewDB. The database uses the server's default character set but uses the `latin1_general_ci` collation. What SQL statement should you use to create the database?

2. You are creating a table in a MySQL database. The table is named Bikes and includes two columns: BikeID and BikeName. The BikeID column must uniquely identify each row in the table, and values must be automatically assigned to each row. In addition, the table should never contain more than 200 models of bikes. The BikeName column must include a descriptive name for each model of bike. The names vary in length but should never exceed 40 characters. In addition, the table never participates in a transaction or foreign key relationship. What SQL statement should you use to create the table?

3. You plan to add a unique index to a table that was defined with the following CREATE TABLE statement:

```
CREATE TABLE ModelTrains
(
ModelID SMALLINT UNSIGNED NOT NULL AUTO_INCREMENT PRIMARY KEY,
ModelName VARCHAR(40) NOT NULL
);
```

   The index should be named un_1 and should be configured on the ModelName column. What `ALTER TABLE` statement should you use to add the index?

4. You now want to drop the un_1 unique index from the ModelTrains table. What `ALTER TABLE` statement should you use to remove the unique index?

5. What SQL statement should you use if you want to view a list of tables in the current database?

Manipulating Data in a MySQL Database

At the heart of every RDBMS is the data stored in that system. The RDBMS is configured and the database is designed for the sole purpose of managing data storage, access, and integrity. Ultimately, the purpose of any RDBMS is to manage data. For this reason, this chapter and the following five chapters focus exclusively on data access and manipulation. You learn how to add and modify data, retrieve data, and use advanced techniques to carry out these operations.

To start you off in the direction of data management, this chapter introduces you to the SQL statements available in MySQL to manipulate data. The statements provide numerous options for effectively inserting data into a database, updating that data, and deleting it once it is no longer useful. By the end of the chapter, you'll be able to populate your database tables according to the restrictions placed on those tables, and you'll be able to access those tables to perform the necessary updates and deletions. Specifically, the chapter covers the following topics:

❑ How to use INSERT and REPLACE statements to add data to tables in a MySQL database

❑ How to use UPDATE statements to modify data in tables in a MySQL database

❑ How to use DELETE and TRUNCATE statements to delete data from tables in a MySQL database

Inserting Data in a MySQL Database

Before you can do anything with the data in a database, the data must exist. For this reason, the first SQL statements that you need to learn are those that insert data in a MySQL database. When you add data to a database, you're actually adding it to the individual tables in that database. Because of this, you must remain aware of how tables relate to each other and whether foreign keys have been defined on any of their columns. For example, in a default configuration of a foreign key, you cannot add a row to a child table if the referencing column of the inserted row contains a value that does not exist in the referenced column of the parent table. If you try to do so, you receive an error. (For more information about foreign keys, refer to Chapter 5.)

MySQL supports two types of statements that insert values in a table: INSERT and REPLACE. Both statements allow you to add data directly to the tables in your MySQL database. MySQL also supports other methods for inserting data in a table, such as copying or importing data. These methods are discussed in Chapter 11.

Using an INSERT Statement to Add Data

An INSERT statement is the most common method used to directly insert data in a table. The statement provides a great deal of flexibility in defining the values for individual rows or for multiple rows. The following syntax defines each element that makes up the INSERT statement:

```
<insert statement>::=
INSERT [LOW_PRIORITY | DELAYED] [IGNORE] [INTO]
{<values option> | <set option> | <select option>}

<values option>::=
<table name> [(<column name> [{, <column name>}...])]
VALUES ({<expression> | DEFAULT} [{, {<expression> | DEFAULT}}...])
   [{, ({<expression> | DEFAULT} [{, {<expression> | DEFAULT}}...])}...]

<set option>::=
<table name>
SET <column name>={<expression> | DEFAULT}
   [{, <column name>={<expression> | DEFAULT}}...]

<select option>::=
<table name> [(<column name> [{, <column name>}...])]
<select statement>
```

You can use the INSERT statement to add data to any table in a MySQL database. When you add data, you must do so on a row-by-row basis, and you must insert exactly one value per column. If you specify fewer values than there are columns, default or null values are inserted for the unspecified values.

Now take a look at the first line of the INSERT statement syntax:

```
INSERT [LOW_PRIORITY | DELAYED] [IGNORE] [INTO]
```

As you can see, the first line includes the required INSERT keyword and a number of options. The first of these options are LOW_PRIORITY and DELAYED. You can include either one of these options, but you cannot include both. If you specify LOW_PRIORITY, the statement is not executed until no other client connections are accessing the same table that the INSERT statement is accessing. This can result in a long delay while you're waiting for the statement to execute. During that time, you cannot take any other actions. If you specify DELAYED, the execution is also delayed, but you can continue to take other actions while the INSERT statement is in queue. The LOW_PRIORITY and DELAYED options can be used only for inserts against MyISAM and ISAM tables.

The next option that you can specify in the INSERT clause is IGNORE. This option applies primarily to INSERT statements that add multiple rows to a table. If you specify IGNORE, inserted rows are ignored if they contain a value that duplicates a primary key or unique index value. The INSERT statement continues to insert the remaining rows. If you do not specify IGNORE, the supplicated values abort the insert process.

The final option in the INSERT clause is the INTO keyword. The keyword has no impact on how the INSERT statement processes, although it is used quite often as a way to provide a sort of roadmap to the statement by indicating the table that is the target of the inserted rows.

Moving on to the next line of syntax in the INSERT statement, you can see that there are three options from which to choose:

```
{<values option> | <set option> | <select option>}
```

Each option refers to a clause in the INSERT statement that helps to define the values to insert in the target table. The remaining part of the syntax defines each INSERT alternative. As you can see from the syntax, a number of elements are common to all three statement options. One of these elements — the <expression> placeholder — is of particular importance to the INSERT statement. An *expression* is a type of formula that helps define the value to insert in a column. In many cases, an expression is nothing more than a *literal value,* which is another way of referring to a value exactly as it will be inserted in a table. In addition to literal values, expressions can also include column names, operators, and functions. An *operator* is a symbol that represents a particular sort of action that should be taken, such as comparing values or adding values together. For example, the plus (+) sign is an arithmetic operator that adds two values together. A *function,* on the other hand, is an object that carries out a predefined task. For example, you can use a function to specify the current date.

You can use expressions in your INSERT statement to help define the data to insert in a particular column. Because operators and functions are not discussed until later chapters (Chapters 8 and 9, respectively), the inclusion of expressions in the example INSERT statements in this chapter, except for the most basic expressions, is minimal. Later in the book, when you have a better comprehension of how to use functions and operators, you'll have a better sense of how to include complex expressions in your INSERT statements.

For now, the discussion moves on to the three INSERT alternatives included in the syntax. Each alternative provides a method for defining the values that are inserted in the target table. The <values option> alternative defines the values in the VALUES clause, the <set option> defines the values in the SET clause, and the <select option> defines the values in a SELECT statement, which is embedded in the INSERT statement. Because SELECT statements are not discussed until later in the book, the <select option> alternative is not discussed until Chapter 11. The following two sections discuss how to create INSERT statements using the other two alternatives.

Using the *<values option>* Alternative of the INSERT Statement

The *<values option>* alternative of the INSERT statement allows you to add one or more rows to a table, as shown in the following syntax:

```
<values option>::=
<table name> [(<column name> [{, <column name>}...])]
VALUES ({<expression> | DEFAULT} [{, {<expression> | DEFAULT}}...])
   [{, ({<expression> | DEFAULT} [{, {<expression> | DEFAULT}}...])}...]
```

As the syntax shows, you must provide a table name and a VALUES clause. You also have the option of specifying one or more columns after the table name. If you specify column names, they must be enclosed in parentheses and separated by commas.

Once you specify the table and optional column names, you must specify a VALUES clause. The clause must include at least one value, which is represented by the <expression> placeholder or the DEFAULT keyword. If you include column names after the table name, the VALUES clause must include a value for each column, in the order that the columns are listed. If you did not specify column names, you must provide a value for every column in the table, in the order that the columns are defined in the table.

If you're uncertain of the names of columns or the order in which they are defined in a table, you can use a DESCRIBE statement to view a list of the columns names. See Chapter 5 for more information about the DESCRIBE statement.

All values must be enclosed in parentheses. If there are multiple values, they must be separated by commas. For columns configured with the AUTO_INCREMENT option or a TIMESTAMP data type, you can specify NULL rather than an actual value, or omit the column and value altogether. Doing so inserts the correct value into those columns. In addition, you can use the DEFAULT keyword in any place that you want the default value for that column inserted in the table. (Be sure to refer back to Chapter 5 for a complete description on how MySQL handles default values.)

Now that you have a basic overview of the syntax, take a look at a few examples of how to create an INSERT statement. The examples are based on the following table definition:

```
CREATE TABLE CDs
(
    CDID SMALLINT UNSIGNED NOT NULL AUTO_INCREMENT PRIMARY KEY,
    CDName VARCHAR(50) NOT NULL,
    Copyright YEAR,
    NumberDisks TINYINT UNSIGNED NOT NULL DEFAULT 1,
    NumberInStock TINYINT UNSIGNED,
    NumberOnReserve TINYINT UNSIGNED NOT NULL,
    NumberAvailable TINYINT UNSIGNED NOT NULL,
    CDType VARCHAR(20),
    RowAdded TIMESTAMP
);
```

You should be well familiar with all the elements in the table definition. If you have any questions about any component, refer back to Chapter 5 for an explanation. Nothing has been used here that you have not already seen.

If you want to create the CDs table (or any of the example tables in this chapter) and try out the example SQL statements, you should use the test database or you should create a database for specifically for this purpose.

The table in this definition, which is named CDs, stores information about compact disks. Suppose that you want to use an INSERT statement to add information about a CD named *Ain't Ever Satisfied: The Steve Earle Collection*. You can set up your statement in a couple of ways. The first is to specify a value for each column, without specifying the name of the columns, as shown in the following INSERT statement:

```
INSERT INTO CDs
VALUES (NULL, 'Ain\'t Ever Satisfied: The Steve Earle Collection',
    1996, 2, 10, 3, NumberInStock-NumberOnReserve, 'Country', NULL);
```

In this statement, the first line contains the mandatory keyword INSERT, the optional keyword INTO, and the name of the table (CDs). The VALUES clause includes a value for each column, entered in the order in which the columns appear in the table definition. The values are enclosed in parentheses and separated with commas.

The first specified value is NULL. The value is used for the CDID column, which is configured with the AUTO_INCREMENT option and is the primary key. By specifying NULL, the next incremented value is auto-matically inserted in that column when you add this row to the table. Because this is the first row added to the table, a value of 1 is inserted in the CDID column.

The next value in the VALUES clause corresponds to the CDName column. Because this value is a string, it is enclosed in parentheses. In addition, the backslash precedes the apostrophe. The backslash is used in a string value to notify MySQL that the following character is a literal value and should not be inter-preted as the ending quote of the string. The backslash is useful for any characters that could be misin-terpreted when executing a statement that contains a string value.

You can also use the backslash to specify other literal values, such as double quotes (\"), a backslash (\\), a percentage sign (\%) or an underscore (_).

The next four values specified in the VALUES clause are date and numerical data that correspond with the columns in the table definition (Copyright = 1996, NumberDisks = 2, NumberInStock = 10, and NumberOnReserve = 3).

The value specified for the NumberAvailable column (NumberInStock-NumberOnReserve) is an expres-sion that uses two column names and the minus (-) arithmetic operator to subtract the value in the NumberOnReserve column from the NumberInStock column to arrive at a total of the number of CDs available for sale. In this case, the total is 7.

The next value specified in the VALUES clause is Country, which is inserted in the CDType column. The final value is NULL, which is used for the RowAdded column. The column is configured as a TIMESTAMP column, which means that the current time and date are inserted automatically in that column.

Another way that you can insert the current date in the table is to use the NOW() function, rather than NULL. The NOW() function can be used in SQL statements to return a value that is equivalent to the current date and time. When used in an INSERT statement, that value can be added to a time/date column. If you want to retrieve only the current date, and not the time, you can use the CURDATE() function. If you want to retrieve only the current time, and not the current date, you can use the CURTIME() function.

In addition to the functions mentioned here, you can use other functions to insert data into a table. Chapter 9 describes many of the functions available in MySQL and how you can use those functions in your SQL statements.

The next example INSERT statement also adds a row to the CDs table. In this statement, the columns names are specified and only the values for those columns are included, as the following statement demonstrates:

```
INSERT LOW_PRIORITY INTO CDs (CDName, Copyright, NumberDisks,
   NumberInStock, NumberOnReserve, NumberAvailable, CDType)
VALUES ('After the Rain: The Soft Sounds of Erik Satie',
   1995, DEFAULT, 13, 2, NumberInStock - NumberOnReserve, 'Classical');
```

In this statement, the CDID column and the RowAdded column are not specified. Because CDID is an AUTO_INCREMENT column, an incremented value is automatically inserted in that column. Because the RowAdded column is a TIMESTAMP column, the current date and time are inserted in the column. Whenever a column is not specified in an INSERT statement, the default value for that column is inserted in the column.

The values that are specified in this INSERT statement are similar to the previous example except for one difference. For the NumberDisks column, DEFAULT is used. This indicates that the default value should be inserted in that column. In this case, that value is 1. Otherwise, the values are listed in a matter similar to what you saw previously. There is one other difference between the two statements, however. The last example includes the LOW_PRIORITY option in the INSERT clause. As a result, this statement is not processed and the client is put on hold until all other client connections have completed accessing the target table.

To demonstrate the types of values that are inserted in the CDID column and the NumberDisks column of the CDs table by the last two example, you can use the following SELECT statement to retrieve data from the CDID, CDName, and NumberDisks of the columns the CDs table:

```
SELECT CDID, CDName, NumberDisks
FROM CDs;
```

The SELECT statement returns results similar to the following

```
+------+------------------------------------------------+-------------+
| CDID | CDName                                         | NumberDisks |
+------+------------------------------------------------+-------------+
|    1 | Ain't Ever Satisfied: The Steve Earle Collection |           2 |
|    2 | After the Rain: The Soft Sounds of Erik Satie  |           1 |
+------+------------------------------------------------+-------------+
2 rows in set (0.00 sec)
```

As you can see, incremented values have been inserted in the CDID column, and a value of 1 has been inserted in the NumberDisks column of the second row.

The next example INSERT statement is much simpler than the rest. It specifies the value for only the CDName column, as shown in the following statement:

```
INSERT INTO CDs (CDName)
VALUES ('Blue');
```

Because the statement specifies only one value, default values are inserted for all other columns. This approach is fine for the CDID, NumberDisks, and RowAdded columns, but it could be problematic for the other columns, unless those are the values you want. For example, because null values are permitted in the Copyright column, NULL was inserted. The NumberInStock and CDType columns also permit null values, so NULL was inserted in those two as well. On the other hand, the NumberOnReserve and NumberAvailable columns do not permit null values, so 0 was inserted into these columns. As a result, whenever you're inserting rows into a table, you must be aware of what the default value is in each column, and you must be sure to specify all the necessary values.

The last example of an INSERT statement that uses the *<values option>* alternative inserts values into multiple rows. The following INSERT statement includes the name of the columns in the INSERT clause and then specifies the values for those columns for three rows:

```
INSERT INTO CDs (CDName, Copyright, NumberDisks,
    NumberInStock, NumberOnReserve, NumberAvailable, CDType)
VALUES ('Mule Variations', 1999, 1, 9, 0,
    NumberInStock-NumberOnReserve, 'Blues'),
('The Bonnie Raitt Collection', 1990, 1, 14, 2,
    NumberInStock-NumberOnReserve, 'Popular'),
('Short Sharp Shocked', 1988, 1, 6, 1,
    NumberInStock-NumberOnReserve, 'Folk-Rock');
```

As the statement demonstrates, when using one INSERT statement to insert values in multiple rows, you must enclose the values for each row in their own set of parentheses, and you must separate the sets of values with a comma. By using this method, you can insert as many rows as necessary in your table, without having to generate multiple INSERT statements.

Using the *<values option>* Alternative to Insert Data in the DVDRentals Database

In Chapter 5, you created the tables for the DVDRentals database. In this chapter you populate those tables with data. The following three Try It Out sections walk you through the steps necessary to add the initial data to each table. Because some dependencies exist between tables — foreign keys have been defined on numerous columns — you must add data to the referenced parent tables before adding data to the referencing child tables. To facilitate this process, first add data to the lookup tables, then to the people tables, and finally those tables configured with foreign keys.

Try It Out   Inserting Data in the Lookup Tables

The lookup tables contain the data that generally changes more infrequently than other data. To insert data in these tables, follow these steps:

1.   Open the mysql client utility, type the following command, and press Enter:

```
use DVDRentals
```

You should receive a message indicating that you switched to the DVDRentals database.

2.   To insert a record int the Formats table, type the following INSERT statement at the mysql command prompt, and then press Enter:

```
INSERT INTO Formats
VALUES ('f1', 'Widescreen');
```

You should receive a response saying that your statement executed successfully, affecting one row.

3.   To insert the next record in the Formats table, type the following INSERT statement at the mysql command prompt, and then press Enter:

```
INSERT INTO Formats (FormID, FormDescrip)
VALUES ('f2', 'Fullscreen');
```

You should receive a response saying that your statement executed successfully, affecting one row.

4. To insert records in the Roles table, type the following INSERT statement at the mysql command prompt, and then press Enter:

```
INSERT INTO Roles
VALUES ('r101', 'Actor'),
('r102', 'Director'),
('r103', 'Producer'),
('r104', 'Executive Producer'),
('r105', 'Co-Producer'),
('r106', 'Assistant Producer'),
('r107', 'Screenwriter'),
('r108', 'Composer');
```

You should receive a response saying that your statement executed successfully, affecting eight rows.

5. To insert records in the MovieTypes table, type the following INSERT statement at the mysql command prompt, and then press Enter:

```
INSERT INTO MovieTypes
VALUES ('mt10', 'Action'),
('mt11', 'Drama'),
('mt12', 'Comedy'),
('mt13', 'Romantic Comedy'),
('mt14', 'Science Fiction/Fantasy'),
('mt15', 'Documentary'),
('mt16', 'Musical');
```

You should receive a response saying that your statement executed successfully, affecting seven rows.

6. To insert records in the Studios table, type the following INSERT statement at the mysql command prompt, and then press Enter:

```
INSERT INTO Studios
VALUES ('s101', 'Universal Studios'),
('s102', 'Warner Brothers'),
('s103', 'Time Warner'),
('s104', 'Columbia Pictures'),
('s105', 'Paramount Pictures'),
('s106', 'Twentieth Century Fox'),
('s107', 'Merchant Ivory Production');
```

You should receive a response saying that your statement executed successfully, affecting seven rows.

7. To insert records in the Ratings table, type the following INSERT statement at the mysql command prompt, and then press Enter:

```
INSERT INTO Ratings
VALUES ('NR', 'Not rated'),
('G', 'General audiences'),
('PG', 'Parental guidance suggested'),
('PG13', 'Parents strongly cautioned'),
('R', 'Under 17 requires adult'),
('X', 'No one 17 and under');
```

You should receive a response saying that your statement executed successfully, affecting six rows.

8.   To insert records in the Status table, type the following INSERT statement at the mysql command prompt, and then press Enter:

```
INSERT INTO Status
VALUES ('s1', 'Checked out'),
('s2', 'Available'),
('s3', 'Damaged'),
('s4', 'Lost');
```

You should receive a response saying that your statement executed successfully, affecting four rows.

How It Works

In this exercise, you added data to the five lookup tables in the DVDRentals database. The first table that you populated was the Formats table. You used the following INSERT statement to add a single row to the table:

```
INSERT INTO Formats
VALUES ('f1', 'Widescreen');
```

Because you did not specify the columns in this statement, you had to specify values for all columns in the table. The table contains only two columns, and the primary key values are not generated automatically, so you were required to specify all the values anyway. As a result, specifying the column names wasn't necessary. In the next step, you did specify the column names, as shown in the following statement:

```
INSERT INTO Formats (FormID, FormDescrip)
VALUES ('f2', 'Fullscreen');
```

As you can see, the results were the same as in the previous steps. Specifying the column names in this case required extra effort but provided no added benefit.

In the remaining steps, you used individual INSERT statements to add multiple rows to each table. For example, you used the following INSERT statement to add data to the Roles table:

```
INSERT INTO Roles
VALUES ('r101', 'Actor'),
('r102', 'Director'),
('r103', 'Producer'),
('r104', 'Executive Producer'),
('r105', 'Co-Producer'),
('r106', 'Assistant Producer'),
('r107', 'Screenwriter'),
('r108', 'Composer');
```

Because the table contains only two columns and both values are provided for each row, you are not required to specify the columns' names. You do need to enclose the values for each row in parentheses and separate each set of values by commas.

The values for the remaining tables were inserted by using the same format as the INSERT statement used for the Roles table. In each case, the columns were not specified, multiple rows were inserted, and both values were provided for each row.

Once you insert the data into the lookup tables, you're ready to add data to the tables that contain information about the people whose participation is recorded in the database, such as employees, customers, and those who make the movies.

Try It Out Inserting Data in the People Tables

To insert data in these tables, follow these steps:

1. If it's not already open, open the mysql client utility, type the following command, and press Enter:

```
use DVDRentals
```

You should receive a message indicating that you switched to the DVDRentals database.

2. To insert records in the Participants table, type the following INSERT statement at the mysql command prompt, and then press Enter:

```
INSERT INTO Participants (PartFN, PartMN, PartLN)
VALUES ('Sydney', NULL, 'Pollack'),
('Robert', NULL, 'Redford'),
('Meryl', NULL, 'Streep'),
('John', NULL, 'Barry'),
('Henry', NULL, 'Buck'),
('Humphrey', NULL, 'Bogart'),
('Danny', NULL, 'Kaye'),
('Rosemary', NULL, 'Clooney'),
('Irving', NULL, 'Berlin'),
('Michael', NULL, 'Curtiz'),
('Bing', NULL, 'Crosby');
```

You should receive a response saying that your statement executed successfully, affecting 11 rows.

3. To insert records in the Employees table, type the following INSERT statement at the mysql command prompt, and then press Enter:

```
INSERT INTO Employees (EmpFN, EmpMN, EmpLN)
VALUES ('John', 'P.', 'Smith'),
('Robert', NULL, 'Schroader'),
('Mary', 'Marie', 'Michaels'),
('John', NULL, 'Laguci'),
('Rita', 'C.', 'Carter'),
('George', NULL, 'Brooks');
```

You should receive a response saying that your statement executed successfully, affecting six rows.

4. To insert records in the Customers table, type the following INSERT statement at the mysql command prompt, and then press Enter:

```
INSERT INTO Customers (CustFN, CustMN, CustLN)
VALUES ('Ralph', 'Frederick', 'Johnson'),
('Hubert', 'T.', 'Weatherby'),
('Anne', NULL, 'Thomas'),
('Mona', 'J.', 'Cavenaugh'),
('Peter', NULL, 'Taylor'),
('Ginger', 'Meagan', 'Delaney');
```

You should receive a response saying that your statement executed successfully, affecting six rows.

How It Works

In this exercise, you used three INSERT statements to insert data in the three people tables (one statement per table). Each statement was identical in structure. The only differences were in the values defined and the number of rows inserted. For example, you used the following statement to insert data in the Participants table:

```
INSERT INTO Participants (PartFN, PartMN, PartLN)
VALUES ('Sydney', NULL, 'Pollack'),
('Robert', NULL, 'Redford'),
('Meryl', NULL, 'Streep'),
('John', NULL, 'Barry'),
('Henry', NULL, 'Buck'),
('Humphrey', NULL, 'Bogart'),
('Danny', NULL, 'Kaye'),
('Rosemary', NULL, 'Clooney'),
('Irving', NULL, 'Berlin'),
('Michael', NULL, 'Curtiz'),
('Bing', NULL, 'Crosby');
```

As you can see, the INSERT clause includes the INTO option, which has no effect on the statement, and the name of the columns. Because the PartID column is configured with the AUTO_INCREMENT option, you don't need to include it here. The new value is automatically inserted in the column. Because these are the first rows to be added to the table, a value of 1 is added to the PartID column of the first row, a value of 2 for the second row, and so on. After you specify the column names, the statement uses a VALUES clause to specify the values for each column. The values for each row are enclosed in parentheses and separated by commas. Commas also separate the sets of values. In addition, you use NULL wherever a value is not known, which in this case is the PartMN column for each row.

You can view the values that you inserted in the Participants table by executing the following SELECT statement:

```
SELECT * FROM Participants;
```

The last tables to add data to are the four configured with foreign keys. Because the data in these tables references data in other tables, you had to populate those other tables first so that they contained the referenced data. Once the referenced tables contain the proper data, you can insert rows in the columns configured with the foreign keys. Because some of these tables have dependencies on each other, they too have to be populated in a specific order.

Try It Out   Inserting Data in the Foreign Key Tables

To insert data in these tables, take the following steps:

1. If it's not already open, open the mysql client utility, type the following command, and press Enter:

```
use DVDRentals
```

You should receive a message indicating that you switched to the DVDRentals database.

2. To insert a record in the DVDs table, type the following INSERT statement at the mysql command prompt, and then press Enter:

```
INSERT INTO DVDs
VALUES (NULL, 'White Christmas', DEFAULT, 2000, 'mt16', 's105', 'NR', 'f1', 's1');
```

You should receive a response saying that your statement executed successfully, affecting one row.

3. To insert the next record in the DVDs table, type the following INSERT statement at the mysql command prompt, and then press Enter:

```
INSERT INTO DVDs
    (DVDName, NumDisks, YearRlsd, MTypeID, StudID, RatingID, FormID, StatID)
VALUES ('What\'s Up, Doc?', 1, 2001, 'mt12', 's103', 'G', 'f1', 's2');
```

You should receive a response saying that your statement executed successfully, affecting one row.

4. To insert additional records in the DVDs table, type the following INSERT statement at the mysql command prompt, and then press Enter:

```
INSERT INTO DVDs
VALUES (NULL, 'Out of Africa', 1, 2000, 'mt11', 's101', 'PG', 'f1', 's1'),
(NULL, 'The Maltese Falcon', 1, 2000, 'mt11', 's103', 'NR', 'f1', 's2'),
(NULL, 'Amadeus', 1, 1997, 'mt11', 's103', 'PG', 'f1', 's2');
```

You should receive a response saying that your statement executed successfully, affecting three rows.

5. To insert the remaining records in the DVDs table, type the following INSERT statement at the mysql command prompt, and then press Enter:

```
INSERT INTO DVDs
    (DVDName, NumDisks, YearRlsd, MTypeID, StudID, RatingID, FormID, StatID)
VALUES
('The Rocky Horror Picture Show', 2, 2000, 'mt12', 's106', 'NR', 'f1', 's2'),
('A Room with a View', 1, 2000, 'mt11', 's107', 'NR', 'f1', 's1'),
('Mash', 2, 2001, 'mt12', 's106', 'R', 'f1', 's2');
```

You should receive a response saying that your statement executed successfully, affecting three rows.

6. To insert records in the DVDParticipant table, type the following INSERT statement at the mysql command prompt, and then press Enter:

```
INSERT INTO DVDParticipant
VALUES (3, 1, 'r102'),
(3, 4, 'r108'),
(3, 1, 'r103'),
(3, 2, 'r101'),
(3, 3, 'r101'),
(4, 6, 'r101'),
(1, 8, 'r101'),
(1, 9, 'r108'),
(1, 10, 'r102'),
(1, 11, 'r101'),
(1, 7, 'r101'),
(2, 5, 'r107');
```

You should receive a response saying that your statement executed successfully, affecting 12 rows.

7. To insert records in the Orders table, type the following INSERT statement at the mysql command prompt, and then press Enter:

```
INSERT INTO Orders (CustID, EmpID)
VALUES (1, 3),
(1, 2),
(2, 5),
(3, 6),
(4, 1),
(3, 3),
(5, 2),
(6, 4),
(4, 5),
(6, 2),
(3, 1),
(1, 6),
(5, 4);
```

You should receive a response saying that your statement executed successfully, affecting 13 rows.

8. To insert records in the Transactions table, type the following INSERT statement at the mysql command prompt, and then press Enter:

```
INSERT INTO Transactions (OrderID, DVDID, DateOut, DateDue)
VALUES (1, 1, CURDATE(), CURDATE()+3),
(1, 4, CURDATE(), CURDATE()+3),
(1, 8, CURDATE(), CURDATE()+3),
(2, 3, CURDATE(), CURDATE()+3),
(3, 4, CURDATE(), CURDATE()+3),
(3, 1, CURDATE(), CURDATE()+3),
(3, 7, CURDATE(), CURDATE()+3),
(4, 4, CURDATE(), CURDATE()+3),
(5, 3, CURDATE(), CURDATE()+3),
(6, 2, CURDATE(), CURDATE()+3),
(6, 1, CURDATE(), CURDATE()+3),
(7, 4, CURDATE(), CURDATE()+3),
(8, 2, CURDATE(), CURDATE()+3),
(8, 1, CURDATE(), CURDATE()+3),
(8, 3, CURDATE(), CURDATE()+3),
(9, 7, CURDATE(), CURDATE()+3),
(9, 1, CURDATE(), CURDATE()+3),
(10, 5, CURDATE(), CURDATE()+3),
(11, 6, CURDATE(), CURDATE()+3),
(11, 2, CURDATE(), CURDATE()+3),
(11, 8, CURDATE(), CURDATE()+3),
(12, 5, CURDATE(), CURDATE()+3);
(13, 7, CURDATE(), CURDATE()+3);
```

You should receive a response saying that your statement executed successfully, affecting 23 rows.

How It Works

In this exercise, you added data to the final four tables in the DVDRentals database. You populated these tables last because each one includes references (through foreign keys) to other tables in the database. In addition, the remaining tables include references to each other, so you had to add data to them in a specific order. You began the process by using the following INSERT statement:

```
INSERT INTO DVDs
    VALUES (NULL, 'White Christmas', DEFAULT, 2000, 'mt16', 's105', 'NR', 'f1', 's1');
```

In this statement, you added one row to the DVDs table. Because you did not specify any columns, you included a value for each column in the table. To ensure that you inserted the correct data in the correct columns, you listed the values in the same order as they are listed in the table definition. For the first column, DVDID, you specified NULL. Because the column is configured with the AUTO_INCREMENT option, the value for this column was determined automatically. For the NumDisks column, you specified DEFAULT. As a result, the value 1 was inserted in this column because that is the default value defined on the column. For all other columns, you specified the values to be inserted in those columns.

The next INSERT statement that you used also inserted one row of data in the DVDs table; however, this statement specified the column names. As a result, the VALUES clause includes values only for the specified columns, as shown in the following statement:

```
INSERT INTO DVDs
    (DVDName, YearRlsd, MTypeID, StudID, RatingID, FormID, StatID)
    VALUES ('What\'s Up, Doc?', 2001, 'mt12', 's103', 'G', 'f1', 's2');
```

By using this approach, you do not have to specify a NULL for the DVDID column or DEFAULT for the NumDiscs column. One other thing to note about this statement is that you used a backslash in the DVDName value to show that the apostrophe should be interpreted as a literal value. Without the backslash, the statement would not execute properly because the apostrophe would confuse the database engine.

The next statement you executed inserted several rows in the DVDs table, as the following statement demonstrates:

```
INSERT INTO DVDs
    VALUES (NULL, 'Out of Africa', 1, 2000, 'mt11', 's101', 'PG', 'f1', 's1'),
    (NULL, 'Maltese Falcon, The', 1, 2000, 'mt11', 's103', 'NR', 'f1', 's2'),
    (NULL, 'Amadeus', 1, 1997, 'mt11', 's103', 'PG', 'f1', 's2');
```

Once again, because you didn't specify the column names, you had to provide NULL for the DVDID column. In addition, you provided a literal value (1) for the NumDisks column, even though that column is configured with a default of 1. Because you had to include a value, the value had to be DEFAULT or it had to be the literal figure.

You could have also created a statement that defined the columns to be inserted. In that case, you could have avoided repeating NULL for each row. Unless the value for the NumDisks column is always the default value, you would have had to include that column either way. The choice of whether to include column names or instead include all values depends on the table and how many rows you need to insert. For tables in which there are many rows of data and an AUTO_INCREMENT primary key, you're usually better off specifying the column names and taking that approach, as you did when you inserted data in the Transactions table and the Orders table.

For example, when you inserted rows in the Transactions table, you specified the column names for every column except TransID, which is the primary key and which is configured with the AUTO_INCREMENT option. The following code shows just the first few rows of data of the INSERT statement that you used for the Transactions table:

```
INSERT INTO Transactions (OrderID, DVDID, DateOut, DateDue)
VALUES (1, 1, CURDATE(), CURDATE()+3),
(1, 4, CURDATE(), CURDATE()+3),
(1, 8, CURDATE(), CURDATE()+3),
(2, 3, CURDATE(), CURDATE()+3),
```

In this case, you can see the advantage of specifying the column names because you did not have to repeat NULL for each row. There is another aspect of this statement, though, that you haven't seen before. The DateOut value is determined by using the CURDATE() function. The function automatically returns the date on which the row is inserted in the table. The function is also used for the DateDue column. A value of 3 is added to the value returned by the function. As a result, the value inserted in the DateDue column is three days after the current date. Functions are very useful when creating expressions and defining values. For this reason, Chapter 9 focuses exclusively on the various functions supported by MySQL.

Using the <set option> Alternative of the INSERT Statement

The <set option> method for creating an INSERT statement provides you with an alternative to the <values option> method when you're adding only one row at a time to a table. The following syntax demonstrates how to use the <set option> alternative to create an INSERT statement:

```
<set option>::=
<table name>
SET <column name>={<expression> | DEFAULT}
   [{, <column name>={<expression> | DEFAULT}}...]
```

As the syntax shows, your INSERT statement must include the name of the table and a SET clause that specifies values for specific columns (all, of course, in addition to the required INSERT clause at the beginning of the statement). Although column names are not specified after the table name, as is the case for some statements that use the <values option> alternative, the column names are specified in the SET clause. For each value, you must specify the column name, an equal (=) sign, and an expression or the DEFAULT keyword. The <expression> option and the DEFAULT keyword work in the same way as they do for the previous INSERT statements that you saw. Also, if you include more than one column/value pair, you must separate them with a comma.

The <set option> alternative is most useful if you're providing values for only some of the columns and allowing default values to be used for the remaining columns. For example, suppose that you want to insert an additional row in the CDs table (the table used in the previous examples). If you used the <values option> method to create an INSERT statement, it would look similar to the following:

```
INSERT INTO CDs (CDName, Copyright, NumberDisks,
   NumberInStock, NumberOnReserve, NumberAvailable, CDType)
VALUES ('Blues on the Bayou', 1998, DEFAULT,
   4, 1, NumberInStock-NumberOnReserve, 'Blues');
```

Notice that each column is specified after the table name and that their respective values are included in the VALUES clause. You could rewrite the statement by using the *<set option>* alternative, as shown in the following example:

```
INSERT DELAYED INTO CDs
SET CDName='Blues on the Bayou', Copyright=1998,
    NumberDisks=DEFAULT, NumberInStock=4, NumberOnReserve=1,
    NumberAvailable=NumberInStock-NumberOnReserve, CDType='Blues';
```

As you can see, the column names, along with their values, are specified in the SET clause. You do not have to enclose them in parentheses, although you do need to separate them with commas. The main advantage to using this method is that it simplifies matching values to column names, without having to refer back and forth between clauses. As a result, you ensure that you always match the proper value to the correct column. If you plan to provide values for each column, you save yourself keystrokes by using the *<values option>* alternative because you don't need to specify column names when values are provided for all columns. In addition, the *<values option>* alternative allows you to insert multiple rows with one statement. The *<set option>* alternative does not.

In the previous Try It Out sections, you used the *<values option>* alternative to insert data in the DVDRentals database. In this exercise, you use the *<set option>* alternative to insert a row in the DVDs table.

Try It Out   **Using the *<set option>* Alternative to Insert Data in the DVDRentals Database**

Follow these steps to insert the data:

1. Open the mysql client utility, type the following command, and press Enter:

```
use DVDRentals
```

You should receive a message indicating that you switched to the DVDRentals database.

2. To insert the record in the DVDs table, type the following INSERT statement at the mysql command prompt, and then press Enter:

```
INSERT INTO DVDs
SET DVDName='Some Like It Hot', YearRlsd=2001, MTypeID='mt12',
    StudID='s108', RatingID='NR', FormID='f1', StatID='s2';
```

You should receive an error message stating that a foreign key constraint failed because the StudID value does not exist in the referenced parent table (Studios).

3. To insert the necessary record in the Studios table, type the following INSERT statement at the mysql command prompt, and then press Enter:

```
INSERT INTO Studios
VALUES ('s108', 'Metro-Goldwyn-Mayer');
```

You should receive a response saying that your statement executed successfully, affecting one row.

4. Now you should be able to insert the record in the DVDs table. Type the following INSERT statement at the mysql command prompt, and then press Enter:

```
INSERT INTO DVDs
SET DVDName='Some Like It Hot', YearRlsd=2001, MTypeID='mt12',
    StudID='s108', RatingID='NR', FormID='f1', StatID='s2';
```

You should receive a response saying that your statement executed successfully and that one row was affected.

How It Works

The first INSERT statement that you used in this exercise attempted to insert a row in the DVDs table in the DVDRentals database, as shown in the following statement:

```
INSERT INTO DVDs
SET DVDName='Some Like It Hot', YearRlsd=2001, MTypeID='mt12',
    StudID='s108', RatingID='NR', FormID='f1', StatID='s2';
```

As you would expect with the <set option> alternative, the column names and values are specified in the SET clause. This INSERT statement failed, though, because you attempted to insert a row that contained a StudID value of s108. As you recall, you defined a foreign key on the StudID column in the DVDs table. The column references the StudID column in the Studios table. Because the Studios table doesn't contain the referenced value of s108 in the StudID column, you could not insert a row in DVDs that includes a StudID value of s108.

To remedy this situation, the following INSERT statement inserts the necessary value in the Studios table:

```
INSERT INTO Studios
VALUES ('s108', 'Metro-Goldwyn-Mayer');
```

Because the Studios table contains only two columns and because you needed to provide values for both those columns, the <values option> alternative adds the row to the Studios table. Once you completed this task, you then used the original INSERT statement to add the same row to the DVDs table. This time the statement succeeded.

Using a REPLACE Statement to Add Data

In addition to using an INSERT statement to add data to a table, you can also use a REPLACE statement. A REPLACE statement is similar to an INSERT statement in most respects. The main difference between the two is in how values in a primary key column or a unique index are treated. In an INSERT statement, if you try to insert a row that contains a unique index or primary key value that already exists in the table, you aren't able to add that row. A REPLACE statement, however, deletes the old row and adds the new row.

Another method that programmers have used to support the same functionality as that of the REPLACE statement is to test first for the existence of a row and then use an UPDATE statement if the row exists or an INSERT statement if the row doesn't exist. The way in which you would implement this method depends on the programming language that you're using. For information on how to set up the conditions necessary to execute the UPDATE and INSERT statements in this way, see the documentation for that particular language.

Despite the issue of primary key and unique index values, the syntax for the REPLACE statement basically contains the same elements as the INSERT statement, as the following syntax shows:

```
<replace statement>::=
REPLACE [LOW_PRIORITY | DELAYED] [INTO]
{<values option> | <set option> | <select option>

<values option>::=
<table name> [(<column name> [{, <column name>}...])]
VALUES ({<expression> | DEFAULT} [{, {<expression> | DEFAULT}}...])
   [{, ({<expression> | DEFAULT} [{, {<expression> | DEFAULT}}...])}...]

<set option>::=
<table name>
SET <column name>={<expression> | DEFAULT}
   [{, <column name>={<expression> | DEFAULT}}...]

<select option>::=
<table name> [(<column name> [{, <column name>}...])]
<select statement>
```

As you can see, the main difference between the INSERT syntax and the REPLACE syntax is that you use the REPLACE keyword rather than the INSERT keyword. In addition, the REPLACE statement doesn't support the IGNORE option. The REPLACE statement does include the same three methods for creating the statement: the *<values option>* alternative, the *<set option>* alternative, and the *<select option>* alternative. As with the INSERT statement, the discussion here includes only the first two alternatives. Chapter 11 discusses the *<select option>* alternative.

> *Although the REPLACE statement and the INSERT statement are nearly identical, the difference between the two can be a critical one. By using the REPLACE statement, you risk overwriting important data. Use caution whenever executing a REPLACE statement.*

Using the *<values option>* Alternative of the REPLACE Statement

As the following syntax shows, the *<values option>* alternative for the REPLACE statement is the same as that alternative for the INSERT statement:

```
<values option>::=
<table name> [(<column name> [{, <column name>}...])]
VALUES ({<expression> | DEFAULT} [{, {<expression> | DEFAULT}}...])
   [{, ({<expression> | DEFAULT} [{, {<expression> | DEFAULT}}...])}...]
```

As you can see, this version of the INSERT statement contains all the same elements, so have a look at a couple of examples to help demonstrate how this statement works. The examples are based on the following table definition:

```
CREATE TABLE Inventory
(
    ProductID SMALLINT UNSIGNED NOT NULL PRIMARY KEY,
    NumberInStock SMALLINT UNSIGNED NOT NULL,
    NumberOnOrder SMALLINT UNSIGNED NOT NULL,
    DateUpdated DATE
);
```

The main characteristic to note about the Inventory table is that the ProductID column is configured as the primary key. It doesn't use the AUTO_INCREMENT option, so you have to provide a value for this column. The following REPLACE statement adds values to each column in the Inventory table:

```
REPLACE LOW_PRIORITY INTO Inventory
VALUES (101, 20, 25, '2004-10-14');
```

You can view the values that you inserted in the Inventory table by executing the following SELECT statement:

```
SELECT * FROM Inventory;
```

Note that the LOW_PRIORITY option, the INTO keyword, the table name, and the values in the VALUES clause are specified exactly as they would be in an INSERT statement. If you were to execute this statement and no rows in the table contain a ProductID value of 101, the statement would be inserted in the table and you would lose no data. Suppose that you then executed the following REPLACE statement:

```
REPLACE LOW_PRIORITY INTO Inventory
VALUES (101, 10, 25, '2004-10-16');
```

This statement also includes a ProductID value of 101. As a result, the original row with that ProductID value would be deleted and the new row would be inserted. Although this might be the behavior that you expected, what if you had meant to insert a different ProductID value? If you had, the original data would be lost and the new data would be inaccurate. For this reason, you should be very cautious when using the REPLACE statement. For the most part, you are better off using an INSERT statement.

In the following exercise, you try out a REPLACE statement by inserting a row in the Studios table.

Try It Out   Using the REPLACE...VALUES Form to Insert Data in the DVDRentals Database

To complete this exercise, follow these steps:

1. Open the mysql client utility, type the following command, and press Enter:

```
use DVDRentals
```

You should receive a message indicating that you switched to the DVDRentals database.

2. To insert the record in the Studios table, type the following REPLACE statement at the mysql command prompt, and then press Enter:

```
REPLACE Studios (StudID, StudDescrip)
VALUES ('s109', 'New Line Cinema, Inc.');
```

You should receive a response saying that your statement executed successfully, affecting one row.

3. Now insert another record in the Studios table. This record includes the same primary key value as the last row you inserted, but the studio name is slightly different. Type the following REPLACE statement at the mysql command prompt, and then press Enter:

```
REPLACE Studios
VALUES ('s109', 'New Line Cinema');
```

You should receive a response saying that your statement executed successfully, affecting two rows.

How It Works

The first REPLACE statement inserted a new row in the Studios table, as shown in the following statement:

```
REPLACE Studios (StudID, StudDescrip)
VALUES ('s109', 'New Line Cinema, Inc.');
```

The new row contained a StudID value of s109 and a StudDescrip value of New Line Cinema, Inc. After executing this statement, you then executed the following REPLACE statement:

```
REPLACE Studios
VALUES ('s109', 'New Line Cinema');
```

For this statement, you did not specify the column names because you inserted a value for each column. You again inserted a row that contained a StudID value of s109. Because the StudID column is configured as the primary key, that last statement replaced the row that the first statement created. As a result, the StudDescrip column now has a value of New Line Cinema.

You can view the values that you inserted in the Studios table by executing the following SELECT statement:

```
SELECT * FROM Studios;
```

Using the *<set option>* Alternative of the REPLACE Statement

As with the *<values option>* alternative, the *<set option>* alternative of the REPLACE statement also includes the same elements that you use in the INSERT statement, as shown in the following syntax:

```
<set option>::=
<table name>
SET <column name>={<expression> | DEFAULT}
   [{, <column name>={<expression> | DEFAULT}}...]
```

The SET clause in the REPLACE statement includes the column names and the values for those columns. Take a look at a couple of examples that help demonstrate this. The following REPLACE statement uses the *<values option>* alternative to add a row to the Inventory table (which is the same table used in the previous REPLACE examples):

```
REPLACE INTO Inventory (ProductID, NumberInStock, DateUpdated)
VALUES (107, 16, '2004-11-30');
```

Notice that values are specified for the ProductID, NumberInStock, and DateUpdated columns, but not for the NumberOnOrder column. Because this column is configured with an integer data type and because the column does not permit null values, a 0 value is added to the column. (When a value is not provided for a column configured with an integer data type, a 0 is inserted if that column does not permit null values and no default is defined for the column. For more information about integer data types, see Chapter 5.)

You could insert the same data shown in the preceding example by using the following REPLACE statement:

```
REPLACE INTO Inventory
SET ProductID=107, NumberInStock=16, DateUpdated='2004-11-30';
```

Notice that a SET clause is used this time, but the column names and values are the same. The SET clause provides the same advantages and disadvantages as using the SET clause in an INSERT statement. The main consideration is, of course, that you do not accidentally overwrite data that you intended to retain.

In the following exercise, you try out the *<set option>* alternative of the REPLACE statement. You use this form of the statement to add two rows to the MovieTypes table.

Try It Out   **Using the *<set option>* Alternative to Insert Data in the DVDRentals Database**

To add these rows, follow these steps:

1. Open the mysql client utility, type the following command, and press Enter:

```
use DVDRentals
```

You should receive a message indicating that you switched to the DVDRentals database.

2. To insert the record in the MovieTypes table, type the following REPLACE statement at the mysql command prompt, and then press Enter:

```
REPLACE MovieTypes
SET MTypeID='mt17', MTypeDescrip='Foreign-subtitled';
```

You should receive a response saying that your statement executed successfully, affecting one row.

3. Now insert another record in the MovieTypes table. This record includes the same primary key value as the last row you inserted, but the name is slightly different. Type the following REPLACE statement at the mysql command prompt, and then press Enter:

```
REPLACE MovieTypes
SET MTypeID='mt17', MTypeDescrip='Foreign';
```

You should receive a response saying that your statement executed successfully, affecting two rows. MySQL reports that two rows are affected because it treats the original row as a deletion and the updated row as an insertion.

How It Works

The first REPLACE statement adds one row to the MovieTypes table, as shown in the following statement:

```
REPLACE MovieTypes
SET MTypeID='mt17', MTypeDescrip='Foreign-subtitled';
```

The added row includes an MTypeID value of mt17 and an MTypeDescrip value of Foreign-subtitled. Because values are defined for both columns in this table, you could just as easily use the *<values option>* alternative of the REPLACE statement. That way, you would not have to specify the column names.

After adding the row to the MovieTypes table, you executed the following REPLACE statement:

```
REPLACE MovieTypes
SET MTypeID='mt17', MTypeDescrip='Foreign';
```

Notice that you've specified the same MTypeID value (mt17), but a slightly different MTypeDescrip value. The question then becomes whether your intent is to replace the original row or to include two rows in the table, one for Foreign films with subtitles and one for other foreign films. Again, this points to the pitfalls of using a REPLACE statement rather than an INSERT statement.

Updating Data in a MySQL Database

Now that you have a foundation in how to insert data in a MySQL database, you're ready to learn how to update that data. The primary statement used to modify data in a MySQL database is the UPDATE statement. The following syntax shows the elements included in an UPDATE statement:

```
<update statement>::=
UPDATE [LOW_PRIORITY] [IGNORE]
<single table update> | <joined table update>

<single table update>::=
<table name>
SET <column name>=<expression> [{, <column name>=<expression>}...]
[WHERE <where definition>]
[ORDER BY <column name> [ASC | DESC] [{, <column name > [ASC | DESC]}...]]
[LIMIT <row count>]

<joined table update>::=
<table name> [{, <table name>}...]
SET <column name>=<expression> [{, <column name>=<expression>}...]
[WHERE <where definition>]
```

The first line of the syntax for the UPDATE statement contains the mandatory UPDATE keyword along with the LOW_PRIORITY option and the IGNORE option, both of which you've seen in the INSERT statement. You should use the LOW_PRIORITY option when you want to delay the execution of the UPDATE statement until no other client connections are accessing that targeted table. You should use the IGNORE option if you want an update to continue even if duplicate primary key and unique index values are found. (The row with the duplicate value is not updated.)

In addition to the UPDATE clause, the syntax for the UPDATE statement specifies two statement alternatives: the *<single table update>* alternative and the *<joined table update>* alternative. A joined table refers to a table that is joined to another table in an SQL statement, such as the UPDATE statement. The join is based on the foreign key relationship established between these two tables. You can use this relationship to access related data in both tables in order to perform an operation on the data in the related tables. Although Chapter 10 discusses joins in greater detail, this chapter includes a brief discussion of joins because they are integral to the *<joined table update>* method of updating a table. Before getting into a discussion about updating joined tables, this chapter first discusses updating a single table.

Using an UPDATE Statement to Update a Single Table

To update a single table in a MySQL database, in which no join conditions are taken into account in order to perform that update, you should create an UPDATE statement that uses the *<single table update>* alternative, which is shown in the following syntax:

```
<single table update>::=
<table name>
SET <column name>=<expression> [{, <column name>=<expression>}...]
[WHERE <where definition>]
[ORDER BY <column name> [ASC | DESC] [{, <column name> [ASC | DESC]}...]]
[LIMIT <row count>]
```

As the syntax shows, you must specify a table name and a SET clause. The SET clause includes, at the very least, a column name and an associated expression, connected by an equal (=) sign. The information sets a value for a particular column. If you want to include more than one column, you must separate the column/expression pairs with commas.

In addition to the of the *<single table update>* alternative's required elements, you can choose to include several additional clauses in your statement. The first of these — the WHERE clause — determines which rows in a table are updated. Without a WHERE clause, all tables are updated, which might some- times be what you want, but most likely you want to use a WHERE clause to qualify your update. The WHERE clause includes one or more conditions that define the extent of the update.

> *Because the WHERE clause is such an integral part of a SELECT statement, it is discussed in detail in Chapter 7; however, this chapter includes information about the clause so that you have a better under- standing of the UPDATE statement. But know that, after you gain a more in-depth knowledge of the WHERE clause in Chapter 7, you'll be able to refine your UPDATE statements to an even greater degree.*

The next optional clause in the UPDATE statement is the ORDER BY clause. The ORDER BY clause allows you to specify that the rows updated by your UPDATE statement are updated in a specified order accord- ing to the values in the column or columns you specify in the clause. If you specify more than one col- umn, you must separate them by a comma, in which case, the rows are updated based on the first column specified, then the second, and so on. In addition, for each column that you include in the clause, you can specify the ASC option or the DESC option. The ASC option means that the rows should be updated in ascending order, based on the column values. The DESC option means that the rows should be updated in descending order. If you specify neither option, the rows are updated in ascending order.

In addition to the ORDER BY clause, you can include a LIMIT clause that limits the number of rows updated to the value specified in the LIMIT clause. For example, if your UPDATE statement would nor- mally update 10 rows in a table, but you specify a LIMIT clause with a value of 5, only the first five rows are updated. Because of a LIMIT clause's nature, it is best suited to use in conjunction with an ORDER BY clause.

To understand how these clauses work, take a look at a few examples. The examples in this section and the next section, which discusses updating joined tables, are based on two tables. The first table is the Books table, which is shown in the following table definition:

```
CREATE TABLE Books
(
    BookID SMALLINT NOT NULL PRIMARY KEY,
    BookName VARCHAR(40) NOT NULL,
    InStock SMALLINT NOT NULL
)
ENGINE=INNODB;
```

The following INSERT statement populates the Books table:

```
INSERT INTO Books
VALUES (101, 'Noncomformity: Writing on Writing', 12),
(102, 'The Shipping News', 17),
(103, 'Hell\'s Angels', 23),
(104, 'Letters to a Young Poet', 32),
(105, 'A Confederacy of Dunces', 6),
(106, 'One Hundred Years of Solitude', 28);
```

The next table is the Orders table, which includes a foreign key that references the Books table, as shown in the following table definition:

```
CREATE TABLE Orders
(
    OrderID SMALLINT NOT NULL PRIMARY KEY,
    BookID SMALLINT NOT NULL,
    Quantity TINYINT (40) NOT NULL DEFAULT 1,
    DateOrdered TIMESTAMP,
    FOREIGN KEY (BookID) REFERENCES Books (BookID)
)
ENGINE=INNODB;
```

The following INSERT statement populates the Orders table:

```
INSERT INTO Orders
VALUES (1001, 103, 1, '2004-10-12 12:30:00'),
(1002, 101, 1, '2004-10-12 12:31:00'),
(1003, 103, 2, '2004-10-12 12:34:00'),
(1004, 104, 3, '2004-10-12 12:36:00'),
(1005, 102, 1, '2004-10-12 12:41:00'),
(1006, 103, 2, '2004-10-12 12:59:00'),
(1007, 101, 1, '2004-10-12 13:01:00'),
(1008, 103, 1, '2004-10-12 13:02:00'),
(1009, 102, 4, '2004-10-12 13:22:00'),
(1010, 101, 2, '2004-10-12 13:30:00'),
(1011, 103, 1, '2004-10-12 13:32:00'),
(1012, 105, 1, '2004-10-12 13:40:00'),
(1013, 106, 2, '2004-10-12 13:44:00'),
(1014, 103, 1, '2004-10-12 14:01:00'),
(1015, 106, 1, '2004-10-12 14:05:00'),
(1016, 104, 2, '2004-10-12 14:28:00'),
(1017, 105, 1, '2004-10-12 14:31:00'),
(1018, 102, 1, '2004-10-12 14:32:00'),
(1019, 106, 3, '2004-10-12 14:49:00'),
(1020, 103, 1, '2004-10-12 14:51:00');
```

Notice that the values added to the BookID column in the Orders table include only values that exist in the BookID column in the Books table. The BookID column in Orders is the referencing column, and the BookID column in Books is the referenced column.

After creating the tables and adding data to those tables, you can modify that data. The following UPDATE statement modifies values in the InStock column of the Books table:

```
UPDATE Books
SET InStock=InStock+10;
```

This statement includes only the required elements of an UPDATE statement. This includes the UPDATE keyword, the name of the table, and a SET clause that specifies one column/expression pair. The expression in this case is made up of the InStock column name, a plus (+) arithmetic operator, and a literal value of 10. As a result, the existing value in the InStock column increases by 10. Because you specify no other conditions in the UPDATE statement, all rows in the table update. This approach might be fine in some cases, but in all likelihood, most of your updates should be more specific than this. As a result, you want to qualify your statements so that only certain rows in the table update, rather than all rows.

The method used to qualify an UPDATE statement is to add a WHERE clause to the statement. The WHERE clause provides the specifics necessary to limit the update. For example, the following UPDATE statement includes a WHERE clause that specifies that only rows with an OrderID value of 1001 should be updated:

```
UPDATE Orders
SET Quantity=2
WHERE OrderID=1001;
```

As you can see, the WHERE clause allows you to be much more specific with your updates. In this case, you specify the OrderID column, followed by an equal (=) sign, and then followed by a value of 1001. As a result, the value in the OrderID column must be 1001 in order for a row to be updated. Because this is the primary key column, only one row contains this value, so that is the only row updated. In addition, the SET clause specifies that the value in the Quantity column be set to 2. The result is that the Quantity column in the row that contains an OrderID value of 1001 is updated, but no other rows are updated.

As you have seen, another method that you can use to update a value in a column is to base the update on the current value in that column. For example, in the following UPDATE statement, the SET clause uses the Quantity column to specify the new value for that column:

```
UPDATE Orders
SET Quantity=Quantity+1
WHERE OrderID=1001;
```

In this statement, the SET clause specifies that the new value for the Quantity column should equal the current value plus one. For example, if the current value is 2, it increases to 3. Also, because the UPDATE statement is qualified by the use of a WHERE clause, only the row with an OrderID value of 1001 increases the value in the Quantity column by a value of 1.

In the last two examples, the WHERE clause specifies that only one record should be updated (OrderID=1001). If the OrderID column were not the primary key and duplicate values were permitted in that column, it would be conceivable that more than one row would be updated, which is often the case in an UPDATE statement. For example, the following statement updates all rows with an InStock value of less than 30:

```
UPDATE LOW_PRIORITY Books
SET InStock=InStock+10
WHERE InStock<30;
```

In this statement, the SET clause specifies that all values in the InStock column should be increased by 10. (The addition [+] operator is used to add 10 to the value in the InStock column.) The WHERE clause limits that update only to those columns that contain an InStock value of less than 30. (The less than [<] operator indicates that the value in the InStock column must be less that 30.) As a result, the number of rows updated equals the number of rows with an InStock value less than 30. (Chapter 8 describes the operators available in MySQL and how to use those operators in your SQL statements.)

An UPDATE statement can be further qualified by the use of the ORDER BY clause and the LIMIT clause. For example, suppose you want to update the Orders table so that orders that contain a BookID value of 103 are increased by 1. You want to limit the increase, though, to the last five orders for that book. You could use the following UPDATE statement to modify the table:

```
UPDATE Orders
SET Quantity=Quantity+1
WHERE BookID=103
ORDER BY DateOrdered DESC
LIMIT 5;
```

By now, you should be familiar with the first three lines of code. In the first line, the UPDATE clause specifies the Orders table. In the second line, the SET clause specifies that the values in the Quantity column should be increased by 1. In the third line, the WHERE clause specifies that only rows that contain a BookID value of 103 should be updated.

The ORDER BY clause then further qualifies the statement by ordering the rows to be updated by the values in the DateOrdered column. Notice the use of the DESC option, which means that the values are sorted in descending order. Because this is a TIMESTAMP column, descending order means that the most recent orders are updated first. Because the LIMIT clause specifies a value of 5, only the first five rows are updated.

As you can see, the ORDER BY and LIMIT clauses are useful only in very specific circumstances, but the WHERE and SET clauses provide a considerable amount of flexibility in defining UPDATE statements.

Now that you have seen examples of how an UPDATE statement works, it's time to try a couple out for yourself. In this exercise you create UPDATE statements that modify values in the DVDs table of the DVDRentals database.

Try It Out   Using UPDATE Statements to Modify Data in a Single Table

Follow these steps to perform updates to the DVDs table:

1. Open the mysql client utility, type the following command, and press Enter:

```
use DVDRentals
```

You should receive a message indicating that you switched to the DVDRentals database.

2. To update the record in the DVDs table, type the following UPDATE statement at the mysql command prompt, and then press Enter:

```
UPDATE DVDs
SET StudID='s110'
WHERE DVDID=9;
```

You should receive an error message stating that a foreign key constraint has failed. This happens because the StudID value does not exist in the referenced parent table (Studios).

3. Now try updating the table in a different way. To update the record in the DVDs table, type the following UPDATE statement at the mysql command prompt, and then press Enter:

```
UPDATE DVDs
SET StatID='s1'
WHERE DVDID=9;
```

This time, you should receive a response saying that your statement executed successfully, affecting one row.

4. To update the same record in the DVDs table, type the following UPDATE statement at the mysql command prompt, and then press Enter:

```
UPDATE DVDs
SET StatID='s3', MTypeID='mt13'
WHERE DVDID=9;
```

You should receive a response saying that your statement executed successfully, affecting one row.

How It Works

In this exercise, you created three UPDATE statements that attempted to update the DVDs table. The first statement tried to update the StudID value in the row that contained a DVDID of 9, as shown in the following statement:

```
UPDATE DVDs
SET StudID='s110'
WHERE DVDID=9;
```

Your attempt to execute this statement failed because you tried to update the StudID value to a value that didn't exist in the referenced column in the parent table (Studios). Had the Studios table contained a row with a StudID value of s110, this statement would have succeeded.

In this next UPDATE statement that you created, you tried to change the StatID value of the row that contains a DVDID value of 9, as shown in the following statement:

```
UPDATE DVDs
SET StatID='s1'
WHERE DVDID=9;
```

The SET clause in this statement specifies that the StatID column should be changed to a value of s1. When you executed the statement, the value changed successfully because the value existed in the referenced column of the parent table (Status). In addition, because the WHERE clause specifies that only rows with a DVDID value of 9 should be updated, only one row changed because the DVDID column is the primary key, so only one row contained that value.

The final UPDATE statement that you created in this exercise updated two values in the DVDs table, as the following statement shows:

```
UPDATE DVDs
SET StatID='s3', MTypeID='mt13'
WHERE DVDID=9;
```

In this statement, you specified that the StatID value should be changed to s3 and that the MTypeID value should be changed to mt13, both acceptable values in the referenced column. Notice that a comma separates the expressions in the SET clause. In addition, as with the previous statement, the updates applied only to the row that contained a DVDID value of 9.

Using an UPDATE Statement to Update Joined Tables

In the example UPDATE statements that you've looked at so far, you updated individual tables without joining them to other tables. Although the tables contained foreign keys that referenced other tables, you specified no join conditions in the UPDATE statements. For a join condition to exist, it must be explicitly defined in the statement.

As you saw earlier in the chapter, the UPDATE statement includes an option that allows you to update joined tables. The following syntax shows the basic elements that are used to create an UPDATE statement that modifies joined tables:

```
<joined table update>::=
<table name> [{, <table name>}...]
SET <column name>=<expression> [{, <column name>=<expression>}...]
[WHERE <where definition>]
```

As you can see, this syntax contains many of the same elements as the syntax used to update a single table that is not specified in a join. One difference, however, is that you can specify more than one table in a statement that uses the <joined table update> alternative. In addition, this method of updating a table does not allow you to specify an ORDER BY clause or a LIMIT clause.

Generally, using an UPDATE statement to modify data in multiple tables is not recommended for InnoDB tables. Instead, you should rely on the ON DELETE and ON CASCADE options specified in the foreign key constraints of the table definitions.

When updating a joined table, you must specify the tables in the join, qualify the column names with table names, and define the join condition in the WHERE clause, as shown in the following UPDATE statement:

```
UPDATE Books, Orders
SET Books.InStock=Books.InStock-Orders.Quantity
WHERE Books.BookID=Orders.BookID
   AND Orders.OrderID=1002;
```

Take a look at this statement one clause at a time. The UPDATE clause includes the name of both the Books table and the Orders table. Although you are updating only the Books table, you must specify both tables because both of them are included in the joined tables. Notice that a comma separates the table names.

The SET clause in this statement uses qualified column names to assign an expression to the InStock column. A *qualified column name* is one that is preceded by the name of the table and a period. This allows MySQL (and you) to distinguish between columns in different tables that have the same name. For example, the first column listed (Books.InStock) refers to the InStock column in the Books table. Qualified names are required whenever column names can be confused.

According to the SET clause, the UPDATE statement should set the value of the Books.InStock column to equal its current value less the value in the Quantity column of the Orders table. For example, if a value in the Books.InStock column is 6 and the value in the Orders.Quantity column is 2, the new value of the Books.InStock column should be 4.

The next clause in the UPDATE statement is the WHERE clause. In this clause, you join the two tables by matching values in the BookID columns in each table: `Books.BookID=Orders.BookID`. By associating the tables through related columns in this way, you are creating a type of join. (A *join* is a condition defined in a SELECT, UPDATE, or DELETE statement that links together two or more tables. You learn more about joins in Chapter 10.)

In the preceding example, the joined columns indicate that values in the Books.BookID column should match values in the Orders.BookID column. As a result, the UPDATE statement affects only rows with matching values. This is how the join condition is defined.

The WHERE clause further qualifies how rows are updated by specifying that the value in the OrderID column of the Orders table must equal 1002. Because the AND keyword connects these two conditions (the `Books.BookID=Orders.BookID` condition and the `Orders.OrderID=1002` condition), a row is updated only if both conditions are met. In other words, the Books.BookID value must equal the Orders.OrderID value *and* the Orders.OrderID value must equal 1002. The Books.InStock value is updated when both these conditions are met.

When you update values in a joined table, you can update more than one value at a time, as the following example demonstrates:

```
UPDATE Books, Orders
SET Orders.Quantity=Orders.Quantity+2,
    Books.InStock=Books.InStock-2
WHERE Books.BookID=Orders.BookID
    AND Orders.OrderID = 1002;
```

In this UPDATE statement, the same conditions hold true as in the previous statement: the Books.BookID value must equal the Orders.OrderID value, *and* the Orders.OrderID value must equal 1002. However, the SET clause is a little different in this statement. If a row meets the conditions specified in the WHERE clause, the Orders.Quantity value is increased by 2, and the Books.InStock value is decreased by 2. As you can see, you can update both tables specified in the join condition.

In the following exercise, you update values in a joined table in the DVDRentals database.

Try It Out   **Using UPDATE Statements to Modify Data in Joined Tables**

The tables you modify include DVDs and Studios, as shown in the following steps.

1. Open the mysql client utility, type the following command, and press Enter:

```
use DVDRentals
```

   You should receive a message indicating that you have switched to the DVDRentals database.

2. To update the record in the DVDs table, type the following UPDATE statement at the mysql command prompt, and then press Enter:

```
UPDATE DVDs, Studios
SET DVDs.StatID='s2'
WHERE DVDs.StudID=Studios.StudID
    AND Studios.StudDescrip='Metro-Goldwyn-Mayer';
```

   You should receive a response saying that your statement executed successfully and that one row was affected.

How It Works

In this exercise, you created the following UPDATE statement to modify values in StatID column of the DVDs table:

```
UPDATE DVDs, Studios
SET DVDs.StatID='s2'
WHERE DVDs.StudID=Studios.StudID
    AND Studios.StudDescrip='Metro-Goldwyn-Mayer';
```

The statement begins with an UPDATE clause that specifies the names of the tables that participate in the join condition. Next, the SET clause specifies that the value in the StatID column of the DVDs table should be set to s2. The last clause in the statement is a WHERE clause that defines the join condition. In this case, the StudID column in the DVDs table is joined to the StudID column of the Studios table.

The join defined in the WHERE clause represents one of two conditions defined in the clause. The second condition — Studios.StudDescrip='Metro-Goldwyn-Mayer' — means that the StudDescrip column of the Studios table must be Metro-Goldwyn-Mayer. This means that, in order for a row to be updated, the value in the DVDs.StudID column must equal the value in the Studios.StudID column *and* the Studios.StudDescrip column must contain the value Metro-Goldwyn-Mayer. If both of these conditions are met, the DVDs.StatID column is set to s2. In practical terms, this statement specifies that the status for any DVD released by Metro-Goldwyn-Mayer should be set to s2, which means that the DVD is available to rent. You might run a statement like this if all your MGM movies have been put on hold for promotional reasons and are now available.

In this exercise, you used an UPDATE statement to modify data in multiple InnoDB tables, even though this method is normally not recommended. The exercise had you perform these updates so that you could try out how these types of UPDATE statements work.

Deleting Data from a MySQL Database

It is inevitable that, after entering data into a database, some of it will have to be deleted. In most cases, you can delete data only if a foreign key column is not referencing it. In that case, you must first delete or modify the referencing value, and then you can delete the row that contains the referenced value.

When you delete data from a table, you must delete one or more entire rows at a time. You cannot delete only a part of a row. MySQL supports two statements that you can use to delete data from a database: the DELETE statement and the TRUNCATE statement.

Using a DELETE Statement to Delete Data

The DELETE statement is the primary statement that you use to remove data from a table. The syntax for the statement is as follows:

```
<delete statement>::=
DELETE [LOW_PRIORITY] [QUICK] [IGNORE]
{<single table delete> | <from join delete> | <using join delete>

<single table delete>::=
FROM <table name>
[WHERE <where definition>]
[ORDER BY <column name> [ASC | DESC] [{, <column name> [ASC | DESC]}...]]
[LIMIT <row count>]

<from join delete>::=
<table name>[.*] [{, <table name>[.*]}...]
FROM <table name> [{, <table name>}...]
[WHERE <where definition>]

<using join delete>::=
FROM <table name>[.*] [{, <table name>[.*]}...]
USING <table name> [{, <table name>}...]
[WHERE <where definition>]
```

The first line of the statement includes the mandatory DELETE keyword, along with the LOW_PRIORITY, QUICK, and IGNORE options. You've seen the LOW_PRIORITY option used in INSERT, REPLACE, and UPDATE statements, and you've seen the IGNORE option used in INSERT and UPDATE statements. If you specify LOW_PRIORITY, the DELETE statement does not execute until no client connections are accessing the target table. If you specify IGNORE, errors are not returned when trying to delete rows; rather, warnings are provided if a row cannot be deleted.

The other option in the DELETE clause is QUICK. This option applies only to MyISAM table. When you use the QUICK option, the MyISAM storage engine does not merge certain components of the index during a delete operation, which may speed up some operations.

The next line of code in the DELETE statement syntax specifies three alternatives that you can use when creating a statement: the <single table delete> alternative, the <from join delete> alternative, and the <using join delete> alternative. The <from join delete> alternative refers to join conditions specified in the statement's FROM clause, and the <using join delete> alternative refers to join conditions that you can specify in the USING clause. The following sections discuss all three alternatives.

Deleting Data from a Single Table

The first type of delete that you can perform is based on the *<single table delete>* alternative. You can use this method to delete rows from a table not defined in a join condition, as shown in the following syntax:

```
<single table delete>::=
FROM <table name>
[WHERE <where definition>]
[ORDER BY <column name> [ASC | DESC] [{, <column name> [ASC | DESC]}...]]
[LIMIT <row count>]
```

As the syntax shows, the *<single table delete>* alternative requires a FROM clause that defines the name of the table. Optionally, you can also add a WHERE, an ORDER BY, or a LIMIT clause. These clauses work the same way they do in an UPDATE statement. The WHERE clause includes one or more conditions that define the extent of the delete operation. The ORDER BY clause sorts rows according to the column or columns specified in the clause. The LIMIT clause limits the number of rows to be deleted to the number specified in the clause.

To better illustrate how to use the DELETE statement, consider a few examples. The first example is a DELETE statement that contains only the required components of the statement, as shown in the following statement:

```
DELETE FROM Orders;
```

As you can see, the statement specifies only the DELETE FROM keywords and the table name. Because a WHERE clause does not qualify the statement, all rows are deleted from the table. Although this might be your intent, it might also result in an unintentional loss of data. As a result, most DELETE statements include a WHERE clause that defines which rows should be deleted. For example, the following statement deletes only rows that contain an OrderID value of 1020:

```
DELETE FROM Orders
WHERE OrderID=1020;
```

There WHERE clause makes the statement much more specific, and now only the applicable rows are deleted. Rows that do not contain an OrderID value of 1020 are left alone.

A DELETE statement can be further qualified by using an ORDER BY and a LIMIT clause, as shown in the following example:

```
DELETE LOW_PRIORITY FROM Orders
WHERE BookID=103
ORDER BY DateOrdered DESC
LIMIT 1;
```

In this statement, the rows to be deleted (those with a BookID of 103) are sorted according to the DateOrdered column, in descending order, meaning that the rows with the most recent dates are deleted first. The LIMIT clause restricts the deletion to only one row. As a result, only the most recent order for the book with the BookID value of 103 is deleted.

Indeed, deleting data from a table that is not joined to another table is a relatively straightforward process, and several examples demonstrate the ease with which you can remove information from a database. The following Try It Out shows you how to use the DELETE statement to remove data from the MovieTypes table in the DVDRentals database.

Try It Out **Using DELETE Statements to Delete Data from a Single Table in the DVDRentals Database**

The following steps walk you though the delete operation:

1. Open the mysql client utility, type the following command, and press Enter:

```
use DVDRentals
```

You should receive a message indicating that you switched to the DVDRentals database.

2. To delete the record in the MovieTypes table, type the following DELETE statement at the mysql command prompt, and then press Enter:

```
DELETE FROM MovieTypes
WHERE MTypeID='mt18';
```

You should receive a response saying that your statement executed successfully but that no rows were affected.

3. To delete the record in the MovieTypes table, type the following DELETE statement at the mysql command prompt, and then press Enter:

```
DELETE FROM MovieTypes
WHERE MTypeID='mt17';
```

You should receive a response saying that your statement executed successfully, affecting one row.

How It Works

The first DELETE statement attempts to remove one row from the MovieTypes table, as shown in the following statement:

```
DELETE FROM MovieTypes
WHERE MTypeID='mt18';
```

The WHERE clause in this statement specifies that any row with an MTypeID value of mt18 should be removed from the table. Because no rows contain an MTypeID value of mt18, no rows are removed. As a result, you executed the following statement:

```
DELETE FROM MovieTypes
WHERE MTypeID='mt17';
```

This time, you specified the MTypeID value of mt17 in the WHERE clause. Because the MovieTypes table contains a row with an MTypeID value of mt17, that row was removed; however, no other rows were removed. Only one row in the table could contain the MTypeID value of mt17 because the MTypeID column is the primary key, so all values in that column are unique.

Deleting Data from Joined Tables

In addition to being able to delete data from an individual table that is not joined to another table, you can delete data from a joined table. The INSERT statement provides two alternatives for deleting data from a joined table: the *<from join delete>* method and the *<using join delete>* method. The *<from join delete>* method refers to the fact that the joined tables are specified in the FROM clause. The *<using join delete>* method refers to the fact that the joined tables are specified in the USING clause.

> *Generally, using a DELETE statement to remove data from joined tables is not recommended for InnoDB tables. Instead, you should rely on the ON DELETE and ON CASCADE options specified in the foreign key constraints of the table definitions.*

Using the *<from join delete>* Alternative of the DELETE Statement

The *<from join delete>* alternative of the DELETE statement is similar to the *<single table delete>* alternative in that it contains a FROM clause and an optional WHERE clause. As the following syntax shows, there are also a number of differences:

```
<from join delete>::=
<table name>[.*] [{, <table name>[.*]}...]
FROM <table name> [{, <table name>}...]
[WHERE <where definition>]
```

One thing that you might notice is that the syntax does not include an ORDER BY clause or a LIMIT clause. In addition, you can specify multiple tables in the DELETE clause *and* in the FROM clause. Tables specified in the DELETE clause are the tables from which data will be removed. Tables specified in the FROM clause are those tables that participate in the join. You specify tables in two separate places because this structure allows you to create a join that contains more tables than the number of tables from which data is actually deleted.

Notice that a period and an asterisk follow the table name. The period and asterisk are optional. MySQL supports their use to provide compatibility with Microsoft Access. They indicate that every column in the specified table will be included. Normally you do not need to include the period and asterisk.

Now take a look at an example of a DELETE statement that deletes data from a joined table. Earlier in the chapter, you saw two tables that demonstrated how the UPDATE statement works: the Books table and the Orders table. Suppose you use the following INSERT statements to add a row to each table:

```
INSERT INTO Books VALUES (107, 'Where I\'m Calling From', 3);
INSERT INTO Orders VALUES (1021, 107, 1, '2003-06-14 14:39:00');
```

Now suppose that you want to delete from the Orders table any order for the book title *Where I'm Calling From*. To delete these Orders, you would use the following DELETE statement:

```
DELETE Orders.*
FROM Books, Orders
WHERE Books.BookID=Orders.BookID
    AND Books.BookName='Where I\'m Calling From';
```

The DELETE clause of this statement specifies the Orders table as the table from which data is deleted. The FROM clause in the DELETE statement then goes on to specify the tables to include in the join, which in this case are the Books and Orders tables. The WHERE clause, as you saw with the UPDATE statement, is where the join is actually defined. The first condition specified in the clause actually defines the join: Books.BookID=Orders.BookID. The WHERE clause also includes a second condition— Books.BookName='Where I\'m Calling From'—which indicates that only orders for this particular book should be deleted. In other words, for a row to be deleted from the Orders table, the BookID value in the Orders table must equal a BookID value in the Books table *and* the BookName value in the Books table must be *Where I'm Calling From*. When a row matches these conditions, it is deleted from the table.

In the following exercise, you attempt to delete two rows from the DVDs table in the DVDRentals database. To delete these rows, you specify a join condition in your DELETE statements.

Try It Out   Using the *<from join delete>* Alternative to Delete Data from the DVDRentals Database

The following steps describe the process you should follow to delete the data from the DVDs table:

1. Open the mysql client utility, type the following command, and press Enter:

```
use DVDRentals
```

   You should receive a message indicating that you switched to the DVDRentals database.

2. To delete a record in the DVDs table, type the following DELETE statement at the mysql command prompt, and then press Enter:

```
DELETE DVDs
FROM DVDs, Studios
WHERE DVDs.StudID=Studios.StudID
   AND Studios.StudDescrip='New Line Cinema';
```

   You should receive a response saying that your statement executed successfully but that no rows were affected.

3. To delete another record in the DVDs table, type the following DELETE statement at the mysql command prompt, and then press Enter:

```
DELETE DVDs
FROM DVDs, Studios
WHERE DVDs.StudID=Studios.StudID
   AND Studios.StudDescrip='Metro-Goldwyn-Mayer';
```

   You should receive a response saying that your statement executed successfully, affecting one row.

How It Works

This exercise had you use two DELETE statements to try to delete two rows from the DVDs table. The statements were identical except for the StudDescrip value that you specified. In the first of the two statements, you specified a StudDescrip value of New Line Cinema, as shown in the following statement:

```
DELETE DVDs
FROM DVDs, Studios
WHERE DVDs.StudID=Studios.StudID
   AND Studios.StudDescrip='New Line Cinema';
```

As the statement shows, the DELETE clause specifies that data should be deleted from the DVDs table. The FROM clause specifies that the DVDs table and the Studios table participate in the join. The join is then defined in the WHERE clause, which specifies that the StudID values in the DVDs table should be matched to the StudID values in the Studios table. In addition, the WHERE clause includes a second condition that specifies that the StudDescrip value in the Studios table must be New Line Cinema. Because New Line Cinema is associated with the StudID value of s109, any rows in the DVDs table that have a StudID value of s109 are deleted. When you executed this statement, no rows were deleted from the DVDs table because no rows met the criteria defined in the WHERE clause.

The next DELETE statement you ran did delete a row because you specified Metro-Goldwyn-Mayer as the StudDescrip value, rather than New Line Cinema. Because Metro-Goldwyn-Mayer is associated with the StudID value of s108 and because the DVDs table included a row that had a StudID value of s108, that row was deleted. For example, you might use a statement such as this if you want to discontinue renting all the current DVDs released by New Line Cinema, perhaps because you plan to sell the DVDs and replace them with new ones.

In this exercise, you used a DELETE statement to remove data from joined InnoDB tables, even though this method is normally not recommended. The exercise had you perform these deletions so that you could try out how these types of DELETE statements work.

Using the <using join delete> Alternative of the DELETE Statement

The <using join delete> alternative of the DELETE statement is very similar to the <from join delete> alternative, as shown in the following syntax:

```
<using join delete>::=
FROM <table name>[.*] [{, <table name>[.*]}...]
USING <table name> [{, <table name>}...]
[WHERE <where definition>]
```

The primary differences between the <using join delete> alternative and the <from join delete> alternative are that, in the <using join delete> alternative, the tables from which data is deleted are specified in the FROM clause, as opposed to the DELETE clause, and the tables that are to be joined are specified in the USING clause, as opposed to the FROM clause. All other aspects of the two alternatives, however, are the same.

For example, suppose you were to rewrite the last example DELETE statement by using the <using join delete> alternative. The new statement would include the Books table in the FROM clause and the Books and Orders tables in the USING clause, as shown in the following example:

```
DELETE FROM Orders
USING Books, Orders
WHERE Books.BookID=Orders.BookID
   AND Books.BookName='Where I\'m Calling From';
```

As you can see in this statement, the DELETE clause doesn't include the name of the table, and the WHERE clause is identical to what you used in the DELETE statement created by using the <from join delete> alternative.

In the following exercise, you create two DELETE statements that use the *<using join delete>* alternative. The statements attempt to delete data from the DVDs table.

Using the *<using join delete>* Alternative to Delete Data from the DVDRentals Database

The following steps walk you through the process of using the *<using join delete>* alternative:

1. Open the mysql client utility, type the following command, and press Enter:

```
use DVDRentals
```

You should receive a message indicating that you switched to the DVDRentals database.

2. To delete the first record in the DVDs table, type the following DELETE statement at the mysql command prompt, and then press Enter:

```
DELETE FROM DVDs
USING DVDs, Studios
WHERE DVDs.StudID=Studios.StudID
   AND Studios.StudDescrip='New Line Cinema';
```

You should receive a response saying that your statement executed successfully but that no rows were affected.

3. To delete the next record in the DVDs table, type the following DELETE statement at the mysql command prompt, and then press Enter:

```
DELETE FROM DVDs
USING DVDs, Studios
WHERE DVDs.StudID=Studios.StudID
   AND Studios.StudDescrip='Metro-Goldwyn-Mayer';
```

You should receive a response saying that your statement executed successfully but that no rows were affected.

4. To delete the records in the Studios table, type the following DELETE statement at the mysql command prompt, and then press Enter:

```
DELETE FROM Studios
WHERE StudID='s108' OR StudID='s109';
```

You should receive a response saying that your statement executed successfully, affecting two rows.

How It Works

In this exercise, you created two DELETE statements that were identical except for the StudDescrip value that you specified. The statements were intended to delete data from the DVDs table. You then used a DELETE statement to delete two rows from the Studios table. In the first DELETE statement, you specified a StudDescrip value of New Line Cinema, as shown in the following statement:

```
DELETE FROM DVDs
USING DVDs, Studios
WHERE DVDs.StudID=Studios.StudID
```

```
        AND Studios.StudDescrip='New Line Cinema';
```

The FROM clause in this statement specifies the DVDs table, which is the table from which data is removed. The USING clause specifies the DVDs and Studios table. These are the tables to be joined. The WHERE clause specifies the join condition, and a second condition that specifies that the StudDescrip value must equal New Line Cinema. The second DELETE statement is the same except that it specifies that the StudDescrip values should be Metro-Goldwyn-Mayer.

When you executed the first two DELETE statements, they were executed successfully; however, neither of them deleted any rows in the DVDs table because no rows existed that met the WHERE clause conditions specified in either statement. Even so, the exercise still demonstrated how to create a DELETE statement that uses the <using join delete> alternative.

After you executed the first two DELETE statements, you created the following DELETE statement to remove rows from the Studios table:

```
DELETE FROM Studios
WHERE StudID='s108' OR StudID='s109';
```

The statement uses the <single table delete> alternative and contains a WHERE clause that contains two conditions. The first condition specifies that the StudID value must equal s108. The second condition specifies that the StudID value should be s109. Because the two conditions are connected by an OR operator, rather than an AND operator, either condition can be met in a row. As a result, any row that contains a StudID value of s108 or s109 is deleted from the table. In this case, two rows were deleted.

As with the last Try It Out section, in this exercise, you used a DELETE statement to remove data from joined InnoDB tables, even though this method is normally not recommended. The exercise had you perform these deletions so that you could try out how these types of DELETE statements work.

Using a TRUNCATE Statement to Delete Data

The final statement that this chapter covers is the TRUNCATE statement. The TRUNCATE statement removes all rows from a table. You cannot qualify this statement in any way. Any rows that exist are deleted from the target table. The following syntax describes how to create a TRUNCATE statement:

```
TRUNCATE [TABLE] <table name>
```

As you can see, you need to specify the TRUNCATE keyword and the table name. You can also specify the TABLE keyword, but it has no effect on how the table works. For example, the following TRUNCATE statement removes all data from the Orders table:

```
TRUNCATE TABLE Orders;
```

The statement includes TRUNCATE, the optional keyword TABLE, and the name of the table. If any rows exist in the table when you execute the statement, those rows are removed. Executing this statement has basically the same effect as issuing the following DELETE statement:

```
DELETE FROM Orders;
```

The most important difference between the TRUNCATE statement and the DELETE statement is that the TRUNCATE statement is not transaction safe. A *transaction* is a set of one or more SQL statements that perform a set of related actions. The statements are grouped together and treated as a single unit whose success or failure depends on the successful execution of each statement in the transaction. You learn more about transactions in Chapter 12.

Another difference between the TRUNCATE statement and the DELETE statement is that the TRUNCATE statement starts the AUTO_INCREMENT count over again, unlike the DELETE statement. TRUNCATE is generally faster than using a DELETE statement as well.

Summary

One of the most important functions of any RDBMS is to support your ability to manipulate data. To this end, you must be able to insert data in a table, modify that data, and then delete whatever data you no longer want to store. To support your ability to perform these operations, MySQL includes a number of SQL statements that allow you to insert, update, and delete data. This chapter provided you with the information you need to create these statements so that you can effectively carry out these operations. You learned how the syntax for each statement is defined and the components that make up those statements. Specifically, this chapter provided you with the information necessary to perform the following tasks:

- ❑ Use INSERT statements to add individual and multiple rows of data into tables
- ❑ Use REPLACE statements to add individual and multiple rows of data into tables
- ❑ Use UPDATE statements to modify data in single tables and joined tables
- ❑ Use DELETE statements to remove data from single tables and joined tables
- ❑ Use TRUNCATE statements to remove all data from a table

When discussing each of these statements, this chapter introduced you to a number of elements that helped to define many of the statement components. For example, the chapter provided examples of expressions, operators, functions, joins, and various statement clauses that played critical roles in defining the different types of statements. In subsequent chapters, you learn more about each of these components, which allows you to create even more robust data manipulation statements so that you can more effectively manage the data in your database and create applications that efficiently add and manipulate data.

Exercises

The following exercises help you become better acquainted with the material covered in this chapter. Be sure to work through each exercise carefully. To view the answers to these questions, see Appendix A.

1. You plan to insert data in the Books table. The table is defined with the following CREATE TABLE statement:

```
CREATE TABLE Books
(
    BookID SMALLINT NOT NULL PRIMARY KEY,
    BookName VARCHAR(50) NOT NULL
);
```

Use the `<values option>` alternative of the INSERT statement to add one row to the Books table. The value for the BookID column is 1001, and the name of the book is *One Hundred Years of Solitude*. Which SQL statement should you use?

2. You decide that you want to use the `<set option>` alternative of the REPLACE statement to add the same values to the Books table that you added in Exercise 1. Which SQL statement should you use?

3. You plan to update data in the CDs table, which is shown in the following table definition:

```
CREATE TABLE CDs
(
    CDID SMALLINT NOT NULL AUTO_INCREMENT PRIMARY KEY,
    CDName VARCHAR(50) NOT NULL,
    CDQuantity SMALLINT NOT NULL
);
```

The following INSERT statement was used to add data to the CDs table:

```
INSERT INTO CDs (CDName, CDQuantity)
VALUES ('Mule Variations', 10),
('Short Sharp Shocked', 3),
('The Bonnie Raitt Collection', 7);
```

You want to increase the CDQuantity value of every row by 3. Which SQL statement should you use?

4. You now want to increase the CDQuantity value in the CDs table by another 3, but this time, the increase should apply only to the CD named *Mule Variations*. Which SQL statement should you use?

5. You decide to delete a row from the CDs table. You want to remove the row that contains a CDID value of 1. Which SQL statement should you use?

Retrieving Data from a MySQL Database

One of the most important functions that a relational database management system (RDBMS) must support is the ability to access data in the databases managed by that system. Data access must extend beyond the mere retrieval of information as it is stored in the tables. You must be able to choose which data you want to view and how that data is displayed. To support this functionality, MySQL provides an SQL statement that is both powerful and flexible in its implementation. The SELECT statement is the primary SQL statement used in MySQL — and in most RDBMSs — to retrieve specific data from one or more tables in a relational database.

By using a SELECT statement, you can specify which columns and which rows to retrieve from one or more tables in your MySQL database. You can also link values together across multiple tables, perform calculations on those values, or group values together in meaningful ways in order to provide summarized information. When you execute a SELECT statement, the values returned by that statement are presented in the form of a *result set*, which is an unnamed temporary table that contains the information retrieved from the tables. In this chapter, you will learn how to create SELECT statements that allow you to retrieve exactly the information that you need. Specifically, the chapter covers the following topics:

❑ The SELECT statement and its syntax, as used in MySQL. You learn how to create statements that retrieve all columns in a table or only specific columns. You also learn how to add expressions and define variables in your SELECT statements.

❑ How to add options to a SELECT statement that determine how the statement is executed.

❑ How to add optional clauses to your SELECT statement that allow you to limit which rows are returned, to group together rows in order to summarize information, and to specify the order in which rows are displayed.

The SELECT Statement

Whenever you want to retrieve data from a MySQL database, you can issue a SELECT statement that specifies what data you want to have returned and in what manner that data should be returned. For example, you can specify that only specific columns or rows be returned. You can also order the rows based on the values in one or more columns. In addition, you can group together rows based on repeated values in a column in order to summarize data.

The SELECT statement is one of the most powerful SQL statements in MySQL. It provides a great deal of flexibility and allows you to create queries that are as simple or as complex as you need to make them. The syntax for a SELECT statement is made up of a number of clauses and other elements, most of which are optional, that allow you to refine your query so that it returns only the information that you're looking for. The following syntax describes the elements that make up a SELECT statement:

```
<select statement>::=
SELECT
[<select option> [<select option>...]]
{* | <select list>}
[<export definition>]
[
    FROM <table reference> [{, <table reference>}...]
    [WHERE <expression> [{<operator> <expression>}...]]
    [GROUP BY <group by definition>]
    [HAVING <expression> [{<operator> <expression>}...]]
    [ORDER BY <order by definition>]
    [LIMIT [<offset>,] <row count>]
    [PROCEDURE <procedure name> [(<argument> [{, <argument>}...])]]
    [{FOR UPDATE} | {LOCK IN SHARE MODE}]
]

<select option>::=
{ALL | DISTINCT | DISTINCTROW}
| HIGH_PRIORITY
| {SQL_BIG_RESULT | SQL_SMALL_RESULT}
| SQL_BUFFER_RESULT
| {SQL_CACHE | SQL_NO_CACHE}
| SQL_CALC_FOUND_ROWS
| STRAIGHT_JOIN

<select list>::=
{<column name> | <expression>} [[AS] <alias>]
[{, {<column name> | <expression>} [[AS] <alias>]}...]

<export definition>::=
INTO OUTFILE '<filename>' [<export option> [<export option>]]
| INTO DUMPFILE '<filename>'

<export option>::=
{FIELDS
    [TERMINATED BY '<value>']
    [[OPTIONALLY] ENCLOSED BY '<value>']
    [ESCAPED BY '<value>']}
| {LINES
```

```
    [STARTING BY '<value>']
    [TERMINATED BY '<value>']}

<table reference>::=
<table name> [[AS] <alias>]
[{USE | IGNORE | FORCE} INDEX <index name> [{, <index name>}...]]

<group by definition>::=
<column name> [ASC | DESC]
[{, <column name> [ASC | DESC]}...]
[WITH ROLLUP]

<order by definition>::=
<column name> [ASC | DESC]
[{, <column name> [ASC | DESC]}...]
```

As you can see from the syntax, a SELECT statement can contain a number of elements. For most of these elements, the chapter discusses each one in detail, providing the necessary examples to illustrate how they work; however, some elements are covered in later chapters. For example, the <export definition> option is discussed in Chapter 11, and the FOR UPDATE and the LOCK IN SHARE MODE options are discussed in Chapter 12. In addition, the PROCEDURE clause, which is used to call C++ procedures, is not discussed; it is beyond the scope of the book. It is included here only to provide you with the complete SELECT statement syntax.

Referring back to the syntax, notice that a SELECT syntax requires only the following clause:

```
SELECT
{* | <select list>}
```

The SELECT clause includes the SELECT keyword and an asterisk (*) or the select list, which is made up of columns or expressions, as shown in the following syntax:

```
<select list>::=
{<column name> | <expression>} [[AS] <alias>]
[{, {<column name> | <expression>} [[AS] <alias>]}...]
```

As you can see, the select list must include at least one column name or one expression. If more than one column/expression element is included, they must be separated by commas. In addition, you can assign an alias to a column name or expression by using the AS subclause. That alias can be then be used in other clauses in the SELECT statement; however, it cannot be used in a WHERE clause because of the way in which MySQL processes a SELECT statement.

As the syntax indicates, the AS keyword is optional when assigning an alias to a column. For the sake of clarity and to avoid confusion with other column names, it is generally recommended that you include the AS keyword.

Although the SELECT clause is the only required element in a SELECT statement, you cannot retrieve data from a table unless you also specify a FROM clause and the appropriate table references. The FROM clause requires one or more table references, separated by commas, as shown in the following syntax:

```
FROM <table reference> [{, <table reference>}...]

<table reference>::=
<table name> [[AS] <alias>]
[{USE | IGNORE | FORCE} INDEX <index name> [{, <index name>}...]]
```

Each table reference is made up of a table name and an optional AS subclause that allows you to assign an alias to a table. The FROM clause can include more than one table reference; however, multiple references are included only if you are joining two or more tables in your SELECT statement. In addition, you would generally assign a table alias or include a {USE | IGNORE | FORCE} INDEX clause only when joining a table. (Table joins are discussed in detail in Chapter 10.) When creating a SELECT statement that does not include joined tables, your FROM clause normally includes only the FROM keyword and the name of the target table.

As the syntax shows, creating a basic SELECT statement that retrieves data from only one table requires few components. To demonstrate how this works, take a look at a few examples. The examples in this chapter are all based on a table named CDs, which is shown in the following table definition:

```
CREATE TABLE CDs
(
    CDID SMALLINT NOT NULL AUTO_INCREMENT PRIMARY KEY,
    CDName VARCHAR(50) NOT NULL,
    InStock SMALLINT UNSIGNED NOT NULL,
    OnOrder SMALLINT UNSIGNED NOT NULL,
    Reserved SMALLINT UNSIGNED NOT NULL,
    Department ENUM('Classical', 'Popular') NOT NULL,
    Category VARCHAR(20) NOT NULL,
    RowUpdate TIMESTAMP NOT NULL
);
```

For the purposes of this chapter, you can assume that the following INSERT statement has been used to add data to the CDs table:

```
INSERT INTO CDs (CDName, InStock, OnOrder, Reserved, Department, Category)
VALUES ('Bloodshot', 10, 5, 3, 'Popular', 'Rock'),
('The Most Favorite Opera Duets', 10, 5, 3, 'Classical', 'Opera'),
('New Orleans Jazz', 17, 4, 1, 'Popular', 'Jazz'),
('Music for Ballet Class', 9, 4, 2, 'Classical', 'Dance'),
('Music for Solo Violin', 24, 2, 5, 'Classical', 'General'),
('Cie li di Toscana', 16, 6, 8, 'Classical', 'Vocal'),
('Mississippi Blues', 2, 25, 6, 'Popular', 'Blues'),
('Pure', 32, 3, 10, 'Popular', 'Jazz'),
('Mud on the Tires', 12, 15, 13, 'Popular', 'Country'),
('The Essence', 5, 20, 10, 'Popular', 'New Age'),
('Embrace', 24, 11, 14, 'Popular', 'New Age'),
('The Magic of Satie', 42, 17, 17, 'Classical', 'General'),
('Swan Lake', 25, 44, 28, 'Classical', 'Dance'),
('25 Classical Favorites', 32, 15, 12, 'Classical', 'General'),
('La Boheme', 20, 10, 5, 'Classical', 'Opera'),
('Bach Cantatas', 23, 12, 8, 'Classical', 'General'),
('Golden Road', 23, 10, 17, 'Popular', 'Country'),
('Live in Paris', 18, 20, 10, 'Popular', 'Jazz'),
('Richland Woman Blues', 22, 5, 7, 'Popular', 'Blues'),
```

```
('Morimur (after J. S. Bach)', 28, 17, 16, 'Classical', 'General'),
('The Best of Italian Opera', 10, 35, 12, 'Classical', 'Opera'),
('Runaway Soul', 15, 30, 14, 'Popular', 'Blues'),
('Stages', 42, 0, 8, 'Popular', 'Blues'),
('Bach: Six Unaccompanied Cello Suites', 16, 8, 8, 'Classical', 'General');
```

As you work your way through the chapter, you might want to refer to this CREATE TABLE statement and INSERT statement to reference the table and its contents as example SELECT statements are presented. Now take a look at a SELECT statement that accesses data in the CDs table:

```
SELECT * FROM CDs;
```

The statement includes a SELECT clause and a FROM clause. The SELECT clause includes the SELECT keyword and an asterisk. The asterisk indicates that the query should return all columns. The FROM clause includes the FROM keyword and the name of the CDs table. When you execute this statement, you should receive results similar to the following:

```
+------+--------------------------------------+---------+---------+----------+-----
| CDID | CDName                               | InStock | OnOrder | Reserved | Depa
+------+--------------------------------------+---------+---------+----------+-----
|    1 | Bloodshot                            |      10 |       5 |        3 | Popu
|    2 | The Most Favorite Opera Duets        |      10 |       5 |        3 | Clas
|    3 | New Orleans Jazz                     |      17 |       4 |        1 | Popu
|    4 | Music for Ballet Class               |       9 |       4 |        2 | Clas
|    5 | Music for Solo Violin                |      24 |       2 |        5 | Clas
|    6 | Cie li di Toscana                    |      16 |       6 |        8 | Clas
|    7 | Mississippi Blues                    |       2 |      25 |        6 | Popu
|    8 | Pure                                 |      32 |       3 |       10 | Popu
|    9 | Mud on the Tires                     |      12 |      15 |       13 | Popu
|   10 | The Essence                          |       5 |      20 |       10 | Popu
|   11 | Embrace                              |      24 |      11 |       14 | Popu
|   12 | The Magic of Satie                   |      42 |      17 |       17 | Clas
|   13 | Swan Lake                            |      25 |      44 |       28 | Clas
|   14 | 25 Classical Favorites               |      32 |      15 |       12 | Clas
|   15 | La Boheme                            |      20 |      10 |        5 | Clas
|   16 | Bach Cantatas                        |      23 |      12 |        8 | Clas
|   17 | Golden Road                          |      23 |      10 |       17 | Popu
|   18 | Live in Paris                        |      18 |      20 |       10 | Popu
|   19 | Richland Woman Blues                 |      22 |       5 |        7 | Popu
|   20 | Morimur (after J. S. Bach)           |      28 |      17 |       16 | Clas
|   21 | The Best of Italian Opera            |      10 |      35 |       12 | Clas
|   22 | Runaway Soul                         |      15 |      30 |       14 | Popu
|   23 | Stages                               |      42 |       0 |        8 | Popu
|   24 | Bach: Six Unaccompanied Cello Suites |      16 |       8 |        8 | Clas
+------+--------------------------------------+---------+---------+----------+-----
24 rows in set (0.00 sec)
```

Because the rows are so long, only a part of each row is displayed here. How these rows would appear on your system varies; however, the basic components should be the same. The important point to remember is that a SELECT clause that contains only an asterisk returns all columns in the table. In addition, all rows are returned as well because the SELECT statement has not been qualified in any way other than adding the optional FROM clause, which defines the table to access.

Although using an asterisk in the SELECT clause is an easy way to retrieve every column from a table, it is not a recommended method to use when embedding a SELECT statement in a programming language. Columns can change or be added or deleted from a table. Consequently, unless you're simply performing an ad hoc query and want to view a table's contents quickly, you should normally specify the column names, as shown in the following SELECT statement:

```
SELECT CDID, CDName, Category
FROM CDs;
```

Notice that, in this case, the query specifies three column names in the SELECT clause: CDID, CDName, and Category. Because these names are specified, only data from these three columns is returned by your query, as shown in the following results:

```
+------+------------------------------------+----------+
| CDID | CDName                             | Category |
+------+------------------------------------+----------+
|    1 | Bloodshot                          | Rock     |
|    2 | The Most Favorite Opera Duets      | Opera    |
|    3 | New Orleans Jazz                   | Jazz     |
|    4 | Music for Ballet Class             | Dance    |
|    5 | Music for Solo Violin              | General  |
|    6 | Cie li di Toscana                  | Vocal    |
|    7 | Mississippi Blues                  | Blues    |
|    8 | Pure                               | Jazz     |
|    9 | Mud on the Tires                   | Country  |
|   10 | The Essence                        | New Age  |
|   11 | Embrace                            | New Age  |
|   12 | The Magic of Satie                 | General  |
|   13 | Swan Lake                          | Dance    |
|   14 | 25 Classical Favorites             | General  |
|   15 | La Boheme                          | Opera    |
|   16 | Bach Cantatas                      | General  |
|   17 | Golden Road                        | Country  |
|   18 | Live in Paris                      | Jazz     |
|   19 | Richland Woman Blues               | Blues    |
|   20 | Morimur (after J. S. Bach)         | General  |
|   21 | The Best of Italian Opera          | Opera    |
|   22 | Runaway Soul                       | Blues    |
|   23 | Stages                             | Blues    |
|   24 | Bach: Six Unaccompanied Cello Suites | General |
+------+------------------------------------+----------+
24 rows in set (0.01 sec)
```

Notice that the same number of rows are returned here as were returned in the previous example; however, only three columns of data are displayed. Later in the chapter, you learn how to use the other optional clauses in the SELECT statement to refine your query even further. For now, return to the SELECT clause. If you refer to the select list syntax, you notice that for each element in the select list you can assign an alias, as shown in the following SELECT statement:

```
SELECT CDName AS Title, OnOrder AS Ordered
FROM CDs;
```

Notice that the CDName column is assigned the alias Title and the OnOrder column is assigned the alias Ordered. When you execute this statement, the alias names are used as column headings in your query results, as shown in the following results:

```
+---------------------------------------+---------+
| Title                                 | Ordered |
+---------------------------------------+---------+
| Bloodshot                             |       5 |
| The Most Favorite Opera Duets         |       5 |
| New Orleans Jazz                      |       4 |
| Music for Ballet Class                |       4 |
| Music for Solo Violin                 |       2 |
| Cie li di Toscana                     |       6 |
| Mississippi Blues                     |      25 |
| Pure                                  |       3 |
| Mud on the Tires                      |      15 |
| The Essence                           |      20 |
| Embrace                               |      11 |
| The Magic of Satie                    |      17 |
| Swan Lake                             |      44 |
| 25 Classical Favorites                |      15 |
| La Boheme                             |      10 |
| Bach Cantatas                         |      12 |
| Golden Road                           |      10 |
| Live in Paris                         |      20 |
| Richland Woman Blues                  |       5 |
| Morimur (after J. S. Bach)            |      17 |
| The Best of Italian Opera             |      35 |
| Runaway Soul                          |      30 |
| Stages                                |       0 |
| Bach: Six Unaccompanied Cello Suites  |       8 |
+---------------------------------------+---------+
24 rows in set (0.02 sec)
```

In a situation like this, in which column names are used rather than expressions and the column names are short and simple, supplying an alias isn't particularly beneficial. As you add expressions to your SELECT clause, create join conditions, or decide to clarify column names, aliases become very useful.

Once you've mastered the SELECT clause and the FROM clause, you can create a basic SELECT statement to query data in any table. In most cases, however, you want to limit the number of rows returned and control how data is displayed. For this, you need to add more clauses. These clauses, which are explained throughout the rest of the chapter, must be added to your statement in the order they are listed in the syntax. MySQL processes the clauses in a SELECT statement in a very specific order, so you must be aware of how clauses are defined in order to receive the results that you expect.

In the following Try It Out exercise, you create three SELECT statements, each of which retrieves data from the Employees table in the DVDRentals database.

Try It Out   **Creating a SELECT Statement**

The following steps describe how to create these statements:

1. Open the mysql client utility, type the following command, and press Enter:

```
use DVDRentals
```

You should receive a message indicating the switch to the DVDRentals database.

2. The first SELECT statement that you create retrieves all columns and all records from the Employees table. To retrieve the records, execute the following SELECT statement at the mysql command prompt:

```
SELECT * FROM Employees;
```

You should receive results similar to the following:

```
+-------+--------+-------+-----------+
| EmpID | EmpFN  | EmpMN | EmpLN     |
+-------+--------+-------+-----------+
|     1 | John   | P.    | Smith     |
|     2 | Robert | NULL  | Schroader |
|     3 | Mary   | Marie | Michaels  |
|     4 | John   | NULL  | Laguci    |
|     5 | Rita   | C.    | Carter    |
|     6 | George | NULL  | Brooks    |
+-------+--------+-------+-----------+
6 rows in set (0.23 sec)
```

3. Next, retrieve values only from the EmpFN and EmpLN columns of the Employees table. To retrieve the values, execute the following SELECT statement at the mysql command prompt:

```
SELECT EmpFN, EmpLN
FROM Employees;
```

You should receive results similar to the following:

```
+--------+-----------+
| EmpFN  | EmpLN     |
+--------+-----------+
| John   | Smith     |
| Robert | Schroader |
| Mary   | Michaels  |
| John   | Laguci    |
| Rita   | Carter    |
| George | Brooks    |
+--------+-----------+
6 rows in set (0.00 sec)
```

4. Now retrieve values from the same columns as the last step, but this time provide aliases for those columns. To retrieve the values, execute the following SELECT statement at the mysql command prompt:

```
SELECT EmpFN AS 'First Name', EmpLN AS 'Last Name'
FROM Employees;
```

You should receive results similar to the following:

```
+------------+-----------+
| First Name | Last Name |
+------------+-----------+
| John       | Smith     |
| Robert     | Schroader |
| Mary       | Michaels  |
| John       | Laguci    |
| Rita       | Carter    |
| George     | Brooks    |
+------------+-----------+
6 rows in set (0.01 sec)
```

How It Works

Whenever you create a SELECT statement that retrieves data from a table in a MySQL database, you must, at the very least, include a SELECT clause and a FROM clause. The SELECT clause determines which columns of values are returned and the FROM clause determines from which tables the data is retrieved. For example, the first SELECT statement that you created retrieves all columns from the Employees table, as shown in the following statement:

```
SELECT * FROM Employees;
```

This statement uses an asterisk to indicate that all columns should be retrieved. Your second SELECT statement specified which columns of data should be returned:

```
SELECT EmpFN, EmpLN
FROM Employees;
```

In this case, the query returns only values in the EmpFN and EmpLN columns because those are the columns specified in the SELECT clause. And as with the first SELECT statement in this exercise, the values were retrieved from the Employees table because that is the table specified in the FROM clause.

The last SELECT statement that you created in this exercise assigns aliases to the columns names, as shown in the following statement:

```
SELECT EmpFN AS 'First Name', EmpLN AS 'Last Name'
FROM Employees;
```

Notice that you assigned the EmpFN column the alias First Name and that you assigned the EmpLN column the alias Last Name. In both cases, you enclosed the aliases in a single quote because they were each made up of more than one word and the quotations were necessary to ensure that both words were considered part of the alias name.

Using Expressions in a SELECT Statement

Recalling from the select list syntax, your select list can include column names or expressions. Up to this point, the example SELECT statements that you've seen have included columns names. Expressions are also very useful in creating robust SELECT statements that can return the data necessary to your applications.

An expression, as you learned in Chapter 6, is a type of formula that helps define the value that the SELECT statement will return. An expression can include column names, literal values, operators, and functions. An operator is a symbol that represents the action that should be taken, such as comparing values or adding values together. For example, the minus (-) sign is an arithmetic operator that is used to subtract one value from another. Another example is the greater than (>) operator, which is a comparison operator used to compare values to determine if one value is greater than the other. (A comparison operator is a type of operator that compares two values.) A function is an object that carries out a predefined task. For example, you can use a function to specify the current date.

Although Chapter 8 discusses operators in greater detail and Chapter 9 discusses functions, both operators and functions are often an integral part of an expression, so some operators and functions are included here so that you can better understand how to use an expression in a SELECT clause. Keep in mind, however, that after you've learned more about operators and functions in Chapters 8 and 9, you will be able to create even more robust expressions in your SELECT clause or anywhere else that you can use expressions.

Now take a look at a SELECT statement that contains an expression in its select list. The statement is based on the table definition for the CDs table that you saw earlier in the chapter. The following statement retrieves information from several columns in the table:

```
SELECT CDName, InStock+OnOrder AS Total
FROM CDs;
```

The first element of the select list is the CDName column, which is included here in the same way that you've seen other column names added to a select list. The second element is an expression, though, rather than a column name. The expression (InStock+OnOrder) adds together the values from the InStock and OnOrder columns for each row returned by the SELECT statement. The expression is assigned the name Total, which is the name used in the query results to display the values, as the following results show:

```
+------------------------------------+-------+
| CDName                             | Total |
+------------------------------------+-------+
| Bloodshot                          |    15 |
| The Most Favorite Opera Duets      |    15 |
| New Orleans Jazz                   |    21 |
| Music for Ballet Class             |    13 |
| Music for Solo Violin              |    26 |
| Cie li di Toscana                  |    22 |
| Mississippi Blues                  |    27 |
| Pure                               |    35 |
| Mud on the Tires                   |    27 |
| The Essence                        |    25 |
| Embrace                            |    35 |
| The Magic of Satie                 |    59 |
| Swan Lake                          |    69 |
```

```
| 25 Classical Favorites                 |    47 |
| La Boheme                              |    30 |
| Bach Cantatas                          |    35 |
| Golden Road                            |    33 |
| Live in Paris                          |    38 |
| Richland Woman Blues                   |    27 |
| Morimur (after J. S. Bach)             |    45 |
| The Best of Italian Opera              |    45 |
| Runaway Soul                           |    45 |
| Stages                                 |    42 |
| Bach: Six Unaccompanied Cello Suites   |    24 |
+----------------------------------------+-------+
24 rows in set (0.00 sec)
```

As you can see, the query returns two columns: the CDName column and the Total column. The values in the Total column are based on the expression defined in the SELECT clause. If you refer back to the original values that you added to the table, you would see that these values are based on the total from the two columns. For example, in the first row, the CDName value is Bloodshot and the Total value is 15. Currently in the CDs table, the InStock value is 10 and the OnOrder value is 5. When added together, the total is 15, which is the amount inserted in the Total column of the result set.

You can also create expressions in your select list that are more complex than the one in the last statement. For example, the following SELECT statement is similar to the last, except that the expression in the select list now subtracts the Reserved value from the total:

```
SELECT CDName, InStock+OnOrder-Reserved AS Total
FROM CDs;
```

To arrive at the value in the Total column, the InStock and OnOrder values are added together, and then the Reserved value is subtracted from this total, as shown in the following results:

```
+----------------------------------------+-------+
| CDName                                 | Total |
+----------------------------------------+-------+
| Bloodshot                              |    12 |
| The Most Favorite Opera Duets          |    12 |
| New Orleans Jazz                       |    20 |
| Music for Ballet Class                 |    11 |
| Music for Solo Violin                  |    21 |
| Cie li di Toscana                      |    14 |
| Mississippi Blues                      |    21 |
| Pure                                   |    25 |
| Mud on the Tires                       |    14 |
| The Essence                            |    15 |
| Embrace                                |    21 |
| The Magic of Satie                     |    42 |
| Swan Lake                              |    41 |
| 25 Classical Favorites                 |    35 |
| La Boheme                              |    25 |
| Bach Cantatas                          |    27 |
| Golden Road                            |    16 |
| Live in Paris                          |    28 |
```

```
| Richland Woman Blues                 |    20 |
| Morimur (after J. S. Bach)           |    29 |
| The Best of Italian Opera            |    33 |
| Runaway Soul                         |    31 |
| Stages                               |    34 |
| Bach: Six Unaccompanied Cello Suites |    16 |
+--------------------------------------+-------+
24 rows in set (0.00 sec)
```

For each row that the SELECT statement returns, the expression is calculated and the result inserted in the Total column. When you use arithmetic operators in an expression, the components of that expression are evaluated according to the basic formulaic principles of mathematics. In Chapter 8, where operators are discussed in greater detail, you learn more about how an expression is evaluated based on the operators used in that expression.

As you have seen, you can specify column names or expressions in the SELECT clause. In the following exercise, you create a SELECT statement that includes an expression.

Try It Out   Adding Expressions to Your Select List

Follow these steps to add expressions to your select list:

1. Open the mysql client utility, type the following command, and press Enter:

```
use DVDRentals
```

You should receive a message indicating that you switched to the DVDRentals database.

2. To retrieve the records from the Employees table, execute the following SELECT statement at the mysql command prompt:

```
SELECT EmpID, EmpFN, EmpLN
FROM Employees;
```

You should receive results similar to the following:

```
+-------+--------+-----------+
| EmpID | EmpFN  | EmpLN     |
+-------+--------+-----------+
|     1 | John   | Smith     |
|     2 | Robert | Schroader |
|     3 | Mary   | Michaels  |
|     4 | John   | Laguci    |
|     5 | Rita   | Carter    |
|     6 | George | Brooks    |
+-------+--------+-----------+
6 rows in set (0.03 sec)
```

How It Works

In this exercise, you created a SELECT statement that included a SELECT clause that contained three select list elements, as shown in the following statement:

```
SELECT EmpID, EmpFN, EmpLN
FROM Employees;
```

The three select list elements consist of the name of columns in the Employees table. Because the columns are included here, the SELECT statement returns values from those columns (as they appear in the Employees table).

Using Variables in a SELECT Statement

One type of expression that you can include in your select list is one that allows you to define a variable. A *variable* is a type of placeholder that holds a value for the duration of a client session. This is useful if you want to reuse a value in later SELECT statements.

You define a variable by using the following structure:

```
@<variable name>:={<column name> | <expression>} [[AS] <alias>]
```

The variable name must always be preceded by the at (@) symbol, and the variable value must always be specified by using the colon/equal sign (:=) symbols. In addition, a variable can be associated with only one value, so your SELECT statement should return only one value per variable. If your SELECT statement returns more than one value for a variable, the last value returned is used by the variable. If you want to define more than one variable in a SELECT statement, you must define each one as a separate select list element. For example, the following SELECT statement defines two variables:

```
SELECT @dept:=Department, @cat:=Category
FROM CDs
WHERE CDName='Mississippi Blues';
```

When you execute this statement, the values from the Department column and the Category column are stored in the appropriate variables. For example, the row in the CDs table that contains a CDName of Mississippi Blues contains a Department value of Popular and a Category value of Blues. As a result, the Popular value is assigned to the @dept variable, and the Blues value is assigned to the @cat variable. When you execute the SELECT statement, you should receive results similar to the following:

```
+------------------+----------------+
| @dept:=Department | @cat:=Category |
+------------------+----------------+
| Popular          | Blues          |
+------------------+----------------+
1 row in set (0.26 sec)
```

As you can see, your result set displays the values assigned to your variables. Once you've assigned values to your variables, you can then use them in other SELECT statements, as shown in the following example:

```
SELECT CDID, CDName, InStock+OnOrder-Reserved AS Available
FROM CDs
WHERE Department=@dept AND Category=@cat;
```

The first thing that you might notice in this SELECT statement is that it contains a WHERE clause. Although WHERE clauses are discussed in greater detail later in the chapter — see the section "The WHERE Clause" — they are used here to demonstrate how to use the variables to refine your SELECT statement. In this case, the WHERE clause includes two conditions. In the first (Department=@dept), the condition specifies that any rows returned must contain a Department value that equals the @dept variable value, which is Popular. The second condition (`Category=@cat`) specifies that any rows returned must also contain a Category value that equals the `@cat` variable value of Blues. When you execute this statement, you should receive results similar to the following:

```
+------+-----------------------+-----------+
| CDID | CDName                | Available |
+------+-----------------------+-----------+
|    7 | Mississippi Blues     |        21 |
|   19 | Richland Woman Blues  |        20 |
|   22 | Runaway Soul          |        31 |
|   23 | Stages                |        34 |
+------+-----------------------+-----------+
4 rows in set (0.07 sec)
```

Notice that four rows are returned. If you refer to the original values that were inserted in the CDs table, you'll find that each of these rows has a Department value of Popular and a Category value of Blues.

Also note that, in addition to a SELECT statement, you can use a SET statement to define a variable. For example, the following SET statement defines the same two variables you saw previously:

```
SET @dept='Popular', @cat='Blues';
```

In this case, rather than setting the variable values based on values returned by a SELECT statement, you can specify the values directly, as shown here. You can then use the variables in subsequent SELECT statements in your client session, as you would variables defined in a SELECT statement. In either case, the variables are usable for only as long as the client session lasts.

In the following Try It Out, you create a SELECT statement that defines a variable, and you then use that variable in a second SELECT statement.

Try It Out   Defining Variables in Your SELECT Statement

To create these statements, follow these steps:

1. Open the mysql client utility, type the following command, and press Enter:

```
use DVDRentals
```

You should receive a message indicating that you switched to the DVDRentals database.

2. You must first define the variable. To define the variable, execute the following SELECT statement at the mysql command prompt:

```
SELECT @rating:=RatingID
FROM DVDs
WHERE DVDName='White Christmas';
```

You should receive results similar to the following:

```
+-------------------+
| @rating:=RatingID |
+-------------------+
| NR                |
+-------------------+
1 row in set (0.00 sec)
```

3. After creating the variable, you can use it in a SELECT statement. To use the variable to retrieve records from the DVDs table, execute the following SELECT statement at the mysql command prompt:

```
SELECT DVDID, DVDName, MTypeID
FROM DVDs
WHERE RatingID=@rating;
```

You should receive results similar to the following:

```
+-------+-----------------------------+---------+
| DVDID | DVDName                     | MTypeID |
+-------+-----------------------------+---------+
|     1 | White Christmas             | mt16    |
|     4 | The Maltese Falcon          | mt11    |
|     6 | The Rocky Horror Picture Show | mt12  |
|     7 | A Room with a View          | mt11    |
+-------+-----------------------------+---------+
4 rows in set (0.00 sec)
```

How It Works

As you have seen, you can use a SELECT statement to define a variable that you can then use in later SELECT statements. In the first SELECT statement that you created in this exercise, you defined the @rating variable, as shown in the following statement:

```
SELECT @rating:=RatingID
FROM DVDs
WHERE DVDName='White Christmas';
```

The @rating variable is assigned a value based on the RatingID value in the DVDs table. Because the WHERE clause specifies that only the row with a DVDName value of White Christmas should be returned, the RatingID value in that row is the one that is assigned to the @rating variable. As a result, @rating is assigned a value of NR. (Had the SELECT statement returned more than one value, the last value returned would have been used by the variable.)

The next SELECT statement uses the @rating variable to specify that only columns that contain a RatingID value equal to the @rating variable value should be returned, as shown in the following SELECT statement:

```
SELECT DVDID, DVDName, MTypeID
FROM DVDs
WHERE RatingID=@rating;
```

Because @rating is assigned a value of NR, this SELECT statement returns only rows that contain a RatingID value of NR.

Using a SELECT Statement to Display Values

When this chapter first introduced you to the SELECT statement syntax, you may have noticed that nearly all elements of the statement are optional. Although your SELECT statements normally include a

FROM clause, along with other optional clauses and options, these elements are all considered optional because you can use a SELECT statement to return values that are not based on data in a table.

When using only the required elements of a SELECT statement, you need to specify only the SELECT keyword and one or more elements of the select list. The select list can contain literal values, operators, and functions, but no column names. For example, the following SELECT statement includes three select list elements:

```
SELECT 1+3, 'CD Inventory', NOW() AS 'Date/Time';
```

The first select list element (1+3) demonstrates how you can use a SELECT statement to perform calculations. The second select list element ('CD Inventory') is a literal value that simply returns the string enclosed in the single quotes. The third select list element (NOW() AS 'Date/Time') uses a NOW() function to return the current date and time. The element also includes an AS subclause that assigns the name Date/Time to the column returned by the statement. If you execute the SELECT statement, you should receive results similar to the following:

```
+-----+--------------+---------------------+
| 1+3 | CD Inventory | Date/Time           |
+-----+--------------+---------------------+
|   4 | CD Inventory | 2004-08-24 11:39:40 |
+-----+--------------+---------------------+
1 row in set (0.00 sec)
```

As you can see, the first select list element is calculated and a value is returned, the second element returns the literal value, and the third element returns the date and time. Notice that the names of the first two columns in the results set are based on the select list elements because you assigned no alias to those expressions.

As you have seen, you can use a SELECT statement to return values that are not tied to a specific table. The following Try It Out describes how to create SELECT statements that return values.

Try It Out   Returning Values from a SELECT Statement

Follow these steps to create a SELECT statement that returns values:

1.   Open the mysql client utility, type the following command, and press Enter:

```
use DVDRentals
```

You should receive a message indicating that you switched to the DVDRentals database.

2.   The first SELECT statement that you create includes one expression. Execute the following SELECT statement at the mysql command prompt:

```
SELECT 1+8+2;
```

You should receive results similar to the following:

```
+-------+
| 1+8+2 |
+-------+
|    11 |
+-------+
1 row in set (0.00 sec)
```

3. The next SELECT statement includes two expressions. Execute the following SELECT statement at the mysql command prompt:

```
SELECT 'DVDRentals Database', NOW();
```

You should receive results similar to the following:

```
+---------------------+---------------------+
| DVDRentals Database | NOW()               |
+---------------------+---------------------+
| DVDRentals Database | 2004-08-25 14:07:07 |
+---------------------+---------------------+
1 row in set (0.03 sec)
```

How It Works

In this exercise, you created two SELECT statements that return values other than data contained in a table. The first table simply added several numbers together to produce a total, as shown in the following statement:

```
SELECT 1+8+2;
```

As you can see, you needed to specify only the SELECT keyword and the select list element, which added the numbers 1, 8, and 2 together. When you executed the statement, you should have received a total value of 11.

The next SELECT statement that you executed included two select list elements, as the following statement shows:

```
SELECT 'DVDRentals Database', NOW();
```

The first select list element was a literal value enclosed in single quotes. The second element was the NOW() function. When you executed the SELECT statement, the results included the literal string value of DVDRentals Database and the current date and time.

The SELECT Statement Options

When you create a SELECT statement, your SELECT clause can include one or more options that are specified before the select list. The options define how a SELECT statement is processed and, for the most part, how it applies to the statement as a whole, rather to the specific data returned. As the following syntax shows, you can include a number of options in a SELECT statement:

```
<select option>::=
{ALL | DISTINCT | DISTINCTROW}
| HIGH_PRIORITY
| {SQL_BIG_RESULT | SQL_SMALL_RESULT}
| SQL_BUFFER_RESULT
| {SQL_CACHE | SQL_NO_CACHE}
| SQL_CALC_FOUND_ROWS
| STRAIGHT_JOIN
```

The following table describes each of the options that you can include in a SELECT statement.

Option	Description
ALL DISTINCT DISTINCTROW	The ALL option specifies that a query should return all rows, even if there are duplicate rows. The DISTINCT and DISTINCTROW options, which have the same meaning in MySQL, specify that duplicate rows should not be included in the result set. If neither option is specified, ALL is assumed.
HIGH_PRIORITY	The HIGH_PRIORITY option prioritizes the SELECT statement over statements that write data to the target table. Use this option only for SELECT statements that you know will execute quickly.
SQL_BIG_RESULT SQL_SMALL_RESULT	The SQL_BIG_RESULT option informs the MySQL optimizer that the result set will include a large number of rows, which helps the optimizer to process the query more efficiently. The SQL_SMALL_RESULT option informs the MySQL optimizer that the result set will include a small number of rows.
SQL_BUFFER_RESULT	The SQL_BUFFER_RESULT option tells MySQL to place the query results in a temporary table in order to release table locks sooner than they would normally be released. This option is particularly useful for large result sets that take a long time to return to the client.
SQL_CACHE SQL_NO_CACHE	The SQL_CACHE option tells MySQL to cache the query results if the cache is operating in demand mode. The SQL_NO_CACHE option tells MySQL not to cache the query results.
SQL_CALC_FOUND_ROWS	You use the SQL_CALC_FOUND_ROWS option in conjunction with the LIMIT clause. The option specifies what the row count of a result set would be if the LIMIT clause were not used.
STRAIGHT_JOIN	You use the STRAIGHT_JOIN option when joining tables in a SELECT statement. The option tells the optimizer to join the tables in the order specified in the FROM clause. You should use this option to speed up a query if you think that the optimizer is not joining the tables efficiently.

To specify an option in a SELECT statement, you must add it after the SELECT keyword, as shown in the following SELECT statement:

```
SELECT ALL Department, Category
FROM CDs;
```

This statement uses the ALL option to specify that all rows should be included in the result set, even if there are duplicates. The select list follows the ALL keyword. The list includes the Department and

Category columns of the CDs table. As a result, all rows are returned from these two columns, as shown in the following results:

```
+------------+----------+
| Department | Category |
+------------+----------+
| Popular    | Rock     |
| Classical  | Opera    |
| Popular    | Jazz     |
| Classical  | Dance    |
| Classical  | General  |
| Classical  | Vocal    |
| Popular    | Blues    |
| Popular    | Jazz     |
| Popular    | Country  |
| Popular    | New Age  |
| Popular    | New Age  |
| Classical  | General  |
| Classical  | Dance    |
| Classical  | General  |
| Classical  | Opera    |
| Classical  | General  |
| Popular    | Country  |
| Popular    | Jazz     |
| Popular    | Blues    |
| Classical  | General  |
| Classical  | Opera    |
| Popular    | Blues    |
| Popular    | Blues    |
| Classical  | General  |
+------------+----------+
24 rows in set (0.00 sec)
```

As you can see, there are duplicate rows in the result set. For example, there are a number of rows that contain a Department value of Popular and a Category value of Blues. You can eliminate these duplicates by using the DISTINCT option, rather then the ALL option, as shown in the following statement:

```
SELECT DISTINCT Department, Category
FROM CDs;
```

As you can see, this SELECT statement is identical to the previous statement except for the DISTINCT option. If you execute this statement, you should receive results similar to the following:

```
+------------+----------+
| Department | Category |
+------------+----------+
| Popular    | Rock     |
| Classical  | Opera    |
| Popular    | Jazz     |
| Classical  | Dance    |
| Classical  | General  |
| Classical  | Vocal    |
| Popular    | Blues    |
| Popular    | Country  |
| Popular    | New Age  |
+------------+----------+
9 rows in set (0.02 sec)
```

Notice that only 9 rows are returned (as opposed to 24 rows in the previous statement). Also notice that the result set no longer contains duplicate rows. Although values are repeated in the Department column, no rows, when the values are taken as a whole, are repeated.

You can also specify multiple options in your SELECT clause, as the following example shows:

```
SELECT DISTINCT HIGH_PRIORITY Department, Category
FROM CDs;
```

Notice that the SELECT clause includes the DISTINCT option and the HIGH_PRIORITY option. Because the HIGH_PRIORITY option has no impact on the values returned, your result set looks the same as the result set in the previous example.

As you have seen, you can add one or more options to your SELECT statement that define the behavior of that statement. For this exercise, you use the ALL and DISTINCT options to return data from the DVDs table of the DVDRentals database.

Try It Out   **Adding Options to Your SELECT Statement**

To create the necessary SELECT statement, use the following steps:

1. Open the mysql client utility, type the following command, and press Enter:

```
use DVDRentals
```

You should receive a message indicating that you switched to the DVDRentals database.

2. In the first SELECT statement, you specify the ALL option to retrieve records from the DVDs table. Execute the following SELECT statement at the mysql command prompt:

```
SELECT ALL RatingID, StatID
FROM DVDs;
```

You should receive results similar to the following:

```
+----------+--------+
| RatingID | StatID |
+----------+--------+
| NR       | s1     |
| G        | s2     |
| PG       | s1     |
| NR       | s2     |
| PG       | s2     |
| NR       | s2     |
| NR       | s1     |
| R        | s2     |
+----------+--------+
8 rows in set (0.00 sec)
```

3. Now execute the same SELECT statement as in the last step, only this time use the DISTINCT option, rather than the ALL option. Execute the following SELECT statement at the mysql command prompt:

```
SELECT DISTINCT RatingID, StatID
FROM DVDs;
```

You should receive results similar to the following:

```
+----------+--------+
| RatingID | StatID |
+----------+--------+
| NR       | s1     |
| G        | s2     |
| PG       | s1     |
| NR       | s2     |
| PG       | s2     |
| R        | s2     |
+----------+--------+
6 rows in set (0.01 sec)
```

How It Works

In this exercise, you created two SELECT statements, one that included the ALL option and one that included the DISTINCT option. The first statement was as follows:

```
SELECT ALL RatingID, StatID
FROM DVDs;
```

By specifying the ALL option, all rows were returned, whether or not there were duplicates. Each row was made up of values from the RatingID column and the StatID column. Overall, eight rows were returned. The second statement, however, included the DISTINCT keyword rather than the ALL keyword, as shown in the following statement.

```
SELECT DISTINCT RatingID, StatID
FROM DVDs;
```

When you executed this statement, only six rows were returned, and no rows were duplicated, although values were duplicated in the individual columns.

The Optional Clauses of a SELECT Statement

As you saw earlier in the chapter, the SELECT statement syntax includes a number of optional clauses that help you define which rows your SELECT statement returns and how those rows display. Of particular importance to creating an effective SELECT statement are the WHERE, GROUP BY, HAVING, ORDER BY, and LIMIT clauses. As you learned earlier, any of these clauses that you include in your SELECT statement must be defined in the order that they are specified in the syntax. The remaining part of the chapter discusses each of these clauses and explains how they must be defined to include them in your SELECT statements.

The WHERE Clause

Earlier in the chapter, you saw how you can use a SELECT clause to identify the columns that a SELECT statement returns and how to use a FROM clause to identify the table from which the data is retrieved. In this section, you look at the WHERE clause, which allows you to specify which rows in your table are returned by your query.

The WHERE clause is made up of one or more conditions that define the parameters of the SELECT statement. Each condition is an expression that can consist of column names, literal values, operators, and functions. The following syntax describes how a WHERE clause is defined:

```
WHERE <expression> [{<operator> <expression>}...]
```

As you can see, a WHERE clause must contain at least one expression that defines which rows the SELECT statement returns. When you specify more than one condition in the WHERE clause, those conditions are connected by an AND or an OR operator. The operators specify which condition or combination of conditions must be met.

Now take a look at an example to help demonstrate how a WHERE clause is defined in a SELECT statement. The following SELECT statement contains a WHERE clause that defines a single condition:

```
SELECT CDName, InStock+OnOrder-Reserved AS Available
FROM CDs
WHERE Category='Blues';
```

The WHERE clause indicates that only rows with a Category value of Blues should be returned as part of the result set. Because the SELECT clause specifies the CDName column and an expression that is assigned the alias Available, only those two columns are included in the result set, as shown in the following results:

```
+----------------------+-----------+
| CDName               | Available |
+----------------------+-----------+
| Mississippi Blues    |        21 |
| Richland Woman Blues |        20 |
| Runaway Soul         |        31 |
| Stages               |        34 |
+----------------------+-----------+
4 rows in set (0.01 sec)
```

Although the Category column is not displayed in the result set, each of these rows has a Category value of Blues. Because only four rows in the table have a Category value of Blues, only four rows are returned.

In this last example, the WHERE clause defined only one condition. You can define multiple conditions in a clause, though, as the following example demonstrates:

```
SELECT CDName, InStock+OnOrder-Reserved AS Available
FROM CDs
WHERE Category='Blues' AND (InStock+OnOrder-Reserved)>30;
```

As you can see, the WHERE clause first specifies that the Category value for each row must be Blues. The WHERE clause also includes a second condition, which contains an expression that adds the values of the InStock and OnOrder columns and then subtracts the value in the Reserved column. This total is then compared to the literal value of 30. The comparison is based on the greater than (>) comparison operator (covered in greater detail in Chapter 8), which indicates that the value on the left must be greater than the value on the right in order for the condition to evaluate to true. Because the two conditions are connected by an AND operator, both conditions must be true in order for a row to be returned. In other words, for each row, the Category value must equal Blues *and* the calculation derived from InStock, OnOrder, and Reserved columns must equal an amount greater than 30.

As you might have noticed, the SELECT clause includes an expression that calculates the same three columns in the same way as they are calculated in the WHERE clause. In addition, the expression in the SELECT clause is assigned the name Available. You would think that, because the same format is used in the WHERE clause, you should be able to refer to the Available expression in the WHERE clause so that you can simply write the expression as Available>30. Because of the way in which MySQL processes SELECT statements, you cannot use column aliases in the WHERE clause. Consequently, you must write out the expression as it is done here.

> *Another alternative is to add a* HAVING *clause to your* SELECT *statement. In that clause, you can use column aliases.* HAVING *clauses are discussed later in the chapter.*

If you were to execute the SELECT statement, you would receive results similar to the following:

```
+--------------+-----------+
| CDName       | Available |
+--------------+-----------+
| Runaway Soul |        31 |
| Stages       |        34 |
+--------------+-----------+
2 rows in set (0.00 sec)
```

In this case, only two rows are returned. For each row, the Category value equals Blues and the calculation of the three columns returns an amount greater than 30.

The next example SELECT statement is similar to the last, except that it adds an additional condition to the WHERE clause and the calculated columns must have a total greater than 20, rather than 30, as shown in the following statement:

```
SELECT CDName, Category, InStock+OnOrder-Reserved AS Available
FROM CDs
WHERE (Category='Blues' OR Category='Jazz')
   AND (InStock+OnOrder-Reserved)>20;
```

As you can see, the WHERE clause now specifies that the Category value can equal Jazz. Because the OR operator is used to connect the first two conditions, either condition can be met in order for a row to be returned. In other words, a row must contain a Category value of Blues, *or* it must contain a Category value of Jazz. In addition, the three calculated columns must include a total greater than 20. When you execute this query, you should receive results similar to the following:

```
+-------------------+----------+-----------+
| CDName            | Category | Available |
+-------------------+----------+-----------+
| Mississippi Blues | Blues    |        21 |
| Pure              | Jazz     |        25 |
| Live in Paris     | Jazz     |        28 |
| Runaway Soul      | Blues    |        31 |
| Stages            | Blues    |        34 |
+-------------------+----------+-----------+
5 rows in set (0.00 sec)
```

For each row included in the results set, the Category value is Blues *or* Jazz, *and* the Available value is greater than 20. One thing to note about the WHERE clause in this statement is that the first two conditions are enclosed in parentheses. This is done to ensure that these conditions are grouped together and processed properly. Without the parentheses, MySQL would interpret this to mean that each row must contain a Category value of Blues, or each row must contain a Category value of Jazz and an Available value greater than 20. This would return a result set that included every row with a Category value of Blues and only those rows that had a Category value of Jazz and an Available value greater than 20. The Available value would apply only to the Jazz rows, not the Blues rows.

In general, when specifying more than two conditions in a WHERE clause, it is often a good idea to use parentheses to make the meaning clear, unless the meaning of the clauses is absolutely certain (for example, if you use three conditions connected by OR operators).

In the following exercise, you create SELECT statements that each contain a WHERE clause that determines which rows are returned from the DVDs table.

Try It Out   Defining a WHERE Clause in Your SELECT Statement

To create these statements, follow these steps:

1. Open the mysql client utility, type the following command, and press Enter:

```
use DVDRentals
```

You should receive a message indicating that you switched to the DVDRentals database.

2. The first SELECT statement includes a WHERE clause that contains one condition. Execute the following SELECT statement at the mysql command prompt:

```
SELECT DVDName, MTypeID
FROM DVDs
WHERE StatID='s2';
```

You should receive results similar to the following:

```
+------------------------------+---------+
| DVDName                      | MTypeID |
+------------------------------+---------+
| What's Up, Doc?              | mt12    |
| The Maltese Falcon           | mt11    |
| Amadeus                      | mt11    |
| The Rocky Horror Picture Show| mt12    |
| Mash                         | mt12    |
+------------------------------+---------+
5 rows in set (0.00 sec)
```

3. Now amend the SELECT statement that you created in the previous step to include multiple conditions in the WHERE clause. Execute the following SELECT statement at the mysql command prompt:

```
SELECT DVDName, MTypeID
FROM DVDs
WHERE StatID='s1' OR StatID='s3' OR StatID='s4';
```

You should receive results similar to the following:

```
+--------------------+---------+
| DVDName            | MTypeID |
+--------------------+---------+
| White Christmas    | mt16    |
| Out of Africa      | mt11    |
| A Room with a View | mt11    |
+--------------------+---------+
3 rows in set (0.00 sec)
```

4. The next SELECT statement also includes multiple conditions in the WHERE clause; this time use an OR and an AND operator. Execute the following SELECT statement at the mysql command prompt:

```
SELECT DVDName, MTypeID
FROM DVDs
WHERE StatID='s2' AND (RatingID='NR' OR RatingID='G');
```

You should receive results similar to the following:

```
+-------------------------------+---------+
| DVDName                       | MTypeID |
+-------------------------------+---------+
| What's Up, Doc?               | mt12    |
| The Maltese Falcon            | mt11    |
| The Rocky Horror Picture Show | mt12    |
+-------------------------------+---------+
3 rows in set (0.00 sec)
```

How It Works

In this exercise, you created three SELECT statements that each contained a WHERE clause. In the first statement the WHERE clause included only one condition, as shown in the following statement:

```
SELECT DVDName, MTypeID
FROM DVDs
WHERE StatID='s2';
```

The condition in this WHERE clause specifies that the query should return only rows with a StatID value of s2. As a result, this query returned only five rows, and each of those rows had a StatID value of s2.

In the next SELECT statement that you created, you included a WHERE clause that specified three conditions, as the following statement shows:

```
SELECT DVDName, MTypeID
FROM DVDs
WHERE StatID='s1' OR StatID='s3' OR StatID='s4';
```

In this case, you connected the three conditions with OR operators. This means that each row returned by the SELECT statement had to contain a StatID value of s1 *or* s3 *or* s4. Because only three rows contained any one of these values, only those rows were returned.

In the final SELECT statement that you created in this exercise, you also included three conditions in the WHERE clause, as shown in the following statement:

```
SELECT DVDName, MTypeID
FROM DVDs
WHERE StatID='s2' AND (RatingID='NR' OR RatingID='G');
```

The first WHERE clause condition specifies that each row returned must have a StatID value of S2. In addition, each row must also have a RatingID value of NR *or* a RatingID value of G. Notice that these two conditions are enclosed in parentheses to ensure that MySQL evaluates the conditions correctly. Another way to look at this is that any row returned by this statement must have a StatID value of s2 and a RatingID value of NR, or the row must have a StatID value of s2 and a RatingID value of G. In this case, only three rows met the conditions specified in the WHERE clause.

The GROUP BY Clause

Up to this point in the chapter, the components of the SELECT statement that you have been introduced to mostly have to do with returning values from columns and rows. Even when your SELECT clause included an expression, that expression usually performed some type of operation on the values in a column. The GROUP BY clause is a little different from the other elements in the SELECT statement in the way that it is used to group values and summarize information.

Take a look at the syntax to see how this works:

```
GROUP BY <group by definition>

<group by definition>::=
<column name> [ASC | DESC]
[{, <column name> [ASC | DESC]}...]
[WITH ROLLUP]
```

The GROUP BY clause includes the GROUP BY keywords and the group by definition. The definition must include at least one column, although it can include more than one. If multiple columns are specified, you must separate them with commas.

When you specify a GROUP BY clause, rows are grouped together according to values in the column or columns specified in the clause. As a result, you should group rows only for those columns that contain repeated values. For example, you would not want to group a primary key column because each value is unique, so the GROUP BY process would have no practical application. Columns that are more general in nature, such as categories or types, make good candidates for GROUP BY operations because you can derive meaningful summary values for these sorts of columns.

After you've seen a few examples of how to use a GROUP BY clause, you'll get a better sense of how this works. Before looking at any examples, return to the syntax. As you can see, for each column that you specify in the GROUP BY clause, you can also specify that the grouped values be returned in ascending order (the ASC option) or descending order (the DESC option). If neither option is specified, the ASC option is assumed.

In addition to a list of the grouped columns, a GROUP BY clause can include the WITH ROLLUP option. This option provides additional rows of summary information, depending on the number of columns specified. The WITH ROLLUP option is best explained through the use of examples. Later in this section, you see how the option can provide additional summary information.

In order to use a GROUP BY clause effectively, you should also include a select list element that contains a function that summarizes the data returned by the SELECT statement. For example, suppose you want to know how many compact disk titles are listed in the CDs table for each category. To find out the number, you can use the following SELECT statement:

```
SELECT Category, COUNT(*) AS Total
FROM CDs
WHERE Department='Popular'
GROUP BY Category;
```

As the example shows, the SELECT clause includes the Category column and the COUNT(*) expression (which is assigned the alias Total). The COUNT() function calculates the number of rows for the specified column or for the table as a whole. Because you use an asterisk instead of a column name, all the rows in the table are counted. If you specify a column name and that column contains NULL values, the rows that contain NULL are not counted. (See Chapter 9 for more information about the COUNT() function and other functions that you can use when working with summarized data.)

After the SELECT clause, the FROM clause specifies the CDs table, and the WHERE clause specifies that only rows with a Department value that equals Popular should be returned. The GROUP BY clause then specifies that the rows should be grouped together according to the values in the Category column. As a result, only one row is returned for each unique Category value, as shown in the following result set:

```
+----------+-------+
| Category | Total |
+----------+-------+
| Blues    |     4 |
| Country  |     2 |
| Jazz     |     3 |
| New Age  |     2 |
| Rock     |     1 |
+----------+-------+
5 rows in set (0.08 sec)
```

As you can see, each Category value is listed only once, and a total is provided for each category. For example, the CDs table contains four Blues compact disks and two Country compact discs. Notice that the values in the Category column are listed in ascending order (alphabetically) because this is the default sort order for grouped columns.

Now take a look at an example that specifies two columns in the GROUP BY clause:

```
SELECT Department, Category, COUNT(*) AS Total
FROM CDs
GROUP BY Department, Category;
```

As you can see, the SELECT clause includes the Department and Category columns and the COUNT(*) expression (assigned the alias Total). The GROUP BY clause also includes the Department and Category columns. As a result, the SELECT statement first groups the result set according to the Department values and then according to the Category column, as shown in the following results:

```
+------------+----------+-------+
| Department | Category | Total |
+------------+----------+-------+
| Classical  | Dance    |     2 |
| Classical  | General  |     6 |
| Classical  | Opera    |     3 |
| Classical  | Vocal    |     1 |
| Popular    | Blues    |     4 |
| Popular    | Country  |     2 |
| Popular    | Jazz     |     3 |
| Popular    | New Age  |     2 |
| Popular    | Rock     |     1 |
+------------+----------+-------+
9 rows in set (0.00 sec)
```

As the result set shows, the Classical department includes four categories, and the Popular department includes five categories. For each category, the number of rows returned by that category is listed in the Total column. For example, the Dance category in the Classical department contains two compact disk titles.

Now take this same statement and add the WITH ROLLUP option to the GROUP BY clause, as shown in the following example:

```
SELECT Department, Category, COUNT(*) AS Total
FROM CDs
GROUP BY Department, Category WITH ROLLUP;
```

When you execute this statement, you should receive results similar to the following:

```
+------------+----------+-------+
| Department | Category | Total |
+------------+----------+-------+
| Classical  | Dance    |     2 |
| Classical  | General  |     6 |
| Classical  | Opera    |     3 |
| Classical  | Vocal    |     1 |
| Classical  | NULL     |    12 |
| Popular    | Blues    |     4 |
| Popular    | Country  |     2 |
| Popular    | Jazz     |     3 |
| Popular    | New Age  |     2 |
| Popular    | Rock     |     1 |
| Popular    | NULL     |    12 |
| NULL       | NULL     |    24 |
+------------+----------+-------+
12 rows in set (0.00 sec)
```

Notice the several additional rows in the result set. For example, the fifth row (the last Classical entry) includes NULL in the Category column and 12 in the Total column. The WITH ROLLUP option provides summary data for the first column specified in the GROUP BY clause, as well as the second column. As this shows, there are a total of 12 Classical compact disks listed in the CDs table. A summarized value is also provided for the Popular department. There are 12 Popular compact disks as well. The last row in the result set provides a total for all compact disks. As the Total value shows, there are 24 compact disks in all.

The type of summarized data included in your result set depends on the summary functions used in the SELECT clause. MySQL supports a number of summary functions that work in conjunction with the GROUP BY clause. Chapter 9 contains detailed information about these and other functions available in MySQL.

In the following exercise, you create several SELECT statements, each of which includes a GROUP BY clause. The first statement groups values by a single column, and the next two statements group values by two columns.

Try It Out   **Defining a GROUP BY Clause in Your SELECT Statement**

The following steps describe how to create these statements:

1. Open the mysql client utility, type the following command, and press Enter:

```
use DVDRentals
```

You should receive a message indicating that you switched to the DVDRentals database.

2. The first SELECT statement groups together the values in the OrderID column. Execute the following SELECT statement at the mysql command prompt:

```
SELECT OrderID, COUNT(*) AS Transactions
FROM Transactions
GROUP BY OrderID;
```

You should receive results similar to the following:

```
+---------+--------------+
| OrderID | Transactions |
+---------+--------------+
|       1 |            3 |
|       2 |            1 |
|       3 |            3 |
|       4 |            1 |
|       5 |            1 |
|       6 |            2 |
|       7 |            1 |
|       8 |            3 |
|       9 |            2 |
|      10 |            1 |
|      11 |            3 |
|      12 |            1 |
|      13 |            1 |
+---------+--------------+
13 rows in set (0.01 sec)
```

3. The next SELECT statement groups together values by the MTypeID and RatingID columns. Execute the following SELECT statement at the mysql command prompt:

```
SELECT MTypeID, RatingID, COUNT(*) AS 'DVD Totals'
FROM DVDs
GROUP BY MTypeID, RatingID;
```

You should receive results similar to the following:

```
+---------+----------+------------+
| MTypeID | RatingID | DVD Totals |
+---------+----------+------------+
| mt11    | NR       |          2 |
| mt11    | PG       |          2 |
| mt12    | G        |          1 |
| mt12    | NR       |          1 |
| mt12    | R        |          1 |
| mt16    | NR       |          1 |
+---------+----------+------------+
6 rows in set (0.00 sec)
```

4. The third SELECT statement is similar to the one in the last step except that you now include the WITH ROLLUP option in the GROUP BY clause. Execute the following SELECT statement at the mysql command prompt:

```
SELECT MTypeID, RatingID, COUNT(*) AS 'DVD Totals'
FROM DVDs
GROUP BY MTypeID, RatingID WITH ROLLUP;
```

You should receive results similar to the following:

```
+---------+----------+------------+
| MTypeID | RatingID | DVD Totals |
+---------+----------+------------+
| mt11    | NR       |          2 |
| mt11    | PG       |          2 |
| mt11    | NULL     |          4 |
| mt12    | G        |          1 |
| mt12    | NR       |          1 |
| mt12    | R        |          1 |
| mt12    | NULL     |          3 |
| mt16    | NR       |          1 |
| mt16    | NULL     |          1 |
| NULL    | NULL     |          8 |
+---------+----------+------------+
10 rows in set (0.00 sec)
```

How It Works

The first SELECT statement that you created in this exercise includes a GROUP BY column that groups data according to the OrderID column of the Transactions table, as shown in the following statement:

```
SELECT OrderID, COUNT(*) AS Transactions
FROM Transactions
GROUP BY OrderID;
```

The SELECT clause in the statement specifies the OrderID column and the COUNT(*) expression, which is assigned the alias Transactions. The GROUP BY clause then specifies that the result set be grouped together based on the OrderID column. The result set returns the number of transactions per order.

The next SELECT statement that you created groups together the values from two columns, as the following SELECT statement shows:

```
SELECT MTypeID, RatingID, COUNT(*) AS 'DVD Totals'
FROM DVDs
GROUP BY MTypeID, RatingID;
```

In this case, the rows are grouped together first by the values in the MTypeID column and then by the RatingID values. For each MTypeID/RatingID pair, a total number of DVDs is provided. For example, for the MTypeID value of mt11, the RatingID value of NR includes two DVDs, and the RatingID value of PG includes two DVDs.

The last SELECT statement that you created is identical to the previous one, except that it includes the WITH ROLLUP option in the GROUP BY clause, as shown in the following statement:

```
SELECT MTypeID, RatingID, COUNT(*) AS 'DVD Totals'
FROM DVDs
GROUP BY MTypeID, RatingID WITH ROLLUP;
```

The WITH ROLLUP option adds rows to the result set that provide additional summary values. In this case, a total is provided for each MTypeID value as well as an overall total.

The HAVING Clause

The HAVING clause is very similar to the WHERE clause in that it consists of one or more conditions that define which rows are included in a result set. The HAVING clause, though, has a couple of advantages over the WHERE clause. For example, you can include aggregate functions in a HAVING clause. An *aggregate function* is a type of function that summarizes data, such as the COUNT() function. You cannot use aggregate functions in expressions in your WHERE clause. In addition, you can use column aliases in a HAVING clause, which you cannot do in a WHERE clause.

Despite the disadvantages of the WHERE clause, whenever an expression can be defined in either a HAVING clause or a WHERE clause, it is best to use the WHERE clause because of the way that MySQL optimizes queries. In general, the HAVING clause is normally best suited to use in conjunction with the GROUP BY clause.

To include a HAVING clause in your SELECT statement, you must include the HAVING keyword and at least one expression, as shown in the following syntax:

```
HAVING <expression> [{<operator> <expression>}...]
```

A HAVING clause is constructed exactly like a WHERE clause, in terms of defining conditions and connecting multiple conditions with operators. For example, the following SELECT statement includes a HAVING clause that contains one condition:

```
SELECT Category, COUNT(*) AS Total
FROM CDs
WHERE Department='Popular'
GROUP BY Category
HAVING Total<3;
```

You should be familiar with most of the elements in this statement. The SELECT clause includes the name of the Category column and the expression COUNT(*), which summarizes the grouped data. The WHERE clause specifies that all returned rows must have a Department value of Popular, and the GROUP BY clause specifies that the rows should be grouped together based on the values in the Category column.

The HAVING clause adds another element to the SELECT statement by specifying that the value in the Total column in the result set must be less than 3. The Total column in the result set shows the values that are returned by the COUNT(*) expression defined in the SELECT clause. The SELECT statement should return the following results:

```
+----------+-------+
| Category | Total |
+----------+-------+
| Country  |     2 |
| New Age  |     2 |
| Rock     |     1 |
+----------+-------+
3 rows in set (0.00 sec)
```

The result set includes only those rows that meet the criteria specified in the SELECT statement. As a result, each row must have a Department value of Popular, the rows must be grouped together according to the values in the Category column, and the result set must include the number of compact disks in each category; however, as a result of the HAVING clause, only those categories that contain fewer than three compact disks are included.

In this exercise, you create two SELECT statements that each include a HAVING clause. The HAVING clauses are used in conjunction with GROUP BY clauses to further refine the search results.

Try It Out   Defining a HAVING Clause in Your SELECT Statement

The following steps describe how to create these statements:

1. Open the mysql client utility, type the following command, and press Enter:

```
use DVDRentals
```

You should receive a message indicating that you switched to the DVDRentals database.

2. The first SELECT statement restricts the rows returned to only those with a Total value greater than 1. Execute the following SELECT statement at the mysql command prompt:

```
SELECT RatingID, COUNT(*) AS Total
FROM DVDs
GROUP BY RatingID
HAVING Total>1;
```

You should receive results similar to the following:

```
+----------+-------+
| RatingID | Total |
+----------+-------+
| NR       |     4 |
| PG       |     2 |
+----------+-------+
2 rows in set (0.00 sec)
```

3. The next SELECT statement includes a HAVING clause that restricts the rows to only those that have an Amount value greater than 2. Execute the following SELECT statement at the mysql command prompt:

```
SELECT EmpID, COUNT(*) AS Amount
FROM Orders
GROUP BY EmpID
HAVING Amount>2;
```

You should receive results similar to the following:

```
+-------+--------+
| EmpID | Amount |
+-------+--------+
|     2 |      3 |
+-------+--------+
1 row in set (0.09 sec)
```

How It Works

In this exercise, you created two SELECT statements, both of which contain GROUP BY and HAVING clauses. In addition, both statements include the COUNT(*) expression in the SELECT clause. For example, the first statement that you created determines the number of DVDs for each RatingID, as shown in the following statement:

```
SELECT RatingID, Count(*) AS Total
FROM DVDs
GROUP BY RatingID
HAVING Total>1;
```

As you can see, the result set is grouped together based on the values in the RatingID column. In addition, the total number of rows for each category is provided in the Total column. The result set includes only rows with a Total value greater than 1.

The second SELECT statement that you created in this exercise is similar to the first one and contains the same elements. The primary difference is that it groups data together in the Orders table, rather than the DVDs table, and the returned rows must have an Amount value greater than 2. Otherwise, the elements between the two statements are the same.

The ORDER BY Clause

In Chapter 6, you were introduced to the ORDER BY clause when you learned about UPDATE and DELETE statements. As you'll recall from both those statements, you could include an ORDER BY clause that allowed you to sort rows that were updated or deleted by one or more columns. The SELECT statement also includes an ORDER BY clause that allows you to determine the order in which rows are returned in a results set. The following syntax describes the elements in an ORDER BY clause:

```
ORDER BY <order by definition>

<order by definition>::=
<column name> [ASC | DESC]
[{, <column name> [ASC | DESC]}...]
```

As the syntax indicates, the ORDER BY clause must include the ORDER BY keywords and at least one column name. You can also specify a column alias in place of the actual name. If you include more than one column, a comma must separate them.

For each column that you include in an ORDER BY clause, you can specify whether the rows are sorted in ascending order (the ASC option) or descending order (the DESC option). If neither option is specified, the ASC option is assumed. In addition, when more than one column is specified, the rows are sorted first by the column that is listed first, then by the next specified column, and so on.

Now take a look at an example that uses the ORDER BY clause. The following SELECT statement includes an ORDER BY clause that sorts the rows in the result set according to the values in the CDName column:

```
SELECT CDName, InStock, OnOrder
FROM CDs
WHERE InStock>20
ORDER BY CDName DESC;
```

Notice that the ORDER BY clause specifies that the values should be sorted in descending order, as shown in the following results:

```
+----------------------------+---------+---------+
| CDName                     | InStock | OnOrder |
+----------------------------+---------+---------+
| The Magic of Satie         |      42 |      17 |
| Swan Lake                  |      25 |      44 |
| Stages                     |      42 |       0 |
| Richland Woman Blues       |      22 |       5 |
| Pure                       |      32 |       3 |
| Music for Solo Violin      |      24 |       2 |
| Morimur (after J. S. Bach) |      28 |      17 |
| Golden Road                |      23 |      10 |
| Embrace                    |      24 |      11 |
| Bach Cantatas              |      23 |      12 |
| 25 Classical Favorites     |      32 |      15 |
+----------------------------+---------+---------+
11 rows in set (0.00 sec)
```

As you can see, the result set includes values from the CDName, InStock, and OnOrder columns. Only rows with an InStock value greater than 20 are included here. In addition, the rows that are included are sorted according to the values in the CDName column.

The next example SELECT statement includes an ORDER BY clause that sorts the result set according to two columns:

```
SELECT Department, Category, CDName
FROM CDs
WHERE (InStock+OnOrder-Reserved)<15
ORDER BY Department DESC, Category ASC;
```

In this case, the returned rows are sorted first by the values in the Department column (in descending order) and then by the values in the Category column (in ascending order). The following results show you what you would expect if you executed this statement:

```
+-------------+----------+-----------------------------+
| Department  | Category | CDName                      |
+-------------+----------+-----------------------------+
| Popular     | Country  | Mud on the Tires            |
| Popular     | Rock     | Bloodshot                   |
| Classical   | Dance    | Music for Ballet Class      |
| Classical   | Opera    | The Most Favorite Opera Duets |
| Classical   | Vocal    | Cie li di Toscana           |
+-------------+----------+-----------------------------+
5 rows in set (0.00 sec)
```

As you can see, the rows that contain a Department value of Popular are listed first, followed by the Classical rows. In addition, for each group of values, the Category values are sorted in ascending order. For example, the Classical rows are sorted by the Category values Dance, Opera, and Vocal, in that order.

You can sort your result sets by as many columns as it is practical; however, this is useful only if the columns listed first have enough repeated values to make sorting additional columns return meaningful results.

In the following Try It Out you create SELECT statements that use the ORDER BY clause to sort the values returned by your queries.

Try It Out   Defining an ORDER BY Clause in Your SELECT Statement

The following steps describe how to create statements that employ the ORDER BY clause:

1.   Open the mysql client utility, type the following command, and press Enter:

```
use DVDRentals
```

You should receive a message indicating that you switched to the DVDRentals database.

2.   The first SELECT statement retrieves rows from the DVDs table and orders those rows according to the values in the DVDName column. Execute the following SELECT statement at the mysql command prompt:

```
SELECT DVDName, MTypeID, RatingID
FROM DVDs
WHERE RatingID!='NR'
ORDER BY DVDName;
```

You should receive results similar to the following:

```
+----------------+---------+----------+
| DVDName        | MTypeID | RatingID |
+----------------+---------+----------+
| Amadeus        | mt11    | PG       |
| Mash           | mt12    | R        |
| Out of Africa  | mt11    | PG       |
| What's Up, Doc? | mt12   | G        |
+----------------+---------+----------+
4 rows in set (0.00 sec)
```

3. The next SELECT statement also retrieves rows from the DVDs table, only this time, the rows are ordered by values in the MTypeID column and the RatingID column. Execute the following SELECT statement at the mysql command prompt:

```
SELECT MTypeID, RatingID, DVDName
FROM DVDs
WHERE RatingID!='NR'
ORDER BY MTypeID, RatingID;
```

You should receive results similar to the following:

```
+---------+----------+----------------+
| MTypeID | RatingID | DVDName        |
+---------+----------+----------------+
| mt11    | PG       | Out of Africa  |
| mt11    | PG       | Amadeus        |
| mt12    | G        | What's Up, Doc?|
| mt12    | R        | Mash           |
+---------+----------+----------------+
4 rows in set (0.00 sec)
```

How It Works

The first SELECT statement that you created in this exercise retrieved data from the DVDs table. The data returned by the statement was sorted according to the values in the DVDName column, as the following statement shows:

```
SELECT DVDName, MTypeID, RatingID
FROM DVDs
WHERE RatingID!='NR'
ORDER BY DVDName;
```

The SELECT statement returns values from the DVDName, MTypeID, and RatingID columns. In addition, the statement returns all rows except those that have a RatingID value of NR. The exclamation point/equal sign (!=) combination acts as a comparison operator that means not equal. In other words, the RatingID value cannot equal NR. The SELECT statement goes on to define a sort order by including an ORDER BY clause that specifies the DVDName column. As a result, the rows returned in the result set are sorted according to the values in the DVDName column. In addition, because you specified no ASC or DESC option in the ORDER BY clause, the rows are sorted in ascending order.

The next statement that you created in this exercise included two columns in the ORDER BY clause:

```
SELECT MTypeID, RatingID, DVDName
FROM DVDs
WHERE RatingID!='NR'
ORDER BY MTypeID, RatingID;
```

In this case, the same columns are displayed as in the previous SELECT statement. The columns are specified in a different order in the SELECT clause, however, and the ORDER BY clause includes two columns. As a result, the rows are sorted first according to the values in the MTypeID column, then sorted according to the values in the RatingID column.

The LIMIT Clause

The final clause to review in this chapter is the LIMIT clause. As with the ORDER BY clause, you also saw this clause used in Chapter 6 when you were introduced to the UPDATE and DELETE statements. As was the case with those statements, the LIMIT clause is used most effectively in a SELECT statement when it is used with an ORDER BY clause.

The LIMIT clause takes two arguments, as the following syntax shows:

```
LIMIT [<offset>,] <row count>
```

The first option, <offset>, is optional and indicates where to begin the LIMIT row count. If no value is specified, 0 is assumed. (The first row in a result set is considered to be 0, rather than 1.) The second argument, <row count> in the LIMIT clause, indicates the number of rows to be returned. For example, the following SELECT statement includes a LIMIT clause that specifies a row count of 4.

```
SELECT CDID, CDName, InStock
FROM CDs
WHERE Department='Classical'
ORDER BY CDID DESC
LIMIT 4;
```

As you can see in this statement, no offset value is specified, so 0 is assumed. The row count value is specified as 4, though, so the first four rows of the result set are returned, as shown in the following results:

```
+------+-------------------------------------------+---------+
| CDID | CDName                                    | InStock |
+------+-------------------------------------------+---------+
|   24 | Bach: Six Unaccompanied Cello Suites      |      16 |
|   21 | The Best of Italian Opera                 |      10 |
|   20 | Morimur (after J. S. Bach)                |      28 |
|   16 | Bach Cantatas                             |      23 |
+------+-------------------------------------------+---------+
4 rows in set (0.00 sec)
```

If you were to specify an offset value, the rows returned would begin with the first row indicated by the offset value and end after the number of rows indicated by the row count is returned. For example, the following SELECT statement includes a LIMIT clause that specifies an offset value of 3 and a row count value of 4:

```
SELECT CDID, CDName, InStock
FROM CDs
WHERE Department='Classical'
ORDER BY CDID DESC
LIMIT 3,4;
```

Because the offset value is 3, the result set begins with the fourth row returned by the results. (Remember that the first row is numbered 0.) The result set then includes the four rows that begin with row number 3, as shown in the following results:

```
+------+------------------------+---------+
| CDID | CDName                 | InStock |
+------+------------------------+---------+
|   16 | Bach Cantatas          |      23 |
|   15 | La Boheme              |      20 |
|   14 | 25 Classical Favorites |      32 |
|   13 | Swan Lake              |      25 |
+------+------------------------+---------+
4 rows in set (0.00 sec)
```

As you can see, the result set includes only four rows, numbers 3 through 6. As you might also notice, the rows returned are based on the sort order defined in the ORDER BY clause, which specifies that the rows should be sorted by the values in the CDID column, in descending order. In other words, the result set is limited only to the most recent orders that have been added to the table, excluding the first three orders.

In this Try It Out, you create a SELECT statement that uses the LIMIT clause, in conjunction with the ORDER BY clause, to limit the number of rows returned by your query.

Try It Out   Defining a LIMIT Clause in Your SELECT Statement

To use the LIMIT clause in a SELECT statement, follow these steps:

1. Open the mysql client utility, type the following command, and press Enter:

```
use DVDRentals
```

You should receive a message indicating that you switched to the DVDRentals database.

2. Now create a SELECT statement that uses an ORDER BY clause and a LIMIT clause to return the last order added to the Orders table. Execute the following SELECT statement at the mysql command prompt:

```
SELECT OrderID, CustID
FROM Orders
ORDER BY OrderID DESC
LIMIT 1;
```

You should receive results similar to the following:

```
+---------+--------+
| OrderID | CustID |
+---------+--------+
|      13 |      5 |
+---------+--------+
1 row in set (0.00 sec)
```

How It Works

In this exercise, you created one SELECT statement that included an ORDER BY clause and a LIMIT clause, as shown in the following statement:

```
SELECT OrderID, CustID
FROM Orders
ORDER BY OrderID DESC
LIMIT 1;
```

The statement retrieves values from the OrderID and CustID columns of the Orders table. The returned rows are sorted in descending order according to the values in the OrderID column. The LIMIT clause limits the returned rows to only the first row of the results returned by the SELECT statement. As a result, this statement returns only the most recent order added to the Orders table.

Summary

As the chapter has demonstrated, the SELECT statement can contain many components, allowing you to create statements as simple or as complex as necessary to retrieve specific data from the tables in your MySQL database. You can specify which columns to retrieve, which rows to retrieve, how the rows should be sorted, whether the rows should be grouped together and summarized, and the number of rows to return in your result set. To provide you with the information you need to create robust SELECT statements, the chapter gave you the information necessary to perform the following tasks:

❑   Create SELECT statements that retrieve all columns and all rows from a table

❑   Create SELECT statements that retrieve specific columns from a table

❑   Assign aliases to column names

❑   Use expressions in the SELECT clauses of your SELECT statements

❑   Use SELECT statements to create variables that can be used in later SELECT statements

❑   Create SELECT statements that return information that is not based on data in a table

❑   Add options to your SELECT statements

❑   Add WHERE clauses to your SELECT statements that determine which rows the statements would return

❑   Add GROUP BY clauses to your SELECT statements to generate summary data

❑   Add HAVING clauses to your SELECT statements to refine the results returned by summarized data

❑   Add ORDER BY clauses to your SELECT statements to sort the rows returned by your statements

❑   Add LIMIT clauses to your SELECT statement to limit the number of rows returned by the statement

In later chapters, you learn how to refine your SELECT statements even further. For example, you learn how to join tables in a SELECT statement or to embed other SELECT statements in a parent SELECT statement. In addition, you also learn more about using operators and functions to create powerful expressions in your statements. To prepare for these chapters, the information in this chapter provided you with the foundation necessary to perform these more advanced tasks. As a result, you might find it useful to refer to this chapter as you progress through the book.

Exercises

The following exercises are provided as a way for you to better acquaint yourself with the material covered in this chapter. The exercises are based on the example CDs table used for the examples in this chapter. To view the answers to these questions, see Appendix A.

1. You are creating a SELECT statement that retrieves data from the CDs table. Your query results should include values from the CDName, InStock, OnOrder, and Reserved columns. In addition, the results should include all rows in the table. What SELECT statement should you create?

2. You want to modify the SELECT statement that you created in Exercise 1 so that the result set includes an additional column. The column should add the values of the InStock and OnOrder columns and then subtract the value in the Reserved column. You want to assign the Total alias to the new column. What SELECT statement should you create?

3. Your next step is to modify the SELECT statement that you created in Exercise 2. You plan to limit the rows returned to those rows that have a Department value of Classical and an InStock value less than 20. What SELECT statement should you create?

4. You now want to create a SELECT statement that summarizes data in the CDs table. The result set should include data that is grouped together by the Department column and then by the Category column. The summary information should include the number of rows for each category, as well as totals for all categories in each department. In addition, the summary column in the result set should be assigned the alias Total, and all grouped columns should be sorted in ascending order. What SELECT statement should you create?

5. You now want to modify the SELECT statement that you created in Exercise 4 to limit the rows returned to those with a Total value less than 3. What SELECT statement should you create?

6. You are creating a SELECT statement that retrieves data from the CDs table. Your query results should include values from the CDName column. The values should be sorted in descending order. What SELECT statement should you create?

Using Operators in Your SQL Statements

In previous chapters, you have seen a number of expressions used within SQL statements to help define the actions taken by those statements. For example, you can use expressions in the WHERE clauses of SELECT, UPDATE, and DELETE statements to help identify which rows in a table or tables should be acted upon. An expression, as you'll recall, is a formula made up of column names, literal values, operators, and functions. Together, these components allow you to create expressions that refine your SQL statements to effectively query and modify data within your MySQL database.

In order to allow the components of an expression to work effectively with each other, operators are used to define those interactions and to specify conditions that limit the range of values permitted in a result set. An *operator* is a symbol or keyword that specifies a specific action or condition between other elements of an expression or between expressions. For example, the addition (+) operator specifies that two elements within an expression should be added together. In this chapter, you learn how to create expressions that use the various operators supported by MySQL. Specifically, this chapter covers the following topics:

❑   Which components make up MySQL expressions, how operators allow expression elements to interact with each other, how operators are prioritized within an expression, and how to use parentheses to group components of an expression together.

❑   Which categories of operators MySQL supports, including arithmetic, comparison, logical, bit, and sort operators, and how to use those operators in expressions contained within SQL statements.

Creating MySQL Expressions

As you have seen throughout the book, expressions can play in important role in any of your SQL data manipulation statements, including SELECT, INSERT, UPDATE, and DELETE statements. Although the complexity of the expression can vary greatly from statement to statement, the basic elements that can make up an expression are the same:

- ❑ **Column names:** When a column name is listed in an expression, it refers to the value contained within the column for the specific row that the SQL statement affects. For example, suppose the InStock column for a specific row contains a value of 14. If the expression references the InStock column, it is replaced with the value 14.

- ❑ **Literal values:** This refers to a value that is used in an expression exactly as entered into that expression. Also referred to as a *literal* or *constant*, a literal value can be a string, number, or date/time value. For example, if an expression contains the value 14, the expression uses that value exactly as written.

- ❑ **Functions:** A function performs a predefined task and returns some type of result, such as a numerical, string, or date/time value. When using a function, you must often supply arguments that provide the function with the information it needs to perform its task. These arguments are usually in the form of column names, literal values, or other expressions.

- ❑ **Operators:** An operator is used in conjunction with column names, literal values, and functions to calculate and compare values within an expression. MySQL supports arithmetic, comparison, logical, bit, and sort operators, which are discussed later in the chapter.

Most expressions consist of at least one argument and one operator, although an expression can consist of nothing more than a function. However, for a typical expression, several elements are included. The term *argument* is generally used to describe the non-operator part of an expression, such as the column name or the literal value. For example, suppose you have an SQL statement that includes the following WHERE clause:

```
WHERE InStock>14
```

The expression in this clause is `InStock>14`. The expression includes two arguments — InStock and 14 — and the greater than (>) comparison operator. When an expression is used in a WHERE clause (or in a HAVING clause in a SELECT statement), the expression is often referred to as a *condition*. This is because each expression is evaluated to determine whether the condition is true, false, or NULL. If a WHERE clause contains multiple expressions, you can say that it has multiple conditions, each of which must be evaluated.

As you progress through this chapter, you see how to use column names, literal values, and operators to create expressions. You even see a couple examples of functions. However, most of the discussion about functions is held off until Chapter 9, where you learn how to incorporate functions into your expressions and see how they work in conjunction with column names, literal values, and operators to create comprehensive, precise expressions in your SQL statements.

Operator Precedence

When an expression in an SQL statement is processed, it is evaluated according to the order in which elements are included in the statement and the precedence in which operators are assigned. MySQL processes expressions according to a very specific operator precedence. The following list shows the operator precedence used when processing expressions in an SQL statement:

1. BINARY, COLLATE
2. NOT (logical negation), ! (logical negation)
3. - (unary minus), ~ (unary bit inversion)

4. ^ (bitwise exclusive OR comparison)

5. * (multiplication), / (division), % (modulo)

6. – (subtraction), + (addition)

7. << (bitwise shift left), >> (bitwise shift right)

8. & (bitwise AND)

9. | (bitwise OR)

10. All comparison operators except BETWEEN and NOT BETWEEN

11. BETWEEN, NOT BETWEEN

12. AND (logical addition), && (logical addition)

13. OR (logical OR comparison), | | (logical OR comparison), XOR (logical exclusive OR comparison)

The operators listed here are shown from the highest precedence to the lowest. For example, the BINARY operator has precedence over the BETWEEN and ampersand (&) operators. However, operators that appear on the same line of the list have the same level of precedence, so they are evaluated in the order in which they appear in the expression. For example, the multiplication (*) and division (/) operators have the same level of precedence so they are evaluated in the order in which they appear.

> *You learn the function of each of these operators as your progress through the chapter. As you start using operators, refer to the preceding list as necessary to understand how a particular operator is prioritized within the order of precedence.*

Grouping Operators

Because of operator precedence, you may often find that, in order to control how expressions and group of expressions are evaluated, you need to group together the appropriate elements within parentheses in order to ensure that those elements are processed as a unit. For example, because the multiplication (*) operator has precedence over the addition (+) operator, the following expression is evaluated as follows:

```
3+4*5=23
```

In this expression, 4 and 5 are multiplied, and *then* 3 is added to the sum. However, you can group together the arguments in an expression to better control your results, as shown in the following example:

```
(3+4)*5=35
```

In this case, the 3+4 calculation is treated as a unit. As a result, 7 and 5 are multiplied, resulting in a total of 35, rather than the 23 in the previous expression. As you learn more about the operators that MySQL supports and how they're used within an expression, you'll get a better sense of how to group elements together. However, as a general rule, it's a good idea to use parentheses whenever any possibility of confusion exists to make certain that your expressions are readable and to ensure that they are correct.

Using Operators in Expressions

MySQL supports a number of different types of operators, which can be divided into the following five categories:

- ❏ **Arithmetic operators:** Perform calculations on the arguments within an expression.

- ❏ **Comparison operators:** Compare the arguments in an expression to test whether a condition is true, false, or NULL.

- ❏ **Logical operators:** Verify the validity of one or more expressions to test whether they return a condition of true, false, or NULL.

- ❏ **Bitwise operators:** Manipulate the bit values associated with numerical values.

- ❏ **Sort operators:** Specify the collation and case-sensitivity of searches and sorting operations.

The rest of the chapter focuses on the operators supported in each of these categories.

Arithmetic Operators

Arithmetic operators are used to calculate arguments within an expression. They are similar to the symbols found in algebraic equations in that they are used to add, subtract, multiply, and divide values. The following table provides a brief description of the arithmetic operators supported by MySQL.

Operator	Description
+ (addition)	Adds the two arguments together.
- (subtraction)	Subtracts the second argument from the first argument.
- (unary)	Changes the sign of the argument.
* (multiplication)	Multiplies the two arguments together.
/ (division)	Divides the first argument by the second argument.
% (modulo)	Divides the first argument by the second argument and provides the remainder from that operation.

In earlier chapters, you saw several examples of arithmetic operators used within SQL statements. Now you take a more thorough look at these types of operators by examining statements that use several of them. The examples in this section are based on a table named Inventory, which is shown in the following table definition:

```
CREATE TABLE Inventory
(
    ProductID SMALLINT NOT NULL PRIMARY KEY,
    InStock SMALLINT NOT NULL,
    OnOrder SMALLINT NOT NULL,
    Reserved SMALLINT NOT NULL
);
```

For the purposes of the examples in this section, you can assume that the Inventory table is populated with the values shown in the following INSERT statement:

```
INSERT INTO Inventory
VALUES (101, 10, 15, 4), (102, 16, 9, 3), (103, 15, 2, 13);
```

As you can see, three rows have been added to the Inventory table. Now suppose that you want to add another row. However, you want the OnOrder value to be based on the InStock value, as shown in the following example:

```
INSERT INTO Inventory
VALUES (104, 16, 25-InStock, 0);
```

As you can see, the third value in the VALUES clause includes the expression 25-InStock. The expression contains two arguments—25 and InStock—and it contains the subtraction (-) operator. As a result, the value from the InStock column, which in this case is 16, is subtracted from 25, giving you a total value of 9. This means that 9 is inserted into the OnOrder column of the Inventory table when the row is added to the table.

Although referencing a column in an expression in the VALUES clause of an INSERT statement can be a handy approach, you can reference a column only if it has already been assigned a value. For example, you would not want to reference the OnOrder column to assign a value to the InStock column because no value has yet been assigned to that column. Be sure that, whenever you plan to reference a column in a VALUES clause, the referenced column is current and contains the correct value.

Now take a look at a SELECT statement that contains an expression that uses arithmetic operators. In the following statement, the second element in the select list includes an expression:

```
SELECT ProductID, InStock+OnOrder-Reserved AS Available
FROM Inventory;
```

The select list in this statement includes two elements. The first is the column name ProductID, and the second is the expression InStock+OnOrder-Reserved. The expression includes three arguments—InStock, OnOrder, and Reserved—and two arithmetic operators—the addition (+) operator and the subtraction (-) operator. Because both operators share the same level of precedence, the values in the InStock and OnOrder columns are added together first, and then, from that sum, the value in the Reserved column is subtracted. The following result set shows how a value has been calculated in the Available column for each row:

```
+-----------+-----------+
| ProductID | Available |
+-----------+-----------+
|       101 |        21 |
|       102 |        22 |
|       103 |         4 |
|       104 |        25 |
+-----------+-----------+
4 rows in set (0.01 sec)
```

The select list in a SELECT statement can also include more than one expression, as the following statement demonstrates:

273

```
SELECT ProductID, InStock+OnOrder-Reserved AS Available,
    InStock+OnOrder*2-Reserved AS DoubleOrder
FROM Inventory;
```

This statement is similar to the previous example except that the result set returned by the modified statement includes a third column named DoubleOrder. The new column is based on an expression that is identical to the first expression except that it doubles the value in the OnOrder column. The result of this is a value that shows how many items would be available if you doubled the number on order. To achieve this, the expression uses the multiplication (*) arithmetic operator to multiply the OnOrder value by two. That amount is then added to the InStock value, and the Reserved value is then subtracted from the total. Because the multiplication operator takes precedence over the subtraction and addition operators, the multiplication operation is carried out first.

Take a look at the first row to help demonstrate how this works. For the row with a ProductID value of 101, the InStock value is 10, the OnOrder value is 15, and the Reserved value is 4. Based on the expression, you must first multiply the OnOrder value by 2, which is 15 x 2, or 30. You then add 30 to the InStock value of 10, to give you 40, and then subtract the Reserved value of 4, which leaves you a total of 36, as the following result set shows:

```
+-----------+-----------+-------------+
| ProductID | Available | DoubleOrder |
+-----------+-----------+-------------+
|       101 |        21 |          36 |
|       102 |        22 |          31 |
|       103 |         4 |           6 |
|       104 |        25 |          34 |
+-----------+-----------+-------------+
4 rows in set (0.00 sec)
```

As you can see, the DoubleOrder column contains the modified totals. The intent of the statement is to calculate the number of available items if the number on order were doubled. However, suppose you want to double the entire amount of available items and you tried to create a statement similar to the following:

```
SELECT ProductID, InStock+OnOrder-Reserved*2 AS Doubled
FROM Inventory;
```

Because of operator precedence, the Reserved value is first doubled, the InStock value is added to the OnOrder value, and then the doubled Reserved value is subtracted from that total. For example, for the row with the ProductID value of 101, the Reserved value is 4, which means that it is doubled to 8. The InStock value of 10 is then added to the OnOrder value of 15, which gives you a total a 25. The double reserved value of 8 is then subtracted from the 25, giving you a final total of 17, as shown in the following result set:

```
+-----------+---------+
| ProductID | Doubled |
+-----------+---------+
|       101 |      17 |
|       102 |      19 |
|       103 |      -9 |
|       104 |      25 |
+-----------+---------+
4 rows in set (0.00 sec)
```

These results are fine if your intent is merely to double the number of items that are on reserve; however, if your intent is to determine how many items you would have if you doubled your availability, you would have to modify your statement as follows:

```
SELECT ProductID, (InStock+OnOrder-Reserved)*2 AS Doubled
FROM Inventory;
```

Notice that part of the expression is now enclosed in parentheses, which means that these arguments and operators are processed as a unit. Only then is the amount multiplied by 2, which provides you with an amount that is double what your availability is, as shown in the following results:

```
+-----------+---------+
| ProductID | Doubled |
+-----------+---------+
|       101 |      42 |
|       102 |      44 |
|       103 |       8 |
|       104 |      50 |
+-----------+---------+
4 rows in set (0.00 sec)
```

You are not limited to INSERT and SELECT statements to use expressions that contain arithmetic operators. For example, the following UPDATE statement contains an expression in the SET clause:

```
UPDATE Inventory
SET OnOrder=OnOrder/2;
```

In this case, the expression (OnOrder/2) uses the division (/) operator to divide the value in the OnOrder column by two. Suppose that, after executing the UPDATE statement, you ran the following SELECT statement:

```
SELECT * FROM Inventory;
```

From this SELECT statement, you would receive results similar to the following:

```
+-----------+---------+---------+----------+
| ProductID | InStock | OnOrder | Reserved |
+-----------+---------+---------+----------+
|       101 |      10 |       7 |        4 |
|       102 |      16 |       4 |        3 |
|       103 |      15 |       1 |       13 |
|       104 |      16 |       4 |        0 |
+-----------+---------+---------+----------+
4 rows in set (0.00 sec)
```

As you can see, the OnOrder values have all been divided by two. However, because this is an integer type column, only whole numbers are used, so the values are rounded off for any of the odd numbers that were divided. For example, the OnOrder value for the row that contains a ProductID value of 101 was rounded off to 7.

In the example above, the OnOrder value has been rounded down from 7.5 (the value returned by 15/2) to 7. Different implementations of the C library might round off numbers in different ways. For example, some might always round numbers up or always down, while others might always round toward zero.

In the following exercise, you create several SQL statements that include expressions that use arithmetic operators. The expressions are used in the select lists of SELECT statements and the SET clause and WHERE clauses of an UPDATE statement. For this exercise, you use the DVDs table in the DVDRentals database.

Try It Out   **Creating Expressions with Arithmetic Operators**

The following steps describe how to create SQL statements that use arithmetic operators:

1. Open the mysql client utility, type the following command, and press Enter:

```
use DVDRentals
```

You should receive a message indicating that you switched to the DVDRentals database.

2. Your first SELECT statement includes an expression in the select list. Execute the following SQL statement at the mysql command prompt:

```
SELECT DVDName, YearRlsd, (YEAR(CURDATE())-YearRlsd) AS YearsAvailable
FROM DVDs;
```

You should receive results similar to the following:

```
+-----------------------------+----------+----------------+
| DVDName                     | YearRlsd | YearsAvailable |
+-----------------------------+----------+----------------+
| White Christmas             |   2000   |              4 |
| What's Up, Doc?             |   2001   |              3 |
| Out of Africa               |   2000   |              4 |
| The Maltese Falcon          |   2000   |              4 |
| Amadeus                     |   1997   |              7 |
| The Rocky Horror Picture Show |  2000   |              4 |
| A Room with a View          |   2000   |              4 |
| Mash                        |   2001   |              3 |
+-----------------------------+----------+----------------+
8 rows in set (0.24 sec)
```

3. In the next SQL statement, you create an INSERT statement that adds a row to the DVDs table. (You use this row to perform an update in the next step.) Execute the following INSERT statement at the mysql command prompt:

```
INSERT INTO DVDs
SET DVDName='The Wizard of Oz', NumDisks=2, YearRlsd=1999,
    MTypeID='mt14', StudID='s102', RatingID='G', FormID='f2', StatID='s2';
```

You should receive a response indicating that the query executed properly, affecting one row.

4. Now you create an UPDATE statement that includes an expression in the SET clause and in the WHERE clause. Execute the following UPDATE statement at the mysql command prompt:

```
UPDATE DVDs
SET NumDisks=NumDisks/2
WHERE DVDName='The Wizard of Oz';
```

You should receive a response indicating that the query executed properly, affecting one row.

5. To return to the DVDs table to its original state, delete the row that you created in Step 3. Execute the following DELETE statement at the mysql command prompt:

```
DELETE FROM DVDs
WHERE DVDName='The Wizard of Oz';
```

You should receive a response indicating that the query executed properly, affecting one row.

How It Works

In this exercise, you created two statements that included expressions that contained arithmetic operators. The first of these was the following SELECT statement, which includes an expression as an element in the select list:

```
SELECT DVDName, YearRlsd, (YEAR(CURDATE())-YearRlsd) AS YearsAvailable
FROM DVDs;
```

As the statement indicates, the select list first includes the DVDName column and the YearRlsd column. These two column names are then followed by an expression (YEAR(CURDATE())-YearRlsd) that subtracts the year value in the YearRlsd column from the current year. The current year is derived by using two functions: the YEAR() function and the CURDATE() function, which is embedded as an argument in the YEAR() function. (Functions are discussed in detail in Chapter 9.) By using these two functions together in this way, you can arrive at the current year. As a result, for each row returned by the SELECT statement, the YearRlsd value is subtracted from the current year and placed in a column named YearsAvailable, which is the alias assigned to the expression. The YearRlsd value is subtracted from the current year by using the subtraction (-) arithmetic operator.

The next statement that includes expressions is the UPDATE statement, which contains an expression in the SET clause and in the WHERE clause, as shown in the following statement:

```
UPDATE DVDs
SET NumDisks=NumDisks/2
WHERE DVDName='The Wizard of Oz';
```

The first expression in this statement is in the SET clause and appears after the first equal sign: NumDisks/2. This expression uses the division (/) operator to divide the value in the NumDisks column by 2. This value is then inserted into the NumDisks column, as indicated by the SET clause. An expression is also used in the WHERE clause to limit which rows are updated. The expression (DVDName='The Wizard of Oz') specifies a condition that must be met in order for the row to be updated. In this case, the equals (=) comparison operator specifies that the DVDName value must equal *The Wizard of Oz*. Comparison operators are discussed in the following section.

Comparison Operators

Comparison operators are used to compare the arguments on either side of the expression and determine whether the condition is true, false, or NULL. If either argument is NULL or if both arguments are NULL, the condition is considered NULL. The only exception to this is the NULL-safe (<=>) operator, which evaluates to true when both arguments are the same, even if they are both NULL. For a condition to be acceptable, it must evaluate to true. For example, suppose you have a SELECT statement that includes the following WHERE clause:

```
SELECT ProductName, ProductType
FROM Products
WHERE ProductType='Boat';
```

The WHERE clause includes the expression ProductType='Boat'. When the table is queried, the ProductType value in each row is compared to the value Boat. If the value equals Boat, the condition is true. If the value does not equal Boat, the condition is false. If the ProductType value is NULL, the condition is NULL. As a result, only rows that contain a ProductType value of Boat meet the condition. In other words, the condition evaluates to true for those rows, and those are the rows returned in the results set.

MySQL supports a number of comparison operators that allow you to define various types of conditions in your SQL statements. The following table describes each of these operators.

Operator	Description
=	Evaluates to true if both arguments are equal, unless both conditions are NULL.
<=>	Evaluates to true if both arguments are equal, even if both conditions are NULL.
<>, !=	Evaluates to true if the two arguments are not equal.
<	Evaluates to true if the value of the first argument is less than the value of the second argument.
<=	Evaluates to true if the value of the first argument is less than or equal to the value of the second argument.
>	Evaluates to true if the value of the first argument is greater than the value of the second argument.
>=	Evaluates to true if the value of the first argument is greater than or equal to the value of the second argument.
IS NULL	Evaluates to true if the argument equals a null value.
IS NOT NULL	Evaluates to true if the argument does not equal a null value.
BETWEEN	Evaluates to true if the value of the argument falls within the range specified by the BETWEEN clause.
NOT BETWEEN	Evaluates to true if the value of the argument does not fall within the range specified by the NOT BETWEEN clause.
IN	Evaluates to true if the value of the argument is specified within the IN clause.
NOT IN	Evaluates to true if the argument is not specified within the NOT IN clause.
LIKE	Evaluates to true if the value of the argument is not specified by the LIKE construction.
NOT LIKE	Evaluates to true if the value of the argument is not specified by the NOT LIKE construction.

Operator	Description
REGEXP	Evaluates to true if the value of the argument is specified by the REGEXP construction.
NOT REGEXP	Evaluates to true if the value of the argument is not specified by the NOT REGEXP construction.

As you can see, there are many comparison operators, and the best way to better understand them is to look at example statements that use these operators. The examples in this section are based on the following table definition:

```
CREATE TABLE CDs
(
    CDID SMALLINT NOT NULL AUTO_INCREMENT PRIMARY KEY,
    CDName VARCHAR(50) NOT NULL,
    InStock SMALLINT UNSIGNED NOT NULL,
    OnOrder SMALLINT UNSIGNED NOT NULL,
    Reserved SMALLINT UNSIGNED NOT NULL,
    Department ENUM('Classical', 'Popular') NOT NULL,
    Category VARCHAR(20)
);
```

For the purposes of the examples in this section, you can assume that the following INSERT statement was used to populate the CDs table:

```
INSERT INTO CDs (CDName, InStock, OnOrder, Reserved, Department, Category)
VALUES ('Bloodshot', 10, 5, 3, 'Popular', 'Rock'),
('The Most Favorite Opera Duets', 10, 5, 3, 'Classical', 'Opera'),
('New Orleans Jazz', 17, 4, 1, 'Popular', 'Jazz'),
('Music for Ballet Class', 9, 4, 2, 'Classical', 'Dance'),
('Music for Solo Violin', 24, 2, 5, 'Classical', NULL),
('Cie li di Toscana', 16, 6, 8, 'Classical', NULL),
('Mississippi Blues', 2, 25, 6, 'Popular', 'Blues'),
('Pure', 32, 3, 10, 'Popular', NULL),
('Mud on the Tires', 12, 15, 13, 'Popular', 'Country'),
('The Essence', 5, 20, 10, 'Popular', 'New Age'),
('Embrace', 24, 11, 14, 'Popular', 'New Age'),
('The Magic of Satie', 42, 17, 17, 'Classical', NULL),
('Swan Lake', 25, 44, 28, 'Classical', 'Dance'),
('25 Classical Favorites', 32, 15, 12, 'Classical', 'General'),
('La Boheme', 20, 10, 5, 'Classical', 'Opera'),
('Bach Cantatas', 23, 12, 8, 'Classical', 'General'),
('Golden Road', 23, 10, 17, 'Popular', 'Country'),
('Live in Paris', 18, 20, 10, 'Popular', 'Jazz'),
('Richland Woman Blues', 22, 5, 7, 'Popular', 'Blues'),
('Morimur (after J. S. Bach)', 28, 17, 16, 'Classical', 'General'),
('The Best of Italian Opera', 10, 35, 12, 'Classical', 'Opera'),
('Runaway Soul', 15, 30, 14, 'Popular', NULL),
('Stages', 42, 0, 8, 'Popular', 'Blues'),
('Bach: Six Unaccompanied Cello Suites', 16, 8, 8, 'Classical', 'General');
```

The first example that you review is a SELECT statement whose WHERE clause contains an expression that uses a comparison operator:

```
SELECT CDName, Department, Category
FROM CDs
WHERE CDID=3;
```

As you can see, an equals (=) comparison operator specifies that the CDID value in each row returned by the query must contain a value equal to 3. The WHERE clause expression includes two arguments—CDID and 3—along with the equals operator. Because the table includes only one row that contains a CDID value of 3, that is the only row for which the WHERE clause condition evaluates to true. As a result, no other row is retuned, as shown in the following result set:

```
+------------------+------------+----------+
| CDName           | Department | Category |
+------------------+------------+----------+
| New Orleans Jazz | Popular    | Jazz     |
+------------------+------------+----------+
1 row in set (0.00 sec)
```

The next example SELECT statement contains a WHERE clause whose expression specifies that the Category column must contain NULL:

```
SELECT CDName, Department, Category
FROM CDs
WHERE Category=NULL
ORDER BY CDName;
```

As you can see, the expression includes two arguments—Category and NULL—and the equals operator. If you return to the original INSERT statement that added data to the CDs table, you see that five rows contain a Category value of NULL. However, if you execute this statement, you should receive the following results:

```
Empty set (0.00 sec)
```

In this case, no rows are returned because, when using an equals (=) comparison operator, neither side is permitted to equal NULL in order for the condition to evaluate to true. As a result, MySQL interprets the condition as NULL, so no rows are returned, even though some rows do indeed contain NULL. One way to get around this is to use the NULL-safe (<=>) comparison operator, as shown in the following statement:

```
SELECT CDName, Department, Category
FROM CDs
WHERE Category<=>NULL
ORDER BY CDName;
```

As you can see, the only difference between this statement and the previous statement is the use of the NULL-safe operator. Now when you execute the statement, you receive the following results:

```
+----------------------+------------+----------+
| CDName               | Department | Category |
+----------------------+------------+----------+
| Cie li di Toscana    | Classical  | NULL     |
| Music for Solo Violin | Classical  | NULL     |
| Pure                 | Popular    | NULL     |
| Runaway Soul         | Popular    | NULL     |
| The Magic of Satie   | Classical  | NULL     |
+----------------------+------------+----------+
5 rows in set (0.00 sec)
```

Another way to work with columns that contain NULL is to use the IS NULL comparison operator, as shown in the following statement:

```
SELECT CDName, Department, Category
FROM CDs
WHERE Category IS NULL
ORDER BY CDName;
```

In this case, the expression has been changed to include only the column name and the IS NULL keywords. When you execute this statement, you should receive the same results as the preceding SELECT statement.

Several of the comparison operators allow you to use the NOT keyword to reverse the meaning of the operator. For example, if you were to rewrite the preceding SELECT statement to include the IS NOT NULL operator, your statement would be as follows:

```
SELECT CDName, Department, Category
FROM CDs
WHERE Category IS NOT NULL
ORDER BY CDName;
```

The only difference between this statement and the preceding one is the addition of the keyword NOT. However, as the following result set shows, the addition of this one element is indeed significant:

```
+---------------------------------------+------------+----------+
| CDName                                | Department | Category |
+---------------------------------------+------------+----------+
| 25 Classical Favorites                | Classical  | General  |
| Bach Cantatas                         | Classical  | General  |
| Bach: Six Unaccompanied Cello Suites  | Classical  | General  |
| Bloodshot                             | Popular    | Rock     |
| Embrace                               | Popular    | New Age  |
| Golden Road                           | Popular    | Country  |
| La Boheme                             | Classical  | Opera    |
| Live in Paris                         | Popular    | Jazz     |
| Mississippi Blues                     | Popular    | Blues    |
| Morimur (after J. S. Bach)            | Classical  | General  |
| Mud on the Tires                      | Popular    | Country  |
| Music for Ballet Class                | Classical  | Dance    |
| New Orleans Jazz                      | Popular    | Jazz     |
| Richland Woman Blues                  | Popular    | Blues    |
| Stages                                | Popular    | Blues    |
| Swan Lake                             | Classical  | Dance    |
| The Best of Italian Opera             | Classical  | Opera    |
| The Essence                           | Popular    | New Age  |
| The Most Favorite Opera Duets         | Classical  | Opera    |
+---------------------------------------+------------+----------+
19 rows in set (0.00 sec)
```

By adding the NOT keyword, the results now include those rows that do *not* contain a Category value of NULL, rather than those that do contain NULL. No rows that contain a Category value of NULL are included in this result set.

Now take a look at another type of comparison operator. In the following example, the WHERE clause includes an expression that compares a calculated value to a value of 20:

```
SELECT CDName, InStock, OnOrder, Reserved
FROM CDs
WHERE (InStock+OnOrder-Reserved)>20
ORDER BY CDName;
```

As you can see, this expression uses arithmetic operators and a comparison operator. The arithmetic operators are used to derive a value from the InStock, OnOrder, and Reserved columns. The operators and columns are enclosed in parentheses to group together the arguments to ensure that the correct value is derived from these columns. The resulting value is then compared to the value of 20. Because the greater than (>) comparison operator is used, the value derived from the three columns must be greater than 20. As a result, only those rows for which this condition evaluates to true are returned by SELECT statement, as shown in the following result set:

```
+----------------------------+---------+---------+----------+
| CDName                     | InStock | OnOrder | Reserved |
+----------------------------+---------+---------+----------+
| 25 Classical Favorites     |      32 |      15 |       12 |
| Bach Cantatas              |      23 |      12 |        8 |
| Embrace                    |      24 |      11 |       14 |
| La Boheme                  |      20 |      10 |        5 |
| Live in Paris              |      18 |      20 |       10 |
| Mississippi Blues          |       2 |      25 |        6 |
| Morimur (after J. S. Bach) |      28 |      17 |       16 |
| Music for Solo Violin      |      24 |       2 |        5 |
| Pure                       |      32 |       3 |       10 |
| Runaway Soul               |      15 |      30 |       14 |
| Stages                     |      42 |       0 |        8 |
| Swan Lake                  |      25 |      44 |       28 |
| The Best of Italian Opera  |      10 |      35 |       12 |
| The Magic of Satie         |      42 |      17 |       17 |
+----------------------------+---------+---------+----------+
14 rows in set (0.02 sec)
```

You can verify that the correct data was returned by sampling one of the rows. For example, the first row contains an InStock value of 32, an OnOrder value of 15, and a Reserved value of 12. According to the expression in the WHERE clause, this would read (32+15-12)>20, or 35>20, which is a true condition.

As you can see, each comparison operator has a very specific meaning. For example, suppose you change the last example simply by changing the comparison operator, as shown in the following SELECT statement:

```
SELECT CDName, InStock, OnOrder, Reserved
FROM CDs
WHERE (InStock+OnOrder-Reserved)<20
ORDER BY CDName;
```

Now the value returned by the InStock, OnOrder, and Reserved columns must equal an amount less than 20. As a result, you would receive the following result set:

```
+----------------------------------------+---------+---------+----------+
| CDName                                 | InStock | OnOrder | Reserved |
+----------------------------------------+---------+---------+----------+
| Bach: Six Unaccompanied Cello Suites   |    16   |    8    |     8    |
| Bloodshot                              |    10   |    5    |     3    |
| Cie li di Toscana                      |    16   |    6    |     8    |
| Golden Road                            |    23   |    10   |    17    |
| Mud on the Tires                       |    12   |    15   |    13    |
| Music for Ballet Class                 |     9   |    4    |     2    |
| The Essence                            |     5   |    20   |    10    |
| The Most Favorite Opera Duets          |    10   |    5    |     3    |
+----------------------------------------+---------+---------+----------+
8 rows in set (0.00 sec)
```

Another comparison operator that can be very useful is the IN operator. In the following example, the expression specifies that the Category value must be Blues or Jazz:

```
SELECT CDName, Category, InStock
FROM CDs
WHERE Category IN ('Blues', 'Jazz')
ORDER BY CDName;
```

The WHERE clause expression—Category IN ('Blues', 'Jazz')—contains several elements. It first specifies the Categories column, then the IN keyword, and then a list of values, which are enclosed in parentheses and separated by a comma. For this SELECT statement to return a row, the Category value must equal Blues or Jazz. The condition evaluates to true only for these rows. Rows that contain other Category values, including NULL, are not returned, as shown in the following result set:

```
+----------------------+----------+---------+
| CDName               | Category | InStock |
+----------------------+----------+---------+
| Live in Paris        | Jazz     |    18   |
| Mississippi Blues    | Blues    |     2   |
| New Orleans Jazz     | Jazz     |    17   |
| Richland Woman Blues | Blues    |    22   |
| Stages               | Blues    |    42   |
+----------------------+----------+---------+
5 rows in set (0.00 sec)
```

MySQL also allows you to use operators to specify a range of values. The following example uses the NOT BETWEEN operator to specify which rows should not be included in the result set:

```
SELECT CDName, InStock, OnOrder, Reserved
FROM CDs
WHERE (InStock+OnOrder-Reserved) NOT BETWEEN 10 AND 20
ORDER BY CDName;
```

The expression used in this case— (InStock+OnOrder-Reserved) NOT BETWEEN 10 AND 20—first uses arithmetic operators to derive a value from the InStock, OnOrder, and Reserved columns. The NOT

BETWEEN operator (along with the AND keyword) defines the range in which values cannot be included. In other words, the value derived from the InStock, OnOrder, and Reserved columns cannot fall within the range of 10 through 20, inclusive, as shown in the follow result set:

```
+-----------------------------+---------+---------+----------+
| CDName                      | InStock | OnOrder | Reserved |
+-----------------------------+---------+---------+----------+
| 25 Classical Favorites      |      32 |      15 |       12 |
| Bach Cantatas               |      23 |      12 |        8 |
| Embrace                     |      24 |      11 |       14 |
| La Boheme                   |      20 |      10 |        5 |
| Live in Paris               |      18 |      20 |       10 |
| Mississippi Blues           |       2 |      25 |        6 |
| Morimur (after J. S. Bach)  |      28 |      17 |       16 |
| Music for Solo Violin       |      24 |       2 |        5 |
| Pure                        |      32 |       3 |       10 |
| Runaway Soul                |      15 |      30 |       14 |
| Stages                      |      42 |       0 |        8 |
| Swan Lake                   |      25 |      44 |       28 |
| The Best of Italian Opera   |      10 |      35 |       12 |
| The Magic of Satie          |      42 |      17 |       17 |
+-----------------------------+---------+---------+----------+
14 rows in set (0.00 sec)
```

If you were to take a row and calculate the InStock, OnOrder, and Reserved columns (according to the how they're calculated in the expression), your total would either be less than 10 or greater than 20, but rows whose totals fall within that range would be returned.

Another useful comparison operator is the LIKE operator, which allows you to search for values similar to a specified value. The LIKE operator supports the use of two wildcards:

❑ **Percentage (%):** Represents zero or more values.

❑ **Underscore (_):** Represents exactly one value.

The following SELECT statement includes a WHERE clause expression that searches for CDName values that contain "bach" somewhere in its title:

```
SELECT CDName, InStock+OnOrder-Reserved AS Available
FROM CDs
WHERE CDName LIKE '%bach%'
ORDER BY CDName;
```

Because the WHERE clause uses the percentage wildcard both before and after the value bach, any characters can fall before and after that value, as shown in the following result set:

```
+-------------------------------------+-----------+
| CDName                              | Available |
+-------------------------------------+-----------+
| Bach Cantatas                       |        27 |
| Bach: Six Unaccompanied Cello Suites|        16 |
| Morimur (after J. S. Bach)          |        29 |
+-------------------------------------+-----------+
3 rows in set (0.01 sec)
```

MySQL supports yet another operator that allows you to locate values similar to a specified value. The REGEXP comparison operator allows you to specify a number of different options and configurations in order to return similar values. The following table lists the primary options that you can use with the REGEXP operator to create expressions in your SQL statements.

Options	Meaning	Example	Acceptable Values
<value>	The tested value must contain the specified value.	'bo'	about, book, abbot, boot
<^>	The tested value must *not* contain the specified value.	'^bo'	abut, took, amount, root
.	The tested value can contain any individual character represented by the period (.).	'b.'	by, be, big, abbey
[<characters>]	The tested value must contain at least one of the characters listed within the brackets.	'[xz]'	dizzy, zebra, x-ray, extra
[<range>]	The tested value must contain at least one of the characters listed within the range of values enclosed by the brackets.	'[1-5]'	15, 3, 346, 50, 22, 791
^	The tested value must begin with the value preceded by the caret (^) symbol.	'^b'	book, big, banana, bike
$	The tested value must end with the value followed by the dollar sign ($) symbol.	'st$'	test, resist, persist
*	The tested value must include zero or more of the character that precedes the asterisk (*).	'^b.*e$'	bake, be, bare, battle

The REGEXP operator can seem confusing at first until you see a couple statements that show how it's used. For example, the following SELECT statement uses the REGEXP operator to return rows that contain a CDName value that begins with the letters a through f:

```
SELECT CDName, InStock+OnOrder-Reserved AS Available
FROM CDs
WHERE CDName REGEXP '^[a-f]'
ORDER BY CDName;
```

The expression—CDName REGEXP '^[a-f]'—first specifies the CDName column, the REGEXP keyword, and the value to be matched. The value is enclosed in single quotes and contains the caret (^) symbol and a bracketed range that specifies the letters a through f. Because the caret is used, the next specified value must appear at the beginning of the column values. In this case, the specified value is actually a bracketed range. This means that, for the condition to evaluate to true for a particular row, the CDName value must begin with the letter a through f, as shown in the following result set:

```
+---------------------------------------+-----------+
| CDName                                | Available |
+---------------------------------------+-----------+
| Bach Cantatas                         |        27 |
| Bach: Six Unaccompanied Cello Suites  |        16 |
| Bloodshot                             |        12 |
| Cie li di Toscana                     |        14 |
| Embrace                               |        21 |
+---------------------------------------+-----------+
5 rows in set (0.00 sec)
```

You can even be more specific with the REGEXP operator by extending the specified value used by the operator, as shown in the following SELECT statement:

```
SELECT CDName, InStock
FROM CDs
WHERE CDName REGEXP '^[mn].*[sz]$'
ORDER BY CDName;
```

In this statement, the REGEXP value again begins with a caret, indicating that the next value must appear at the beginning of the column value. However, in this case, a range of values is not specified in the brackets, but rather two specific characters: m and n. As a result, the CDName value must begin with an m or an n. In addition, the REGEXP value includes the period/asterisk (.*) construction. The period (.) indicates that any single character can be included, and the asterisk (*) indicates that the preceding character can be repeated zero or more times. In another words, any character can be repeated any number of times. The REGEXP value then ends with the bracketed s and z, followed by a dollar ($) sign. As a result, the returned CDName value must end in an s or a z, as shown in the follow result set:

```
+-----------------------+---------+
| CDName                | InStock |
+-----------------------+---------+
| Mississippi Blues     |       2 |
| Mud on the Tires      |      12 |
| Music for Ballet Class|       9 |
| New Orleans Jazz      |      17 |
+-----------------------+---------+
4 rows in set (0.00 sec)
```

As you can see in the results, each CDName value begins with an m or an n and ends with an s or a z, and any characters can be included between the beginning and ending letters. These four rows were the only rows that met the condition specified by the WHERE clause. In other words, these were the only rows for which the WHERE clause expression evaluated to true.

As you saw in this section, comparison operators provide a great deal of flexibility in allowing you to create SQL statements that are both flexible and very specific. The following exercise has you create a number of SELECT statements that use comparison operators in the WHERE clause to define which rows your query returns. You query tables in the DVDRentals database.

Try It Out   Creating Expressions with Comparison Operators

The following steps describe how to create SELECT statements employing comparison operators in the WHERE clause:

1. Open the mysql client utility, type the following command, and press Enter:

```
use DVDRentals
```

You should receive a message indicating that you switched to the DVDRentals database.

2. The first SELECT statement requests information from the DVDs table. Your statement returns only those rows that have a StatID value of s2 (Available). Execute the following SELECT statement at the mysql command prompt:

```
SELECT DVDName, StatID
FROM DVDs
WHERE StatID='s2'
ORDER BY DVDName;
```

You should receive results similar to the following:

```
+------------------------------+--------+
| DVDName                      | StatID |
+------------------------------+--------+
| Amadeus                      | s2     |
| Mash                         | s2     |
| The Maltese Falcon           | s2     |
| The Rocky Horror Picture Show | s2    |
| What's Up, Doc?              | s2     |
+------------------------------+--------+
5 rows in set (0.01 sec)
```

3. The next SELECT statement that you create is similar to the last, except that you will return only those rows that do *not* have a StatID value of s2. Execute the following SELECT statement at the mysql command prompt:

```
SELECT DVDName, StatID
FROM DVDs
WHERE StatID<>'s2'
ORDER BY DVDName;
```

You should receive results similar to the following:

```
+---------------------+--------+
| DVDName             | StatID |
+---------------------+--------+
| A Room with a View  | s1     |
| Out of Africa       | s1     |
| White Christmas     | s1     |
+---------------------+--------+
3 rows in set (0.00 sec)
```

4. The next SELECT statement that you create retrieves those rows for DVDs that have been released after the year 2000. Execute the following SELECT statement at the mysql command prompt:

```
SELECT DVDName, YearRlsd, StatID
FROM DVDs
WHERE YearRlsd>2000
ORDER BY DVDName;
```

You should receive results similar to the following:

```
+-----------------+----------+--------+
| DVDName         | YearRlsd | StatID |
+-----------------+----------+--------+
| Mash            |     2001 | s2     |
| What's Up, Doc? |     2001 | s2     |
+-----------------+----------+--------+
2 rows in set (0.01 sec)
```

5. The next SELECT statement returns results from the Employees table. Only those rows that do not contain an EmpMN value of NULL should be included in the result set. Execute the following SELECT statement at the mysql command prompt:

```
SELECT EmpFN, EmpMN, EmpLN
FROM Employees
WHERE EmpMN IS NOT NULL;
```

You should receive results similar to the following:

```
+-------+-------+----------+
| EmpFN | EmpMN | EmpLN    |
+-------+-------+----------+
| John  | P.    | Smith    |
| Mary  | Marie | Michaels |
| Rita  | C.    | Carter   |
+-------+-------+----------+
3 rows in set (0.00 sec)
```

6. Now you query data in the Transactions table. Your SELECT statement should return only these rows that have a DVDID of 2, 5, or 8. Execute the following SELECT statement at the mysql command prompt:

```
SELECT OrderID, TransID, DVDID
FROM Transactions
WHERE DVDID IN (2, 5, 8)
ORDER BY OrderID, TransID;
```

You should receive results similar to the following:

```
+---------+---------+-------+
| OrderID | TransID | DVDID |
+---------+---------+-------+
|       1 |       3 |     8 |
|       6 |      10 |     2 |
|       8 |      13 |     2 |
|      10 |      18 |     5 |
|      11 |      20 |     2 |
|      11 |      21 |     8 |
|      12 |      22 |     5 |
+---------+---------+-------+
7 rows in set (0.01 sec)
```

7. In the next SELECT statement, you query the DVDs table and return any rows that contain the word "horror" anywhere within the DVDName value. Execute the following SELECT statement at the mysql command prompt:

```
SELECT DVDName, StatID, RatingID
FROM DVDs
WHERE DVDName LIKE '%horror%'
ORDER BY DVDName;
```

You should receive results similar to the following:

```
+-----------------------------+--------+----------+
| DVDName                     | StatID | RatingID |
+-----------------------------+--------+----------+
| The Rocky Horror Picture Show | s2   | NR       |
+-----------------------------+--------+----------+
1 row in set (0.01 sec)
```

8. The final SELECT statement that you create in this exercise returns any row with a DVDName value that contains the letters "ro" anywhere within the name. Execute the following SELECT statement at the mysql command prompt:

```
SELECT DVDName, StatID, RatingID
FROM DVDs
WHERE DVDName REGEXP 'ro'
ORDER BY DVDName;
```

You should receive results similar to the following:

```
+-----------------------------+--------+----------+
| DVDName                     | StatID | RatingID |
+-----------------------------+--------+----------+
| A Room with a View          | s1     | NR       |
| The Rocky Horror Picture Show | s2   | NR       |
+-----------------------------+--------+----------+
2 rows in set (0.00 sec)
```

How It Works

In this exercise, you created seven SELECT statements that retrieved data from tables in the DVDRentals database. The first statement included a WHERE clause expression that specified the value of the StatID column.

```
SELECT DVDName, StatID
FROM DVDs
WHERE StatID='s2'
ORDER BY DVDName;
```

For this statement to return a row, the StatID value must equal s2. For each row that contains a StatID value of s2, the condition specified in the WHERE clause expression evaluates to true. All other rows evaluate to false. No rows evaluate to NULL because null values are not permitted in this column.

The next SELECT statement that you created was identical to the first except that you used a not equal (<>) operator to specify that the StatID value should not equal s2, as shown in the following statement:

```
SELECT DVDName, StatID
FROM DVDs
WHERE StatID<>'s2'
ORDER BY DVDName;
```

As a result of this statement, the only rows that meet the WHERE clause condition were those that contain a non-NULL value other than s2. All other rows evaluate to false.

Your next SELECT statement used the greater than (>) comparison operator to compare the YearRlsd values in the DVDs table to the year 2000, as shown in the following statement:

```
SELECT DVDName, YearRlsd, StatID
FROM DVDs
WHERE YearRlsd>2000
ORDER BY DVDName;
```

The only rows that return a true condition are those for DVDs that were released after the year 2000. All other rows fail to meet the condition specified by the WHERE expression.

You then created the following SELECT statement, which uses the IS NOT NULL operator to determine which rows to return:

```
SELECT EmpFN, EmpMN, EmpLN
FROM Employees
WHERE EmpMN IS NOT NULL;
```

The expression in this statement specifies the EmpMN column and the IS NOT NULL operator. As a result, only rows that contain an EmpMN value other than NULL are included in the result set. In other words, only employees who listed a middle name are included in the result set.

Next you created a SELECT statement that retrieved data from the Transactions table. The statement retrieved rows with DVDID values of 2, 5, or 8, as shown in the following statement:

```
SELECT OrderID, TransID, DVDID
FROM Transactions
WHERE DVDID IN (2, 5, 8)
ORDER BY OrderID, TransID;
```

The expression in this case includes the name of the DVDID column, the IN keyword, and three values that are enclosed in parentheses and separated by commas. In order for a condition to be true, a row must have a DVDID value that is equal to one of the values specified as an argument for the IN operator. As a result, only rows with a DVDID value of 2, 5, or 8 are returned.

Next you created a SELECT statement that used the LIKE operator to return rows, as shown in the following statement:

```
SELECT DVDName, StatID, RatingID
FROM DVDs
WHERE DVDName LIKE '%horror%'
ORDER BY DVDName;
```

The WHERE clause expression shown here specifies the DVDName column, the LIKE keyword, and a value enclosed in single quotes. The value uses percentage (%) wildcards to indicate that any characters can appear before or after the word horror. As a result, only rows with a DVDName value that contains the word horror are included in the result set, which in this case is only one row.

The final SELECT statement that you created also used an operator to define a value to be used to match patterns, as shown in the following statement

```
SELECT DVDName, StatID, RatingID
FROM DVDs
WHERE DVDName REGEXP 'ro'
ORDER BY DVDName;
```

In this statement, the REGEXP operator searches for any values in the DVDName column that contains the letters "ro," in that order. However, the letters can appear anywhere within the DVDName value. In this case, only two rows are returned because only two DVDName values return a WHERE clause condition of true.

Logical Operators

Logical operators allow you to test the validity of one or more expressions. Through the use of these operators, you can associate expressions to determine whether the conditions, when taken as a whole, evaluate to true, false, or NULL. For a condition or set of conditions to be acceptable, they must evaluate to true. The following table describes the logical operators available in MySQL.

Operator	Description
AND	Evaluates to true if both of the two arguments or expressions evaluate to true. You can use double ampersands (&&) in place of the AND operator.
OR	Evaluates to true if either of the two arguments or expressions evaluates to true. You can use the double vertical pipes (||) in place of the OR operator
XOR	Evaluates to true if exactly one of the two arguments or expressions evaluates to true.
NOT, !	Evaluates to true if the argument or expression evaluates to false. You can use an exclamation point (!) in place of the NOT operator.

To better understand how to use logical operators, take a look at a few examples. These examples are based on the following table definition:

```
CREATE TABLE Books
(
    BookID SMALLINT NOT NULL PRIMARY KEY,
    BookName VARCHAR(40) NOT NULL,
    Category VARCHAR(15),
    InStock SMALLINT NOT NULL,
    OnOrder SMALLINT NOT NULL
);
```

For the purposes of these examples, you can assume that the following INSERT statement has been used to insert data into the Books table:

```
INSERT INTO Books
VALUES (101, 'Noncomformity: Writing on Writing', 'Nonfiction', 12, 13),
(102, 'The Shipping News', 'Fiction', 17, 20),
(103, 'Hell\'s Angels', 'Nonfiction', 23, 33),
(104, 'Letters to a Young Poet', 'Nonfiction', 32, 12),
(105, 'A Confederacy of Dunces', 'Fiction', 6, 35),
(106, 'One Hundred Years of Solitude', 'Fiction', 28, 14),
(107, 'Where I\'m Calling From', NULL, 46, 3);
```

The first example is a SELECT statement that includes a WHERE clause that contains two expressions (conditions):

```
SELECT BookName, Category, InStock, OnOrder
FROM Books
WHERE Category='Fiction' AND (InStock+OnOrder)>40
ORDER BY BookName;
```

The first expression in the WHERE clause specifies that the Category column must contain the value Fiction. The second expression specifies that the sum derived from the InStock and OnOrder columns must be greater than 40. The two expressions are connected by the AND logical operator. As a result, both expressions must evaluate to true in order for the conditions, when taken as a whole, to evaluate to true. In other words, each row returned by the SELECT statement must contain a Category value of Fiction *and* an (InStock+OnOrder) value greater than 40, as shown in the following result set:

```
+--------------------------------+----------+---------+---------+
| BookName                       | Category | InStock | OnOrder |
+--------------------------------+----------+---------+---------+
| A Confederacy of Dunces        | Fiction  |       6 |      35 |
| One Hundred Years of Solitude  | Fiction  |      28 |      14 |
+--------------------------------+----------+---------+---------+
2 rows in set (0.00 sec)
```

The next SELECT statement also includes two expressions within the WHERE clause, only this time the two expressions are connected by an OR logical operator, as shown in the following statement:

```
SELECT BookName, Category, InStock, OnOrder
FROM Books
WHERE InStock>30 OR OnOrder>30
ORDER BY BookName;
```

The first expression specifies that the InStock column must contain a value greater than 30, and the second expression specifies that the OnOrder value must be greater than 30. Because an OR operator connects these two conditions, only one of the expressions must evaluate to true. In other words, the InStock value must be greater than 30 *or* the OnOrder value must be greater than 30, as the following result set demonstrates:

```
+--------------------------+------------+---------+---------+
| BookName                 | Category   | InStock | OnOrder |
+--------------------------+------------+---------+---------+
| A Confederacy of Dunces  | Fiction    |       6 |      35 |
| Hell's Angels            | Nonfiction |      23 |      33 |
| Letters to a Young Poet  | Nonfiction |      32 |      12 |
| Where I'm Calling From   | NULL       |      46 |       3 |
+--------------------------+------------+---------+---------+
4 rows in set (0.00 sec)
```

You can also use an XOR logical operator between two expressions in an SQL statement, as the following example shows:

```
SELECT BookName, Category, InStock, OnOrder
FROM Books
WHERE Category='Fiction' XOR InStock IS NULL
ORDER BY BookName;
```

When you use an XOR operator to compare expressions, the expressions, when taken as a whole, evaluate to true if exactly one of the expressions evaluates to true. In other words, one expression can evaluate to true, but not both. As a result, either the Category column must contain a value of Fiction *or* the InStock column must contain a value of NULL. However, both conditions cannot be true, as shown in the following result set:

```
+--------------------------------+----------+---------+---------+
| BookName                       | Category | InStock | OnOrder |
+--------------------------------+----------+---------+---------+
| A Confederacy of Dunces        | Fiction  |       6 |      35 |
| One Hundred Years of Solitude  | Fiction  |      28 |      14 |
| The Shipping News              | Fiction  |      17 |      20 |
+--------------------------------+----------+---------+---------+
3 rows in set (0.01 sec)
```

The following SELECT statement includes three expressions connected with an AND operator and an OR operator:

```
SELECT BookName, Category, InStock, OnOrder
FROM Books
WHERE InStock>20 AND (Category IS NULL OR NOT (Category='Fiction'))
ORDER BY BookName;
```

The first expression in this statement specifies that the InStock column must contain a value greater than 20. The next two expressions, which are connected by an OR operator, are enclosed in parentheses, so they're evaluated together. The first of these conditions specifies that the Category column must contain a NULL value. The NOT operator precedes the second of these two conditions, which means that the Category column must *not* contain the value Fiction. Because these two expressions are connected by an OR operator, either condition can evaluate to true. As a result, for a row to be returned, the InStock value must be greater than 20 *and* the Category column must contain a value of NULL or a value other than Fiction, as shown in the following result set:

```
+-------------------------+------------+---------+---------+
| BookName                | Category   | InStock | OnOrder |
+-------------------------+------------+---------+---------+
| Hell's Angels           | Nonfiction |      23 |      33 |
| Letters to a Young Poet | Nonfiction |      32 |      12 |
| Where I'm Calling From  | NULL       |      46 |       3 |
+-------------------------+------------+---------+---------+
3 rows in set (0.00 sec)
```

As the example SELECT statements demonstrate, you can use logical operators to create complex statements that allow you to include multiple expressions in your statements in order to specify the exact rows that you want to return. You can also use logical operators the WHERE clauses of your UPDATE and DELETE statements to specify which rows should be modified in your MySQL tables.

In the following exercise, you create several SELECT statements that include expressions that contain logical operators that create conditions made up of multiple expressions. In the statements, you query data from the DVDs table in the DVDRentals database.

Try It Out   Creating Expressions with Logical Operators

The following steps describe how to create the statements containing logical operators:

1.   Open the mysql client utility, type the following command, and press Enter:

```
use DVDRentals
```

You should receive a message indicating that you switched to the DVDRentals database.

2.   The first SELECT statement that you create includes two WHERE clause expressions that are linked together with an OR logical operator. Execute the following SELECT statement at the mysql command prompt:

```
SELECT DVDName, MTypeID, RatingID
FROM DVDs
WHERE RatingID='G' OR RatingID='PG'
ORDER BY DVDName;
```

You should receive results similar to the following:

```
+-----------------+----------+----------+
| DVDName         | MTypeID  | RatingID |
+-----------------+----------+----------+
| Amadeus         | mt11     | PG       |
| Out of Africa   | mt11     | PG       |
| What's Up, Doc? | mt12     | G        |
+-----------------+----------+----------+
3 rows in set (0.04 sec)
```

3. Next, create a SELECT statement that includes three expressions in the WHERE clause. The clause includes an AND operator and an OR operator. Execute the following SELECT statement at the mysql command prompt:

```
SELECT DVDName, MTypeID, RatingID
FROM DVDs
WHERE StatID='s2' AND (RatingID='G' OR RatingID='PG')
ORDER BY DVDName;
```

You should receive results similar to the following:

```
+-----------------+----------+----------+
| DVDName         | MTypeID  | RatingID |
+-----------------+----------+----------+
| Amadeus         | mt11     | PG       |
| What's Up, Doc? | mt12     | G        |
+-----------------+----------+----------+
2 rows in set (0.02 sec)
```

4. The next SELECT statement also includes three expressions connected by an AND operator and an OR operator. In addition, use the NOT operator to reverse one of sets of conditions. Execute the following SELECT statement at the mysql command prompt:

```
SELECT DVDName, MTypeID, RatingID
FROM DVDs
WHERE StatID='s2' AND NOT (RatingID='G' OR RatingID='PG')
ORDER BY DVDName;
```

You should receive results similar to the following:

```
+------------------------------+----------+----------+
| DVDName                      | MTypeID  | RatingID |
+------------------------------+----------+----------+
| Mash                         | mt12     | R        |
| The Maltese Falcon           | mt11     | NR       |
| The Rocky Horror Picture Show| mt12     | NR       |
+------------------------------+----------+----------+
3 rows in set (0.01 sec)
```

How It Works

The first SELECT statement includes two expressions in the WHERE clause, as shown in the following statement:

```
SELECT DVDName, MTypeID, RatingID
FROM DVDs
WHERE RatingID='G' OR RatingID='PG'
ORDER BY DVDName;
```

The first expression specifies that the RatingID value must be G, and the second expression specifies that the RatingID value must be PG. Because you used an OR logical operator to connect the two expressions, either expression can evaluate to true in order for a row to be included in the result set.

The next SELECT statement that you created included three expressions:

```
SELECT DVDName, MTypeID, RatingID
FROM DVDs
WHERE StatID='s2' AND (RatingID='G' OR RatingID='PG')
ORDER BY DVDName;
```

The first expression specifies that the StatID value must be s2, the second expression specifies that the RatingID value must be G, and the third expression specifies that the RatingID value must be PG. However, the last two expressions are enclosed in parentheses and they are connected by an OR logical operator, so only one of these two conditions must evaluate to true. However, because these conditions are connected to the first condition by an AND operator, the first condition must also evaluate to true. In other words, the StatID value must be s2 and the RatingID value must be G or PG.

The last SELECT statement that you created in this exercise is nearly identical to the previous one, except that you added the NOT logical operator before the parentheses that enclose the last to expressions:

```
SELECT DVDName, MTypeID, RatingID
FROM DVDs
WHERE StatID='s2' AND NOT (RatingID='G' OR RatingID='PG')
ORDER BY DVDName;
```

Because you included the NOT operator, the condition specified within the parentheses (the last two expressions) is negated, so the opposite condition must be met. As a result, the StatID value must be s2, and the RatingID value *cannot* be G or PG.

Bitwise Operators

Bitwise operators are a special type of operator that allow you to compare and modify the bit values associated with numerical values stored in your database. The following table lists the bitwise operators available in MySQL.

Operator	Description
&	The bitwise AND operator that compares bits and returns 1 when each bit equals 1. Otherwise, 0 is returned.
|	The bitwise OR operator that compares bits and returns 1 when at least one of the bits equals 1. Otherwise, 0 is returned.
^	The bitwise XOR operator that compares bits and returns 1 if exactly one of the bits equals 1. Otherwise, 0 is returned.
~	The bitwise negation operator that inverts all bits in a specified number. All 0 bits are converted to 1, and all 1 bits are converted to 0.
<<	The bitwise shift left operator that shifts all bits to the left by the specified number of positions.
>>	The bitwise shift right operator that shifts all bits to the right by the specified number of positions.

You can use the bitwise operators to work directly with numerical values stored within a table. For example, suppose that your database includes a table that stores the attribute settings for specific users of an application. The following table definition provides an example of this type of table:

```
CREATE TABLE Attributes
(
    UserID SMALLINT NOT NULL PRIMARY KEY,
    Settings TINYINT UNSIGNED NOT NULL
);
```

Each row within the table stores the attributes for a specific user. The the UserID column, which is the primary key, indicates the user, and the Settings column stores the application attributes for each user. The Settings column is configured with an unsigned TINYINT data type, so it stores one byte of data, which ranges from 0 through 255. Now suppose that you use the following INSERT statement to add the attribute settings for three users:

```
INSERT INTO Attributes
VALUES (101, 58), (102, 73), (103, 45);
```

For each set of values added to the table, the first value is the UserID value and the second value is the Settings value. Because bitwise operators are concerned with working with bit values, each Settings value is associated with one byte, as shown in Figure 8-1. For example, user 101 contains a Settings value of 58. The byte that represents this number is 00111010 (bit 32 + bit 16+ bit 8 + bit 2 = 58). This means that for user 101, bits 32, 16, 8, and 2 have been set to 1, and all other bits within the byte have been set to 0. Figure 8-1 also shows the bit settings for users 102 and 103.

UserID	Settings	128	64	32	16	8	4	2	1
101	58	0	0	1	1	1	0	1	0
102	73	0	1	0	0	1	0	0	1
103	45	0	0	1	0	1	1	0	1

Figure 8-1

Now suppose that you want to update the settings for user 101 so that bit 1 is also set to 1, as is the case for users 102 and 103. To update row 101, you can use the following UPDATE statement:

```
UPDATE Attributes
SET Settings=Settings | 1
WHERE UserID=101;
```

The UPDATE statement specifies that the bit value in the Settings column (for the row with a UserID value of 101) should be compared to the value of 1 and updated appropriately. Because you use the bitwise OR (|) operator, each bit within the byte is compared. Any bit position that includes a bit value of 1 returns a value of 1. Any bit position that contains only bit values of 0 returns a 0. Figure 8-2 demonstrates how this works. The byte associated with the value 58 is 00111010. The byte that is associated with the value 1 is 00000001. The last row in Figure 8-2 shows the results of the comparisons between the two bytes. For example, bit 16 is set to 1 for value 58 and set to 0 for value 1, so the bitwise OR operator returns a value of 1 for bit 16. As a result, the new value inserted into the Settings column is 59 (bit 32 + bit 16+ bit 8+ bit 2 + bit 1 = 59).

Settings	128	64	32	16	8	4	2	1
58	0	0	1	1	1	0	1	0
1	0	0	0	0	0	0	0	1
59	0	0	1	1	1	0	1	1

Figure 8-2

You can confirm that the correct change has been made to the Attributes table by running the following SELECT statement:

```
SELECT * FROM Attributes;
```

When you execute the statement, you should receive the following result set:

```
+--------+----------+
| UserID | Settings |
+--------+----------+
|    101 |       59 |
|    102 |       73 |
|    103 |       45 |
+--------+----------+
3 rows in set (0.00 sec)
```

As you can see, the Settings value for the row with a UserID value of 101 is now set to 59.

As you saw earlier in this section, you can also use bitwise operators to manipulate bits in other ways. For example, the following UPDATE statement moves each bit to the left one position:

```
UPDATE Attributes
SET Settings=Settings << 1;
```

The bitwise shift left (<<) operator indicate that the bits should be shifted to the left. The value to the right of the carets indicates how many positions the bits should be moved. Figure 8-3 demonstrates what the bits look like after they've been moved to the left one position. Notice that the Settings values have now been modified to reflect the new bit settings. For example, the value for user 101 is now 118 (bit 64 + bit 32 + bit 16+ bit 4+ bit 2 = 118).

UserID	Settings
101	118
102	146
103	90

128	64	32	16	8	4	2	1
0	1	1	1	0	1	1	0
1	0	0	1	0	0	1	0
0	1	0	1	1	0	1	0

Figure 8-3

You can verify the new settings by running the following SELECT statement:

```
SELECT * FROM Attributes;
```

The following result set shows the new values that have been inserted into the Settings column of the Attributes table:

```
+--------+----------+
| UserID | Settings |
+--------+----------+
|    101 |      118 |
|    102 |      146 |
|    103 |       90 |
+--------+----------+
3 rows in set (0.00 sec)
```

As you can see, each Settings value has been updated as a result of using the bitwise operator in your UPDATE statement.

The examples that you have seen in this section are based on only eight bits (one byte) of data. However, bitwise operators support calculations up to 64 buts. As a result, you can perform a bitwise shift left operation as long as there are bits to the left, but you cannot go beyond the 64th bit. For example, if you were to repeat the UPDATE statement shown in the previous example, the bits for user 102 would be shifted out of the first byte into the byte to the left. This would place a bit in bit position 9 (bit 1 of the second byte). As a result, your calculation would begin with bit 1 in the second byte and move to the right accordingly.

In the following Try It Out exercise, you create several SELECT statements that demonstrate how you can use bitwise operators to convert numerical values that represent bit values. The SELECT statements that you create are made up only of SELECT clauses, without specifying any tables or other clauses. The purpose of this exercise is only to demonstrate how the bitwise operators work.

Try It Out   Creating Expressions with Bitwise Operators

To create these statements using bitwise operators, follow these steps:

1. Open the mysql client utility.

2. In the first SELECT statement, you use the bitwise AND (&) operator to manipulate the bit values. Execute the following SELECT statement at the mysql command prompt:

```
SELECT 8 & 8, 8 & 10, 8 & 16;
```

You should receive results similar to the following:

```
+-------+--------+--------+
| 8 & 8 | 8 & 10 | 8 & 16 |
+-------+--------+--------+
|     8 |      8 |      0 |
+-------+--------+--------+
1 row in set (0.03 sec)
```

3. In the next SELECT statement, you use the bitwise OR (|) operator to manipulate the bit values. Execute the following SELECT statement at the mysql command prompt:

```
SELECT 8 | 8, 8 | 10, 8 | 16;
```

You should receive results similar to the following:

```
+-------+--------+--------+
| 8 | 8 | 8 | 10 | 8 | 16 |
+-------+--------+--------+
|     8 |     10 |     24 |
+-------+--------+--------+
1 row in set (0.00 sec)
```

4. The final SELECT statement that you create in this exercise uses the bitwise XOR (^) operator to manipulate the bit values. Execute the following SELECT statement at the mysql command prompt:

```
SELECT 8 ^ 8, 8 ^ 10, 8 ^ 16;
```

You should receive results similar to the following:

```
+-------+--------+--------+
| 8 ^ 8 | 8 ^ 10 | 8 ^ 16 |
+-------+--------+--------+
|     0 |      2 |     24 |
+-------+--------+--------+
1 row in set (0.02 sec)
```

How It Works

For this exercise, you created several SELECT statements that used bitwise operators to calculate numerical values based on manipulating the underlying bit values. The first SELECT statement used the bitwise AND operator, as shown in the following statement:

```
SELECT 8 & 8, 8 & 10, 8 & 16;
```

The SELECT statement is made up only of a SELECT clause that includes three expressions. Each expression contains two arguments, which are numerical values and the bitwise AND operator. The bitwise AND operator compares each bit in the two values and returns 1 if both compared bits are 1 and returns 0 if either of the compared bits or both of those bits is 0. Figure 8-4 demonstrates how bits are compared for the values in each expression.

Value	128	64	32	16	8	4	2	1
8	0	0	0	0	1	0	0	0
8	0	0	0	0	1	0	0	0
8	0	0	0	0	1	0	0	0
8	0	0	0	0	1	0	0	0
10	0	0	0	0	1	0	1	0
8	0	0	0	0	1	0	0	0
8	0	0	0	0	1	0	0	0
16	0	0	0	1	0	0	0	0
0	0	0	0	0	0	0	0	0

Figure 8-4

For example, the second expression uses the bitwise AND operator to compare a value of 8 to a value of 10. The byte that represents the value 8 includes a 1 in the bit 8 position and a 0 in each of the other positions. The byte that represents the value 10 has a 1 in the bit 8 position, a 1 in the bit 2 position, and a 0 in each of the other bit positions. Because both bit 8 positions contain 1, a 1 is returned. Because only one bit 2 position contains a 1, a 0 is returned. However, because all other bit positions are 0, a 0 is returned for those positions. As a result, the value produced by the comparison contains a 1 only in the bit 8 position and nowhere else, which means that the expression produces a value of 8.

The next SELECT statement that you created in this exercise is nearly identical to the last statement, except that you used a bitwise OR operator, rather than an ampersand, as shown in the following statement.

```
SELECT 8 | 8, 8 | 10, 8 | 16;
```

As you can see, this statement also contains three expressions. However, when the bits are compared in each expression, a 1 is returned if one or both bits contain a value of 1, as shown in Figure 8-5. For example, the second expression compares a 10 to 8. Because both values contain a 1 in the bit 8 position, a 1 is returned. In addition, because the second value contains a value of 1 in the bit 2 position, a 1 is returned for that position as well. All other bit positions return a 0 because the compared bits each contain a 0. As a result, the value produced by this expression contains a 1 in the bit 8 position and a 1 in the bit 2 position, which results in a numerical value of 10.

The final SELECT statement that you created is also like the previous statements, except that it uses the bitwise XOR operator, as shown in the following SELECT statement:

```
SELECT 8 ^ 8, 8 ^ 10, 8 ^ 16;
```

Value	128	64	32	16	8	4	2	1
8	0	0	0	0	1	0	0	0
8	0	0	0	0	1	0	0	0
8	0	0	0	0	1	0	0	0
8	0	0	0	0	1	0	0	0
10	0	0	0	0	1	0	1	0
10	0	0	0	0	1	0	1	0
8	0	0	0	0	1	0	0	0
16	0	0	0	1	0	0	0	0
24	0	0	0	1	1	0	0	0

Figure 8-5

In this case, when the bits are compared, a value of 1 is returned only if one of the two bits contains a value of 1, as shown in Figure 8-6. As you can see, if both bits contain a 1, a 0 value is returned. If both bits contain a 0 value, a 0 is again returned. However, if one bit contains a 1 and the other contains a 0, a 1 is returned. For example, in the second expression, bit 2 contains a 0 for the first value and a 1 for the second value, so a 1 is returned. However, bit 8 contains a 1 for both values, so a 0 is returned. In addition, all other bit positions contain a 0 for each value, so a 0 is returned for each of these bit positions. As a result, the value produced by the expression contains a 1 only in bit 2, so the numerical value returned by that expression is 2.

Value	128	64	32	16	8	4	2	1
8	0	0	0	0	1	0	0	0
8	0	0	0	0	1	0	0	0
0	0	0	0	0	0	0	0	0
8	0	0	0	0	1	0	0	0
10	0	0	0	0	1	0	1	0
2	0	0	0	0	0	0	1	0
8	0	0	0	0	1	0	0	0
16	0	0	0	1	0	0	0	0
24	0	0	0	1	1	0	0	0

Figure 8-6

Sort Operators

The final type of operators covered in this chapter are the sort operators, which are used to define a pattern that is compared to values within a column. The rows returned are based on whether the compared values match the specified pattern. The following table describes each of the sort operators.

Operator	Description
BINARY	Converts a string to a binary string so that comparing and sorting data is case-sensitive.
COLLATE	Specifies that a particular collation be used to compare and sort string data.

The best way to understand each of these operators is to look at examples. The examples are based on the following table definition:

```
CREATE TABLE ProductColors
(
    ProdID SMALLINT NOT NULL PRIMARY KEY,
    ProdColor VARCHAR(15) NOT NULL
);
```

For these examples, you can assume that the following INSERT statement was used to populate the ProductColors table:

```
INSERT INTO ProductColors
VALUES (101, 'Red'), (102, 'red'), (103, 'RED'), (104, 'REd'), (105, 'reD'),
    (106, 'Blue'), (107, 'blue'), (108, 'BLUE'), (109, 'BLue'), (110, 'blUE');
```

Notice that the values added to the table include only the primary key values for the first column and some form of the values red or blue for the second columns. The values are added in this way merely to demonstrate how sort operators work.

The first sort operator discussed is the BINARY operator. However, before you see an example of a statement that includes a BINARY operator, take a look at the following SELECT statement:

```
SELECT * FROM ProductColors
WHERE ProdColor='red';
```

As you can see, the statement is a basic SELECT statement that retrieves rows from the ProductColors table. The rows returned are only those that contain a ProdColor value of red, as shown in the following results:

```
+--------+-----------+
| ProdID | ProdColor |
+--------+-----------+
|    101 | Red       |
|    102 | red       |
|    103 | RED       |
|    104 | REd       |
|    105 | reD       |
+--------+-----------+
5 rows in set (0.00 sec)
```

As the result set demonstrates, all variations of the red value are returned, regardless of the capitalization used in each value. This is because MySQL, when retrieving data, ignores the case of that data. However, you can override this default behavior by adding the BINARY operator to your expression, as shown in the following SELECT statement:

```
SELECT * FROM ProductColors
WHERE ProdColor = BINARY 'red';
```

As you can see, this statement is nearly identical to the preceding example, except for the addition of the keyword BINARY directly before the value. As a result, the ProdColor column must match the case of the specified value, as well as matching the value itself. As a result, this statement only returns one row, as shown in the following result set:

```
+--------+-----------+
| ProdID | ProdColor |
+--------+-----------+
|    102 | red       |
+--------+-----------+
1 row in set (0.01 sec)
```

As you can see, the value listed in the ProdColor column of the result set is an exact match to the value specified in the WHERE clause expression.

The next sort operator supported by MySQL is the COLLATE operator, which allows you ro specify a collation in your expression. For example, the following SELECT statement specifies that the latin1_german2_ci collation be used when determining which rows to retrieve:

```
SELECT * FROM ProductColors
WHERE ProdColor COLLATE latin1_german2_ci = 'red';
```

As you can see, the WHERE clause expression in this statement includes the COLLATE keyword and the name of the collation (latin1_german2_ci). By specifying the collation, the comparison operator (the equals operator in this case) compares values based on the specified collation. If you execute this statement, you receive the following results:

```
+--------+-----------+
| ProdID | ProdColor |
+--------+-----------+
|    101 | Red       |
|    102 | red       |
|    103 | RED       |
|    104 | REd       |
|    105 | reD       |
+--------+-----------+
5 rows in set (0.00 sec)
```

As you may have noticed, the results returned are the same as the results returned when you didn't specify the collation. This is because the specified collation and the default collation treat these particular values the same way when sorting and comparing values. Whenever you specify a collation, you should be well aware of how that collation differs from the default that is used; otherwise you might end up with results you were not looking for. In addition, any collation that you do specify must be supported by the character set being used.

This next exercise allows you to try out the BINARY sort operator in a SELECT statement that retrieves data from the DVDs table in the DVDRentals database. You actually create two SELECT statements in this exercise, one that does not use the BINARY operator and one that does.

Try It Out   **Creating Expressions with Sort Operators**

To create these statements that employ sort operators, follow these steps:

1. Open the mysql client utility, type the following command, and press Enter:

```
use DVDRentals
```

You should receive a message indicating that you switched to the DVDRentals database.

2. The first SELECT statement that you create does not use the BINARY operator. Execute the following SELECT statement at the mysql command prompt:

```
SELECT DVDName, StatID, RatingID
FROM DVDs
WHERE DVDName REGEXP 'W'
ORDER BY DVDName;
```

You should receive results similar to the following:

```
+-----------------------------+--------+----------+
| DVDName                     | StatID | RatingID |
+-----------------------------+--------+----------+
| A Room with a View          | s1     | NR       |
| The Rocky Horror Picture Show | s2   | NR       |
| What's Up, Doc?             | s2     | G        |
| White Christmas             | s1     | NR       |
+-----------------------------+--------+----------+
4 rows in set (0.00 sec)
```

3. Now create a SELECT statement nearly identical to the one that you created in Step 2, except that the new statement includes the BINARY operator. Execute the following SELECT statement at the mysql command prompt:

```
SELECT DVDName, StatID, RatingID
FROM DVDs
WHERE DVDName REGEXP BINARY 'W'
ORDER BY DVDName;
```

You should receive results similar to the following:

```
+-----------------+--------+----------+
| DVDName         | StatID | RatingID |
+-----------------+--------+----------+
| What's Up, Doc? | s2     | G        |
| White Christmas | s1     | NR       |
+-----------------+--------+----------+
2 rows in set (0.05 sec)
```

How It Works

In this statement, you created two SELECT statements. The statements were nearly identical except that the first one did not contain the BINARY operator and the second one did, as shown in the following statement:

```
SELECT DVDName, StatID, RatingID
FROM DVDs
WHERE DVDName REGEXP BINARY 'W'
ORDER BY DVDName;
```

As you can see, the WHERE clause includes an expression that uses the REGEXP operator to compare the letter W to the values in the DVDName clause. The first SELECT statement returned any row that contains a DVDName value that included a W. However, adding the BINARY operator ensured that only those rows that contain an uppercase W were returned.

Summary

As you have seen in this chapter, operators are critical to your ability to create effective expressions, and expressions are essential to creating flexible, robust SQL statements. Operators allow you to perform calculations on the values derived from individual arguments as well as allow you to compare those values. You can also use operators to join the values derived from individual expressions in order to specify a unified condition, and you can specify comparison and sorting criteria in your expressions. Specifically, this chapter provided you the background information and examples necessary to perform the following tasks:

- ❑ Use arithmetic operators to perform calculations on the elements within an expression.

- ❑ Use comparison operators to compare arguments within an expression in order to test values to determine whether they return a result of true, false, or NULL.

- ❑ Use logical operators to join multiple expressions to test whether the expressions, when taken as a whole, return a result of true, false, or NULL.

- ❑ Use bitwise operators to compare the actual bit value associated with a numerical value in order to manipulate those bits.

- ❑ Use sort operators to specify the collation and case-sensitivity of searching and sorting operations.

Each type of operation can play a critical role in creating effective expressions. However, operators are not the only components that can play a significant part in an expression. Functions provide powerful tools for creating expressions that, when used in conjunction with operators, allow you to manipulate column and literal values to create dynamic data management statements that are precise, flexible, and very effective. For that reason, the next chapter introduces you to the functions that MySQL supports and explains how you can incorporate them into your SQL statements.

Exercises

For these exercises, you create a number of SQL statements that use various types of operators to return results or update rows. The exercises are based on the following table definition:

```
CREATE TABLE Produce
(
    ProdID SMALLINT UNSIGNED NOT NULL PRIMARY KEY,
    ProdName VARCHAR(40) NOT NULL,
    Variety VARCHAR(40) NULL,
    InStock SMALLINT UNSIGNED NOT NULL,
    OnOrder SMALLINT UNSIGNED NOT NULL,
    SeasonAttr TINYINT UNSIGNED NOT NULL
);
```

You can assume that the following INSERT statement has been used to populate the Produce table:

```
INSERT INTO Produce
VALUES (101, 'Apples', 'Red Delicious', 2000, 1000, 4),
(102, 'Apples', 'Fuji', 1500, 1200, 4),
(103, 'Apples', 'Golden Delicious', 500, 1000, 4),
(104, 'Apples', 'Granny Smith', 300, 800, 4),
(105, 'Oranges', 'Valencia', 1200, 1600, 15),
(106, 'Oranges', 'Seville', 1300, 1000, 15),
(107, 'Grapes', 'Red seedless', 3500, 1500, 4),
(108, 'Grapes', 'Green seedless', 3500, 1500, 4),
(109, 'Carrots', NULL, 4500, 1500, 6),
(110, 'Broccoli', NULL, 800, 2500, 6),
(111, 'Cherries', 'Bing', 2500, 2500, 2),
(112, 'Cherries', 'Rainier', 1500, 1500, 2),
(113, 'Zucchini', NULL, 1000, 1300, 2),
(114, 'Mushrooms', 'Shitake', 800, 900, 15),
(115, 'Mushrooms', 'Porcini', 400, 600, 15),
(116, 'Mushrooms', 'Portobello', 900, 1100, 15),
(117, 'Cucumbers', NULL, 2500, 1200, 2);
```

Use the Produce table to complete the following exercises. You can find the answers to these exercises in Appendix A.

1. Create a SELECT statement that retrieves data from the ProdName, InStock, and OnOrder columns. In addition, the result set should include a column named Total that contains the values of the InStock column added to the OnOrder column. The result set should also be ordered according to the values in the ProdName column.

2. Create a SELECT statement that retrieves data from the ProdName, Variety, InStock, and OnOrder columns. The result set should include only rows whose InStock plus OnOrder values are greater than or equal to 5000. The result set should also be ordered according to the values in the ProdName column.

3. Create a SELECT statement that retrieves data from the ProdName, Variety, and InStock columns. The rows returned should have an InStock value greater than or equal to 1000. In addition, the rows should contain a ProdName value of Apples or Oranges. The result set should also be ordered according to the values in the ProdName column.

4. Create an UPDATE statement that modifies the rows that have a ProdName value of Grapes. The SeasonAttr values within those rows should be modified so that the bit 2 position is set to one, without affecting any of the other bit positions.

5. Create a SELECT statement that retrieves data from the ProdName, Variety, and InStock columns. The rows returned should contain a ProdName value that includes the "Ch" pattern anywhere within that value. The pattern's case should be preserved when matching product names. In addition, the result set should be ordered according to the values in the ProdName column.

Using Functions in Your SQL Statements

In earlier chapters, you learned how to use expressions in your SQL statements to make those statements more robust and specific. As you recall, one of the elements that you can use in an expression is a function. Each function performs a specific task and then returns a value that represents the output resulting from the performance of that task. For many functions, you must provide one or more arguments that supply the parameters used by the functions to perform the necessary tasks. These tasks can include calculating numeric data, manipulating string data, returning system data, converting and extracting data, and performing numerous other operations.

In this chapter, you learn about many of the functions included in MySQL. The chapter explains the purpose of each of these functions, describes the results you can expect when a statement includes a function, and provides numerous examples that demonstrate how to use each function. Although this chapter doesn't describe every function included with MySQL, it covers many of them, focusing on those that you're most likely to use when creating SQL statements. Specifically, the chapter covers the following types of functions:

❑   Comparison, control flow, and cast functions that allow you to compare and convert data

❑   String, numeric, and date/time functions that allow you to manipulate, calculate, convert, extract, and concatenate data

❑   Aggregate functions that you can use in SELECT statements to summarize data that has been grouped together by a GROUP BY clause

❑   Encryption, system-related, and query and insert functions that allow you to perform system operations

Comparing and Converting Data

MySQL provides three types of functions that allow you to compare and convert data. These include comparison functions, control flow functions, and cast functions. In this section, you learn about these types of functions and review examples that demonstrate how they're used.

> *The functions included as part of the MySQL installation are referred to as built-in functions. These are the type of functions that you learn about in this chapter. MySQL also supports the creation of user-defined functions, which are functions that you can write in C or C++ and then use in MySQL SQL statements. To use user-defined functions, you must compile the mysqld server program dynamically, not statically, and your operating system must support dynamic loading. Because user-defined functions are beyond scope of this book, you should refer to the MySQL product documentation for more information about how to create and use them.*

Comparison Functions

Comparison functions are similar to the comparison operators that you saw in Chapter 8. These functions allow you to compare different values and, from those comparisons, return one of the values or return a condition of true, false, or NULL. If either argument or both arguments in a comparison are NULL, NULL is returned. This section covers many of the more common comparison functions supported by MySQL.

GREATEST() and LEAST() Functions

Two functions that are useful for comparing values are the GREATEST() and LEAST() functions, which allow you to compare two or more values and return the value that is either the highest or lowest, depending on the function used. The values specified can be numeric, string, or date/time values and are compared based on the current character set. The GREATEST() function uses the following syntax:

```
GREATEST(<value1>, <value2> [{, <value>}...])
```

When you use this function, you must specify at least two values, although you can specify as many additional values as necessary. As with most arguments in a function, the arguments are separated by commas.

One other thing to note about this and any function is that the arguments are enclosed by parentheses and the opening parenthesis follows directly after the function name. A space after the function name is not permitted. For example, a basic SELECT statement might use the GREATEST() function as follows:

```
SELECT GREATEST(4, 83, 0, 9, -3);
```

If you were to execute this statement, the value 83 would be returned because it is the highest number in the set of values. Of course, you do not need to use the GREATEST() function to see that the highest number is 83. The example here merely demonstrates the format used when including the GREATEST() function in your SQL statement. In actuality, you would probably pass the function arguments to the statement through your application or through variables. For example, suppose that you are working with a database that includes a table that lists books and another table that lists publishers. Now suppose that you had used SELECT statements to assign PublisherID values to several variables. You can then use the GREATEST() function to compare the values represented by those variables. For example, the following SELECT statement uses the GREATEST() function in the WHERE clause:

```
SELECT BookID, BookTitle, PublisherID
FROM Books
WHERE PublisherID=GREATEST(@id1, @id2, @id3, @id4, @id5)
ORDER BY BookTitle;
```

This statement retrieves only those books that have the highest PublisherID value. To retrieve those books, you don't have to know the PublisherID values because those values were assigned to the variables in a separate process.

For the purposes of this chapter, the majority of the function examples shown are based on the most basic SELECT statement, where only the SELECT clause is included. This is done for the sake of brevity and in order to cover as many functions as reasonably possible. Keep in mind, though, that you may find that these functions provide you with far greater value when used in other ways in your SQL statements, as this chapter's Try It Out sections demonstrate.

Now take a look at the LEAST() function. As the following syntax shows, the function is identical to the GREATEST() function except that the LEAST keyword is used rather than GREATEST:

```
LEAST(<value1>, <value2> [{, <value>}...])
```

Again, you must include at least two values and separate those values with a comma, as shown in the following example:

```
SELECT LEAST(4, 83, 0, 9, -3);
```

As you would expect, this statement returns a value of -3. If you specify string values, then the lowest value alphabetically (for example, a before b) is returned, and if you specify date/time values, the earliest date is returned.

COALESCE() and ISNULL() Functions

The COALESCE() function returns the first value in the list of arguments that is not NULL. If all values are NULL, then NULL is returned. The following syntax shows how this function is used:

```
COALESCE(<value> [{, <value>}...])
```

For the COALESCE() function, you must specify at least one value, although the function is more useful if multiple values are provided, as shown in the following example:

```
SELECT COALESCE(NULL, 2, NULL, 3);
```

In this case, the value 2 is returned because it is the first value that is not NULL. The ISNULL() function is also concerned with null values, although the output is not one of the specified values. Instead, ISNULL() returns a value of 1 if the expression evaluates to NULL; otherwise, the function returns a value of 0. The syntax for the ISNULL() function is as follows:

```
ISNULL(<expression>)
```

When using this function, you must specify an expression in the parentheses, as shown in the following example:

```
SELECT ISNULL(1*NULL);
```

The expression in this statement is 1*NULL. As you recall, an expression evaluates to NULL if either argument is NULL. Because the expression evaluates to NULL, the ISNULL() function returns a value of 1, rather than 0.

A function such as ISNULL() can be handy when developing an application if your application includes conditional logic that needs to determine whether a value is NULL before taking an action. For example, suppose that you have a form that updates data in a table. You want the form to ask for a user's date of birth only if that user already hasn't provided a date of birth. You can use the ISNULL() function to check the appropriate column in the database table to determine whether a value exists. If a value of 1 is returned, then your application should ask the user for a date of birth. If a value of 0 is returned, the user should not be asked.

INTERVAL() and STRCMP() Functions

The INTERVAL() function compares the first integer listed as an argument to the integers that follow the first integer. The following syntax shows how to use this function:

```
INTERVAL(<integer1>, <integer2> [{, <integer>}...])
```

Starting with <integer2>, the values must be listed in ascending order. If <integer1> is less than <integer2>, a value of 0 is returned. If <integer1> is less than <integer3>, a value of 1 is returned. If <integer1> is less than <integer4>, a value of 2 is returned, and so on. The following SELECT statement demonstrates how the INTERVAL() function works:

```
SELECT INTERVAL(6, -2, 0, 4, 7, 10, 12);
```

In this case, <integer1> is greater than <integer2>, <integer3>, and <integer4>, but less than <integer5>, so a value of 3 is returned, which represents the position of <integer5>. In other words, 7 is the first value in the list that 6 is less than.

The STRCMP() is different from the INTERVAL() function in that it compares string values that can be literal values or derived from expressions, as shown in the following syntax:

```
STRCMP(<expression1>, <expression2>)
```

As the syntax shows, the STRCMP() function compares exactly two values. The function returns a 0 if <expression1> equals <expression2> and returns -1 if <expression1> is smaller than <expression2>. If <expression1> is larger than <expression2>, or if a NULL is returned by the comparison, the function returns a 1. For example, the following SQL statement compares two literal values:

```
SELECT STRCMP('big', 'bigger');
```

The values are compared based on the current character set. Because big is smaller than bigger (it is first alphabetically), the statement returns a -1.

In the following exercise, you create two SELECT statements that each define a variable based on a DVDID value in the DVDs table of the DVDRentals database. Once you've assigned values to the variables, you include them in a SELECT statement that uses the LEAST() comparison function to compare values stored in the variables.

Try It Out   **Passing Values to a Comparison Function**

The following steps describe how to create statements that use comparison functions:

1.   Open the mysql client utility, type the following command, and press Enter:

```
use DVDRentals
```

You should receive a message indicating that you switched to the DVDRentals database.

2.   The first SELECT statement that you create assigns a value to the @dvd1 variable. Execute the following SQL statement at the mysql command prompt:

```
SELECT @dvd1:=DVDID
FROM DVDs
WHERE DVDName='White Christmas';
```

You should receive results similar to the following:

```
+--------------+
| @dvd1:=DVDID |
+--------------+
|            1 |
+--------------+
1 row in set (0.05 sec)
```

3.   Next assign a value to the @dvd2 variable. Execute the following SQL statement at the mysql command prompt:

```
SELECT @dvd2:=DVDID
FROM DVDs
WHERE DVDName='Out of Africa';
```

You should receive results similar to the following:

```
+--------------+
| @dvd2:=DVDID |
+--------------+
|            3 |
+--------------+
1 row in set (0.00 sec)
```

4.   Now use the variables that you created in steps 2 and 3 in the WHERE clause of a SELECT statement. Execute the following SQL statement at the mysql command prompt:

```
SELECT OrderID, TransID, DVDID
FROM Transactions
WHERE DVDID=LEAST(@dvd1, @dvd2)
ORDER BY OrderID, TransID;
```

You should receive results similar to the following:

```
+----------+----------+--------+
| OrderID  | TransID  | DVDID  |
+----------+----------+--------+
|        1 |        1 |      1 |
|        3 |        6 |      1 |
|        6 |       11 |      1 |
|        8 |       14 |      1 |
|        9 |       17 |      1 |
+----------+----------+--------+
7 rows in set (0.10 sec)
```

How It Works

In Chapter 7, you learned how to create SELECT statements that assigned values to variables. You were then able to use those variables in other SQL statements executed in the same user session. To complete this exercise, you created the same type of SELECT statements so that the LEAST() comparison function could use variables to compare values in the WHERE clause of the following SELECT statement:

```
SELECT OrderID, TransID, DVDID
FROM Transactions
WHERE DVDID=LEAST(@dvd1, @dvd2)
ORDER BY OrderID, TransID;
```

In this statement, @dvd1 and @dvd2 are used as arguments in the LEAST() function. Because you assigned the @dvd1 variable a value of 1 and the @dvd2 variable a value of 3, the LEAST() function compares the value of 1 to the value of 3. As a result, the WHERE clause expression is interpreted as DVDID=1 because 1 is the lower of the two values. The rest of the SELECT statement is then executed as other SELECT statements you have seen. The SELECT list indicates that the result set should include only the OrderID, TransID, and DVDID columns. The WHERE clause indicates that the only rows returned should be those that contain a DVDID value of 1. The ORDER BY clause indicates that the result set should be ordered first by the values in the OrderID column and then by the values in the TransID column.

Control Flow Functions

The types of functions that you look at next are those that return a result by comparing conditions. The returned value is determined by which condition is true.

IF() Function

The IF() function compares three expressions, as shown in the following syntax:

```
IF(<expression1>, <expression2>, <expression3>)
```

If <expression1> evaluates to true, then the function returns <expression2>; otherwise, the function returns <expression3>. Take a look at an example to demonstrate how this works. The following SELECT statement evaluates the first expression and then returns one of the two literal values:

```
SELECT IF(10>20, 'expression correct', 'expression incorrect');
```

In this statement, literal values are used for the second and third expressions. Because the first expression (10>20) evaluates to false, the third expression is returned. This function is useful if you want to return a specific response based on the value returned by the IF() function. For example, suppose that you're developing an application for a bookstore. The application should be able to check the database to determine whether requested books are in stock. If the book is in stock, the results should return the department in which the book can be found. If the book is not in stock, the results should return the International Standard Book Number (ISBN) of the book so that it can be ordered. You can use the IF() function to check a column that retrieves the number of books in stock. Based on the value returned, the function can then return either a value from a column that specifies the department where the book can be found or a value from a different column that specifies the book's ISBN.

IFNULL() and NULLIF() Functions

The IFNULL() function returns a value based on whether a specified expression evaluates to NULL. The function includes two expressions, as shown in the following syntax:

```
IFNULL(<expression1>, <expression2>)
```

The function returns <expression1> if it is not NULL; otherwise, it returns <expression2>. For example, the following SELECT statement includes an IFNULL() function whose first expression is NULL:

```
SELECT IFNULL(10*NULL, 'expression incorrect');
```

Because the first expression (10*NULL) evaluates to NULL, the NULL value is not returned. Instead, the second expression is returned. In this case, the second expression is a literal value, so that is the value returned.

To get a better idea of how this function works, suppose that you are developing an application that tracks profile information about a company's customers. The profile data is stored in a database that includes a table for contact information. The table includes a column for a home phone number and a column for a cell phone number. Along with other details about the employee, the application should display the customer's home phone number if that is known. If not, the application should display the cell phone number. You can use the IFNULL() function to specify that the home number should be returned unless that value is NULL, in which case the cell phone number should be returned.

The NULLIF() function is a little different from the IFNULL() function. The NULLIF() function returns NULL if <expression1> equals <expression2>; otherwise, it returns <expression1>. The syntax for the NULLIF() function is as follows:

```
NULLIF(<expression1>, <expression2>)
```

The following SELECT statement demonstrates how this works:

```
SELECT NULLIF(10*20, 20*10);
```

As you can see, the statement specifies two expressions. Because they are equal (they both return a value of 200), NULL is returned, rather than the value of 200 returned by the first expression.

CASE() Function

The CASE() function is a little more complicated than the previous control flow functions that you looked at. This function, though, provides far more flexibility in terms of the number of conditions that you can evaluate and the type of results that you can provide.

The CASE() function supports two slightly different formats. The first of these is shown in the following syntax:

```
CASE WHEN <expression> THEN <result>
    [{WHEN <expression> THEN <result>}...]
    [ELSE <result>]
END
```

As the syntax shows, you must specify the CASE keyword, followed by at least one WHEN...THEN clause. The WHEN...THEN clause specifies the expression to be evaluated and the results to be returned if that expression evaluates to true. You can specify as many WHEN...THEN clauses as necessary. The next clause is the ELSE clause, which is also optional. The ELSE clause provides a default result in case none of the expressions in the WHEN...THEN clauses evaluate to true. Finally, the CASE() function construction must be terminated with the END keyword.

The following SELECT statement demonstrates how this form of the CASE() function works:

```
SELECT CASE WHEN 10*2=30 THEN '30 correct'
    WHEN 10*2=40 THEN '40 correct'
    ELSE 'Should be 10*2=20'
END;
```

As you can see, the first WHEN...THEN clause specifies an expression (10*2=30) and a result ('30 correct'). The result is returned if the expression evaluates to true. The statement includes two WHEN...THEN clauses; if the expression in the first one evaluates to true, that result is returned. If the expression in the second WHEN...THEN clause evaluates to true, that result is returned. If neither clause evaluates to true, the result in the ELSE clause is returned. In this case, the result in the ELSE clause is returned because neither WHEN...THEN clause expression evaluates to true.

The next version of the CASE() function is slightly different from the first, as shown in the following syntax:

```
CASE <expression>
    WHEN <value> THEN <result>
    [{WHEN <value> THEN <result>}...]
    [ELSE <result>]
END
```

The main difference in this version of the CASE() function is that the expression is specified after the keyword CASE, and the WHEN...THEN clauses include the possible values that result from that expression. The following example demonstrates how this form of the CASE() function works:

```
SELECT CASE 10*2
    WHEN 20 THEN '20 correct'
    WHEN 30 THEN '30 correct'
    WHEN 40 THEN '40 correct'
END;
```

As you can see, the CASE() function includes the expression (10*2) after the CASE keyword. Three WHEN...THEN clauses follow the CASE keyword, each of which contains a possible value that represents the value returned by the expression. In this case, the first WHEN...THEN clause evaluates to true because it contains the correct value (20) returned by the expression. Also notice that the CASE() function doesn't include an ELSE clause. The assumption here is that one of the WHEN...THEN clauses contains the correct values. If you do include an ELSE clause, it works the same way as the ELSE clause in the previous form of the CASE() function. The ELSE clause provides a default result in case none of the expressions in the WHEN...THEN clauses evaluates to true.

The CASE() function is similar to the logic found in application languages. By using the CASE(), you're switching the conditional logic from the application side to the database side. This can be useful if you want to shift some of the business logic to the back end, helping to minimize some of the front-end processing. In this way, the database determines what value to return, rather than the application itself.

For example, suppose that you are developing an application that retrieves data about different car models. If a model is available in different editions, a list of the editions should be returned, as well as the basic details about the model; otherwise, only basic details should be returned. You can use the CASE() function to first determine how many editions are available for a model. If the amount is greater than one, then the list of editions should be included in the results; otherwise, no edition information should be included.

In the next exercise you try out some of the control flow functions that you learned about in this section. To use these functions, you create SELECT statements that retrieve data from the DVDs table in the DVDRentals database.

Try It Out   Using Control Flow Functions in a SELECT Statement

The following steps describe how to create statements that use control flow functions:

1. Open the mysql client utility, type the following command, and press Enter:

```
use DVDRentals
```

You should receive a message indicating that you switched to the DVDRentals database.

2. The first SELECT statement uses the IF() function in the SELECT clause to retrieve data. Execute the following SQL statement at the mysql command prompt:

```
SELECT DVDName AS Title, StatID AS Status, RatingID AS Rating,
    IF(NumDisks>1, 'Check for extra disks!', 'Only 1 disk.') AS Verify
FROM DVDs
ORDER BY Title;
```

You should receive results similar to the following:

```
+-------------------------------+--------+--------+------------------------+
| Title                         | Status | Rating | Verify                 |
+-------------------------------+--------+--------+------------------------+
| A Room with a View            | s1     | NR     | Only 1 disk.           |
| Amadeus                       | s2     | PG     | Only 1 disk.           |
| Mash                          | s2     | R      | Check for extra disks! |
| Out of Africa                 | s1     | PG     | Only 1 disk.           |
| The Maltese Falcon            | s2     | NR     | Only 1 disk.           |
| The Rocky Horror Picture Show | s2     | NR     | Check for extra disks! |
```

```
| What's Up, Doc?              | s2     | G      | Only 1 disk.           |
| White Christmas              | s1     | NR     | Only 1 disk.           |
+-----------------------------+--------+--------+------------------------+
8 rows in set (0.00 sec)
```

3. Now try out the CASE() function. Execute the following SQL statement at the mysql command prompt:

```
SELECT DVDName, RatingID AS Rating,
    CASE
        WHEN RatingID='R' THEN 'Under 17 requires an adult.'
        WHEN RatingID='X' THEN 'No one 17 and under.'
        WHEN RatingID='NR' THEN 'Use discretion when renting.'
        ELSE 'OK to rent to minors.'
    END AS Policy
FROM DVDs
ORDER BY DVDName;
```

You should receive results similar to the following:

```
+-----------------------------+--------+------------------------------------+
| DVDName                     | Rating | Policy                             |
+-----------------------------+--------+------------------------------------+
| A Room with a View          | NR     | Use discretion when renting.       |
| Amadeus                     | PG     | OK to rent to minors.              |
| Mash                        | R      | Under 17 requires an adult.        |
| Out of Africa               | PG     | OK to rent to minors.              |
| The Maltese Falcon          | NR     | Use discretion when renting.       |
| The Rocky Horror Picture Show | NR   | Use discretion when renting.       |
| What's Up, Doc?             | G      | OK to rent to minors.              |
| White Christmas             | NR     | Use discretion when renting.       |
+-----------------------------+--------+------------------------------------+
8 rows in set (0.01 sec)
```

4. In the next statement, you also use the CASE() function, but you use a different form of that function. Execute the following SQL statement at the mysql command prompt:

```
SELECT DVDName, RatingID AS Rating,
    CASE RatingID
        WHEN 'R' THEN 'Under 17 requires an adult.'
        WHEN 'X' THEN 'No one 17 and under.'
        WHEN 'NR' THEN 'Use discretion when renting.'
        ELSE 'OK to rent to minors.'
    END AS Policy
FROM DVDs
ORDER BY DVDName;
```

You should receive the same results that you received when you executed the statement in Step 3.

How It Works

You should be well familiar with most of the elements in the SELECT statement that you created in this exercise. If you have any questions about how the statement is used, refer back to Chapter 7 for an explanation of SELECT statements. These statements include functions that you have not used before, so individual examinations of each one follow. In the first SELECT statement that you created, you included the IF() function:

```
SELECT DVDName AS Title, StatID AS Status, RatingID AS Rating,
    IF(NumDisks>1, 'Check for extra disks!', 'Only 1 disk.') AS Verify
FROM DVDs
ORDER BY Title;
```

The IF() function is used as one of the elements in the SELECT list. The function includes three arguments. The first argument is an expression (NumDisks>1) that determines whether the second or third argument in the function is returned. For each row in which the NumDisks value is greater than 1, the first message is returned. For all other rows, the second message is returned. Notice that the column in the result set that includes the data returned by the IF() function is named Verify. You can assign aliases to select list elements constructed with functions as you would any other select list element. (For details about assigning an alias to an element in the select list, see Chapter 7.)

The next SELECT statement that you created uses a CASE() function to specify a set of results to return depending on the value in the RatingID column:

```
SELECT DVDName, RatingID AS Rating,
    CASE
        WHEN RatingID='R' THEN 'Under 17 requires an adult.'
        WHEN RatingID='X' THEN 'No one 17 and under.'
        WHEN RatingID='NR' THEN 'Use discretion when renting.'
        ELSE 'OK to rent to minors.'
    END AS Policy
FROM DVDs
ORDER BY DVDName;
```

The CASE() function includes three WHEN...THEN clauses and one ELSE clause. This means that the function can return four possible results, depending on the value in the RatingID column. Specific results are assigned to the values R, X, and NR, but all other RatingID values are assigned the result in the ELSE clause. Notice that the CASE() function is one of the elements in the select list of the SELECT clause. Also notice that it is assigned the name Policy. For each row returned by the SELECT statement, the Policy column includes one of the four results returned by the CASE() function.

The last SELECT statement that you created in this exercise uses a different form of the CASE() function than you used in the previous statement; however, the outcome is the same. In the updated SELECT statement, the expression is specified after the CASE keyword:

```
SELECT DVDName, RatingID AS Rating,
    CASE RatingID
        WHEN 'R' THEN 'Under 17 requires an adult.'
        WHEN 'X' THEN 'No one 17 and under.'
        WHEN 'NR' THEN 'Use discretion when renting.'
        ELSE 'OK to rent to minors.'
    END AS Policy
FROM DVDs
ORDER BY DVDName;
```

As you can see, the expression specified after CASE is made up only of the RatingID column name. No other elements are necessary to qualify as an expression. In addition, the WHEN...THEN clauses no longer contain expressions, but contain only the values returned by the RatingID column.

Cast Functions

Cast functions allow you to convert values to a specific type of data or to assign a character set to a value. The first of these functions is the CAST() function, which is shown in the following syntax:

```
CAST(<expression> AS <type>)
```

The function converts the value returned by the expression to the specified conversion type, which follows the AS keyword. The CAST() function supports a limited number of conversion types. These types are similar to data types, but they are specific to the CAST() function (and the CONVERT() function) and serve a slightly different purpose, which is to specify how the data is converted. Data types, on the other hand, specify the type of data that can be inserted in a column. (For more information about data types, see Chapter 5.)

The conversion types available to the CAST() function are as follows:

❑ BINARY

❑ CHAR

❑ DATE

❑ DATETIME

❑ SIGNED [INTEGER]

❑ TIME

❑ UNSIGNED [INTEGER]

For example, you might have a numeric value (either a literal value or one returned by an expression) that you want converted to the DATE conversion type. The following SELECT statement demonstrates how you might do this:

```
SELECT CAST(20041031 AS DATE);
```

As you can see, the value is specified, followed by the AS keyword, and then followed by the DATE conversion type. The value returned by this function will be in a DATE format (2004-10-31).

The CONVERT() function allows you to convert dates in the same way as the CAST() function, only the format is a little different, as shown in the following syntax:

```
CONVERT(<expression>, <type>)
```

Notice that you need to specify only the expression and the conversion type, without the AS keyword, but you must separate the two by a comma. The conversion types you can use in the CONVERT() function are the same as those you can use for the CAST() function. For example, the following SELECT statement produces the same results as the last example:

```
SELECT CONVERT(20041031, DATE);
```

Notice that you need to specify only the numeric value and the DATE conversion type. The CONVERT() function, however, also includes another form, as shown in the following syntax:

```
CONVERT(<expression> USING <character set>)
```

This form is used to assign a character set to the specified expression. For example, the following SELECT statement converts a string to the latin2 character set:

```
SELECT CONVERT('cats and dogs' USING latin2);
```

In this statement, the CONVERT() function includes the expression (which is a literal string), followed by the USING keyword and the name of the character set (latin2). The value returned is the string value in the new character set. (In this case, the value is the same as it appears in the function.)

The CAST() and CONVERT() functions are particularly useful when you want to convert data stored in a MySQL database to a format that can be used by an application. For example, suppose that you have a table in a MySQL database that includes a DATETIME column. You also have an application that needs to use those values, but it cannot work with them as DATETIME values. As a result, you need to convert those values to numerical (UNSIGNED INTEGER) values that can be used by the application. To achieve this conversion, you can use the CAST() or CONVERT() function as you're retrieving data from the database. This next exercise allows you to try out the CAST() and CONVERT() functions in SELECT statements. You convert a date value to an integer.

Try It Out   Converting Data to Different Types

To create statements that convert values, follow these steps:

1. Open the mysql client utility, type the following command, and press Enter:

```
use DVDRentals
```

You should receive a message indicating that you switched to the DVDRentals database.

2. The first SELECT statement that you create includes the CAST() function. Execute the following SQL statement at the mysql command prompt:

```
SELECT OrderID, TransID, DVDID,
    CAST(DateOut AS UNSIGNED INTEGER) AS DateOut_INT
FROM Transactions
WHERE DVDID=4 OR DVDID=5 OR DVDID=7
ORDER BY OrderID, TransID, DVDID;
```

You should receive results similar to the following:

```
+---------+---------+-------+-------------+
| OrderID | TransID | DVDID | DateOut_INT |
+---------+---------+-------+-------------+
|       1 |       2 |     4 |    20041007 |
|       3 |       5 |     4 |    20041007 |
|       3 |       7 |     7 |    20041007 |
|       4 |       8 |     4 |    20041007 |
|       7 |      12 |     4 |    20041007 |
|       9 |      16 |     7 |    20041007 |
|      10 |      18 |     5 |    20041007 |
|      12 |      22 |     5 |    20041007 |
|      13 |      23 |     7 |    20041007 |
+---------+---------+-------+-------------+
9 rows in set (0.10 sec)
```

3. Next modify the SELECT statement to use the CONVERT() function. Execute the following SQL statement at the mysql command prompt:

```
SELECT OrderID, TransID, DVDID,
    CONVERT(DateOut, UNSIGNED) AS DateOut_INT
FROM Transactions
WHERE DVDID=4 OR DVDID=5 OR DVDID=7
ORDER BY OrderID, TransID, DVDID;
```

You should receive the same results that you received when you executed the SELECT statement in Step 2.

How It Works

In this exercise, you created two SELECT statements. The first of these included the CAST() function as an element in the select list of the SELECT clause:

```
SELECT OrderID, TransID, DVDID,
    CAST(DateOut AS UNSIGNED INTEGER) AS DateOut_INT
FROM Transactions
WHERE DVDID=4 OR DVDID=5 OR DVDID=7
ORDER BY OrderID, TransID, DVDID;
```

The CAST() function extracts the values from the DateOut column in the Transactions table and converts them to UNSIGNED INTEGER values. The converted values are included in the result set in the DateOut_INT column.

The next SELECT statement that you created produces the same results as the first, only this time you used the CONVERT() function:

```
SELECT OrderID, TransID, DVDID,
    CONVERT(DateOut, UNSIGNED) AS DateOut_INT
FROM Transactions
WHERE DVDID=4 OR DVDID=5 OR DVDID=7
ORDER BY OrderID, TransID, DVDID;
```

As you can see, the DateOut column is again specified as the first argument; however, the second argument consists only of the keyword UNSIGNED. When you specify UNSIGNED, it is the same as specifying UNSIGNED INTEGER. You do not need to include the keyword INTEGER in this case.

Managing Different Types of Data

MySQL includes functions that allow you to manage string, numeric, and date/time data. Unlike the functions that you've already looked at, the next set of functions is specific to a type of data. You can use these functions in conjunction with the functions you've already seen. In many cases, a function can be embedded as an argument in other functions, which makes the use of functions all the more powerful. In several of the Try It Out sections that follow, you see how to embed functions as arguments in other functions.

String Functions

As you would guess, string functions allow you to manipulate and extract string values. MySQL supports numerous string functions. This section covers those that you're most likely to use in your applications and provides examples of each of them.

ASCII() and ORD() Functions

The ASCII() function allows you to identify the numeric value of the first character in a string. The syntax for the function is as follows:

```
ASCII(<string>)
```

To use the ASCII() function, you need only to identify the string, as shown in the following example:

```
SELECT ASCII('book');
```

The SELECT statement returns the numeric value for the first character, which is the letter b. The numeric value for the letter b is 98.

The ASCII() function works only for single-byte characters (with values from 0 to 255). For multi-byte characters, you should use the ORD() function, which is shown in the following syntax:

```
ORD(<string>)
```

The ORD() function works just like the ASCII() function except that it also supports multibyte characters. To use the ORD() function, specify a string (which can include numerals), as shown in the following example:

```
SELECT ORD(37);
```

As with the ASCII() function, the ORD() function returns the numeric value of the first character. For the number 3, the numeric value is 51. If you specify a number, rather than a regular string, you do not need to include the single quotes. In addition, if the function argument is a single-byte character, the results are the same as what you would see when using the ASCII() function.

CHAR_LENGTH(), CHARACTER_LENGTH(), and LENGTH() Functions

The CHAR_LENGTH() and CHARACTER_LENGTH() functions, which are synonymous, return the number of characters in the specified string. The following syntax shows how to use either function:

```
CHAR_LENGTH(<string>)
```

As you can see, you need only to specify the string to determine the length of that string, as shown in the following example:

```
SELECT CHAR_LENGTH('cats and dogs');
```

The statement returns a value of 13, which is the number of characters in the string, including spaces.

The LENGTH() function also returns the length of a string, only the length is measured in bytes, rather than characters. The syntax for the LENGTH() function is similar to the CHAR_LENGTH() and CHARACTER_LENGTH functions:

```
LENGTH(<string>)
```

If you use the LENGTH() function with single-byte characters, the results are the same as with the CHAR_LENGTH() function, as shown in the following example:

```
SELECT LENGTH('cats and dogs');
```

In this case, the result is once again 13. If this were a double-byte character string, though, the result would be 26 because the LENGTH() function measures in bytes, not characters.

The CHAR_LENGTH() and LENGTH() functions can be useful if you need to return values that are greater than or less than a specific length. For example, suppose that you have a table that includes a list of pet-related products. The table includes a Description column that provides a brief description of each product. You want all descriptions to be no longer than 50 characters; however, some descriptions exceed this amount, so you plan to cut content in those columns. To determine which columns exceed 50 characters, you can use the CHAR_LENGTH() function to retrieve those rows whose Description value is greater than 50 characters.

CHARSET() and COLLATION() Functions

The CHARSET() function identifies the character set used for a specified string, as shown in the following syntax:

```
CHARSET(<string>)
```

For example, the following SELECT statement uses the CHARSET() function to return the character set used for the 'cats and dogs' string:

```
SELECT CHARSET('cats and dogs');
```

If you are running a default installation of MySQL, the SELECT statement returns a value of latin1.

You can also identify the collation used for a string by using the COLLATION() function, shown in the following syntax:

```
COLLATION(<string>)
```

As with the CHARSET() function, you need only to specify the string, as the following SELECT statement demonstrates:

```
SELECT COLLATION('cats and dogs');
```

In this case, if working with a default installation of MySQL, the SELECT statement returns a value of latin1_swedish_ci.

Using the CHARSET() and COLLATION() functions to identify the character set or collation of a string can be useful when you want to find this information quickly, without having to search column, table, database, and system settings. By simply using the appropriate function when you retrieve the data, you can avoid the possibility of having to take numerous steps to find the information you need, allowing you to determine exactly what you need with one easy step.

CONCAT() and CONCAT_WS() Functions

MySQL provides two very useful functions that allow you to concatenate data. The first of these is the CONCAT() function, which is shown in the following syntax:

```
CONCAT(<string1>, <string2> [{, <string>}...])
```

As the syntax demonstrates, you must specify two or more string values, which are separated by commas. For example, the following statement concatenates five values:

```
SELECT CONCAT('cats', ' ', 'and', ' ', 'dogs');
```

Notice that the second and fourth values are spaces. This ensures that a space is provided between each of the three words. As a result, the output from this function (cats and dogs) is shown correctly. Another way you can include the spaces is by using the CONCAT_WS() function, which allows you to define a separator as one of the arguments in the function, as shown in the following syntax:

```
CONCAT_WS(<separator>, <string1>, <string2> [{, <string>}...])
```

By using this function, the separator is automatically inserted between the values. If one of the values is NULL, the separator is not used. Except for the separator, the CONCAT_WS() function is the same as the CONCAT() function. For example, the following SELECT statement concatenates the same words as in the last example:

```
SELECT CONCAT_WS(' ', 'cats', 'and', 'dogs');
```

Notice that the CONCAT_WS() function identifies the separator (a space) in the first argument and that the separator is followed by the string values to be concatenated. The output from this function (cats and dogs) is the same as the output you saw in the CONCAT() example.

The CONCAT() and CONCAT_WS functions can be useful in a number of situations. For example, suppose that you have a table that displays employee first names and last names in separate columns. You can use one of these functions to display the names in a single column, while still sorting them according to the last names. You can also use the functions to join other types of data, such as a color to a car model (for instance, red Honda) or a flavor to a food (for instance, chocolate ice cream). There are no limits to the types of string data that you can put together.

INSTR() and LOCATE() Functions

The INSTR() function takes two arguments, a string and a substring, as shown in the following syntax:

```
INSTR(<string>, <substring>)
```

The function identifies where the substring is located in the string and returns the position number. For example, the following INSTR() function returns the position of dogs in the string:

```
SELECT INSTR('cats and dogs', 'dogs');
```

In this case, the substring dogs begins in the tenth position, so the function returns a value of 10. You can achieve the same results by using the LOCATE() function, shown in the following syntax:

```
LOCATE(<substring>, <string>)
```

As you can see, the syntax for the LOCATE() and INSTR() functions is similar except that, with LOCATE(), the substring is listed first, as shown in the following example:

```
SELECT LOCATE('dogs', 'cats and dogs');
```

Again, the function returns a value of 10. The LOCATE() function, however, provides another alternative, as the following syntax demonstrates:

```
LOCATE(<substring>, <string>, <position>)
```

The function includes a third argument, <position>, which identifies a starting position in the function. This is the position at which the function should start looking for the substring. For example, suppose that you create the following SELECT statement:

```
SELECT LOCATE('dogs', 'cats and dogs and more dogs', 15);
```

Notice that the LOCATE() function includes a third argument: 15. This is the position at which the function should begin looking for the substring dogs. As a result, the function disregards the first occurrence of dogs because it is before position 15 and returns a value of 24, which is where the second dogs begins.

LCASE(), LOWER(), UCASE(), and UPPER() Functions

MySQL also includes functions that allow you to change string values to upper or lowercase. For example, the LCASE() and LOWER() functions, which are synonymous, change the case of the specified string, as shown in the following syntax:

```
LOWER(<string>)
```

As you can see, you need to include the string as a function argument. For example, the following SELECT statement uses the LOWER() function to remove the initial capitalizations from the string:

```
SELECT LOWER('Cats and Dogs');
```

The output from this statement is cats and dogs. Notice that the string value now includes no uppercase letters. You can also change lowercase to uppercase by using the UPPER() or UCASE() functions, which are also synonymous. The following syntax shows the UPPER() function:

```
UPPER(<string>)
```

Notice that, as with the LOWER() function, you need only to supply the string, as shown in the following example:

```
SELECT UPPER('cats and dogs');
```

By using the UPPER() function, all characters in the string are returned as uppercase (CATS AND DOGS).

The LOWER() and UPPER() functions are useful whenever you need to change the case of a value. For example, suppose that you have an application that allows customers to register online for product information. The registration information is stored in a table in your database. When the customers enter their e-mail addresses, the addresses are stored as they are entered by the customers, so some are stored as all lowercase, some all uppercase, and some mixed case. When you retrieve those e-mail addresses, you want them displayed as all lowercase. You can use the LOWER() function when you retrieve the e-mail addresses to provide a uniform display.

LEFT() and RIGHT() Functions

MySQL also provides functions that return only a part of a string value. For example, you can use the LEFT() function to return only a specific number of characters from a value, as shown in the following syntax:

```
LEFT(<string>, <length>)
```

The <length> value determines how many characters are returned, starting at the left end of the string. For example, the following SELECT statement returns only the first four characters of the string:

```
SELECT LEFT('cats and dogs', 4);
```

Because the value 4 is specified in the function arguments, the function returns the value cats.

You can also specify which characters are returned starting at the right end of the string by using the following RIGHT() function:

```
RIGHT(<string>, <length>)
```

Notice that the syntax is similar to the LEFT() function. You must again specify the length of the substring that is returned. For example, the following SELECT statement returns only the last four characters of the specified string:

```
SELECT RIGHT('cats and dogs', 4);
```

In this case, the statement returns the value dogs.

The LEFT() and RIGHT() functions are useful when you want to use only part of values from multiple columns. For example, suppose that you want to create a user ID for your employees based on their first and last names. You can use the LEFT() function to take the first three letters of their first names and the first four letters of their last names and then use the CONCAT() function to join these extracted values together.

REPEAT() and REVERSE() Functions

The REPEAT() function, shown in the following syntax, is used to repeat a string a specific number of times:

```
REPEAT(<string>, <count>)
```

To use this function, you must first specify the string and then the number of times that the string should be repeated. The values are then concatenated and returned. For example, the following SELECT statement uses the REPEAT() function to repeat CatsDogs three times:

```
SELECT REPEAT('CatsDogs', 3);
```

The result from this function is CatsDogsCatsDogsCatsDogs.

In addition to repeating string values, you can reverse their order by using the following REVERSE() function:

```
REVERSE(<string>)
```

In this case, you need to specify only the string, as the following SELECT statement shows:

```
SELECT REVERSE('dog');
```

The value returned by this function is god, which, as anyone with a dog will tell you, is exactly what you should expect.

SUBSTRING() Function

The final string function that you examine in this section is the SUBSTRING() function. The function, which includes several forms, returns a substring from the identified string. The first form of the SUBSTRING() function is shown in the following syntax:

```
SUBSTRING(<string>, <position>)
```

In this form of the SUBSTRING() function, you must specify the string and the starting position. The function then returns a substring that includes the rest of the string value, starting at the identified position. You can achieve the same results by using the following syntax:

```
SUBSTRING(<string> FROM <position>)
```

In this case, you must separate the two arguments with the FROM keyword, rather than a comma; however, either method works. For example, you can use the following SELECT statement to return the substring dog, which starts at the tenth position.

```
SELECT SUBSTRING('cats and dogs', 10);
```

As you might have noticed, the SUBSTRING() function, when used this way, is a little limiting because it provides only a starting position but no ending position. MySQL does support another form of the SUBSTRING() function:

```
SUBSTRING(<string>, <position>, <length>)
```

This form includes the <length> argument, which allows you to specify how long (in characters) the substring should be. You can also use the following format to specify the length:

```
SUBSTRING(<string> FROM <position> FOR <length>)
```

In this case, instead of using commas to separate the arguments, you use the FROM and FOR keywords, but the results are the same. The following example demonstrates how to specify a length:

```
SELECT SUBSTRING('cats and dogs and more dogs', 10, 4);
```

Notice that, after defining the string, the function arguments identify the starting position (10) and the length of the substring (4). As a result, the function returns a value of dogs.

As you have seen, string functions allow you to manipulate and extract string values. In the following Try It Out, you try out several of these functions by creating SELECT statements that retrieve data from the DVDRentals database.

Try It Out **Using String Functions in Your SQL Statements**

To create statements employing string functions, follow these steps:

1. Open the mysql client utility, type the following command, and press Enter:

```
use DVDRentals
```

You should receive a message indicating that you switched to the DVDRentals database.

2. The first statement that you create uses the CHAR_LENGTH() function to specify the length of a retrieved value. Execute the following SQL statement at the mysql command prompt:

```
SELECT DVDName, CHAR_LENGTH(DVDName) AS CharLength
FROM DVDs
WHERE CHAR_LENGTH(DVDName)>10
ORDER BY DVDName;
```

You should receive results similar to the following:

```
+-------------------------------+------------+
| DVDName                       | CharLength |
+-------------------------------+------------+
| A Room with a View            |         18 |
| Out of Africa                 |         13 |
| The Maltese Falcon            |         18 |
| The Rocky Horror Picture Show |         29 |
| What's Up, Doc?               |         15 |
| White Christmas               |         15 |
+-------------------------------+------------+
6 rows in set (0.00 sec)
```

3. The next SELECT statement that you create uses the CONCAT_WS() function to concatenate the employee names. Execute the following SQL statement at the mysql command prompt:

```
SELECT EmpID, CONCAT_WS(' ', EmpFN, EmpMN, EmpLN) AS Name
FROM Employees
ORDER BY EmpLN;
```

You should receive results similar to the following:

```
+--------+----------------------+
| EmpID  | Name                 |
+--------+----------------------+
|     6  | George Brooks        |
|     5  | Rita C. Carter       |
|     4  | John Laguci          |
|     3  | Mary Marie Michaels  |
|     2  | Robert Schroader     |
|     1  | John P. Smith        |
+--------+----------------------+
6 rows in set (0.00 sec)
```

4. Next, use the CONCAT() and LEFT() functions to create registration codes for the employees. Execute the following SQL statement at the mysql command prompt:

```
SELECT EmpID, CONCAT(LEFT(EmpFN, 2), LEFT(EmpLN, 3), EmpID) AS RegID
FROM Employees
ORDER BY EmpID;
```

You should receive results similar to the following:

```
+--------+---------+
| EmpID  | RegID   |
+--------+---------+
|     1  | JoSmi1  |
|     2  | RoSch2  |
|     3  | MaMic3  |
|     4  | JoLag4  |
|     5  | RiCar5  |
|     6  | GeBro6  |
+--------+---------+
6 rows in set (0.00 sec)
```

5. Now create a SELECT statement that uses the UPPER(), CONCAT_WS(), CONCAT(), LOWER(), and LEFT() functions to manipulate retrieved data from the Employees table. Execute the following SQL statement at the mysql command prompt:

```
SELECT EmpID, UPPER(CONCAT_WS(' ', EmpFN, EmpMN, EmpLN)) AS Name,
    CONCAT(LOWER(LEFT(EmpFN, 2)), LOWER(LEFT(EmpLN, 3)), EmpID) AS RegID
FROM Employees
ORDER BY EmpID;
```

You should receive results similar to the following:

```
+--------+----------------------+---------+
| EmpID  | Name                 | RegID   |
+--------+----------------------+---------+
|     1  | JOHN P. SMITH        | josmi1  |
|     2  | ROBERT SCHROADER     | rosch2  |
|     3  | MARY MARIE MICHAELS  | mamic3  |
|     4  | JOHN LAGUCI          | jolag4  |
|     5  | RITA C. CARTER       | ricar5  |
|     6  | GEORGE BROOKS        | gebro6  |
+--------+----------------------+---------+
6 rows in set (0.00 sec)
```

6. Your final SELECT statement includes the UPPER(), CONCAT_WS(), CONCAT(), LOWER(), and SUBSTRING() functions to use on data from the Employees table. Execute the following SQL statement at the mysql command prompt:

```
SELECT EmpID, UPPER(CONCAT_WS(' ', EmpFN, EmpMN, EmpLN)) AS Name,
    CONCAT(LOWER(SUBSTRING(EmpFN, 2, 2)),
    LOWER(SUBSTRING(EmpLN, 2, 3)), EmpID) AS RegID
FROM Employees
ORDER BY EmpID;
```

You should receive results similar to the following:

```
+-------+---------------------+--------+
| EmpID | Name                | RegID  |
+-------+---------------------+--------+
|     1 | JOHN P. SMITH       | ohmit1 |
|     2 | ROBERT SCHROADER    | obchr2 |
|     3 | MARY MARIE MICHAELS | arich3 |
|     4 | JOHN LAGUCI         | ohagu4 |
|     5 | RITA C. CARTER      | itart5 |
|     6 | GEORGE BROOKS       | eoroo6 |
+-------+---------------------+--------+
6 rows in set (0.00 sec)
```

How It Works

The first statement that you created uses the CHAR_LENGTH() function, as shown in the following statement:

```
SELECT DVDName, CHAR_LENGTH(DVDName) AS CharLength
FROM DVDs
WHERE CHAR_LENGTH(DVDName)>10
ORDER BY DVDName;
```

The function appears as one of the elements of the select list in the SELECT clause and in an expression in the WHERE clause. The function retrieves the number of characters in a value. Notice that, in this case, the <string> argument is the name of the DVDName column. As a result, the string values are taken from that column. In addition, the WHERE clause specifies that the result set should include only those DVDName values with a length greater than 10.

The next statement that you created uses the CONCAT_WS() function to concatenate the employee names:

```
SELECT EmpID, CONCAT_WS(' ', EmpFN, EmpMN, EmpLN) AS Name
FROM Employees
ORDER BY EmpLN;
```

The function contains four arguments. The first argument is the separator, which in this case is a space. As a result, a space is added between all concatenated values, except those that are NULL. The next three arguments are the names of the columns from which the string values are extracted. For each row the SELECT statement returns, the employee's first name, middle name (in some cases), and last name appear together, with a space between values.

In the next statement, you used a CONCAT() function to concatenate the employee names and IDs. As the following statement shows, you used only part of the first and last names:

```
SELECT EmpID, CONCAT(LEFT(EmpFN, 2), LEFT(EmpLN, 3), EmpID) AS RegID
FROM Employees
ORDER BY EmpID;
```

The LEFT() function extracts only part of the first and last names. In the first usage, a 2 is specified as the second argument, so only the first two characters are retrieved from the first name. In the second usage of the LEFT() function, a 3 is specified as the second argument, so only the first three characters are retrieved. The retrieved characters are then concatenated to create one value made up of the first two letters of the first name, the first three letters of the last name, and the employee ID.

One thing to notice about the last statement is that you embedded one function as an argument within another function. You can embed functions to as many levels as necessary. For example, in the next statement that you created, you embedded functions to an additional level:

```
SELECT EmpID, UPPER(CONCAT_WS(' ', EmpFN, EmpMN, EmpLN)) AS Name,
    CONCAT(LOWER(LEFT(EmpFN, 2)), LOWER(LEFT(EmpLN, 3)), EmpID) AS RegID
FROM Employees
ORDER BY EmpID;
```

In the second element of the select clause, you used the familiar CONCAT_WS() construction to concatenate the employee name. Then you embedded the function as an argument in the UPPER() function so that the value returns in upper case. In the third element of the select list, you first used LEFT() functions to retrieve the first two letters from the first name and the first three letters from the last name. You then embedded each of these functions as an argument in a LOWER() function. As a result, the values retrieved by the LEFT() function changed to all lowercase. From these values, you used the CONCAT() function to concatenate the three arguments. As a result, one value is created that consists of the first two letters of the first name (in lowercase), the first three letters of the last name (in lowercase), and the employee ID.

The last SELECT statement that you created deviated from the previous statement by using a SUB-STRING() function rather than a LEFT() function:

```
SELECT EmpID, UPPER(CONCAT_WS(' ', EmpFN, EmpMN, EmpLN)) AS Name,
    CONCAT(LOWER(SUBSTRING(EmpFN, 2, 2)),
    LOWER(SUBSTRING(EmpLN, 2, 3)), EmpID) AS RegID
FROM Employees
ORDER BY EmpID;
```

Because you used the SUBSTRING() function, you can be more specific about which characters are retrieved from the first name and last name. For the first name, you retrieved two characters starting with the character in the second position. For the last name, you retrieved three characters starting with the character in the second position. The SUBSTRING() functions were then embedded in the LOWER() functions, which were then embedded as arguments for the CONCAT() function. The result is a value for each employee that is made up of the second and third letters of the first name (in lowercase), the second, third, and fourth letters of the last name (in lowercase), and the employee ID.

Numeric Functions

Now that you've had a good sampling of how string functions work, it's time to look at numeric functions. Numeric functions allow you to perform calculations on numeric values. MySQL supports various numeric functions that allow you to perform advanced mathematical operations. This section covers many of the more common numeric functions.

CEIL(), CEILING(), and FLOOR() Functions

The CEIL() and CEILING() functions, which are synonymous, return the smallest integer that is not less than the specified number. As the following syntax shows, to use this function, you need to specify only the number:

```
CEILING(<number>)
```

For example, the following SELECT statement returns a value of 10:

```
SELECT CEILING(9.327);
```

The value 10 is returned because it is the smallest integer that is not less than 9.327. However, if you want to retrieve the largest integer that is not greater than a specified value, you can use the FLOOR() function:

```
FLOOR(<number>)
```

The FLOOR() function is similar to the CEILING() function in the way that it is used. For example, the following SELECT statement uses the FLOOR() function:

```
SELECT FLOOR(9.327);
```

Notice that the same value is specified as in the previous example. Because the FLOOR() function retrieves the largest integer not greater than the specified value, a value of 9 is returned, rather than 10.

COT() Functions

MySQL includes numerous functions that allow you to calculate specific types of equations. For example, you can use the COT() function to determine the cotangent of a number:

```
COT(<number>)
```

As you can see, you need to provide only the number whose cotangent you want to find. For example, suppose you want to find the cotangent of 22. You can use the following SELECT statement:

```
SELECT COT(22);
```

MySQL returns a value of 112.97321035643, which is the cotangent of 22.

MOD() Function

The MOD() function is similar to the percentage (%) arithmetic operator you saw in Chapter 8. The function returns the remainder derived by dividing two numbers. The following syntax shows how to use a MOD() function:

```
MOD(<number1>, <number2>)
```

As you can see, you must specify the numbers that you want to divide as arguments, separated by a comma. The first argument that you specify is divided by the second argument, as shown in the following example.

```
SELECT MOD(22, 7);
```

In this statement, the MOD() function divides 22 by 7 and then returns the remainder. As a result, the function returns a value of 1.

PI() Function

The PI() function returns the value of PI. As the following syntax shows, you do not specify any arguments when using this function:

```
PI()
```

You can use the function to retrieve the value of PI to use in your SQL statement. At its simplest, you can use a basic SELECT statement to retrieve PI:

```
SELECT PI();
```

The PI() function returns a value of 3.141593.

POW() and POWER() Functions

The POW() and POWER() functions, which are synonymous, raise the value of one number to the power of the second number, as shown in the following syntax:

```
POW(<number>, <power>)
```

In the first argument, you must specify the root number. This is followed by the second argument (separated from the first by a comma) that specifies the power by which you should raise the root number. For example, the following SELECT statement raises the number 4 by the power of 2:

```
SELECT POW(4, 2);
```

The POW() function returns a value of 16.

ROUND() and TRUNCATE() Functions

There will no doubt be times when retrieving data from a MySQL database when you want to round off numbers to the nearest integer. MySQL includes the following function to allow you to round off numbers:

```
ROUND(<number> [, <decimal>])
```

To round off a number, you must specify that number as an argument of the function. Optionally, you can round off a number to a fractional value by specifying the number of decimal places that you want the returned value to include. For example, the following SELECT statement rounds off a number to two decimal places:

```
SELECT ROUND(4.27943, 2);
```

In this case, the ROUND() function rounds off 4.27943 to 4.28. As you can see, the number is rounded up. Different implementations of the C library, however, might round off numbers in different ways. For example, some might always round numbers up or always down. If you want to have more control over how a number is rounded, you can use the FLOOR() or CEILING() functions, or you can use the TRUNCATE() function, which is shown in the following syntax:

```
TRUNCATE(<number>, <decimal>)
```

The TRUNCATE() function takes the same arguments as the ROUND() function, except that <decimal> is not optional in TRUNCATE() functions. You can declare the decimal value as zero, which has the same effect as not including the argument. The main functional difference between TRUNCATE() and ROUND() is that TRUNCATE() always rounds a number toward zero. For example, suppose you modify the last example SELECT statement to use TRUNCATE(), rather than ROUND(), as shown in the following example:

```
SELECT TRUNCATE(4.27943, 2);
```

This time, the value 4.27 is returned, rather than 4.28, because the original value is rounded toward zero, which means, for positive numbers, it is rounded down, rather than up.

SQRT() Function

The SQRT() function returns to the square root of a specified number:

```
SQRT(<number>)
```

To use the function, you need to specify the original number as an argument of the function. For example, the following SELECT statement uses the SQRT() function to find the square root of 36:

```
SELECT SQRT(36);
```

The statement returns a value of 6.

The following exercise allows you to try out several of the numeric functions that you learned about in this section. Because the DVDRentals database doesn't include any tables that are useful to test out these functions, you first must create a table named Test and then add values to that table. From there, you can create SELECT statements that use numeric functions to calculate data in the Test table.

Try It Out   Using Numeric Functions in Your SQL Statements

Follow these steps to create and populate the Test table and then use SELECT statements that employ numeric functions:

1. Open the mysql client utility, type the following command, and press Enter:

```
use DVDRentals
```

> You should receive a message indicating that you switched to the DVDRentals database.

2. First, you create the Test table. Execute the following SQL statement at the mysql command prompt:

```
CREATE TABLE Test
(
    TestID SMALLINT NOT NULL PRIMARY KEY,
    Amount SMALLINT NOT NULL
);
```

> You should receive a message indicating that the statement executed successfully.

3. Next, add values to the Test table. Execute the following SQL statement at the mysql command prompt:

```
INSERT INTO Test
VALUES (101, 12), (102, 1), (103, 139), (104, -37), (105, 0), (106, -16);
```

> You should receive a message indicating that the statement executed successfully, affecting five rows.

4. The first SELECT statement that you create includes the COT() function, which calculates the cotangent of the values in the Amount column. Execute the following SQL statement at the mysql command prompt:

```
SELECT TestID, Amount, COT(Amount) AS Cotangent
FROM Test
ORDER BY TestID;
```

> You should receive results similar to the following:

```
+--------+--------+------------------+
| TestID | Amount | Cotangent        |
+--------+--------+------------------+
|    101 |     12 | -1.5726734063977 |
|    102 |      1 | 0.64209261593433 |
|    103 |    139 | 1.0314388663087  |
|    104 |    -37 | 1.1893841441106  |
|    105 |      0 |             NULL |
|    106 |    -16 | -3.3263231956354 |
+--------+--------+------------------+
6 rows in set (0.00 sec)
```

5. The next statement that you create builds on the previous statement by adding a column to the result set that rounds off the cotangent. Execute the following SQL statement at the mysql command prompt:

```
SELECT TestID, Amount, COT(Amount) AS Cotangent, ROUND(COT(Amount)) AS Rounded
FROM Test
ORDER BY TestID;
```

You should receive results similar to the following:

```
+--------+--------+------------------+---------+
| TestID | Amount | Cotangent        | Rounded |
+--------+--------+------------------+---------+
|    101 |     12 | -1.5726734063977 |      -2 |
|    102 |      1 | 0.64209261593433 |       1 |
|    103 |    139 | 1.0314388663087  |       1 |
|    104 |    -37 | 1.1893841441106  |       1 |
|    105 |      0 |             NULL |    NULL |
|    106 |    -16 | -3.3263231956354 |      -3 |
+--------+--------+------------------+---------+
6 rows in set (0.00 sec)
```

6. In the next SELECT statement, you use the MOD() function to divide the Amount values by 10 and then return the remainder from that division. Execute the following SQL statement at the mysql command prompt:

```
SELECT TestID, Amount, MOD(Amount, 10) AS Modulo
FROM Test
ORDER BY TestID;
```

You should receive results similar to the following:

```
+--------+--------+--------+
| TestID | Amount | Modulo |
+--------+--------+--------+
|    101 |     12 |      2 |
|    102 |      1 |      1 |
|    103 |    139 |      9 |
|    104 |    -37 |     -7 |
|    105 |      0 |      0 |
|    106 |    -16 |     -6 |
+--------+--------+--------+
6 rows in set (0.00 sec)
```

7. Next you create a SELECT statement that uses the POW() function to raise the Amount values by a power of 2. Execute the following SQL statement at the mysql command prompt:

```
SELECT TestID, Amount, POW(Amount, 2) AS Raised2
FROM Test
ORDER BY TestID;
```

You should receive results similar to the following:

```
+--------+--------+---------+
| TestID | Amount | Raised2 |
+--------+--------+---------+
|    101 |     12 |     144 |
|    102 |      1 |       1 |
|    103 |    139 |   19321 |
|    104 |    -37 |    1369 |
|    105 |      0 |       0 |
|    106 |    -16 |     256 |
+--------+--------+---------+
6 rows in set (0.00 sec)
```

8.   Execute the following SQL statement at the mysql command prompt:

```
DROP TABLE Test;
```

You should receive a message indicating that the statement executed successfully.

How It Works

The first SELECT statement that you created includes the COT() function:

```
SELECT TestID, Amount, COT(Amount) AS Cotangent
FROM Test
ORDER BY TestID;
```

The function is used as one of the elements in the select list. The Amount column is specified as the argument used by the COT() function. As a result, for each row returned, the cotangent of the Amount value is calculated and returned in the Cotangent column.

The next SELECT statement that you created is similar to the previous one, except that it includes an additional column in the result set:

```
SELECT TestID, Amount, COT(Amount) AS Cotangent, ROUND(COT(Amount)) AS Rounded
FROM Test
ORDER BY TestID;
```

The Rounded column takes the cotangent for each value and rounds the number to an integer. Notice that the COT() function is embedded as an argument in the ROUND() function. This demonstrates that numeric functions, like other functions, can be embedded to as many layers as necessary.

In the next SELECT statement that you created, you used a MOD() function on the Amount column:

```
SELECT TestID, Amount, MOD(Amount, 10) AS Modulo
FROM Test
ORDER BY TestID;
```

For each row returned by this statement, the Amount value is divided by 10. The remainder from this value is then returned in the Modulo column.

The final statement that you created is similar to the last statement except that it uses the POW() function, rather than the MOD() function:

```
SELECT TestID, Amount, POW(Amount, 2) AS Raised2
FROM Test
ORDER BY TestID;
```

In this case, for each row returned by the SELECT statement, the value in the Amount column is raised by a power of 2 and then returned in the Rasied2 column.

Date/Time Functions

The next set of functions covered are those related to date and time values. These functions are handy for comparing and calculating dates and times as well as returning the current dates and times. MySQL supports numerous date/time functions, and this section covers many of those.

ADDDATE(), DATE_ADD(), SUBDATE(), DATE_SUB(), and EXTRACT() Functions

The ADDDATE() and DATE_ADD() functions, which are synonymous, allow you to add date-related intervals to your date values, as shown in the following syntax:

```
ADDDATE(<date>, INTERVAL <expression> <type>)
```

As you can see from the syntax, the function includes two arguments, the <date> value and the INTERVAL clause. The <date> value can be any date or date/time literal value or value derived from an expression. This value acts as the root value to which time is added. The INTERVAL clause requires an <expression>, which must be a time value in an acceptable format, and a <type> value. The following table lists the types that you can specify in the INTERVAL clause and the format for the expression used with that type:

<type>	<expression> format
MICROSECOND	<microseconds>
SECOND	<seconds>
MINUTE	<minutes>
HOUR	<hours>
DAY	<days>
MONTH	<months>
YEAR	<years>
SECOND_MICROSECOND	'<seconds>.<microseconds>'
MINUTE_MICROSECOND	'<minutes>.<microseconds>'
MINUTE_SECOND	'<minutes>:<seconds>'

Table continued on following page

<type>	<expression> format
HOUR_MICROSECOND	'<hours>.<microseconds>'
HOUR_SECOND	'<hours>:<minutes>:<seconds>'
HOUR_MINUTE	'<hours>:<minutes>'
DAY_MICROSECOND	'<days>.<microseconds>'
DAY_SECOND	'<days> <hours>:<minutes>:<seconds>'
DAY_MINUTE	'<days> <hours>:<minutes>'
DAY_HOUR	'<days> <hours>'
YEAR_MONTH	'<years>-<months>'

The best way to understand how the types and expression formats work is to look at an example. The following SELECT statement uses the ADDDATE() function to add 10 hours and 20 minutes to the specified date/time value:

```
SELECT ADDDATE('2004-10-31 13:39:59', INTERVAL '10:20' HOUR_MINUTE);
```

As you can see, the first argument in the ADDDATE() function is the base date/time value, and the second argument is the INTERVAL clause. In this clause, the expression used ('10:20') is consistent with the type used (HOUR_MINUTE). If you refer back to the table, notice that the expression is in the format acceptable for this type. As a result, the value returned by this statement is 2004-10-31 23:59:59, which is 10 hours and 20 minutes later than the original date/time value.

The ADDDATE() function also includes a second form, which is shown in the following syntax:

```
ADDDATE(<date>, <days>)
```

This form of the ADDDATE() syntax allows you to specify a date value as the first argument and a number of days as the second argument. These are the number of days that are to be added to the specified date. For example, the following SELECT statement adds 31 days to the date in the first argument:

```
SELECT ADDDATE('2004-11-30 23:59:59', 31);
```

The statement returns a result of 2004-12-31 23:59:59, which is 31 days after the original date. Notice that the time value remains the same.

In addition to being able to add to a date, you can also subtract from a date by using the SUBDATE() or DATE_SUB() functions, which are synonymous, as shown in the following syntax:

```
SUBDATE(<date>, INTERVAL <expression> <type>)
```

The arguments used in this syntax are the same as those used for the ADDDATE() syntax. For example, the following statement subtracts 12 hours and 10 minutes from the specified date:

```
SELECT SUBDATE('2004-10-31 23:59:59', INTERVAL '12:10' HOUR_MINUTE);
```

The statement returns a value of `2004-10-31 11:49:59`, which is 12 hours and 10 minutes earlier than the original date.

The `SUBDATE()` function also includes a second form, which allows you to subtract a specified number of days from a date:

```
SUBDATE(<date>, <days>)
```

For example, the following `SELECT` statement subtracts 31 days from the specified date:

```
SELECT SUBDATE('2004-12-31 23:59:59', 31);
```

The value returned by this statement is `2004-11-30 23:59:59`, 31 days earlier than the original date.

Functions like `ADDDATE()` and `SUBDATE()` are useful when you need to change a date value stored in a database but you don't know the new value, only the interval change of that value. For example, suppose that you are building an application for a company that rents computers. You want the application to include a way for users to be able to add days to the date that the equipment must be returned. For example, suppose that the equipment is due back on November 8, but you want to add three days to that date so that the due date is changed to November 11. You can use the `ADDDATE()` function along with the `DAY` interval type and set up the application to allow users to enter the number of days. The value returned by the `ADDDATE()` function can then be inserted in the appropriate column.

Another useful time-related function is the `EXTRACT()` function, which is shown in the following syntax:

```
EXTRACT(<type> FROM <date>)
```

The function uses the same `<type>` values that are used for the `ADDDATE()`, `DATE_ADD()`, `SUBDATE()`, and `DATE_SUB()` functions. In this case, the type extracts a specific part of the date/time value. In addition, when using an `EXTRACT()` function, you must specify the `FROM` keyword and a date value. For example, the following `SELECT` statement extracts the year and month from the specified date:

```
SELECT EXTRACT(YEAR_MONTH FROM '2004-12-31 23:59:59');
```

The `EXTRACT()` function in this statement includes the type `YEAR_MONTH`. As a result, the year (`2004`) and month (`12`) are extracted from the original value and returned as `200412`.

The `EXTRACT()` function is handy if you have an application that must display only part of a date. For example, suppose that a table in your database includes a `TIMESTAMP` column. Your application should display only the date portion of the column value. You can use the `EXTRACT()` function to retrieve only the date portion of the value and use that date portion in your application.

CURDATE(), CURRENT_DATE(), CURTIME(), CURRENT_TIME(), CURRENT_TIMESTAMP(), and NOW() Functions

MySQL includes a number of functions that allow you to retrieve current date and time information. The first of these are the `CURDATE()` and `CURRENT_DATE()` functions, which are synonymous. As the following syntax shows, the functions do not require any arguments:

```
CURDATE()
```

To use this function, you simply specify the function in your statement. For example, if you want to retrieve the current date, you can use the following SELECT statement:

```
SELECT CURDATE();
```

The statement retrieves a value similar to 2004-09-08. Notice that the value includes first the year, then the month, and then the day.

You can retrieve the current time by using the CURTIME() or CURRENT_TIME functions, which are also synonymous:

```
CURTIME()
```

Again, you do not need to supply any arguments, as shown in the following SELECT statement:

```
SELECT CURTIME();
```

As you can see, you simply use the function as is to retrieve the information. The date returned is in the same format as the following value: 16:07:46. The time value is listed by hour, then by minute, and then by second.

In addition to retrieving only the date or only the time, you can retrieve both in one value by using the NOW() or CURRENT_TIMESTAMP() functions, which are also synonymous:

```
NOW()
```

The function is used just like CURDATE() or CURTIME(), as shown in the following SELECT statement:

```
SELECT NOW();
```

The value returned by this function is in the same format as the following value: 2004-09-08 16:08:00. The value contains two parts, first the date and then the time. The date value includes first the year, then the month, and then the day. The time value includes first the hour, then the minute, and then the second.

The CURDATE(), CURTIME(), and NOW() functions are particularly useful if you need to insert a date in a column that is based on the current date or time. For example, suppose that your application includes a table that tracks when a user has checked a book out of the library and when that book is due back. You can use the CURDATE() function to determine the current date and insert that function in the column that tracks today's date. You can then use the same function to calculate when the book is due back by adding the correct number of days to today's date. For example, if the book is due back 21 days from today, you can add 21 to CURDATE() to return a date 21 days from today.

DATE(), MONTH(), MONTHNAME(), and YEAR() Functions

MySQL also includes a set of functions that allow you to extract specific information from a date or time value. For example, you can use the following function to extract just the date:

```
DATE(<date>)
```

In this function, the `<date>` value usually represents a date/time value from which you want to extract only the date, as in the following statement:

```
SELECT DATE('2004-12-31 23:59:59');
```

This statement retrieves the full date value of 2004-12-31. You can extract only the month by using the `MONTH()` function:

```
MONTH(<date>)
```

If you were to update the last SELECT statement to include `MONTH()` rather than `DATE()`, the statement would be as follows:

```
SELECT MONTH('2004-12-31 23:59:59');
```

This SELECT statement retrieves only the month number, which is 12. If you prefer to retrieve the actual month name, you would use the following function:

```
MONTHNAME(<date>)
```

As you can see, you simply use the keyword `MONTHNAME` rather than `MONTH`, as shown in the following SELECT statement:

```
SELECT MONTHNAME('2004-12-31 23:59:59');
```

Now your result is the value December, instead of 12.

You can also extract the year from a date value by using the `YEAR()` function:

```
YEAR(<date>)
```

The function returns the year from any date or date/time value, as the following SELECT statement demonstrates:

```
SELECT YEAR('2004-12-31 23:59:59');
```

The statement returns the value 2004.

The `DATE()`, `MONTH()`, `MONTHNAME()`, and `YEAR()` functions are helpful when you want to retrieve a portion of a date or a related value based on the date and use it in your application. For example, suppose that you are developing an application that displays individual orders that your company has processed. For each order processed, you want to display the name of the month that the order was taken. You can use the `MONTHNAME()` function to extract the name of the month from the order date, as it's recorded in the database. That way, you don't have to store all the month names in your database, but they're readily available when you retrieve an order.

DATEDIFF() and TIMEDIFF() Functions

You can also use functions to determine the differences between dates and times. For example, the following function calculates the number of dates that separates two dates:

```
DATEDIFF(<date>, <date>)
```

To use the function, you must specify the dates as arguments. For example, the following SELECT statement specifies two dates that are exactly one year apart:

```
SELECT DATEDIFF('2004-12-31 23:59:59', '2003-12-31 23:59:59');
```

The statement returns a value of 366 (because 2004 is a leap year). Notice that the most recent date is specified first. You can specify them in any order, but if the less recent date is specified first, your results are a negative number because of the way dates are compared.

You can also compare time values by using the TIMEDIFF() function:

```
TIMEDIFF(<time>, <time>)
```

This function works similarly to the way that the DATEDIFF() function works. You must specify two time or date/time values, as shown in the follow SELECT statement:

```
SELECT TIMEDIFF('2004-12-31 23:59:59', '2004-12-30 23:59:59');
```

This time, the time difference is returned as 24:00:00, indicating that the time difference between the two is exactly 24 hours.

The DATEDIFF() and TIMEDIFF() functions are useful when you have a table that includes two time/date columns. For example, suppose that you have a table that tracks project delivery dates. The table includes the date that the project started and the date that the project was completed. You can use the TIMEDIFF() function to calculate the number of days that each project took. You can then use that information in your applications or reports or however you want to use it.

DAY(), DAYOFMONTH(), DAYNAME(), DAYOFWEEK(), and DAYOFYEAR() Functions

MySQL also allows you to pull day-related values out of date or date/time values. For example, the DAY() and DAYOFMONTH() functions, which are synonymous, extract the day of the month out of a value. The DAY() function is shown in the following syntax:

```
DAY(<date>)
```

As you can see, only one argument is required. For example, the following SELECT statement includes a DAY() function with a time/date value as an argument:

```
SELECT DAY('2004-12-31 23:59:59');
```

The day in this case is 31, which is the value returned by this statement. You can also return the name of the day by using the following function:

```
DAYNAME(<date>)
```

You can use the DAYNAME() function with any date or date/time value, as shown in the following example:

```
SELECT DAYNAME('2004-12-31 23:59:59');
```

In this example, the function calculates which day is associated with the specified date and returns that day as a value. In this case, the value returned is Friday. If you want to return the day of the week by number, you would use the following function:

```
DAYOFWEEK(<date>)
```

The function returns a value from 1 through 7, with Sunday being 1. For example, the following SELECT statement calculates the day of the week for December 31, 2004.

```
SELECT DAYOFWEEK('2004-12-31 23:59:59');
```

The day in this case is Friday. Because Friday is the sixth day, the statement returns a value of 6. In addition, you can calculate a numerical value for the day, as it falls in the year, by using the DAYOFYEAR() function:

```
DAYOFYEAR(<date>)
```

In this case, the day is based on the number of days in the year, starting with January 1. For example, the following statement calculates the day of year for the last day of 2004:

```
SELECT DAYOFYEAR('2004-12-31 23:59:59');
```

Because 2004 is a leap year, the statement returns the value 366.

The DAY(), DAYOFMONTH(), DAYNAME(), DAYOFWEEK(), and DAYOFYEAR() functions can be useful if you want to extract specific types of information from a date. For example, suppose that you are developing an application that tracks employee sick days. When the application pulls dates from the database, it should also display the day of the week that the employee was sick. You can use the DAYOFWEEK() function when retrieving the date value from the database to display the day of the week in your application.

SECOND(), MINUTE(), HOUR(), and TIME() Functions

You can also use functions to extract time parts from a time or date/time value. For example, the following function extracts the seconds from a time value:

```
SECOND(<time>)
```

As you would expect, the SECOND() function determines the seconds based on the value specified as an argument in the function. For example, the following SELECT statement extracts 59 from the specified value.

```
SELECT SECOND('2004-12-31 23:59:59');
```

You can also extract the minutes by using the MINUTE() function:

```
MINUTE(<time>)
```

If you were to modify the last statement to use the MINUTE() function, it would extract the minutes from the specified date. For example, the following statement would extract 59 from the time value:

```
SELECT MINUTE('2004-12-31 23:59:59');
```

The following function allows you to extract the hour from the time value:

```
HOUR(<time>)
```

As shown in the following SELECT statement, the HOUR() function extracts 23 from the time value:

```
SELECT HOUR('2004-12-31 23:59:59');
```

You can also extract the entire time value by using the TIME() function:

```
TIME(<time>)
```

Using this function returns the hour, minutes, and seconds. For example, the following SELECT statement includes a date/time value as an argument in the TIME() function:

```
SELECT TIME('2004-12-31 23:59:59');
```

In this case, the function returns the value 23:59:59.

The SECOND(), MINUTE(), HOUR(), and TIME() functions are similar to the DAY(), DAYOFMONTH(), DAYNAME(), DAYOFWEEK(), and DAYOFYEAR() functions in how they can be used in your applications. For example, suppose that you are creating an application to track orders. The order data is stored in a table in your database. Each time an order is added to the table, a value is automatically inserted in the TIMESTAMP column. For tracking purposes, you want your application to display the hour that each order was taken as a field separate from the rest of the TIMESTAMP value. You can use the TIME() function to extract only the time from the TIMESTAMP value and use that time value in your application.

Now that you've seen how to use many of the date/time functions in MySQL, you're ready to try some out. This exercise uses a number of SELECT statements to retrieve date- and time-related data from the DVDRentals database as well as to retrieve current date and time date.

Try It Out — Using Date/Time Functions in Your SQL Statements

The following steps describe how to create statements that include date/time functions:

1. Open the mysql client utility, type the following command, and press Enter:

```
use DVDRentals
```

You should receive a message indicating that you switched to the DVDRentals database.

2. The first SELECT statement that you create uses the DATEDIFF() function to determine the difference between DateOut and DateDue values in the Transactions table. Execute the following SQL statement at the mysql command prompt:

```
SELECT DVDID, DateOut, DateDue, DATEDIFF(DateDue, DateOut) AS TotalDays
FROM Transactions
WHERE TransID=11;
```

You should receive results similar to the following:

```
+-------+------------+------------+-----------+
| DVDID | DateOut    | DateDue    | TotalDays |
+-------+------------+------------+-----------+
|     1 | 2004-09-06 | 2004-09-09 |         3 |
+-------+------------+------------+-----------+
1 row in set (0.00 sec)
```

3. Next you use the DAYNAME() function to retrieve the name of a day for a specific date. Execute the following SQL statement at the mysql command prompt:

```
SELECT DVDID, DateDue, DAYNAME(DateDue) AS DayDue
FROM Transactions
WHERE TransID=11;
```

You should receive results similar to the following:

```
+-------+------------+----------+
| DVDID | DateDue    | DayDue   |
+-------+------------+----------+
|     1 | 2004-09-09 | Thursday |
+-------+------------+----------+
1 row in set (0.00 sec)
```

4. In the next SELECT statement, you use the YEAR() function to extract the year from a date value. Execute the following SQL statement at the mysql command prompt:

```
SELECT TransID, YEAR(DateOut) AS YearOut
FROM Transactions
WHERE TransID>15
ORDER BY TransID;
```

You should receive results similar to the following:

```
+---------+---------+
| TransID | YearOut |
+---------+---------+
|      16 |    2004 |
|      17 |    2004 |
|      18 |    2004 |
|      19 |    2004 |
|      20 |    2004 |
|      21 |    2004 |
|      22 |    2004 |
|      23 |    2004 |
+---------+---------+
8 rows in set (0.00 sec)
```

5. Next, use the DATE_ADD() function to add four days to a DateDue value in the Transactions table. Execute the following SQL statement at the mysql command prompt:

```
SELECT TransID, DateDue, DATE_ADD(DateDue, INTERVAL 4 DAY) AS Add4Days
FROM Transactions
WHERE TransID=11;
```

You should receive results similar to the following:

```
+---------+------------+------------+
| TransID | DateDue    | Add4Days   |
+---------+------------+------------+
|      11 | 2004-09-09 | 2004-09-13 |
+---------+------------+------------+
1 row in set (0.00 sec)
```

6. Your last SELECT statement retrieves the current date and time from your system. Execute the following SQL statement at the mysql command prompt:

```
SELECT CURDATE(), CURTIME(), NOW();
```

You should receive results similar to the following:

```
+------------+-----------+---------------------+
| CURDATE()  | CURTIME() | NOW()               |
+------------+-----------+---------------------+
| 2004-09-08 | 16:26:42  | 2004-09-08 16:26:42 |
+------------+-----------+---------------------+
1 row in set (0.00 sec)
```

How It Works

The first SELECT statement that you created includes the DATEDIFF() function as an element in the select list:

```
SELECT DVDID, DateOut, DateDue, DATEDIFF(DateDue, DateOut) AS TotalDays
FROM Transactions
WHERE TransID=11;
```

The function uses the values in the DateDue and DateOut columns of the Transactions table to provide date values as arguments in the function. The difference in days is then displayed in the TotalDays column of the result set.

In the next SELECT statement, you used the DAYNAME() function to retrieve the name of the day from a date in the DateDue column of the Transactions table:

```
SELECT DVDID, DateDue, DAYNAME(DateDue) AS DayDue
FROM Transactions
WHERE TransID=11;
```

The DAYNAME() function is used as an argument in the select list to return the name of the day to the DayDue column of the result set.

Next, you created a SELECT statement that includes a YEAR() function as an element in the select list:

```
SELECT TransID, YEAR(DateOut) AS YearOut
FROM Transactions
WHERE TransID>15
ORDER BY TransID;
```

The YEAR() function extracts the year from the DateOut values of the Transactions table and displays those years in the YearOut column of the result set.

In the next SELECT statement, you used the DATE_ADD() function to add four days to the value in the DateDue column:

```
SELECT TransID, DateDue, DATE_ADD(DateDue, INTERVAL 4 DAY) AS Add4Days
FROM Transactions
WHERE TransID=11;
```

As with the other functions used in this exercise, the DATE_ADD() function is an element in the select list. The function's first argument is the base date value, which is pulled from the DateDue column of the Transactions table. The function's second argument is the INTERVAL clause, which specifies that four days should be added to the date. The new day is then displayed in the Add4Days columns of the result set.

Finally, the last SELECT statement that you created retrieved current date and time information from your system:

```
SELECT CURDATE(), CURTIME(), NOW();
```

The statement includes three functions: CURDATE(), CURTIME(), and NOW(). Each function is an element in the select list. The CURDATE() function returns the current date, the CURTIME() function returns the current time, and the NOW() function returns both.

Summarizing Data

In Chapter 7, you learned how you can add the GROUP BY clause to a SELECT statement in order to summarize data. To provide effective summarizing capabilities, MySQL includes a number of functions — referred to as *aggregate* functions — that calculate or compare values based on the columns specified in the GROUP BY clause. In this section, you learn about many of the aggregate functions and how they're used in a SELECT statement. The examples in this section are based on the following table definition:

```
CREATE TABLE Classes
(
    ClassID SMALLINT NOT NULL PRIMARY KEY,
    Dept CHAR(4) NOT NULL,
    Level ENUM('Upper', 'Lower') NOT NULL,
    TotalStudents TINYINT UNSIGNED NOT NULL
);
```

For the purposes of these examples, you can assume that the following INSERT statement populated the Classes table:

```
INSERT INTO Classes
VALUES (1001, 'ANTH', 'Upper', 25),
(1002, 'ANTH', 'Upper', 25),
(1003, 'MATH', 'Upper', 18),
(1004, 'ANTH', 'Lower', 19),
(1005, 'ENGL', 'Upper', 28),
(1006, 'MATH', 'Lower', 23),
(1007, 'ENGL', 'Upper', 25),
(1008, 'MATH', 'Lower', 29),
(1009, 'ANTH', 'Upper', 25),
(1010, 'ANTH', 'Lower', 30),
(1011, 'ENGL', 'Lower', 26),
(1012, 'MATH', 'Lower', 22),
(1013, 'ANTH', 'Upper', 27),
(1014, 'ANTH', 'Upper', 21),
(1015, 'ENGL', 'Lower', 25),
(1016, 'ENGL', 'Upper', 32);
```

This section uses the Classes table to demonstrate how to add aggregate functions to your SELECT statements. For the purposes of this discussion, the functions have been divided into two broad categories: basic summary functions and bit functions.

Summary Functions

Summary functions are the basic functions that you're most likely to use when using a GROUP BY clause to group together columns of data. The summary functions allow you to perform such tasks as determining the average of a group of values or adding those values together.

AVG() Function

The first aggregate function that you learn about is the AVG() function, which averages the values returned by a specified expression. The following syntax shows how to use the function:

```
AVG(<expression>)
```

Nearly all aggregate functions use similar syntax. Each one requires that you specify some type of expression. In most cases, the expression is simply the name of a column that is significant in terms of how data is being grouped together in the GROUP BY clause. For example, the following SELECT statement uses the AVG() function to average the values in the TotalStudents column:

```
SELECT Dept, Level, ROUND(AVG(TotalStudents)) AS Average
FROM Classes
GROUP BY Dept, Level WITH ROLLUP;
```

As you can see, the statement includes a GROUP BY clause that specifies that the results be grouped together first by the Dept column and then by the Level column. The AVG() function then calculates the values in the TotalStudents column. The TotalStudents column is the only column significant to the way that the data is being grouped together. Finding the average of the ClassID column (the only other column in the Classes table) would have no meaning in this sense; however, the number of students is meaningful to the groups. As a result, the values returned by the SELECT statement include an average number of students for each department at each level, as shown in the following result set:

```
+------+-------+---------+
| Dept | Level | Average |
+------+-------+---------+
| ANTH | Upper |      25 |
| ANTH | Lower |      24 |
| ANTH | NULL  |      25 |
| ENGL | Upper |      28 |
| ENGL | Lower |      25 |
| ENGL | NULL  |      27 |
| MATH | Upper |      18 |
| MATH | Lower |      25 |
| MATH | NULL  |      23 |
| NULL | NULL  |      25 |
+------+-------+---------+
10 rows in set (0.00 sec)
```

As you can see, an average is provided for each group. For example, the average class size for an Upper level ANTH class is 25, but the average class size for a Lower level ANTH class is 24.

One thing you might have also noticed is that the statement uses the ROUND() function to round the values returned by the AVG() function. If you had not used the ROUND() function, the values in the Average column would have been fractional. Another aspect of the statement that you might have noticed is the use of the WITH ROLLUP option in the GROUP BY clause. As a result, averages are provided for the departments as a whole and for all classes added together. For example, the ANTH department has an average class size of 25 students per class, while the ENGL department has an average class size of 27 students.

SUM() Function

The next aggregate function is the SUM() function, which is shown in the following syntax:

```
SUM(<expression>)
```

The SUM() function returns the sum of the expression. In most cases, this means that the values in a column are added together, based on how columns are grouped together in the GROUP BY clause. For example, suppose you modify the last SELECT statement to include the SUM() function rather than the AVG() and ROUND() functions:

```
SELECT Dept, Level, SUM(TotalStudents) AS Total
FROM Classes
GROUP BY Dept, Level WITH ROLLUP;
```

By using the SUM() function, the values in the TotalStudents column are added together, as shown in the following result set:

```
+------+-------+-------+
| Dept | Level | Total |
+------+-------+-------+
| ANTH | Upper |   123 |
| ANTH | Lower |    49 |
| ANTH | NULL  |   172 |
| ENGL | Upper |    85 |
| ENGL | Lower |    51 |
| ENGL | NULL  |   136 |
| MATH | Upper |    18 |
| MATH | Lower |    74 |
| MATH | NULL  |    92 |
| NULL | NULL  |   400 |
+------+-------+-------+
10 rows in set (0.00 sec)
```

Now each grouping includes the total number of students. For example, the total number of students that attend the Upper level ANTH classes is 123, compared to 49 for the Lower level.

MIN() and MAX() Functions

In addition to calculating averages and sums, you can also find the minimum or maximum value in a column. For example, the following aggregate function returns the minimum value from a group of values:

```
MIN(<expression>)
```

If you modify the last SELECT statement to use MIN() instead of SUM(), your statement reads as follows:

```
SELECT Dept, Level, MIN(TotalStudents) AS Minimum
FROM Classes
GROUP BY Dept, Level WITH ROLLUP;
```

Notice that nothing has changed in the statement except the function keyword and the name assigned to the column. Now the results include the minimum value for each group, as shown in the following result set:

```
+------+-------+---------+
| Dept | Level | Minimum |
+------+-------+---------+
| ANTH | Upper |      21 |
| ANTH | Lower |      19 |
| ANTH | NULL  |      19 |
| ENGL | Upper |      25 |
| ENGL | Lower |      25 |
| ENGL | NULL  |      25 |
| MATH | Upper |      18 |
| MATH | Lower |      22 |
| MATH | NULL  |      18 |
| NULL | NULL  |      18 |
+------+-------+---------+
10 rows in set (0.00 sec)
```

As the results show, the minimum number of students in an Upper level anthropology class is 21. You can also calculate the maximum value by using the MAX() function:

```
MAX(<expression>)
```

You can then modify your SELECT statement as follows:

```
SELECT Dept, Level, MAX(TotalStudents) AS Maximum
FROM Classes
GROUP BY Dept, Level WITH ROLLUP;
```

Now your result set includes the maximum number of students in each type of class:

```
+------+-------+---------+
| Dept | Level | Maximum |
+------+-------+---------+
| ANTH | Upper |      27 |
| ANTH | Lower |      30 |
| ANTH | NULL  |      30 |
| ENGL | Upper |      32 |
| ENGL | Lower |      26 |
| ENGL | NULL  |      32 |
| MATH | Upper |      18 |
| MATH | Lower |      29 |
| MATH | NULL  |      29 |
| NULL | NULL  |      32 |
+------+-------+---------+
10 rows in set (0.00 sec)
```

As you can see, the largest ANTH class size is in the Lower level, with 30 students in that class.

COUNT() Function

Another very useful aggregate function is COUNT(), which is shown in the following syntax:

```
COUNT([DISTINCT] {<expression> | *})
```

The COUNT() function is the only aggregate function that deviates from the basic syntax used by the other aggregate functions. As you can see, there are two differences. You can include the DISTINCT keyword, and you can specify an asterisk (*) rather than an expression. You should use the DISTINCT keyword if you want to eliminate duplicates from the count. The asterisk is useful if you want to count all the rows, whether or not they contain NULL values. If you specify a column rather than an asterisk, and that column contains NULL values, the rows that contain the NULL values are not included in the count. If the column contains no NULL values, then the results are the same whether you specify a column name or an asterisk.

Return to the example SELECT statement and replace the MAX() function with the COUNT() function:

```
SELECT Dept, Level, COUNT(*) AS NumberClasses
FROM Classes
GROUP BY Dept, Level WITH ROLLUP;
```

Notice that the statement uses the asterisk rather than specifying a column name. By using the COUNT() function, the statement now returns the number of classes in each group, as shown in the following result set:

```
+------+-------+--------------+
| Dept | Level | NumberClasses |
+------+-------+--------------+
| ANTH | Upper |            5 |
| ANTH | Lower |            2 |
| ANTH | NULL  |            7 |
| ENGL | Upper |            3 |
| ENGL | Lower |            2 |
| ENGL | NULL  |            5 |
| MATH | Upper |            1 |
| MATH | Lower |            3 |
| MATH | NULL  |            4 |
| NULL | NULL  |           16 |
+------+-------+--------------+
10 rows in set (0.01 sec)
```

As you can see, the COUNT() function adds together the number of rows in each group. For example, the number of rows in the ANTH/Upper group is 5. Because each row in the table represents one class, the ANTH/Upper group contains five classes.

Bit Functions

The bit aggregate functions work in the same way that bit operators work. (Refer to Chapter 8 for more information about bit operators.) When values in a grouped column are calculated using a bit function, the bits are compared and a value is returned. The way in which the bits are compared depends on the bit function being used.

The first bit aggregate function is the BIT_AND() function. The function uses the following syntax:

```
BIT_AND(<expression>)
```

The BIT_AND() function is similar to the bitwise AND (&) comparison operator in the way in which the function compares bits. For any two or more values, the bits in each bit position are compared. Based on the comparison, a 1 is returned if all bits in a bit position equal 1; otherwise, a 0 is returned. For example, suppose that the Classes table that you have been using in this section includes an additional column that tracks attributes that describe the class, such as room requirements or special equipment. You are developing an application that uses the Attributes column to determine class-specific needs. The following SELECT statement uses the BIT_AND() function to compare bits in the Attributes column:

```
SELECT Dept, Level, BIT_AND(Attributes) AS BitwiseAND
FROM Classes
GROUP BY Dept, Level WITH ROLLUP;
```

As the statement shows, the BIT_AND() function takes the TotalStudents column as an argument. Your application can then use this information to form a bigger picture of the class attributes. For example, these results would tell you if every class is going to need special equipment of some type. As a result, the bits for each value in this column are compared, and the following results are returned:

```
+------+-------+------------+
| Dept | Level | BitwiseAND |
+------+-------+------------+
| ANTH | Upper |         17 |
| ANTH | Lower |         18 |
| ANTH | NULL  |         16 |
| ENGL | Upper |          0 |
| ENGL | Lower |         24 |
| ENGL | NULL  |          0 |
| MATH | Upper |         18 |
| MATH | Lower |         20 |
| MATH | NULL  |         16 |
| NULL | NULL  |          0 |
+------+-------+------------+
10 rows in set (0.00 sec)
```

The next bit aggregate function is the BIT_OR() function, which is shown in the following syntax:

```
BIT_OR(<expression>)
```

This function is similar to the bitwise OR (|) bit operator. The function compares bits in each bit position and returns 1 if at least one bit is 1; otherwise, 0 is returned. You can use the BIT_OR() function as you use the BIT_AND() function:

```
SELECT Dept, Level, BIT_OR(TotalStudents) AS BitwiseOR
FROM Classes
GROUP BY Dept, Level WITH ROLLUP;
```

By using the BIT_OR() function, your results are now similar to the following:

```
+------+-------+-----------+
| Dept | Level | BitwiseOR |
+------+-------+-----------+
| ANTH | Upper |        31 |
| ANTH | Lower |        31 |
| ANTH | NULL  |        31 |
| ENGL | Upper |        61 |
| ENGL | Lower |        27 |
| ENGL | NULL  |        63 |
| MATH | Upper |        18 |
| MATH | Lower |        31 |
| MATH | NULL  |        31 |
| NULL | NULL  |        63 |
+------+-------+-----------+
10 rows in set (0.01 sec)
```

As with bit operators, bit functions also provide an exclusive OR (XOR) function, as shown in the following syntax:

```
BIT_XOR(<expression>)
```

This function is similar to the bitwise exclusive XOR (^) bit operator in that it compares bits and returns 1 only if exactly one of the bit equals 1; otherwise, 0 is returned. For example, suppose that you update your SELECT statement to include the BIT_XOR() function:

```
SELECT Dept, Level, BIT_XOR(TotalStudents) AS BitwiseXOR
FROM Classes
GROUP BY Dept, Level WITH ROLLUP;
```

Now your results are different from either the BIT_AND() function or the BIT_OR() function, as shown in the following result set:

```
+------+-------+------------+
| Dept | Level | BitwiseXOR |
+------+-------+------------+
| ANTH | Upper |         23 |
| ANTH | Lower |         13 |
| ANTH | NULL  |         26 |
| ENGL | Upper |         37 |
| ENGL | Lower |          3 |
| ENGL | NULL  |         38 |
| MATH | Upper |         18 |
| MATH | Lower |         28 |
| MATH | NULL  |         14 |
| NULL | NULL  |         50 |
+------+-------+------------+
10 rows in set (0.00 sec)
```

As illustrated in this section, aggregate functions are a useful way to summarize data that's been grouped together. In the following example, you try out a couple of these functions by creating SELECT statements that group together data in the DVDRentals database.

Try It Out   Using Aggregate Functions to Group Data

The following steps describe how to use aggregate functions in your SELECT statements:

1. Open the mysql client utility, type the following command, and press Enter:

```
use DVDRentals
```

You should receive a message indicating that you switched to the DVDRentals database.

2. First, use the MAX() function to return the maximum value in the NumDisks column of the DVDs table. Execute the following SQL statement at the mysql command prompt:

```
SELECT MTypeID, MAX(NumDisks) AS MaxDisks
FROM DVDs
GROUP BY MTypeID;
```

You should receive results similar to the following:

```
+---------+----------+
| MTypeID | MaxDisks |
+---------+----------+
| mt11    |        1 |
| mt12    |        2 |
| mt16    |        1 |
+---------+----------+
3 rows in set (0.00 sec)
```

3. Now use the COUNT() function to determine the number of rows in each RatingID/MTypeID group in the DVDs table. Execute the following SQL statement at the mysql command prompt:

```
SELECT RatingID, MTypeID, COUNT(*) AS Total
FROM DVDs
GROUP BY RatingID, MTypeID WITH ROLLUP;
```

You should receive results similar to the following:

```
+----------+---------+-------+
| RatingID | MTypeID | Total |
+----------+---------+-------+
| G        | mt12    |     1 |
| G        | NULL    |     1 |
| NR       | mt11    |     2 |
| NR       | mt12    |     1 |
| NR       | mt16    |     1 |
| NR       | NULL    |     4 |
| PG       | mt11    |     2 |
| PG       | NULL    |     2 |
| R        | mt12    |     1 |
| R        | NULL    |     1 |
| NULL     | NULL    |     8 |
+----------+---------+-------+
11 rows in set (0.01 sec)
```

How It Works

The first aggregate function that you used in this exercise is the MAX() function, as shown in the following statement:

```
SELECT MTypeID, MAX(NumDisks) AS MaxDisks
FROM DVDs
GROUP BY MTypeID;
```

In this statement, you grouped together data based on the values in the MTypeID column. You then used the MAX() function to retrieve the maximum value from the NumDisks column in each group. For example, one of the groups of data is based on the MTypeID value of mt12. For this group, the maximum value in the NumDisks column is 2, so that is the value the MAX() function returns.

In the next SELECT statement that you created, you grouped data together first by the RatingID column and then by the MTypeID column:

```
SELECT RatingID, MTypeID, COUNT(*) AS Total
FROM DVDs
GROUP BY RatingID, MTypeID WITH ROLLUP;
```

You then used the COUNT() function to return the number of rows in each group. For example, one group is made up of the NR value in the RatingID column and the mt11 value in the MTypeID column. This group is made up of two rows, so the COUNT() functions returns a value of 2. In other words, two rows contain a RatingID value of NR and an MTypeID value of mt11.

Performing System Operations

The functions examined so far in this chapter have been specific to the data itself; however, a number of functions are related to system operations. For example, you can use function to encrypt and decrypt data, return system-related information, or provide details about executed query and insert operations. This section covers many of these functions and provides examples that demonstrate how they are used.

Encryption Functions

The encryption functions are used to encrypt and decrypt data. These functions are useful when securing the data in your database. You can use these functions in conjunction with MySQL security to secure your database. (For more information about database security, see Chapter 14.)

ENCODE() and DECODE() Functions

The first encryption function that you look at is the ENCODE() function, which encrypts a specified string. To use the function, you must specify two arguments, the string to be encrypted and a key (password), as shown in the following syntax:

```
ENCODE(<string>, <key>)
```

When you use the ENCODE() function to encrypt a string, the string is stored in a column as a binary string that is the same length as the original string value. To better understand how this function works, take a look at an example, which is based on the following table definition:

```
CREATE TABLE UserAccounts
(
    UserID SMALLINT NOT NULL PRIMARY KEY,
    Password VARCHAR(20) NOT NULL
);
```

Suppose that you want to insert a row in the UserAccounts table, but you want to encrypt the Password value. To encrypt the Password value, you can use an INSERT statement similar to the following:

```
INSERT INTO UserAccounts
VALUES (101, ENCODE('pw101', 'key101'));
```

In this statement, the ENCODE() function defines the second value in the VALUES clause. The function contains two arguments. The first (pw101) is the string that is to be encrypted. The second (key101) is the password that decrypts the string value if necessary. Once the row is inserted, you can use the following SELECT statement to view the values in the new row:

```
SELECT * FROM Users;
```

The SELECT statement returns something similar to the following results:

```
+--------+----------+
| UserID | Password |
+--------+----------+
|    101 | ¢-*'_    |
+--------+----------+
1 row in set (0.00 sec)
```

The result set shows that the Password value is encrypted. The only way that you can read the actual string value is to use the DECODE() function, which is shown in the following syntax:

```
DECODE(<encrypted string>, <key>)
```

As you can see, you must supply the encrypted value as well as the password that you used to encrypt that value. For example, you can use the following SELECT statement to display the actual Password value:

```
SELECT UserID, DECODE(Password, 'key101') AS Password
FROM UserAccounts;
```

Notice that the DECODE() function serves as the second element in the select list. The first argument in the function is the Password column, and the second argument is the password. The statement returns the following results:

```
+--------+----------+
| UserID | Password |
+--------+----------+
|    101 | pw101    |
+--------+----------+
1 row in set (0.00 sec)
```

As you can see, the original string value is displayed in the result set. The value, however, is still stored in the Users table in its encrypted state.

PASSWORD(), MD5(), SHA(), and SHA1() Functions

MySQL provides several functions that support one-way hashing encryption, as opposed to the ENCODE() function, which facilitates two-way encryption. The advantage to one-way encryption over two-way is that a one-way is less likely to be compromised as a result of a key value being discovered. In addition, one-way encryption eliminates the need to track the decryption key.

The first of these one-way hashing encryption functions is the PASSWORD() function. The PASSWORD() function, which is shown in the following syntax, encrypts a specified string as a 41-byte hash value:

```
PASSWORD(<string>)
```

For this function, you need to provide only one argument: the string value to be encrypted. You can test how this function works by using a SELECT statement similar to the following:

```
SELECT PASSWORD('MyPassword');
```

The PASSWORD() function encrypts the MyPassword string value and returns the following results:

```
+------------------------------------------+
| PASSWORD('MyPassword')                   |
+------------------------------------------+
| *ACE88B25517D0F22E5C3C643944B027D56345D2D |
+------------------------------------------+
1 row in set (0.00 sec)
```

MySQL uses the PASSWORD() function to encrypt passwords that are stored in the user grant table. These are the passwords that are associated with specific MySQL user accounts. You should use this function if you plan to modify those passwords directly, after a user account has been created. (You learn more about setting passwords in Chapter 14.) If you're planning to build an application that uses a MySQL database, and you store the passwords that are used for that application in the database, you should use the MD5() or SHA() functions, rather than the PASSWORD() function, because the MD5() and SHA() functions conform to widely accepted standards that are supported on multiple platforms. If you use the PASSWORD() function to encrypt the passwords, the platform on which your application is running might not support that particular format, preventing users from using the application.

You can use the MD5() function to create a 128-bit encrypted value that is based on the specified string. You use the MD5() function just like the PASSWORD() function, as shown in the following syntax.

```
MD5(<string>)
```

As with the PASSWORD() function, you can try out the MD5() function by using a SELECT statement similar to the following:

```
SELECT MD5('MyPassword');
```

The following result set shows the value returned by using the MD5() to encrypt the MyPassword string value:

```
+----------------------------------+
| MD5('MyPassword')                |
+----------------------------------+
| 48503dfd58720bd5ff35c102065a52d7 |
+----------------------------------+
1 row in set (0.00 sec)
```

If you want to create a 160-bit encrypted value based on a specified string, you can use the SHA() or SHA1() functions, which are synonymous. The SHA() function is shown in the following syntax:

```
SHA(<string>)
```

You can use the SHA() function just as you use the MD5() function:

```
SELECT SHA('MyPassword');
```

When you use the SHA() function to encrypt the MyPassword string value, the following value is returned:

```
+------------------------------------------+
| SHA('MyPassword')                        |
+------------------------------------------+
| daa1f31819ed4928fd00e986e6bda6dab6b177dc |
+------------------------------------------+
1 row in set (0.00 sec)
```

Now that you have an overview of how encryption functions work, you're ready to learn about system-related functions that provide you with information about the MySQL operation.

System-Related Functions

The system-related functions return information about the current users on the system, the connection ID being used, and the current database. You can also use system-related functions to convert IP addresses to numerical values and numerical values to IP addresses.

CURRENT_USER(), SESSION_USER(), SYSTEM_USER(), and USER() Functions

The CURRENT_USER(), SESSION_USER(), SYSTEM_USER(), and USER() functions all return the username and the hostname under which the current session is authenticated. In each case, the functions take no arguments. For example, the syntax for the USER() function is as follows:

```
USER()
```

You can use the functions in any SELECT statement to return the username and hostname, as shown in the following example:

```
SELECT USER();
```

The value returned by these functions is in the form of *<username>@<hostname>*, such as root@localhost.

> *Note that, under some circumstances, the CURRENT_USER() function can sometimes return a value different from the other three functions. For example, if a client specifies a username, but the client is authenticated anonymously, a difference can occur. For more information about these functions, see the MySQL product documentation.*

CONNECTION_ID(), DATABASE(), and VERSION() Functions

MySQL also provides functions that return information about the current connection, database, and MySQL version. For example, the following function returns the current connection ID:

```
CONNECTION_ID()
```

As you can see, the function takes no arguments. If you invoke this function through a SELECT statement such as the following, the value returned is a digit that represents the connection ID:

```
SELECT CONNECTION_ID();
```

You can also retrieve the name of the current database by using the DATABASE() function:

```
DATABASE()
```

Again, you can use the function in an SQL statement to retrieve the name of the database. For example, the following SELECT statement returns the name of the current database:

```
SELECT DATABASE();
```

If you are using the mysql client tool but are not working in the context of a specific database, a NULL is returned.

MySQL also allows you to check which version of MySQL that you're working on:

```
VERSION()
```

Once again, no arguments are required, as shown in the following SELECT statement:

```
SELECT VERSION();
```

The statement returns the current version number.

INET_ATON() and INET_NTOA() Functions

If you want to convert a network address to a numeric value, you can use the following INET_ATON() function:

```
INET_ATON(<network address>)
```

The function takes one argument, which is the network address. For example, the following SELECT statement returns the numeric value for the address 127.0.0.1:

```
SELECT INET_ATON('127.0.0.1');
```

When you execute the statement, MySQL returns the value of 2130706433. You can also take a numeric value such as this and convert it to an IP address by using the following function:

```
INET_NTOA(<network integer>)
```

This function also takes only one argument, which is the numeric representation of a network address. For example, the following SELECT statement converts the value 2130706433 to an IP address:

```
SELECT INET_NTOA(2130706433);
```

The statement returns an IP address of 127.0.0.1.

The INET_ATON() and INET_NTOA() functions are useful if you want to store IP addresses as numerical values, rather than string values. Storing IP addresses as numerical values requires only 4 bytes of storage per value, whereas storing them as string values requires up to 15 bytes.

As you have seen, you can use system-related functions to return information about users, connections, and databases. Now you can examine functions that can be used in conjunction with your query and insert operations.

Query and Insert Functions

The query and insert functions are used for specific types of queries and inserts. They include two functions: the FOUND_ROWS() function and the LAST_INSERT_ID() function.

FOUND_ROWS() Function

The FOUND_ROWS() function is used in conjunction with the LIMIT clause of a SELECT statement. Recalling from Chapter 7, the LIMIT clause specifies the number of rows to be returned in a result set.

There might be times, though, when you want to know how many rows would have been returned had you not used the LIMIT. The FOUND_ROWS() function allows you to determine the number of the entire result set. The function is shown in the following syntax:

```
FOUND_ROWS()
```

As you can see, the FOUND_ROWS() function requires no arguments. To use the function, the SELECT statement that includes the LIMIT clause must also include the SQL_CALC_FOUND_ROWS option. (The SQL_CALC_FOUND_ROWS option is a SELECT statement option that specifies what the row count of a result set would be if the LIMIT clause were not used.) Once you execute that SELECT statement, you can execute a second SELECT statement that calls the FOUND_ROWS() function, as shown in the following example:

```
SELECT FOUND_ROWS();
```

Executing this statement displays the number of rows that would have been returned by the original SELECT statement, had you not used the LIMIT clause.

LAST_INSERT_ID() Function

The LAST_INSERT_ID() function allows you to retrieve the last value that was inserted in an AUTO_INCREMENT column. For example, suppose you insert a row in a table whose primary key column is configured with the AUTO_INCREMENT option. When you insert that row, a value is automatically added to the primary key value. The value increments by one, based on the highest value that already exists in the column. Once you insert a row, you might want to know the value that was inserted in the primary key column. You can use the following function to retrieve that value:

```
LAST_INSERT_ID()
```

As you can see, the function takes no argument. You simply call the function after your last insert operation, as shown in the following SELECT statement:

```
SELECT LAST_INSERT_ID();
```

The value retrieved by the LAST_INSERT_ID() function is specific to a client connection. This way, you won't retrieve an AUTO_INCREMENT value that another client added. You can retrieve only the last value that you generated, not one that someone else generated.

In the following Try It Out exercise, you use several of the system-related functions that you learned about in this last section. To use the functions, you create a number of SELECT statements that include the functions as elements in the select lists of those statements.

Try It Out   Using Functions to Perform System-Related Operations

The following steps describe how to create the SELECT statements that use functions to perform system-related operations:

1.   Open the mysql client utility, type the following command, and press Enter:

```
use DVDRentals
```

You should receive a message indicating that you switched to the DVDRentals database.

2. First, create a SELECT statement that retrieves information about the current user. Execute the following SQL statement at the mysql command prompt:

```
SELECT USER();
```

You should receive results similar to the following:

```
+----------------+
| USER()         |
+----------------+
| root@localhost |
+----------------+
1 row in set (0.00 sec)
```

3. Now retrieve the name of the current database. Execute the following SQL statement at the mysql command prompt:

```
SELECT DATABASE();
```

You should receive results similar to the following:

```
+------------+
| DATABASE() |
+------------+
| dvdrentals |
+------------+
1 row in set (0.00 sec)
```

4. Next, create a SELECT statement that returns the connection ID. Execute the following SQL statement at the mysql command prompt:

```
SELECT CONNECTION_ID();
```

You should receive results similar to the following (with a connection ID specific to your connection):

```
+-----------------+
| CONNECTION_ID() |
+-----------------+
|              12 |
+-----------------+
1 row in set (0.01 sec)
```

5. Now try out the FOUND_ROWS() function. Before you do that, you must create a SELECT statement that includes the SQL_CALC_FOUND_ROWS option and the LIMIT clause. Execute the following SQL statement at the mysql command prompt:

```
SELECT SQL_CALC_FOUND_ROWS DVDName
FROM DVDs
WHERE StatID='s2'
ORDER BY DVDName
LIMIT 2;
```

You should receive results similar to the following:

```
+---------+
| DVDName |
+---------+
| Amadeus |
| Mash    |
+---------+
2 rows in set (0.00 sec)
```

6. Now you can create a SELECT statement that includes the FOUND_ROWS() function. Execute the following SQL statement at the mysql command prompt:

```
SELECT FOUND_ROWS();
```

You should receive results similar to the following:

```
+--------------+
| FOUND_ROWS() |
+--------------+
|            5 |
+--------------+
1 row in set (0.00 sec)
```

How It Works

The first SELECT statement that you created includes the USER() function, which returns the name of the current user and host:

```
SELECT USER();
```

The next SELECT statement that you created includes the DATABASE() function, which returns the name of the current database:

```
SELECT DATABASE();
```

The third SELECT statement that you created includes the CONNECTION_ID() function, which returns the current connection ID:

```
SELECT CONNECTION_ID();
```

Next you created a SELECT statement that includes the SQL_CALC_FOUND_ROWS option and a LIMIT clause:

```
SELECT SQL_CALC_FOUND_ROWS DVDName
FROM DVDs
WHERE StatID='s2'
ORDER BY DVDName
LIMIT 2;
```

The SQL_CALC_FOUND_ROWS option stores the number of actual rows that would have been returned had you not used the LIMIT clause. Because you used the SQL_CALC_FOUND_ROWS option, you can now use the FOUND_ROWS() function:

```
SELECT FOUND_ROWS();
```

The SELECT statement returns the value that was stored as a result of specifying the SQL_CALC_FOUND_ROWS option. In this case, five rows would have been returned had not the LIMIT clause limited the result set to two rows.

Summary

This chapter introduced you to a number of functions that you can use to retrieve, extract, calculate, and summarize data. The chapter also provided numerous examples that demonstrated how to use the functions. Although the majority of these examples were SELECT statements, you can use most functions in any statement or statement clause that supports expressions. In addition, you can often use expressions as arguments in the functions themselves. The way in which you can use a function depends on the function itself. For this reason, the chapter provided a description of a variety of functions supported by MySQL. Specifically, the chapter described how to use functions to perform any of the following tasks:

❑ Use comparison functions to compare values in an expression and use cast functions to convert data to a different type.

❑ Use control flow functions to return results based on specifications in the functions.

❑ Use data-specific functions to perform operations on string, numerical, and date/time data.

❑ Use aggregate functions to summarize data grouped together in a SELECT statement.

❑ Use system-related functions to encrypt and decrypt data, view system information, and retrieve information about query and insert operations.

Although you learned how to use numerous types of functions in this chapter, you should consider reviewing the MySQL product documentation for additional information on any functions that you include in your code. In addition, whenever you upgrade to a newer version of MySQL, you should verify that the functions still perform as you would expect them to perform. Subtle differences can exist between versions of MySQL. Despite the difference, the basic functionality supported by the functions described in this chapter is fairly consistent from one version to the next. Chapter 10 covers accessing data in multiple tables through the use of joins, subqueries, and unions.

Exercises

For these exercises, you create a series of SELECT statements that use several of the functions described in this chapter. The statements are based on the Produce table, which is shown in the following table definition:

```
CREATE TABLE Produce
(
    ProdID SMALLINT UNSIGNED NOT NULL PRIMARY KEY,
    ProdName VARCHAR(40) NOT NULL,
    Variety VARCHAR(40) NULL,
    InStock SMALLINT UNSIGNED NOT NULL,
    OnOrder SMALLINT UNSIGNED NOT NULL,
    DateOrdered DATE NOT NULL
);
```

You can assume that the following INSERT statement populated the Produce table:

```
INSERT INTO Produce
VALUES (101, 'Apples', 'Red Delicious', 2000, 1000, '2004-10-12'),
(102, 'Apples', 'Fuji', 1500, 1200, '2004-10-11'),
(103, 'Apples', 'Golden Delicious', 500, 1000, '2004-10-12'),
(104, 'Apples', 'Granny Smith', 300, 800, '2004-10-12'),
(105, 'Oranges', 'Valencia', 1200, 1600, '2004-10-11'),
(106, 'Oranges', 'Seville', 1300, 1000, '2004-10-12'),
(107, 'Grapes', 'Red seedless', 3500, 1500, '2004-10-13'),
(108, 'Grapes', 'Green seedless', 3500, 1500, '2004-10-12'),
(109, 'Carrots', NULL, 4500, 1500, '2004-10-15'),
(110, 'Broccoli', NULL, 800, 2500, '2004-10-15'),
(111, 'Cherries', 'Bing', 2500, 2500, '2004-10-11'),
(112, 'Cherries', 'Rainier', 1500, 1500, '2004-10-12'),
(113, 'Zucchini', NULL, 1000, 1300, '2004-10-09'),
(114, 'Mushrooms', 'Shitake', 800, 900, '2004-10-10'),
(115, 'Mushrooms', 'Porcini', 400, 600, '2004-10-11'),
(116, 'Mushrooms', 'Portobello', 900, 1100, '2004-10-13'),
(117, 'Cucumbers', NULL, 2500, 1200, '2004-10-14');
```

Use the Produce table to complete the following exercises. You can find the answers to these exercises in Appendix A.

1. Create a SELECT statement that retrieves data from the ProdName and InStock columns. The result set should also include a column named Signage whose values depend on the values in the ProdName column. For apples, the Signage column should display a value that reads "On Sale!" For oranges, the Signage column should display a value that reads "Just Arrived!" For all other produce, the Signage column should display a value that reads "Fresh Crop!" In addition, the result set should include only those rows whose InStock value is greater than or equal to 1000, and the result set should be sorted according to the values in the ProdName column.

2. Create a SELECT statement that retrieves data from the ProdName, Variety, and InStock columns. The values in the InStock column should be converted to a CHAR type, and the column should be named InStock_CHAR. In addition, the result set should include only those rows whose InStock value is greater than or equal to 1000, and the result set should be sorted according to the values in the ProdName column.

3. Create a SELECT statement that retrieves data from the ProdName, Variety, and InStock columns. The values in the ProdName and Variety column should be concatenated and displayed in a column named ProduceVariety. The values in the column should be in the format <ProdName> (<Variety>). In addition, the result set should include only those rows whose InStock value is greater than or equal to 1000 and those rows whose Variety value is not NULL. Also, the result set should be sorted according to the values in the ProdName column.

4. Create a SELECT statement that is identical to the one in Exercise 3, only return the ProdName and Variety values in all uppercase.

5. Create a SELECT statement that retrieves data from the Variety, OnOrder, and DateOrdered columns. The result set should also include a column named DeliveryDate, which should include values that add four days to the DateOrdered values. In addition, the result set should include only rows for apples, and the rows should be sorted according to the variety of the apples.

6. Create a SELECT statement that retrieves data from the ProdName, InStock, and OnOrder columns. The result set should be grouped together according to the ProdName column. In addition, the values in the InStock column should be added together to create a total for each group. The name of the column should be TotalInStock. Also, the values in the OnOrder column should be added together to create a total for each group. The name of the column should be TotalOrdered.

Accessing Data in Multiple Tables

In earlier chapters, you learned how to use SELECT statements to retrieve data from a database. As you recall, MySQL supports a number of options that allow you to create statements that are as precise as you need them to be. You can retrieve specific rows and columns, group and summarize data, or use expressions that include literal values, operators, functions, and column names. In learning about these options, most of the examples that you looked at retrieved data from only one table. MySQL also allows you to retrieve data from multiple tables and then produce one result set, as you would see when retrieving data from a single table. In fact, you can also access multiple tables from within UPDATE and DELETE statements.

MySQL supports several methods that you can use to access multiple tables in a single SQL statement. The first of these is to create a join in the statement that defines the tables to be linked together. Another method that you can use is to embed a subquery in your statement so that you can use the data returned by the subquery in the main SQL statement. In addition, you can create a union that joins together two SELECT statements in order to produce a result set that contains data retrieved by both statements. In this chapter, you learn about all three methods for accessing data in multiple tables. This chapter covers the following topics:

❑ Using full and outer joins in SELECT, UPDATE, and DELETE statements that link together two or more tables

❑ Adding subqueries to your SELECT, UPDATE, and DELETE statements that retrieve data that can be used by those statements

❑ Create unions that join together two SELECT statements

Creating Joins in Your SQL Statements

In a normalized database, groups of data are stored in individual tables, and relationships are established between those tables to link related data. As a result, often when creating SELECT, UPDATE, or DELETE statements, you want to be able to access data in different tables to carry out an operation affected by those relationships.

To support the capability to access data in multiple tables, MySQL allows you to create joins in a statement that define how data is accessed in multiple tables. A *join* is a condition defined in a SELECT, UPDATE, or DELETE statement that links together two or more tables. In this section, you learn how to create joins in each of these types of statements. Although much of the discussion focuses on creating joins in a SELECT statement, which is where you will most commonly use joins, many of the elements used in a SELECT join are the same elements used for UPDATE and DELETE joins.

Joining Tables in a SELECT Statement

As you're creating your SELECT statements for your applications, you may want to create statements that return data stored in different tables. The result set, though, cannot contain data that appears arbitrary in nature. In other words, the result set must be displayed in a way that suggests that the data could have been retrieved from one table. The data must be integrated and logical, despite the fact that it might come from different tables.

To achieve this integration, MySQL allows you to add joins to your SELECT statements that link together two or more tables. To illustrate how to add joins to a SELECT statement, return to the SELECT statement syntax that you first saw in Chapter 7:

```
<select statement>::=
SELECT
[<select option> [<select option>...]]
{* | <select list>}
[
    FROM {<table reference> | <join definition>}
    [WHERE <expression> [{<operator> <expression>}...]]
    [GROUP BY <group by definition>]
    [HAVING <expression> [{<operator> <expression>}...]]
    [ORDER BY <order by definition>]
    [LIMIT [<offset>,] <row count>]
]

<join definition>::=
{<table reference>, <table reference> [{, <table reference>}...]}
| {<table reference> [INNER | CROSS ] JOIN <table reference> [<join condition>]}
| {<table reference> STRAIGHT_JOIN <table reference>}
| {<table reference> LEFT [OUTER] JOIN <table reference> [<join condition>]}
| {<table reference> RIGHT [OUTER] JOIN <table reference> [<join condition>]}
| {<table reference> NATURAL [{LEFT | RIGHT} [OUTER]] JOIN <table reference>}

<table reference>::=
<table name> [[AS] <alias>]
[{USE | IGNORE | FORCE} INDEX <index name> [{, <index name>}...]]

<join condition>::=
ON <expression> [{<operator> <expression>}...]
| USING (<column> [{, <column>}...])
```

The syntax is not presented in its entirety and contains only those elements that are relevant to defining a join in a SELECT statement. (Refer to Chapter 7 for more information about the SELECT statement.) In addition, the syntax includes elements that you have not seen before. These elements are based on the

FROM clause, which has been modified from the original definition. As you can see, the FROM clause syntax is now as follows:

```
FROM {<table reference> | <join definition>}
```

When you originally learned about the SELECT statement syntax in Chapter 7, the clause was quite different:

```
FROM <table reference> [{, <table reference>}...]
```

Originally, the clause included only the `<table reference>` placeholders, and there was no mention of the `<join definition>` placeholder. This was done for the sake of brevity and to avoid presenting too much information at one time. As a result, the original syntax suggested that the FROM clause could include only one or more table references. Another way to describe the FROM clause is by also including the `<join definition>` placeholder, which defines how to add joins to a SELECT statement.

As you can see from the updated syntax of the FROM clause, the clause can include either a table reference or a join definition. You've already seen numerous examples of SELECT statements that use the `<table reference>` format. These are the SELECT statements that include only one table name in the FROM clause. If you plan to reference multiple tables in your FROM clause, you are defining some type of join, in which case the `<join definition>` placeholder applies.

The `<join definition>` placeholder refers to a number of different types of joins, as the following syntax shows:

```
<join definition>::=
{<table reference>, <table reference> [{, <table reference>}...]}
| {<table reference> [INNER | CROSS ] JOIN <table reference> [<join condition>]}
| {<table reference> STRAIGHT_JOIN <table reference>}
| {<table reference> LEFT [OUTER] JOIN <table reference> [<join condition>]}
| {<table reference> RIGHT [OUTER] JOIN <table reference> [<join condition>]}
| {<table reference> NATURAL [{LEFT | RIGHT} [OUTER]] JOIN <table reference>}
```

The first of these is the basic join, which is made up of only table references separated by commas. The other joins are the inner and cross joins, the straight join, the left join, the right join, and the natural join. Later in this section, you learn about each type of join. For now, the most important point to know is that you can define a FROM clause with a table reference or with one of several join definitions. It's also worth noting that each join definition includes one or two `<table reference>` placeholders. This is the same `<table reference>` placeholder used when the FROM clause includes no join definition. The following syntax describes the table reference:

```
<table reference>::=
<table name> [[AS] <alias>]
[{USE | IGNORE | FORCE} INDEX <index name> [{, <index name>}...]]
```

As you recall from Chapter 7, the `<table reference>` placeholder refers not only to the table name, but also to the syntax used to assign an alias to that table or define index-related options. You use table references in your joins in the same way you use a table reference directly in a FROM clause. At the very least, you must provide a table name, but you can also use any of the other options.

As you move through this section, you learn how to create each type of join. To demonstrate how to create joins, the section provides a number of examples. The examples are based on three tables: Books, Authors, and AuthorBook. The table definition for the Books table is as follows:

```
CREATE TABLE Books
(
    BookID SMALLINT NOT NULL PRIMARY KEY,
    BookTitle VARCHAR(60) NOT NULL,
    Copyright YEAR NOT NULL
)
ENGINE=INNODB;
```

For the purposes of the examples, you can assume that the following INSERT statement populated the Books table:

```
INSERT INTO Books
VALUES (12786, 'Letters to a Young Poet', 1934),
(13331, 'Winesburg, Ohio', 1919),
(14356, 'Hell\'s Angels', 1966),
(15729, 'Black Elk Speaks', 1932),
(16284, 'Noncomformity', 1996),
(17695, 'A Confederacy of Dunces', 1980),
(19264, 'Postcards', 1992),
(19354, 'The Shipping News', 1993);
```

The Authors table is the next that you use, which is shown in the following CREATE TABLE statement:

```
CREATE TABLE Authors
(
    AuthID SMALLINT NOT NULL PRIMARY KEY,
    AuthFN VARCHAR(20),
    AuthMN VARCHAR(20),
    AuthLN VARCHAR(20)
)
ENGINE=INNODB;
```

The following INSERT statement shows the values that have been inserted in the Authors table:

```
INSERT INTO Authors
VALUES (1006, 'Hunter', 'S.', 'Thompson'),
(1007, 'Joyce', 'Carol', 'Oates'),
(1008, 'Black', NULL, 'Elk'),
(1009, 'Rainer', 'Maria', 'Rilke'),
(1010, 'John', 'Kennedy', 'Toole'),
(1011, 'John', 'G.', 'Neihardt'),
(1012, 'Annie', NULL, 'Proulx'),
(1013, 'Alan', NULL, 'Watts'),
(1014, 'Nelson', NULL, 'Algren');
```

Finally, the table definition for the AuthorBook table is as follows:

```
CREATE TABLE AuthorBook
(
    AuthID SMALLINT NOT NULL,
```

```
      BookID SMALLINT NOT NULL,
      PRIMARY KEY (AuthID, BookID),
      FOREIGN KEY (AuthID) REFERENCES Authors (AuthID),
      FOREIGN KEY (BookID) REFERENCES Books (BookID)
   )
ENGINE=INNODB;
```

The following INSERT statement has been used to add data to the AuthorBook table:

```
INSERT INTO AuthorBook
VALUES (1006, 14356), (1008, 15729), (1009, 12786), (1010, 17695),
   (1011, 15729), (1012, 19264), (1012, 19354), (1014, 16284);
```

Now that you've seen the table definitions for the Books, Authors, and AuthorBook tables, take a look at Figure 10-1, which illustrates how these three tables are related to one another. Notice that a one-to-many relationship exists between the Books and AuthorBook tables, and one exists between the Authors and AuthorBook tables. What this implies is that each book may have been written by one or more authors and that each author may have written one or more books.

Figure 10-1

As you learn more about each type of join, you might want to refer to these table definitions and the illustration as a reference. In the meantime, take a look at the different types of joins supported by MySQL. You can divide these joins into two broad categories: full joins and outer joins. Full joins and outer joins are distinguished from one another in the way that they match rows in the tables that are being joined. In a full join, the SELECT statement returns only rows that match the join condition. In an outer join, the rows that match the join condition are returned as well as additional rows. As you work your way through the chapter, you better understand how the two types of joins differ from one another. Keep in mind, however, that the term "full join" is used here only as a way to group together similar types of nonouter joins. The term used to describe these types of joins varies greatly in different documentation and in different RDBMS products. In some cases, the two types of joins are differentiated by referring to inner joins and outer joins. Because one type of full join that MySQL supports is referred to as an inner join, categorizing the joins in this way can lead to confusion. The important point to remember is that the terms "full join" and "outer join" are based on the results returned by the SELECT statement, with full joins being the more common of the two.

Creating Full Joins

MySQL supports several types of full joins: the basic join, the inner and cross joins, and the straight join. Of these, the basic join is the one most commonly used, so that is where the discussion begins.

Creating Basic Joins

In some of the examples provided earlier in the book, you saw how to use basic joins. As you recall, you simply specified a FROM clause, along with multiple table names, separated by commas. The following syntax shows how a basic join is defined in the FROM clause:

```
<table reference>, <table reference> [{, <table reference>}...]
```

As you can see, the basic join must include at least two table references, but you can add as many table references as necessary. Just remember that commas must separate the table references. For example, the following SELECT statement creates a join on the Books and AuthorBook tables:

```
SELECT BookTitle, Copyright, AuthID
FROM Books, AuthorBook
ORDER BY BookTitle;
```

This statement is very similar to many of the SELECT statements that you've already seen, except that the FROM clause includes two tables: Books and AuthorBook. Because the FROM clause references the Books and the AuthorBook tables, these are the tables that are joined together.

Now take a look at the SELECT clause. The clause references three columns: BookTitle, Copyright, and AuthID. The first two columns, BookTitle and Copyright, are in the Books table, and the third column, AuthID, is in the Authors table.

The only other clause in the SELECT statement is the ORDER BY clause, which specifies that the query results be sorted according to the values in the BookTitle column.

In the previous example SELECT statement, a join is defined on two tables; however, the join is not qualified in any other way. (The columns referenced in the SELECT clause or the column referenced in the ORDER BY clause do not affect how the join itself is defined.) When a basic join is not qualified in any way, it returns a result set that matches every row in one table to every row in the joined table. This type of result set is referred to as a *Cartesian product*. For example, the previous SELECT statement returns the following Cartesian product:

```
+------------------------------+-----------+--------+
| BookTitle                    | Copyright | AuthID |
+------------------------------+-----------+--------+
| A Confederacy of Dunces      |      1980 |   1008 |
| A Confederacy of Dunces      |      1980 |   1009 |
| A Confederacy of Dunces      |      1980 |   1010 |
| A Confederacy of Dunces      |      1980 |   1011 |
| A Confederacy of Dunces      |      1980 |   1012 |
| A Confederacy of Dunces      |      1980 |   1012 |
| A Confederacy of Dunces      |      1980 |   1014 |
| A Confederacy of Dunces      |      1980 |   1006 |
| Black Elk Speaks             |      1932 |   1012 |
| Black Elk Speaks             |      1932 |   1012 |
| Black Elk Speaks             |      1932 |   1014 |
| Black Elk Speaks             |      1932 |   1006 |
| Black Elk Speaks             |      1932 |   1008 |
| Black Elk Speaks             |      1932 |   1009 |
| Black Elk Speaks             |      1932 |   1010 |
```

```
| Black Elk Speaks        |        1932 |    1011 |
| Hell's Angels           |        1966 |    1014 |
| Hell's Angels           |        1966 |    1006 |
| Hell's Angels           |        1966 |    1008 |
```

The results shown here are only part of the rows returned by the SELECT statement. The statement returns 64 rows in all. This is based on the fact that each table named in the FROM clause contains 8 rows. If each row in the Books table is matched to each row in the AuthorBook table, there are 8 AuthorBook rows for each Books row, or a total of 64 rows. For example, in the previous result set, you can see that the first 8 rows have a BookTitle value of A Confederacy of Dunces. Each of these rows is matched with 1 row from the AuthorBook table. Because the SELECT clause specifies that the AuthID value from the AuthorBook table should be displayed, that value from each row is displayed.

Using a join to return a Cartesian product is normally not very useful, and it could potentially return a great many rows. For example, if you joined 3 tables that each included 100 rows (relatively small tables in today's world of databases), the Cartesian product returned by joining these tables would be made up of 1 million rows (100 x 100 x 100). As a result, most joins must be qualified in some way to limit the number of rows returned and to ensure that the result set contains only data that is both useful and manageable.

When using a basic join to retrieve data from multiple tables, you can qualify the join by adding the necessary conditions in the WHERE clause. For example, the following SELECT statement is similar to the last, except for the addition of a WHERE clause:

```
SELECT BookTitle, Copyright, AuthID
FROM Books AS b, AuthorBook AS ab
WHERE b.BookID=ab.BookID
ORDER BY BookTitle;
```

The WHERE clause includes a condition that defines the join's limitations. In this case, the values in the BookID column in the Books table (b.BookID) are matched to the values in the BookID column of the AuthorBook table (ab.BookID). As a result, the only rows that are returned are those in which the BookID values in both tables are equal.

Notice that the Books and AuthorBook tables have been assigned alias names, b and ab, respectively. Aliases are assigned to table names to make referencing those tables easier in other parts of the statement. For example, each BookID reference in the WHERE clause is qualified with the alias for the table name. The aliases are assigned to the table names in the FROM clause. Thereafter, any references to the tables are through the use of the aliases. If there is no chance of confusing a column name with another column, you do not need to qualify the column name. If the same column name is used in more than one table, the name must be qualified so that MySQL knows which column is being referenced.

By adding the WHERE clause to the statement, the number of rows returned by the statement is drastically reduced, as shown in the following result set:

```
+----------------------------+-----------+---------+
| BookTitle                  | Copyright | AuthID  |
+----------------------------+-----------+---------+
| A Confederacy of Dunces    |      1980 |    1010 |
| Black Elk Speaks           |      1932 |    1008 |
| Black Elk Speaks           |      1932 |    1011 |
| Hell's Angels              |      1966 |    1006 |
| Letters to a Young Poet    |      1934 |    1009 |
```

```
| Noncomformity              |     1996 |   1014 |
| Postcards                  |     1992 |   1012 |
| The Shipping News          |     1993 |   1012 |
+----------------------------+----------+--------+
8 rows in set (0.00 sec)
```

As you can see, this is a very different result from the Cartesian product returned by the first example you looked at. Now only rows that have the same BookID value in both columns are returned. For example, the row in the Books table that contains a BookTitle value of A Confederacy of Dunces is matched to the row in the AuthorBook table that contains an AuthID value of 1010. The rows in both tables have the same BookID value, which is 17695.

In addition to the WHERE clause containing a condition that specifies the extent of the join, the WHERE clause can include additional logical operators and expressions that further limit the results returned by the SELECT statement. For example, the following SELECT statement returns only those rows that contain a Copyright value less than 1980:

```
SELECT BookTitle, Copyright, ab.AuthID
FROM Books AS b, AuthorBook AS ab
WHERE b.BookID=ab.BookID AND Copyright<1980
ORDER BY BookTitle;
```

As you can see, this SELECT statement is identical to the preceding one, except for the addition of an expression in the WHERE clause. Now the statement returns only those rows with matching BookID values *and* whose Copyright value is less than 1980, as shown in the following query results:

```
+----------------------------+----------+--------+
| BookTitle                  | Copyright | AuthID |
+----------------------------+----------+--------+
| Black Elk Speaks           |     1932 |   1008 |
| Black Elk Speaks           |     1932 |   1011 |
| Hell's Angels              |     1966 |   1006 |
| Letters to a Young Poet    |     1934 |   1009 |
+----------------------------+----------+--------+
4 rows in set (0.00 sec)
```

As you can see, the statement returns only 4 rows, which is quite a difference from the 64 rows returned by the first statement. As this last example demonstrates, the more specific you can be in your SELECT statement, the more precise the results.

In the last few examples that you've seen, the SELECT statements included joins that linked two tables together. As you can see from the query results, returning only an AuthID value might not always be very useful. Wouldn't it be better to know the author's name for that book?

Fortunately, MySQL allows you to join more than two tables together. The basic statement is similar to what you've already seen; only a few supplemental elements are added to bring in the additional table, as shown in the following SELECT statement:

```
SELECT BookTitle, Copyright, CONCAT_WS(' ', AuthFN, AuthMN, AuthLN) AS Author
FROM Books AS b, AuthorBook AS ab, Authors AS a
WHERE b.BookID=ab.BookID AND ab.AuthID=a.AuthID AND Copyright<1980
ORDER BY BookTitle;
```

Now the FROM clause includes three tables: Books, AuthorBook, and Authors. Each table is assigned an alias, which is then used in the WHERE clause. The WHERE clause also contains an additional element, which is a condition that specifies that the AuthID value in the AuthorBook table must match the AuthID value in the Authors table. When all the conditions in the WHERE clause are taken together, the result is that, for each row returned by the result set, the BookID value in the Books table must equal the BookID value in the AuthorBook table *and* the AuthID value in the AuthorBook table must equal the AuthID value in the Authors table *and* the Copyright value must be less than 1980, as shown in the following query results:

```
+-------------------------+-----------+---------------------+
| BookTitle               | Copyright | Author              |
+-------------------------+-----------+---------------------+
| Black Elk Speaks        |      1932 | Black Elk           |
| Black Elk Speaks        |      1932 | John G. Neihardt    |
| Hell's Angels           |      1966 | Hunter S. Thompson  |
| Letters to a Young Poet |      1934 | Rainer Maria Rilke  |
+-------------------------+-----------+---------------------+
4 rows in set (0.00 sec)
```

As you can see, the query results now show the name of the author rather than the AuthID value. The author's first, middle, and last names are taken from the Authors table and concatenated in one value. As a result, the query returns information that is far more useful than you saw in the preceding statements, and you no longer have to try to decipher primary key values to determine who the author is.

Creating Inner Joins and Cross Joins

When it comes to joins, MySQL provides numerous ways to accomplish the same results. For example, you can create inner joins and cross joins that produce identical result sets as those generated by the basic joins you saw in the previous section. As you recall from the Introduction, there are a number of reasons why MySQL provides different methods for achieving the same results. For example, as MySQL has tried to conform to the SQL standard, statements have evolved from one version of MySQL to the next; however, the original statement is supported for legacy systems. In addition, by supporting different ways to achieve different results, your code can be more portable in an application. For instance, one version of the SQL statement might be supported in another RDBMS, so the statement can be used to retrieve data from two different database systems. If you're creating an application that accesses only a MySQL database and that database is managed by a current version of MySQL, you're usually safe using the simplest statement available. For more complex joins, you might want to try different types of joins to determine whether one performs better than the other. Normally, though, this isn't necessary.

Now take a look at how an inner or cross join is created. The following syntax shows you how to add an inner or cross join to your SELECT statement:

```
<table reference> [INNER | CROSS ] JOIN <table reference> [<join condition>]

<join condition>::=
ON <expression> [{<operator> <expression>}...]
| USING (<column> [{, <column>}...])
```

As the syntax illustrates, you must include a table reference, the optional INNER or CROSS keyword, the JOIN keyword, the second table reference, and an optional join condition. The join condition can consist of an ON clause or a USING clause. The join condition defines the circumstances of the join. In the basic join, the circumstances are defined in the WHERE clause, but in the inner and cross joins, this is accomplished through the join condition.

For all practical purposes, specifying the INNER or CROSS keywords produces the same results as not specifying either. (When neither the INNER nor the CROSS keywords are specified, the join is usually referred to as a cross join.) In addition, if you don't qualify the join in any way, the results produce the same Cartesian product as their basic join counterpart. For example, the following four statements produce the same results:

```
SELECT BookTitle, AuthID FROM Books, AuthorBook;
SELECT BookTitle, AuthID FROM Books JOIN AuthorBook;
SELECT BookTitle, AuthID FROM Books INNER JOIN AuthorBook;
SELECT BookTitle, AuthID FROM Books CROSS JOIN AuthorBook;
```

Each statement returns 64 rows. Each row in the Books table is matched to each row in the AuthorBook table. As a result, the join must be qualified in order to produce useful results. To qualify the inner or cross join, you can use the ON or USING clause rather than the WHERE clause. For example, the following SELECT statement uses an ON clause to qualify the join condition:

```
SELECT BookTitle, Copyright, ab.AuthID
FROM Books AS b JOIN AuthorBook AS ab
    ON b.BookID=ab.BookID
ORDER BY BookTitle;
```

As you can see, the FROM clause defines the join. Rather than separating the joined tables with a comma, the statement uses the JOIN keyword. In addition, the ON clause specifies that the BookID values in the Books and AuthorBook tables must be equal in order for a row to be returned. By defining a join condition in an ON clause, the results are limited to eight rows, as shown in the following result set:

```
+-------------------------+-----------+--------+
| BookTitle               | Copyright | AuthID |
+-------------------------+-----------+--------+
| A Confederacy of Dunces |      1980 |   1010 |
| Black Elk Speaks        |      1932 |   1008 |
| Black Elk Speaks        |      1932 |   1011 |
| Hell's Angels           |      1966 |   1006 |
| Letters to a Young Poet |      1934 |   1009 |
| Noncomformity           |      1996 |   1014 |
| Postcards               |      1992 |   1012 |
| The Shipping News       |      1993 |   1012 |
+-------------------------+-----------+--------+
8 rows in set (0.00 sec)
```

You can produce the same results by using a USING clause to qualify the join, as shown in the following statement:

```
SELECT BookTitle, Copyright, ab.AuthID
FROM Books JOIN AuthorBook AS ab
    USING (BookID)
ORDER BY BookTitle;
```

As you can see, the USING clause requires only that you specify the joined columns (in parentheses). You can use this technique only when the joined columns in each table share the same name. If you create a join that is based on more than one column, you must specify all those columns and separate them with a comma.

As is the case with the basic join, you can also further qualify an inner or full join by specifying a condition in the WHERE clause, as shown in the following statement:

```
SELECT BookTitle, Copyright, ab.AuthID
FROM Books AS b JOIN AuthorBook AS ab
    ON b.BookID=ab.BookID
WHERE Copyright<1980
ORDER BY BookTitle;
```

When defining inner or cross joins, you should specify the linked columns in the ON or USING clause and any other conditions in the WHERE clause. You can also specify the join conditions in the WHERE clause, as you do in a basic join, and not use ON or USING clauses. Your statements are generally easier to read, however, if you use ON or USING clauses.

Returning now to the preceding SELECT statement, if you execute this statement, it produces the same results as its basic join counterpart, as shown in the following result set:

```
+-------------------------+-----------+--------+
| BookTitle               | Copyright | AuthID |
+-------------------------+-----------+--------+
| Black Elk Speaks        |      1932 |   1008 |
| Black Elk Speaks        |      1932 |   1011 |
| Hell's Angels           |      1966 |   1006 |
| Letters to a Young Poet |      1934 |   1009 |
+-------------------------+-----------+--------+
4 rows in set (0.00 sec)
```

You can also create inner and cross joins on more than two tables. As with the preceding example, you should specify the necessary join conditions in an ON or USING clause. For example, the following SELECT statement includes two ON clauses:

```
SELECT BookTitle, Copyright, CONCAT_WS(' ', AuthFN, AuthMN, AuthLN) AS Author
FROM Books AS b CROSS JOIN AuthorBook AS ab ON b.BookID=ab.BookID
    CROSS JOIN Authors AS a ON ab.AuthID=a.AuthID
WHERE Copyright<1980
ORDER BY BookTitle;
```

In this statement, the FROM clause first joins the Books table to the AuthorBook table. The join is qualified through the use of an ON clause that matches the values in the BookID column of each table. The FROM clause then goes on to join the AuthorBook table to the Authors table. The second join is qualified through the use of an ON clause that matches the values of the AuthID column of the Authors table and the AuthorBook table. Consequently, the following results are produced:

```
+-------------------------+-----------+--------------------+
| BookTitle               | Copyright | Author             |
+-------------------------+-----------+--------------------+
| Black Elk Speaks        |      1932 | Black Elk          |
| Black Elk Speaks        |      1932 | John G. Neihardt   |
| Hell's Angels           |      1966 | Hunter S. Thompson |
| Letters to a Young Poet |      1934 | Rainer Maria Rilke |
+-------------------------+-----------+--------------------+
4 rows in set (0.00 sec)
```

Finally, you can achieve the same results in the preceding statement by using two USING clauses, rather than ON clauses, as shown in the following statement:

```
SELECT BookTitle, Copyright, CONCAT_WS(' ', AuthFN, AuthMN, AuthLN) AS Author
FROM Books JOIN AuthorBook USING (BookID)
    JOIN Authors USING (AuthID)
WHERE Copyright<1980
ORDER BY BookTitle;
```

As you can see, the USING clause is a little simpler to create and read because you have to specify the linking columns only once. The USING clause is also handy because it often eliminates the need to use aliases.

Creating Straight Joins

Another type of join that you can create is the straight join, which is similar to a basic join in most respects. The primary difference is that a straight join allows you to specify that the join optimizer read the table on the left before the table on the right. (The join optimizer is a component of the MySQL server that tries to determine the best way to process a join.) You would use a straight join in those cases in which you believe that the join optimizer is not processing your SELECT statement as efficiently as it could. In most cases, though, you should rely on the optimizer.

To create a straight join, you can use the following syntax in your FROM clause:

```
<table reference> STRAIGHT_JOIN <table reference>
```

As you can see, you must specify a table reference, followed by the STRAIGHT_JOIN keyword, which is then followed by another table reference. For example, the following SELECT statement produces the same results that you saw in the previous two examples:

```
SELECT BookTitle, Copyright, CONCAT_WS(' ', AuthFN, AuthMN, AuthLN) AS Author
FROM Books AS b STRAIGHT_JOIN AuthorBook AS ab STRAIGHT_JOIN Authors AS a
WHERE b.BookID=ab.BookID AND ab.AuthID=a.AuthID AND Copyright<1980
ORDER BY BookTitle;
```

One thing to notice about the straight join is that, like the basic join, the join is qualified in the WHERE clause, not in an ON or USING clause. In fact, the only difference between a straight join and a basic join, in terms of syntax, is that in a straight join you use the STRAIGHT_JOIN keyword to separate the table references, rather than a comma.

MySQL provides another method that you can use to create a straight join. Instead of using the straight join syntax in the FROM clause, you use the basic join syntax and you specify the STRAIGHT_JOIN table option in the SELECT clause, as shown in the following example:

```
SELECT STRAIGHT_JOIN BookTitle, Copyright,
    CONCAT_WS(' ', AuthFN, AuthMN, AuthLN) AS Author
FROM Books AS b, AuthorBook AS ab, Authors AS a
WHERE b.BookID=ab.BookID AND ab.AuthID=a.AuthID AND Copyright<1980
ORDER BY BookTitle;
```

As you can see, the table references in the FROM clause are separated by commas, which is typical of a basic join. In addition, the SELECT clause includes the STRAIGHT_JOIN select option. This statement returns the same results that you saw in the preceding three examples.

So far in this chapter, you have learned how to create SELECT statements that use full joins to retrieve data from two or more tables. In this Try It Out section you create your own SELECT statements that retrieve data from multiple tables in the DVDRentals database.

Try It Out   Using Full Joins to Retrieve Data

Follow these steps to create statements that use full joins:

1.   Open the mysql client utility, type the following command, and press Enter:

```
use DVDRentals
```

You should receive a message indicating that you switched to the DVDRentals database.

2.   The first SELECT statement that you create uses a basic join to retrieve DVDName values from the DVDs table and MTypeDescrip values from the MovieTypes table. Execute the following SQL statement at the mysql command prompt:

```
SELECT DVDName, MTypeDescrip As MovieType
FROM DVDs AS d, MovieTypes AS mt
WHERE d.MTypeID=mt.MTypeID AND StatID='s2'
ORDER BY DVDName;
```

You should receive results similar to the following:

```
+-------------------------------+-----------+
| DVDName                       | MovieType |
+-------------------------------+-----------+
| Amadeus                       | Drama     |
| Mash                          | Comedy    |
| The Maltese Falcon            | Drama     |
| The Rocky Horror Picture Show | Comedy    |
| What's Up, Doc?               | Comedy    |
+-------------------------------+-----------+
5 rows in set (0.00 sec)
```

3. The next SELECT statement that you create is similar to the preceding one except that you also retrieve data from the Ratings table. Execute the following SQL statement at the mysql command prompt:

```
SELECT DVDName, MTypeDescrip As MovieType,
    CONCAT(d.RatingID, ': ', r.RatingDescrip) AS Rating
FROM DVDs AS d, MovieTypes AS mt, Ratings AS r
WHERE d.MTypeID=mt.MTypeID AND d.RatingID=r.RatingID
    AND StatID='s2'
ORDER BY DVDName;
```

You should receive results similar to the following:

```
+------------------------------+-----------+---------------------------------+
| DVDName                      | MovieType | Rating                          |
+------------------------------+-----------+---------------------------------+
| Amadeus                      | Drama     | PG: Parental guidance suggested |
| Mash                         | Comedy    | R: Under 17 requires adult      |
| The Maltese Falcon           | Drama     | NR: Not rated                   |
| The Rocky Horror Picture Show| Comedy    | NR: Not rated                   |
| What's Up, Doc?              | Comedy    | G: General audiences            |
+------------------------------+-----------+---------------------------------+
5 rows in set (0.00 sec)
```

4. Now retrieve the same data that your retrieved in the preceding SELECT statement, only this time, use a cross join. Execute the following SQL statement at the mysql command prompt:

```
SELECT DVDName, MTypeDescrip AS MovieType,
    CONCAT(d.RatingID, ': ', r.RatingDescrip) AS Rating
FROM MovieTypes AS mt CROSS JOIN DVDs AS d USING (MTypeID)
    CROSS JOIN Ratings AS r USING (RatingID)
WHERE StatID='s2'
ORDER BY DVDName;
```

You should receive results similar to those you received in the preceding statement.

5. In the next SELECT statement that you create, you use an inner join to retrieve customer names and the transactions IDs for those transactions that involve the DVD with a DVDID value of 4. Execute the following SQL statement at the mysql command prompt:

```
SELECT CONCAT_WS(' ', CustFN, CustMN, CustLN) AS Customer, TransID
FROM Customers INNER JOIN Orders USING (CustID)
    INNER JOIN Transactions USING (OrderID)
WHERE DVDID=4
ORDER BY CustLN;
```

You should receive results similar to the following:

```
+------------------------+---------+
| Customer               | TransID |
+------------------------+---------+
| Ralph Frederick Johnson|       2 |
| Peter Taylor           |      12 |
| Anne Thomas            |       8 |
| Hubert T. Weatherby    |       5 |
+------------------------+---------+
4 rows in set (0.01 sec)
```

6. Next, use a basic join in a SELECT statement to join together four tables in order to display the names of movie participants, the movies that they participated in, and the roles they played in those movies. Execute the following SQL statement at the mysql command prompt:

```
SELECT CONCAT_WS(' ', PartFN, PartMN, PartLN) AS Participant, DVDName,
    RoleDescrip AS Role
FROM DVDs AS d, DVDParticipant AS dp, Participants AS p, Roles AS r
WHERE d.DVDID=dp.DVDID AND p.PartID=dp.PartID AND r.RoleID=dp.RoleID
ORDER BY PartLN;
```

You should receive results similar to the following:

```
+------------------+--------------------+--------------+
| Participant      | DVDName            | Role         |
+------------------+--------------------+--------------+
| John Barry       | Out of Africa      | Composer     |
| Irving Berlin    | White Christmas    | Composer     |
| Humphrey Bogart  | The Maltese Falcon | Actor        |
| Henry Buck       | What's Up, Doc?    | Screenwriter |
| Rosemary Clooney | White Christmas    | Actor        |
| Bing Crosby      | White Christmas    | Actor        |
| Michael Curtiz   | White Christmas    | Director     |
| Danny Kaye       | White Christmas    | Actor        |
| Sydney Pollack   | Out of Africa      | Producer     |
| Sydney Pollack   | Out of Africa      | Director     |
| Robert Redford   | Out of Africa      | Actor        |
| Meryl Streep     | Out of Africa      | Actor        |
+------------------+--------------------+--------------+
12 rows in set (0.02 sec)
```

How It Works

In this exercise, you created five SELECT statements that each use a different type of join to integrate data from more than one table in a single result set. In this first statement, you defined a basic join that integrated data from the DVDs table and the MovieTypes table:

```
SELECT DVDName, MTypeDescrip As MovieType
FROM DVDs AS d, MovieTypes AS mt
WHERE d.MTypeID=mt.MTypeID AND StatID='s2'
ORDER BY DVDName;
```

The join is defined in the FROM clause. By including more than one table in the clause, you're specifying that a join be created. Because this is a basic join, the join is qualified by adding a condition to the WHERE clause that specifies that the MTypeID values in both tables be equal. The WHERE clause also contains a second condition that specifies that the StatID value must be s2. As a result, any row returned by this statement must have equal values in the MTypeID columns of both tables *and* the StatID value in the DVDs table must equal s2.

The next SELECT statement is similar to the preceding one except that you added a third table to the statement:

```
SELECT DVDName, MTypeDescrip As MovieType,
    CONCAT(d.RatingID, ': ', r.RatingDescrip) AS Rating
FROM DVDs AS d, MovieTypes AS mt, Ratings AS r
```

```
WHERE d.MTypeID=mt.MTypeID AND d.RatingID=r.RatingID
    AND StatID='s2'
ORDER BY DVDName;
```

The FROM clause now includes the Ratings table in addition to the DVDs and MovieTypes tables. In addition, you added a third condition to the WHERE clause that specifies that the RatingID values in the DVDs table and the Ratings table must be equal. As a result, any row returned by this statement must have equal values in the MTypeID columns of the DVDs and MovieTypes tables *and* values in the RatingID columns of the DVDs and Ratings tables *and* the StatID value in the DVDs table must equal s2. In addition, the updated SELECT statement also includes a third column in the result set that concatenates the RatingID value and the RatingDescrip value for each returned row.

You then created a SELECT statement that retrieved the same results as the preceding statement. The next statement, however, uses a cross join rather than a basic join:

```
SELECT DVDName, MTypeDescrip AS MovieType,
    CONCAT(d.RatingID, ': ', r.RatingDescrip) AS Rating
FROM MovieTypes AS mt CROSS JOIN DVDs AS d USING (MTypeID)
    CROSS JOIN Ratings AS r USING (RatingID)
WHERE StatID='s2'
ORDER BY DVDName;
```

As the statement shows, the FROM clause now includes the join definitions and the USING clauses. The MovieTypes table is joined to the DVDs table, and that join is qualified through the USING clause, which specifies the MTypeID column. The Orders DVDs table is then joined to the Ratings table, and that join is qualified through the USING clause, which specifies the RatingID column.

In the next SELECT statement that you created, you defined an inner join on the Customers, Orders, and Transactions table:

```
SELECT CONCAT_WS(' ', CustFN, CustMN, CustLN) AS Customer, TransID
FROM Customers INNER JOIN Orders USING (CustID)
    INNER JOIN Transactions USING (OrderID)
WHERE DVDID=4
ORDER BY TransID;
```

The Customers table is joined to the Orders table, and that join is qualified through the USING clause, which specifies the CustID column. The Orders table is then joined to the Transactions table, and that join is qualified through the USING clause, which specifies the Order ID column. The statement returns the customer name (concatenated) from the Customers table and the TransID value from the Transactions table. Only rows that have a DVDID value of 4 are returned, as specified by the WHERE clause.

The final SELECT statement that you created joined the DVDs, DVDParticipant, Participants, and Roles table:

```
SELECT CONCAT_WS(' ', PartFN, PartMN, PartLN) AS Participant, DVDName,
    RoleDescrip AS Role
FROM DVDs AS d, DVDParticipant AS dp, Participants AS p, Roles AS r
WHERE d.DVDID=dp.DVDID AND p.PartID=dp.PartID AND r.RoleID=dp.RoleID
ORDER BY PartLN;
```

The statement creates a basic join and defines the join conditions in the WHERE clause, which states that the DVDID values in the DVDs and DVDParticipant tables must be equal, the PartID values in the Participants and DVDParticipant tables must be equal, and the RoleID values in the Roles and DVDParticipant tables must be equal. The result set includes a list of the participants (from the Participants table), the names of the movies in which they participated (from the DVDs table), and the roles they played (from the Roles table). The link among these three tables is defined through the DVDParticipant table, which is why all tables must join to that table.

As you have seen, MySQL supports a number of full joins. There might be times when you want to display results that include rows in addition to those that match the join condition. To include additional rows in your result sets, you can use the outer join.

Creating Outer Joins

Except for the joins that returned Cartesian products, the joins that you have seen so far have been those that returned only rows that contained matching values in the specified columns. Suppose that you want to include details that do not fit these conditions, yet at the same time, you don't want to return large result sets of unnecessary information. For example, in the statements that you looked at when learning about full joins, you saw joins that were based on the Books, AuthorBook, and Authors tables (shown in Figure 10-1). Some of the joins that were created allowed you to match authors to books so that you were able to view books and their authors together. What if the Books table contains books for which no authors are listed in the Authors table? Or authors are listed in the Authors table that do not have books listed in the Books table?

MySQL allows you to view these authors or books by using outer joins. You can create one of two types of outer joins: a left join or a right join. A left join pulls all values from the table on the left, and a right join pulls all values from the table listed on the right. To help illustrate this point, Figure 10-2 shows a Venn diagram that represents the left outer join. The circle on the left represents the Books table, and the circle on the right represents the Authors table. The Venn diagram illustrates what will happen when these tables are joined together. The values on the left side of the join are taken from the Books table, and the values on the right side of the join are taken from the Authors table. In a full join, only the values that are matched by the join are returned. These are the values that appear in the section where the two circles intersect. As you can see, each title is matched with one or more authors.

Figure 10-2 shows something else. The book *Winesburg, Ohio* cannot be matched with an author because no author exists in the Authors table for that book. In a full join, this book is not included in the results set. Because this is a left outer join, the book is still returned, but it is matched with a value of NULL.

If this were a right outer join, any authors that do not match a book in the Books table are paired with NULL values, as is the case of the books for which no authors are listed. The following sections examine each type of outer join to better illustrate how they work.

Books   Authors

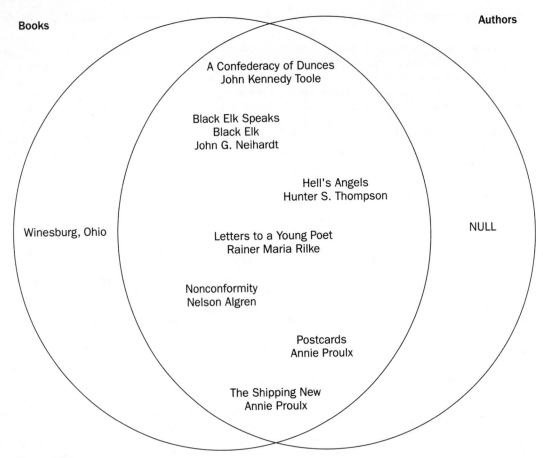

A Confederacy of Dunces
John Kennedy Toole

Black Elk Speaks
Black Elk
John G. Neihardt

Hell's Angels
Hunter S. Thompson

Winesburg, Ohio

Letters to a Young Poet
Rainer Maria Rilke

NULL

Nonconformity
Nelson Algren

Postcards
Annie Proulx

The Shipping New
Annie Proulx

Figure 10-2

Creating Left Joins

The syntax for a left outer join is similar to an inner or cross join, except that you must include the LEFT keyword, as shown in the following syntax:

```
<table reference> LEFT [OUTER] JOIN <table reference> [<join condition>]

<join condition>::=
ON <expression> [{<operator> <expression>}...]
| USING (<column> [{, <column>}...])
```

As you can see, you first specify a table reference, followed by the LEFT keyword, the optional OUTER keyword, and then the JOIN keyword. This is all followed by another table reference and an optional join condition, which can be an ON clause or a USING clause. For example, the following SELECT statement defines a left outer join on the Books and AuthorBook tables:

```
SELECT BookTitle, Copyright, AuthID
FROM Books AS b LEFT JOIN AuthorBook AS ab
    ON b.BookID=ab.BookID
ORDER BY BookTitle;
```

As you can see, the FROM clause first references the Books table and then references the AuthorBook table. As a result, all results are returned from the Books table (the left table), and only the results that meet the condition specified in the ON clause are returned from the AuthorBook table (the right table), as shown in the following result set:

```
+------------------------+-----------+--------+
| BookTitle              | Copyright | AuthID |
+------------------------+-----------+--------+
| A Confederacy of Dunces |     1980 |   1010 |
| Black Elk Speaks       |      1932 |   1008 |
| Black Elk Speaks       |      1932 |   1011 |
| Hell's Angels          |      1966 |   1006 |
| Letters to a Young Poet |     1934 |   1009 |
| Noncomformity          |      1996 |   1014 |
| Postcards              |      1992 |   1012 |
| The Shipping News      |      1993 |   1012 |
| Winesburg, Ohio        |      1919 |   NULL |
+------------------------+-----------+--------+
9 rows in set (0.00 sec)
```

If you refer to the last row, you can see that a NULL value has been returned for the AuthID column. A NULL is returned because the book *Winesburg, Ohio* is listed in the Books table, but no author is listed in the Authors table. Whenever a value in the left table doesn't have an associated value in the right table, NULL is returned for the left table.

You can receive the same results as the preceding statement by replacing the ON clause with the USING clause, as shown in the following statement:

```
SELECT BookTitle, Copyright, AuthID
FROM Books LEFT JOIN AuthorBook
    USING (BookID)
ORDER BY BookTitle;
```

You can also use a left join to link more than two tables. For example, the following SELECT statement defines a left join on the Books, AuthorBook, and Authors tables:

```
SELECT BookTitle, Copyright, CONCAT_WS(' ', AuthFN, AuthMN, AuthLN) AS Author
FROM Books AS b LEFT JOIN AuthorBook AS ab ON b.BookID=ab.BookID
    LEFT JOIN Authors AS a ON ab.AuthID=a.AuthID
ORDER BY BookTitle;
```

As you can see, the FROM clause includes an additional left join definition. Because of this, the result set can now include the actual author's name, rather than an ID, while preserving the left join, as shown in the following results:

```
+------------------------+-----------+---------------------+
| BookTitle              | Copyright | Author              |
+------------------------+-----------+---------------------+
| A Confederacy of Dunces|      1980 | John Kennedy Toole  |
| Black Elk Speaks       |      1932 | Black Elk           |
| Black Elk Speaks       |      1932 | John G. Neihardt    |
| Hell's Angels          |      1966 | Hunter S. Thompson  |
| Letters to a Young Poet|      1934 | Rainer Maria Rilke  |
| Noncomformity          |      1996 | Nelson Algren       |
| Postcards              |      1992 | Annie Proulx        |
| The Shipping News      |      1993 | Annie Proulx        |
| Winesburg, Ohio        |      1919 |                     |
+------------------------+-----------+---------------------+
9 rows in set (0.00 sec)
```

As you probably noticed, the Author column for the last row is now blank because you used the CON-CAT_WS() function to concatenate the author names. Because the function cannot concatenate a value that doesn't exist, MySQL does not know to return NULL, so no value is inserted in the Author column. The results still tell you that *Winesburg, Ohio* is listed in the Books table, but no matching author is listed in the Authors table.

If you were to modify the preceding SELECT statement to remove the CONCAT_WS() function, your statement would now look similar to the following:

```
SELECT BookTitle, Copyright, AuthFN, AuthMN, AuthLN
FROM Books AS b LEFT JOIN AuthorBook AS ab ON b.BookID=ab.BookID
    LEFT JOIN Authors AS a ON ab.AuthID=a.AuthID
ORDER BY BookTitle;
```

Now MySQL interprets the columns as it would any column in the right table of a left join, as shown in the following result set:

```
+------------------------+-----------+--------+--------+----------+
| BookTitle              | Copyright | AuthFN | AuthMN | AuthLN   |
+------------------------+-----------+--------+--------+----------+
| A Confederacy of Dunces|      1980 | John   | Kennedy| Toole    |
| Black Elk Speaks       |      1932 | Black  | NULL   | Elk      |
| Black Elk Speaks       |      1932 | John   | G.     | Neihardt |
| Hell's Angels          |      1966 | Hunter | S.     | Thompson |
| Letters to a Young Poet|      1934 | Rainer | Maria  | Rilke    |
| Noncomformity          |      1996 | Nelson | NULL   | Algren   |
| Postcards              |      1992 | Annie  | NULL   | Proulx   |
| The Shipping News      |      1993 | Annie  | NULL   | Proulx   |
| Winesburg, Ohio        |      1919 | NULL   | NULL   | NULL     |
+------------------------+-----------+--------+--------+----------+
9 rows in set (0.00 sec)
```

As you can see, NULL is inserted in the AuthFN, AuthMN, and AuthLN columns of the last row of the result set.

Creating Right Joins

A right join is simply the counterpart to the left join and works the same as a left join, except that all values are retrieved from the table on the right. The following syntax shows how to define a right join in your FROM clause:

```
<table reference> RIGHT [OUTER] JOIN <table reference> [<join condition>]

<join condition>::=
ON <expression> [{<operator> <expression>}...]
| USING (<column> [{, <column>}...])
```

As you can see, the language is the same as with a left join, except for the keyword RIGHT. Now take a look at an example of a right join to demonstrate how to retrieve data from the joined tables. The following SELECT statement joins the Books table to the AuthorBook table, and the AuthorBook table to the Authors table:

```
SELECT BookTitle, Copyright, CONCAT_WS(' ', AuthFN, AuthMN, AuthLN) AS Author
FROM Books AS b RIGHT JOIN AuthorBook AS ab ON b.BookID=ab.BookID
    RIGHT JOIN Authors AS a ON ab.AuthID=a.AuthID
ORDER BY BookTitle;
```

As the statement shows, the first join condition is specified on the BookID column, and the second join condition is specified on the AuthID column. Although three tables are joined, the statement takes data only from the Books table and the Authors table, and the AuthorBook table is what links the other two tables together, with the Books table on the left side of the join condition and the Authors table on the right side. As a result, all authors are retrieved from the Authors table, but only books with matching BookID values (in Books and AuthorBook) are retrieved, as shown in the following result set:

```
+-------------------------+-----------+---------------------+
| BookTitle               | Copyright | Author              |
+-------------------------+-----------+---------------------+
| NULL                    |      NULL | Joyce Carol Oates   |
| NULL                    |      NULL | Alan Watts          |
| A Confederacy of Dunces |      1980 | John Kennedy Toole  |
| Black Elk Speaks        |      1932 | John G. Neihardt    |
| Black Elk Speaks        |      1932 | Black Elk           |
| Hell's Angels           |      1966 | Hunter S. Thompson  |
| Letters to a Young Poet |      1934 | Rainer Maria Rilke  |
| Noncomformity           |      1996 | Nelson Algren       |
| Postcards               |      1992 | Annie Proulx        |
| The Shipping News       |      1993 | Annie Proulx        |
+-------------------------+-----------+---------------------+
10 rows in set (0.00 sec)
```

As you can see, the BookTitle and Copyright values in the first two rows are set to NULL. Because both columns are part of the Books table, the left table, only matched rows are retrieved. The Author column, which comes from the right table, includes all authors, even the two with no matching books in the Books table. If you had wanted, you could have reversed the order in which the tables are joined in the FROM clause and then changed the join definition to a left join, and you would have received the same results.

Now that you know how to create outer joins, in the following Try It Out you create a SELECT statement that uses a left join to retrieve data from the Employees table and the Orders table in the DVDRentals database.

Try It Out   Using Outer Joins to Retrieve Data

Follow these steps to test out a left outer join:

1. Open the mysql client utility, type the following command, and press Enter:

```
use DVDRentals
```

You should receive a message indicating that you switched to the DVDRentals database.

2. In order to fully test a left join, you must first add data to the Employees table that provides you with results that demonstrate how a left join operates. Execute the following SQL statement at the mysql command prompt:

```
INSERT INTO Employees
VALUES (NULL, 'Rebecca', 'T.', 'Reynolds'),
(NULL, 'Charlie', 'Patrick', 'Waverly');
```

You should receive a message indicating that the statement executed successfully, affecting two rows.

3. Now create a left outer join on the Employees and Order tables. Because the Employees table is named first in the join condition, all rows are retrieved from that table, whether or not any associated records exist in the Orders table. Execute the following SQL statement at the mysql command prompt:

```
SELECT CONCAT_WS(' ', EmpFN, EmpMN, EmpLN) AS Employee, OrderID
FROM Employees LEFT JOIN Orders USING (EmpID)
ORDER BY EmpLN;
```

You should receive results similar to the following:

```
+-------------------------+---------+
| Employee                | OrderID |
+-------------------------+---------+
| George Brooks           |       4 |
| George Brooks           |      12 |
| Rita C. Carter          |       3 |
| Rita C. Carter          |       9 |
| John Laguci             |       8 |
| John Laguci             |      13 |
| Mary Marie Michaels     |       1 |
| Mary Marie Michaels     |       6 |
| Rebecca T. Reynolds     |    NULL |
| Robert Schroader        |       2 |
| Robert Schroader        |       7 |
| Robert Schroader        |      10 |
| John P. Smith           |       5 |
| John P. Smith           |      11 |
| Charlie Patrick Waverly |    NULL |
+-------------------------+---------+
15 rows in set (0.00 sec)
```

4. Now you should delete the rows that you added to the Employees table. Execute the following SQL statement at the mysql command prompt:

```
DELETE FROM Employees
WHERE EmpLN='Reynolds' OR EmpLN='Waverly';
```

You should receive a message indicating that the statement executed successfully, affecting two rows.

How It Works

In this exercise, you created a SELECT statement that defined a left join on the Employees and Orders tables, as shown in the following statement:

```
SELECT CONCAT_WS(' ', EmpFN, EmpMN, EmpLN) AS Employee, OrderID
FROM Employees LEFT JOIN Orders USING (EmpID)
ORDER BY EmpLN;
```

The join is defined in the FROM clause, which first lists the Employees table, the LEFT JOIN keywords, the Orders table, and the USING clause, which specifies that the join be defined on the EmpID column in both tables. Because the Employees table is listed first — on the left side of the join — all rows are retrieved from the Employees table, whether or not a matching order exists in the Orders table. On the other hand, the Orders table is on the right side of the join, so only rows with an EmpID value that equals the EmpID value in the Employees table are returned. As the result set shows, only two employees — Charlie Patrick Waverly and Rebecca T. Reynolds — are not linked with any orders in the Orders table.

Creating Natural Joins

Another type of join that you can specify in a SELECT statement is the natural join. This type of join can be specified as a full join, left join, or right join. The following syntax shows how to define a natural join in your FROM clause:

```
<table reference> NATURAL [{LEFT | RIGHT} [OUTER]] JOIN <table reference>
```

As you can see in the syntax, you do not define a join condition. A natural join automatically joins the columns in both tables that are common to each other. For example, if you were joining the Books table to the AuthorBook table, the natural join would automatically define that join on the BookID column, which is common to both tables.

To create a natural join, your FROM clause must include a table reference, the NATURAL JOIN keywords, and then a second table reference. If you include only these elements, you're creating a natural full join. If you also specify the LEFT or LEFT OUTER keywords, you're creating a natural left join. If you specify the RIGHT or RIGHT OUTER keywords, you're creating a natural right join.

First take a look at a natural full join to demonstrate how this works. In the following SELECT statement, the FROM clause defines a natural full join on the Books, AuthorBook, and Authors tables:

```
SELECT BookTitle, Copyright,
    CONCAT_WS(' ', AuthFN, AuthMN, AuthLN) AS Author
FROM Books AS b NATURAL JOIN AuthorBook AS ab
    NATURAL JOIN Authors AS a
WHERE Copyright<1980
ORDER BY BookTitle;
```

As you can see, this statement defines no join condition. There are no ON clauses or USING clauses, and the WHERE clause contains only an expression that limits rows to those whose Copyright value is less than 1980. There are no join conditions specified in the WHERE clause. When you execute this statement, you receive results similar to the following:

```
+--------------------------+-----------+---------------------+
| BookTitle                | Copyright | Author              |
+--------------------------+-----------+---------------------+
| Black Elk Speaks         |      1932 | Black Elk           |
| Black Elk Speaks         |      1932 | John G. Neihardt    |
| Hell's Angels            |      1966 | Hunter S. Thompson  |
| Letters to a Young Poet  |      1934 | Rainer Maria Rilke  |
+--------------------------+-----------+---------------------+
4 rows in set (0.00 sec)
```

As you can see, the natural join automatically matches the BookID values in the Books and AuthorBook tables and matches the AuthID values in the Authors and AuthorBook tables. The natural join is similar to full joins in that it returns only matched rows, unlike outer joins that return unmatched values from either the left or right table.

If you want to create an outer join, rather than a full join, you simply add the LEFT or RIGHT keyword, as appropriate. For example, the following SELECT statement is similar to the preceding one, except for the addition of the LEFT keyword to each join definition:

```
SELECT BookTitle, Copyright,
    CONCAT_WS(' ', AuthFN, AuthMN, AuthLN) AS Author
FROM Books AS b NATURAL LEFT JOIN AuthorBook AS ab
    NATURAL LEFT JOIN Authors AS a
WHERE Copyright<1980
ORDER BY BookTitle;
```

As with the preceding statement, the BookID values and AuthID values are automatically matched. In addition, unmatched rows in the left table (the Books table) are also returned, as shown in the following result set:

```
+--------------------------+-----------+---------------------+
| BookTitle                | Copyright | Author              |
+--------------------------+-----------+---------------------+
| Black Elk Speaks         |      1932 | Black Elk           |
| Black Elk Speaks         |      1932 | John G. Neihardt    |
| Hell's Angels            |      1966 | Hunter S. Thompson  |
| Letters to a Young Poet  |      1934 | Rainer Maria Rilke  |
| Winesburg, Ohio          |      1919 |                     |
+--------------------------+-----------+---------------------+
5 rows in set (0.00 sec)
```

As you can see, the book *Winesburg, Ohio* has no matching author in the Authors table, so a blank is displayed. As you recall, a blank is displayed, rather than NULL, because the CONTACT_WS() function concatenates the values in that column.

Joining Tables in an UPDATE Statement

In Chapter 6, you learned how to create an UPDATE statement that joins multiple tables in that statement. Basic joins were demonstrated in that chapter. MySQL allows you to use any join definition in your UPDATE statement. To reflect the ability to use different types of join definitions, the syntax for the UPDATE statement must be modified a bit from what you saw in Chapter 6. The updated syntax now shows how you can use different join definitions:

```
<update statement>::=
UPDATE [LOW_PRIORITY] [IGNORE]
<single table update> | <joined table update>

<joined table update>::=
<join definition>
SET <column name>=<expression> [{, <column name>=<expression>}...]
[WHERE <where definition>]
```

The syntax here shows only those components relevant to a multiple-table update. (For more information about the UPDATE statement, see Chapter 6.) The original syntax didn't use the `<join definition>` placeholder. Instead, you saw only the syntax for a basic join:

```
<table name> [{, <table name>}...]
```

By replacing this with `<join definition>`, you can see how to insert other types of joins in this part of the syntax. To demonstrate how this works, take a look at a couple of examples. First, assume that the following INSERT statements have been used to insert data in the Books table and the AuthorBook table:

```
INSERT INTO Books VALUES (21356, 'Tao: The Watercourse Way', 1975);
INSERT INTO AuthorBook VALUES (1013, 21356);
```

The author for this book (Alan Watts) is already listed in the Authors table, so that author is now linked to a book in the Books table. You can now perform an update based on that link. For example, the following UPDATE statement updates the last name of the author, based on the name of the book:

```
UPDATE Authors AS a, AuthorBook AS ab, Books AS b
SET AuthLN='Wats'
WHERE a.AuthID=ab.AuthID AND ab.BookID=b.BookID
   AND BookTitle='Tao: The Watercourse Way';
```

In this statement, the join is defined in the UPDATE clause. The statement uses a basic join, similar to the type of join used in the examples in Chapter 6. Notice that the join condition is specified in the WHERE clause. The AuthID values are linked, and the BookID values are linked. In addition, the WHERE clause includes an expression that specifies that the BookTitle value must be *Tao: The Watercourse Way*. As a result, all three conditions in the WHERE clause must be met in order for a row to be updated. In other words, for any updated row, the AuthID value in the Authors and AuthorBook tables must be equal, the BookID value in the Books and BookTitle table must be equal, and the BookTitle value must equal *Tao: The Watercourse Way*. When all three conditions are met, the AuthLN value is changed to Wats.

The author's name is being intentionally misspelled here, but it is corrected in the next example UPDATE *statement.*

You can modify the UPDATE statement so that a different join is defined in the UPDATE clause. For example, the following statement defines a CROSS join rather than a basic join:

```
UPDATE Authors CROSS JOIN AuthorBook USING (AuthID)
   CROSS JOIN Books USING (BookID)
SET AuthLN='Watts'
WHERE BookTitle='Tao: The Watercourse Way';
```

As you can see, two cross joins are now defined in the UPDATE clause. In addition, the USING clause specifies that the first join should be created on the AuthID column, and the second USING clause specifies that the second join should be created on the BookID column. This statement produces the same results as the previous UPDATE statement, except that the author's name is now correctly spelled.

MySQL product documentation recommends against performing multiple-table updates against InnoDB *tables joined through foreign key constraints because you cannot always predict how the join optimizer might process tables. If an update is not performed in the correct order, the statement could fail. For* InnoDB *tables, it is generally recommended that you rely on the* ON UPDATE *options provided by* InnoDB *tables to modify the data.*

Joining Tables in a DELETE Statement

As you also saw in Chapter 6, you can define a join condition in a DELETE statement, and you can use any of the join definitions you saw for the SELECT statement. As a result, the syntax for the DELETE statement must be slightly modified to reflect its support for any join definition, as shown in the following syntax:

```
<delete statement>::=
DELETE [LOW_PRIORITY] [QUICK] [IGNORE]
{<single table delete> | <from join delete> | <using join delete>

<from join delete>::=
<table name>[.*] [{, <table name>[.*]}...]
FROM <join definition>
[WHERE <where definition>]

<using join delete>::=
FROM <table name>[.*] [{, <table name>[.*]}...]
USING <join definition>
[WHERE <where definition>]
```

Only the elements specific to joining tables in a DELETE statement are shown here. (For more information about the DELETE statement, see Chapter 6.) Also, in the original syntax, the <join definition> placeholder wasn't used. Instead, you saw the following syntax for the <from join delete> option:

```
FROM <table name> [{, <table name>}...]
```

For the <using join delete> option, the following syntax was used:

```
USING <table name> [{, <table name>}...]
```

In both cases, a basic join is reflected by the syntax. As the `<join definition>` placeholder demonstrates, you can use any join definition in these clauses. The following couple of examples help explain how the join definitions work. The first example uses a basic join to delete data from the AuthorBook and Authors tables:

```
DELETE ab
FROM AuthorBook AS ab, Authors AS a
WHERE ab.AuthID=a.AuthID AND AuthLN='Watts';
```

As you can see, the AuthorBook table is joined to the Authors table (in the FROM clause), and the join condition is defined in the WHERE clause (ab.AuthID=a.AuthID). The WHERE clause also identifies the name of the author, which is used to find the AuthID value for that author. As a result, the only rows deleted from the AuthorBook table are those whose AuthID values are the same in the AuthorBook and Authors tables whose AuthLN value is Watt.

You can also delete rows from multiple tables, as shown in the following example:

```
DELETE ab, b
FROM Authors AS a, AuthorBook AS ab, Books AS b
WHERE a.AuthID=ab.AuthID AND ab.BookID=b.BookID
   AND AuthLN='Watts';
```

In this case, a basic join is created on the Authors, AuthorBook, and Books table, and rows are deleted from the AuthorBook and Books tables. The join conditions are specified in the WHERE clause, along with a third condition that limits the rows deleted to those associated with the author whose last name is Watts. As a result, any rows that reference books written by Alan Watts are deleted from the AuthorBook and Books tables; the author is not deleted from the Authors table.

You can rewrite this statement to use an inner join, rather than a basic join, as shown in the following statement:

```
DELETE ab, b
FROM Authors AS a INNER JOIN AuthorBook AS ab ON a.AuthID=ab.AuthID
   INNER JOIN Books AS b ON ab.BookID=b.BookID
WHERE AuthLN='Watts';
```

Now the join conditions are specified in the ON clause of each inner join definition, but the WHERE clause still includes the expression that specifies that the AuthLN value must be Watts.

> *MySQL product documentation recommends against performing multiple-table deletions against* InnoDB *tables that are joined through foreign key constraints because you cannot always predict how the join optimizer might process tables. If an update is not performed in the correct order, the statement could fail. For* InnoDB *tables, it is generally recommended that you rely on the* ON UPDATE *options provided by* InnoDB *tables to modify the data.*

As you have seen, MySQL provides a number of different ways to join tables. Joins, however, are not the only method you can use to access multiple tables in a single statement. MySQL also supports the use of subqueries in your statements.

Creating Subqueries in Your SQL Statements

Another useful method that you can use to access multiple tables from within your SQL statement is to include a subquery in that statement. A *subquery*, also referred to as a *subselect*, is a SELECT statement that is embedded in another SQL statement. The results returned by the subquery — the inner statement — are then used by the outer statement in the same way a literal value would be used.

You can add subqueries to SELECT, UPDATE, and DELETE statements. In addition, you can embed subqueries in your statement to multiple levels. For example, one subquery can be embedded in another subquery, which is then embedded in still another subquery. In this section, you learn how you can add subqueries to your SELECT, UPDATE and DELETE statements.

> Note that you can include SELECT statements in your INSERT and CREATE TABLE statements, but these SELECT statements are not considered subqueries. For a discussion of how to add SELECT statements to your INSERT and CREATE TABLE statements, see Chapter 11.

Adding Subqueries to Your SELECT Statements

The most common way to include a subquery in a SELECT statement is to add it as an element of the WHERE clause to help restrict which rows the outer SELECT statement returns. When adding a subquery to a WHERE clause, you can use a comparison operator to introduce the subquery or you can use a subquery operator. In addition, you can use subqueries when using a GROUP BY clause in your SELECT statement. In this case, you can add the subquery to the HAVING clause of the statement. The following sections examine the different ways that you can use subqueries.

Working with Comparison Operators

One of the easiest ways to use a subquery in your SELECT statement is to include it as part of an expression in the WHERE clause of your statement. The subquery is included as one of the elements of expression and is introduced by a comparison operator. For example, the following SELECT statement uses a subquery to return an AuthID value:

```
SELECT CONCAT_WS(' ', AuthFN, AuthMN, AuthLN) AS Author
FROM Authors
WHERE AuthID=
    (
        SELECT ab.AuthID
        FROM AuthorBook AS ab, Books AS b
        WHERE ab.BookID=b.BookID AND BookTitle='Noncomformity'
    );
```

As you can see, the WHERE clause of the outer statement includes an expression that specifies that the AuthID value should equal the subquery. The subquery is the portion of the expression enclosed in parentheses. Subqueries must always be enclosed in parentheses. The subquery itself is a typical SELECT statement. Whenever a comparison operator precedes a subquery, the subquery must return a single value. That value is then compared to the first part of the expression.

> Note that the example is based on the same three tables that you saw earlier in the chapter, as they were originally populated. The three tables — Books, AuthorBook, and Authors — are shown in Figure 10-1. You can also refer to the table definitions and INSERT statements that precede the figure to see how these tables are set up.

Now take a look at the subquery itself to better understand how this works. Suppose you were to execute the subquery as an independent SELECT statement, as shown in the following statement:

```
SELECT ab.AuthID
FROM AuthorBook AS ab, Books AS b
WHERE ab.BookID=b.BookID AND BookTitle='Noncomformity';
```

The statement uses a join to retrieve the AuthID value from the AuthorBook table. If you were to execute this statement, you would receive the following results:

```
+--------+
| AuthID |
+--------+
|   1014 |
+--------+
1 row in set (0.00 sec)
```

Notice that the result set includes only one column and one value for that column. If your query were to return more that one value, you would receive an error when you tried to execute the outer SELECT statement. Because only one value is returned, the outer statement can now use that value. As a result, the WHERE clause in the outer statement now has a value to work with. The expression can now be interpreted as AuthID=1014. Once the subquery returns the value, the outer statement can be processed and can return the name of the author with an AuthID value of 1014, as shown in the following results.

```
+---------------+
| Author        |
+---------------+
| Nelson Algren |
+---------------+
1 row in set (0.01 sec)
```

An important point to make about subqueries is that they can often be rewritten as joins. For example, you can retrieve the same results as the preceding statement by using the following SELECT statement:

```
SELECT DISTINCT CONCAT_WS(' ', AuthFN, AuthMN, AuthLN) AS Author
FROM Authors AS a JOIN AuthorBook AS ab ON a.AuthID=ab.AuthID
    JOIN Books AS b ON ab.BookID=b.BookID
WHERE BookTitle='Noncomformity';
```

In this case, rather than using a subquery to retrieve the data, you use a join. In some cases, joins perform better than subqueries, so it's often more efficient to rewrite a subquery as a join when possible. If you're joining numerous tables and a subquery can bypass many of those joins, performance might be better with a subquery. When creating complex statements that retrieve large numbers of rows, it is sometimes best to create both types of statements, then compare the performance of each.

Another advantage of using a join in this case, rather than a subquery, is that the subquery fails if more than one author has written the specified book. For example, suppose you modify your subquery to specify a different book:

```
SELECT CONCAT_WS(' ', AuthFN, AuthMN, AuthLN) AS Author
FROM Authors
WHERE AuthID=
   (
```

```
    SELECT ab.AuthID
    FROM AuthorBook AS ab, Books AS b
    WHERE ab.BookID=b.BookID AND BookTitle='Black Elk Speaks'
);
```

As it turns out, two authors wrote *Black Elk Speaks*, so the statement would return an error similar to the following:

```
ERROR 1242 (21000): Subquery returns more than 1 row
```

Despite some of the limitations of using subqueries, they can often provide an efficient method for retrieving data, so take a look at some more examples of how they're used. In the last example, the equals (=) comparison operator is used in the WHERE clause expression of the outer statement to compare the results of the subquery. You can use other types of comparison operators. For example, the following statement uses a not equal (<>) comparison operator in the WHERE clause to introduce the subquery:

```
SELECT DISTINCT CONCAT_WS(' ', AuthFN, AuthMN, AuthLN) AS Author
FROM Authors
WHERE AuthID<>
    (
        SELECT ab.AuthID
        FROM AuthorBook AS ab, Books AS b
        WHERE ab.BookID=b.BookID AND BookTitle='Noncomformity'
    )
ORDER BY AuthLN;
```

Now rows returned by the outer SELECT statement *cannot* contain an AuthID value that is the same as the AuthID value assigned to author of *Noncomformity*. In other words, AuthID cannot equal 1014. As a result, the outer SELECT statement returns the following result set:

```
+--------------------+
| Author             |
+--------------------+
| Black Elk          |
| John G. Neihardt   |
| Joyce Carol Oates  |
| Annie Proulx       |
| Rainer Maria Rilke |
| Hunter S. Thompson |
| John Kennedy Toole |
| Alan Watts         |
+--------------------+
8 rows in set (0.00 sec)
```

Now look at another way that you can use a subquery. In the following example, the subquery uses an aggregate function to arrive at a value that the outer statement can use:

```
SELECT BookTitle, Copyright
FROM Books
WHERE Copyright<(SELECT MAX(Copyright)-50 FROM Books)
ORDER BY BookTitle;
```

In this statement, the subquery uses the MAX() aggregate function to determine the most recent year in the Copyright column and then subtracts 50 from that year. You can see what this value would be by executing the following subquery SELECT statement separately from the outer statement:

```
SELECT MAX(Copyright)-50 FROM Books;
```

The subquery returns the following result set:

```
+-------------------+
| MAX(Copyright)-50 |
+-------------------+
|              1946 |
+-------------------+
1 row in set (0.03 sec)
```

The subquery takes the highest value in the Copyright column (1996), subtracts 50, and returns a value of 1946. That value is then used in the WHERE clause expression of the outer statement. The expression can be interpreted as Copyright<1946. As a result, only rows with a copyright value that is less than 1946 are included in the result set, as shown in the following results:

```
+-------------------------+-----------+
| BookTitle               | Copyright |
+-------------------------+-----------+
| Black Elk Speaks        |      1932 |
| Letters to a Young Poet |      1934 |
| Winesburg, Ohio         |      1919 |
+-------------------------+-----------+
3 rows in set (0.00 sec)
```

An interesting aspect of the subquery used in the previous statement is that it retrieves a value from the same table as the outer statement. A subquery can provide a handy way to calculate a value that the outer statement can then use to specify which rows are returned.

Working with Subquery Operators

In the examples that you have looked at so far, each subquery had to return a single value in order to be used by the outer statement. MySQL provides a set of operators that allows you to work with subqueries that return multiple values. When using these operators, the subquery must still return a single column of values, but that column can contain more than one value.

The ANY and SOME Operators

The ANY and SOME operators, which are synonymous, allow you to create an expression that compares a column to any of the values returned by a subquery. For the expression to evaluate to true, any value returned by the subquery can be used. For example, the following statement returns book information about any books that have a copyright date greater than any books written by Proulx:

```
SELECT BookTitle, Copyright
FROM Books
WHERE Copyright > ANY
    (
        SELECT b.copyright
```

```
        FROM Books AS b JOIN AuthorBook AS ab USING (BookID)
            JOIN Authors AS a USING (AuthID)
        WHERE AuthLN='Proulx'
    )
ORDER BY BookTitle;
```

In this case, the subquery returns a list of Copyright values (1992 and 1993) for the books written by the author Proulx. Those values are used in the WHERE clause expression, which can be interpreted as Copyright > ANY (1992, 1993). Because the statement uses the ANY operator, a value in the Copyright column must be greater than either 1992 or 1993, so the expression can now be interpreted as Copyright>1992 OR Copyright>1993. As a result, the outer query returns two rows, as shown in the following result set:

```
+--------------------+-----------+
| BookTitle          | Copyright |
+--------------------+-----------+
| Noncomformity      |      1996 |
| The Shipping News  |      1993 |
+--------------------+-----------+
2 rows in set (0.00 sec)
```

As you might have realized, the second row returned, *The Shipping News,* is written by Annie Proulx. Because the book has a copyright value of 1993, which is greater than 1992, it is included in the result set, even though it is one of the values returned by the subquery.

The ALL Operator

The ALL operator is different from the ANY and SOME operators because it requires that all values returned by the subquery must cause the expression to evaluate to true before the outer statement can return a row. For example, modify the previous example to use the ALL operator rather than the ANY operator:

```
SELECT BookTitle, Copyright
FROM Books
WHERE Copyright > ALL
    (
        SELECT b.copyright
        FROM Books AS b JOIN AuthorBook AS ab USING (BookID)
            JOIN Authors AS a USING (AuthID)
        WHERE AuthLN='Proulx'
    )
ORDER BY BookTitle;
```

The subquery still returns the same values (1992 and 1993); however, the values in the Copyright column must now be greater than all the values returned by the subquery. In other words, the Copyright value must be greater than 1992 and greater than 1993. As a result, you can interpret the WHERE clause expression as Copyright> 1992 AND Copyright>1993. Now the result set includes only one row, as shown in the following:

```
+----------------+-----------+
| BookTitle      | Copyright |
+----------------+-----------+
| Noncomformity  |      1996 |
+----------------+-----------+
1 row in set (0.00 sec)
```

The IN and NOT IN Operators

The IN and NOT IN operators provide the most flexibility when comparing values to the results returned by a subquery. To demonstrate how this works, replace the ALL operator and the comparison operator with the IN operator, as shown in the following statement:

```
SELECT BookTitle, Copyright
FROM Books
WHERE Copyright IN
    (
        SELECT b.copyright
        FROM Books AS b JOIN AuthorBook AS ab USING (BookID)
            JOIN Authors AS a USING (AuthID)
        WHERE AuthLN='Proulx'
    )
ORDER BY BookTitle;
```

Now the copyright value must equal either 1992 or 1993 because these are the two values returned by the subquery. As a result, the outer statement returns the following rows:

```
+-------------------+-----------+
| BookTitle         | Copyright |
+-------------------+-----------+
| Postcards         |      1992 |
| The Shipping News |      1993 |
+-------------------+-----------+
2 rows in set (0.00 sec)
```

You would return the same results if you were to use the equals comparison operator along with the ANY operator, as in Copyright = ANY, but the IN operator provides a simpler construction.

Now revise the SELECT statement to use the NOT IN operator:

```
SELECT BookTitle, Copyright
FROM Books
WHERE Copyright NOT IN
    (
        SELECT b.copyright
        FROM Books AS b JOIN AuthorBook AS ab USING (BookID)
            JOIN Authors AS a USING (AuthID)
        WHERE AuthLN='Proulx'
    )
ORDER BY BookTitle;
```

The results are now the opposite of those generated by the previous statement. The outer statement returns only those rows whose Copyright value is not equal to 1992 or 1993, as shown in the following result set:

```
+-------------------------+-----------+
| BookTitle               | Copyright |
+-------------------------+-----------+
| A Confederacy of Dunces |      1980 |
| Black Elk Speaks        |      1932 |
| Hell's Angels           |      1966 |
```

```
| Letters to a Young Poet |      1934 |
| Noncomformity           |      1996 |
| Winesburg, Ohio         |      1919 |
+-------------------------+-----------+
6 rows in set (0.00 sec)
```

Although the IN and NOT IN operators are very useful for comparing values returned by a subquery, you might find that you simply need to determine whether a subquery returns a value. The actual value is not important. To allow you to test for the existence of a value, MySQL provides the EXISTS and NOT EXISTS operators.

The EXISTS and NOT EXISTS Operators

The EXISTS and NOT EXISTS operators are very different from the previous subquery operators that you have seen. The EXISTS and NOT EXISTS operators are used only to test whether a subquery does or does not produce any results. If you use the EXISTS operator, and the subquery returns results, then the condition evaluates to true; otherwise, it is evaluates to false. If you use the NOT EXISTS operator, and the subquery returns results, the condition evaluates to false; otherwise, it evaluates to true.

The EXISTS and NOT EXISTS operators are useful primarily when trying to correlate conditions in the subquery with the outer statement. This is best explained through an example. Suppose that you want to retrieve information from the Books table about only those books associated with authors listed in the Authors table. Because the AuthorBook table already tells you whether a book is associated with an author, you can use that table to help you determine which book titles to return, as shown in the following SELECT statement:

```
SELECT BookID, BookTitle
FROM Books AS b
WHERE EXISTS
    (
        SELECT BookID
        FROM AuthorBook AS ab
        WHERE b.BookID=ab.BookID
    )
ORDER BY BookTitle;
```

The first thing to look at is the WHERE clause of the subquery. This is an unusual construction because it shows a join condition even though the subquery doesn't define a join. This is how the subquery is correlated with the outer table. The BookID value of the AuthorBook table, which is specified in the subquery, must equal the BookID value in the Books table, which is specified in the outer statement. As a result, the subquery returns a row only if that row contains a BookID value that correlates to a BookID value of the outer table. If a row is returned, the condition specified in the WHERE clause evaluates to true. If a row is not returned, the condition evaluates to false. As a result, the outer statement returns only those rows whose BookID values exist in the AuthorBook table, as shown in the following result set:

```
+--------+-------------------------+
| BookID | BookTitle               |
+--------+-------------------------+
|  17695 | A Confederacy of Dunces |
|  15729 | Black Elk Speaks        |
|  14356 | Hell's Angels           |
|  12786 | Letters to a Young Poet |
```

```
|   16284 | Noncomformity            |
|   19264 | Postcards                |
|   19354 | The Shipping News        |
+---------+--------------------------+
7 rows in set (0.00 sec)
```

For each book returned, a BookID exists in the AuthorBook table. If a book is listed in the Books table and the BookID value for that book is not included in the AuthorBook table, the book is not displayed.

You can use the NOT EXISTS operator in the same way as the EXISTS operator, only the opposite results are returned. The following SELECT statement is identical to the preceding one except that the WHERE clause of the outer statement now includes the NOT keyword:

```
SELECT BookID, BookTitle
FROM Books AS b
WHERE NOT EXISTS
    (
        SELECT BookID
        FROM AuthorBook AS ab
        WHERE b.BookID=ab.BookID
    )
ORDER BY BookTitle;
```

As you would expect, the results returned by this statement include any books whose BookID value is not listed in the AuthorBook table. In other words, any book not associated with an author is returned, as shown in the following result set:

```
+---------+-----------------+
| BookID  | BookTitle       |
+---------+-----------------+
|   13331 | Winesburg, Ohio |
+---------+-----------------+
1 row in set (0.00 sec)
```

Working with Grouped Data

The subqueries that you have seen so far have been used in the WHERE clauses of various SELECT statements. You can also use subqueries in a HAVING clause when you group data together. For the most part, adding subqueries to your HAVING clause is similar to using them in the WHERE clause, except that you're working with grouped data. To demonstrate how this works, take a look at a couple of examples. The examples use the same three tables (Books, AuthorBook, and Authors) that have been used in the previous examples. Yu also need an additional table, which is shown in the following table definition:

```
CREATE TABLE BookOrders
(
    OrderID SMALLINT NOT NULL,
    BookID SMALLINT NOT NULL,
    Quantity SMALLINT NOT NULL,
    PRIMARY KEY (OrderID, BookID),
    FOREIGN KEY (BookID) REFERENCES Books (BookID)
)
ENGINE=INNODB;
```

For these exercises, you can assume that the following INSERT statement populated the table:

```
INSERT INTO BookOrders
VALUES (101, 13331, 1), (101, 12786, 1), (101, 16284, 2), (102, 19354, 1),
(102, 15729, 3), (103, 12786, 2), (103, 19264, 1), (103, 13331, 1),
(103, 14356, 2), (104, 19354, 1), (105, 15729, 1), (105, 14356, 2),
(106, 16284, 2), (106, 13331, 1), (107, 12786, 3), (108, 19354, 1),
(108, 16284, 4), (109, 15729, 1), (110, 13331, 2), (110, 12786, 2),
(110, 14356, 2), (111, 14356, 2);
```

Figure 10-3 shows you how the four tables are related.

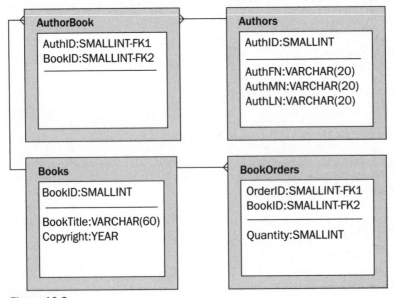

Figure 10-3

Now take a look at an example. Suppose that you want to retrieve the total number of books sold for each order listed in the BookOrders table. To do so, you would group together the data based on the OrderID column and then use the SUM() function to retrieve the number of books for each group. Now suppose that you want the result set to include only those groups whose total number of books sold is greater than the average number of books sold for each title in each order. You can use a subquery to find that average, then use the average in the HAVING clause of the outer statement, as shown in the following statement:

```
SELECT OrderID, SUM(Quantity) AS Total
FROM BookOrders
GROUP BY OrderID
HAVING Total>(SELECT AVG(Quantity) FROM BookOrders);
```

As you can see, the statement includes a GROUP BY clause that specifies which column should be grouped together and a HAVING clause that specifies which rows of grouped data to return. Notice that the expression in the having clause is made up of the Total column (defined in the SELECT clause), the greater than (>) comparison operator, and a subquery. The subquery returns that average value of the Quantity column of the BookOrders table, which is a value of 1.7273. In other words, the average number of books sold for each title in an order is 1.7273.

The outer statement then uses this value in the HAVING clause. As a result, the HAVING expression can be interpreted as Total>1.7273. This means that every order that has sold more that 1.7273 books is included in the result set, as shown in the following:

```
+---------+-------+
| OrderID | Total |
+---------+-------+
|     101 |     4 |
|     102 |     4 |
|     103 |     6 |
|     105 |     3 |
|     106 |     3 |
|     107 |     3 |
|     108 |     5 |
|     110 |     6 |
|     111 |     2 |
+---------+-------+
9 rows in set (0.00 sec)
```

As you can see, no orders are listed that contain fewer than two books. Now suppose that you want to determine how many books have been ordered for authors who have more than one book listed in the Books table. Because you don't need to know the name of the author, you can go directly to the AuthorBook table to determine which authors are associated with more than one book. From there, you can determine the BookID value for those books, then use that value to determine which books in the BookOrders table to include in the result set. The following SELECT statement shows you how this can be accomplished:

```
SELECT BookID, SUM(Quantity) AS Total
FROM BookOrders
GROUP BY BookID
HAVING BookID IN
    (SELECT BookID FROM AuthorBook WHERE AuthID IN
        (
            SELECT AuthID FROM AuthorBook
            GROUP BY AuthID
            HAVING COUNT(*)>1
        )
    )
);
```

The first thing that you might notice is that a subquery is embedded in another subquery. So take a look at the most deeply embedded subquery first:

```
SELECT AuthID FROM AuthorBook
GROUP BY AuthID
HAVING COUNT(*)>1;
```

If you were to execute this statement separately from the other parts of the statement, you would receive the following results:

```
+--------+
| AuthID |
+--------+
|   1012 |
+--------+
1 row in set (0.00 sec)
```

The subquery is requesting the AuthID value for any group of AuthID values that have a value greater than 1. In this case, only author 1012 is associated with more than one BookID value in the AuthorBook table. Now that you have retrieved the AuthID value that you need, you can use it in the second subquery, as shown in the following:

```
SELECT BookID FROM AuthorBook WHERE AuthID IN
    (
        SELECT AuthID FROM AuthorBook
        GROUP BY AuthID
        HAVING COUNT(*)>1
    );
```

Notice that the WHERE clause in the outer subquery includes an expression specifying that the AuthID value must be one of the values returned by the inner subquery. In this case, only one value (1012) is returned, so any rows returned by the outer subquery must have an AuthID value of 1012. If you were to execute the outer and inner subqueries together, you would receive the following results:

```
+--------+
| BookID |
+--------+
|  19264 |
|  19354 |
+--------+
2 rows in set (0.00 sec)
```

Notice that two BookID values are returned. The values represent the two books that were written by the author with the AuthID value of 1012. The outer SELECT statement can then use these values in the HAVING clause expression to determine which rows are returned. Because of the HAVING clause, only groups that have a BookID value of 19264 or 19354 are returned, along with the total number of books sold, as shown in the following result set:

```
+--------+-------+
| BookID | Total |
+--------+-------+
|  19264 |     1 |
|  19354 |     3 |
+--------+-------+
2 rows in set (0.01 sec)
```

Had more than one author written more than one book, those rows would appear here as well. By using subqueries in the HAVING clause, you can be very specific about exactly which groups to include in the result set.

In the following Try It Out exercise, you create several SELECT statements that include subqueries that retrieve data that the outer SELECT statements can then use.

Including Subqueries in Your SELECT Statements

The following steps explain how to include subqueries in SELECT statements:

1. Open the mysql client utility, type the following command, and press Enter:

```
use DVDRentals
```

You should receive a message indicating that you switched to the DVDRentals database.

2. The first SELCT statement that you create retrieves data from the DVDs table. The SELECT statement uses a subquery to return a value from the Status value, which the outer statement then uses. Execute the following SQL statement at the mysql command prompt:

```
SELECT DVDName
FROM DVDs
WHERE StatID<>
    (SELECT StatID FROM Status WHERE StatDescrip='Available')
ORDER BY DVDName;
```

You should receive results similar to the following:

```
+--------------------+
| DVDName            |
+--------------------+
| A Room with a View |
| Out of Africa      |
| White Christmas    |
+--------------------+
3 rows in set (0.00 sec)
```

3. The next SELECT statement that you create retrieves data from the DVDs and MovieTypes tables. The statement also contains a subquery in the WHERE clause of the outer statement that retrieves a value from the Status table, which the outer statement then uses. Execute the following SQL statement at the mysql command prompt:

```
SELECT DVDName, MTypeDescrip As MovieType
FROM DVDs AS d, MovieTypes AS mt
WHERE d.MTypeID=mt.MTypeID AND StatID=
    (SELECT StatID FROM Status WHERE StatDescrip='Available')
ORDER BY DVDName;
```

You should receive results similar to the following:

```
+-----------------------------+-----------+
| DVDName                     | MovieType |
+-----------------------------+-----------+
| Amadeus                     | Drama     |
| Mash                        | Comedy    |
| The Maltese Falcon          | Drama     |
| The Rocky Horror Picture Show | Comedy  |
| What's Up, Doc?             | Comedy    |
+-----------------------------+-----------+
5 rows in set (0.00 sec)
```

4. The next SELECT statement that you create is similar to the last, except that the WHERE clause of the outer statement uses the IN operator to compare values to those returned by the subquery. Execute the following SQL statement at the mysql command prompt:

```
SELECT DVDName, MTypeDescrip As MovieType
FROM DVDs AS d, MovieTypes AS mt
WHERE d.MTypeID=mt.MTypeID AND StatID IN
    (SELECT StatID FROM Status WHERE StatDescrip<>'Available')
ORDER BY DVDName;
```

You should receive results similar to the following:

```
+---------------------+-----------+
| DVDName             | MovieType |
+---------------------+-----------+
| A Room with a View  | Drama     |
| Out of Africa       | Drama     |
| White Christmas     | Musical   |
+---------------------+-----------+
3 rows in set (0.01 sec)
```

5. The last SELECT statement that you create uses a GROUP BY clause to group data together. In addition, the statement includes a HAVING clause that contains a subquery that returns data from the MovieTypes table. Execute the following SQL statement at the mysql command prompt:

```
SELECT MTypeID, RatingID, COUNT(*) AS TotalDVDs
FROM DVDs
GROUP BY MTypeID, RatingID
HAVING MTypeID IN
    (SELECT MTypeID FROM MovieTypes WHERE MTypeDescrip<>'Documentary');
```

You should receive results similar to the following:

```
+---------+----------+-----------+
| MTypeID | RatingID | TotalDVDs |
+---------+----------+-----------+
| mt11    | NR       |         2 |
| mt11    | PG       |         2 |
| mt12    | G        |         1 |
| mt12    | NR       |         1 |
| mt12    | R        |         1 |
| mt16    | NR       |         1 |
+---------+----------+-----------+
6 rows in set (0.00 sec)
```

How It Works

The first SELECT statement that you created in this exercise includes a subquery in the WHERE clause:

```
SELECT DVDName
FROM DVDs
WHERE StatID<>
    (SELECT StatID FROM Status WHERE StatDescrip='Available')
ORDER BY DVDName;
```

The WHERE clause in the outer SELECT statement includes an expression that is made up of the StatID column, the not equal (<>) comparison operator, and the following subquery:

```
SELECT StatID FROM Status WHERE StatDescrip='Available';
```

If you were to execute the subquery independently of the rest of the statement, you would receive the following results:

```
+--------+
| StatID |
+--------+
| s2     |
+--------+
1 row in set (0.00 sec)
```

The outer SELECT statement uses those results to complete the expression in the WHERE clause. As a result, only rows that have a StatID value of s2 are included in the result set.

The next SELECT statement that you created is similar to the last one except that it now includes a join definition in the outer statement:

```
SELECT DVDName, MTypeDescrip As MovieType
FROM DVDs AS d, MovieTypes AS mt
WHERE d.MTypeID=mt.MTypeID AND StatID=
    (SELECT StatID FROM Status WHERE StatDescrip='Available')
ORDER BY DVDName;
```

The FROM clause in the outer statement joins together the DVDs table and the MovieTypes table. In addition, MTypeDescrip values are now included in the result set. Like the previous SELECT statement, only rows with a StatID value of s2 are included in the result set because that is the value returned by the subquery.

The next SELECT statement that you created is a little different from the last one in that it uses an IN operator in the outer WHERE clause to introduce the subquery:

```
SELECT DVDName, MTypeDescrip As MovieType
FROM DVDs AS d, MovieTypes AS mt
WHERE d.MTypeID=mt.MTypeID AND StatID IN
    (SELECT StatID FROM Status WHERE StatDescrip<>'Available')
ORDER BY DVDName;
```

The IN operator is used because the subquery has been modified and now returns multiple values. The subquery returns the StatID value of all rows in the Status table whose StatDescrip value does not equal Available, as shown in the following result set:

```
+--------+
| StatID |
+--------+
| s1     |
| s3     |
| s4     |
+--------+
3 rows in set (0.00 sec)
```

These values are then compared to the StatID value in the DVDs table. Any rows that have a StatID value that matches the values returned by the subquery are included in the result set.

The next SELECT statement that you created groups together data in the DVDs table according to the MTypeID and RatingID columns:

```
SELECT MTypeID, RatingID, COUNT(*) AS TotalDVDs
FROM DVDs
GROUP BY MTypeID, RatingID
HAVING MTypeID IN
    (SELECT MTypeID FROM MovieTypes WHERE MTypeDescrip<>'Documentary');
```

The statement includes a HAVING clause that contains a subquery. The subquery returns the MTypeID value for all rows in the MovieTypes table that do not have a MTypeDescrip value of Documentary, as shown in the following query results:

```
+---------+
| MTypeID |
+---------+
| mt10    |
| mt11    |
| mt12    |
| mt13    |
| mt14    |
| mt16    |
+---------+
6 rows in set (0.00 sec)
```

The HAVING clause then uses the subquery results to limit the groups returned in the result set to those that have an MTypeID value for any movie type except Documentary. Because you used the IN operator in the HAVING clause, the result set includes any MTypeID value that equals one of the values returned by the subquery.

Adding Subqueries to Your UPDATE Statements

Up to this point, you have used subqueries in SELECT statements. You can also include subqueries in your UPDATE statements. You can use subqueries in the SET clause to help define the new values to be inserted in a table, or you can use them in the WHERE clause to help define which rows should be updated. Take a look at an example to illustrate how to use a subquery in an UPDATE statement. For this example, assume that the following INSERT statements have been used to add data to the Books and AuthorBook table:

```
INSERT INTO Books VALUES (21356, 'Tao: The Watercourse Way', 1975);
INSERT INTO AuthorBook VALUES (1013, 21356);
```

Now take a look at an UPDATE statement that contains a subquery in its WHERE clause:

```
UPDATE Books
SET BookTitle='The Way of Zen', Copyright=1957
WHERE BookID=
    (
```

```
        SELECT ab.BookID
        FROM Authors AS a, AuthorBook AS ab
        WHERE a.AuthID=ab.AuthID AND a.AuthLN='Watts'
);
```

The statement updates a row in the Books table. The subquery determines which row should be updated. In this case, the subquery returns a BookID value based on an author with a last name of Watts. The subquery defines a join condition that joins the Authors and AuthorBook tables and then retrieves the BookID value for the book written by Watts. The WHERE expression then uses that value in the outer statement to limit the updated rows. Only the row that has a BookID value that matches the value returned by the subquery is updated. As a result, the row in the Books table with a BookID value of 21356 and a BookTitle value of *Tao: The Watercourse Way* has been changed so that the BookTitle value is now *The Way of Zen*.

Also, you should keep in mind that the subquery must return only one value when it is used in a comparison as it is used here. If you had specified Proulx as the author (in the WHERE clause of the subquery), two BookID values would have been returned, which would have made the outer UPDATE statement fail.

Adding Subqueries to Your DELETE Statements

You can also add subqueries to the WHERE clause of a DELETE statement, just as you can with UPDATE and SELECT statements. The subquery helps to determine which rows should be deleted from a table. For example, the subquery in the following DELETE statement returns the AuthID value for the author with last name of Watts:

```
DELETE ab, b
FROM AuthorBook AS ab, Books AS b
WHERE ab.BookID=b.BookID
    AND ab.AuthID=(SELECT AuthID FROM Authors WHERE AuthLN='Watts');
```

One of the expressions in the WHERE clause of the outer statement uses the value returned by the subquery to specify which rows are deleted. Because the DELETE statement joins together the AuthorBook table and the Books table, only those rows whose BookID values are equal and whose AuthID value equals the value returned by the subquery are deleted from the tables. In other words, those rows in the AuthorBook table and the Books table that contains a BookID value associated with Alan Watts are deleted.

As this section illustrates, you can use subqueries in UPDATE and DELETE statements to determine which values should be modified in a table. In the next Try It Out exercise, you create both an UPDATE statement and a DELETE statement that use subqueries.

Try It Out **Including Subqueries in Your UPDATE and DELETE Statements**

To complete this exercise, follow these steps:

1. Open the mysql client utility, type the following command, and press Enter:

```
use DVDRentals
```

You should receive a message indicating that you switched to the DVDRentals database.

2. In order to demonstrate how to use subqueries in your UPDATE and DELETE statements, you should first add a row to the Employees table. Execute the following SQL statement at the mysql command prompt:

```
INSERT INTO Employees
VALUES (NULL, 'Rebecca', 'T.', 'Reynolds');
```

You should receive a message indicating that the statement executed successfully, affecting one row.

3. When you inserted the row in the Employees table, a value was automatically inserted in the primary key column. Now use the LAST_INSERT_ID() function to retrieve the primary key value. Execute the following SQL statement at the mysql command prompt:

```
SELECT LAST_INSERT_ID();
```

You should receive results similar to the following:

```
+-----------------+
| last_insert_id() |
+-----------------+
|               7 |
+-----------------+
1 row in set (0.01 sec)
```

Note that you will not necessarily receive a value of 7. Depending on whether you inserted any other rows in the table (whether or not they still exist) or whether you re-created the database or the table, the value might be anywhere from 7 on up. Whatever the actual value is, you should remember that value for use in later statements. For the purposes of this exercise, the value 7 is assumed.

4. Now you need to insert a row in the Orders table. Execute the following SQL statement at the mysql command prompt:

```
INSERT INTO Orders (CustID, EmpID) VALUES (6, 5);
```

You should receive a message indicating that the statement executed successfully, affecting one row.

5. Again, you need to retrieve the last value inserted in the primary key column. Execute the following SQL statement at the mysql command prompt:

```
SELECT LAST_INSERT_ID();
```

You should receive results similar to the following:

```
+-----------------+
| last_insert_id() |
+-----------------+
|              14 |
+-----------------+
1 row in set (0.01 sec)
```

Once again, the value returned might vary, depending on previous modifications to the table. The value that you receive will be anything from 14 on up. For the purposes of this exercise, the value 14 is assumed.

6. Now you create an UPDATE statement that updates the Orders table. The statement uses a subquery in the SET clause to retrieve the EmpID value from the Employees table. Execute the following SQL statement at the mysql command prompt:

```
UPDATE Orders
SET EmpID=(SELECT EmpID FROM Employees WHERE EmpLN='Reynolds')
WHERE OrderID=14;
```

You should receive a message indicating that the statement executed successfully, affecting one row.

7. Execute the following SQL statement at the mysql command prompt:

```
DELETE FROM Orders
WHERE EmpID=(SELECT EmpID FROM Employees WHERE EmpLN='Reynolds');
```

You should receive a message indicating that the statement executed successfully, affecting one row.

8. Finally, delete the row that you added to the Employees table. Execute the following SQL statement at the mysql command prompt:

```
DELETE FROM Employees
WHERE EmpLN='Reynolds';
```

You should receive a message indicating that the statement executed successfully, affecting one row.

How It Works

In this exercise, you created an UPDATE statement that updated a row in the Orders table:

```
UPDATE Orders
SET EmpID=(SELECT EmpID FROM Employees WHERE EmpLN='Reynolds')
WHERE OrderID=14;
```

The row updated had an OrderID value of 14. For this row, the EmpID value was changed to the value returned by the subquery. The subquery returns the EmpID value associated with the employee whose last name is Reynolds. Because the value returned is 7, the EmpID value in the Orders table is set to 7.

Next, you created a DELETE statement that deleted the row that you just updated:

```
DELETE FROM Orders
WHERE EmpID=(SELECT EmpID FROM Employees WHERE EmpLN='Reynolds');
```

The DELETE statement includes a subquery in the WHERE clause that retrieves the employee ID for Reynolds. Because the subquery returns a value of 7, any rows in the Orders table with an EmpID value of 7 are deleted from the table.

Creating Unions That Join SELECT Statements

Times might arise when you want to combine the results of multiple SELECT statements in one result set. An easy way to do this is to use the UNION operator to connect the statements, as shown in the following syntax:

```
<select statement> UNION <select statement>
```

To join two statements in this way, the statements must return the same number of values, and the data types for the returned values must correspond to each other. For example, suppose that you are joining two SELECT statements. The first statement returns two columns: ColA and ColB. ColA is configured with an INT data type, and ColB is configured with a CHAR data type. As a result, the second query must also return two columns, and those columns must be configured with an INT data type and CHAR data type, respectively.

Now take a look at an example to demonstrate how this works. Suppose that a second table is added to the set of example tables that have been used in this chapter. The table is named Authors2 and is defined by the following CREATE TABLE statement:

```
CREATE TABLE Authors2
(
    AuthID SMALLINT NOT NULL PRIMARY KEY,
    AuthFN VARCHAR(20),
    AuthMN VARCHAR(20),
    AuthLN VARCHAR(20)
);
```

Now assume that the following INSERT statement populated the Authors2 table:

```
INSERT INTO Authors2
VALUES (1006, 'Mark', NULL, 'Twain'),
(2205, 'E.', 'M.', 'Forster'),
(2206, 'Gabriel', 'Garcia', 'Marquez'),
(2207, 'Raymond', NULL, 'Carver'),
(2208, 'Mary', NULL, 'Shelley'),
(2209, 'Albert', NULL, 'Camus');
```

Once you have similar tables from which to retrieve data, you can use the UNION operator to join SELECT statements, as shown in the following statement:

```
SELECT AuthFN, AuthMN, AuthLN FROM Authors
UNION
SELECT AuthFN, AuthMN, AuthLN FROM Authors2;
```

As you can see, using a UNION operator is very simple, as long as the number of columns and their data types match. When you execute the statement, the following results are returned:

```
+---------+---------+----------+
| AuthFN  | AuthMN  | AuthLN   |
+---------+---------+----------+
| Hunter  | S.      | Thompson |
| Joyce   | Carol   | Oates    |
| Black   | NULL    | Elk      |
| Rainer  | Maria   | Rilke    |
| John    | Kennedy | Toole    |
| John    | G.      | Neihardt |
| Annie   | NULL    | Proulx   |
| Alan    | NULL    | Watts    |
| Nelson  | NULL    | Algren   |
| Mark    | NULL    | Twain    |
| E.      | M.      | Forster  |
| Gabriel | Garcia  | Marquez  |
| Raymond | NULL    | Carver   |
| Mary    | NULL    | Shelley  |
| Albert  | NULL    | Camus    |
+---------+---------+----------+
15 rows in set (0.00 sec)
```

As you can see, the data from Authors and Authors 2 have been added together in one result set. You might want to sort the result set in a specific order. To do this, you can use the ORDER BY clause, as shown in the following example:

```
(SELECT AuthFN, AuthMN, AuthLN FROM Authors)
UNION
(SELECT AuthFN, AuthMN, AuthLN FROM Authors2)
ORDER BY AuthLN;
```

To use the ORDER BY clause, you must enclose each SELECT statement in a set of parentheses and then add the ORDER BY clause at the end of the statement. Now when you execute the statement, you should receive results similar to the following:

```
+---------+---------+----------+
| AuthFN  | AuthMN  | AuthLN   |
+---------+---------+----------+
| Nelson  | NULL    | Algren   |
| Albert  | NULL    | Camus    |
| Raymond | NULL    | Carver   |
| Black   | NULL    | Elk      |
| E.      | M.      | Forster  |
| Gabriel | Garcia  | Marquez  |
| John    | G.      | Neihardt |
| Joyce   | Carol   | Oates    |
| Annie   | NULL    | Proulx   |
| Rainer  | Maria   | Rilke    |
| Mary    | NULL    | Shelley  |
| Hunter  | S.      | Thompson |
| John    | Kennedy | Toole    |
| Mark    | NULL    | Twain    |
| Alan    | NULL    | Watts    |
+---------+---------+----------+
15 rows in set (0.00 sec)
```

In this section, you learned how to create a union to join two SELECT statements together to produce one set of query results. In the Try It Out exercise that follows, you create your own union statement.

Try It Out   **Using Unions to Join SELECT Statements**

The following steps explain how to use a union to join two SELECT statements:

1. Open the mysql client utility, type the following command, and press Enter:

```
use DVDRentals
```

You should receive a message indicating that you switched to the DVDRentals database.

2. Before you can create a union, you must add one more table to the DVDRentals database that is similar to the original Employees table. Execute the following SQL statement at the mysql command prompt:

```
CREATE TABLE Employees2
   (
   EmpID SMALLINT NOT NULL AUTO_INCREMENT PRIMARY KEY,
   EmpFN VARCHAR(20) NOT NULL,
   EmpLN VARCHAR(20) NOT NULL
   )
ENGINE=INNODB;
```

You should receive a message indicating that the statement executed successfully.

3. Now add two rows to the new table. Execute the following SQL statement at the mysql command prompt:

```
INSERT INTO Employees2
VALUES (NULL, 'Rebecca', 'Reynolds'),
(NULL, 'Charlie', 'Waverly');
```

You should receive a message indicating that the statement executed successfully, affecting two rows.

4. You can now use a union to join the Employees and Employees2 tables. Execute the following SQL statement at the mysql command prompt:

```
(SELECT EmpLN, EmpFN FROM Employees)
UNION
(SELECT EmpLN, EmpFN FROM Employees2)
ORDER BY EmpLN;
```

You should receive results similar to the following:

```
+----------+---------+
| EmpLN    | EmpFN   |
+----------+---------+
| Brooks   | George  |
| Carter   | Rita    |
| Laguci   | John    |
| Michaels | Mary    |
| Reynolds | Rebecca |
```

```
| Schroader  | Robert  |
| Smith      | John    |
| Waverly    | Charlie |
+------------+---------+
8 rows in set (0.00 sec)
```

5. Finally, remove the Employees2 table from the DVDRentals database. Execute the following SQL statement at the mysql command prompt:

```
DROP TABLE Employees2;
```

You should receive a message indicating that the statement executed successfully.

How It Works

In this exercise, you used a UNION operator to join together two SELECT statements:

```
(SELECT EmpLN, EmpFN FROM Employees)
UNION
(SELECT EmpLN, EmpFN FROM Employees2)
ORDER BY EmpLN;
```

The first SELECT statement retrieves the EmpLN and EmpFN values from the Employees table. The second SELECT statement retrieves the EmpLN and EmpFN values from the Employees2 table. You might have noticed that the Employees2 table contains a different number of columns than the Employees table. This does not affect the union query as long as each SELECT statement retrieves the same number of columns and those columns are configured with the same data type.

The statement also uses an ORDER BY clause to sort the query results according to the EmpLN values. As a result, each SELECT statement is enclosed in its own set of parentheses.

Summary

As you learned in this chapter, you can create SQL statements that allow you to access multiple tables in a single statement. This is useful when you need to access related data stored in different tables. For example, you can use a SELECT statement to join together multiple tables and then extract the data you need from any of those tables. The data you retrieve depends on how that data is related and on how you define the join in the SELECT statement. MySQL provides several methods for accessing multiple tables in your SQL statements. These include joins, subqueries, and unions. In this chapter, you learned how to use all three methods to access data in multiple tables. Specifically, you learned how to do the following:

❑ Create basic, inner, and straight joins that retrieve matched data from two or more tables

❑ Create left and right joins that retrieve matched data from two or more tables, plus additional data from one of the joined tables

❑ Create natural, full, and outer joins that automatically match data from one or more tables without having to specify a join condition

❑ Add subqueries to your SELECT, UPDATE, and DELETE statements

❑   Use subqueries in SELECT statements that group and summarize data

❑   Use the UNION operator to join SELECT statements together in order to return one result set

As the chapter demonstrated, joins, subqueries, and unions provide powerful tools for accessing related data in multiple tables. As you build applications that retrieve data from a MySQL database, you will use these methods often to access data. This is especially true of SELECT statements that define joins in those statements. In fact, for many applications, this is the most commonly used type of SQL statement. As a result, it is well worth your time to experiment with the SELECT statements that include different types of joins. The more you use these statements, the greater your understanding of their flexibility and precision. Once you're comfortable with joining tables, adding subqueries to your statements, and creating unions, you're ready to move beyond accessing data in multiple tables and creating statements that access multiple tables in managing data that extends beyond those tables. In Chapter 11, you learn how to export, copy, and import data.

Exercises

For these exercises, you create several SELECT statements that use joins, subqueries, and unions. You use the same tables that have been used for the examples throughout the chapter. These include the Books, AuthorBook, Authors, BookOrders, and Authors2 tables (shown in Figure 10-4). Refer back to the table definitions and their related INSERT statements as necessary if you have any questions about the tables. You can find the answers to these exercises in Appendix A.

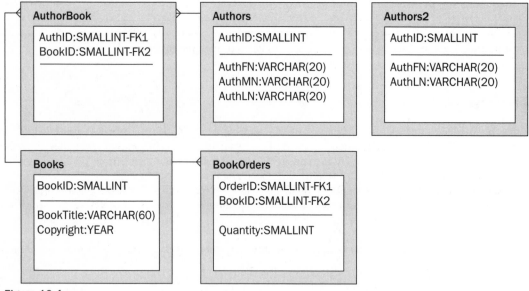

Figure 10-4

1. Create a SELECT statement that uses a basic join to retrieve the name of books in the Books table and the name of the authors in the Authors table who wrote those books. The author names should be concatenated with a space between names. In addition, the result set should be sorted according to the book titles.

2. Create a SELECT statement that is similar to the statement that you created in Step 1. The new statement should use a cross join to join the tables, and the rows returned should be limited to those books that were written by authors whose last names begin with Toole or Thompson.

3. Create a SELECT statement that uses a right outer join to retrieve the name of books in the Books table and the name of the authors in the Authors table who wrote those books. The Authors table should be on the right side of the join. The author names should be concatenated with a space between names. In addition, the result set should be sorted according to the book titles.

4. Create a SELECT statement similar to the one that you created in Step 3. The new statement should use a natural right join to join the tables.

5. Create a SELECT statement that retrieves book titles from the Books table. The result set should include only those books whose BookID value is equal to one of the values returned by a subquery. The subquery should return BookID values from the BookOrders table for those books that sold more than two books in an order. The result set should be sorted according to the book titles.

6. Create a SELECT statement that retrieves OrderID, BookID, and Quantity values from the BookOrders table for the book *Letters to a Young Poet*. The statement should use a subquery to retrieve the BookID value associated with the book.

7. Use a UNION operator to join two SELECT statements. The first SELECT statement should retrieve the AuthLN column from the Authors table. The second SELECT statement should retrieve the AuthLN column from the Authors2 table. The names returned by the statement should be sorted alphabetically, in ascending order.

Exporting, Copying, and Importing Data

Up to this point in the book, the process of managing data has been confined to the manipulation of data in your database. For example, to add data to your tables, you manually created INSERT statements that targeted specific tables. To view data, you manually created SELECT statements that retrieved data from specific tables. In each case, the data was added to the tables by specifying those values to be inserted, or the data was retrieved by executing the applicable SELECT statement each time you wanted to view that data. At no time was data copied to or from files outside the database, nor was data copied between tables in the database.

The limitations of these approaches become apparent when you want to add large quantities of data to a database or manage large quantities of data outside the database. MySQL supports a number of SQL statements and commands that allow you to export data into files outside the database, copy data between tables in a database, and import data into the database. By using these statements and commands, you can easily work with large amounts of data that must be added to and retrieved from a database or data that must be copied from one table to the next. This chapter discusses how to use these statements and commands and provides examples of each. Specifically, the chapter explains how to perform the following tasks:

- ❑ Create SELECT statements that export data to out files and dump files

- ❑ Create INSERT and REPLACE statements that copy data into existing tables and create CREATE TABLE statements that copy data into new tables

- ❑ Create LOAD DATA statements and execute mysql and mysqlimport commands that import data into existing tables

Exporting Data Out of a Table

There might be times when you want to export data in a MySQL database to text files stored outside the database. MySQL allows you to export this data by using SELECT statements that include the appropriate export definitions. To understand how to add an export definition to a SELECT statement, return to the SELECT statement syntax that you were introduced to in Chapter 7:

```
<select statement>::=
SELECT
[<select option> [<select option>...]]
{* | <select list>}
[<export definition>]
[
    FROM <table reference> [{, <table reference>}...]
    [WHERE <expression> [{<operator> <expression>}...]]
    [GROUP BY <group by definition>]
    [HAVING <expression> [{<operator> <expression>}...]]
    [ORDER BY <order by definition>]
    [LIMIT [<offset>,] <row count>]
    [PROCEDURE <procedure name> [(<argument> [{, <argument>}...])]]]
    [{FOR UPDATE} | {LOCK IN SHARE MODE}]
]

<export definition>::=
INTO OUTFILE '<filename>' [<export option> [<export option>]]
| INTO DUMPFILE '<filename>'

<export option>::=
{FIELDS
    [TERMINATED BY '<value>']
    [[OPTIONALLY] ENCLOSED BY '<value>']
    [ESCAPED BY '<value>']}
| {LINES
    [STARTING BY '<value>']
    [TERMINATED BY '<value>']}
```

The syntax shown here includes only the basic elements that make up a SELECT statement and those elements specific to exporting data. (For a detailed explanation of the SELECT statement, refer to Chapter 7.) Notice that the <export definition> placeholder precedes the FROM clause. To export data, you must include an export definition that specifies whether the data is imported to an out file or a dump file. An *out file* is a text file (such as a .txt or .sql file) that contains one or more rows of exported data in a delimited format. A *delimited* format is one in which the values and rows are separated and enclosed by specific types of characters. For example, a tab is commonly used to separate values in the same row, and a line break (also known as newline) is often used to separate rows. In contrast to an out file, a *dump file* is a text file that contains only one row that is not delimited. Dump files are used primarily for large values, such as a value from a column configured with a BLOB data type.

In this section, you learn about how to export data to an out file and to a dump file. To demonstrate how to export data, the table shown in the following table definition is used:

```
CREATE TABLE CDs
(
    CDID SMALLINT NOT NULL PRIMARY KEY,
    CDName VARCHAR(50) NOT NULL,
    InStock SMALLINT UNSIGNED NOT NULL,
    Category VARCHAR(20)
);
```

In addition to using the CDs table to demonstrate how to export data, the table is also used later in the chapter for examples that show how to copy and import. For all examples in this chapter, you can assume that the following INSERT statement has been used to populate the CDs table:

```
INSERT INTO CDs
VALUES (101, 'Bloodshot', 10, 'Rock'),
(102, 'New Orleans Jazz', 17, 'Jazz'),
(103, 'Music for Ballet Class', 9, 'Classical'),
(104, 'Music for Solo Violin', 24, NULL),
(105, 'Mississippi Blues', 2, 'Blues'),
(106, 'Mud on the Tires', 12, 'Country'),
(107, 'The Essence', 5, 'New Age'),
(108, 'The Magic of Satie', 42, 'Classical'),
(109, 'La Boheme', 20, 'Opera'),
(110, 'Ain\'t Ever Satisfied', 23, 'Country'),
(111, 'Live in Paris', 18, 'Jazz'),
(112, 'Richland Woman Blues', 22, 'Blues'),
(113, 'Stages', 42, 'Blues');
```

Now take a look how to export data to out files and dump files.

Exporting Data to an Out File

As you saw in the previous section, the elements in the SELECT statement syntax that are specific to exporting to an out file are as follows:

```
INTO OUTFILE '<filename>' [<export option> [<export option>]]

<export option>::=
{FIELDS
    [TERMINATED BY '<value>']
    [[OPTIONALLY] ENCLOSED BY '<value>']
    [ESCAPED BY '<value>']}
| {LINES
    [STARTING BY '<value>']
    [TERMINATED BY '<value>']}
```

When exporting data to an out file, you must specify the INTO OUTFILE clause after the select list and before the FROM clause. The INTO OUTFILE clause includes a filename, enclosed in single quotes, and one or two export options. The export options can include a FIELDS clause, a LINES clause, or both. If you include both, then the FIELDS clause must come before the LINES clause. In addition, for each clause that you specify, you must specify at least one of the subclauses available for that clause. For example, if you specify a LINES clause, you must also specify a STARTING BY subclause, a TERMINATED BY subclause, or both.

Now take a close look at the FIELDS clause, which includes three optional subclauses:

```
FIELDS
    [TERMINATED BY '<value>']
    [[OPTIONALLY] ENCLOSED BY '<value>']
    [ESCAPED BY '<value>']
```

As you can see in the syntax, the FIELDS clause includes the following three subclauses:

- **TERMINATED BY:** Specifies the character or characters to be used to separate each value returned by a row of data. By default, a tab is used, which is indicated by \t.

- **ENCLOSED BY:** Specifies the character to be used to enclose each value returned by a row of data. By default, no characters are used.

- **ESCAPED BY:** Specifies the character to be used to escape special characters. By default, a back-slash is used, which is indicated by \\.

In general, you would use these subclauses only when you have a special requirement for the way data is retrieved from the file. Otherwise, the default values are normally adequate. One thing to note, how-ever, is that the TERMINATED BY clause allows you to specify more than one character to use to separate values in a row. The other subclauses allow you to specify only one character.

For the most part, the TERMINATED BY and ENCLOSED BY clauses are fairly straightforward. Whatever values you specify in these clauses are the values that are used. It's worth taking a closer look at the ESCAPED BY subclause. This clause is used to escape any characters in the data that are also used in the FIELDS subclauses. In other words, the characters in the data values are treated literally, rather than the way they are treated between values or rows. The ESCAPED BY subclause escapes the following charac-ters when they appear in a value:

- The first character in the FIELDS TERMININATED BY and LINES TERMINATED BY subclauses

- The character in the ENCLOSED BY subclause

- The character in the ESCAPED BY subclause

- Uppercase N, when used to represent NULL

Whenever any of these characters appear in a data value, the character specified in the ESCAPED BY sub-clause precedes the character. As a result, when you import data from the out file, you have a way to ensure that specified characters are treated appropriately, depending on where they appear in the text file. Later in this section, you see an example of how this works.

Now take a look at the LINES clause, shown in the following syntax:

```
LINES
    [STARTING BY '<value>']
    [TERMINATED BY '<value>']
```

As you can see, the LINES clause supports the following two subclauses:

- **STARTED BY:** Specifies the character or characters to be used to begin each row of data. By default, no characters are used.

- **TERMINATED BY:** Specifies the character or characters to be used to end each row of data. By default, a newline is used, which is shown as \n.

When you're specifying the values that can be inserted in any of the FIELDS or LINES subclauses, you can use a literal value, or you can use one of the special values supported by the subclauses. Whenever you use a special value, it must be preceded by a backslash. The following table provides the meanings for the primary special values that you can use in your FIELDS and LINES subclauses.

Value	Meaning
\'	Single quote
\\	Backslash
\n	Newline
\r	Carriage return
\s	Space
\t	Tab

Whenever you specify one of the special values, that character is used for the purpose specified by the subclause. For example, if you specify that a space (\s) be used to separate values (the FIELDS TERMINATED BY subclause), a space is used between each value in each row.

Now that you have an overview of the components that make up an export definition, you can examine an example of a SELECT statement that includes a basic definition. In the following SELECT statement, values are retrieved from the CDs table and exported to a file named CDsOut.txt:

```
SELECT CDName, InStock, Category
    INTO OUTFILE 'CDsOut.txt'
FROM CDs;
```

As you can see, the statement includes an INTO OUTFILE clause directly after the select list and preceding the FROM clause. Because the INTO OUTFILE clause is used, a file is created and the values are added to that file, rather than a result set being generated. Any values that you would expect to see in the result set are copied to the file. If a file by that name already exists, the SELECT statement fails.

The file is saved to the location of the database folder that corresponds to the database in which you're working. For example, if you're working in the test database, the file is saved to the test folder in your data directory. To save the file to a different location, you must specify a path for that file.

Once an out file has been created, you can open the file and view its contents. For example, if you were to view the contents of the CDsOut.txt file, you would see results similar to the following:

```
Bloodshot        10       Rock
New Orleans Jazz 17       Jazz
Music for Ballet Class  9    Classical
Music for Solo Violin   24   \N
Mississippi Blues       2    Blues
Mud on the Tires 12      Country
The Essence      5       New Age
The Magic of Satie      42   Classical
La Boheme        20      Opera
Ain't Ever Satisfied    23   Country
Live in Paris    18      Jazz
Richland Woman Blues    22   Blues
Stages    42     Blues
```

As you can see, the results that you would expect to have been generated by the result set are added to the file. Note that tabs separate the values and that each row is on its own line. In addition, the values are not enclosed in any specific character. These are the results you would expect when you generate an out file without specifying any FIELDS or LINES subclauses.

In some text programs, the rows might not be shown as being separated into different lines, but rather separated by a symbol that looks like a small rectangle. As a result, the rows run together in one line that wraps down your document. If you were to copy and paste the results into a word processing program, you would find that they are displayed with each row on a separate line, as they are in the preceding example.

One thing that you might notice is that, in the fourth row, the Category value is \N. This indicates that the query returned a NULL. By default, whenever a value is NULL, an uppercase N is returned, preceded by a backslash. If the ESCAPED BY option specifies a character other than a backslash, that character precedes the N.

The next example SELECT statement is similar to the last except that two FIELDS subclauses are specified, as shown in the following statement:

```
SELECT CDName, InStock, Category INTO OUTFILE 'CDsOut.txt'
    FIELDS
        TERMINATED BY ','
        ENCLOSED BY '"'
FROM CDs;
```

In this case, the values are saved to a file named CDsOut.txt, the values are separated by commas (as specified in the TERMINATED BY subclause), and the values are enclosed in double quotes (as specified in the ENCLOSED BY subclause).

If you try to create an out file and that file already exists, you receive an error. If the file already exists, you should rename the original out file or delete it before attempting to create the new file.

The following results show the contents of the CDsOut.txt file:

```
"Bloodshot","10","Rock"
"New Orleans Jazz","17","Jazz"
"Music for Ballet Class","9","Classical"
"Music for Solo Violin","24",\N
"Mississippi Blues","2","Blues"
"Mud on the Tires","12","Country"
"The Essence","5","New Age"
"The Magic of Satie","42","Classical"
"La Boheme","20","Opera"
"Ain't Ever Satisfied","23","Country"
"Live in Paris","18","Jazz"
"Richland Woman Blues","22","Blues"
"Stages","42","Blues"
```

As you can see, commas have replaced the tabs and each value is enclosed in double quotes. Now modify this statement even further by adding an ESCAPED BY subclause:

```
SELECT CDName, InStock, Category INTO OUTFILE 'CDsOut.txt'
    FIELDS
```

```
            TERMINATED BY ','
            ENCLOSED BY '\"'
            ESCAPED BY '\''
    FROM CDs;
```

The ESCAPED BY value specifies that a single quote be used to escape the subclause values. As a result, each comma, double quote, and single quote that appears in a value is preceded by a single quote. The following results show the contents of the CDsOut.txt file:

```
"Bloodshot","10","Rock"
"New Orleans Jazz","17","Jazz"
"Music for Ballet Class","9","Classical"
"Music for Solo Violin","24",'N
"Mississippi Blues","2","Blues"
"Mud on the Tires","12","Country"
"The Essence","5","New Age"
"The Magic of Satie","42","Classical"
"La Boheme","20","Opera"
"Ain''t Ever Satisfied","23","Country"
"Live in Paris","18","Jazz"
"Richland Woman Blues","22","Blues"
"Stages","42","Blues"
```

First, notice that the uppercase N is now preceded by a single quote, rather than a backslash. In addition, the single quote (used as an apostrophe) in the tenth row is also preceded by a single quote because a single quote is one of the values specified in the FIELDS subclauses. As a result, the second single quote is treated as a literal value when importing data from this file.

Now that you've seen several examples of how to use FIELDS subclauses, you can take a look at an example of LINES subclauses. The following statement is similar to the last, only now it includes LINES subclauses rather than FIELD subclauses:

```
SELECT CDName, InStock, Category INTO OUTFILE 'CDsOut.txt'
    LINES
        STARTING BY '*'
        TERMINATED BY '**'
FROM CDs
WHERE Category='Blues' OR Category='Jazz';
```

The export definition in this statement now specifies that each row should begin with an asterisk (*) and each row should end with double asterisks (**). The following results show the contents of the CDsOut.txt file:

```
*New Orleans Jazz      17      Jazz***Mississippi Blues     2       Blues***Live
in Paris 18     Jazz***Richland Woman Blues   22      Blues***Stages 42
Blues**
```

As you can see, each row is no longer on its own line, and the rows appear to be separated by three asterisks, making it difficult to distinguish where one row ends and where the other begins. To put the rows on separate lines, you must modify the TERMINATED BY subclause, as shown in the following SELECT statement:

```
SELECT CDName, InStock, Category INTO OUTFILE 'CDsOut.txt'
    LINES
        STARTING BY '*'
        TERMINATED BY '**\n'
FROM CDs
WHERE Category='Blues' OR Category='Jazz';
```

Notice that the TERMINATED BY clause now includes the newline (\n) value, as well as the double asterisks. As a result, the contents of the CDsOut.txt file now appear similar to the following:

```
*New Orleans Jazz       17      Jazz**
*Mississippi Blues      2       Blues**
*Live in Paris   18     Jazz**
*Richland Woman Blues   22      Blues**
*Stages  42      Blues**
```

As you can see, each row is on a separate line, begins with an asterisk, and ends with double asterisks. You're not limited to only symbols in your TERMINATED BY subclauses. The following SELECT statement terminates each line with <<end>>:

```
SELECT CDName, InStock, Category INTO OUTFILE 'CDsOut.txt'
    FIELDS
        TERMINATED BY ','
        ENCLOSED BY '\"'
    LINES
        TERMINATED BY '<<end>>\n'
FROM CDs
WHERE Category='Blues' OR Category='Jazz';
```

Now when you view the contents of the CDsOut.txt file, you see the following results:

```
"New Orleans Jazz","17","Jazz"<<end>>
"Mississippi Blues","2","Blues"<<end>>
"Live in Paris","18","Jazz"<<end>>
"Richland Woman Blues","22","Blues"<<end>>
"Stages","42","Blues"<<end>>
```

As you can see, you can be quite imaginative with the values in your FIELDS and LINES subclauses; however, you should use these clauses only if it's necessary to set up the file in a specific way. Most of the time, the default settings are adequate.

In the following exercise, you create several SELECT statements that each include an export definition that creates an out file. Because you are exporting data from the DVDRentals database, the files are saved to the DVDRentals folder in the data directory.

Try It Out   Exporting DVDRentals Data to an Out File

The following steps describe how to create the SELECT statements:

1.   Open the mysql client utility, type the following command, and press Enter:

```
use DVDRentals
```

You should receive a message indicating that you switched to the DVDRentals database.

2. The first SELECT statement exports data from joined tables in the DVDRentals database to a text file named AvailDVDs.txt. Execute the following SQL statement at the mysql command prompt:

```
SELECT DVDName, MTypeDescrip, FormDescrip, d.RatingID
   INTO OUTFILE 'AvailDVDs.txt'
FROM DVDs AS d, MovieTypes AS m, Formats AS f
WHERE d.MTypeID=m.MTypeID AND d.FormID=f.FormID
   AND StatID='s2'
ORDER BY DVDName;
```

You should receive a message indicating that the statement executed successfully, affecting five rows.

3. Go to the DVDRentals folder of your data directory, and open the AvailDVDs.txt file. The file should contain the following values in a format similar to what is shown here:

```
Amadeus  Drama   Widescreen       PG
Mash        Comedy  Widescreen       R
The Maltese Falcon       Drama    Widescreen       NR
The Rocky Horror Picture Show    Comedy  Widescreen       NR
What's Up, Doc? Comedy  Widescreen       G
```

4. In the next SELECT statement, you add the FIELDS TERMINATED BY and LINES TERMINATED BY subclauses. Execute the following SQL statement at the mysql command prompt:

```
SELECT DVDName, MTypeDescrip, FormDescrip, d.RatingID
   INTO OUTFILE 'AvailDVDs2.txt'
   FIELDS TERMINATED BY '*,*'
   LINES TERMINATED BY '**\n'
FROM DVDs AS d, MovieTypes AS m, Formats AS f
WHERE d.MTypeID=m.MTypeID AND d.FormID=f.FormID
   AND StatID='s2'
ORDER BY DVDName;
```

You should receive a message indicating that the statement executed successfully, affecting five rows.

5. Go to the DVDRentals folder of your data directory and open the AvailDVDs2.txt file. The file should contain the following values in a format similar to what is shown here:

```
Amadeus*,*Drama*,*Widescreen*,*PG**
Mash*,*Comedy*,*Widescreen*,*R**
The Maltese Falcon*,*Drama*,*Widescreen*,*NR**
The Rocky Horror Picture Show*,*Comedy*,*Widescreen*,*NR**
What's Up, Doc?*,*Comedy*,*Widescreen*,*G**
```

How It Works

The first SELECT statement that you created includes a basic export definition:

```
SELECT DVDName, MTypeDescrip, FormDescrip, d.RatingID
   INTO OUTFILE 'AvailDVDs.txt'
FROM DVDs AS d, MovieTypes AS m, Formats AS f
WHERE d.MTypeID=m.MTypeID AND d.FormID=f.FormID
   AND StatID='s2'
ORDER BY DVDName;
```

The export definition is made up of the INTO OUTFILE keywords and the name of the new file, enclosed in single quotes. Because you specified no FIELDS or LINES subclauses, the values are added using the default format. As a result, values are separated with tabs, the values are not enclosed in any characters, and special characters are escaped by the use of a backslash. In addition, each row is on its own line, and no characters precede each row.

The next statement that you created is similar to the last, except that it includes the FIELDS TERMINATED BY and LINES TERMINATED BY subclauses:

```
SELECT DVDName, MTypeDescrip, FormDescrip, d.RatingID
    INTO OUTFILE 'AvailDVDs2.txt'
    FIELDS TERMINATED BY '*,*'
    LINES TERMINATED BY '**\n'
FROM DVDs AS d, MovieTypes AS m, Formats AS f
WHERE d.MTypeID=m.MTypeID AND d.FormID=f.FormID
    AND StatID='s2'
ORDER BY DVDName;
```

Because you added the subclauses to the export definition, the fields are now separated by an asterisk, a comma, and another asterisk, and the rows end in double asterisks, although they are still each on their own lines.

Exporting Data to a Dump File

Exporting data to a dump file is much simpler than an out file because you cannot specify any FIELDS or LINES subclauses. As a result, the syntax for a dump file export definition is very simple, as shown in the following:

```
INTO DUMPFILE '<filename>'
```

As you can see, you need to specify only the INTO DUMPFILE keywords and the filename, enclosed in single quotes. As with an out file, the dump file export definition is placed after the SELECT list and before the FROM clause of the SELECT statement, as shown in the following example:

```
SELECT CDName, InStock, Category
    INTO DUMPFILE 'CDsOut.txt'
FROM CDs
WHERE CDID=110;
```

In this statement, the data extracted from the CDs table is exported to the CDsOut.txt file. Notice that the SELECT statement returns only one row of data. Your SELECT statement must return exactly one row if you want to save data to a dump file. In addition, the values are not in any way delimited. For example, the preceding statement returns the row for the CD named *Ain't Ever Satisfied*. When added to the file, all values from that row are run together, as shown in the following results:

```
Ain't Ever Satisfied23Country
```

As you can see, the only spaces are those that are between the words in a value, but there is nothing that separates the individual values from one another. Normally, you would create a dump file if you want to store a value from a BLOB column in a file.

In this Try It Out exercise, you create a SELECT statement that includes an export definition. The statement extracts data from joined tables in the DVDRentals database and adds that data to a dump file.

Exporting DVDRentals Data to a Dump File

The following steps describe how to create the SELECT statement:

1. Open the mysql client utility, type the following command, and press Enter:

```
use DVDRentals
```

You should receive a message indicating that you switched to the DVDRentals database.

2. In this statement, you extract data about the DVD *Out of Africa* and place it in a dump file. Execute the following SQL statement at the mysql command prompt:

```
SELECT DVDName, MTypeDescrip, FormDescrip, d.RatingID
    INTO DUMPFILE 'DVD3.txt'
FROM DVDs AS d, MovieTypes AS m, Formats AS f
WHERE d.MTypeID=m.MTypeID AND d.FormID=f.FormID
    AND DVDID=3;
```

You should receive a message indicating that the statement executed successfully, affecting one row.

3. Go to the DVDRentals folder of your data directory, and open the DVD3.txt file. The file should contain the following values in a format similar to what is shown here:

```
Out of AfricaDramaWidescreenPG
```

How It Works

The SELECT statement that you included in this exercise includes an export definition that exports data to a dump file:

```
SELECT DVDName, MTypeDescrip, FormDescrip, d.RatingID
    INTO DUMPFILE 'DVD3.txt'
FROM DVDs AS d, MovieTypes AS m, Formats AS f
WHERE d.MTypeID=m.MTypeID AND d.FormID=f.FormID
    AND DVDID=3;
```

In this statement, one row of data is retrieved from joined tables in the DVDRentals database. When the statement was executed, a dump file named DVD3.txt was created and the data retrieved by the SELECT statement was inserted in the dump file. The values added to the file were not delimited in any way, so the values ran together. The only spaces anywhere in the text were those that are part of the *Out of Africa* value retrieved from the DVDName column.

Copying Data into a Table

MySQL provides two primary methods for copying existing data into a table. You can add data to a new table when the table is created, or you can add data to an existing table. In this section, you learn how to use a CREATE TABLE statement to add data to a new table and how to use an INSERT statement to add data to an existing table.

Copying Data into a New Table

When you learned about how to create tables in Chapter 5, you were introduced to the syntax used for table definitions. The basic syntax for a table definition is as follows:

```
<table definition>::=
CREATE TABLE <table name>
(<table element> [{, <table element>}...])
[<table option> [<table option>...]]
[<select statement>]
```

The syntax here includes an element that you did not see in Chapter 5, the `<select statement>` placeholder. (For an explanation of the other components of a CREATE TABLE statement, see Chapter 5.) As the placeholder indicates, you can add a SELECT statement to the end of your table definition. The values returned by that statement are automatically inserted in the new table. To add a SELECT statement, the statement must return results that can be inserted naturally in the statement. This means that the values must be compatible with the data types of the columns in the new table, and each row must contain the correct number of values, one for each column of the new table.

For example, the following CREATE TABLE statement extracts data from the CDs table and adds it to the new CDs2 table:

```
CREATE TABLE CDs2
(
    CDID SMALLINT NOT NULL PRIMARY KEY,
    CDName VARCHAR(50) NOT NULL,
    InStock SMALLINT UNSIGNED NOT NULL
)
SELECT CDID, CDName, InStock
FROM CDs
WHERE Category='Blues' OR Category='Jazz';
```

The first part of the statement is a standard table definition. The table named CDs2 includes three columns: CDID, CDName, and InStock. The next part of the table definition (the last three rows) includes the SELECT statement that retrieves the values to be inserted in the new table.

Once the table has been created, you can run the following SELECT statement:

```
SELECT * FROM CDs2;
```

Your statement should return results similar to the following:

```
+------+---------------------+---------+
| CDID | CDName              | InStock |
+------+---------------------+---------+
|  102 | New Orleans Jazz    |      17 |
|  105 | Mississippi Blues   |       2 |
|  111 | Live in Paris       |      18 |
|  112 | Richland Woman Blues|      22 |
|  113 | Stages              |      42 |
+------+---------------------+---------+
5 rows in set (0.00 sec)
```

As you can see, these are the same results that you would have received if you executed the SELECT statement separately from the CREATE TABLE statement. By adding the SELECT statement to the CREATE TABLE statement, you save yourself the trouble of first creating the table and then using an INSERT statement to add data to that table.

Keep in mind that when you create a table, the columns must be defined with data types compatible with the data that you're retrieving from an existing table. This refers not only to the type of data (for example, INT versus CHAR), but also to the length of the data (for example, CHAR(4) versus CHAR(40)). If you use an incorrect data type or specify the size too small for the data type, MySQL truncates the data. This means that the data is shortened or another value is inserted in the column. For example, suppose that you use the following CREATE TABLE statement to create a table:

```
CREATE TABLE CDs2a
(
    CDID SMALLINT NOT NULL PRIMARY KEY,
    CDName VARCHAR(5) NOT NULL,
    InStock SMALLINT UNSIGNED NOT NULL
)
SELECT CDID, CDName, InStock
FROM CDs
WHERE Category='Blues' OR Category='Jazz';
```

Notice that the CDName column of the new table is defined with a VARCHAR(5) data type. The data that is retrieved for that column comes from a column with a VARCHAR(50) data type, and values in that column all exceed five characters. As a result, when you try to insert data it is truncated. For example, if you retrieve all the data from the CDs3 table, you receive results similar to the following:

```
+------+--------+---------+
| CDID | CDName | InStock |
+------+--------+---------+
|  102 | New O  |      17 |
|  105 | Missi  |       2 |
|  111 | Live   |      18 |
|  112 | Richl  |      22 |
|  113 | Stage  |      42 |
+------+--------+---------+
5 rows in set (0.00 sec)
```

As you can see, each CDName value has been truncated, which means that only the first five characters of the name are displayed.

In this Try It Out, you create a table named DVDs2 in the DVDRentals database. The table is populated with data returned by a SELECT statement that joins several tables in the database.

Try It Out   Copying Data to a New Table in the DVDRentals Database

Follow these steps to create the table definition:

1. Open the mysql client utility, type the following command, and press Enter:

```
use DVDRentals
```

You should receive a message indicating that you switched to the DVDRentals database.

2. Now create a table definition that includes a SELECT statement that retrieves data from the DVDs, MovieTypes, and Formats tables. Execute the following SQL statement at the mysql command prompt:

```
CREATE TABLE DVDs2
(
    DVDName VARCHAR(60) NOT NULL,
    MTypeDescrip VARCHAR(30) NOT NULL,
    FormDescrip VARCHAR(15) NOT NULL,
    RatingID VARCHAR(4) NOT NULL
)
SELECT DVDName, MTypeDescrip, FormDescrip, d.RatingID
FROM DVDs AS d, MovieTypes AS m, Formats AS f
WHERE d.MTypeID=m.MTypeID AND d.FormID=f.FormID
    AND StatID='s2'
ORDER BY DVDName;
```

You should receive a message indicating that the statement executed successfully, affecting five rows.

3. Next, view the contents of the DVDs2 table. Execute the following SQL statement at the mysql command prompt:

```
SELECT * FROM DVDs2;
```

You should receive results similar to the following:

```
+-----------------------------+--------------+-------------+----------+
| DVDName                     | MTypeDescrip | FormDescrip | RatingID |
+-----------------------------+--------------+-------------+----------+
| Amadeus                     | Drama        | Widescreen  | PG       |
| Mash                        | Comedy       | Widescreen  | R        |
| The Maltese Falcon          | Drama        | Widescreen  | NR       |
| The Rocky Horror Picture Show | Comedy     | Widescreen  | NR       |
| What's Up, Doc?             | Comedy       | Widescreen  | G        |
+-----------------------------+--------------+-------------+----------+
5 rows in set (0.01 sec)
```

Be sure not to delete the DVDs2 table from the DVDRentals database because you use it for Try It Out sections later in the chapter.

How It Works

In this exercise, you created a table definition that includes a SELECT statement at the end of the definition:

```
CREATE TABLE DVDs2
(
    DVDName VARCHAR(60) NOT NULL,
    MTypeDescrip VARCHAR(30) NOT NULL,
    FormDescrip VARCHAR(15) NOT NULL,
    RatingID VARCHAR(4) NOT NULL
)
SELECT DVDName, MTypeDescrip, FormDescrip, d.RatingID
FROM DVDs AS d, MovieTypes AS m, Formats AS f
```

```
WHERE d.MTypeID=m.MTypeID AND d.FormID=f.FormID
   AND StatID='s2'
ORDER BY DVDName;
```

The statement first creates the actual table, which is named DVDs2 and which contains four columns: DVDName, MTypeDescrip, FormDescrip, and RatingID. After the table is defined, the table definition then includes a SELECT statement that retrieves data from the DVDs, MovieTypes, and Formats tables. The data retrieved by the SELECT statement is inserted in the DVDs2 table. Notice that each row returned by the SELECT statement contains the same number of values as there are columns in the new table. In addition, the data returned by the SELECT statement is made up of values that are consistent with the column types of the new table.

Copying Data into an Existing Table

MySQL provides two methods that you can use to copy data into an existing table: the INSERT statement and the REPLACE statement. (You learned about both these statements in Chapter 6.) Both statements are used to add data to a table. The main difference between the two is in how values in a primary key column or a unique index are treated. In an INSERT statement, if you try to insert a row that contains a unique index or primary key value that already exists in the table, you won't be able to add that row. With a REPLACE statement, the old row is deleted and the new row is added. In all other respects, the statements are the same.

Using the INSERT Statement to Copy Data

When Chapter 6 introduced you to the INSERT statement, it provided you with the statement syntax. The following syntax provides you with an abbreviated version of what you saw in Chapter 6:

```
<insert statement>::=
INSERT [LOW_PRIORITY | DELAYED] [IGNORE] [INTO]
{<values option> | <set option> | <select option>}

<select option>::=
<table name> [(<column name> [{, <column name>}...])]
<select statement>
```

As you can see, the main part of the statement includes three options: the <values option>, the <set option>, and the <select option>. Of these three, the <select option> is the only one shown here. For an explanation of the other two options, see Chapter 6.

The <select option> allows you to define a SELECT statement in your INSERT statement. The values returned by the SELECT statement are then inserted in the table specified by the main part of the INSERT statement. For example, the following INSERT statement adds data from the CDs table to the CDs2 table:

```
INSERT INTO CDs2
SELECT CDID, CDName, InStock FROM CDs
WHERE Category='Country' OR Category='Rock';
```

In this statement, the INSERT clause includes the name of the target table (CDs2). (This is the table that you created when learning about adding data to a new table.) As you can see, the SELECT statement follows the INSERT clause. In this case, the statement retrieves data from the CDID, CDName, and InStock columns of the CDs table and returns three rows (with CDID values of 101, 106, and 110). The SELECT statement must return the same number of columns specified in the INSERT clause. If no columns are specified in the INSERT clause, the SELECT statement must return the same number of columns that exist in the target table. In addition, the values retrieved by the SELECT statement must be compatible with the data types of the targeted columns.

Once you execute the INSERT statement, you can use the following SELECT statement to view the contents of the CDs2 table:

```
SELECT * FROM CDs2;
```

The SELECT statement returns the following result set:

```
+------+----------------------+---------+
| CDID | CDName               | InStock |
+------+----------------------+---------+
|  102 | New Orleans Jazz     |      17 |
|  105 | Mississippi Blues    |       2 |
|  111 | Live in Paris        |      18 |
|  112 | Richland Woman Blues |      22 |
|  113 | Stages               |      42 |
|  101 | Bloodshot            |      10 |
|  106 | Mud on the Tires     |      12 |
|  110 | Ain't Ever Satisfied |      23 |
+------+----------------------+---------+
8 rows in set (0.00 sec)
```

As you can see, the CDs2 table now contains the rows added when the table was created and the rows returned by the SELECT statement specified in the INSERT statement.

Using the REPLACE Statement to Copy Data

The REPLACE statement syntax is essentially the same as that of the INSERT statement, as shown in the following:

```
<replace statement>::=
REPLACE [LOW_PRIORITY | DELAYED] [INTO]
{<values option> | <set option> | <select option>}

<select option>::=
<table name> [(<column name> [{, <column name>}...])]
<select statement>
```

To use a REPLACE statement to insert values returned by a SELECT statement, you should add the SELECT statement after the REPLACE clause, in the same way as you did with the INSERT statement. For example, the following REPLACE statement is identical to the INSERT statement in the previous example, except that it now uses the keyword REPLACE:

```
REPLACE INTO CDs2
SELECT CDID, CDName, InStock
FROM CDs
WHERE Category='Country' OR Category='Rock';
```

The SELECT statement returns the same results that it returned in the INSERT statement, and those values are inserted in the CDs2 table.

In this Try It Out section, you create an INSERT statement that adds data to the DVDs2 table that you created in the last Try It Out section. The INSERT statement uses data retrieved from several joined tables in the DVDRentals database.

Try It Out Copying Data to an Existing Table in the DVDRentals Database

The following steps describe how to create the INSERT statement:

1. Open the mysql client utility, type the following command, and press Enter:

```
use DVDRentals
```

You should receive a message indicating that you switched to the DVDRentals database.

2. Now create the INSERT statement, which includes the necessary SELECT statement. Execute the following SQL statement at the mysql command prompt:

```
INSERT INTO DVDs2
SELECT DVDName, MTypeDescrip, FormDescrip, d.RatingID
FROM DVDs AS d, MovieTypes AS m, Formats AS f
WHERE d.MTypeID=m.MTypeID AND d.FormID=f.FormID
    AND StatID='s1'
ORDER BY DVDName;
```

You should receive a message indicating that the query executed successfully, affecting five rows.

3. Now view the contents of the DVDs2 table to verify that the new data has been added. Execute the following SQL statement at the mysql command prompt:

```
SELECT * FROM DVDs2;
```

You should receive results similar to the following:

```
+------------------------------+--------------+-------------+----------+
| DVDName                      | MTypeDescrip | FormDescrip | RatingID |
+------------------------------+--------------+-------------+----------+
| Amadeus                      | Drama        | Widescreen  | PG       |
| Mash                         | Comedy       | Widescreen  | R        |
| The Maltese Falcon           | Drama        | Widescreen  | NR       |
| The Rocky Horror Picture Show| Comedy       | Widescreen  | NR       |
| What's Up, Doc?              | Comedy       | Widescreen  | G        |
| A Room with a View           | Drama        | Widescreen  | NR       |
| Out of Africa                | Drama        | Widescreen  | PG       |
| White Christmas              | Musical      | Widescreen  | NR       |
+------------------------------+--------------+-------------+----------+
8 rows in set (0.00 sec)
```

How It Works

In this exercise, you created an INSERT statement that included an INSERT clause and a SELECT statement:

```
INSERT INTO DVDs2
SELECT DVDName, MTypeDescrip, FormDescrip, d.RatingID
```

```
FROM DVDs AS d, MovieTypes AS m, Formats AS f
WHERE d.MTypeID=m.MTypeID AND d.FormID=f.FormID
    AND StatID='s1'
ORDER BY DVDName;
```

The INSERT clause includes only the INSERT INTO keywords and the name of the target table, DVDs2. The rest of the statement is a SELECT statement that retrieves data from the DVDs, MovieTypes, and Formats tables. The retrieved data is inserted in the DVDs2 table. When data is added to a table in this way, it is inserted after the existing data.

Importing Data into a Table

In addition to allowing you to export and copy data, MySQL allows you to import data from text files. To import data, you can use the mysql client utility or you can use the mysqlimport client utility. In this section, you learn how to use both tools to copy data into your database.

Using the mysql Utility to Import Data

The mysql client utility provides a number of options that you can use to import data into your database:

❑ **The LOAD DATA statement:** You can use the LOAD DATA statement at the mysql command prompt to import delimited values directly from a text file.

❑ **The source command:** You can use the source command at the mysql command prompt to run SQL statements and mysql commands that are saved in a text file. The statements can include INSERT statements that define values to be added to your tables.

❑ **The mysql command:** You can use the mysql command at your operating system's command prompt to run SQL statements and mysql commands that are saved in a text file. The mysql command is the same command that you use to launch the mysql client utility. You can also use the command to execute statements in a text file, without actually launching the utility, and these statements can include INSERT statements that define values to be added to your tables.

Now that you know the basics, take a closer look at each one of these options.

Using the LOAD DATA Statement to Import Data

Of the three options available for using the mysql client utility to import data, the LOAD DATA statement is the only one that allows you to import values directly from a delimited text file. (These are the type of files that are created when you export data from a MySQL database.) The following syntax describes how a LOAD DATA statement is created:

```
<load data statement>::=
LOAD DATA [LOW_PRIORITY | CONCURRENT] [LOCAL] INFILE '<filename>'
[REPLACE | IGNORE]
INTO TABLE <table name>
[<import option> [<import option>]]
[IGNORE <number> LINES]
[(<column name> [{, <column name>}...])]
```

```
<import option>::=
{FIELDS
    [TERMINATED BY '<value>']
    [[OPTIONALLY] ENCLOSED BY '<value>']
    [ESCAPED BY '<value>']}
| {LINES
    [STARTING BY '<value>']
    [TERMINATED BY '<value>']}
```

As you can see, the LOAD DATA statement includes a number of elements; however, relatively few of these elements are actually required. The following syntax shows the bare-bones components that make up a basic LOAD DATA statement:

```
LOAD DATA INFILE '<filename>'
INTO TABLE <table name>
```

At the very least, you must specify two clauses: the LOAD DATA clause, which takes a filename as an argument, and the INTO TABLE clause, which takes a table name as an argument. The syntax demonstrates how simple the LOAD DATA statement can be. The statement can include a number of optional elements, however, so take a look at each line of the full syntax so that you have a complete picture of how the LOAD DATA statement works.

The first line of syntax is as follows:

```
LOAD DATA [LOW_PRIORITY | CONCURRENT] [LOCAL] INFILE '<filename>'
```

As the syntax shows, you must start with the LOAD DATA keywords, which introduce the LOAD DATA clause. The keywords are followed by the LOW_PRIORITY and CONCURRENT options. You can specify only one of the options. Use LOW_PRIORTY if you want to wait to load the data into the table until no clients are reading from the table. Use CONCURRENT (for MyISAM tables only) if you want to permit clients to retrieve data while rows are being added to the table.

By default, the LOAD DATA statement retrieves data from files stored on the MySQL server host. If you are accessing MySQL from that host, then the file is read from the local location. If you're accessing MySQL from a client computer and the target file is located on that computer, you can specify the LOCAL keyword to direct MySQL to look for the file on the client computer rather than the server host.

Once you specify any option that you want to include in the LOAD DATA clause, you must specify the INFILE keyword, followed by the name of the target file, enclosed in single quotes. If only a filename is specified, and no directory path, MySQL looks for the file in the folder associated with the current database (which is located in the data directory). You can also specify a full path, in which case MySQL looks in the specified location for the file.

The next set of options that you can add to your LOAD DATA statement is shown in the following syntax:

```
[REPLACE | IGNORE]
```

The two options refer to values that are duplicated in a unique index when you try to insert data. If neither option is specified, you receive an error if you try to insert a row in which a value in a unique index would be duplicated. You can override this behavior by using one of the two options. Use the REPLACE option if you want to replace the existing rows with new rows. Use the IGNORE option if you do not want to replace the existing rows, but you do want the insert process to continue.

If you specify the LOCAL option, file transmission cannot be interrupted. As a result, the default behavior is the same as if the IGNORE option were specified.

Next in the LOAD DATA syntax is the following INTO TABLE clause:

```
INTO TABLE <table name>
```

As you can see, this clause requires only that you specify the name of the table to which data will be added. After the INTO TABLE clause, you can specify one or two import options, as shown in the following syntax:

```
[<import option> [<import option>]]

<import option>::=
{FIELDS
   [TERMINATED BY '<value>']
   [[OPTIONALLY] ENCLOSED BY '<value>']
   [ESCAPED BY '<value>']}
| {LINES
   [STARTING BY '<value>']
   [TERMINATED BY '<value>']}
```

No doubt, much of this syntax looks familiar to you. The import options of the LOAD DATA statement work just like the export options in a SELECT statement. You can specify a FIELDS clause, a LINES clause, or both. If you specify both, you must specify the FIELDS clause before the LINES clause. In addition, you must include at least one subclause for each clause you include.

The subclauses in the FIELDS and LINES clauses use the same defaults as are used when exporting data. As a result, if you use the default values when you export a file, you can use the default values when you import a file. If you're importing files that are generated outside MySQL, you can use the FIELDS and LINES subclauses as appropriate to match how the target files have been formatted. (Refer back to the section "Exporting Data to an Out File" for more information on the FIELDS and LINES clauses and their subclauses.)

For text files created in some Windows applications, you might find that you have to specify the LINES TERMINATED BY '\r\n' subclause in a LOAD DATA statement in which you would normally use the default setting because of the way that those applications handle new lines.

The next optional component of the LOAD DATA statement is the IGNORE clause, which is shown in the following syntax:

```
[IGNORE <number> LINES]
```

The IGNORE clause allows you to specify that a certain number of rows are ignored when the values are added to the table. The rows discarded are the first ones to be returned by the LOAD DATA statement. For example, if you specify IGNORE 10 LINES, the first 10 rows are ignored, and the rest of the data is added to the table.

After the IGNORE clause, you can specify one or more columns from the target table, as shown in the following syntax:

```
[(<column name> [{, <column name>}...])]
```

As you can see, if more than one column name is included, they must be separated by commas. If you specify column names, each row returned by the LOAD DATA statement must include one value for each specified column. If you don't specify any column names, each row returned must include one value for each column in the table.

Now take a look at a couple of examples of how the LOAD DATA statement works. These examples are based on the CDs table used in earlier examples and the CDs3 table, which is shown in the following table definition:

```
CREATE TABLE CDs3
(
    CDName VARCHAR(50) NOT NULL,
    InStock SMALLINT UNSIGNED NOT NULL,
    Category VARCHAR(20)
);
```

For the purposes of these examples, assume that data has been exported out of the CDs table by using the following SELECT statement:

```
SELECT CDName, InStock, Category INTO OUTFILE 'CDsBlues.sql'
FROM CDs WHERE Category='Blues';
```

Now suppose that you want to import data from the CDsBlues.sql file. To do so, you can use the following LOAD DATA statement:

```
LOAD DATA INFILE 'CDsBlues.sql'
INTO TABLE CDs3;
```

As you can see, the statement includes only the required components. The LOAD DATA clause includes the INFILE keyword and the filename, and the INTO TABLE clause includes the table name. Once you execute this statement, you can use the following SELECT statement to view the contents of the CDs3 table:

```
SELECT * FROM CDs3;
```

The statement should return a result set similar to the following:

```
+----------------------+---------+----------+
| CDName               | InStock | Category |
+----------------------+---------+----------+
| Mississippi Blues    |       2 | Blues    |
| Richland Woman Blues |      22 | Blues    |
| Stages               |      42 | Blues    |
+----------------------+---------+----------+
3 rows in set (0.00 sec)
```

The CDs3 table now contains the data that was first exported to the CDsBlues.sql file and then imported from the file.

> *Be sure that each row in the file that contains the data to be imported includes the correct number of values. The number of values should match the number of columns, and the values should be of a type compatible with the columns. If you try to insert too few or too many values per row, you will receive undesired results. MySQL attempts to insert the data in the order that it appears in the files. For example, if your file includes three values per row and your table includes five columns, MySQL attempts to place the first three values in the first three columns in the order that the values are specified, and no values are inserted in the remaining two columns. If a value cannot be inserted in a targeted column, the value is truncated or ignored.*

The next example to examine uses data from the CDsCountry.sql file, which has been created by using the following SELECT statement:

```
SELECT CDName, InStock, Category INTO OUTFILE 'CDsCountry.sql'
    FIELDS
        TERMINATED BY ','
        ENCLOSED BY '"'
FROM CDs WHERE Category='Country';
```

Notice that the values are separated by a comma and enclosed by double quotes. As a result, you need to specify these characters when you import the data, as shown in the following LOAD DATA statement:

```
LOAD DATA INFILE 'CDsCountry.sql'
INTO TABLE CDs3
FIELDS
    TERMINATED BY ','
    ENCLOSED BY '"';
```

The statement contains the same required elements contained in the previous LOAD DATA example; however, the new statement also contains a FIELDS clause that specifies two subclauses. The subclauses are used because the values in the targeted file are separated with commas and enclosed in double quotes.

If, after running the LOAD DATA statement, you were to use a SELECT statement to retrieve all the content that is now contained in the CDs3 table, you would see a result set similar to the following:

```
+----------------------+---------+----------+
| CDName               | InStock | Category |
+----------------------+---------+----------+
| Mississippi Blues    |       2 | Blues    |
| Richland Woman Blues |      22 | Blues    |
| Stages               |      42 | Blues    |
| Ain't Ever Satisfied |      23 | Country  |
| Mud on the Tires     |      12 | Country  |
+----------------------+---------+----------+
5 rows in set (0.01 sec)
```

As you can see, two new rows have been added to the CDs3 table.

This Try It Out exercise has you import data into the DVDs2 table that you created in an earlier Try It Out section. You import data from files that you created when you exported data from the DVDRentals database.

Try It Out   **Using the LOAD DATA Statement to Import Data into the DVDRentals Database**

The following steps describe how to import the data:

1. Open the mysql client utility, type the following command, and press Enter:

```
use DVDRentals
```

You should receive a message indicating that you switched to the DVDRentals database.

2. First, you should remove the data currently stored in the DVDs2 table. Execute the following SQL statement at the mysql command prompt:

```
TRUNCATE DVDs2;
```

You should receive a message indicating that your query executed successfully, affecting no rows.

3. Now import data from the AvailDVDs.txt file into the DVDs2 table. Execute the following SQL statement at the mysql command prompt:

```
LOAD DATA INFILE 'AvailDVDs.txt'
INTO TABLE DVDs2;
```

You should receive a message indicating that your query executed successfully, affecting five rows.

4. Your next step is to view the contents of the DVDs2 table. Execute the following SQL statement at the mysql command prompt:

```
SELECT * from DVDs2;
```

You should receive results similar to the following:

```
+------------------------------+--------------+-------------+----------+
| DVDName                      | MTypeDescrip | FormDescrip | RatingID |
+------------------------------+--------------+-------------+----------+
| Amadeus                      | Drama        | Widescreen  | PG       |
| Mash                         | Comedy       | Widescreen  | R        |
| The Maltese Falcon           | Drama        | Widescreen  | NR       |
| The Rocky Horror Picture Show| Comedy       | Widescreen  | NR       |
| What's Up, Doc?              | Comedy       | Widescreen  | G        |
+------------------------------+--------------+-------------+----------+
5 rows in set (0.00 sec)
```

5. In order to try out another LOAD DATA statement, you should delete the records from the DVDs2 table once more. Execute the following SQL statement at the mysql command prompt:

```
TRUNCATE DVDs2;
```

You should receive a message indicating that your query executed successfully, affecting no rows.

6. Next, import data from the AvailDVDs2.txt file into the DVDs2 table. Execute the following SQL statement at the mysql command prompt:

```
LOAD DATA INFILE 'AvailDVDs2.txt'
INTO TABLE DVDs2
FIELDS TERMINATED BY '*,*'
LINES TERMINATED BY '**\n';
```

You should receive a message indicating that your query executed successfully, affecting five rows.

7. Once more, you should view the contents of the DVDs2 table. Execute the following SQL statement at the mysql command prompt:

```
SELECT * from DVDs2;
```

You should receive the same results as you received in Step 4.

How It Works

The first LOAD DATA statement that you created includes only the required elements:

```
LOAD DATA INFILE 'AvailDVDs.txt'
INTO TABLE DVDs2;
```

The LOAD DATA clause includes the INFILE keyword and the name of the file (AvailDVDs.txt) that contains the data to be imported. The INTO TABLE clause contains the name of the table (DVDs2) in which data from the file is added. Because data had been exported to the file by using default formatting values, no FIELDS or LINES clause is required. The next statement that you created, however, required both clauses:

```
LOAD DATA INFILE 'AvailDVDs2.txt'
INTO TABLE DVDs2
FIELDS TERMINATED BY '*,*'
LINES TERMINATED BY '**\n';
```

The statement includes the required elements plus the optional FIELDS and LINES clauses. The FIELDS TERMINATED BY subclause specifies that the values in each row (in the AvailDVDs2.txt file) are separated by an asterisk, a comma, and another asterisk (*,*). The LINES TERMINATED BY subclause specifies that the rows are terminated by double asterisks and a newline symbol (**\n).

Using the source Command to Import Data

You can use the source command at the mysql command prompt to run SQL statements and commands that are stored in a text file. To use the source command, you need only to specify the path and filename of the file that contains the statements and command. For example, assume that you have created a file named CDsJazz.sql and added the following SQL statement to the file:

```
INSERT INTO CDs3
VALUES ('New Orleans Jazz', 17, 'Jazz'),
('Live in Paris', 18, 'Jazz');
```

As you can see, the file adds values to the CDs3 table, which is the table used in the examples in the last section. You can specify multiple statements and commands in a file, as long as each statement and command is terminated by a semi-colon so that MySQL knows where one ends and the other begins.

Once your text file is created, you can use the `source` command to run the statements and commands in the file, as shown in the following example:

```
source c:\program files\mysql\mysql server 4.1\data\test\CDsJazz.sql
```

As you can see, you need to specify only the `source` command and the path and filename. When you run this command, the SQL statements and MySQL commands in the file are executed. You can also use the following convention to use the source command:

```
\. c:\program files\mysql\mysql server 4.1\data\test\CDsJazz.sql
```

In this case, the backslash and period (\ .) replace the word source, but the path and filename are still specified. Once you run the `source` command, you can verify the results by using a SELECT statement to retrieve all the contents from the CDs3 table, which should be similar to the following:

```
+----------------------+---------+----------+
| CDName               | InStock | Category |
+----------------------+---------+----------+
| Mississippi Blues    |       2 | Blues    |
| Richland Woman Blues |      22 | Blues    |
| Stages               |      42 | Blues    |
| Ain't Ever Satisfied |      23 | Country  |
| Mud on the Tires     |      12 | Country  |
| Live in Paris        |      18 | Jazz     |
| New Orleans Jazz     |      17 | Jazz     |
+----------------------+---------+----------+
7 rows in set (0.00 sec)
```

As you can see, the new rows have been added to the CDs3 table.

In the following exercise, you try out the `source` command to add data to the DVDs2 table that you created in an earlier Try It Out section.

Try It Out   **Using the source Command to Import Data into the DVDRentals Database**

To try out the `source` command, you should first create a text file that contains the necessary INSERT statement. The following steps describe how to test the `source` command:

1. Create a text file in a text editor (such as Notepad) and name it DVD_1.sql. Add the following statement to the file, and save the file in the DVDRentals folder of your data directory:

```
INSERT INTO DVDs2
VALUES ('A Room with a View', 'Drama', 'Widescreen', 'NR');
```

2. Open the mysql client utility, type the following command, and press Enter:

```
use DVDRentals
```

You should receive a message indicating that you switched to the DVDRentals database.

3. Next, use the `source` command to execute the `INSERT` statement in the DVD_1.sql file. Execute the following command at the mysql command prompt:

```
source <path>DVD_1.sql
```

The `<path>` placeholder refers to the DVDRentals folder in your data directory, which is where the text file should be stored. Be sure to enter the entire path, followed by the filename. When you execute the command, you should receive a message indicating that the command executed successfully and that one row was affected.

4. Now you should view the contents of the DVDs2 table. Execute the following SQL statement at the mysql command prompt:

```
SELECT * FROM DVDs2;
```

You should receive results similar to the following:

```
+-----------------------------+--------------+------------+----------+
| DVDName                     | MTypeDescrip | FormDescrip | RatingID |
+-----------------------------+--------------+------------+----------+
| Amadeus                     | Drama        | Widescreen | PG       |
| Mash                        | Comedy       | Widescreen | R        |
| The Maltese Falcon          | Drama        | Widescreen | NR       |
| The Rocky Horror Picture Show | Comedy     | Widescreen | NR       |
| What's Up, Doc?             | Comedy       | Widescreen | G        |
| A Room with a View          | Drama        | Widescreen | NR       |
+-----------------------------+--------------+------------+----------+
6 rows in set (0.00 sec)
```

How It Works

After you created a text file that contains an `INSERT` statement, you used the following `source` command to retrieve data from that file:

```
source <path>DVD_1.sql
```

As you can see, the command required only the `source` keyword, followed by a path and filename. When you ran this command, the `INSERT` statement in the DVD_1.sql file was executed and data was added to the DVDs2 table.

Using the mysql Command to Import Data

You can also use the `mysql` command at your operating system's command prompt to execute SQL statements and mysql commands in a text file. To do so, you must enter the `mysql` command, followed by the name of the database, the less than (<) symbol, and the path and filename of the file that contains the statements and command.

Take a look at an example to demonstrate how this works. For this example, assume that a file named CDsRock.sql has been created and that the following `INSERT` statement has been added to the file.

```
INSERT INTO CDs3
VALUES ('Bloodshot', 10, 'Rock');
```

You can now exit the mysql client utility and execute that statement from your operating system's command prompt. For example, the following command executes the INSERT statement in the CDsRock.sql file:

```
mysql test < "c:\program files\mysql\mysql server 4.1\data\test\CDsRock.sql"
```

When specifying a path and filename in a MySQL command at your operating system's command prompt, you must enclose the path and filename in double quotes if either name contains spaces. For example, in the preceding command, the pathname includes spaces in the Program Files directory and the MySQL Server 4.1 directory.

As the statement shows, you must first specify the mysql command and then specify the database (test), the less than (<) symbol, and the path and filename (c:\program files\mysql\mysql server 4.1\data\test\CDsRock.sql). Once you run the mysql command statement, you can run a SELECT statement to retrieve the contents of the CDs3 table in order to verify that the command executed successfully. Your SELECT statement should return a result set similar to the following:

```
+----------------------+---------+----------+
| CDName               | InStock | Category |
+----------------------+---------+----------+
| Mississippi Blues    |       2 | Blues    |
| Richland Woman Blues |      22 | Blues    |
| Stages               |      42 | Blues    |
| Ain't Ever Satisfied |      23 | Country  |
| Mud on the Tires     |      12 | Country  |
| Live in Paris        |      18 | Jazz     |
| New Orleans Jazz     |      17 | Jazz     |
| Bloodshot            |      10 | Rock     |
+----------------------+---------+----------+
8 rows in set (0.00 sec)
```

Notice that the new row has been added to the CDs3 table.

Now that you've learned how to import data at your operating system's command prompt, you can try it out. In this exercise, you create a text file that includes an INSERT statement; then you use the mysql command to run that statement.

Try It Out   Using the mysql Command to Import Data into the DVDRentals Database

Follow these steps to test the mysql command:

1. Open the mysql client utility, type the following command, and press Enter:

```
use DVDRentals
```

You should receive a message indicating that you switched to the DVDRentals database.

2. Create a text file in a text editor (such as Notepad), and name it DVD_2.sql. Add the following statement to the file, and save the file in the DVDRentals folder of your data directory:

```
INSERT INTO DVDs2
VALUES ('Out of Africa', 'Drama', 'Widescreen', 'PG');
```

3. At your operating system's command prompt, execute the following command:

```
mysql dvdrentals < <path>DVD_2.sql
```

The *<path>* placeholder refers to the DVDRentals folder in your data directory, which is where the text file should be stored. Be sure to enter the entire path, followed by the filename.

4. Open the mysql client utility, type the following command, and press Enter:

```
use DVDRentals
```

You should receive a message indicating that you switched to the DVDRentals database.

5. Next, view the contents of the DVDs2 table. Execute the following SQL statement at the mysql command prompt:

```
SELECT * FROM DVDs2;
```

You should receive results similar to the following:

```
+-------------------------------+--------------+-------------+----------+
| DVDName                       | MTypeDescrip | FormDescrip | RatingID |
+-------------------------------+--------------+-------------+----------+
| Amadeus                       | Drama        | Widescreen  | PG       |
| Mash                          | Comedy       | Widescreen  | R        |
| The Maltese Falcon            | Drama        | Widescreen  | NR       |
| The Rocky Horror Picture Show | Comedy       | Widescreen  | NR       |
| What's Up, Doc?               | Comedy       | Widescreen  | G        |
| A Room with a View            | Drama        | Widescreen  | NR       |
| Out of Africa                 | Drama        | Widescreen  | PG       |
+-------------------------------+--------------+-------------+----------+
7 rows in set (0.00 sec)
```

How It Works

In this exercise, you first created a text file that includes an INSERT statement. The statement adds a row of data to the DVDs2 table in the DVDRentals database. Once the file was created, you executed the following mysql command statement:

```
mysql dvdrentals < <path>DVD_2.sql
```

In the command, you specified the mysql command, followed by the name of the DVDRentals database. After the database name, you added a less than (<) symbol and then the path and filename. When you executed the command, the INSERT statement in the DVD_2.sql file was executed and a row was added to the DVDs2 table.

Using the mysqlimport Utility to Import Data

MySQL includes a utility that allows you to import delimited data in a text file, without having to launch the mysql client utility. The mysqlimport utility supports many of the same functions as the LOAD DATA statement. To use the mysqlimport utility, you must specify the mysqlimport command, followed by any options that you want to include. Next, you must specify the name of the database and the path and filename of the file that contains the data to be inserted.

The mysqlimport command statement does not include the name of the target table. Instead, the table is determined by the name of the file. MySQL assumes that the filename will be the same as the table name (not counting any file extensions). For example, if you're inserting data in the Authors table, the file must be named Authors.txt, Authors.sql, or something similar to that.

Now take a look at a couple of examples that demonstrate how this works. The first example imports data from a file named CDs3.sql, which has been created by using the following SELECT statement:

```
SELECT CDName, InStock, Category INTO OUTFILE 'CDs3.sql'
FROM CDs WHERE Category='New Age';
```

Notice that the name of the file, not including the extension, is CDs3. As a result, you can insert data only in a table named CDs3, as shown in the following example:

```
mysqlimport --user=root --password=pw1 test "c:\program files\mysql\mysql server
4.1\data\test\CDs3.sql"
```

In this command statement (which is run from your operating system's command prompt), the mysqlimport command is specified, followed by the optional --user and --password arguments. After the arguments comes the name of the table (test) and the path and filename (c:\program files\mysql\mysql server 4.1\data\test\CDs3.sql). The user and password that are provided in the command statement are those that you would normally use when you access the MySQL databases.

You can verify whether the data has been successfully added to the table by starting the mysql client utility and running a SELECT statement that retrieves the contents of the CDs3 table. The SELECT statement should retrieve a result set similar to the following:

```
+----------------------+---------+----------+
| CDName               | InStock | Category |
+----------------------+---------+----------+
| Mississippi Blues    |       2 | Blues    |
| Richland Woman Blues |      22 | Blues    |
| Stages               |      42 | Blues    |
| Ain't Ever Satisfied |      23 | Country  |
| Mud on the Tires     |      12 | Country  |
| Live in Paris        |      18 | Jazz     |
| New Orleans Jazz     |      17 | Jazz     |
| Bloodshot            |      10 | Rock     |
| The Essence          |       5 | New Age  |
+----------------------+---------+----------+
9 rows in set (0.00 sec)
```

As the result set shows, a New Age row has been added to the table.

Now take a look at another example. This time, when the CDs3 file is created, a FIELDS clause is included in the export definition:

```
SELECT CDName, InStock, Category INTO OUTFILE 'CDs3.sql'
    FIELDS
        TERMINATED BY ','
        ENCLOSED BY '*'
FROM CDs WHERE Category='Classical';
```

Remember, you cannot create an out file that already exists. If one does exist, rename the old file or delete it.

As the statement shows, the values are now separated by a comma and enclosed by asterisks. As a result, when you run the mysqlimport command, you must specify these formatting characters in the command statement, as shown in this example:

```
mysqlimport --user=root --password=pw1 --fields-terminated-by="," --fields-
enclosed-by="*" test "c:\program files\mysql\mysql server 4.1\data\test\CDs3.sql"
```

As you can see, two more arguments have been added to the command statement: --fields-terminated-by="," and --fields-enclosed-by="*". The mysqlimport utility supports arguments that are counterparts to the FIELDS and LINES subclauses of a LOAD DATA statement. For example, the FIELDS TERMINATED BY subclause in the LOAD DATA statement is the same as the --fields-terminated-by argument in the mysql import utility. Each of the FIELDS and LINES subclauses follows the same format. (For details on all the mysqlimport arguments, see the MySQL product documentation.)

Now if you were to retrieve data from the CDs3 table, your result set would include Classical CDs, so you should receive results similar to the following:

```
+------------------------+---------+-----------+
| CDName                 | InStock | Category  |
+------------------------+---------+-----------+
| Mississippi Blues      |       2 | Blues     |
| Richland Woman Blues   |      22 | Blues     |
| Stages                 |      42 | Blues     |
| Ain't Ever Satisfied   |      23 | Country   |
| Mud on the Tires       |      12 | Country   |
| Live in Paris          |      18 | Jazz      |
| New Orleans Jazz       |      17 | Jazz      |
| Bloodshot              |      10 | Rock      |
| The Essence            |       5 | New Age   |
| Music for Ballet Class |       9 | Classical |
| The Magic of Satie     |      42 | Classical |
+------------------------+---------+-----------+
11 rows in set (0.00 sec)
```

In this Try It Out exercise, you use a SELECT statement to export data to the DVDs2.txt file. You then use the mysqlimport command to add data to the DVDs2 table.

Try It Out   Using the mysqlimport Utility to Import Data into the DVDRentals Database

The following steps describe how to carry out these tasks:

1. Open the mysql client utility, type the following command, and press Enter:

```
use DVDRentals
```

You should receive a message indicating that you switched to the DVDRentals database.

2. Create a text file in a text editor (such as Notepad) and name it DVDs2.txt. Add the following statement to the file and save the file in the DVDRentals folder of your data directory:

```
SELECT DVDName, MTypeDescrip, FormDescrip, d.RatingID
   INTO OUTFILE 'DVDs2.txt'
FROM DVDs AS d, MovieTypes AS m, Formats AS f
WHERE d.MTypeID=m.MTypeID AND d.FormID=f.FormID
   AND DVDID=1;
```

You should receive a message indicating that the statement executed successfully, affecting one row.

3. Type the following command at the mysql command prompt, and press Enter:

```
exit
```

You are returned to your operating system's command prompt.

4. At your operating system's command prompt, execute the following command:

```
mysqlimport --user=root --password=pw1 dvdrentals <path>DVDs2.txt
```

The *<path>* placeholder refers to the DVDRentals folder in your data directory, which is where the text file should be stored. Be sure to enter the entire path, followed by the filename. If your pathname includes spaces, be sure to enclose the entire path and filename in double quotes. You should receive a message indicating that the one record in the DVDs2 table of the DVDRentals database has been affected.

5. Open the mysql client utility, type the following command, and press Enter:

```
use DVDRentals
```

You should receive a message indicating that you switched to the DVDRentals database.

6. Now view the contents of the DVDs2 table to verify that the data has been added. Execute the following SQL statement at the mysql command prompt:

```
SELECT * FROM DVDs2;
```

You should receive results similar to the following:

```
+-----------------------------+--------------+-------------+----------+
| DVDName                     | MTypeDescrip | FormDescrip | RatingID |
+-----------------------------+--------------+-------------+----------+
| Amadeus                     | Drama        | Widescreen  | PG       |
| Mash                        | Comedy       | Widescreen  | R        |
| The Maltese Falcon          | Drama        | Widescreen  | NR       |
```

```
| The Rocky Horror Picture Show | Comedy     | Widescreen   | NR        |
| What's Up, Doc?               | Comedy     | Widescreen   | G         |
| A Room with a View            | Drama      | Widescreen   | NR        |
| Out of Africa                 | Drama      | Widescreen   | PG        |
| White Christmas               | Musical    | Widescreen   | NR        |
+-------------------------------+------------+--------------+----------+
8 rows in set (0.00 sec)
```

7. Finally, you should drop the DVDs2 table from the DVDRentals database. Execute the following SQL statement at the mysql command prompt:

```
DROP TABLE DVDs2;
```

You should receive a message indicating that the query executed successfully and that no rows were affected.

How It Works

In this exercise, you used a SELECT statement to join tables in the DVDRentals database and then export data retrieved by the statement to a file named DVDs2.sql. You then used the mysqlimport utility to import data from the file into the DVDs2 table, as shown in the following statement:

```
mysqlimport --user=root --password=pw1 dvdrentals <path>DVDs2.txt
```

In this command statement, you specified the mysqlimport command and the --user and --password arguments. The user (root) and password (pw1) are the user and password that you use to launch the mysql client utility. (These are the values that should be stored in your configuration file.) After you defined the two arguments, you specified the name of the DVDRentals database and the path and file-name that contained the data to be imported. When you ran the mysqlimport command, the values in the DVDs2.sql file were added to the DVDs2 table. MySQL inserted the values in the table with the same name as the file.

Summary

As the chapter has demonstrated, MySQL provides a number of SQL statements and commands that allow you to export, copy, and import data in a database. As a result, you can work with large quantities of data that can be copied between tables in the database or copied to or from files outside the database. In this chapter, you learned how to use the following SQL statements and MySQL commands to export, copy, and import data:

❑ The SELECT statement, in order to export data into out files and dump files

❑ The CREATE TABLE statement, in order to copy data into a new table as you're creating that table

❑ The INSERT statement, in order to copy data into an existing table

❑ The REPLACE statement, in order to copy data into an existing table

❑ The LOAD DATA statement, in order to import data into a table

❑ The source, mysql, and mysqlimport commands, in order to import data into a table

Being able to import and export data is particularly useful when working with other applications or database products that require the exchange of data. For example, suppose that you want to import data from a database other than MySQL. To do so, you can simply export the data out of the other database into text files and then import the data into the MySQL database from the text files. Nearly any data that can be saved to text files and clearly delimited can be imported into MySQL, and any application or database product that can import data from a text file can import data from MySQL. As a result, you can easily manage large quantities of data from different data sources. In Chapter 12, you learn how to manage transactions to ensure safe data access by multiple users, as well as how to use transactions to manage the execution of SQL statements.

Exercises

For these exercises, you use SQL statements and MySQL commands to export, copy, and import data. The statements and commands are based on the Produce table in the test database. The Produce table is based on the following table definition:

```
CREATE TABLE Produce
(
    ProdID SMALLINT UNSIGNED NOT NULL PRIMARY KEY,
    ProdName VARCHAR(40) NOT NULL,
    Variety VARCHAR(40) NULL,
    InStock SMALLINT UNSIGNED NOT NULL
);
```

You can assume that the following INSERT statement has populated the Produce table:

```
INSERT INTO Produce
VALUES (101, 'Apples', 'Red Delicious', 2000),
(102, 'Apples', 'Fuji', 1500),
(103, 'Apples', 'Golden Delicious', 500),
(104, 'Apples', 'Granny Smith', 300),
(105, 'Oranges', 'Valencia', 1200),
(106, 'Oranges', 'Seville', 1300),
(107, 'Cherries', 'Bing', 2500),
(108, 'Cherries', 'Rainier', 1500),
(109, 'Mushrooms', 'Shitake', 800),
(110, 'Mushrooms', 'Porcini', 400),
(111, 'Mushrooms', 'Portobello', 900);
```

Use the Produce table to complete the following exercises. You can find the answers to these exercises in Appendix A.

1. Create an SQL statement that exports data from the Produce table to a text file named Apples.txt. The file should be saved to the folder associated with the test database. The rows exported should include only the ProdName, Variety, and InStock columns and only those rows that contain a ProdName value of Apples. The exported data should be copied to the text file in a default format.

2. Create an SQL statement that exports data from the Produce table to a text file named Oranges.txt. The file should be saved to the folder associated with the test database. The rows exported should include only the ProdName, Variety, and InStock columns and only those rows that contain a ProdName value of Oranges. The exported data should be copied to the text file in a default format, except that the fields should be terminated by a comma (,) and should be enclosed by an asterisk (*).

3. Create an SQL statement that creates a table named Produce2. The table should be identical to the Produce table, except that it should not include the ProdID column. When creating the table, copy data from the Produce table to the Produce2 table. The copied data should include only the ProdName, Variety, and InStock columns and only those rows that contain a ProdName value of Cherries.

4. Create an SQL statement that adds data to the Produce2 table that you created in Step 3. The data should be made up of ProdName, Variety, and InStock values from the Produce table. In addition, the data should include only those rows that contain a ProdName value of Mushrooms.

5. Create an SQL statement that adds data to the Produce2 table that you created in Step 3. The data should be retrieved from the Apples.txt file that you created in Step 1.

6. Create an SQL statement that adds data to the Produce2 table that you created in Step 3. The data should be retrieved from the Oranges.txt file that you created in Step 2.

Managing Transactions

As you have worked your way through this book, you have executed a number of SQL statements that have performed various actions in your MySQL database. The statements were executed interactively in an isolated environment in which you ran one statement at a time, without competing for data access with other users or connections. As a result, you continuously maintained control over the database, the tables in the database, and the data in those tables.

In the real world, databases seldom exist in an isolated state, nor is access limited to one user working interactively with the database. In fact, numerous applications and users attempting to access and manipulate data at the same time often share databases. As a result, MySQL supports the use of transactions to ensure safe data access by multiple users. In this chapter, you learn how to use transactions to manage the execution of SQL statements. Specifically, this chapter covers the following topics:

- ❑ Understanding what a transaction is and the characteristics of a transaction
- ❑ Performing basic transactions and adding savepoints to your transactions
- ❑ Setting the autocommit mode for your session and setting the transaction isolation levels
- ❑ Locking and unlocking nontransactional tables

Introducing Transactions

When developing an application that accesses data in a MySQL database, you must take into account whether multiple users will attempt to view and modify data at the same time. If users try to perform these operations simultaneously, the result can be data that is inconsistent and inaccurate. To avoid these types of problems, you can use transactions to isolate each operation in order to ensure the accuracy and consistency of data.

In the context of SQL and relational databases, a *transaction* is a set of one or more SQL statements that perform a set of related actions. The statements are grouped together and treated as a single unit whose success or failure depends on the successful execution of each statement in the transaction. For example, suppose that you have a database that supports the online sale of compact disks. The database includes the Inventory table, which tracks the number of CDs in stock, and the Sales table, which tracks each CD sale. Every time a CD sells, it must be added to the Sales table and subtracted from the Inventory table. Both actions should be performed as a unit to ensure that the data in the tables is accurate. By placing the necessary statements in a transaction, each action must be executed successfully in order for any data to be modified; otherwise, all statements are rolled back and the database remains unchanged. In other words, if the UPDATE statement is executed successfully, but the INSERT statement is not, all changes to the databases are undone and the data is returned to its original state at the beginning of the transaction.

In addition to ensuring the proper execution of a set of SQL statements, a transaction locks the tables involved in the transaction so that other users cannot modify any rows that are involved in the transaction. For example, suppose you have an application that does not use transactions, and two users attempt to purchase the same CD, but there is only one in stock. When the first user initiates the sale, an INSERT statement is issued against the Sales table to add the CD order to the table. The application then experiences a delay before trying to issue an UPDATE statement against the Inventory table to subtract the CD from the inventory. Between the time when the INSERT statement is executed and the UPDATE statement is waiting to be executed, a second user initiates a sale for the same CD. As a result, a second INSERT statement is issued against the Sales table for that CD, and a second UPDATE statement is issued against the Inventory table, subtracting that CD from the inventory before the first user completes the order process.

The first user then attempts to complete the order process by issuing an UPDATE statement against the Inventory table. Depending on how the Inventory table is configured, the UPDATE statement issued by the first user either fails or the number of CDs is changed to a negative number (-1), and an order now exists in the Sales table for a CD that doesn't exist. If the application were to use transactions, the rows involved in the first transaction would have been locked, so the second transaction could not have been initiated until the first transaction had completed. As a result, the second user could not have completed an order for a CD that was already spoken for.

In order for an operation in a relational database to qualify as a transaction, it must pass what is referred to as the *ACID* test. ACID is an acronym for the four properties that describe a transaction — atomic, consistent, isolated, and durable — which are described here:

❑ **Atomic:** The statements in a transaction are treated as a single unit. Either all the designated operations are performed, or none are performed. Only when all operations are performed successfully are the results of that transaction applied to the database.

❑ **Consistent:** Each transaction must leave the database in the same consistent state that it was in at the beginning of the transaction. Even if only some of the statements are executed and the transaction fails before it is completed, the database should end up in a consistent state. In other words, the transaction cannot do anything to the database that would cause data to be inaccurate or inconsistent.

❑ **Isolated:** A transaction must be isolated from other transactions so that no users outside the transaction can access data that becomes temporarily inconsistent during the execution of the transaction. In other words, no transaction can affect another transaction.

❑ **Durable:** Once any changes that result from a transaction are committed to the database, those changes must be preserved permanently in the database, despite any hardware or software errors that might occur.

MySQL supports transactions for only two table types: InnoDB and BDB. All other MySQL table types are considered nontransactional. Considering that an InnoDB table is the only type that supports full foreign key functionality, it is clearly the best choice for the transactional-safe relational database.

Performing a Transaction

Now that you have a basic overview of the characteristics of a transaction, take a look at how you actually implement a transaction. In this section, you first look at how to create a basic transaction that isolates SQL statements as a unit in the context of that transaction. From there, you learn how to add savepoints to your transaction. A *savepoint* is marker that indicates where a rollback point exists in a transaction, allowing you to roll back a specific portion of your transaction to that savepoint, rather than rolling back the entire transaction.

In order to demonstrate the concepts described in this section, use the Books table. The definition for this table is slightly different from what you've seen previously in this book, as the following table definition shows:

```
CREATE TABLE Books
(
    BookID SMALLINT NOT NULL PRIMARY KEY,
    BookTitle VARCHAR(60) NOT NULL,
    Copyright YEAR NOT NULL
)
ENGINE=INNODB;
```

As you can see, the table is configured as an InnoDB table, which together with BDB tables are the only tables that support transactions. Now take a look at how to create a basic transaction.

Performing a Basic Transaction

In a basic transaction, SQL statements are executed as a unit. If one of the statements fails, the entire transaction should be rolled back; otherwise, any changes made by the statements are saved to the database. To support the creation of a transaction, MySQL provides the START TRANSACTION, COMMIT, and ROLLBACK statements. The START TRANSACTION statement begins the transaction, the COMMIT statement commits changes to the database, and the ROLLBACK statement undoes any changes made by the statement and returns the database to the state it was in when the transaction began.

Normally the three transaction-related statements are used in conjunction with the conditional structure of a programming language that specifies what happens if an SQL statement returns a particular result. Figure 12-1 provides an overview of the logic used to create a basic transaction. The transaction-related statements are written in bold.

The transaction begins with the START TRANSACTION statement, which notifies MySQL that the statements that follow should be treated as a unit, until the transaction has been ended. The transaction then includes two INSERT statements. If those statements succeed, a COMMIT statement is issued and the changes are saved to the database. If either of the INSERT statements fails, then a ROLLBACK statement is issued, and the database is returned to its original state. Now examine the statements individually.

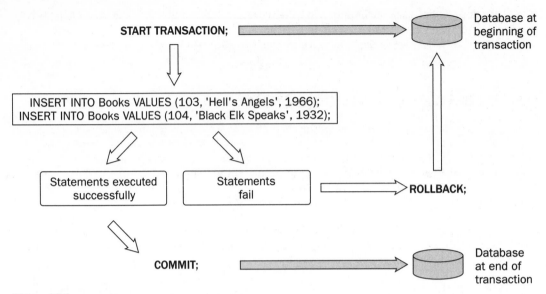

Figure 12-1

The START TRANSACTION Statement

The START TRANSACTION statement, shown in the following syntax, requires no clauses or options other than the START TRANSACTION keywords:

```
START TRANSACTION
```

As you can see, you simply specify START TRANSACTION. When the statement is executed, MySQL isolates any statements that follow in a transactional unit. The statements are treated as part of the transaction until the transaction is specifically committed to the database or until the transaction is rolled back, in which case no changes are committed to the database.

Note that you can use a BEGIN statement to start a transaction. The BEGIN statement is the same as START TRANSACTION and was at one time the only statement that you could use in MySQL to explicitly start a transaction.

The COMMIT Statement

The COMMIT statement is used to terminate a transaction and to save all changes made by the transaction to the database. The COMMIT statement, like the START TRANSACTION statement, includes no additional clauses or options, as shown in the following syntax:

```
COMMIT
```

As you can see, you merely specify the COMMIT keyword. For example, the following transaction includes two INSERT statements, followed by a COMMIT statement:

```
START TRANSACTION;
INSERT INTO Books VALUES (101, 'Letters to a Young Poet', 1934);
INSERT INTO Books VALUES (102, 'Winesburg, Ohio', 1919);
COMMIT;
```

In this example, the transaction is initiated by the use of the START TRANSACTION statement. Two INSERT statements are then executed, followed by a COMMIT statement. Assuming that both INSERT statements are executed successfully, the COMMIT statement saves the changes to the database, and the rows are added to the Books table. You can use the following SELECT statement to verify that the rows have been added:

```
SELECT * FROM BOOKS;
```

The SELECT statement should return results similar to the following:

```
+--------+------------------------+-----------+
| BookID | BookTitle              | Copyright |
+--------+------------------------+-----------+
|    101 | Letters to a Young Poet |     1934 |
|    102 | Winesburg, Ohio        |      1919 |
+--------+------------------------+-----------+
2 rows in set (0.04 sec)
```

The ROLLBACK Statement

In addition to using a COMMIT statement to terminate a transaction, you can use a ROLLBACK statement. Unlike the COMMIT statement, though, the ROLLBACK statement does not save any of the changes to the database. To roll back a transaction, you simply specify the ROLLBACK keyword, as shown in the following syntax:

```
ROLLBACK
```

As you can see, the ROLLBACK statement also takes no clauses or arguments. For example, the following transaction uses a ROLLBACK statement to undo the INSERT statements also included in the transaction:

```
START TRANSACTION;
INSERT INTO Books VALUES (103, 'Hell\'s Angels', 1966);
INSERT INTO Books VALUES (104, 'Black Elk Speaks', 1932);
ROLLBACK;
```

Now if you were to use a SELECT statement to view the contents of the Books table, you would find that the two new rows have not been added, as shown in the following result set:

```
+--------+------------------------+-----------+
| BookID | BookTitle              | Copyright |
+--------+------------------------+-----------+
|    101 | Letters to a Young Poet |     1934 |
|    102 | Winesburg, Ohio        |      1919 |
+--------+------------------------+-----------+
2 rows in set (0.04 sec)
```

As you can see, the ROLLBACK statement rolled back the changes made by the transaction's two INSERT statements.

If a transaction ends before it is explicitly terminated, which would happen if a connection is ended or if there is a hardware or software failure, the transaction is rolled back automatically.

Statements That Automatically Commit Transactions

MySQL includes a number of statements that should not be included in a transaction. If you issue one of these statements in a transaction, the statement automatically commits that transaction; then the statement itself is executed. The following list provides a brief description of the statements that should not be included in an expression:

- ❏ **ALTER TABLE:** Modifies a table definition.
- ❏ **CREATE INDEX:** Creates an index on a table.
- ❏ **DROP DATABASE:** Removes a database from a MySQL server.
- ❏ **DROP INDEX:** Removes an index on a table.
- ❏ **DROP TABLE:** Removes a table from a database.
- ❏ **LOCK TABLES:** Prevents concurrent access to tables.
- ❏ **RENAME TABLES:** Renames a table.
- ❏ **SET AUTOCOMMIT=1:** Sets the autocommit mode to on.
- ❏ **START TRANSACTION:** Begins a transaction.
- ❏ **TRUNCATE TABLE:** Removes data from a table.
- ❏ **UNLOCK TABLES:** Unlocks locked tables.

Issuing one of these statements has the same effect as issuing a COMMIT statement: The transaction is terminated, and all applicable changes are saved to the database. Only then is the statement executed. In addition, none of these statements can be rolled back.

Now that you've been introduced to the SQL statements that allow you to create a transaction, you can try out those statements in your own transactions. In this Try It Out exercise, you create two transactions. The first one you roll back, and the second one you commit.

Try It Out   Creating a Transaction

To create the transactions, follow these steps:

1. Open the mysql client utility, type the following command, and press Enter:

```
use DVDRentals
```

You should receive a message indicating that you switched to the DVDRentals database.

2. The first step is to begin your transaction. Execute the following SQL statement at the mysql command prompt:

```
START TRANSACTION;
```

You should receive a message indicating that the statement executed successfully, affecting no rows.

3. Now create an INSERT statement that adds a row to the Employees table. Execute the following SQL statement at the mysql command prompt:

```
INSERT INTO Employees
VALUES (NULL, 'Rebecca', 'T.', 'Reynolds');
```

You should receive a message indicating that the statement executed successfully and that the statement affected one row.

4. Next, roll back the INSERT statement that you created in the last step. Execute the following SQL statement at the mysql command prompt:

```
ROLLBACK;
```

You should receive a message indicating that the statement executed successfully, affecting no rows.

5. To verify that the INSERT statement has been rolled back, you should view a list of last names in the Employees table to ensure that Reynolds has not been added. Execute the following SQL statement at the mysql command prompt:

```
SELECT EmpLN FROM EMPLOYEES;
```

You should receive results similar to the following:

```
+-----------+
| EmpLN     |
+-----------+
| Smith     |
| Schroader |
| Michaels  |
| Laguci    |
| Carter    |
| Brooks    |
+-----------+
6 rows in set (0.00 sec)
```

6. Now start a second transaction. Execute the following SQL statement at the mysql command prompt:

```
START TRANSACTION;
```

You should receive a message indicating that the statement executed successfully and that the statement affected no rows.

7. Now attempt to add the same row to the Employees table that you tried to add in Step 3. Execute the following SQL statement at the mysql command prompt:

```
INSERT INTO Employees
VALUES (NULL, 'Rebecca', 'T.', 'Reynolds');
```

You should receive a message indicating that the statement executed successfully and that the statement affected one row.

8. Finally, you must commit your transaction so that the changes take effect. Execute the following SQL statement at the mysql command prompt:

```
COMMIT;
```

You should receive a message indicating that the statement executed successfully, affecting no rows.

9. To verify that the changes have been made to the table, execute the following SQL statement at the mysql command prompt:

```
SELECT EmpLN FROM EMPLOYEES;
```

You should receive results similar to the following:

```
+-----------+
| EmpLN     |
+-----------+
| Smith     |
| Schroader |
| Michaels  |
| Laguci    |
| Carter    |
| Brooks    |
| Reynolds  |
+-----------+
7 rows in set (0.00 sec)
```

10. Now you should delete the row that you added to the Employees table to return the table to its original state. Execute the following SQL statement at the mysql command prompt:

```
DELETE FROM Employees
WHERE EmpLN='Reynolds';
```

You should receive a message indicating that the statement executed successfully and that the statement affected one row.

How It Works

In this exercise, you created two transactions. To begin each transaction, you used the follow SQL statement:

```
START TRANSACTION;
```

By using the START TRANSACTION statement, you indicated to MySQL that any SQL statements that followed were part of the transaction, until the transaction was committed or rolled back. After you started the first transaction, you executed an INSERT statement that added a row of data to the Employees table. After you executed the statement, you used the following statement to roll back the statement:

```
ROLLBACK;
```

Because you used the ROLLBACK statement, the INSERT statement was rolled back and the database returned to its original state. In addition, the transaction was terminated. You then verified that the statement was rolled back by using a SELECT statement to retrieve data from the Employees table. You then started a second transaction by initiating another START TRANSACTION statement. From there, you executed the same INSERT statement a second time. In this case, though, you followed the INSERT statement with the following SQL statement:

```
COMMIT;
```

The COMMIT statement committed the changes to the database and ended the transaction. As a result, the new row was added to the Employees table, which you verified by using a SELECT statement.

Adding Savepoints to Your Transaction

Now that you know how to use the START TRANSACTION, COMMIT, and ROLLBACK statements to create a basic transaction, you're ready to use the SAVEPOINT and ROLLBACK TO SAVEPOINT statements to isolate portions of your transaction. The SAVEPOINT statement allows you to define a savepoint in a transaction, and the ROLLBACK TO SAVEPOINT statement allows you to roll back a transaction to a specified savepoint.

As with other transaction-related statements, SAVEPOINT and ROLLBACK TO SAVEPOINT statements are used in conjunction with the conditional structure of a programming language that specifies what happens if an SQL statement returns a particular result. In Figure 12-2, you can see an example of how a savepoint can be added to a transaction. As with any transaction, you should use the START TRANSACTION statement to start the statement, the ROLLBACK statement to terminate the transaction and roll back the database to its original state, and the COMMIT statement to commit changes to the database.

Figure 12-2 contains two elements that you did not see in Figure 12-1: the SAVEPOINT statement and the ROLLBACK TO SAVEPOINT statement. The SAVEPOINT statement is added to the transaction after the first two INSERT statements. If the statements are executed successfully, the savepoint is defined. If the statements fail, the database is rolled back to its original statement. Once the savepoint is defined, two more INSERT statements are executed. If the statements are executed successfully, the changes are committed to the database. If either of the INSERT statements fails, however, the database is rolled back to the savepoint, undoing the changes made by the second set of INSERT statements, but preserving the changes made by the first two INSERT statements. Any changes made before the savepoint are saved. Now take a closer look at the SAVEPOINT and ROLLBACK TO SAVEPOINT statements.

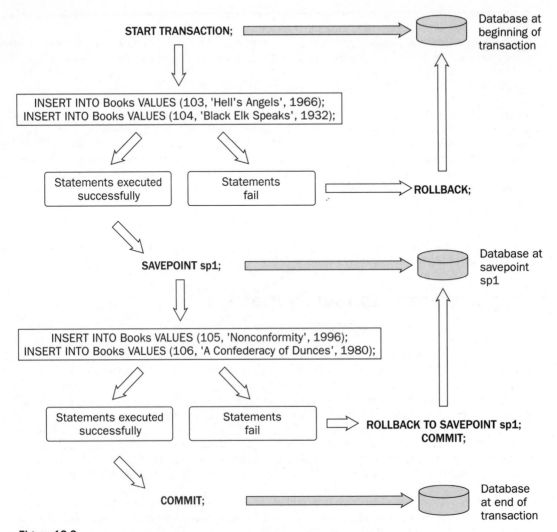

Figure 12-2

The SAVEPOINT Statement

You can add a savepoint anywhere in a transaction. When you roll back to that savepoint, any changes made to the database after the savepoint are discarded, and any changes made prior to the savepoint are saved. To create a savepoint, you must use the SAVEPOINT statement, which is shown in the following syntax:

```
SAVEPOINT <savepoint name>
```

As the syntax shows, when you create a savepoint, you must assign it a name. For example, the following set of statements shows the beginning of a transaction:

```
START TRANSACTION;
INSERT INTO Books VALUES (103, 'Hell\'s Angels', 1966);
INSERT INTO Books VALUES (104, 'Black Elk Speaks', 1932);
SAVEPOINT sp1;
```

As you can see, the transaction begins with the START TRANSACTION statement, followed by two INSERT statements. After the INSERT statements, a SAVEPOINT statement is used to define a savepoint with the name sp1. That savepoint then becomes a permanent marker in the transaction.

The ROLLBACK TO SAVEPOINT Statement

In order for a savepoint to be effective, it must be used in conjunction with one or more ROLLBACK TO SAVEPOINT statements. When using a ROLLBACK TO SAVEPOINT statement, you must provide a savepoint name, as shown in the following syntax:

```
ROLLBACK TO SAVEPOINT <savepoint name>
```

To demonstrate how this statement works, take a look at an example of a transaction. In the following transaction, a savepoint is defined and a ROLLBACK TO SAVEPOINT statement is used to roll back to the savepoint:

```
START TRANSACTION;
INSERT INTO Books VALUES (103, 'Hell\'s Angels', 1966);
INSERT INTO Books VALUES (104, 'Black Elk Speaks', 1932);
SAVEPOINT sp1;
INSERT INTO Books VALUES (105, 'Noncomformity', 1996);
INSERT INTO Books VALUES (106, 'A Confederacy of Dunces', 1980);
ROLLBACK TO SAVEPOINT sp1;
INSERT INTO Books VALUES (107, 'Postcards', 1992);
INSERT INTO Books VALUES (108, 'The Shipping News', 1993);
COMMIT;
```

As you can see, a savepoint named sp1 is defined after the first two INSERT statements. Then, after the second two INSERT statements, a ROLLBACK TO SAVEPOINT statement is used to roll back the transaction to savepoint sp1. Following the ROLLBACK TO SAVEPOINT statement, two more INSERT statements are included in the transaction, followed by a COMMIT statement. If you were now to use a SELECT statement to view the contents of the Books table, you would see a result set similar to the following:

```
+--------+----------------------------+-----------+
| BookID | BookTitle                  | Copyright |
+--------+----------------------------+-----------+
|    101 | Letters to a Young Poet    |      1934 |
|    102 | Winesburg, Ohio            |      1919 |
|    103 | Hell's Angels              |      1966 |
|    104 | Black Elk Speaks           |      1932 |
|    107 | Postcards                  |      1992 |
|    108 | The Shipping News          |      1993 |
+--------+----------------------------+-----------+
6 rows in set (0.00 sec)
```

As the result set shows, the rows with a BookID value of 103, 104, 107, and 108 have been added to the table, but no rows with a value of 105 or 106. The first two and last two INSERT statements were committed to the database, but not the middle two. The middle two were rolled back because the ROLLBACK TO SAVEPOINT statement was used to roll back the transaction to the savepoint. Any statements executed between the SAVEPOINT statement and the ROLLBACK TO SAVEPOINT statement were rolled back, and the rows were not added to the table.

In this section, you learned how to add savepoints to your transactions. Now you can create a transaction that includes a savepoint and a rollback to that savepoint.

Try It Out   **Using Savepoints in Your Transactions**

The following steps describe how to create a transaction that includes savepoints:

1. Open the mysql client utility, type the following command, and press Enter:

```
use DVDRentals
```

You should receive a message indicating that you switched to the DVDRentals database.

2. Your first step in creating the transaction is to start the transaction. Execute the following SQL statement at the mysql command prompt:

```
START TRANSACTION;
```

You should receive a message indicating that the statement executed successfully and that the statement affected no rows.

3. Next, insert a row in the Employees table. Execute the following SQL statement at the mysql command prompt:

```
INSERT INTO Employees
VALUES (NULL, 'Rebecca', 'T.', 'Reynolds');
```

You should receive a message indicating that the statement executed successfully, affecting one row.

4. Now create a savepoint named sp1 in your transaction. Execute the following SQL statement at the mysql command prompt:

```
SAVEPOINT sp1;
```

You should receive a message indicating that the statement executed successfully, affecting no rows.

5. Next, insert another row in the Employees table. Execute the following SQL statement at the mysql command prompt:

```
INSERT INTO Employees
VALUES (NULL, 'Fred', NULL, 'Paulson');
```

You should receive a message indicating that the statement executed successfully and that the statement affected one row.

6. Now roll back the last INSERT statement to the savepoint that you created in Step 4. Execute the following SQL statement at the mysql command prompt:

```
ROLLBACK TO SAVEPOINT sp1;
```

You should receive a message indicating that the statement executed successfully and that the statement affected no rows.

7. Your next step is to commit that part of the transaction that has not been rolled back. Execute the following SQL statement at the mysql command prompt:

```
COMMIT;
```

You should receive a message indicating that the statement has executed successfully, affecting no rows.

8. Finally, you should verify what data was inserted in the Employees table. Execute the following SQL statement at the mysql command prompt:

```
SELECT EmpLN FROM EMPLOYEES;
```

You should receive results similar to the following:

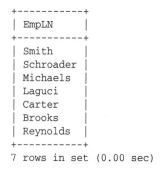

```
+-----------+
| EmpLN     |
+-----------+
| Smith     |
| Schroader |
| Michaels  |
| Laguci    |
| Carter    |
| Brooks    |
| Reynolds  |
+-----------+
7 rows in set (0.00 sec)
```

9. Now delete the Reynolds row from the Employees table. Execute the following SQL statement at the mysql command prompt:

```
DELETE FROM Employees
WHERE EmpLN='Reynolds';
```

You should receive a message indicating that the statement executed successfully and that the statement affected one row.

How It Works

In this exercise, you created a transaction that included one savepoint. To begin the transaction, you used the following SQL statement:

```
START TRANSACTION;
```

By executing the START TRANSACTION statement, you're telling MySQL that all SQL statements to follow are part of that transaction, until the transaction is committed or rolled back. Once you started the transaction, you used an INSERT statement to add a row to the Employees table, and then you used the following SQL statement to create a savepoint after the first INSERT statement:

```
SAVEPOINT sp1;
```

The savepoint provides a marker that indicates the point to which you can roll back a transaction. This allows you to roll back the transaction to this point, without having to undo the entire transaction. After you created the savepoint, you used a second INSERT statement to add another row to the Employees table. Then you issued the following SQL statement to roll back the transaction to the savepoint:

```
ROLLBACK TO SAVEPOINT sp1;
```

The ROLLBACK TO SAVEPOINT statement rolls back the transaction to the savepoint named sp1. As a result, the second INSERT statement was undone. Because the first INSERT statement was executed prior to the savepoint, that change was not undone, although it has not yet been committed to the database. To commit the first INSERT statement, you used the following SQL statement:

```
COMMIT;
```

The COMMIT statement saves any modifications that are not undone by the ROLLBACK TO SAVEPOINT command. In this case, the first INSERT statement was committed to the database, but the second was not, because the transaction was rolled back to the savepoint.

Setting the Autocommit Mode and Transaction Isolation Level

To support the use of transactions, MySQL allows you to configure the autocommit mode and the transaction isolation level, both of which affect transaction behavior. In this section, you learn how to configure both of these options.

Setting the Autocommit Mode

By default, whenever you execute a single SQL statement, that statement is automatically committed to the database. At the same time, MySQL prevents multiple statements from modifying any one table at the same time. As a result, you can think of each statement as a transaction that is implicitly initiated whenever you execute a single statement, except that you don't have to use the START TRANSACTION statement before you execute a single statement, and you don't have to use the COMMIT statement to save any changes to the database.

The ability of MySQL to commit an individual statement automatically is controlled through the autocommit mode. For a statement to be committed automatically, the autocommit mode must be set to on. To prevent individual statements from committing automatically, the autocommit mode must be set to off. The autocommit mode is turned on by default, which is why individual statements are committed automatically when you begin a mysql session.

> *The autocommit mode applies only to transactional tables. All statement that are issued against a nontransactional table are committed automatically, and you cannot override that behavior.*

If the autocommit mode is set to off, all statements that follow are considered part of a transaction. You must then manually commit your statements by using the COMMIT statement or roll back your statements by using the ROLLBACK statement. If you fail to commit your statements before you end the session, they are automatically rolled back and you lose your changes.

To set the autocommit mode, you must use a SET statement along with the AUTOCOMMIT argument. The AUTOCOMMIT argument can be set with one of two values. The first value is 0, which sets the autocommit mode to off. For example, the following SET statement sets the autocommit mode to off:

```
SET AUTOCOMMIT=0;
```

Once you execute this statement, all statements that follow must be explicitly committed to the database. If you fail to commit them before ending a session, the statements will be rolled back.

The autocommit mode stays off until you end the current session or you explicitly turn the autocommit mode back on, which you can do by setting the AUTOCOMMIT argument to 1 (the default setting). To set the mode to on, you should use the following SET statement:

```
SET AUTOCOMMIT=1;
```

When you set the autocommit mode to on, all statements that precede the SET clause are committed to the database, as if you had executed a COMMIT statement, and individual statements that follow are each committed automatically. Once the autocommit mode is set to on, you must explicitly start your transactions if they include more than one statement that you want treated as a unit.

If the autocommit mode has been set to off in a session and you end that session, the autocommit mode is automatically set to on when you start a new session.

In addition to allowing you to set the autocommit mode, MySQL provides the @@autocommit system variable that allows you to view the current autocommit mode setting. To use the system variable, simply include it in a SELECT statement, as shown in the following statement:

```
SELECT @@autocommit;
```

When you execute this statement, MySQL returns the current autocommit mode. For example, if your autocommit mode is set to on, you receive results similar to the following:

```
+--------------+
| @@autocommit |
+--------------+
|            1 |
+--------------+
1 row in set (0.00 sec)
```

Now that you're acquainted with the autocommit mode, you can look at a hands-on example. In this Try It Out exercise, you first set the autocommit mode to off, verify the autocommit setting, and then test the impact that this configuration has on executed statements.

Try It Out   Configuring the Autocommit Mode

To complete these tasks, follow these steps:

1. Open the mysql client utility, type the following command, and press Enter:

```
use DVDRentals
```

You should receive a message indicating that you switched to the DVDRentals database.

2. To begin, you must override the default autocommit mode by setting the mode to off. Execute the following SQL statement at the mysql command prompt:

```
SET AUTOCOMMIT=0;
```

You should receive a message indicating that the statement executed successfully and that the statement affected no rows.

3. Next, use the @@autocommit system variable to retrieve the current autocommit mode. Execute the following SQL statement at the mysql command prompt:

```
SELECT @@autocommit;
```

You should receive results similar to the following:

```
+--------------+
| @@autocommit |
+--------------+
|            0 |
+--------------+
1 row in set (0.02 sec)
```

4. Now insert a row in the Employees table. Execute the following SQL statement at the mysql command prompt:

```
INSERT INTO Employees
VALUES (NULL, 'Rebecca', 'T.', 'Reynolds');
```

You should receive a message indicating that the statement executed successfully, affecting one row.

5. Next, use a SELECT statement to verify that the Reynolds row has been added to the Employees table. Execute the following SQL statement at the mysql command prompt:

```
SELECT EmpLN FROM EMPLOYEES;
```

You should receive results similar to the following:

```
+-----------+
| EmpLN     |
+-----------+
| Smith     |
| Schroader |
| Michaels  |
| Laguci    |
| Carter    |
| Brooks    |
| Reynolds  |
+-----------+
7 rows in set (0.00 sec)
```

6. Now you must exit the mysql client utility in order to end your current session. Execute the following SQL statement at the mysql command prompt:

```
exit
```

You should be returned to your operating system's command prompt.

7. Now you should launch the mysql client utility and go directly to the DVDRentals database. At your operating system's command prompt, type the following command, and press Enter:

```
mysql DVDRentals
```

If you did not add the user=<username> and password=<password> options to the [mysql] section of your option file (which you set up in Chapter 3), be sure to include the correct parameters when launching the mysql client utility. When the utility is launched, the DVDRentals database is the active database.

8. At the mysql command prompt, execute the same SELECT statement that you executed in Step 5:

```
SELECT EmpLN FROM EMPLOYEES;
```

You should receive results similar to the following:

```
+-----------+
| EmpLN     |
+-----------+
| Smith     |
| Schroader |
| Michaels  |
| Laguci    |
| Carter    |
| Brooks    |
+-----------+
6 rows in set (0.01 sec)
```

9. Finally, use the @@autocommit system variable to view the autocommit mode once more. Execute the following SQL statement at the mysql command prompt:

```
SELECT @@autocommit;
```

You should receive results similar to the following:

```
+--------------+
| @@autocommit |
+--------------+
|            1 |
+--------------+
1 row in set (0.00 sec)
```

How It Works

One of the first steps that you took in this exercise was to use the following SET statement to set the autocommit mode to 0 (off):

```
SET AUTOCOMMIT=0;
```

By setting the autocommit mode to off, individual SQL statements are no longer committed automatically to the database. To verify that the autocommit mode has been set to 0, you used the following SELECT statement to view the current autocommit mode:

```
SELECT @@autocommit;
```

The SELECT statement uses the @@autocommit system variable to return the current autocommit status. In this case, a 0 is returned, indicating that the autocommit mode is set to off. If it were set to on, a 1 would have been returned.

Once you verified the autocommit mode, you executed an INSERT statement that added a row to the Employees table. You then used a SELECT statement to verify that the row had been added. Although the result set indicated that the row had been added, when you ended your current session by exiting the mysql client utility, the INSERT statement was rolled back because the modification to the Employees table was never committed to the database. To verify this, you relaunched the mysql utility and queried the Employees table, which indicated that the Reynolds row was not committed to the database. Next, you again used the @@autocommit system variable to view the autocommit mode. As you discovered, the mode is turned back on automatically when you start a new session, which means that individual statements are automatically committed to the database.

Setting the Transaction Isolation Level

In addition to being able to set the autocommit mode, MySQL also allows you to set the transaction isolation level, which specifies how isolated your transactions will be from other transactions. To set the transaction isolation level, you must use the SET TRANSACTION statement, which is shown in the following syntax:

```
SET [GLOBAL | SESSION] TRANSACTION ISOLATION LEVEL
{READ UNCOMMITTED | READ COMMITTED | REPEATABLE READ | SERIALIZABLE}
```

At a minimum, the statement requires that you specify the SET TRANSACTION ISOLATION LEVEL keywords and one of the four isolation levels — READ UNCOMMITTED, READ COMMITTED, REPEATABLE READ, SERIALIZABLE. (The isolation levels are discussed in detail later in this section.) In addition to these elements, you can specify the GLOBAL or SESSION keywords. If GLOBAL is specified, the SET TRANSACTION statement applies to all new connections to the database, but no current connections are affected. If SESSION is specified, the SET TRANSACTION statement applies to all new transactions started during the current connection, but no other connections are affected. If neither GLOBAL nor SESSION is specified, the SET TRANSACTION statement applies only to the next transaction.

Data Anomalies in a Transaction

As you saw in the syntax for the SET TRANSACTION statement, you must specify one of the four isolation levels for the statement to be complete. To understand the differences among the isolation levels, though, you should first have an overview of some of the problems that can arise in a transaction, depending on how isolated that transaction is from other transactions. Depending on the level of isolation, you can experience one of several problems when multiple transactions are initiated at the same time. These problems include dirty reads, nonrepeatable reads, and phantom reads.

Dirty Reads

One problem that can occur when multiple transactions try to access the same table at the same time or near to the same time is the *dirty read*. A dirty read can occur when one transaction modifies data in a table, a second transaction reads the table before those modifications are committed to the database, and then the first transaction rolls back the modification, returning the database to its original statement. The second transaction might then try to modify the table based on its initial read, which is no longer accurate.

To better understand how a dirty read can occur, take a look at the BookInventory table in Figure 12-3 as it progresses through two transactions. The first transaction (the one on the left) starts and reads data from the BookInventory table. Next, the transaction updates the table by modifying the InStock values. After the update, a second transaction starts and reads the BookInventory table. The first transaction then rolls back the update, returning the BookInventory table to its original state. The second transaction, however, then tries to take an action based on its initial read. For example, it might create an order for 10 copies of the book *Letters to a Young Poet*, the user believing that there are 13 copies available, rather than 8. Because of the dirty read, the second transaction is working with inaccurate data.

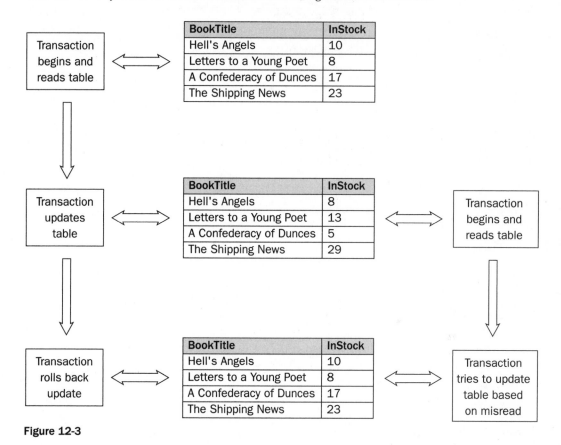

Figure 12-3

Nonrepeatable Reads

In addition to dirty reads, multiple transactions can experience what is referred to as a *nonrepeatable read*. A nonrepeatable read can occur when one transaction reads from a table, and then a second transaction updates the table. If the first transaction then tries to read from the table again — after the update — the transaction experiences a nonrepeatable read. In other words, the data is now different from what was originally viewed.

To better understand how a nonrepeatable read can occur, take a look at Figure 12-4. Suppose that a user initiates the first transaction. The user reads the data from the BookInventory table and then pauses the transaction. The user might be considering the information or waiting for a response from a client or delayed for another reason. Shortly after the first transaction is initiated, another user initiates a second transaction, reads from the table, and then immediately updates the table. When the first user returns to the transaction, the data in the BookInventory table is now different from what it was originally, and the transaction experiences a nonrepeatable read.

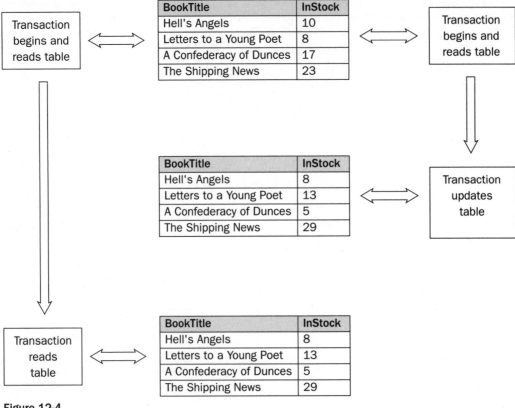

Figure 12-4

Phantom Reads

A *phantom read* is similar to a nonrepeatable read, except that it is more specific, with regard to the data retrieved from a table. Your transaction can experience a phantom read when the first transaction reads data based on a specified search condition, a second transaction updates the table, and then the first transaction reads from the table once more, using the same search condition. Because the table has changed, different results are returned to the first transaction.

To understand how a phantom read can occur, take a look at Figure 12-5. Suppose that the first transaction retrieves only those rows with an InStock value greater than 10 (WHERE InStock>10). The query will return *A Confederacy of Dunces* and *The Shipping News*. Now suppose that after the first transaction retrieves this data, a second transaction reads the table and then updates the data. If the first transaction were then to retrieve data from the table, it would now see the books *Letters to a Young Poet* and *The Shipping News*. A different set of values has been returned, which indicates that a phantom read has occurred.

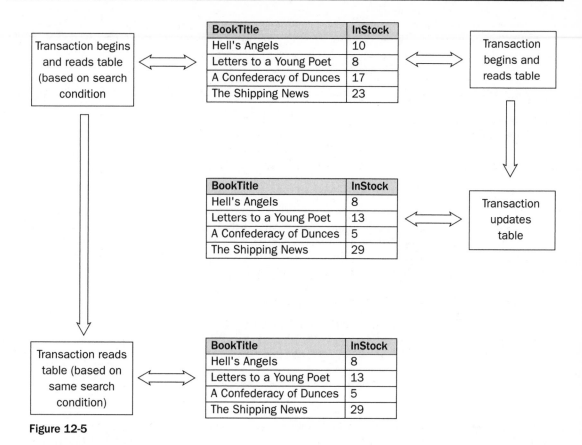

Figure 12-5

Transaction Isolation Levels

Now that you've learned about the different types of data anomalies that can occur between transactions, you can examine how you set transaction isolation levels, which determine which anomalies are prevented. As discussed earlier in this section, the SET TRANSACTION statement allows you to specify one of four transaction isolation levels:

- ❑ **READ UNCOMMITTED:** The least restrictive of the isolation levels, READ UNCOMMITTED permits dirty reads, nonrepeatable reads, and phantom reads. You should use this isolation level only for transactions that return general information, such as statistical data that does not have to be specific.

- ❑ **READ COMMITTED:** This transaction isolation level is a bit more restrictive than READ UNCOMMITTED. The READ COMMITTED isolation level permits nonrepeatable reads and phantom reads, but it prevents dirty reads.

- ❑ **REPEATABLE READ:** More restrictive than the previous two isolation levels, REPEATABLE READ permits phantom reads, but it prevents dirty reads and nonrepeatable reads. This is the default transaction isolation level for InnoDB tables.

- ❑ **SERIALIZABLE:** The most restrictive of the transaction isolation levels, SERIALIZABLE prevents dirty reads, nonrepeatable reads, and phantom reads. When SERIALIZABLE is specified, transactions are fully isolated from one another and are processed sequentially. This is the only transaction isolation level available for BDB tables.

As you can see, the transaction isolation level determines which data anomalies are prevented and which are permitted. For your convenience, the following table summarizes which data anomalies are permitted by which isolation levels.

Isolation level	Dirty reads	Nonrepeatable reads	Phantom reads
READ UNCOMMITTED	Yes	Yes	Yes
READ COMMITTED	No	Yes	Yes
REPEATABLE READ	No	No	Yes
SERIALIZABLE	No	No	No

To determine which isolation level to use, you must balance the need to ensure the accuracy of the data retrieved by a transaction against the trade-offs in performance. The more restrictive the isolation level, the greater the impact on performance. For data whose precision is always critical, such as in financial transactions, you should use the SERIALIZABLE isolation level.

Using the SET TRANSACTION Statement

Now that you have an understanding of how the transaction isolation levels differ from one another, you can use the SET TRANSACTION statement to set the isolation level. For example, the following SET TRANSACTION statement sets the isolation level to READ COMMITTED:

```
SET TRANSACTION ISOLATION LEVEL READ COMMITTED;
```

As you can see, the statement includes the keywords SET TRANSACTION ISOLATION LEVEL and the READ COMMITTED isolation level option. In addition, because neither the GLOBAL OPTION nor the SESSION option is specified, the transaction isolation level applies only to the next transaction that is initiated in the current session and to no other transactions.

You can view the current setting for the global transaction isolation level by using the @@global.tx_isolation system variable, as shown in the following SELECT statement:

```
SELECT @@global.tx_isolation;
```

The variable returns the setting that applies to all new connections when they are established. For example, if the default transaction isolation level is being used, the variable returns results similar to the following:

```
+-----------------------+
| @@global.tx_isolation |
+-----------------------+
| REPEATABLE-READ       |
+-----------------------+
1 row in set (0.00 sec)
```

As you can see, REPEATABLE-READ is specified, which means that the REPEATABLE READ isolation level is applied to transactions in any new connections that are established, unless another isolation level is explicitly specified.

You can also check the session isolation level by using the @@tx_isolation system variable, as shown in the following SELECT statement:

```
SELECT @@tx_isolation;
```

The variable returns the isolation level that is set for the current session. For example, if the isolation level for the current session is READ COMMITTED, results similar to the following are returned:

```
+----------------+
| @@tx_isolation |
+----------------+
| READ-COMMITTED |
+----------------+
1 row in set (0.00 sec)
```

For this Try It Out exercise, you set the transaction isolation level to SERIALIZABLE for the current session only. You then verify the transaction isolation level settings.

Try It Out   Configuring the Isolation Levels of Your Transactions

To perform these tasks, follow these steps:

1. Open the mysql client utility.

2. First use the SET TRANSACTION statement to set the isolation level to SERIALIZABLE for the current session. Execute the following SQL statement at the mysql command prompt:

```
SET SESSION TRANSACTION ISOLATION LEVEL SERIALIZABLE;
```

   You should receive a message indicating that the statement executed successfully and that the statement affected no rows.

3. Next, use the @@global.tx_isolation system variable to view the current global transaction isolation level. Execute the following SQL statement at the mysql command prompt:

```
SELECT @@global.tx_isolation;
```

   You should receive results similar to the following:

```
+-----------------------+
| @@global.tx_isolation |
+-----------------------+
| REPEATABLE-READ       |
+-----------------------+
1 row in set (0.00 sec)
```

4. Now use the `@@tx_isolation` system variable to view the current session transaction isolation level. Execute the following SQL statement at the mysql command prompt:

```
SELECT @@tx_isolation;
```

You should receive results similar to the following:

```
+----------------+
| @@tx_isolation |
+----------------+
| SERIALIZABLE   |
+----------------+
1 row in set (0.00 sec)
```

5. To end the current session, you should exit the mysql client utility. Execute the following SQL statement at the mysql command prompt:

```
exit
```

You should be returned to your operating system's command prompt.

6. Now relaunch the mysql client utility in order to start a new session. Be sure to enter your username and password if necessary. At your operating system's command prompt, type the following command, and press Enter:

```
mysql
```

The mysql utility is launched.

7. Once again, use the `@@global.tx_isolation` system variable to view the current global transaction isolation level. Execute the following SQL statement at the mysql command prompt:

```
SELECT @@global.tx_isolation;
```

You should receive results similar to the following:

```
+-----------------------+
| @@global.tx_isolation |
+-----------------------+
| REPEATABLE-READ       |
+-----------------------+
1 row in set (0.00 sec)
```

8. Again, use the `@@tx_isolation` system variable to view the current session transaction isolation level. Execute the following SQL statement at the mysql command prompt:

```
SELECT @@tx_isolation;
```

You should receive results similar to the following:

```
+----------------+
| @@tx_isolation |
+----------------+
| REPEATABLE-READ |
+----------------+
1 row in set (0.00 sec)
```

How It Works

In this exercise, you used the following SET TRANSACTION statement to change the transaction isolation level for the current statement:

```
SET SESSION TRANSACTION ISOLATION LEVEL SERIALIZABLE;
```

The SET TRANSACTION statement includes the SESSION option and the SERIALIZABLE option. As a result, the new transaction isolation level applies only to the current session. In addition, because you specified the SERIALIZABLE option, each transaction in the current session is processed with the maximum level of isolation, which means that each transaction is fully isolated from all other transactions. As a result, the transactions avoid dirty reads, nonrepeatable reads, and phantom reads.

After you set the transaction isolation level, you used the following SELECT statement to verify the setting for the global transaction isolation level:

```
SELECT @@global.tx_isolation;
```

The statement uses the @@global.tx_isolation system variable to return the current transaction isolation level used for all new sessions that are started. In this case, REPEATABLE READ is specified as the transaction isolation level. As a result, the transaction in all new sessions will not experience dirty reads and nonrepeatable reads, but phantom reads are still possible.

Next, you used the following SELECT statement to verify the setting for the session transaction isolated level:

```
SELECT @@tx_isolation;
```

As you would expect, the @@tx_isolation system variable indicated that the current session was set to SERIALIZABLE. You then exited the mysql client utility to end the session, and then you relaunched the utility. From there, you used the @@global.tx_isolation and @@tx_isolation system variables to view the settings for the global and session transaction isolation levels. In both cases, the default level of REPEATABLE READ was returned by the variables. Because you had specified that the SERIALIZABLE transaction isolation level applies only to the current session, the new session reverted back to the default isolation level.

Locking Nontransactional Tables

As stated earlier in the chapter, MySQL supports the use of transactions only for InnoDB and BDB tables. There might be times, though, when you want to lock other types of tables that are included in your database. By locking nontransactional tables manually, you can group SQL statements together and set up a transaction-like operation in order to prevent anyone from changing the tables that participate in your operation. To lock a nontransactional table, you must use the LOCK TABLES statement. Once you've completed updating the tables, you should use the UNLOCK TABLES statement to release them. In this section, you learn how to both lock and unlock tables.

The LOCK TABLES Statement

To lock a table in a MySQL database, you should use the LOCK TABLES statement, as shown in the following syntax:

```
LOCK {TABLE | TABLES}
  <table name> [AS <alias>] {READ [LOCAL] | [LOW_PRIORITY] WRITE}
  [{, <table name> [AS <alias>] {READ [LOCAL] | [LOW_PRIORITY] WRITE}}...]
```

To use the statement, you must specify the LOCK keyword, the TABLE or TABLES keyword, one or more tables, and the type of lock for each table. The TABLE and TABLES keywords are synonymous, and you can use either one, whether you're locking one table or multiple tables. Generally, TABLE is used for one table, and TABLES is used for multiple tables, but either can be used in either situation.

For each table that you specify, you have the option of providing an alias for the table. In addition, you must specify a READ lock type or a WRITE lock type. If you specify READ, any connection can read from the table, but no connection can write to the table. If you specify READ LOCAL, nonconflicting INSERT statements can be executed by any connection. If you specify WRITE, the current connection can read or write to the table, but no other connections can access the table until the lock has been removed. If you specify LOW_PRIORITY WRITE, other connections can obtain READ locks while the current session is waiting for the WRITE lock.

Once you lock a table, it remains locked until you explicitly unlock the table with the UNLOCK TABLES statement (described in the text that follows) or end your current session.

Now take a look at an example of a LOCK TABLE statement. The following statement places a lock on the Books table:

```
LOCK TABLE Books READ;
```

As you can see, a READ lock has been placed on the table. Now only read access is available to all connections. You are not limited, however, to placing a lock on only one table. For example, the following LOCK TABLES statement places locks on the Books and BookOrders tables:

```
LOCK TABLES Books READ, BookOrders WRITE;
```

In this case, a READ lock is placed on the Books table, and a WRITE lock is placed on the BookOrders table. As a result, other connections can read from the Books table, but they cannot access the BookOrders table.

The UNLOCK TABLES Statement

Once you've completed accessing a locked table, you should explicitly unlock the table or end your current session. To unlock one or more locked tables, you must use the UNLOCK TABLES statement, shown in the following syntax:

```
UNLOCK {TABLE | TABLES}
```

As you can see, you must specify the UNLOCK keyword along with the TABLE or TABLES keyword. As with the LOCK TABLES statement, the TABLE and TABLES keywords are synonymous, which means that you can use either one, regardless of the number of tables that you're unlocking.

One thing to notice about the UNLOCK TABLES statement is that no table names are specified. When you use this statement, all tables that have been locked from within the current session are unlocked. For example, to unlock the Books and BookOrders tables, you would use a statement similar to the following:

```
UNLOCK TABLES;
```

If only one table is locked, you can still use this statement, although you can also use the TABLE keyword, rather than TABLES. Either way, any locked tables are now unlocked.

In general, you should try to use InnoDB tables when setting up your system to support transactions. In the case of the DVDRentals database, all tables are defined as InnoDB. Should you ever run into a situation in which you want to lock another type of table manually, you can use the LOCK TABLES and UNLOCK TABLES statements. In this Try It Out exercise, you try both types of statements.

Try It Out   Locking Your Nontransactional Tables

Follow these steps to complete this exercise:

1. Open the mysql client utility, type the following command, and press Enter:

```
use test
```

You should receive a message indicating that you switched to the test database.

2. To demonstrate how to lock a table, you should first create the table in the test database. Execute the following SQL statement at the mysql command prompt:

```
CREATE TABLE t1 (ID INT NOT NULL);
```

You should receive a message indicating that the statement executed successfully and that the statement affected no rows.

3. Now you can specify a READ lock on the t1 table. Execute the following SQL statement at the mysql command prompt:

```
LOCK TABLE t1 READ;
```

You should receive a message indicating that the statement executed successfully, affecting no rows.

4. Next, you should try to insert a row in the t1 table to demonstrate that placing a READ lock prevents you from adding data to the table. Execute the following SQL statement at the mysql command prompt:

```
INSERT INTO t1 VALUES (101);
```

You should receive a message indicating that the table has been locked with a READ lock and cannot be updated.

5. Now you can specify a WRITE lock on the t1 table. Execute the following SQL statement at the mysql command prompt:

```
LOCK TABLE t1 WRITE;
```

You should receive a message indicating that the statement executed successfully and that the statement affected no rows.

6. Next, you should insert a row in the t1 table to demonstrate that placing a WRITE lock does not prevent you from adding data to the table. Execute the following SQL statement at the mysql command prompt:

```
INSERT INTO t1 VALUES (101);
```

You should receive a message indicating that the statement executed successfully, affecting one row.

7. Now you should unlock the table. Execute the following SQL statement at the mysql command prompt:

```
UNLOCK TABLES;
```

You should receive a message indicating that the statement has executed successfully and that the statement affected no rows.

8. Finally, you should remove the table from the test database. Execute the following SQL statement at the mysql command prompt:

```
DROP TABLE t1;
```

You should receive a message indicating that the statement executed successfully, affecting no rows.

How It Works

One of the first steps that you took in this exercise was to create a table named t1. From there, you used the following LOCK TABLE statement to set a READ lock on the table:

```
LOCK TABLE t1 READ;
```

As you can see, the statement includes the LOCK TABLE keywords, the name of the table (t1), and the READ option. Because you specified a READ lock, any sessions that try to access the t1 table can only read from that table, but no one can write to the table. In order to demonstrate this, you executed an INSERT statement, but you received an error indicating that you could not write to this table.

To address this situation, you used the following LOCK TABLE statement to change the lock to a WRITE lock:

```
LOCK TABLE t1 WRITE;
```

Because you specified a WRITE lock, only the current session could read from or write to the table. No other sessions could access the table until the lock was removed. After you locked the table with a WRITE lock, you tested your ability to write to the table by executing the INSERT statement a second time. This time you were able to write to the table successfully. After you inserted the row, you used the following SQL statement to unlock the table:

```
UNLOCK TABLES;
```

When you executed this statement, the lock was removed from the t1 table and other sessions were able to access the table.

Summary

As this chapter has demonstrated, transactions provide an effective way to help ensure the safe execution of your SQL statements and the integrity of your data. Transactions allow multiple statements to be treated as a unit so that data in the process of being modified is isolated in such a way as to prevent data inconsistencies and inaccuracies. In this chapter, you learned how to use transactions to control how statements are executed in order to protect your data. You also learned how to lock and unlock nontransactional tables. Specifically, the chapter described how to use the following SQL statements to perform transactions and lock tables:

❑   The START TRANSACTIONS statement, in order to begin a transaction

❑   The COMMIT and ROLLBACK statements, in order to end a transaction

❑   The SAVEPOINT and ROLLBACK TO SAVEPOINT statements, in order to use savepoints in your transactions

❑   The SET AUTOCOMMIT statement, in order to set the autocommit mode

❑   The SET TRANSACTION statement, in order to set the transaction isolation levels

❑   The LOCK TABLES and UNLOCK TABLES statements, in order lock nontransactional tables

As you begin developing applications that access data in a MySQL database, you may find that transactions are often necessary to allow users to access the data concurrently, while ensuring that each user updates only consistent and accurate data. To use transactions effectively, your application should include logic that specifies when a transaction should be committed and when it should be rolled back. Because that logic is written in the application language, you should refer to that language's documentation for more information on how to set up the necessary conditions. From there, you can create transactions that are both effective and safe. Chapter 13 deals with MySQL administration and introduces you to such topics as modifying default settings, setting system variables, and implementing logging.

Exercises

The following exercises are provided as a way for you to better acquaint yourself with the material covered in this chapter. Be sure to work through each exercise carefully. To view the answers to these questions, see Appendix A.

1.   You are setting up a transaction that first inserts data in one table and then updates data in a second table. The autocommit mode is set to on, so you must begin the transaction manually. Create an SQL statement that begins the transaction.

2.   For the transaction that you created in Step 1, you want any changes committed to the database if the INSERT and UPDATE statements execute successfully. Create an SQL statement that commits the transaction.

3.   For the transaction that you created in Step 1, you want all changes to the database rolled back if either the INSERT or UPDATE statement fails. Create an SQL statement that rolls back the transaction.

4.   For the transaction that you created in Step 1, you want to add a savepoint to the transaction after the INSERT statement. The name of the savepoint is save1. Create an SQL statement that creates the savepoint.

5.   For the transaction that you created in Step 1, you want to add a statement that rolls back the transaction to the savepoint. Create an SQL statement that rolls back the transaction to the savepoint.

6.   You want to turn the autocommit mode for the current session to off. Create an SQL statement that changes the autocommit mode to off.

7.   You want to set the transaction isolation level to SERIALIZABLE. You want the new level to apply to all sessions. Create an SQL statement that changes the isolation level to SERIALIZABLE.

8.   You want to lock two MyISAM tables: Produce and Orders. You want to set a READ lock on the Produce table and a WRITE lock on the Orders table. Create an SQL statement that locks the two tables.

Administering MySQL

In previous chapters, you learned how to install MySQL on Linux and Windows operating systems, maneuver through the MySQL installation, implement relational databases in the MySQL environment, and execute SQL statements that insert, update, delete, and retrieve data from those databases. In this chapter and the next several chapters, you learn how to perform administrative tasks that allow you to determine how MySQL runs, who can access the MySQL server, and how to replicate your system and prepare for database disaster.

This chapter introduces you to MySQL administration and describes how to modify default MySQL settings, set system variables, and implement logging. Chapter 14 explains how to manage security, and Chapter 15 describes how to optimize performance. In Chapter 16, you learn how to back up and restore your MySQL databases as well as set up replication. This chapter, then, provides the starting point from which you begin to perform basic administrative tasks. Specifically, the chapter covers the following topics:

❑ Using the mysqladmin client utility to verify system settings and perform server-related operations

❑ Using the SHOW VARIABLES, SELECT, and SHOW STATUS statements to retrieve system variable settings and using start-up options, option files, and the SET statement to set system variables

❑ Managing error, query, and binary logging

Performing Administrative Tasks

Once you install MySQL, you might find that you want to view information about the MySQL server, such as status or version information. You might also find that you want to perform administrative tasks such as stopping the server or flushing the host's cache. To allow you to perform these tasks, the MySQL installation includes the mysqladmin client utility, which provides an administrative interface to the MySQL server. Using this tool, you can perform a variety of administrative tasks, such as obtaining information about the MySQL configuration, setting passwords, starting the server, creating and dropping databases, and reloading privileges.

You use the mysqladmin client utility at a command prompt, as you use the mysql client utility. When launching mysqladmin, you can specify zero or more program options and one or more commands, as shown in the following syntax:

```
mysqladmin [<program option> [<program option>...]]
<command> [<command option>] [{<command> [<command option>]}...]
```

The program options define how to connect to the MySQL server and how to run the mysqladmin utility. For example, you can use program options to specify the user account to use when connecting to the MySQL server, the password for that account, and the port to use when establishing the connection.

Many of the program options provide two forms that you can use when specifying that option. For example, the --force option can also be specified as the -f option. The following table describes many of the program options that you can use with the mysqladmin utility and, when applicable, provides both the long and short form of the option. (When two options are provided, they're separated by a vertical pipe [|].) Note, however, that program options can vary from one release of MySQL to the next, so it's always a good idea to check the latest MySQL product documentation for current information about options as well as information about other options available to mysqladmin. (For additional information about specifying program options, see Chapter 3.)

Option syntax	Description
--character-set-dir=<path>	Specifies the directory where the character sets are stored.
--compress	-C	Compresses the data that is sent between the server and the client. Both the server and client must support compression.
--connect_timeout=<seconds>	Specifies the number of seconds to wait before timing out when trying to connect to the server.
--count=<number>	-c <number>	Specifies the number of iterations to make when the --sleep option is used to execute the mysqladmin command repeatedly.
--force	-f	Causes mysqladmin to execute the drop <database> command without asking for confirmation. Also forces the execution of multiple mysqladmin commands even if an error is caused by one of the commands. (Normally, mysqladmin would exit if one of the specified commands caused an error.)
--help	-?	Displays information about the options available to mysqladmin.
--host=<host name>	-h <host name>	Specifies the name of the host where the MySQL server is running.

Option syntax	Description
`--password[=<password>] | -p[<password>]`	Specifies the password to use when connecting to the MySQL server. When using the -p alternative to specify a password, the password must follow immediately after the option. (There should be no space.) For either option, if the password is not specified, MySQL prompts you for a password.
`--port=<port number> | -P <port number>`	Specifies the port number to use when connecting to the MySQL server.
`--protocol=` `  {TCP | SOCKET | PIPE | MEMORY}`	Specifies the connection protocol to use when connecting to the MySQL server.
`--silent | -s`	Exits without providing output if mysqladmin cannot connect to the server.
`--sleep=<seconds> | -i <seconds>`	Specifies that the mysqladmin command (along with any defined options) should be executed repeatedly. The specified number of seconds represents the length of delay between executions. The --sleep command can be used in conjunction with the --count command.
`--user=<username> | -u <username>`	Specifies the user account to use when connecting to the MySQL server.
`--version | -V`	Displays version number and other information about mysqladmin as well as information about the MySQL server.
`--wait[=<number>] | -w[<number>]`	Retries to connect to the MySQL server if a connection cannot be established. The optional <number> placeholder indicates the number of times to retry. If no value is provided, a 1 is assumed. When using the -w alternative to specify this option, there should be no space between the -w and the number.

In addition to specifying program options when using the mysqladmin client utility, you must specify one or more commands. The commands define the actions that mysqladmin should take when the mysqladmin program is executed. For example, you can verify whether the MySQL server is running or reload the grant tables. In some cases, a command takes a command option. It is usually evident when an option is required. For instance, you can use mysqladmin to create a database. To do so, you must supply a name for the new database. The database name is the command option.

The following table describes many of the commands that you can use with the mysqladmin utility. As with program options, commands can vary from one release of MySQL to the next, so be sure to check the latest MySQL product documentation for current information about a command as well as information about other commands available to mysqladmin.

Command syntax	Description
create <database >	Creates a new database with the specified name.
drop <database>	Removes a database with the specified name.
extended-status	Displays the names and values of the server status variables.
flush-hosts	Flushes the host's cache.
flush-logs	Closes and then reopens the log files. For some log file types, MySQL creates a new file.
flush-privileges	Reloads the grant tables. This command is equivalent to the reload command.
flush-status	Clears the status variables and resets several counters to zero.
flush-tables	Flushes the table cache.
flush-threads	Flushes the thread cache.
kill <thread ID> [<thread ID>...]	Kills the specified threads. Each thread is associated with a single connection, so when you kill a thread, you're terminating that connection. You can use the processlist command to display a list of active threads.
password <new password>	Assigns a password to the MySQL user account currently being used to invoke mysqladmin. If a password already exists for the user account, the new password is applied *after* the execution of the mysqladmin command, which means that you must supply the original password for the --password program option.
ping	Verifies whether the MySQL server is running.
processlist	Displays a list of the active server threads. Each thread is assigned an ID, which you can use along with the kill command to terminate the thread.
reload	Reloads the grant tables. This command is equivalent to the flush-privileges command.
refresh	Flushes the table cache, closes and then reopens the log files, and reloads the grant tables.
shutdown	Stops the MySQL server.
start-slave	Starts replication on the slave server.

Command syntax	Description
`status`	Displays current status information about the MySQL server.
`stop-slave`	Stops replication on the slave server.
`variables`	Displays the names and values of the server variables.
`version`	Displays version information about the current MySQL server.

Now that you have an overview of the program options and commands that you can use with the mysqladmin client utility, take a look at a few examples that demonstrate the various tasks that you can perform by using this tool. The first example demonstrates how to use the `--help` program option to retrieve information about the options and commands that you can use with the mysqladmin utility:

```
mysqladmin --help
```

As you can see, you need to specify only the mysqladmin utility name and the `--help` program option. Even if a username and password are required to connect to the MySQL server, you do not have to specify them here, because the purpose of the `--help` option is to allow you to find the information that you need in order to use the tool for other tasks. When you execute the command, you receive information similar to the following:

```
mysqladmin  Ver 8.40 Distrib 4.1.5-gamma, for Win95/Win98 on i32
Copyright (C) 2000 MySQL AB & MySQL Finland AB & TCX DataKonsult AB
This software comes with ABSOLUTELY NO WARRANTY. This is free software,
and you are welcome to modify and redistribute it under the GPL license

Administration program for the mysqld daemon.
Usage: mysqladmin [OPTIONS] command command....
  -c, --count=#          Number of iterations to make. This works with -i
                         (--sleep) only.
  -#, --debug[=name]     Output debug log. Often this is 'd:t:o,filename'.
  -f, --force            Don't ask for confirmation on drop database; with
                         multiple commands, continue even if an error occurs.
  -C, --compress         Use compression in server/client protocol.
  --character-sets-dir=name
                         Directory where character sets are.
  -?, --help             Display this help and exit.
  -h, --host=name        Connect to host.
  -p, --password[=name]
```

The results shown here represent only a part of what is returned when you specify the `--help` option. As you can see, each program option is listed here, along with a brief description of how it is used. The `--help` command also lists and describes the commands that are available to mysqladmin.

The next example that you look at combines program options and a command, as shown in the following:

```
mysqladmin -u root -p version
```

In this case, the `mysqladmin` command includes the -u program option followed by the name of the user account, which is root. Next comes the -p program option. The -p program option is different from other program options that require a value because it allows you to specify that value separately from the main `mysqladmin` command. When you specify -p, without a password value, you're prompted for a password when you execute the command. When you then enter your password, each letter of the password appears as an asterisk at the command line, rather than the actual character. MySQL recommends this method as a way to keep your password secure.

In addition to the two program options, the preceding example also includes the `version` command. The `version` command displays version information about the MySQL server, as shown in the following results:

```
mysqladmin  Ver 8.40 Distrib 4.1.6-gamma, for Win95/Win98 on i32
Copyright (C) 2000 MySQL AB & MySQL Finland AB & TCX DataKonsult AB
This software comes with ABSOLUTELY NO WARRANTY. This is free software,
and you are welcome to modify and redistribute it under the GPL license

Server version         4.1.6-gamma-nt
Protocol version       10
Connection             localhost via TCP/IP
TCP port               3306
Uptime:                2 hours 15 min 1 sec

Threads: 1  Questions: 24  Slow queries: 0  Opens: 26  Flush tables: 1  Open tab
les: 0  Queries per second avg: 0.003
```

As you can see, the results include version-related information, plus information about the protocol version, the connection, the port used to connect to MySQL, and the amount of time that the MySQL server has been running. The `version` command also returns status-related information, which is described in the following table.

Status variable	Description
Threads	The number of currently open connections.
Questions	The number of queries that have been sent to the server since the server has been running.
Slow queries	The number of queries that have taken more time to execute than the time specified in the `long_query_time` system variable.
Opens	The number of tables that have been opened since the server has been running.
Flush tables	The number of flush, refresh, and reload commands that have been executed since the server has been running.
Open tables	The number of current open tables. These are tables that are currently being accessed.
Queries per second avg	The average number of queries per second.

As you may recall from earlier in this chapter, you can use a long form or a short form to specify many of the program options. In the previous example, the short form of each program option is used. You can achieve the same effect, though, by using the long form, as shown in the following command:

```
mysqladmin --user=root --password version
```

As you can see, the command uses `--user=root` instead of `-u root` and `--password` instead of `-p`.

In addition to executing mysqladmin commands that return information, you can execute commands that take a specific action. For instance, the following mysqladmin example includes the reload command:

```
mysqladmin -u root -p reload
```

The `reload` command reloads the grant tables so that any changes made to the grant tables are immediately applied. The grant tables determine who can access the MySQL server and what type of access they have. (For more information about the grant tables and MySQL security, see Chapter 14.)

The mysqladmin client utility also allows you to specify multiple commands when running the utility. For example, the following command reloads the grant table and returns version-related information:

```
mysqladmin -u root -p reload version
```

When you execute this command, MySQL reloads the grant tables and returns the same information that you saw in an earlier example, when only the version command was specified.

Now that you have seen examples of how to use the mysqladmin client utility to perform administrative tasks, you can test the tool for yourself. In the following exercise, you try out the mysqladmin client utility by viewing the MySQL server's current status and process list. You then use the utility to create a database and then delete the database from your system

Try It Out   Using mysqladmin to Administer MySQL

The following steps describe how to use the mysqladmin client utility to perform several administrative tasks:

1. The first command that you create returns current status information about the MySQL server. At your operating system's command prompt, execute the following command:

```
mysqladmin -u root -p status
```

When prompted, type in your password, and then press Enter. You should receive status information about the MySQL server, similar to the following:

```
Uptime: 8859  Threads: 1  Questions: 25  Slow queries: 0  Opens: 26  Flush table
s: 1  Open tables: 0  Queries per second avg: 0.003
```

2. The next command that you create returns status information and a process list. At your operating system's command prompt, execute the following command:

```
mysqladmin -u root -p status processlist
```

When prompted, type your password, and then press Enter. You should receive status information about the MySQL server, followed by a list of active server threads, similar to the following:

```
Uptime: 8870  Threads: 1  Questions: 26  Slow queries: 0  Opens: 26  Flush table
s: 1  Open tables: 0  Queries per second avg: 0.003
+----+------+----------------+----+---------+------+-------+------------------+
| Id | User | Host           | db | Command | Time | State | Info             |
+----+------+----------------+----+---------+------+-------+------------------+
| 18 | root | localhost:2695 |    | Query   | 0    |       | show processlist |
+----+------+----------------+----+---------+------+-------+------------------+
```

3. The next command is similar to the previous, except that the order of the status and processlist options is reversed. At your operating system's command prompt, execute the following command:

```
mysqladmin -u root -p processlist status
```

When prompted, type in your password, and then press Enter. You should receive a list of active server threads, followed by status information about the MySQL server, similar to the following:

```
+----+------+----------------+----+---------+------+-------+------------------+
| Id | User | Host           | db | Command | Time | State | Info             |
+----+------+----------------+----+---------+------+-------+------------------+
| 19 | root | localhost:2698 |    | Query   | 0    |       | show processlist |
+----+------+----------------+----+---------+------+-------+------------------+
Uptime: 8880  Threads: 1  Questions: 29  Slow queries: 0  Opens: 26  Flush table
s: 1  Open tables: 0  Queries per second avg: 0.003
```

4. The next command creates a database named db1. At your operating system's command prompt, execute the following command:

```
mysqladmin -u root -p create db1
```

When prompted, type your password, and then press Enter. You should be returned to your operating system's command prompt.

5. To view whether the database has been created, open the mysql client utility. At your operating system's command prompt, execute the following command:

```
mysql
```

The mysql client utility is launched.

6. Next, view a list of databases that currently exist on your system. At the mysql command prompt, execute the following command:

```
SHOW DATABASES;
```

At a minimum, your results should include the db1, mysql, and test tables, as shown in the following result set:

```
+----------+
| Database |
+----------+
| db1      |
| mysql    |
| test     |
+----------+
3 rows in set (0.00 sec)
```

7. Now close the mysql client utility by executing the following command:

```
exit
```

You should be returned to your operating system's command prompt.

8. The final command that you create removes the db1 database from your system. At your operating system's command prompt, execute the following command:

```
mysqladmin -u root -p -f drop db1
```

When prompted, type your password, and then press Enter. You should receive a message indicating that the db1 database has been dropped.

How It Works

In this exercise, you created a series of commands to perform various administrative tasks. The commands are based on the mysqladmin client utility. The first administrative task that you performed was to use the following command to return the current MySQL server status:

```
mysqladmin -u root -p status
```

The mysqladmin command includes several options. The first option (-u) specifies that the root user account should be used to connect to MySQL. The second option (-p) specifies that a password should be used. When you specify the -p option in this way, without supplying the password, you're prompted for the password when you execute the command. Note that you can use --user=root instead of -u root and --password instead of -p.

The third option included in the preceding example is the status command. The status command displays the current status information about the MySQL server. This includes such information as uptime, active threads, number of queries that have been processed, and other status-related data. The status-related information is, for the most part, similar to the status information returned by the version command. The main difference is that, for the version command, the uptime is displayed in hours, minutes, and seconds. For the status command, the uptime is displayed in seconds.

The next mysqladmin command that you created was similar to the last command, except that it also included the processlist option, as shown in the following command:

```
mysqladmin -u root -p status processlist
```

The processlist option displays a list of the active server threads. Because the command includes the status and processlist options, information returned by both options is displayed in the results, in the order that the options are specified in the commands. If you reverse the options, as you did in the following command, the results are reversed:

```
mysqladmin -u root -p processlist status
```

Now the results first display the process list and then display the status information.

The next command that you created adds the db1 database to your system, as shown in the following mysqladmin command:

```
mysqladmin -u root -p create db1
```

The command includes the create option, followed by the name of the new database (db1). After you executed this command, you opened the mysql client utility and viewed a list of databases to verify that the database has been added. You then exited from the mysql utility and used the following command to remove the database:

```
mysqladmin -u root -p -f drop db1
```

The command includes the drop option and the name of the database. As a result, the db1 database is removed from your system. Notice that the command also includes the -f option. This is also referred to as the --force option, which causes mysqladmin to execute the drop command without asking for confirmation. As a result, the db1 database is removed from the system as soon as you execute the command, and you're not prompted to confirm the command.

Managing System Variables

When MySQL starts up, it uses default and user-defined settings that determine how the MySQL server runs. To a great degree, these settings determine the environment in which MySQL operates and how users can connect to the system. The settings are stored in system variables that specify such details as connection timeouts, where the data directory is located, whether logging is enabled, the maximum number of connections allowed, cache sizes, and numerous other settings.

All system variables are configured with default settings. You can override default variable settings by specifying new settings at server startup in command-line options or in option files. You can also specify a number of variable settings at runtime by using SET statements. (You learn more about these three options later in the chapter.)

MySQL system variables are either global variables or session variables. Global system variables apply to the entire server operation. Session system variables apply to specific client connections. When the server starts, it initializes all global system variables to their default and, when applicable, user-defined settings (those settings specified at startup). When a connection is established, MySQL initializes a set of session variables for that connection.

Most session variables correspond to global variables. The values initially assigned to those session variables are based on the current values of their global counterparts at the time the connection is established. For example, if the wait_timeout global variable is set to 600 when a connection is established, the wait_timeout session variable associated with that connection is set to 600. (The wait_timeout system variable specifies the number of seconds to wait for activity on a connection before closing that connection.) Some session variables do not correspond to global variables. In this case, MySQL assigns a default value to these session variables.

Not all session variables are the same in terms of the function they perform or whether they can be updated. MySQL supports the following three types of system variables:

❑ **Server system variables:** A set of system variables that determines how MySQL should run and how clients should interact with the server. Essentially, server system variables refer to all system variables that are not explicitly used to return status information.

❑ **Dynamic system variables:** A subset of server system variables whose settings can be modified at runtime.

❑ **Server status variables:** A set of system variables whose primary purpose is to provide status-related information about the server's operation. All status variables are considered global variables.

MySQL provides different methods for viewing the three types of system variables. In the next section, you learn how to view each type of variable and its current settings.

Retrieving System Variable Settings

The method that you use to view system variable settings depends on the type of system variable. For server system variables, you use a SHOW VARIABLES statement. For dynamic system variables, you use a SELECT statement. And for server status variables, you use a SHOW STATUS statement.

MySQL supports hundreds of system variables, many more than can be described here. As a result, whenever you need information about a specific system variable or you want to determine what variables are supported, you're encouraged to use one of the statements described in the following sections and to refer to the MySQL product documentation.

Using the SHOW VARIABLES Statement to Retrieve Server System Variable Settings

The SHOW VARIABLES statement allows you to view most of the server system variables and their current settings from within the mysql client utility. (The statement does not display some dynamic system variables. For those, you must use SELECT statements, which are described later in the chapter.) You can view global or session system variables, and you can qualify your SHOW VARIABLES statement by adding a LIKE clause, as shown in the following syntax:

```
SHOW [GLOBAL | SESSION] VARIABLES [LIKE '<value>']
```

As you can see, the only required elements in this statement are the SHOW VARIABLES keywords. You can also specify either the GLOBAL keyword or the SESSION keyword. If you specify GLOBAL, MySQL displays global system variables. If you specify SESSION, MySQL displays session system variables. If you don't specify either option, session variables are displayed if they exist, and global variables are displayed if session variables don't exist.

The SHOW VARIABLES syntax also supports the optional LIKE clause. The LIKE clause allows you to specify an exact value in order to return a specific system variable or to specify an approximate value (by using wildcards) in order to return system variables with names that contain a certain pattern.

Later in this section, you see an example of how to use the LIKE clause, but first take a look at a simple example of a SHOW VARIABLES statement. The following statement returns all global variables and their settings:

```
SHOW GLOBAL VARIABLES;
```

As you can see, the statement includes the required SHOW VARIABLES keywords and the optional GLOBAL keyword. When you execute this statement, you should receive results similar to the following:

```
+----------------------------+--------------------------------------------------+
| Variable_name              | Value                                            |
+----------------------------+--------------------------------------------------+
| back_log                   | 50                                               |
| basedir                    | C:\Program Files\MySQL\MySQL Server 4.1\          |
| binlog_cache_size          | 32768                                            |
| bulk_insert_buffer_size    | 8388608                                          |
| character_set_client       | latin1                                           |
| character_set_connection   | latin1                                           |
| character_set_database     | latin1                                           |
| character_set_results      | latin1                                           |
| character_set_server       | latin1                                           |
| character_set_system       | utf8                                             |
```

The results shown here represent only a partial list of the server system variables. Normally, the statement returns nearly 180 system variables. If you want to return the session system variables, you would use the following statement:

```
SHOW SESSION VARIABLES;
```

The results returned by this statement are normally similar to the results returned by the statement when the GLOBAL keyword is used. As you can see, you most likely want to trim down the number of rows that are returned by these statements, which is where the LIKE clause comes in. The LIKE clause allows you to specify a value that is compared to the variable names. For example, suppose that you want to view all variables that are related to database queries. You might want to specify a value in the LIKE clause that includes the string *query*, as shown in the following statement:

```
SHOW VARIABLES LIKE '%query%';
```

As you can see, the LIKE clause specifies the string, surrounded by the percentage (%) wildcards. As a result, the variable name can begin or end with any character, as long as query is included somewhere in the name. When you execute this statement, you should receive results similar to the following:

```
+----------------------------+---------+
| Variable_name              | Value   |
+----------------------------+---------+
| ft_query_expansion_limit   | 20      |
| have_query_cache           | YES     |
| long_query_time            | 10      |
| query_alloc_block_size     | 8192    |
| query_cache_limit          | 1048576 |
| query_cache_min_res_unit   | 4096    |
| query_cache_size           | 0       |
| query_cache_type           | ON      |
| query_cache_wlock_invalidate | OFF   |
| query_prealloc_size        | 8192    |
+----------------------------+---------+
10 rows in set (0.00 sec)
```

The table displays the variables and their settings only for those variables whose name contains *query*. For information about the meaning of each variable, check out the MySQL product documentation. Now take a look at how a SELECT statement is used to retrieve the settings of a dynamic system variable.

Using the SELECT Statement to Retrieve Dynamic System Variable Settings

Like all system variables, MySQL supports dynamic system variables that are either global or specific to a session. Many dynamic system variables exist as both, while others are either global or session, but not both. For example, the `autocommit` variable (which specifies the autocommit mode) is session specific, but the `binlog_cache_size` variable (which specifies the size of the cache to use for the binary logging process) is global and does not apply to the individual session. The `wait_timeout` variable applies at a global level as well as at a session level, however, and the settings for each can be different.

You can use a SELECT statement to retrieve the current setting for a dynamic session variable, whether it applies globally or to a session. For individual variables, this is an easier method to use than the SHOW VARIABLES statement. For session variables that are not returned by SHOW VARIABLES statement, however, this is the only method available for viewing dynamic variable settings.

The following syntax shows how to use a SELECT statement to retrieve a dynamic variable setting:

```
SELECT @@[global.]<variable> [{, @@[global.]<variable>}...]
```

As you can see, you must specify the SELECT keyword, the double at symbols (@@), and the variable name. If you're retrieving the value of a global variable, you must also precede the variable name with the global keyword, followed by a period, as shown in the following example:

```
SELECT @@global.max_binlog_size;
```

In this SELECT statement, a value is retrieved from the `global max_binlog_size` variable, a variable that determines the maximize size in bytes to which a binary log can grow. When you execute this statement, you should receive results similar to the following:

```
+--------------------------+
| @@global.max_binlog_size |
+--------------------------+
|               1073741824 |
+--------------------------+
1 row in set (0.00 sec)
```

Because this variable is one of the system variables returned by the SHOW VARIABLES statement, you can also use that statement to retrieve the same results, as shown in the following statement:

```
SHOW GLOBAL VARIABLES LIKE 'max_binlog_size';
```

As you can see, the LIKE clause includes a specific value and not wildcards. The statement produces results similar to the following:

```
+-----------------+------------+
| Variable_name   | Value      |
+-----------------+------------+
| max_binlog_size | 1073741824 |
+-----------------+------------+
1 row in set (0.00 sec)
```

Although the results appear in a different form from those returned by the SELECT statement, the information is essentially the same. Remember, however, that this method works only for those system variables that are returned by the SHOW VARAIBLES statement.

If you want to retrieve a value for a session variable, rather than a global variable, you simply omit the global keyword and the period, as shown in the following example:

```
SELECT @@tx_isolation;
```

In this case, the SELECT statement retrieves the value of the tx_isolation session variable, which determines the current connection's isolation level, as shown in the following results:

```
+------------------+
| @@tx_isolation   |
+------------------+
| REPEATABLE-READ  |
+------------------+
1 row in set (0.01 sec)
```

As you can see, the isolation level is REPEATABLE READ. (For more information about isolation levels, see Chapter 12.)

If you refer back to the preceding syntax, notice that you can specify more than one dynamic system variable in your SELECT statement. For example, the following SELECT statement returns the isolation level for the current session and the maximum permitted size of the binary log file:

```
SELECT @@tx_isolation, @@global.max_binlog_size;
```

When you execute this statement, the settings from both variables are displayed, as shown in the following results:

```
+------------------+--------------------------+
| @@tx_isolation   | @@global.max_binlog_size |
+------------------+--------------------------+
| REPEATABLE-READ  |               1073741824 |
+------------------+--------------------------+
1 row in set (0.00 sec)
```

The SELECT statement, like the SHOW VARIABLES statement, is a handy method for viewing system variables; however, neither method displays the settings of the server status variables. For that, you need the SHOW STATUS statement.

Using the SHOW STATUS Statement to Retrieve Server Status Variable Settings

Most server status variables are essentially counters set to zero when the MySQL server is started. From there, they count the number of times that a particular event has occurred. For example, the Connections status variable provides a total of the number of connections that have been attempted since the server was started, and the Bytes_sent variable tracks the total number of bytes sent to all clients. In addition to the status variables that count events, some status variables provide other types of information, such as the amount of memory available for the query cache or the number of open tables. To view the current status variable settings, you can use the SHOW STATUS statement, which is shown in the following syntax:

```
SHOW STATUS [LIKE '<value>']
```

As the syntax shows, you must include the SHOW STATUS keywords. In addition, you can include a LIKE clause. The LIKE clause in this statement works the same way as the LIKE clause in the SHOW VARIABLES statement, as you see later in this section.

Returning now to the syntax, you can see that a basic SHOW STATUS statement is very straightforward, as shown in the following example:

```
SHOW STATUS;
```

When you execute this statement, all status variables and their current settings are returned. The following result set shows part of the results that you can expect from the SHOW STATUS statement:

```
+--------------------------+-------+
| Variable_name            | Value |
+--------------------------+-------+
| Aborted_clients          | 0     |
| Aborted_connects         | 0     |
| Binlog_cache_disk_use    | 0     |
| Binlog_cache_use         | 0     |
| Bytes_received           | 993   |
| Bytes_sent               | 879   |
| Com_admin_commands       | 0     |
| Com_alter_db             | 0     |
| Com_alter_table          | 0     |
| Com_analyze              | 0     |
| Com_backup_table         | 0     |
| Com_begin                | 0     |
| Com_change_db            | 0     |
| Com_change_master        | 0     |
| Com_check                | 0     |
| Com_checksum             | 0     |
| Com_commit               | 0     |
| Com_create_db            | 0     |
| Com_create_function      | 0     |
| Com_create_index         | 0     |
| Com_create_table         | 4     |
| Com_dealloc_sql          | 0     |
```

In all, there are more than 150 status variables in MySQL. For this reason, the LIKE clause is a handy tool to use to trim down your results. For example, the following SHOW STATUS statement returns all those status variables whose name contains the string *select*:

```
SHOW STATUS LIKE '%select%';
```

When you execute this statement, you should receive results similar to the following:

```
+-------------------------+--------+
| Variable_name           | Value  |
+-------------------------+--------+
| Com_insert_select       | 0      |
| Com_replace_select      | 0      |
| Com_select              | 44     |
| Select_full_join        | 0      |
| Select_full_range_join  | 0      |
| Select_range            | 0      |
| Select_range_check      | 0      |
| Select_scan             | 42     |
+-------------------------+--------+
8 rows in set (0.00 sec)
```

As you can see, the statement returns only status variables that contain the string *select* somewhere in the variable name.

Now that you have an overview of the various SQL statements that you can use to view system variables and their settings, you can begin to use these statements. In the following exercise, you try out the SHOW VARIABLES, SELECT, and SHOW STATUS statements in order to view the settings assigned to specified system variables.

Try It Out   Viewing System Settings

The following steps describe how to use various SQL statements to view the settings assigned to system variables:

1. Open the mysql client utility.

2. Create a SHOW VARIABLES statement that returns global variables with the string *log* contained anywhere in the variable name. Execute the following SQL statement at the mysql command prompt:

```
SHOW GLOBAL VARIABLES LIKE '%log%';
```

   You should receive results similar to the following:

```
+---------------------------------+------------+
| Variable_name                   | Value      |
+---------------------------------+------------+
| back_log                        | 50         |
| binlog_cache_size               | 32768      |
| expire_logs_days                | 0          |
| innodb_locks_unsafe_for_binlog  | OFF        |
| innodb_flush_log_at_trx_commit  | 1          |
| innodb_log_arch_dir             |            |
| innodb_log_archive              | OFF        |
| innodb_log_buffer_size          | 1048576    |
| innodb_log_file_size            | 10485760   |
| innodb_log_files_in_group       | 2          |
| innodb_log_group_home_dir       | .\         |
| innodb_mirrored_log_groups      | 1          |
| log                             | ON         |
| log_bin                         | ON         |
```

```
| log_error            | .\ws01.err |
| log_slave_updates    | OFF        |
| log_slow_queries     | OFF        |
| log_update           | OFF        |
| log_warnings         | 1          |
| max_binlog_cache_size | 4294967295 |
| max_binlog_size      | 1073741824 |
| max_relay_log_size   | 0          |
| relay_log_purge      | ON         |
| sync_binlog          | 0          |
+-----------------------------+------------+
24 rows in set (0.00 sec)
```

3. Create a SELECT statement that returns a value for the max_connections global system variable. The max_connections variable determines the maximum number of simultaneous connections that are permitted. Execute the following SQL statement at the mysql command prompt:

```
SELECT @@global.max_connections;
```

You should receive results similar to the following:

```
+--------------------------+
| @@global.max_connections |
+--------------------------+
|                      100 |
+--------------------------+
1 row in set (0.00 sec)
```

4. Create a SHOW STATUS statement that returns status variables with the string *thread* contained anywhere in the variable name. Execute the following SQL statement at the mysql command prompt:

```
SHOW STATUS LIKE '%thread%';
```

You should receive results similar to the following:

```
+------------------------+-------+
| Variable_name          | Value |
+------------------------+-------+
| Delayed_insert_threads | 0     |
| Slow_launch_threads    | 0     |
| Threads_cached         | 0     |
| Threads_connected      | 1     |
| Threads_created        | 1     |
| Threads_running        | 1     |
+------------------------+-------+
6 rows in set (0.00 sec)
```

How It Works

The first SQL statement that you created in this exercise was the following SHOW VARIABLES statement:

```
SHOW GLOBAL VARIABLES LIKE '%log%';
```

The statement includes the mandatory SHOW VARIABLES keyword along with the GLOBAL option. As a result, this statement returns only global variables and their settings. In addition, the statement uses a

LIKE clause to specify that any variables returned must include the string *log* somewhere in the name of the variable. (The % wildcards indicates that zero or more of any characters can precede or follow the string.)

The next SQL statement that you created in this exercise was the following SELECT statement:

```
SELECT @@global.max_connections;
```

The SELECT statement retrieves the value in the max_connections variable. Because the variable name is prefixed with global, the statement applies to the global variable, rather than the session variable. To view the value for the session variable, you must remove the global prefix.

The next statement that you created in this exercise was the following SHOW STATUS statement:

```
SHOW STATUS LIKE '%thread%';
```

In addition to including the mandatory SHOW STATUS keywords, the statement includes a LIKE clause that specifies that the status variables returned by the statement must contain the string *thread* somewhere in the name of the variable.

Modifying the Server Configuration

In Chapter 3, you learned how you can specify options when you start up a MySQL program, including the MySQL server. Of these methods, the two most commonly used are specifying options at a command prompt when you start up the program or specifying the options in an option file. Most of the options that you can specify at a command prompt or in an option file are the system variables that affect how the server runs. Once the server is running, you can modify the settings of dynamic system variables by using a SET statement. In this section, you review how to specify options at server startup; then you learn how to use a SET statement to set system variables at runtime.

This section touches only briefly on the subjects of specifying options at a command prompt or in an option file. Chapter 3 covers each topic in far greater detail. The information is included here in order to provide a cohesive overview of setting variable values.

Specifying System Settings at the Command Line

As discussed in Chapter 3, you can specify options when you start the MySQL server. When assigning a value to a variable, you precede the variable name by double dashes (--) and then use an equal sign after the variable name to assign the value. For example, the following command assigns a value to the query_cache_limit system variable:

```
mysqld --query_cache_limit=1000000
```

The query_cache_limit variable limits the size (in bytes) of a result set that can be cached. Any result set larger than the specified size is not cached. By setting a value for the query_cache_limit at the command line, you're overriding the default limit, which is 1048576 bytes.

You can also specify multiple options at the command line, as shown in the following example:

```
mysqld --query_cache_limit=1000000 --wait_timeout=600
```

When the server starts, the query cache limit is set to 1000000 bytes, and the connection timeout is set to 600. Despite your ability to set these variables and other variables at the command line, the preferable way to specify startup options is to use an option file.

Specifying System Settings in an Option File

The advantage of using an option file over using command-line options is that, with an option file, you have to enter the optional settings only once. With specifying options at a command line, you must specify the options each time you start the server. The only time that specifying options at the command line is useful is when you want your setting to apply only to a single server startup, and not to each server startup. Otherwise, the option file is the better choice.

To specify settings for system variables in an option file, you must add the settings to the [mysqld] section of your option file. For example, the following entries demonstrate how to set values for two system variables:

```
[mysqld]
query_cache_limit=1000000
wait_timeout=600
```

When you specify the system variables in an option file, you do not need to precede the variable name with double dashes, as you do when specifying variables in a command line. You do, however, have to use an equal sign and then specify the appropriate value.

When specifying server-related variable settings in a Windows option file, you have to be aware of where the MySQL service looks for an option file. By default, the service looks for the my.ini *file in the* C:\Program Files\MySQL\MySQL Server <version> *directory for the server-related options when starting the server. The MySQL client utilities look for the* my.ini *file in the* C:\WINDOWS *directory for client-related settings. One option is to remove the current MySQL service and then re-create the service so that it points to the same option file used by the MySQL client utilities. This way, you need to maintain only one option file. (This process is described in a Try It Out section later in the chapter.) Otherwise, you can maintain two option files.*

Specifying System Settings at Runtime

Once your server is running, you might find that you want to modify the system variable settings, either at a global level or at the session level. If you make the change at the global level, the change affects all clients. However, the change does not affect corresponding session variables for current connections, only for new connections initiated. If you make a change at the session level, the change affects only the connection in which the change has been made. No other connections are affected.

To set a dynamic system variable at runtime, you can use the SET statement, which is shown in the following syntax:

```
SET [GLOBAL | SESSION] <variable setting>
```

The statement must include the SET keyword and the variable setting, which usually includes a variable name followed by the equal sign and the new value. If you specify the GLOBAL keyword, MySQL assigns the new value to the specified global variable. If you specify the SESSION or neither of the optional keywords, MySQL assigns the new value to the specified session variable.

For a list of dynamic system variables and whether those variables apply at the global level, at the session level, or both, see the MySQL product documentation.

For example, if you want to set the query_cache_limit variable to 1000000 at the global level, use the following SET statement:

```
SET GLOBAL QUERY_CACHE_LIMIT=1000000;
```

As you can see, the statement includes the SET GLOBAL keywords, the name of the variable, an equal sign, and the new value. When you execute this statement, the new setting is applied at the global level, and all connections are affected. As a result, the query cache limit is now smaller than the default.

To set a session-level variable, you can either specify the SESSION keyword or omit it, as shown in the following example:

```
SET WAIT_TIMEOUT=600;
```

As you can see, the statement sets the wait_timeout variable to 600 seconds, much less than the default of 28800 seconds.

Now that you have an understanding of how to use a SET statement to set the values of dynamic system variables, you can try out one of these statements. In the following exercise, you use a SET statement to set the value of the foreign_key_checks system variable. The variable determines whether foreign key references on InnoDB tables are checked when data is modified. If the value is set to 1, foreign key references are checked. If set to 0, they are not checked. By default, the variable is set to 1.

Try It Out   Managing System Settings at Runtime

The following steps describe how to set the value of the foreign_key_checks system variable:

1. Open the mysql client utility.

2. First, use a SELECT statement to determine the current setting of the foreign_key_checks system variable. Execute the following SQL statement at the mysql command prompt:

```
SELECT @@foreign_key_checks;
```

You should receive results similar to the following:

```
+----------------------+
| @@foreign_key_checks |
+----------------------+
|                    1 |
+----------------------+
1 row in set (0.00 sec)
```

3. To turn off foreign key checking, set the `foreign_key_checks` variable to 0. Execute the following SQL statement at the mysql command prompt:

```
SET FOREIGN_KEY_CHECKS=0;
```

You should receive a message indicating the successful execution of the statement.

4. Once again use a `SELECT` statement to determine the current setting of the `foreign_key_checks` system variable. Execute the same SQL statement that you executed in Step 2. You should receive results similar to the following:

```
+----------------------+
| @@foreign_key_checks |
+----------------------+
|                    0 |
+----------------------+
1 row in set (0.00 sec)
```

5. Next, end your MySQL session by closing the mysql client utility, then start a new session by relaunching the utility.

6. Finally, verify the current `foreign_key_checks` setting one last time. Execute the following SQL statement at the mysql command prompt:

```
SELECT @@foreign_key_checks;
```

You should receive results similar to the following:

```
+----------------------+
| @@foreign_key_checks |
+----------------------+
|                    1 |
+----------------------+
1 row in set (0.00 sec)
```

How It Works

At several different points in this exercise, you used the following `SELECT` statement to verify the current setting for the `foreign_key_checks` system variable:

```
SELECT @@foreign_key_checks;
```

You can use this method to return a value of a dynamic system variable. As the statement shows, you must include the `SELECT` keyword followed by the variable name. The variable name must be preceded by the double at symbols (@@). In addition, because the variable name is not preceded by the `global` prefix, the value for the session variable is returned.

When you checked the `foreign_key_checks` variable the first time, the value was set to 1. You then used the following `SET` statement to change the value to 0:

```
SET FOREIGN_KEY_CHECKS=0;
```

You then checked the `foreign_key_checks` setting again and verified that it was now set to 0. From there, you ended your session and opened a new session. When you checked the `foreign_key_checks` setting this time, you verified that it was now set to 1. When you set the `foreign_key_checks` value, you did not include the GLOBAL keyword, so the session variable was set. As a result, when you ended your session and then started a new session, the global setting was applied.

Managing Log Files

When you install MySQL, it automatically sets up error log files, whether you install MySQL on Linux or on Windows. You can also implement other types of logging, such as query logging and binary logging. In this section, you learn how to work with error logs, query logs, and binary logs. For information about other types of logging available in MySQL, see the MySQL product documentation.

Note that, by default, all log files are stored in the MySQL data directory for your specific installation.

Working with Error Log Files

The error log is a text file that records information about when the MySQL server was started and stopped, as well as error-related information. You can view the error log through a text editor such as Notepad or Vim. By default, the error log is saved to the data directory. In Linux, the file is saved as `<host>.err`. You can specify a different path and filename by adding the following command to the `[mysqld]` section of the option file:

```
log-error=<path/filename>
```

In Windows, the error file is saved as `mysql.err`. You cannot change the path or filename. MySQL also creates a file named `<host>.err`. This file, though, contains only a subset of the information in the `mysql.err` file and currently is not of much use. Based on MySQL documentation, it appears that the `<host>.err` file might eventually replace the `mysql.err` file and that you may be able to rename the file and specify a new path, but this is not how the error logging in Windows currently works.

When you view the error file, you see entries similar to the following:

```
c:\program files\mysql\mysql server 4.1\bin\mysqld-nt: ready for connections.
Version: '4.1.5-gamma-nt'  socket: ''  port: 3306  Source distribution
041002 10:33:29  [ERROR] DROP USER: Can't drop user: 'user1'@'%'; No such user
041006  9:04:10  [NOTE] c:\program files\mysql\mysql server 4.1\bin\mysqld-nt:
Normal shutdown

041006  9:04:10  InnoDB: Starting shutdown...
041006  9:04:13  InnoDB: Shutdown completed; log sequence number 0 84629
041006  9:04:13  [NOTE] c:\program files\mysql\mysql server 4.1\bin\mysqld-nt:
Shutdown complete
```

The first two lines shown here are what you would typically see when a server startup is recorded. The information is related specifically to the server and includes such details as the path and server filename, the version, and the port number. The third line shows an error that occurred on October 2, 2004 (041002). In this case, the error results from trying to drop a user that did not exist. Whenever an error occurs, a line is added to the log. The remaining lines are all related to shutting down the server. Whenever you start or stop the server, you see information in the error log similar to what you see here.

Enabling Query and Binary Logging

Unlike error logging, you must enable query and binary logging in order to implement it on your system. This section explains how to implement each of these types of logging and how to view those log files once logging is implemented.

Setting Up Query Logging

The query log, also referred to as the general query log, records all connections to the server, SQL statements executed against the server, and other events such as server startup and shutdown. Query logging is not enabled when you install MySQL. To enable query logging, you should add the following command to the [mysqld] section of your option file:

```
log[=<path/filename>]
```

If you do not specify a path and filename, the query log is stored in the data directory and is assigned the name `<host>.log`. Because the query log is a text file, you can use a text editor such as Notepad or Vim to view its contents. MySQL writes queries to the log in the order in which the server receives them. (This might be different from the order in which the statements are executed.) Each query is entered as a line in the log. For example, the following two entries in a query log are for a SELECT statement and a SET statement:

```
041006 14:59:58       16 Query       SELECT @@foreign_key_checks
041006 15:00:08       16 Query       SET FOREIGN_KEY_CHECKS=0
```

The query log can be especially useful when you want to track who is connecting to the server, where the user is connecting from, and what statements that user is executing. This can be helpful in troubleshooting or debugging a system because it allows you to pinpoint exactly where the statement is originating and how the statement is created. Because the query log records every statement that is executed, in addition to connection and other information, the logs can grow quite large and can affect performance. As a result, you might prefer to use binary logging, rather than query logging.

Setting Up Binary Logging

The binary log stores logged data in a more efficient binary format than the query log and records only statements that update or potentially update data. For example, a DELETE statement that affects no rows would be recorded in the log because it could potentially update the data. Like query logging, binary logging is not enabled when you install mysql. To enable binary logging, you should add the following command to the [mysqld] section of your option file:

```
log-bin[=<path/filename>]
```

If you do not specify a path and filename, the file is stored in the data directory and is assigned the name `<host>-bin.000001`. If a binary log file already exists, the file extension is incremented by 1, based on the highest file number. In addition, when you set up binary logging, a file named `<host>-bin.index` is created. The index file tracks the binary log files. You can change the name of the index file and its location by adding the following command to the [mysqld] section of your option file:

```
log-bin-index[=<path/filename>]
```

If you specify a filename for either the log file or the index file and that filename includes an extension, MySQL automatically drops the extension and adds a numerical extension to the log file and the .index extension to the index file.

Because the log files and index files are created as binary files, you should use the `mysqlbinlog` client utility to view the contents of the file. To use `mysqlbinlog`, you must specify the utility name, followed by the name of the file, as shown in the following syntax:

```
mysqlbinlog <host>-bin.<numeric suffix>
```

For example, suppose that you want to view the contents of a binary log file named `Server21-bin.000001`. To do so, you would use the following command:

```
mysqlbinlog Server21-bin.000001
```

MySQL adds information for each event that is tracked by binary logging. For example, the following binary log entry shows that data was inserted in the t1 table:

```
# at 138
#041006  9:09:57 server id 1  log_pos 138  Query  thread_id=1  exec_time=0  error_
SET TIMESTAMP=1097078997;
INSERT INTO t1 VALUES (12);
```

As you can see, the information includes identifying information about the log entry and the statement execution, a timestamp, and the actual `INSERT` statement. (Note that, in the results shown here, the second line is cut off after `error_`, but you might see the line wrapped around or cut off at a different point.) Each time an event is recorded, an entry similar to this is added to the log file. If you restart your server or flush the logs, a new log file is created, with the numeric suffix incremented by one. (When you flush logs, MySQL closes and reopens the log files. In the case of the binary log files, a new log file is also created. To flush the logs, you can execute a `FLUSH LOG` statement or use the `flush-logs` command of the mysqladmin utility.)

> *Flushing logs is part of a larger process of log file maintenance. When any type of logging is enabled, the log files can grow quite large. As a result, administrators must often devise a comprehensive maintenance strategy to manage the log files. Planning this sort of maintenance is beyond the scope of this book; however, if you ever become responsible for this task, you should refer to the MySQL product documentation as well as other MySQL-related documentation for information on log flushing, log rotation, age-based expiration, and other aspects of log file maintenance.*

Now that you have an overview of how to implement query and binary logging, you can implement logging on your system. The next two Try It Out sections have you try out how to enable query and binary logging on Linux and Windows. The first Try It Out section focuses on Linux logging, and the second one focuses on Windows logging. In both cases, you stop and restart the MySQL server and modify the option file. Because MySQL is installed as a service on Windows, you also take the extra step of removing the service and then re-creating it so that it points to the correct option file.

Try It Out   Enabling Query and Binary Logging on Linux

The following steps describe how to set up query and binary logging on Linux:

1. Open a Terminal window (if you're working in a GUI environment) or use the shell's command prompt. In either case, you should be at the root directory.

2. First, you must add the necessary options to the option file. To do this, use the Vim text editor to edit the .my.cnf configuration file. To edit the file, execute the following command:

```
vi .my.cnf
```

The `vi` command opens the Vim text editor in Linux, which allows you to edit text files.

3. In order to edit the files, you must change the Vim utility to insert mode by typing the following letter:

```
i
```

As soon as you type this command, you are placed in Insert mode.

4. Scroll down to the section that begins with `[mysqld]`, and add a blank line beneath the `[mysqld]` heading.

5. To set up query and binary logging, add the following code beneath the `[mysqld]` heading:

```
log
log-bin
```

6. Press the Escape button to get out of Insert mode.

7. To indicate to the Vim utility that you have completed your edit, you must type the following command:

```
:
```

When you type this command, a colon is inserted at the bottom of the screen and your cursor is moved to the position after the colon.

8. At the colon, type the following command, and press Enter:

```
wq
```

The `w` option tells the Vim utility to save the edits on exiting, and the `q` option tells Vim to exit the program. When you execute this command, you're returned to the command prompt (at the root).

9. In order for the changes to the option file to take effect, you must shut down the MySQL server and then start it up again. To shut down the server, execute the following command:

```
mysqladmin -u root -p shutdown
```

Enter a password when prompted, and then press Enter. Depending on your Linux installation, you might receive a message indicating that the server has been shut down.

10. Now you must restart the MySQL server. Execute the following command:

```
mysqld_safe -u mysql &
```

You should receive a message indicating that the server has started. If, after you execute the `mysqld_safe` command, you're not returned to the command prompt right away, press Enter to display the prompt.

11. At the command prompt, change to the data directory for your installation, and verify that the following three files have been added to the data directory:

- ❏ *<host>*.log
- ❏ *<host>*-bin.000001
- ❏ *<host>*-bin.index

12. The next part of this process is to verify that changes are being logged to the log files. Use the following command to open the mysql utility with the test database active:

```
mysql test
```

You should be connected to MySQL, and the mysql prompt should be displayed.

13. Next, create a table, add a row to the table, drop the table, and exit the mysql client utility. Execute the following statements:

```
CREATE TABLE t1 (c1 INT);
INSERT INTO t1 VALUES (12);
SELECT * FROM t1;
DROP TABLE t1;
exit
```

You're returned to your shell's command prompt (at the data directory).

14. Use the Vim text editor to view the <host>.log file. Execute the following command:

```
vi <host>.log
```

In addition to version, port, and socket information, the file should include the following details:

```
Time                    Id Command    Argument
041001      4:33:09      1 Connect    root@localhost on test
041001      4:33:49      1 Query      CREATE TABLE t1 (c1 INT)
041001      4:34:01      1 Query      INSERT INTO t1 VALUES (12)
041001      4:34:10      1 Query      SELECT * FROM t1
041001      4:34:17      1 Query      DROP TABLE t1
041001      4:34:22      1 Quit
```

15. Once you finish viewing the contents of the log file, type the following command:

```
:
```

When you type this command, a colon is inserted at the bottom of the screen, and your cursor is moved to the position after the colon.

16. At the colon, type the following command, and press Enter:

```
q
```

You're returned to the command prompt (at the data directory).

17. Use the mysqlbinlog utility to view the <host>-bin.000001 file. Execute the following command:

```
mysqlbinlog <host>-bin.000001
```

In addition to version and connection information, the file should include the following details:

```
# at 79
#041005 18:40:08 server id 1  log_pos 79  Query  thread_id=1  exec_time=0  error_
use test;
SET TIMESTAMP=1097026808;
```

510

```
CREATE TABLE t1 (c1 INT);
# at 138
#041005 18:40:08 server id 1   log_pos 138   Query   thread_id=1   exec_time=0   error_
SET TIMESTAMP=1097026808;
INSERT INTO t1 VALUES (12);
# at 199
#041005 18:40:08 server id 1   log_pos 199   Query   thread_id=1   exec_time=0   error_
SET TIMESTAMP=1097026808;
DROP TABLE t1;
```

Note that, depending on the viewing capacity of your command window, longer lines might be cut off or wrapped around at different places.

How It Works

To set up logging on Linux, you had to first edit the option file, which is stored in the root directory. (You created the .my.cnf option file in Chapter 3. For details about the file, see that chapter.) You edited the option file by adding the following commands to the [mysqld] section:

```
log
log-bin
```

The log command implements query logging and creates the <host>.log. The log-bin command implements binary logging and creates the <host>-bin.000001 file and the <host>-bin.index file. If a binary log file already exists, the file extension is incremented by one, based on the highest file number.

After you modified and saved the .my.cnf option file, you used the following command to shut down the MySQL server:

```
mysqladmin -u root -p shutdown
```

The command uses the mysqladmin utility and the shutdown option to shut down MySQL. The command also specifies the root user account and prompts for a password. Once the server was shut down, you immediately started it up again by using the following command:

```
mysqld_safe -u mysql &
```

The command uses the mysqld_safe shell script to start the server and monitor it. The user specified is the mysql account that was created when you installed MySQL. (See Chapter 2 for information about that account.) The ampersand (&) at the end of the command is specific to Linux and indicates that the script should run as a process in the background to support the script's monitoring capabilities.

After restarting the MySQL server, you viewed the contents of the data directory to verify that the three new log files had been added. From there, you used the mysql client utility to execute several SQL statements; then you used the Vim text editor to view the contents of the <host>.log file. The log file should have contained the four SQL statements that you executed, as well as the time and date of when they were executed.

Next, you used the following command to view the contents of the <host>-bin.000001 file:

```
mysqlbinlog <host>-bin.000001
```

Chapter 13

The `mysqlbinlog` command allows you to view the contents of the binary log and index files. The log file should have contained the SQL statements that affect data (CREATE TABLE, INSERT, and DROP TABLE), but not the SELECT statement.

Try It Out   **Enabling Query and Binary Logging on Windows**

The following steps describe how to set up query and binary logging on Windows:

1. Because the default MySQL service points to a different option file than the client utilities use, you can delete the current service and re-create it to point to the `my.ini` file. To remove the MySQL service, you must first stop it. Open a Command Prompt window, and at the command prompt, execute the following command:

```
net stop mysql
```

You should receive a message verifying that the MySQL service has been stopped.

2. Next, remove the MySQL service by executing the following command:

```
mysqld-nt --remove
```

You should receive a message verifying that the service has been removed.

3. You must now add the MySQL service back to Windows, only now the service should point to the `my.ini` file. Execute the following command:

```
"c:\program files\mysql\mysql server 4.1\bin\mysqld-nt" --install MySQL --defaults-file="c:\windows\my.ini"
```

You should receive a message that verifies that the service has been successfully installed.

4. Before you can use MySQL, you must start the service. Execute the following command:

```
net start mysql
```

You should receive a message that indicates that the MySQL service has been started.

5. The next step is to set up logging in the `my.ini` option file. Open the `C:\WINDOWS\my.ini` file in a text editor such as Notepad. Scroll down to the section that begins with `[mysqld]`, and add a blank line beneath the `[mysqld]` heading.

6. Add the following code beneath the `[mysqld]` heading:

```
log
log-bin
```

7. Save and close the `my.ini` file.

8. To implement the changes added to the `my.ini` file, you should first stop the MySQL service and then restart it. To stop the service, execute the following command:

```
net stop mysql
```

You should receive a message that indicates that the service has been stopped.

You could have waited to start up the service until after you modified the option file, thus skipping steps 4 and 8. By restarting the service before modifying the option file, though, you're ensuring that the service has been properly added to the Windows environment and that it starts up properly. If you wait to start up the service until after you modify the option file and you run into a problem when starting the service, you do not know if the problem is because of the service configuration or because of the change you made to the option file.

9. To start the MySQL service, execute the following command:

```
net start mysql
```

You should receive a message that verifies that the service has been started.

10. At the command prompt, change to the `C:\Program Files\MySQL\MySQL Server 4.1\data` directory, and then verify that the following three files have been added to the data directory:

- ❑ *<host>*.log
- ❑ *<host>*-bin.000001
- ❑ *<host>*-bin.index

11. You use the mysql client utility to verify that the log files have been properly initiated. Execute the following command:

```
mysql test
```

You should be connected to MySQL, and the mysql prompt should be displayed.

12. Next, create a table, add a row to the table, drop the table, and exit the mysql client utility. Execute the following SQL statements:

```
CREATE TABLE t1 (c1 INT);
INSERT INTO t1 VALUES (12);
SELECT * FROM t1;
DROP TABLE t1;
exit
```

Each statement should be executed and should return the appropriate message. You're then returned to the command prompt (at the data directory).

13. Use a text editor such as Notepad to view the contents of the *<host>*.log. In addition to version, port, and socket information, the file should include the following details:

```
Time              Id Command      Argument
041001    4:33:09  1 Connect      root@localhost on test
041001    4:33:49  1 Query        CREATE TABLE t1 (c1 INT)
                   1 Query        INSERT INTO t1 VALUES (12)
                   1 Query        SELECT * FROM t1
                   1 Query        DROP TABLE t1
                   1 Quit
```

14. Once you finish viewing the contents of the log file, close the file.

15. Use the `mysqlbinlog` utility to view the `<host>-bin.000001` file. At the command prompt, execute the following command:

```
mysqlbinlog <host>-bin.000001
```

In addition to version and connection information, the file should include the following details:

```
# at 79
#041005 18:40:08 server id 1  log_pos 79  Query  thread_id=1  exec_time=0  error_
use test;
SET TIMESTAMP=1097026808;
CREATE TABLE t1 (c1 INT);
# at 138
#041005 18:40:08 server id 1  log_pos 138  Query  thread_id=1  exec_time=0  error_
SET TIMESTAMP=1097026808;
INSERT INTO t1 VALUES (12);
# at 199
#041005 18:40:08 server id 1  log_pos 199  Query  thread_id=1  exec_time=0  error_
SET TIMESTAMP=1097026808;
DROP TABLE t1;
```

How It Works

To consolidate your commands into one option file, you had to first delete the MySQL service and then re-create the service. The first step, then, was to use the following command to stop the MySQL service:

```
net stop mysql
```

The command stops the service, which means that you can no longer access the MySQL server. You had to stop the service before you could remove it. Once it was stopped, you executed the following command:

```
mysqld-nt --remove
```

The `mysqld-nt` command (the MySQL server normally implemented in a Windows environment) uses the `--remove` option to remove the service from Windows. Once the service was removed, you added a new service by using the following command:

```
"c:\program files\mysql\mysql server 4.1\bin\mysqld-nt" --install MySQL --defaults-
file="c:\windows\my.ini"
```

The command first specifies the path and filename of the `mysqld-nt` server file, the `--install` option, and the `--defaults-file` option. The `--install` option specifies that the new service be named MySQL, and the `--defaults-file` option specifies that the `my.ini` option file, which is located in the `C:\WINDOWS` directory, should be referenced when starting the service.

After you created the MySQL service, you then used the following command to start the service:

```
net start mysql
```

Starting the service now allows you to verify that it has been successfully installed. To test that installation, you can try to open the mysql client utility, which works only if a connection to the server can be established (which means that the service is installed and running).

Once the new service had been installed, your next step was to set up logging. In order to do so, you had to edit first the option file, which is stored in the C:\WINDOWS directory. (You created the my.ini option file in Chapter 3. For details about the file, see that chapter.) You edited the option file by adding the following commands to the [mysqld] section:

```
log
log-bin
```

The log command implements query logging and creates the <host>.log. The log-bin command implements binary logging and creates the <host>-bin.000001 file and the <host>-bin.index file. If a binary log file already exists, the file extension is incremented by one, based on the highest file number.

After the option file had been modified, you again stopped and then restarted the MySQL service. From there, you viewed the contents of the data directory to verify that the three new log files had been added. Then you used the mysql client utility to execute several SQL statements. After you exited the mysql utility, you used a text editor to view the contents of the <host>.log file. The log file should have contained the four SQL statements that you executed, as well as the time and date of when they were executed.

Next, you used the following command to view the contents of the <host>-bin.000001 file:

```
mysqlbinlog <host>-bin.000001
```

The mysqlbinlog command allows you to view the contents of the binary log and index files. The log file should have contained the SQL statements that affect data (CREATE TABLE, INSERT, and DROP TABLE), but not the SELECT statement.

Summary

This chapter covered a number of topics related to administering the MySQL server. You learned how to view and modify system settings, take specific actions that affect how MySQL runs, and implement logging. Specifically, you learned how to perform the following administrative tasks:

- ❑ Use the mysqladmin client utility to view system information and modify server-related processes
- ❑ Use the SHOW VARIABLES statement to view server system variables
- ❑ Use the SELECT statement to view dynamic system variable settings
- ❑ Use the SHOW STATUS statement to retrieve server status variable settings
- ❑ Specify system settings at server startup
- ❑ Specify system settings in an option file
- ❑ Specify system settings at runtime
- ❑ View the error log file
- ❑ Implement query logging and view query log files
- ❑ Implement binary logging and view binary log files

Now that you have an overview of how to perform basic administrative tasks in MySQL, you're ready to move on to the next topic — security. By understanding how to set up your system's security, you can protect the data in your databases and permit access only to specified users, preventing all other users from viewing or modifying that data. From there, you move on to optimizing performance, implementing replications, backing up your databases, and restoring those databases should it become necessary. Fortunately, much of what you've learned in this chapter provides you with the foundation you need to perform the administrative tasks described in subsequent chapters.

Exercises

In this chapter, you learned how to perform a number of administrative tasks. To help you build on your ability to carry out these tasks, the following exercises are provided. To view solutions to these exercises, see Appendix A.

1. Create a command that flushes the table cache, closes and then reopens the log files, and reloads the grant tables. In addition, the command must return status information about the MySQL server. You must use the command as the user myadmin, and the command must prompt you for your password.

2. Create an SQL statement that displays all global server system variables and their values for those variables whose name contains the string *max* anywhere in the name.

3. Create an SQL statement that displays the current session setting for the dynamic system variable named `query_cache_limit`.

4. Create an SQL statement that displays all server status variables and their values for those variables whose name contains the string *cache* anywhere in the name.

5. Create an SQL statement that sets the session value of the `max_tmp_tables` dynamic system variable to 24.

6. Add the necessary commands to an option file in order to enable binary logging and create the necessary binary log and index files. The files should be stored in the data directory.

7. Create a command that displays the contents of the `Server21-bin.000327` binary log file.

Managing MySQL Security

An important component of administering any database is ensuring that only those users that you want to be able to access the database can do so, while preventing access by all other users. Not only should you be able to control who can log on to the MySQL server, but you should be able to determine what actions authenticated users can take once they connect to the server. All RDBMS products support some level of security in order to protect the data stored in their systems' databases — and MySQL is no exception.

When a user logs on to a MySQL server, MySQL permits the user to perform only approved operations. MySQL security is managed through a set of tables and privileges that determine who can establish a connection to the MySQL server, from what host that connection can be established, and what actions the user (from the specified host) can take. In this chapter, you learn how this system is set up and how you can add user accounts or remove them from the tables. You also learn how to permit users to perform certain actions, while preventing them from taking other actions. To facilitate your ability to configure MySQL security, this chapter provides information about the following topics:

- ❑ The MySQL grant tables, including the user, db, host, tables_priv, and columns_priv tables

- ❑ The process used to authenticate connections to the MySQL server and to verify the privileges necessary to perform various operations

- ❑ The statements necessary to manage MySQL user accounts, including the GRANT, SHOW GRANTS, SET PASSWORD, FLUSH PRIVILEGES, REVOKE, and DROP USER statements

The Access Privilege System

In Chapter 3, you were introduced to the mysql database created by default when you install MySQL. As you learned in that chapter, the mysql database is an administrative database that contains tables related to securing the MySQL installation, storing user-defined functions, and providing data related to the MySQL help system and to time-zone functionality. Of particular concern to preventing unauthorized access to the MySQL server are the security-related tables, which are referred to as the *grant tables*. The grant tables are a set of five tables in the mysql database used to control access to the MySQL server and to the databases managed by that server. The grant tables define which users can access MySQL, from which computers that access is supported, what actions those users can perform, and on which database components those actions can be performed. For example, the grant tables allow you to specify which users can view data in a particular table and which users can actually update that data. In this section, you learn about each of the five grant tables and how those tables are used to authenticate users and determine what operations they can perform.

Working with the grant tables and MySQL security is only one aspect of securing a MySQL installation. You should also ensure the security of the MySQL-related files and the network used to access data in the MySQL databases. A discussion about security specific to your operating system or your network is beyond the scope of this book. For information about system and network security, consult the appropriate product and system documentation.

MySQL Grant Tables

When you install MySQL, five grant tables are added to the mysql database. These tables — user, db, host, tables_priv, and columns_priv — each perform a specific role in either authenticating users or determining whether a particular action can be carried out. Each table contains two types of columns:

❑   **Scope columns:** Columns in a grant table that determine who has access to the MySQL server and the extent, or scope, of that access. Depending on the grant table, the scope columns can include the user account name, the host from which that user connects, the user account's password, or, when appropriate, the name of a specific database, table, or column.

❑   **Privilege columns:** Columns in a grant table that determine what operations can be performed by the user identified in the scope columns. For most grant tables, the privilege columns define the level of access a user account has to the data and the extent to which the user can manipulate that data or allow others to access and manipulate that data. The user table also includes privilege columns that permit administrative operations, require encrypted connections, and specify limits on connections. The default value for most privilege columns is N (for *no*, or *false*). When a privilege is assigned to a user, the value in the related privilege column is set to Y (for *yes*, or *true*).

Through the use of privileges, all five tables participate in the process of determining whether a user can perform a particular operation. (An operation refers to an event such as issuing a SELECT statement to view data in a table or a CREATE TABLE statement to create a table.) Later in the chapter, in the section MySQL Privileges, you learn about the different types of privileges and how they're supported by the grant tables. After that (in the section MySQL Access Control), you learn how the grant tables and privileges are used to authenticate connections to the MySQL server and to permit various types of operations. First, though, you take a closer look at each grant table.

The user Table

The user table is the primary grant table in the mysql database. The table controls who can connect to MySQL, from which hosts they can connect, and what global privileges they have. A global privilege is one that applies to the MySQL server or to any database in the system. For example, a global privilege might be used to allow a user to view data in every table in every database or to allow the user to display a list of the current processes running.

In MySQL, a user is identified not only by the user account name, but also by the host from which the user connects. For example, user1@domain1.com *is considered a different user from* user1@domain2.com. *MySQL uses this method so that users with the same name but from different domains are not treated as the same user. When you come across a reference to a user in MySQL, that reference is usually referring to that user in association with a particular host (or with any host, if that is how the user account is set up). As you progress through this chapter, you learn how this user/host association is used in authenticating a user and in authorizing certain operations.*

As with the other grant tables, the user table contains scope columns and privilege columns. Unlike the other grant tables, though, the user table is the only table that contains different types of privilege columns. The following list describes the different types of columns in the user table:

❑ **Scope columns:** Includes the Host, User, and Password columns. When a connection is initiated, the connection must be made from the host specified in the Host column. In addition, the user account name used for the connection must match the value in the User column, and the password provided when the connection is initiated must match the value in the Password column. A connection is permitted only if all three values match.

❑ **Data-related privilege columns:** Includes those privilege columns that permit data-related operations that are global in scope. There are 11 data-related privilege columns. A privilege granted at this level applies to all tables in all databases. There are also two additional data-related privilege columns that are not currently supported, but they should be supported in later releases of MySQL.

❑ **Administrative privilege columns:** Includes those privilege columns that permit administrative operations to the MySQL server. There are eight administrative privilege columns.

❑ **Encryption-related privilege columns:** Includes the ssl_type, ssl_cipher, x509_issuer, and x509_subject columns, which define whether a user account requires a secure connection and define the nature of that connection.

❑ **Connection-related privilege columns:** Includes the max_questions, max_updates, and max_connections columns, which define whether a limit should be placed on the number of queries, the number of data updates, and the number of connections that can be made in an hour.

To give you an idea of how the user table is configured, assume that you have a user account named user1 that can connect from the domain1.com domain. You can execute a SELECT statement similar to the following to view how that user is listed in the user table:

```
SELECT Host, User, Select_priv, Process_priv, ssl_type, max_updates
FROM user
WHERE User='user1';
```

The SELECT statement retrieves values from two of the scope columns (Host and User) and several of the privilege columns. The Select_priv column assigns a data-related privilege, the Process_priv column assigns an administrative privilege, the ssl_type assigns an encryption privilege, and the max_updates column assigns a connection-related privilege. (You learn more about these privileges later in the chapter.) When you execute this statement, you receive results similar to the following:

```
+--------------+-------+-------------+--------------+----------+-------------+
| Host         | User  | Select_priv | Process_priv | ssl_type | max_updates |
+--------------+-------+-------------+--------------+----------+-------------+
| domain1.com  | user1 | N           | N            | ANY      |           0 |
+--------------+-------+-------------+--------------+----------+-------------+
1 row in set (0.01 sec)
```

There are, of course, many more privileges than are shown here, but this should give you an idea of how MySQL stores user account information in the user table. As you can see, the host from which the user should connect, the name of the user account, and the columns for each privilege that can be applied globally are listed.

Every MySQL user is listed in the user table, whether or not he or she is assigned privileges in that table or any other grant table. The user table provides the widest scope in a MySQL implementation, followed by the db and host tables. If a user is not listed in the user table, that user cannot connect to MySQL.

The db Table

The purpose of the db table is to assign database-specific privileges to users. Any privileges applied in the db table are specific to the specified database. If privileges are assigned to a user for multiple databases, a row is added to the db table for each database, and privileges are then assigned for that row. (If the privileges should apply to all databases, the privileges are assigned in the user table.)

As with the other grant tables, the db table includes scope columns and privilege columns. The following list provides an overview of these columns:

❑   **Scope columns:** Includes the Host, Db, and User columns. For the privileges in this table to apply, the connection must be made from the host specified in the Host column, and the user account name used for the connection must match the value in the User column. If the host column is blank, then the privileges also defined in the host table are applied. Any privileges assigned in the db table apply only to the database specified in the Db column.

❑   **Privilege columns:** Includes those privileges that can be applied at the database level. These are the 11 data-related privileges (the same as those you see in the user table) used to permit data-related operations. There is an additional data-related privilege column that is not currently supported, but it should be supported in later releases of MySQL.

To get a better sense of the db table, assume that the user1 account has been assigned privileges specifically on the test database. You can then use a SELECT statement to view information about that user account:

```
SELECT Host, Db, User, Select_priv, Update_priv
FROM db
WHERE User='user1';
```

The statement retrieves information from the three scope columns (Host, Db, and User) and from two of the privilege columns (Select_priv and Update_priv), as shown in the following results:

```
+--------------+------+-------+-------------+-------------+
| Host         | Db   | User  | Select_priv | Update_priv |
+--------------+------+-------+-------------+-------------+
| domain1.com  | test | user1 | Y           | N           |
+--------------+------+-------+-------------+-------------+
1 row in set (0.00 sec)
```

As you can see, the Host value is domain1.com, the Db value is test, and the User value is User1. As a result, the privileges assigned in this row are applied to the user1 account when that account connects from domain1.com. In addition, the privileges apply only to the test database. You can, of course, retrieve more privilege columns than those shown here. If a privilege is assigned to the account, a value of Y is displayed in the columns; otherwise, a value of N is displayed.

The db table works in conjunction with the host table. If the Host column in the db table is blank, MySQL checks the host table to determine whether any privileges apply to a specific database from a specific host.

The host Table

The host table is associated with the db table and is checked only when a user is listed in the db table but the Host column is blank. The combination of these two tables allows you to apply privileges to a user who connects from multiple hosts. For example, if a user named SarahW connects to MySQL from big.domain1.com and little.domain1.com, you can add the user to the db table, with a blank host value, and then add the two hosts to the host table, specifying the same database name in the SarahW row of the db table and in the big.domain1.com and little.domain1.com rows of the host table. When MySQL sees the blank host value in the db table, it looks in the host table for a Host value that matches the hostname of the connection. If there's a match, the privileges from the db table and the host table are compared to determine whether an operation is permitted. The matching privileges in both tables must be set to Y for the operation to be permitted. (You learn more about this process in the section "MySQL Access Control" later in the chapter.)

The host table, as with other grant tables, includes scope columns and privilege columns. Because the host table works in conjunction with the db table, it is the only grant table that does not include a User column. The following list describes the columns in the db table:

- ❑ **Scope columns:** Includes the Host and Db columns. For the privileges in this table to apply, the Host column in the db table must be blank, and the connection must be made from the host specified in the Host column of the host table. Any privileges assigned in the host table apply only to the database specified in the Db column of the host table.

- ❑ **Privilege columns:** Includes those privileges that can be applied at the database level for user accounts accessing the databases from specific hosts. These are the same 11 data-related privilege columns that you find in the user and db tables. The privileges are combined with the applicable privileges in the db table to permit authorized operations. There is an additional data-related privilege column that is not currently supported, but it should be supported in later releases of MySQL.

To better understand how user accounts are added to the host table, suppose that you want to allow user1 to connect from the host host1.domain1.com or from host2.domain1.com domains. You add a row for each host in the host table. To then view the rows added to the table, you can use a SELECT statement similar to the following:

```
SELECT Host, Db, Select_priv, Update_priv
FROM host
WHERE Host='host1.domain1.com' OR Host='host2.domain1.com';
```

As you can see, the SELECT statement retrieves values from the two scope columns (Host and Db) and two of the privilege columns, as shown in the following results:

```
+-------------------+------+------------+------------+
| Host              | Db   | Select_priv | Update_priv |
+-------------------+------+------------+------------+
| host1.domain1.com | test | Y          | N          |
| host2.domain1.com | test | Y          | N          |
+-------------------+------+------------+------------+
2 rows in set (0.01 sec)
```

The results include only the Host and Db scope columns, but not a User scope column because one isn't included in the host table. The host table contains the same 11 data-related privilege columns that are in the db and user tables (12 data-related columns if you include the unsupported column).

The host table is different from other grant tables in that user account information and privilege settings are not configured in the same way as the other tables. Later in the chapter you learn that the GRANT statement is the primary method that you should use to add users to your system and to assign privileges. At the same time, the REVOKE statement is the primary method that you should use to revoke privileges. The host table, however, is not affected by the GRANT statement or the REVOKE statement, which means that, if you plan to use the host table, you must set up the privileges manually, which is a less efficient method to use than the GRANT and REVOKE statements and which is more prone to errors.

This problem can be exacerbated if multiple users connect from the same hosts. You must ensure that the entries in the host table can be applied to all users in such a way that, when those privileges are compared with the privileges in the db table, each user can perform the necessary operations, without being able to perform unauthorized operations. As a result of these issues, few MySQL implementations use the host table.

The tables_priv Table

The tables_priv table is specific to table-level privileges. Any privileges assigned in this table apply only to the table specified in the tables_priv table. The following list describes the columns in the tables_priv table:

❑ **Scope columns:** Includes the Host, Db, User, and Table_name columns. For the privileges in this table to apply, the connection must be made from the host specified in the Host column, and the user account name used for the connection must match the value in the User column. Any privileges assigned in the tables_priv table apply only to the table specified in the Table_name column, as it exists in the database specified in the Db column.

❑ **Privilege columns:** Includes the Table_priv column and the Column_priv column. The Table_priv column defines the privileges applied at the table level. The Column_priv column defines the privileges applied at the column level.

Note that the tables_priv table also includes the Grantor and Timestamp columns, but they are currently unused. It is assumed that future releases of MySQL will make use of these columns.

To better understand how the tables_priv table stores user account data, assume that user1 has been assigned table- and column-level privileges. You can use a SELECT statement similar to the following to retrieve data from the tables_priv table about that user:

```
SELECT Host, Db, User, Table_name, Table_priv, Column_priv
FROM tables_priv
WHERE User='user1';
```

The statement includes the four scope columns (Host, Db, User, and Table_name) and the two privilege columns (Table_priv and Column_priv). As you learn in the next section, the privilege columns in the tables_priv and columns_priv tables work differently from the privilege columns in the other grant tables. When you execute the SELECT statement, your results should be similar to the following:

```
+-------------+------+-------+------------+------------+-------------+
| Host        | Db   | User  | Table_name | Table_priv | Column_priv |
+-------------+------+-------+------------+------------+-------------+
| domain1.com | test | user1 | Books      | Select     | Update      |
+-------------+------+-------+------------+------------+-------------+
1 row in set (0.00 sec)
```

As you can see, the scope columns include not only the host, user, and database (as you saw in the db table) but also the name of the table. As a result, any privileges assigned to this user account in this table are specifically for the Books table.

The tables_priv table works in conjunction with the columns_priv table. If the Column_priv column in the tables_priv table contains a value, MySQL checks the columns_priv table for specifics about the privileges that apply to the individual columns.

The columns_priv Table

The columns_priv table shows the privileges associated with individual columns. When a user is listed in the tables_priv table and the columns_priv table, the privileges specified in the Column_priv column of the columns_priv table are applied to the columns, and the privileges specified in the Table_priv column of the tables_priv table are applied to the table as a whole. The following list describes the columns in the columns_priv table:

❏ **Scope columns:** Includes the Host, Db, User, Table_name, and Column_name columns. For the privileges in this table to apply, the connection must be made from the host specified in the Host column, and the user account name used for the connection must match the value in the User column. Any privileges assigned in the columns_priv table apply only to the column specified in the Column_name column, as it exists in the table specified in the Table_name column, which exists in the database specified in the Db column.

❏ **Privilege columns:** Includes the Column_priv column, which defines the privileges applied at the column level.

Note that the columns_priv table also includes the Timestamp column, but is currently unused. It is assumed that future releases of MySQL will make use of this column.

In the previous example, you saw how the user1 account appears in the tables_priv table. Now you can use a SELECT statement to retrieve information about that account in the columns_priv table:

```
SELECT Host, Db, User, Table_name, Column_name, Column_priv
FROM columns_priv
WHERE User='user1';
```

As you can see, the statement retrieves data from the scope columns (Host, Db, User, Table_name, and Column_name) and the privilege column (Column_priv), as shown in the following results:

```
+-------------+------+-------+------------+-------------+-------------+
| Host        | Db   | User  | Table_name | Column_name | Column_priv |
+-------------+------+-------+------------+-------------+-------------+
| domain1.com | test | user1 | books      | BookTitle   | Update      |
| domain1.com | test | user1 | books      | Copyright   | Update      |
+-------------+------+-------+------------+-------------+-------------+
2 rows in set (0.00 sec)
```

Each row in the columns_priv table assigns privileges to a specific column. The columns_priv table is the most granular of all the tables, in terms of assigning privileges to users. When MySQL authorizes a user to perform an operation, however, all applicable grant tables are examined, starting with the user table and working down to the columns_priv table. For example, if a user is granted select privileges on a table, but update privileges on only one column in the table, the user can still retrieve data from the entire table, but update data only in that one column. The following section takes a closer look at the different privileges supported by MySQL.

MySQL Privileges

The user, db, and host tables contain columns that each represent individual privileges. All three tables include the data-related privileges, which deal specifically with managing data. As you saw previously, only the user table contains privileges that are specific to administration and connectivity. The following table describes the privileges that can be assigned in the user, db, and host tables, and it shows which tables contain which privileges.

Column	Type	Allows user to	user table	db table	host table
Select_priv	Data-related	Query data in a database.	X	X	X
Insert_priv	Data-related	Insert data in a database.	X	X	X
Update_priv	Data-related	Update data in a database.	X	X	X
Delete_priv	Data-related	Delete data from a database.	X	X	X
Create_priv	Data-related	Create a table in a database.	X	X	X
Drop_priv	Data-related	Remove a table from a database.	X	X	X
Reload_priv	Administrative	Reload the data in the grant tables in MySQL.	X		

Column	Type	Allows user to	user table	db table	host table
Shutdown_priv	Administrative	Shut down the MySQL server.	X		
Process_priv	Administrative	View a list of MySQL processes.	X		
File_priv	Administrative	Export data from a database into a file.	X		
Grant_priv	Data-related	Grant privileges on database objects.	X	X	X
Index_priv	Data-related	Create and delete indexes in a database.	X	X	X
Alter_priv	Data-related	Alter database objects.	X	X	X
Show_db_priv	Administrative	View all databases.	X		
Super_priv	Administrative	Perform advanced administrative tasks.	X		
Create_tmp_table_priv	Data-related	Create temporary tables.	X	X	X
Lock_tables_priv	Data-related	Place locks on tables.	X	X	X
Repl_slave_priv	Administrative	Read binary logs for a replication master.	X		
Repl_client_priv	Administrative	Request information about slave and master servers used for replication.	X		
ssl_type	Encryption-related	Specifies whether a secure connection is required. If required, the column specifies the type of secure connection.	X		
ssl_cipher	Encryption-related	Specifies the cipher method that should be used for a connection. If the column is blank, no special cipher method is required.	X		

Table continued on following page

Column	Type	Allows user to	user table	db table	host table
x509_issuer	Encryption-related	Specifies the name of the certificate authority that issues the x509 certificate. The name should be used for an x509 connection. If the column is blank, the issuer name is not required.	X		
x509_subject	Encryption-related	Specifies the subject that should be included on the x509 certificate when establishing a secure connection. If the column is blank, the subject is not required.	X		
max_questions	Connection-related	Specifies the number of queries that an account can issue in an hour. If set to 0, the user account can issue an unlimited number of queries.	X		
max_updates	Connection-related	Specifies the number of data updates that an account can perform in an hour. If set to 0, the user account can perform an unlimited number of updates.	X		
max_connections	Connection-related	Specifies the number of connections that an account can establish in an hour. If set to 0, the user account can connect an unlimited number of times.	X		

The privileges are listed in this table in the order they appear in the user table. Because permissions in the user table are applied globally, it is the only table that contains all privileges. The more granular the privileges, the fewer privileges there are, which is reflected in the grant tables. For example, the user table has more privilege columns than the db table, which is more granular than the user table.

Some of the grant tables also include the Execute_priv and the References_priv, neither of which are currently supported. It appears that the Execute_priv will be related to stored procedures when they're implemented in MySQL, and the References_priv will be related to foreign keys.

All the data-related and administrative privilege columns in the user, db, and host tables are configured with the ENUM data type and assigned the values N or Y, with N being the default. When a permission is granted to an account, the value is changed to Y. For the encryption-related and connection-related columns, the data types vary, depending on the type of data that can be inserted in those columns. In the "Managing MySQL User Accounts" section later in the chapter, you learn how to use the GRANT statement to insert values in these columns.

Privileges are assigned differently in the tables_priv and columns_priv tables than they're assigned in the user, db, and host tables. The tables_priv table includes the Table_priv and Column_priv columns, and the columns_priv table includes only the Column_priv column. Each of these columns is configured with the SET data type, which means that a set of values is defined for each column. One or more of those values can be inserted in the columns. The following table lists the values included with each column.

Column	Privilege values
Table_priv	Select, Insert, Update, Delete, Create, Drop, Grant, Index, Alter
Column_priv	Select, Insert, Update

Both columns also include a References privilege, but that privilege currently is not used by MySQL.

The values in the Table_priv and Column_priv columns have their counterparts with some of the data-related privilege columns you find in the user, db, and host tables. The names of the values clearly indicate to which privileges they are related. For example, the Select value has its counterpart with the Select_priv column in the user, db, and host tables. In both cases, the privilege allows the specified user to retrieve data from a database.

MySQL Access Control

When MySQL permits a user to conduct various operations in the MySQL environment, it first authenticates those connections to allow access to the MySQL server, and then it verifies the privileges assigned to that user account to determine whether the requested operations are permitted.

Authenticating Connections

The first step in allowing a user to access the MySQL server is to ensure that the user has that access. If access is permitted, MySQL authenticates the connection. The connection is authenticated only if the Host value in the user table matches the name of the host from which the connection is being established. In addition, the username used for the connection must match the value in the User column, and if a password is required, the password supplied for the connection must match the value in the Password column. If the parameters supplied by the connection match all the applicable values in the user table, the connection is permitted.

If a Host value in the user table contains the percentage (%) wildcard, the user can connect from any host. If the User column is blank, any user can connect to the server from the specified host. (These types of users are referred to as anonymous users.) If the Host value is the percentage wildcard and the User column is blank, any user from any host can connect to the server. The Password column can also be blank.

This does not mean, though, that any password is acceptable. It means that the user must supply a blank password. For example, if the user specifies the -p option when launching MySQL and then is prompted for a password, the user should simply press Enter and not enter any password.

If you expect to allow anonymous users or plan to allow users to connect from any host, you must plan your user table carefully to ensure that the right user is associated with the correct privileges. To plan your user accounts, you should keep in mind how MySQL accesses the user table:

1. When the MySQL server starts, data from the user table is copied to memory in sorted order.

2. When a client attempts to log on to the server, the user account is checked against the sorted user data in memory.

3. The server uses the first applicable entry to authenticate a user, based first on the Host value and then on the User value.

MySQL first sorts the user table according to the Host column and then according to the User column. For the Host column, specific values are listed first, followed by less specific values, such as those that use the percentage wildcard. Rows that have the same value in the Host column are then sorted according to the value in the User column, again, with the specific values listed first and the least specific (a blank) last.

This sorting is important because MySQL, when authenticating a user, first checks the Host column for a match and then checks the User column. Whichever row in the user table provides the first match, that is the user account used to authenticate the user and subsequently assign privileges to that user. If there are no wildcards in the host column and no blanks in the User column, MySQL simply matches the host-name and username to the Host and User values and authenticates the user. The use of wildcards and blanks in the Host and User column, however, can result in a user being incorrectly authenticated.

To help illustrate the implications of the user table sorting, take a look at the following result set, which shows the Host and User values from the user table in a MySQL installation:

```
+-------------+-------+
| Host        | User  |
+-------------+-------+
| %           | root  |
| domain1.com | user1 |
| localhost   |       |
| %           |       |
+-------------+-------+
4 row in set (0.01 sec)
```

As you saw earlier, when the user table is copied to memory, the data is sorted according to the Host and User columns, as shown in the following result set:

```
+-------------+-------+
| Host        | User  |
+-------------+-------+
| domain1.com | user1 |
| localhost   |       |
| %           | root  |
| %           |       |
+-------------+-------+
4 row in set (0.01 sec)
```

Notice that the rows that contain the percentage wildcard in the Host column are the last rows. The percentage represents the least specific type of host, so it appears last. Now suppose that the root user attempts to log in from the local computer. According to the user table, there is only one entry for the root account: root@%. In theory, this would mean that the root account can log in from any host, including the local computer. When the user logs on, MySQL first checks the Host column and finds the first match, which is the localhost value. MySQL then checks the User column and finds only a blank value, indicating that anonymous users are permitted, which is also a match. As a result, the root account is logged on as an anonymous user, rather than the primary administrator. This means that the root user is now operating under the privileges granted to the anonymous user rather than to the root user.

One way to get around this situation is to create two entries in the user table for a specified user, as is done for the root user when you install MySQL. In Windows, the root user can log on as root@localhost or as root@%, and in Linux, the root user can log on as root@localhost or as root@<host>, where <host> is the name of the local computer. This way, even if the percentage wildcard is used for the Host value or a blank is used for the User value, MySQL can still identify the root account. By including an entry specifically for localhost, anonymous users can be permitted, but the specified accounts are still protected. As a result, when the root user logs on, there are now two rows for localhost. These two rows are then sorted first by the root user and then by the anonymous users. A blank value is always at the end of the list. The root user is then logged on with the correct privileges.

> *If anonymous accounts are allowed to access the MySQL server, normally passwords would not be permitted. This can even further complicate the user who is inadvertently treated as an anonymous user. For example, if a user tries to log on as root and supplies a password, but MySQL treats that user as anonymous, the password is interpreted as an incorrect value because MySQL is expecting a blank password. As a result, the connection is denied.*

By ensuring that the user table has the necessary entries for each user, users can be correctly logged on to the MySQL server. The operations that the user can perform are still limited to those permitted by the privileges associated with that user account.

Verifying Privileges

After MySQL authenticates a user, it checks the privileges associated with that user account to determine what operations the user can perform. When verifying privileges, MySQL first checks the user table. If privileges have not been granted to the account in the user table, MySQL checks the db table and, if appropriate, the host table. If privileges have not been granted at the database level, MySQL checks the tables_priv table, and, if appropriate, the columns_priv table. If, after checking all applicable tables, the operation is not permitted, the operation fails.

> *MySQL drills down through the grant tables (from the user table down to the columns_priv table) only as far as necessary. For example, if a user logs on to the MySQL server and tries to perform an administrative action, MySQL checks only the user table because only that table contains administrative privileges.*

Figure 14-1 illustrates the process that MySQL uses to authorize users to perform the requested operation. The figures show the process only as far as it goes to checking the tables_priv and columns_priv tables. (Figure 14-2 covers those two tables.) Figure 14-1 assumes that the requested operation is one that could potentially require permissions as far down as those that can be assigned in the tables_priv and columns_priv tables. Of course, if any operation does not require that MySQL drill down through the grant tables that far, the operation either is permitted or fails at whatever point MySQL no longer needs to continue checking tables.

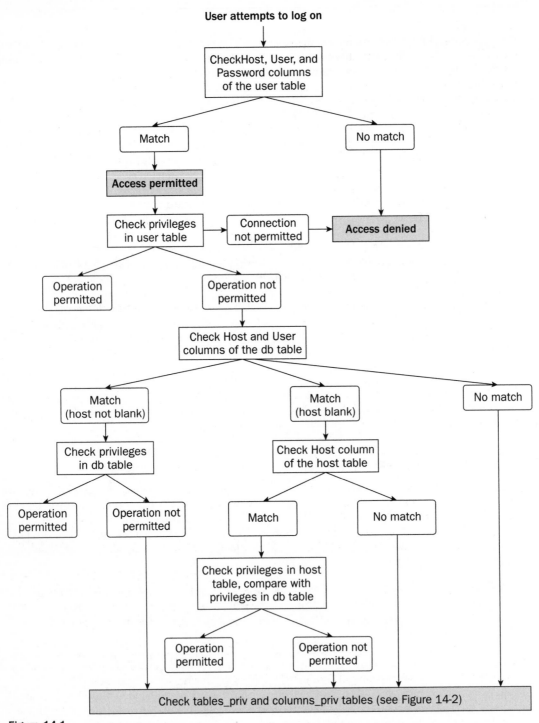

Figure 14-1

The following steps describe the process that MySQL follows when verifying privileges:

1. The user or the application initiates a connection, supplying a hostname, username, and password, if a password has been assigned to the user account. For users or applications attempting to log on anonymously, only the hostname is provided.

2. If no match is found in the Host, User, and Password columns of the user table, access is denied. If a match is found, access to the MySQL server is permitted.

3. MySQL then checks the privileges in the user table. If the connection exceeds the connections-per-hour limit, access is denied. If the connection does not meet any encryption-related privileges assigned to the connection, access is denied. Otherwise, the operation being requested by the connection is compared to the data-related and administrative privileges defined in the user table. For example, if the connection attempts to execute a SELECT statement, the SELECT privilege is checked to see whether a SELECT statement operation is permitted.

4. If the privileges permit the operation, MySQL carries out that operation. If the privileges do not permit the operation, MySQL checks the db table:

    ❑   If the connection hostname and username match the values in the Host and User columns of the db table, MySQL checks the privileges in that table. If the privileges permit the operation for the specified database, MySQL carries out that operation. If the privileges do not permit the operation, MySQL checks the tables_priv and columns_priv tables. (See Figure 14-2.)

    ❑   If the username matches the value in the User column of the db table and the Host column for that table is blank, MySQL checks the Host column of the host table. If the connection hostname matches the value in the Host column, MySQL checks the privileges in the host table and compares them to the privileges in the db table. If the privileges permit the operation for the specified database, MySQL carries out that operation. If the privileges do not permit the operation, MySQL checks the tables_priv and columns_priv tables. If the connection hostname does not match the value in the Host column of the host table, MySQL checks the tables_priv and columns_priv tables.

    ❑   If the connection hostname and username do not match the values in the Host and User columns of the db table, MySQL checks the tables_priv and columns_priv tables.

If, after checking the db and host tables, MySQL reaches a point when it still cannot determine whether to permit the operation, it checks the tables_priv table and, if necessary, the columns_priv table. Figure 14-2 illustrates the process that MySQL uses to check these two tables. This process is a continuation of the privilege checking shown in Figure 14-1.

MySQL first checks to see whether the connection hostname and username are listed in the Host and User columns of the tables_priv table. If there is a match, MySQL checks the privileges in that table. If there is no match, the operation fails.

If MySQL does match the hostname and username to the values in the tables_priv table, MySQL takes one of the following steps:

    ❑   If the privileges in the Table_priv column of the tables_priv table permit the operation, MySQL carries out the operation.

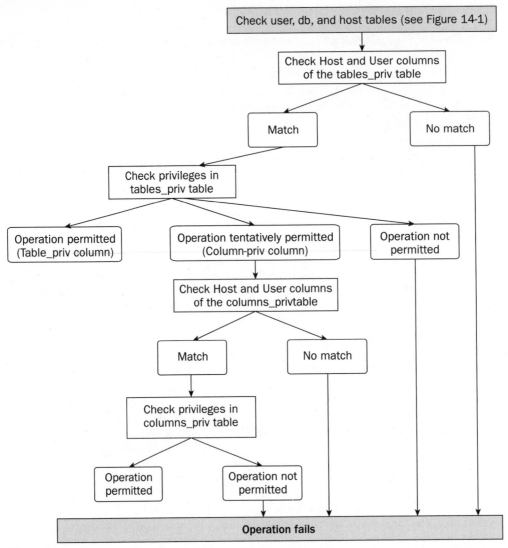

Figure 14-2

❑ If the privileges in the Column_priv column of the tables_priv table permit the operation, MySQL checks the columns_priv table:

    ❑ If the hostname and username match the values in the Host and User columns of the columns_priv table, MySQL checks the privileges in the Column_priv column of the columns_priv table. If the privileges permit the operation, MySQL carries out the operation. If the privileges do not permit the operation, the operation fails.

    ❑ If the hostname and username do not match the values in the Host and User columns of the columns_priv table, the operation fails.

❑ If the privileges in the tables_priv table don't permit the operation, the operation fails.

As you can see, there are many places in the authorization process at which an operation can succeed or fail. As a result, it's important that you set up your user accounts with great care to ensure that those users who should have access can log on to the server and perform the necessary operations and that those users who should not have access are prevented from logging on to the MySQL server or viewing or modifying data in the MySQL databases.

Managing MySQL User Accounts

MySQL provides a number of SQL statements that allow you to manage your user accounts. By using these statements, you can add user accounts to your system and grant privileges to those accounts. You can also view the privileges that have been assigned to a user account, or you can change the password for that account. In addition, the statements allow you to revoke privileges and drop users from your system. In this section, you learn about these SQL statements and how they can be used to secure your MySQL installation effectively.

Adding Users and Granting Privileges

You can add a user account to your system and assign privileges to that account by using the GRANT statement, which allows you to perform both operations in a single statement. Although you can insert account information directly in the grant tables, the GRANT statement is easier and is less likely to result in errors that can occur if information is added in different grant tables that conflict with each other. Once you have added a user account and assigned privileges to that account, you can use the SHOW GRANTS statement to view details about that account.

Using the GRANT Statement

Now that you have an overview of how the grant tables are used to authenticate users and associate privileges with those users, you're ready to look at how you actually create a user account and assign privileges to the account. To perform both operations, you should use the GRANT statement, which is shown in the following syntax:

```
GRANT <privilege> [(<column> [{, <column>}...])]
    [{, <privilege> [(<column> [{, <column>}...])]}...]
ON {<table> | * | *.* | <database>.*}
TO '<user>'@'<host>' [IDENTIFIED BY [PASSWORD] '<new password>']
    [{, '<user>'@'<host>' [IDENTIFIED BY [PASSWORD] '<new password>']}...]
[REQUIRE {NONE | SSL | X509 | {<require definition>}]
[WITH <with option> [<with option>...]]

<require definition>::=
<require option> [[AND] <require option>] [[AND] <require option>]

<require option>::=
{CIPHER '<string>'}
| {ISSUER '<string>'}
| {SUBJECT '<string>'}

<with option>::=
{GRANT OPTION}
| {MAX_QUERIES_PER_HOUR <count>}
| {MAX_UPDATES_PER_HOUR <count>}
| {MAX_CONNECTIONS_PER_HOUR <count>}
```

As with other SQL statements, the GRANT statement is made up of multiple clauses and options, some of which are optional and some of which are required. As you're learning about each of these clauses and you start creating your own GRANT statements, you should keep in mind that the MySQL server treats some scope column values as case sensitive (whether or not they're treated this way by your operating system). The following table shows the case sensitivity of each scope column.

Column	Case sensitive?
Host	No
User	Yes
Password	Yes
Db	Yes
Table_name	Yes
Column_name	No

When working with the GRANT statement, you want to ensure that you enter User, Password, Db, and Table_name values exactly as you intend for them to be treated once the account is created.

When you use the GRANT statement to set up a user account, the statement adds the necessary data to the grant tables. Whenever you create an account, a row is added to the user table. Whether rows are added to other grant tables depends on the level at which the privileges are being granted (for example, a global level versus a database level). In addition to using the GRANT statement to add the necessary rows to the grant tables, you can also use INSERT statements to add the necessary data. Using INSERT statements can be far more cumbersome and prone to error. For that reason, using a GRANT statement is the recommended method for adding user accounts to your system. Now take a look at how to create the required clauses in your GRANT statement.

Defining the Mandatory Clauses of the GRANT Statement

If you refer back to the GRANT statement syntax, notice that there are three required clauses: the GRANT clause, the ON clause, and the TO clause. In this section, you learn how to define each of these clauses.

Defining the GRANT Clause

The GRANT clause determines the type of privileges that should be assigned to the user account. As the following syntax shows, you can specify one or more privileges, and you can specify one or more column names with each privilege:

```
GRANT <privilege> [(<column> [{, <column>}...])]
    [{, <privilege> [(<column> [{, <column>}...])]}...]
```

Each privilege is associated with a privilege column in the user, db, or host table or with one of the privileges listed in the Table_priv or Column_priv columns of the tables_priv and columns_priv tables. The following table describes all the privileges that you can use (in place of the <privilege> placeholder) available to the GRANT statement. The table also shows the privilege column that is associated with that privilege. For the tables_priv and columns_priv table, the privilege name is associated with the appropriate option in the Table_priv and Column_priv columns. For example, the INSERT privilege is associated with the Insert column option.

Privilege syntax	Columns set to Y	Actions permitted
ALL [PRIVILEGES]	All columns (at the level that the GRANT statement applies to), except the Grant_priv column	Execute all statements except GRANT, REVOKE, and DROP USER statements.
ALTER	Alter_priv	Execute ALTER TABLE statements.
CREATE	Create_priv	Execute CREATE TABLE statements.
CREATE TEMPORARY TABLES	Create_tmp_table_priv	Execute CREATE TEMPORARY TABLE statements.
DELETE	Delete_priv	Execute DELETE statements.
DROP	Drop_priv	Execute DROP TABLE statements.
FILE	File_priv	Execute SELECT...INTO OUTFILE and LOAD DATA INFILE statements.
INDEX	Index_priv	Execute CREATE INDEX and DROP INDEX statements.
INSERT	Insert_priv	Execute INSERT statements.
GRANT OPTION	Grant_priv	Execute GRANT, REVOKE, and DROP USER statements.
LOCK TABLES	Lock_tables_priv	Execute LOCK TABLES statements. (User must also have SELECT privilege.)
PROCESS	Process_priv	Execute SHOW FULL PROCESSLIST statements.
RELOAD	Reload_priv	Execute FLUSH statements.
REPLICATION CLIENT	Repl_client_priv	Locate slave and master replication servers.
REPLICATION SLAVE	Repl_slave_priv	Read binary log events from master replication servers.
SELECT	Select_priv	Execute SELECT statements.
SHOW DATABASES	Show_db_priv	Execute SHOW DATABASES statements.
SHUTDOWN	Shutdown_priv	Use shutdown option of the mysqladmin client utility

Table continued on following page

Privilege syntax	Columns set to Y	Actions permitted
SUPER	Super_priv	Execute CHANGE MASTER, KILL, PURGE MASTER LOGS, and SET GLOBAL statements; use the debug command of the mysqladmin client utility; and connect to MySQL server even if max_connections system variable limit has been reached.
UPDATE	Update_priv	Execute UPDATE statements.
USAGE	No columns affected	No actions permitted. Option used to add user with no privileges or to update user options not related to privileges.

You might have noticed that not all privileges are represented here. The encryption-related and connection-related privileges are assigned in different clauses, which are described later in the chapter.

When you specify privileges in the GRANT clause, you simply include the privilege name and, if applicable, the column names, enclosed in the parentheses. If you include more than one privilege, they must be separated with commas. If you include more than one column for a privilege, the column names must be separated by commas.

Defining the ON Clause

After you define the GRANT clause, you can define the ON clause, shown in the following syntax:

```
ON {<table> | * | *.* | <database>.*}
```

The ON clause specifies to which tables or database the GRANT statement applies. As you can see, the clause includes four options. The option you choose determines the level at which the privileges are applied. The following list describes how the options can be used for each level:

❑ **Global:** Use the double wildcard (*.*) option to specify that the privileges should apply to the MySQL server and to all databases and their tables. You can also use the single wildcard (*) option if no database is active when executing the GRANT statement; otherwise, the single wildcard option applies only to the active database.

❑ **Database:** Use the <database>.* option to specify that the privileges should apply to the specified database as a whole and to all tables in that database. You can also use the single wildcard (*) option if a database is active; otherwise, the single wildcard option applies globally.

❑ **Table:** Use the <table> option to specify that the privileges should apply only to that table. The option is usually preceded by the database name and a period. For example, the books table in the test database is referred to as test.books.

❑ **Column:** Use the <table> option to specify that the privileges should apply only to that table, as is the case when assigning table-level privileges. To make the GRANT table column-specific, the <table> option should be used in conjunction with the columns specified in the GRANT clause.

You can use a single GRANT statement if you want to grant privileges at both the table level and at the column level. To do so, specify column names in the GRANT clause only for those columns that should be associated with privileges at the column level. Do not specify column names for the other privileges so that those privileges are applied to the table as a whole. If you want to grant privileges that combine other levels (for example, a SELECT privilege at a global level and a DELETE privilege at a table level), you should use separate GRANT statements.

Defining the TO Clause

The final required clause that you must include in your GRANT statement is the TO clause, which is shown in the following syntax:

```
TO '<user>'@'<host>' [IDENTIFIED BY [PASSWORD] '<new password>']
   [{, '<user>'@'<host>' [IDENTIFIED BY [PASSWORD] '<new password>']}...]
```

As the syntax illustrates, you can assign privileges to one or more users, as long as you separate each pair of user definitions with a comma. For each user account, you must specify a username, hostname, and optionally a password. When assigning values in the TO clause, keep the following guidelines in mind:

❑   **Host:** The host from which the user will be connecting. You can specify a hostname, an IP address, or localhost. You can use the percentage (%) and underscore (_) wildcards in your hostname. The percentage wildcard indicates that any number of any character can be used. The underscore wildcard indicates that any single character can be used. You can use the percentage wildcard with no other values to indicate that any host is acceptable.

❑   **User:** The username associated with the user account that is being created. You cannot use wildcards, but you can use a blank, which indicates that anonymous users are permitted access.

❑   **Password:** The password associated with the user account that is being created. You cannot use wildcards, but you can use a blank. If a blank is used, users must supply a blank password when logging on to the server. When you use a GRANT statement to create a password, the password is automatically encrypted when it is saved to the user table.

When you assign a password to a user, you must precede the password with the IDENTIFIED BY subclause. In addition, the password, just like the user and host values, should be enclosed in single quotes.

Now that you have seen how the syntax is defined for the GRANT, ON, and TO clauses, you're ready to take a look at some examples that put all these clauses together.

Creating a Basic GRANT Statement

The first example GRANT statement creates a user account and grants global-level privileges to that account:

```
GRANT ALL
ON *.*
TO 'user1'@'domain1.com' IDENTIFIED BY 'pw1';
```

In this statement, the GRANT clause includes one privilege (ALL). The ALL privileges grants all privileges to the user except those that allow the user to grant and revoke privileges. The ON clause includes the double wildcard (*.*) option, which indicates that the privileges being assigned to this user are at the global level. The TO clause specifies the username (user1) and the hostname (domain1.com). The clause also includes the IDENTIFIED BY subclause, which defines the password pw1 on the user account.

In order to grant privileges to another user, you must have the necessary privileges. This means that, when you're user account was created, it must have been created with the GRANT OPTION. This option is discussed later in the chapter.

To sum up the GRANT statement, you can say that user1, connecting from domain1.com, can perform all tasks on all tables and databases except for granting and revoking privileges. In addition, user1 must supply the pw1 password when logging on to the MySQL server. If you want to view how this account would be added to the user table (the table associated with global privileges), you can use a SELECT statement similar to the following:

```
SELECT host, user, select_priv, update_priv FROM user WHERE user='user1';
```

The statement retrieves only two of the privilege columns, both of which are data-related privileges, as shown in the following results:

```
+--------------+-------+-------------+-------------+
| host         | user  | select_priv | update_priv |
+--------------+-------+-------------+-------------+
| domain1.com  | user1 | Y           | Y           |
+--------------+-------+-------------+-------------+
1 row in set (0.00 sec)
```

The next example is far more limited in scope than the previous example. The GRANT statement grants SELECT and UPDATE privileges on all tables in the test database, as shown in the following statement:

```
GRANT SELECT, UPDATE
ON test.*
TO 'user1'@'domain1.com' IDENTIFIED BY 'pw1';
```

Note that user1 is used as the name in all the example GRANT statements in this chapter, but you can assume that, for the purpose of these examples, that a new account is being created when each GRANT statement is issued.

As you can see, the GRANT clause includes the SELECT and UPDATE privileges, the ON clause specifies that the entire test database is affected, and the TO clause identifies user1@domain1.com. A password has also been assigned to this account. The statement, then, allows user1 to connect to the MySQL server from the domain1.com host. The user must supply the pw1 password and can issue only SELECT and UPDATE statements against the tables in the test database.

Because the GRANT statement is specific to a database, you can use the following SELECT statements to see how the user account would be added to the user and db tables:

```
SELECT host, user, select_priv, update_priv FROM user WHERE user='user1';
SELECT host, db, user, select_priv, update_priv FROM db WHERE user='user1';
```

The SELECT statements return results similar to the following:

```
+-------------+-------+-------------+-------------+
| host        | user  | select_priv | update_priv |
+-------------+-------+-------------+-------------+
| domain1.com | user1 | N           | N           |
+-------------+-------+-------------+-------------+
1 row in set (0.00 sec)

+-------------+------+-------+-------------+-------------+
| host        | db   | user  | select_priv | update_priv |
+-------------+------+-------+-------------+-------------+
| domain1.com | test | user1 | Y           | Y           |
+-------------+------+-------+-------------+-------------+
1 row in set (0.00 sec)
```

As you can see, user1 is listed in the user table but is assigned no privileges. (Each privilege column has an N as a value.) The user, however, is also listed in the db table, which shows that the user has been assigned privileges on the test table. (Each privilege column has Y as a value.) Next you look at an example that creates table-level privileges. The table used in the example is shown in the following table definition:

```
CREATE TABLE Books
(
    BookID SMALLINT NOT NULL PRIMARY KEY,
    BookTitle VARCHAR(60) NOT NULL,
    Copyright YEAR NOT NULL
)
ENGINE=INNODB;
```

You can assume that the Books table has been added to the test database. Now take a look at a GRANT statement that assigns table-level privileges on the Books table:

```
GRANT SELECT, UPDATE
ON test.Books
TO 'user1'@'domain1.com' IDENTIFIED BY 'pw1';
```

As you can see, the example is nearly identical to the previous example GRANT statement; however, the ON clause now specifies a table as well as a database, so the statement is now applied at the table level, rather than the database level. As a result, the user account is added to the tables_priv table rather than the db table. To view how the user account is added to the grant tables, you can use a SELECT statement similar to the following:

```
SELECT host, user, select_priv, update_priv FROM user WHERE user='user1';
SELECT host, db, user, table_name, table_priv, column_priv
    FROM tables_priv WHERE user='user1';
```

The statements return results similar to the following:

```
+-------------+-------+-------------+-------------+
| host        | user  | select_priv | update_priv |
+-------------+-------+-------------+-------------+
| domain1.com | user1 | N           | N           |
+-------------+-------+-------------+-------------+
1 row in set (0.00 sec)
```

```
+-------------+------+-------+------------+---------------+-------------+
| host        | db   | user  | table_name | table_priv    | column_priv |
+-------------+------+-------+------------+---------------+-------------+
| domain1.com | test | user1 | books      | Select,Update |             |
+-------------+------+-------+------------+---------------+-------------+
1 row in set (0.00 sec)
```

As you can see, the user table is unchanged from the results returned by the previous example, but notice the results returned from the tables_priv table. The table includes the hostname, database name, username, and table name. In addition, the Table_priv column includes the two privilege values (Select and Update) as they were assigned in the GRANT statement. As the results indicate, the user can execute SELECT and UPDATE statements against the Books table in the test database.

Now take a look at an example GRANT statement that assigns column-level privileges:

```
GRANT SELECT, UPDATE (BookTitle, Copyright)
ON test.Books
TO 'user1'@'domain1.com' IDENTIFIED BY 'pw1';
```

The only difference between this statement and the previous example is that the UPDATE privilege includes columns names (BookTitle and Copyright). This means that the user can update only those columns and no other columns in the table. As a result, the user has now been added to the columns_priv table. To demonstrate this, you can use the following SELECT statements to retrieve data from the user, tables_priv, and columns_priv tables:

```
SELECT host, user, select_priv, update_priv FROM user WHERE user='user1';
SELECT host, db, user, table_name, table_priv, column_priv
    FROM tables_priv WHERE user='user1';
SELECT host, db, user, table_name, column_name, column_priv
    FROM columns_priv WHERE user='user1';
```

The statements should return results similar to the following:

```
+-------------+-------+-------------+-------------+
| host        | user  | select_priv | update_priv |
+-------------+-------+-------------+-------------+
| domain1.com | user1 | N           | N           |
+-------------+-------+-------------+-------------+
1 row in set (0.00 sec)
+-------------+------+-------+------------+------------+-------------+
| host        | db   | user  | table_name | table_priv | column_priv |
+-------------+------+-------+------------+------------+-------------+
| domain1.com | test | user1 | books      | Select     | Update      |
```

```
+-------------+------+-------+------------+-------------+-------------+
1 row in set (0.00 sec)
```

```
+-------------+------+-------+------------+-------------+-------------+
| host        | db   | user  | table_name | column_name | column_priv |
+-------------+------+-------+------------+-------------+-------------+
| domain1.com | test | user1 | books      | BookTitle   | Update      |
| domain1.com | test | user1 | books      | Copyright   | Update      |
+-------------+------+-------+------------+-------------+-------------+
2 rows in set (0.00 sec)
```

Once again, the results returned from the user table remain unchanged from the previous two examples. Notice that the Column_priv column of the tables_priv table now includes the Update value. (The value has been removed from the Table_priv column.) In addition, two rows have been added to the columns_priv table, one for each column. As you can see, the Update privilege has been assigned to each column, but the user still retains the Select privilege at the table level.

Defining the REQUIRE Clause

The REQUIRE clause determines whether a secure connection is required when connecting to the MySQL server and, if so, the degree to which that connection should be secured. Secure connections are implemented in MySQL through the use of the Secure Sockets Layer (SSL) protocol, which is a protocol that uses encryption algorithms to protect data that is sent over unsecured connections, such as the Internet. To make connections even more secure, MySQL supports the use of the x509 standard, an industry standard that relies on the use of certificates to help authenticate the identity of a user trying to connect to a MySQL server. Companies referred to as *certificate authorities* issue the certificates that verify the authenticity of the user trying to establish a connection.

> *To support secure connections between clients and the MySQL server, your system must be configured to support the SSL protocol and the x509 standard, as necessary. A discussion of these topics is beyond the scope of this book. The purpose of this section is merely to demonstrate how to create user accounts that require secure connections. For specific system configuration information, refer to the appropriate product documentation as well as the MySQL Web site (www.mysql.com).*

To use the REQUIRE clause in your GRANT statement, you must specify one or more options, as shown in the following syntax:

```
[REQUIRE {NONE | SSL | X509 | {<require definition>}]

<require definition>::=
<require option> [[AND] <require option>] [[AND] <require option>]

<require option>::=
{CIPHER '<string>'}
| {ISSUER '<string>'}
| {SUBJECT '<string>'}
```

As you can see, you can specify NONE, SSL, X509, or one or more of the options available to the <require definition> placeholder. The following list describes each of these options:

❑ **NONE:** Indicates that a secure connection is not required. This option is associated with the ssl_type column in the user table. If the NONE option is used in the REQUIRE clause, a blank value is added to the column, which is the default value. Specifying this option is the equivalent of not specifying a REQUIRE clause in your GRANT statement.

- ❑ **SSL:** Specifies that a secure connection is required, but that it can be any type of SSL connection. This option is associated with the ssl_type column in the user table. If the SSL option is used in the REQUIRE clause, the ANY value is added to the column.

- ❑ **X509:** Specifies that a secure connection is required and that the connection requires a valid x509 certificate. This option is associated with the ssl_type column in the user table. If the X509 option is used in the REQUIRE clause, the x509 value is added to the column.

- ❑ **CIPHER '<string>':** Specifies the cipher method that should be used for the SSL connection. Cipher methods are based on standards that specify how data is to be encrypted. This option is associated with the ssl_type and ssl_cipher columns in the user table. If the CIPHER '<string>' option is used in the REQUIRE clause, the SPECIFIED value is added to the ssl_type column, and the <string> value is added to the ssl_cipher column.

- ❑ **ISSUER '<string>':** Specifies the name of the certificate authority that issues the x509 certificate. The name should be used for an x509 connection. This option is associated with the ssl_type and x509_issuer columns in the user table. If the ISSUER '<string>' option is used in the REQUIRE clause, the SPECIFIED value is added to the ssl_type column, and the <string> value is added to the x509_issuer column.

- ❑ **SUBJECT '<string>':** Specifies the subject that should be included on the x509 certificate when establishing a secure connection. This option is associated with the ssl_type and x509_subject columns in the user table. If the SUBJECT '<string>' option is used in the REQUIRE clause, the SPECIFIED value is added to the ssl_type column, and the <string> value is added to the x509_subject column.

If you specify the NONE, SSL, or X509 option, you can specify only one of these options. For the last three options (CIPHER, ISSUER, and STRING), you can specify one or more, in any order. Optionally, if you specify more than one of these three options, you can separate them with the AND keyword. If you don't separate them with the AND keyword, then you simply separate them with a space or line break (no comma). Now take a look at an example of a GRANT statement that uses a REQUIRE clause:

```
GRANT SELECT, UPDATE (BookTitle, Copyright)
ON test.Books
TO 'user1'@'domain1.com' IDENTIFIED BY 'pw1'
REQUIRE SSL;
```

As you can see, the REQUIRE clause includes the SSL option, which indicates that an SSL connection is required, but there are no restrictions placed on the nature of the SSL connection. Once you execute the GRANT statement, you can use the following SELECT statement to view the user account information that is added to the user table:

```
SELECT user, ssl_type, ssl_cipher, x509_issuer, x509_subject
FROM user WHERE user='user1';
```

The statement returns results similar to the following:

```
+-------+----------+------------+-------------+--------------+
| user  | ssl_type | ssl_cipher | x509_issuer | x509_subject |
+-------+----------+------------+-------------+--------------+
| user1 | ANY      |            |             |              |
+-------+----------+------------+-------------+--------------+
1 row in set (0.00 sec)
```

As the results show, the encryption-related permission columns are empty except for the ssl_type column, which contains a value of ANY. Now take a look at what happens if you modify the GRANT statement:

```
GRANT SELECT, UPDATE (BookTitle, Copyright)
ON test.Books
TO 'user1'@'domain1.com' IDENTIFIED BY 'pw1'
REQUIRE SUBJECT 'test client cert.'
  AND ISSUER 'Test C.A.';
```

Now the REQUIRE clause includes the SUBJECT and ISSUER items. If you run the SELECT statement again, you should see results similar to the following:

```
+-------+-----------+------------+-------------+-------------------+
| user  | ssl_type  | ssl_cipher | x509_issuer | x509_subject      |
+-------+-----------+------------+-------------+-------------------+
| user1 | SPECIFIED |            | Test C.A.   | test client cert. |
+-------+-----------+------------+-------------+-------------------+
1 row in set (0.00 sec)
```

As you can see, the ssl_type column contains the SPECIFIED value, and the x509_issuer and the x509_subject columns include the string values that you specified in the GRANT statement.

Defining the WITH Clause

The last clause in the GRANT statement is the WITH clause, which allows you to specify whether a user can grant and revoke privileges as well as allowing you to specify connection-related privileges, as shown in the following syntax:

```
[WITH <with option> [<with option>...]]

<with option>::=
{GRANT OPTION}
| {MAX_QUERIES_PER_HOUR <count>}
| {MAX_UPDATES_PER_HOUR <count>}
| {MAX_CONNECTIONS_PER_HOUR <count>}
```

As the syntax shows, the WITH clause can include from one to four options. The following list describes each of these options:

❑ **GRANT OPTION:** Specifies that users can execute GRANT, REVOKE, and DROP USER statements. Using this option in this clause has the same effect as using the option in the GRANT clause. Grant privileges are applied to the user at the level that the GRANT statement is applied (as defined in the ON clause) and to the limit that the grantor is permitted access to the system. This option sets the Grant_priv column in the user, db, or host table or adds the Grant value to the Table_priv column of the tables_priv table. (Using the GRANT OPTION in the WITH clause achieves the same results as using the GRANT OPTION as a privilege in the GRANT clause.)

❑ **MAX_QUERIES_PER_HOUR <count>:** The number of queries permitted in an hour. The number is added to the max_questions column of the user table. If the option is not specified, the default value is 0, which indicates that an unlimited number of queries are permitted.

❑ **`MAX_UPDATES_PER_HOUR <count>`:** The number of data modifications permitted in an hour. The number is added to the max_updates column of the user table. If the option is not specified, the default value is 0, which indicates that an unlimited number of updates are permitted.

❑ **`MAX_CONNECTIONS_PER_HOUR <count>`:** The number of connections permitted in an hour. The number is added to the max_connections column of the user table. If the option is not specified, the default value is 0, which indicates that an unlimited number of connections are permitted.

When you create a GRANT statement that includes the WITH clause, you simply specify the options and, if appropriate, specify a value. You do not need to separate the options with a comma. For example, the following GRANT statement specifies the MAX_QUERIES_PER_HOUR and MAX_UPDATES_PER_HOUR options, setting the value of each to 50:

```
GRANT SELECT, UPDATE
ON test.*
TO 'user1'@'domain1.com' IDENTIFIED BY 'pw1'
WITH GRANT OPTION MAX_QUERIES_PER_HOUR 50 MAX_UPDATES_PER_HOUR 50;
```

As the statement shows, the connection-related values are added to the applicable columns in the user table. The other privileges are assigned at the database level. To verify this, you can run the following SELECT statements:

```
SELECT user, grant_priv, max_questions, max_updates, max_connections
    FROM user WHERE user='user1';
SELECT user, grant_priv FROM db WHERE user='user1';
```

The statements return results similar to the following:

```
+-------+------------+---------------+-------------+-----------------+
| user  | grant_priv | max_questions | max_updates | max_connections |
+-------+------------+---------------+-------------+-----------------+
| user1 | N          |            50 |          50 |               0 |
+-------+------------+---------------+-------------+-----------------+
1 row in set (0.00 sec)

+-------+------------+
| user  | grant_priv |
+-------+------------+
| user1 | Y          |
+-------+------------+
1 row in set (0.00 sec)
```

As you can see, the account as it appears in the user table has not been granted the GRANT OPTION privilege, but the max_questions and max_updates columns each contain 50. If the user tries to exceed this number of queries or updates, the operations are not allowed. The results returned by the SELECT statement also show that the user has been added to the db table, where the GRANT OPTION privilege has been assigned.

Once you add a user to your system, it is often useful to view what privileges have been assigned to that user. This is helpful in troubleshooting connections and in changing privileges — or revoking them. To view the privileges that have been assigned to a user, you can use SELECT statements to retrieve all columns for all grant tables, which is a very cumbersome process. However, you can also use the SHOW GRANTS statement, which is a far more efficient method to use to display a user's privileges.

Using the SHOW GRANTS Statement

The SHOW GRANTS statement displays information about a specific user account. To use the statement, you must include the SHOW GRANTS FOR keywords, followed by the username and hostname, as shown in the following syntax:

```
SHOW GRANTS FOR '<user>'@'<host>'
```

As you can see, the syntax for a SHOW GRANTS statement is very basic. You want to be sure that, when specifying the username and hostname, you enclose each name in single quotes and you separate the names with the at symbol (@). For example, the following SHOW GRANTS statement displays the user account information for user1@domain1.com:

```
SHOW GRANTS FOR 'user1'@'domain1.com';
```

When you execute this statement, you should receive results similar to the following:

```
+--------------------------------------------------------------------------------+
| Grants for user1@domain1.com                                                   |
+--------------------------------------------------------------------------------+
| GRANT USAGE ON *.* TO 'user1'@'domain1.com' IDENTIFIED BY PASSWORD
'*2B602296A79E0A8784ACC5C88D92E46588CCA3C3' WITH MAX_QUERIES_PER_HOUR 50
MAX_UPDATES_PER_HOUR 50                                                          |
| GRANT SELECT, UPDATE ON 'test'.* TO 'user1'@'domain1.com' WITH GRANT OPTION    |
+--------------------------------------------------------------------------------+
2 rows in set (0.00 sec)
```

The first row returned by the SHOW GRANTS statements displays information from the user table. In the previous results, this row is broken over three lines, but what you actually see depends on your system. In this case, the row begins with the GRANT USAGE ON keywords. Usage is a privilege option that indicates that no privileges have been set for that account. Whenever a user account has not been assigned global data-related or administrative privileges, the USAGE option is used. If global privileges have been granted, those privilege options are displayed. The first row also displays the username, hostname, and encrypted password. If encryption-related or connection-related privileges have been assigned to an account, they're displayed after the username, hostname, and password. For this user, the MAX_QUERIES_PER_HOUR and MAX_UPDATES_PER_HOUR privileges are displayed, which are associated with the max_questions and max_updates columns, respectively.

If the SHOW GRANTS statement returns more than one row, those additional rows display details about nonglobal privileges. For example, the second row returned by the preceding SHOW GRANTS statement indicates that the SELECT and UPDATE privileges have been granted on the test database (test.*) and that the GRANT OPTION has been assigned at the database level. If table or column level privileges had been assigned to this user, they would also be returned by the SHOW GRANTS statement.

Now that you have seen how to add users to your MySQL environment, configure privileges for those users, and display user account information, you're ready to try it out for yourself. In the following exercise, you use the GRANT statement to add users to the DVDRentals database and assign privileges to those users, and you use the SHOW GRANTS statement to verify that those privileges have been correctly assigned.

Try It Out   Adding Users to the DVDRentals Database

The following steps describe how to add users to the DVDRentals database and assign privileges to those users:

1. Open the mysql client utility. If the mysql database is not the active database, type the following command, and press Enter:

```
use mysql
```

   You should receive a message indicating that you switched to the mysql database.

2. The first user account that you create is named myuser1, which is allowed to connect only from the local computer. Execute the following SQL statement at the mysql command prompt:

```
GRANT SELECT, UPDATE (EmpFN, EmpMN, EmpLN)
ON DVDRentals.Employees
TO 'myuser1'@'localhost' IDENTIFIED BY 'mypw1'
WITH MAX_CONNECTIONS_PER_HOUR 25;
```

   You should receive a message indicating that the statement successfully executed.

3. When you created the myuser1 user account, the user should have been added to the user, tables_priv, and columns_priv tables. Retrieve data from those tables to verify that the user has been added. Execute the following SQL statements at the mysql command prompt:

```
SELECT host, user, select_priv, update_priv FROM user WHERE user='myuser1';
SELECT host, db, user, table_name, table_priv, column_priv
   FROM tables_priv WHERE user='myuser1';
SELECT host, db, user, table_name, column_name, column_priv
   FROM columns_priv WHERE user='myuser1';
```

   You should receive results similar to the following:

```
+-----------+---------+-------------+-------------+
| host      | user    | select_priv | update_priv |
+-----------+---------+-------------+-------------+
| localhost | myuser1 | N           | N           |
+-----------+---------+-------------+-------------+
1 row in set (0.00 sec)
```

```
+-----------+------------+---------+------------+------------+-------------+
| host      | db         | user    | table_name | table_priv | column_priv |
+-----------+------------+---------+------------+------------+-------------+
| localhost | dvdrentals | myuser1 | employees  | Select     | Update      |
+-----------+------------+---------+------------+------------+-------------+
1 row in set (0.00 sec)
```

```
+-----------+------------+---------+------------+-------------+-------------+
| host      | db         | user    | table_name | column_name | column_priv |
+-----------+------------+---------+------------+-------------+-------------+
| localhost | dvdrentals | myuser1 | employees  | EmpMN       | Update      |
| localhost | dvdrentals | myuser1 | employees  | EmpLN       | Update      |
| localhost | dvdrentals | myuser1 | employees  | EmpFN       | Update      |
+-----------+------------+---------+------------+-------------+-------------+
3 rows in set (0.00 sec)
```

4. Now use the SHOW GRANTS statement to display the privileges assigned to the myuser1 user account. Execute the following SQL statement at the mysql command prompt:

```
SHOW GRANTS FOR 'myuser1'@'localhost';
```

You should receive results similar to the following:

```
+-------------------------------------------------------------------------------------+
| Grants for myuser1@localhost                                                        |
+-------------------------------------------------------------------------------------+
| GRANT USAGE ON *.* TO 'myuser1'@'localhost' IDENTIFIED BY PASSWORD
'*129A95F81EAFD64723D26F1872A8F27B22A25B48' WITH MAX_CONNECTIONS_PER_HOUR 25          |
| GRANT SELECT, UPDATE (EmpFN, EmpLN, EmpMN) ON `dvdrentals`.`employees` TO
'myuser1'@'localhost'                                                                 |
+-------------------------------------------------------------------------------------+
2 rows in set (0.00 sec)
```

5. To verify that the myuser1 user account has been properly added to your system, exit the mysql client utility and then relaunch the utility as the new user. Close the mysql client utility by executing the following command:

```
exit
```

You should be returned to your operating system's command prompt.

6. Now execute the following command at your operating system's command prompt:

```
mysql -u myuser1 -p DVDRentals
```

When prompted, type the password mypw1, and then press Enter. You should now be at the mysql command prompt.

7. Next, try to retrieve data from the Employees table. Execute the following SQL statements at the mysql command prompt:

```
SELECT * FROM Employees;
```

You should receive results similar to the following:

```
+-------+--------+-------+-----------+
| EmpID | EmpFN  | EmpMN | EmpLN     |
+-------+--------+-------+-----------+
|     1 | John   | P.    | Smith     |
|     2 | Robert | NULL  | Schroader |
|     3 | Mary   | Marie | Michaels  |
|     4 | John   | NULL  | Laguci    |
|     5 | Rita   | C.    | Carter    |
|     6 | George | NULL  | Brooks    |
+-------+--------+-------+-----------+
6 rows in set (0.04 sec)
```

8. Now try to insert data in the Employees table. Execute the following SQL statements at the mysql command prompt:

```
INSERT INTO Employees VALUES ('Sarah', 'Louise', 'Peterson');
```

You should receive an error message indicating that you cannot perform this operation.

9. Close the mysql client utility by executing the following command:

```
exit
```

You should be returned to your operating system's command prompt.

10. Log back in the mysql client utility as the root user, with the mysql database as the active database.

11. Next, create the mysqlapp user account, which is permitted to access the MySQL server from the local computer. Execute the following SQL statement at the mysql command prompt:

```
GRANT SELECT, INSERT, UPDATE, DELETE
ON DVDRentals.*
TO 'mysqlapp'@'localhost' IDENTIFIED BY 'pw1';
```

You should receive a message indicating that the statement successfully executed.

12. To verify that the mysqlapp user account has been added to the user and db tables, execute the following SQL statement at the mysql command prompt:

```
SELECT host, user, select_priv, update_priv FROM user WHERE user='mysqlapp';
SELECT host, db, user, select_priv, update_priv FROM db WHERE user='mysqlapp';
```

You should receive results similar to the following:

```
+-----------+----------+-------------+-------------+
| host      | user     | select_priv | update_priv |
+-----------+----------+-------------+-------------+
| localhost | mysqlapp | N           | N           |
+-----------+----------+-------------+-------------+
1 row in set (0.00 sec)

+-----------+------------+----------+-------------+-------------+
| host      | db         | user     | select_priv | update_priv |
+-----------+------------+----------+-------------+-------------+
| localhost | dvdrentals | mysqlapp | Y           | Y           |
+-----------+------------+----------+-------------+-------------+
1 row in set (0.03 sec)
```

13. Now display the privileges that are assigned to the mysqlapp user account. Execute the following SQL statement at the mysql command prompt:

```
SHOW GRANTS FOR 'mysqlapp'@'localhost';
```

You should receive results similar to the following:

```
+-------------------------------------------------------------------------------+
| Grants for mysqlapp@localhost                                                 |
+-------------------------------------------------------------------------------+
| GRANT USAGE ON *.* TO 'mysqlapp'@'localhost' IDENTIFIED BY PASSWORD
'*2B602296A79E0A8784ACC5C88D92E46588CCA3C3'                                     |
| GRANT SELECT, INSERT, UPDATE, DELETE ON 'dvdrentals'.* TO 'mysqlapp'@'localhost'|
+-------------------------------------------------------------------------------+
2 rows in set (0.00 sec)
```

14. To verify that the user account can connect to the MySQL server, you must exit the mysql client utility and then relaunch the utility as the new user. Close the mysql client utility by executing the following command:

```
exit
```

You should be returned to your operating system's command prompt.

15. Now execute the following command at your operating system's command prompt:

```
mysql DVDRentals -u mysqlapp -p
```

When prompted, type the password pw1, and then press Enter. You should now be at the mysql command prompt.

16. Close the mysql client utility by executing the following command:

```
exit
```

You should be returned to your operating system's command prompt.

How It Works

To create the first user account in this exercise, you used the following GRANT statement:

```
GRANT SELECT, UPDATE (EmpFN, EmpMN, EmpLN)
ON DVDRentals.Employees
TO 'myuser1'@'localhost' IDENTIFIED BY 'mypw1'
WITH MAX_CONNECTIONS_PER_HOUR 25;
```

The first clause in this statement is the GRANT clause, which grants the SELECT privilege and the UPDATE privilege. The UPDATE privilege is specific to the EmpFN, EmpMN, and EmpLN columns of the Employees table. The ON clause specifies the database name (DVDRentals) and the table (Employees). As a result, the privileges apply only to the Employees table. The TO clause specifies the name of the user (myuser1) and the host from which the user can connect to the MySQL server (localhost). The TO clause also includes an IDENTIFIED BY clause, which specifies that the password mypw1 will be assigned to the account. The GRANT statement also includes a WITH clause that contains the MAX_CONNECTIONS_PER_HOUR option. The user account is permitted up to 25 connections per hour.

After you executed the GRANT statement, you executed three SELECT statements that retrieved data from the user, tables_priv, and columns_priv tables. The first SELECT statement retrieved the values in the Host, User, Select_priv, and Update_priv columns of the user table. The results showed that a user named myuser1 had been created and that the account could log on to the MySQL server from the local computer. The results also showed that the user did not have SELECT or UPDATE privileges at the global level, which is to be expected because the privileges are assigned at a table and column level.

The second SELECT statement retrieved data from the Host, Db, User, Table_name, Table_priv, and Column_priv columns of the tables_priv table. As you would expect, the user account and host are listed. In addition, the account is assigned SELECT table privileges and UPDATE column privileges on the Employees table of the DVDRentals database. Because the Column_priv column includes the Update value, you would expect the columns_priv table to contain the applicable privilege for each column specified in the GRANT clause of the GRANT statement.

To verify this, the third SELECT statement retrieved the Host, Db, User, Table_name, Column_name, and Column_priv columns from the columns_priv table. The results show that a row has been added to the table for each column specified in the GRANT statement, indicating that the user can update the EmpFN, EmpMN, and EmpLN columns of the Employees table.

You also used the SHOW GRANTS statement to confirm that the new user account was assigned the appropriate privileges:

```
SHOW GRANTS FOR 'myuser1'@'localhost';
```

The statement specifies the user account name and the host from which the user account can connect. When you executed the statement, you received a result set that contained one column and two rows. The first row shows the global settings and privileges that are assigned to the user account. In this case, the user can log on to the MySQL server from the localhost. The user must supply a password and cannot initiate more than 25 connections in an hour. The user, though, is not assigned any global privileges, as indicated by the USAGE privilege.

The second row of the results returned by the SHOW GRANTS statement indicates that the SELECT privilege and UPDATE privilege have been assigned to the user for the Employees table of the DVDRentals database. The UPDATE privilege applies only to the specified columns in the Employees table.

After you viewed the privileges assigned to the myuser1 account, you exited the MySQL client utility and then relaunched the utility as the new user. You then tried to execute a SELECT statement against the Employees table and then an INSERT statement. As you would expect, you were able to retrieve data from the table, but not add data to the table. However, if you had tried to update any part of an employee's name, you would have been permitted to do so because the UPDATE privilege was also assigned to this user account.

After you tested the connection for the new user account, you exited mysql and then logged back in as the root user. From there, you executed the following GRANT statement:

```
GRANT SELECT, INSERT, UPDATE, DELETE
ON DVDRentals.*
TO 'mysqlapp'@'localhost' IDENTIFIED BY 'pw1';
```

The GRANT statement assigns the SELECT, INSERT, UPDATE, and DELETE privileges for all tables in the DVDRentals database. The statement also creates a user account named mysqlapp. The user can connect only from the local computer. To connect to the MySQL server, the user must supply the pw1 password.

After you executed the GRANT statement, you used two SELECT statements to verify that the user and db tables contained the correct data. As you would expect, the user table includes the account, but no privileges have been assigned because the privileges are assigned at a database level, not a global level. The second SELECT statement verifies this. The data returned by that statement shows that privileges have been granted to that user on the DVDRentals database. Although only two of the four privileges were returned by the SELECT statement, you were able to verify that all privileges had been granted to the account by running the following SHOW GRANTS statement:

```
SHOW GRANTS FOR 'mysqlapp'@'localhost';
```

The results returned by the statement indicate that the user can log on to the MySQL server, that no global privileges have been granted, and that the SELECT, INSERT, UPDATE, and DELETE privileges have been granted to this account.

Setting Passwords for MySQL User Accounts

There might be times when, after a user account has been created, you want to add a password to the user account or change the existing password. MySQL provides the SET PASSWORD statement for setting a user account password; however, setting the new password doesn't mean that the password is immediately implemented. After setting a new password, you should use the FLUSH PRIVILEGES statement to reload the grant tables in your system's memory to ensure that the most current user information (including the new password) is being used.

Using the SET PASSWORD Statement

The SET PASSWORD statement can be used to set the password of another user account or of your own user account. The syntax for the SET PASSWORD statement is as follows:

```
SET PASSWORD [FOR '<user>'@'<host>'] = PASSWORD('<new password>')
```

As you can see, you must specify the SET PASSWORD keywords, the equal sign, and the PASSWORD() function, using the new password as an argument in the function. You can also include the optional FOR clause in your statement. If you're setting the password for the user account under which you're currently logged on to the system, you don't need to use the FOR clause. For example, the following statement allows you to change your password to pw2:

```
SET PASSWORD = PASSWORD('pw2');
```

As you can see, you have to specify only the required statement elements to change your own password. Notice that the new password is included as an argument in the PASSWORD() function and that the new password is enclosed in single quotes. If you are setting a password for a user account other than the one you used to log on to the system, you can use a statement similar to the following:

```
SET PASSWORD FOR 'user1'@'domain1.com' = PASSWORD('pw3');
```

The statement includes a FOR clause, which identifies the user account as user1@domain1.com. All other aspects of the statement are the same as the previous example (except that the new password is now pw3). Once you set a password for an account, it takes effect when you restart the MySQL server or you flush the privileges, which means that you reload the grant tables in your system's memory. To flush the privileges, you can use the FLUSH PRIVILEGES statement.

Using the FLUSH PRIVILEGES Statement

The FLUSH PRIVILEGES statement includes no options or clauses other than the FLUSH PRIVILEGES keywords. As a result, to reload the grant tables into memory, all you need to do is execute the following statement:

```
FLUSH PRIVILEGES;
```

As soon as you execute this statement, the grant tables are reloaded and any new user account information is put into effect.

Now that you know how to assign a password to a user account and reload the grant tables in your system's memory, you're ready to try out the SET PASSWORD and FLUSH PRIVILEGES statements. In the following exercise you change the password of the myuser1 account that you created in the last Try It Out section.

Try It Out   Changing a User Account Password

The following steps describe how to change the password for the myuser1 account:

1. Open the mysql client utility as the root user.

2. To change the password of the myuser1 account, execute the following SQL statement at the mysql command prompt:

```
SET PASSWORD FOR 'myuser1'@'localhost' = PASSWORD('mypw2');
```

You should receive a message indicating that the statement successfully executed.

3. Once you change the password, you should reload the grant tables in your system's memory to ensure that the new password takes effect. Execute the following SQL statement at the mysql command prompt:

```
FLUSH PRIVILEGES;
```

You should receive a message indicating that the statement successfully executed.

4. Next, try out the new password by exiting the mysql client utility and then relaunching the utility as the myuser1 account. Close the mysql client utility by executing the following command:

```
exit
```

You should be returned to your operating system's command prompt.

5. Execute the following SQL statement at the mysql command prompt:

```
mysql DVDRentals -u myuser1 -p
```

When prompted, type the password mypw2, and then press Enter. You should now be at the mysql command prompt.

6. Close the mysql client utility by executing the following command:

```
exit
```

You should be returned to your operating system's command prompt.

How It Works

To set the password for the muuser1 account, you used the following SET PASSWORD statement:

```
SET PASSWORD FOR 'myuser1'@'localhost' = PASSWORD('mypw2');
```

The statement specifies the SET PASSWORD FOR keywords, followed by the name of the user account (myuser1) and the host (localhost) from which the user is permitted to connect to the MySQL server. The statement then uses the PASSWORD() function to encrypt and set the new password (mypw2).

Because a password already existed for the user account, the new password simply replaced the old password in the user table. If a password had not existed for that account, the new password would have been added to the user table.

Once you assigned the new password to the myuser1 account, you used the following statement to reload the grant tables in your system's memory:

```
FLUSH PRIVILEGES;
```

The FLUSH PRIVILEGES statement ensures that the most current user account information is applied when a user logs into the MySQL server.

Dropping Users and Revoking Privileges

Quite often you will find that, once you've created a user account, you want to remove that account from your system or modify the account's privileges. Removing an account often includes three steps:

1. Using the SHOW GRANTS statement to view the user account's current privileges.

2. Using the REVOKE statement to revoke the privileges from the user account.

3. Using the DROP USER statement to remove the user from the system.

All privileges must have been revoked from a user account before you can use the DROP USER statement to remove the user; however, you do not always need to take each step described here. For example, if you know what privileges have been granted to the user, you don't have to use the SHOW GRANTS statement to view those privileges. In addition, if you know that no privileges have been granted to the user, you do not have to use the REVOKE statement before using the DROP USER statement. You might also find that you want to revoke certain privileges but not remove the user from the system. In that case, you need to use only the SHOW GRANTS statement and the REVOKE statement.

Now that you have an overview of how the user account modification and removal process works, you can take a close look at the statement used to modify the accounts. You've already seen how you can use the SHOW GRANTS statement to display privilege information. Now take a look at the REVOKE and DROP USER statements.

Using the REVOKE Statement

The REVOKE statement allows you to remove privileges for a user account. When you revoke privileges, the user account record is removed from db, host, tables_priv, and columns_priv tables, whichever are applicable, and all privileges are revoked from the user table. But the user account is still listed in the user table. (To remove the account from the user table, you must use the DROP USER statement, which is described in the text that follows.)

Before you can actually drop the user account from the user table, you should use the REVOKE statement to revoke all privileges. The REVOKE statement takes two forms. The first form removes all privileges from the user account. This is the simplest method to use if you're simply going to drop the user from the system and are not going to revoke only specific privileges. The following syntax describes how the first form of the REVOKE statement is defined:

```
REVOKE ALL PRIVILEGES, GRANT OPTION
FROM '<user>'@'<host>' [{, '<user>'@'<host>'}...]
```

As you can see, you must specify the REVOKE clause and the FROM clause. The FROM clause identifies one or more user accounts. To illustrate how the REVOKE statement works, take a look at an example based on a user account created with the following GRANT statement:

```
GRANT SELECT, UPDATE
ON test.*
TO 'user1'@'domain1.com' IDENTIFIED BY 'pw1'
WITH GRANT OPTION MAX_QUERIES_PER_HOUR 50 MAX_UPDATES_PER_HOUR 50;
```

The user1 account has been granted SELECT and UPDATE privileges on the test database. The account has also been assigned two connection-related privileges. To use the first form of the REVOKE statement to remove this account, you can use the following statement:

```
REVOKE ALL PRIVILEGES, GRANT OPTION
FROM 'user1'@'domain1.com';
```

Notice that the statement includes only the REVOKE clause and the FROM clause, which identifies the user1@domain1.com user account. You can also revoke the privileges from the user1 account by using a long form of the REVOKE statement, which is shown in the following syntax:

```
REVOKE <privilege> [(<column> [{, <column>}...])]
    [{, <privilege> [(<column> [{, <column>}...])]}...]
ON {<table> | * | *.* | <database>.*}
FROM '<user>'@'<host>' [{, '<user>'@'<host>'}...]
```

As you can see, the REVOKE clause now includes <privilege> and <column> placeholders. The clause is defined exactly as it is defined in the GRANT clause of the GRANT statement. You must specify each privilege that you want to revoke. If privileges are assigned at the column level, then you must also identify those columns. The ON clause of the long version of the REVOKE statement is also the same as the ON clause of the GRANT statement. The same options are available, and the option you pick depends on the scope of the privileges.

The long form of the REVOKE statement also includes a FROM clause, which works the same as the FROM clause in the short form of the statement. For example, if you want to use the long form of the statement to revoke the privileges of the user1 account, you would use the following REVOKE statement:

```
REVOKE SELECT, UPDATE, GRANT OPTION
ON test.*
FROM 'user1'@'domain1.com';
```

As you can see, the REVOKE clause includes all the privileges that have been granted to the user account (including the GRANT OPTION privilege), the ON clause specifies the test database, and the FROM clause identifies the user account.

The primary advantage of the long form of the REVOKE statement over the short form is that the long form allows you to revoke all privileges or only certain privileges, whereas the short form allows you to revoke all privileges only.

When you revoke all the privileges from a user account, that account is removed from all grant tables except the user table. In addition, any privileges that had been set in the user table are also revoked. To remove the user account from the user table after all privileges have been revoked, you must use the DROP USER statement.

The REVOKE statement does not remove a user account from grant tables other than the user table if that user account is not listed in the user table. For example, if the db table includes a user account that is not in the user table, the REVOKE statement does not remove the user from the db table. In a case like this, you must use a DELETE statement to remove that row from the table.

Using the DROP USER Statement

The DROP USER statement requires only the DROP USER keywords and one or more user accounts, as shown in the following syntax:

```
DROP USER '<user>'@'<host>' [{, '<user>'@'<host>'}...]
```

If you specify multiple accounts, you must separate them by a comma. Remember, to drop the accounts, there can be no privileges assigned to the account. If you try to execute a DROP USER statement and it fails, use the SHOW GRANTS statement to determine whether any privileges still exist for that account.

Now take a look at an example of a DROP USER statement. The following statement shows how you would drop the user1@domain1.com user account:

```
DROP USER 'user1'@'domain1.com';
```

As you can see, the statement includes only the DROP USER keywords, along with the username and hostname, each enclosed in single quotes and separated by the at (@) symbol.

Now that you've learned how to revoke privileges and drop users from your system, you're ready to try it out for yourself. In the following exercise, you revoke the privileges of the myuser1 account that you created in an earlier Try It Out section, and then you remove this account from your system.

Try It Out   Removing Users from the DVDRentals Database

The following steps describe how to revoke the privileges of the myuser1 account and then drop that user from your system:

1. Open the mysql client utility. If the mysql database is not the active database, execute the following command:

```
use mysql
```

You should receive a message indicating that you switched to the DVDRentals database.

2. Before revoking the privileges of the myuser1 account, you should view the current privileges. Execute the following SQL statement at the mysql command prompt:

```
SHOW GRANTS FOR 'myuser1'@'localhost';
```

You should receive results similar to the following:

```
+--------------------------------------------------------------------------------+
| Grants for myuser1@localhost                                                   |
+--------------------------------------------------------------------------------+
| GRANT USAGE ON *.* TO 'myuser1'@'localhost' IDENTIFIED BY PASSWORD             |
'*B7F1931E8F564F69038DB9132AB2ED7F144D8414' WITH MAX_CONNECTIONS_PER_HOUR 25     |
| GRANT SELECT, UPDATE (EmpFN, EmpMN, EmpLN) ON `dvdrentals`.`employees` TO       |
'myuser1'@'localhost'                                                           |
+--------------------------------------------------------------------------------+
2 rows in set (0.00 sec)
```

3.   You can use the information returned by the SHOW GRANTS statement to create a REVOKE statement. Execute the following SQL statement at the mysql command prompt:

```
REVOKE SELECT, UPDATE (EmpFN, EmpMN, EmpLN)
ON DVDRentals.Employees
FROM 'myuser1'@'localhost';
```

You should receive a message indicating that the statement successfully executed.

4.   Once you have revoked all the permissions from the myuser1 account, you should drop the user from your system. Execute the following SQL statement at the mysql command prompt:

```
DROP USER 'myuser1'@'localhost';
```

You should receive a message indicating that the statement successfully executed.

5.   Now that you have learned how to remove users from your system, you should remove any anonymous users that are created when you installed MySQL. For Linux, you should remove the anonymous users from the user table. For Windows and Linux, you should remove the anonymous users in the db table. If you're working in a Windows environment, skip ahead to Step 7. If you're working in a Linux environment, execute the following SQL statement at the mysql command prompt:

```
DROP USER ''@'localhost';
```

You should receive a message indicating that the statement successfully executed.

6.   If you're working in a Linux environment, execute the following SQL statement at the mysql command prompt:

```
DROP USER ''@'<host>';
```

The *<host>* placeholder refers to the name of the local computer. Once you execute the statement, you should receive a message indicating that the statement successfully executed.

7.   For both Windows and Linux environments, execute the following SQL statement at the mysql command prompt:

```
DELETE FROM db WHERE user='';
```

You should receive a message indicating that the statement successfully executed and that two rows were affected.

8.   Exit the mysql client utility.

How It Works

The first step that you took in deleting the myuser1 account from your system was to execute the following SHOW GRANTS table:

```
SHOW GRANTS FOR 'myuser1'@'localhost';
```

The results returned by the statement indicated that the myuser1 account had been granted no global data-related or administrative privileges but was configured with the MAX_CONNECTIONS_PER_HOUR option set to 25. In addition, the user was granted SELECT and UPDATE privileges on the Employees table of the DVDRentals database. The user, though, could update only the EmpFN, EmpMN, and EmpLN columns of the Employees table.

From the information returned by the SHOW GRANTS statement, you were able to create a REVOKE statement that revokes the applicable permissions:

```
REVOKE SELECT, UPDATE (EmpFN, EmpMN, EmpLN)
ON DVDRentals.Employees
FROM 'myuser1'@'localhost';
```

In this statement, the REVOKE clause specifies SELECT and UPDATE privileges. The statement specifies the UPDATE privilege on the EmpFN, EmpMN, and EmpLN columns only. The ON clause specifies that the privileges apply to the Employees table of the DVDRentals database, and the FROM clause specifies that the privileges be revoked from the myuser1 account associated with the local host.

This exercise used the long form of the REVOKE statement to revoke the privileges in order to demonstrate how the more complicated form of the statement works. You could have also used the short form, in which case, you could have used the following statement:

```
REVOKE ALL PRIVILEGES, GRANT OPTION
FROM 'myuser1'@'localhost';
```

When you executed the REVOKE statement, rows related to the user were removed from the tables_priv and columns_priv tables. In addition, any privileges granted in the user table were revoked. You then used the following statement to remove the user from your system:

```
DROP USER 'myuser1'@'localhost';
```

The statement includes the DROP USER keywords, the name of the user (myuser1), and the name of the host (localhost). When you executed this statement, the myuser1 account was removed from the user table.

Once you dropped the myuser1 account from your system, you dropped anonymous user accounts from your system. These are the user accounts that have a blank value in the User column. By dropping the anonymous accounts, you are preventing anonymous users from being able to log on to the MySQL server. Even if no privileges are assigned to an account, any account that is listed in the user table can log on to the server. In addition, because anonymous user accounts were added to the user table only for the Linux installation, you had to use the DROP USER statements only for the Linux environment. Note, however, that you did not have to revoke permissions before deleting the accounts because no privileges had been assigned to the anonymous accounts.

In addition to anonymous accounts existing in the user table of a Linux installation, the db table for both Linux and Windows installations contained anonymous accounts. Because these accounts have no accounts associated with them in the user table, you cannot use the REVOKE statement or the DROP USER statement on the account, but instead must use a DELETE statement to remove the users. To drop the anonymous users from the db table in your installation, you created a DELETE statement whose WHERE clause specified a blank user (WHERE user=''). When you executed the statement, the user accounts were removed from the table. The only user account that should now be listed in your db table is the mysqlapp account, which you created in an earlier Try It Out section.

Summary

As the chapter has demonstrated, MySQL allows you to control who has access to the MySQL server and allows you to assign privileges to individual user accounts. You can assign these privileges at a global level, database level, table level, or column level, and you can mix the level for individual users. For example, you can allow a user to view data from all tables in a database, permit the user to add data to only one table in the database, and restrict the user to being able to update only one column in that table. To support your ability to administer MySQL security, this chapter covered the following topics:

❑   Understanding how the user, db, host, tables_priv, and columns_priv tables provide security

❑   Learning how users are authenticated to access the MySQL server and authorized to perform specific operations

❑   Using GRANT statements to create user accounts and assign privileges

❑   Using SHOW GRANTS statements to display user privileges

❑   Using SET PASSWORD statements to assign or change user account passwords

❑   Using FLUSH PRIVILEGES statements to reload the grant tables in your system's memory

❑   Using REVOKE statements to revoke privileges assigned to user accounts

❑   Using DROP USER statements to remove a user account from MySQL

Although MySQL provides an effective infrastructure for protecting the data in the databases, your security strategies should not be limited to the MySQL environment alone. Be sure to implement the security necessary to protect the MySQL-related files stored in your directories so that no unauthorized users can access or copy those files. Also be sure that your network is protected from unauthorized access. To carry out these measures, you should work closely with your system and network administrators and consult the applicable documentation. For current information on MySQL security, be sure to consult the MySQL Web site (www.mysql.com). You should take every step necessary to ensure the security of your MySQL installation before you implement MySQL in a production environment. Once you're confident that your system is secure, you can start looking at ways to optimize your system's performance. In Chapter 15, you learn how you can improve the performance of your queries so that you can retrieve and modify data as efficiently as possible.

Exercises

In this chapter, you learned how to create user accounts, assign privileges to those accounts, revoke those privileges, and remove the user accounts from your system. The following exercises help you build on your ability to perform these tasks. The exercises are based on the following database and table definitions:

```
CREATE DATABASE Books;
use Books;
CREATE TABLE Publishers
(
   PubID INT PRIMARY KEY,
   PubName VARCHAR(40) NOT NULL,
   City VARCHAR(20)
);
```

To view solutions to these exercises, see Appendix A.

1. Create a user account for a user named mgr1. The user account should be able to connect from the local computer, using the password mgr1pw. Grant the user account SELECT and INSERT privileges on the Publishers table. In addition, grant the user UPDATE privileges on the PubName and City columns of the Publishers table.

2. Create an SQL statement that changes the mgr1 user account password to mgr2pw.

3. Create an SQL statement that flushes the grant tables and reloads them in your system's memory.

4. Create an SQL statement that displays the privileges assigned to the mgr1 user account.

5. Create an SQL statement that revokes the privileges assigned to the mgr1 user account.

6. Create an SQL statement that removes the mgr1 user account from your system.

Optimizing Performance

In many examples throughout this book, you have seen SQL statements executed against small tables that contain relatively few rows. As a result, the performance of these statements has not been an issue because it takes relatively little time for MySQL to return information or modify data. This is often not the case, however, in the real world. If you're accessing tables that contain thousands of rows of data (or more), you might find that certain SQL statements are slow and take a relatively long time to be processed, despite how efficiently you think that statement should run. As a result, whenever you're setting up a database or creating SQL statements to execute against the database, you should take into consideration how well those statements perform when they are executed.

When you begin working with tables that contain large quantities of data, there are several steps that you can take to optimize the performance of your SQL statements. By optimizing performance, you're maximizing the speed and efficiency at which those statements are executed. For example, in order to ensure that your SELECT statements retrieve data as quickly as possible, you can ensure that your tables have been properly indexed. In this chapter, you learn about various steps that you can take to optimize your system's performance. Specifically, the chapter covers the following topics:

❑   Advantages and disadvantages of indexing and when you should use indexing

❑   Determining how effectively your queries are being executed and steps you can take to improve your data-related operations

❑   Modifying table definitions to improve query performance

❑   Enabling your system's query cache

Optimizing MySQL Indexing

In MySQL, the most useful step that you can take to maximize performance is to ensure that your tables are properly indexed. Indexes provide an effective way to access data in your tables and speed up searches. An index provides an organized list of pointers to the actual data. As a result, when MySQL executes a query, it can scan the index to locate the correct data, rather than having to scan the entire table.

Figure 15-1 helps to illustrate how this works. The figure shows a table named Parts, which includes the PartID column, the PartName column, and the ManfID column. The Parts table, as with any table, is basically a collection of rows. Although in this case the rows are ordered by the PartID values, they can be in any order.

Parts

PartID	PartName	ManfID
101	DVD burner	abc123
102	CD drive	jkl123
103	80-GB hard disk	mno456
104	Mini-tower	ghi789
105	Power supply	def456
106	LCD monitor	mno456
107	Zip drive	ghi789
109	Floppy drive	jkl123
109	Network adapter	def456
110	Network hub	jkl123
111	Router	mno456
112	Sound card	ghi789
113	Standard keyboard	mno456
114	PS/2 mouse	jkl123
115	56-K modem	ghi789
116	Display adapter	mno456
117	IDE controller	def456

Figure 15-1

Assume for now that no indexes have been defined on the Parts table. Now imagine that you want to run the following SELECT statement:

```
SELECT PartName FROM Parts
WHERE ManfID='jkl123';
```

When you execute the statement, MySQL must search through each row in the Parts table to find those rows that have a ManfID value of jkl123. If the table includes a large number of rows, this process can be slow and very inefficient. Now take a look at Figure 15-2, which shows that same table, only this time an index is defined on the ManfID column. The index contains exactly the same values as the ManfID column; however, the values are sorted in ascending order. In addition, each value in the index contains a pointer to the applicable row in the Parts column.

Now when you execute the SELECT statement, MySQL searches the index, rather than searching the entire table row by row and, as a result, can find the ManfID value of jkl123 much faster. Searches are faster in indexes because indexes are sorted. Identical values are grouped together and organized in an easy-to-locate order. In addition, because of this sorting, MySQL knows when to stop searching. As soon as it reaches the end of the matching rows, it discontinues the search. For example, if you refer to the index in Figure 15-2, you can see that all the jkl123 values are grouped together. This means that they can all be located with one search and that the last one is easy to identify. The process is made even more efficient because MySQL uses a special positioning algorithm that locates the first matching entry, without having to start the scan at the beginning of the index.

Parts

PartID	PartName	ManfID
101	DVD burner	abc123
102	CD drive	jkl123
103	80-GB hard disk	mno456
104	Mini-tower	ghi789
105	Power supply	def456
106	LCD monitor	mno456
107	Zip drive	ghi789
109	Floppy drive	jkl123
109	Network adapter	def456
110	Network hub	jkl123
111	Router	mno456
112	Sound card	ghi789
113	Standard keyboard	mno456
114	PS/2 mouse	jkl123
115	56-K modem	ghi789
116	Display adapter	mno456
117	IDE controller	def456

Index
abc123
def456
def456
def456
ghi789
ghi789
ghi789
ghi789
jkl123
jkl123
jkl123
jkl123
mno456
mno456
mno456
mno456
mno456

Figure 15-2

The benefit of indexes becomes even more apparent for queries that join multiple tables. As you recall from Chapter 10, when you join two or more tables, rows in each table are matched together based on the specified join condition. If the tables are not indexed, MySQL must compare each row in each table with each row in each other table to determine which rows contain the values that meet the join criteria. This means that MySQL must try every possible combination in the joined tables to determine which rows meet the join criteria.

For example, suppose you execute a SELECT statement that joins tables A, B, and C, none of which are configured with indexes. Each row in table A is combined with each row in tables B and C to determine whether each combination matches the join condition. In other words, the first row in table A is combined with the first row in table B and the first row in table C. The first row in table A is then combined with the first row in table B and the second row in table C. The first row in table A is then combined with the first row in table B and the third row in table C. The process is repeated until each row in table C is covered. The process begins again as the first row in table A is combined with the second row in table B and the first row in table C. The first row in table A is then combined with the second row in table B and the second row in table C. This continues until all possible combinations are compared, which can result in excessively large searches. For example, if each table contains 100 rows, MySQL must compare one million rows (100 x 100 x 100) to determine which rows match the join condition.

Indexes, though, eliminate the need to compare all the rows in all the tables. Returning to tables A, B, and C, assume that the columns specified in the join condition are now indexed. When you execute your SELECT statement, MySQL uses an index to locate the first applicable row in table A. MySQL then uses an index on table B to match the row in table A to the appropriate row in table B. From there, MySQL uses a table C index to match the row in table B to the appropriate row in table C. Each step of the way, MySQL uses indexes to locate values in order to match rows according to how the join condition has been defined. As a result, the number of rows that must be searched is significantly reduced, which results in a dramatic improvement in performance.

Despite the clear advantages of using indexes, there are some drawbacks. For example, indexes can require a great deal of storage. The larger the tables and greater the number of indexes, the more storage you need to hold those indexes. You must allow for file size and potential growth whenever you implement an index. Another disadvantage to indexes is that, while they speed up data retrieval, they can slow down data inserts and deletes, as well as updates to columns that are indexed. Any change made to rows in an indexed table must also be made to the index (unless the change is an update that doesn't affect the value in the index).

Despite these drawbacks, indexing provides the most beneficial tool for improving the performance of your SELECT statements. You should not, however, index every column in a table. The following list provides several guidelines that you can use in determining when to implement indexing:

❑ **Index columns that appear in search conditions.** As a general rule, you should consider defining an index on any column that you commonly use in WHERE, GROUP BY, or HAVING clauses. Because these columns define the limitations of a query, they are good candidates for improving performance because they allow MySQL to identify quickly which rows should be included in a search and which should not.

❑ **Index columns that appear in join conditions.** Index any columns that appear in a join condition. Because join conditions are often based on foreign key columns that reference primary key columns, MySQL creates the indexes automatically when you define the primary keys and foreign keys.

❑ **Do not index columns that appear only in the SELECT clause.** If a column appears in the SELECT clause of a SELECT statement, but does not appear in WHERE, GROUP BY, or HAVING clauses, you usually shouldn't index these columns because indexing them provides no performance benefit but does require additional storage. Indexing columns in the SELECT clause provides no benefit because the SELECT clause is one of the last parts of a SELECT statement to be processed. MySQL conducts searches based on the other clauses. After MySQL identifies which rows to return, it then consults the SELECT clause to determine which columns from the identified rows to return.

❑ **Do not index columns that contain only a few different values.** If a column contains many duplicated values, indexing that column provides little benefit. For example, suppose that your column is configured to accept only Y and N values. Because of the way in which MySQL accesses an index and uses that index to locate the rows in the tables, many duplicated values can actually cause the process to take longer than if no index is used. In fact, when MySQL finds that a value occurs in more than 30 percent of a table's rows, it usually doesn't use the index at all.

❑ **Specify prefixes for indexes on columns that contain large string values.** If you're adding an index to a string column, consider defining a prefix on that index so that your index includes only part of the entire values, as they're stored in the table. For example, if your table includes a CHAR(150) column, you might consider indexing only the first 10 or 15 bytes, or whatever number provides enough unique values without having to store the entire values in the index.

❑ **Create only the indexes that you need.** Never create more indexes than you need. If a column is rarely used in a search or join condition, don't index that column. You want to index only those columns that are frequently used to identify the rows being searched.

Once you determine whether to index a column you must decide which type of index to use. In Chapter 5, you learned how to use the CREATE TABLE statement to add tables to your MySQL database. As you recall from that chapter, you can define one or more indexes as part of that statement. MySQL supports five types of indexes:

- ❏ **Primary key:** Requires that each value or set of values be unique in the columns on which the primary key is defined. In addition, NULL values are not allowed. A table can include only one primary key.

- ❏ **Foreign key:** Enforces the relationship between the referencing columns in the child table where the foreign key is defined and the referenced columns in the parent table.

- ❏ **Regular:** Provides a basic index that permits duplicate values and NULL values in the columns on which the index is defined.

- ❏ **Unique:** Requires that each value or set of values be unique in the columns on which the index is defined. Unlike primary key indexes, NULL values are allowed.

- ❏ **Full-text:** Supports full-text searches of the values in the columns on which the index is defined. A full-text index permits duplicate values and NULL values in those columns. A full-text index can be defined only on MyISAM tables and only on CHAR, VARCHAR, and TEXT columns.

Refer to Chapter 5 for more details about each type of index and how they're defined on a table in a MySQL database.

The type of index you should use depends on your particular requirements. Because primary key and foreign key indexes provide such specific purposes, their use is fairly evident. You should configure every table with one primary key, and you should use foreign keys whenever columns in one table reference columns in another table. In many cases, the use of these keys alone is enough to meet your indexing needs. Should you require additional indexes, you should try to use a unique index over regular and full-text indexes because indexes that contain unique values provide the best performance. MySQL must locate only one value and that value is matched to exactly one row. As soon as MySQL finds that value, the search is complete.

Once you have defined the necessary indexes on your table, you may have addressed many of the performance issues that you experience when running queries against a MySQL database. Even a well-indexed table can experience performance problems. As a result, you should also consider other methods that you can use to optimize your queries.

Optimizing SQL Queries

When you're setting up your database or configuring system settings, you're likely to perform a number of operations such as creating tables, granting privileges to users, or setting the values of system variables. Once your MySQL server and databases have been set up the way you want them, most of the access to the server and database is through applications that retrieve and modify data, which means that statements such as SELECT, INSERT, UPDATE, and DELETE represent the most common operations performed. As a result, you should ensure that your system is fully optimized to support these operations. To do so, you must take into account not only methods that you can use to improve data retrieval, but also methods that improve inserting data, updating data, and deleting data.

Optimizing Data Retrieval

Of all the operations performed against a MySQL database, data retrieval operations, through the use of different types of SELECT statements, are the most common. When you execute a SELECT statement, MySQL uses the query optimizer to analyze the statement and perform the query as effectively as possible. The optimizer is a MySQL component whose sole purpose is to ensure the best performance possible for each query by planning out the execution of that query.

The optimizer's primary goal is to try to use indexes whenever possible to process the statement. As you saw earlier in the chapter, an index can provide the most efficient method for locating rows that are accessed by the statement. The optimizer tries to determine which indexes benefit the execution of the statement and which ones don't. In some cases, the optimizer determines that it is better to bypass the index, rather than use it, such as when there are too many duplicate values.

The optimizer also tries to determine the greatest number of rows that can be eliminated from the search. To better understand how this works, take a look at the following SELECT statement:

```
SELECT BookTitle FROM Books
WHERE InStock>20 AND OnOrder>10;
```

Assume that the statement returns 20 rows, with each row meeting the conditions specified by the two expressions in the WHERE clause. When the optimizer first looks at the statement, it tests each of these expressions in order to estimate the number of rows that must be examined to meet the conditions specified by the expressions. You can also assume that, in this case, the optimizer estimates that 600 rows need to be examined for the first expression. If only 20 of the 600 rows meet both search conditions, MySQL has to search through 570 rows that don't meet both search conditions. The optimizer, however, also estimates that only 100 rows have to be examined for the second expression, which means that only 80 rows fail to meet both search conditions.

Based on the results of its initial tests of the two conditions, the query optimizer decides that it is best to process the second expression first and then, from those results, process the first expression. This way, fewer rows have to be processed, which means that the SELECT statement requires less processing time and fewer disk I/O operations than if the first expression is processed first.

The optimizer includes other capabilities that lend to the optimization of a statement; however, despite how efficient the optimizer can be, you might try to execute statements that you believe are not performing as well as they could. As a result, you must sometimes analyze your SELECT statements to determine what steps you can take to improve performance. The most effective method that you can use to analyze your SELECT statement is to use the EXPLAIN statement.

Using the EXPLAIN Statement

The EXPLAIN statement provides an analysis of a specified SELECT statement. To use the EXPLAIN statement, simply include the EXPLAIN keyword, followed by the SELECT statement, as shown in the following syntax:

```
EXPLAIN <select statement>
```

You should include your SELECT statement after the EXPLAIN keyword exactly as you would use the SELECT statement in a query. The EXPLAIN statement then returns results that provide details about how the SELECT statement will be executed. From these details, you can determine whether indexes are being used effectively, whether you should add new indexes, or whether you should specify the order of how tables are joined together.

You can also use the EXPLAIN *statement to return details about a table. To view table details, use the following syntax:* EXPLAIN <table name>. *As you can see, the name of the table follows the* EXPLAIN *keyword. Using the* EXPLAIN *statement in this way produces the same results as using the* DESCRIBE <table name> *statement.*

The best way to understand the EXPLAIN statement is to look at an example. The example is based on a SELECT statement that joins two tables: Manufacturers and Parts. The following table definition describes how the Manufacturers table is created:

```
CREATE TABLE Manufacturers
(
    ManfID CHAR(8)NOT NULL PRIMARY KEY,
    ManfName VARCHAR(30) NOT NULL
)
ENGINE=INNODB;
```

For the purpose of the example, you can assume that the following INSERT statement has populated the Manufacturers table:

```
INSERT INTO Manufacturers
VALUES ('abc123', 'ABC Manufacturing'),
('def456', 'DEF Inc.'),
('ghi789', 'GHI Corporation'),
('jkl123', 'JKL Limited'),
('mno456', 'MNO Company');
```

The following table definition describes how the Parts table is created:

```
CREATE TABLE Parts
(
    PartID SMALLINT NOT NULL PRIMARY KEY,
    PartName VARCHAR(30) NOT NULL,
    ManfID CHAR(8) NOT NULL
)
ENGINE=INNODB;
```

The Parts table shown in this definition is the same Parts table shown in Figure 15-1. As you can see, no foreign key is defined on this table. In reality, you would probably define a foreign key on the ManfID column of the Parts table that references the ManfID column of the Manufacturers table, but it is not done here in order to demonstrate how to analyze a SELECT statement.

Now assume that the following INSERT statement has been used to populate the Parts table:

```
INSERT INTO Parts
VALUES (101, 'DVD burner', 'abc123'),
(102, 'CD drive', 'jkl123'),
(103, '80-GB hard disk', 'mno456'),
(104, 'Mini-tower', 'ghi789'),
(105, 'Power supply', 'def456'),
(106, 'LCD monitor', 'mno456'),
(107, 'Zip drive', 'ghi789'),
(108, 'Floppy drive', 'jkl123'),
(109, 'Network adapter', 'def456'),
(110, 'Network hub', 'jkl123'),
(111, 'Router', 'mno456'),
(112, 'Sound card', 'ghi789'),
(113, 'Standard keyboard', 'mno456'),
(114, 'PS/2 mouse', 'jkl123'),
(115, '56-K modem', 'ghi789'),
(116, 'Display adapter', 'mno456'),
(117, 'IDE controller', 'def456');
```

Once the tables are created and populated, you can execute SELECT statements against the tables in order to retrieve data in those tables. For example, you might execute the following SELECT statement:

```
SELECT PartName, ManfName
FROM Parts AS p, Manufacturers as m
WHERE p.ManfID = m.ManfID
ORDER BY PartName;
```

The SELECT statement returns results similar to the following:

```
+-------------------+-------------------+
| PartName          | ManfName          |
+-------------------+-------------------+
| 56-K modem        | GHI Corporation   |
| 80-GB hard disk   | MNO Company       |
| CD drive          | JKL Limited       |
| Display adapter   | MNO Company       |
| DVD burner        | ABC Manufacturing |
| Floppy drive      | JKL Limited       |
| IDE controller    | DEF Inc.          |
| LCD monitor       | MNO Company       |
| Mini-tower        | GHI Corporation   |
| Network adapter   | DEF Inc.          |
| Network hub       | JKL Limited       |
| Power supply      | DEF Inc.          |
| PS/2 mouse        | JKL Limited       |
| Router            | MNO Company       |
| Sound card        | GHI Corporation   |
| Standard keyboard | MNO Company       |
| Zip drive         | GHI Corporation   |
+-------------------+-------------------+
17 rows in set (0.12 sec)
```

After executing the statement, you might decide that the statement's performance could be better. Although this might not be apparent when each table contains so few rows, it would become so if the tables contained thousands of rows. As a result, you decide to analyze this statement to see whether any bottlenecks exist and, if so, where they might be. To analyze the SELECT statement, you simply precede it with the EXPLAIN keyword, as shown in the following statement:

```
EXPLAIN SELECT PartName, ManfName
FROM Parts AS p, Manufacturers as m
WHERE p.ManfID = m.ManfID
ORDER BY PartName;
```

When you execute this statement, you should receive results similar to the following:

```
+----+-------------+-------+------+---------------+------+---------+------+------+-
| id | select_type | table | type | possible_keys | key  | key_len | ref  | rows |
+----+-------------+-------+------+---------------+------+---------+------+------+-
|  1 | SIMPLE      | p     | ALL  | NULL          | NULL |    NULL | NULL |   17 |
|  1 | SIMPLE      | m     | ALL  | PRIMARY       | NULL |    NULL | NULL |    4 |
+----+-------------+-------+------+---------------+------+---------+------+------+-
2 rows in set (0.00 sec)
```

The results returned by the EXPLAIN statement include a row for each table that participates in the query. The results shown here represent only a part of the entire results. The results that you can expect also include a column named Extra. In the preceding statement, the Extra column displays the value Using temporary; Using filesort for the first row and displays the value Using where in the second row.

Each column returned by the EXPLAIN statement provides specific information about how the optimizer plans to execute the SELECT statement. The following table describes each column returned by the EXPLAIN statement and provides information about the values displayed in the previous results set.

Column	Description
id	An identifier for the SELECT statement that is being analyzed. If the statement doesn't include subqueries or unions, the id value is 1 for each row, as is the case in the preceding example results set.
select_type	The type of SELECT statement. The SIMPLE value indicates that the statement doesn't include subqueries or unions. Other values indicate how the statement participates in a subquery or union.
table	The table being analyzed by the row. If an alias is used for the table name, the column displays the alias, rather than the actual table name.
type	The method used to match rows in different tables when the SELECT statement joins two or more tables. If ALL is specified, MySQL conducts a full table scan for each combination of rows from the current table and the joined table. Generally, you should avoid ALL in all but the first row.
possible_keys	The indexes that MySQL can use to find rows. If NULL, no indexes can be used. In the previous example, the primary key in the Manufacturers table can potentially be used to process the SELECT statement. This index would be considered because it is one of the columns specified in the join condition.

Table continued on following page

Column	Description
key	The indexes that MySQL actually uses to return rows. If NULL, no indexes are used.
key_len	The length of the index used to retrieve rows. This is most useful in determining how many parts of a multicolumn index are used. For example, if an index is made up of two columns that are each configured as CHAR(4) columns and the key_len column value is 4, you know that only the first column in the index is used. The key_len value is NULL if the key value is NULL.
ref	The column used in conjunction with the index specified in the key column. This usually refers to the column referenced in a foreign key. If NULL, no columns are used.
rows	The number of rows that MySQL plans to examine in order to execute the query. This column is normally your best indicator of the efficiency of the column. The more rows that must be examined, the less efficient the query.
Extra	Additional information about the query. For example, if a query can be executed by referring only to the index, the value Using index is displayed. The Using filesort value is displayed if MySQL must make an additional pass to retrieve rows in a sorted order. The Using temporary value is displayed if MySQL will create a temporary table to execute the query. The Using where value indicates that the WHERE clause will be used to restrict which rows to retrieve.

This table includes only the basic information that you need to understand the results returned by an EXPLAIN statement. For more information about the results returned by the statement, see the MySQL product documentation.

As the EXPLAIN statement results in the preceding example indicate, the SELECT statement will be processed by examining 17 rows in the Parts table and 4 rows in the Manufacturers table. In addition, because ALL is specified as the scan type, you know that a full-table scan will be conducted on both tables. To arrive at how many rows will actually be examined, you should multiply the values in the rows column. In this case, 68 rows will be examined. As you'll recall from the query results for this statement, only 17 rows are actually returned. As the EXPLAIN statement results also show, no indexes are being used to process the SELECT statement.

The first step that you should take is to try to determine whether you should add any more indexes to the table. As you would expect, the place to start is to add a foreign key to the Parts table. The foreign key not only provides referential integrity but creates an index on that column, which is important because that column is specified in the join condition. You can add the foreign key by using the following ALTER TABLE statement:

```
ALTER TABLE Parts
ADD FOREIGN KEY (ManfID) REFERENCES Manufacturers (ManfID);
```

After you modify the Parts table, you can use the same EXPLAIN statement that you saw in the preceding example. You should now receive results similar to the following:

```
+----+-------------+-------+------+---------------+------+---------+------+------+-
| id | select_type | table | type | possible_keys | key  | key_len | ref  | rows |
+----+-------------+-------+------+---------------+------+---------+------+------+-
|  1 | SIMPLE      | m     | ALL  | PRIMARY       | NULL |    NULL | NULL |    5 |
|  1 | SIMPLE      | p     | ALL  | ManfID        | NULL |    NULL | NULL |   13 |
+----+-------------+-------+------+---------------+------+---------+------+------+-
2 rows in set (0.00 sec)
```

The results shown here are similar to the results displayed the first time you executed the EXPLAIN statement. However, the new results show that 5 rows in the Manufacturers table and 13 in the Parts table will be scanned. When you multiply these values, you find that 65 rows will be examined to execute this query, not a very big improvement over the last time. One reason for this is that, although the ManfID index is listed in the possible_keys column, it is not being used. As a result, MySQL will still do a full-table scan on both tables.

The SELECT statement has not seen a great improvement in performance because the cardinality of the index is improperly set when you use the ALTER TABLE statement to create that index. Index *cardinality* refers to the number of unique values in an index. For example, suppose that you have a column that permits only three values. If you create an index on the column, the cardinality for that index is 3, no matter how many rows are in that table. In general, MySQL does not use an index with a low cardinality because this is not an efficient use of indexes. As a result, when you add an index to a table or modify it significantly in any other way, you should ensure that the cardinality is correctly represented to the query optimizer. The easiest way to do this is to execute an OPTIMIZE TABLE statement.

You can view a table's cardinality by using the SHOW INDEX statement on that table. Viewing the cardinality does not necessarily tell you whether that setting is improperly set, so you still might want to run the OPTIMIZE TABLE statement.

Using the OPTIMIZE TABLE Statement

The OPTIMIZE TABLE statement performs a number of functions. For example, it defragments the table and sorts the table's indexes. It also updates the internal table statistics. One of these statistics is the cardinality of its indexes. If you add an index to an existing table, you might have to use the OPTIMIZE TABLE statement to ensure that the table statistics are accurate when read by the query optimizer. The following syntax shows how to create an OPTIMIZE TABLE statement:

```
OPTIMIZE [LOCAL | NO_WRITE_TO_BINLOG] TABLE <table name> [{, <table name>}...]
```

As the syntax shows, you must, at a minimum, specify the OPTIMIZE TABLE keywords and the name of the table. In addition, you can specify the LOCAL option or the NO_WRITE_TO_BIN_LOG option (which are synonymous) to prevent the optimization process from being written to the binary log. In addition, you can specify more than one table.

Now return to the examples from the previous section. Because you added an index to the Parts table, you should run the OPTIMIZE TABLE statement on that table, as shown in the following example:

```
OPTIMIZE TABLE Parts;
```

When you execute this statement, you should receive results similar to the following:

```
+-------------+----------+----------+----------+
| Table       | Op       | Msg_type | Msg_text |
+-------------+----------+----------+----------+
| test.parts  | optimize | status   | OK       |
+-------------+----------+----------+----------+
1 row in set (0.35 sec)
```

Basically, these results are telling you that the parts table has been optimized. Now when you run an EXPLAIN statement (against the same example SELECT statement used previously), your results should be similar to the following:

```
------+------+---------------+--------+---------+----------------+------+-----------
table | type | possible_keys | key    | key_len | ref            | rows | Extra
------+------+---------------+--------+---------+----------------+------+-----------
m     | ALL  | PRIMARY       | NULL   | NULL    | NULL           |    5 | Using temp
p     | ref  | ManfID        | ManfID |       8 | test.m.ManfID  |    1 |
------+------+---------------+--------+---------+----------------+------+-----------
2 rows in set (0.00 sec)
```

Again, these results show only a part of the entire results. The id and select_type columns are not included, but they show the same results as in the earlier examples. The id value for both rows is 1, and the select_type value for both rows is SIMPLE. In addition, only part of the Extra column is shown in these results. The entire Extra value for the row about the Manufacturers table is Using temporary; Using filesort, indicating that a temporary table is used in processing the SELECT statement and an additional pass is made to retrieve the rows in a sorted order.

Although the id and select_type values are the same as in the previous example, there are a number of differences. First, the type column for the Parts table shows a value of ref, rather than ALL, indicating that the rows from this table are read based on index values that are matched according to the join condition, rather than performing a full-table scan. In addition, the optimizer now uses the index defined on the ManfID column of the Parts table, in conjunction with the ManfID column of the Manufacturers table, as shown in the ref column. The most important statistics in these results are in the rows column, which shows that 5 rows will be searched in the Manufacturers table and 1 row searched in the Parts table, indicating that only 5 rows will be examined to process this query, rather than 65.

At this point, you may wonder how it's possible that so few rows can be examined when you know that 17 rows are returned by the SELECT statement. The problem is that the values that are shown in the rows column are only estimates of the number of rows that the optimizer believes must be processed in order to execute the query. Because of the method the optimizer uses to arrive at these estimates, the smaller the table, the more inaccurate the estimates can be. And in reality, if you are working with tables as small as the ones shown in these examples, you do not need to be too concerned about optimizing your queries. As your tables grow and they contain thousands of rows, or even millions, optimization becomes critical. Regardless of the exact amount shown in the rows column, your goal should still be to get that total row count down as low as possible, and the steps shown here are a good way to start.

Adding indexes and executing OPTIMIZE TABLE statements are not the only methods that you can use to optimize query performance. MySQL also recommends other steps that you can take to maximize performance.

Understanding the SELECT Statement Guidelines

As stated earlier, proper indexing should still be your first strategy in optimizing your system so that you can retrieve data as efficiently as possible. There are several other steps that you can take to improve performance, as described in the following guidelines:

❑ **Do not use unnecessary wildcards in LIKE clauses.** Use wildcards only when you need them. For example, if you are looking for values that begin with "Cha," don't specify a wildcard at the beginning of your value, as in LIKE '%cha%'. Instead, omit the first wildcard. (For more information about using the LIKE clause, see Chapter 8.)

❑ **Isolate indexed columns in comparison expressions.** MySQL cannot use an index on a column if that column appears as an argument in a function or an arithmetic expression. For example, suppose your WHERE clause includes the expression YEAR(DateJoined)>1999, where DateJoined is a column that contains date values. If DateJoined is an indexed column, you might want to rewrite the WHERE clause to something similar to the following: DateJoined>'1999-12-31'. (For information about using functions, see Chapter 9. For information about expressions, see Chapter 8.)

❑ **Turn subqueries into joins.** In some cases, you can rewrite a subquery into a join. MySQL processes joins more efficiently than subqueries, so if using a join is an alternative, you should try that. (For more information about joins and subqueries, see Chapter 10.)

❑ **Try using the FORCE INDEX clause.** At times the query optimizer chooses to process a SELECT statement without using a particular index. You can try adding the FORCE INDEX clause to your SELECT statement to force the statement to use the specified index. (You add the FORCE INDEX clause to the table reference in your SELECT statement. For more information about how to include this option in your SELECT statement, see Chapter 7.)

❑ **Try using the STRAIGHT_JOIN option.** When the query optimizer analyzes a SELECT statement, it determines the order in which tables will be joined. In some cases, you might find that forcing the optimizer to join tables in the order specified in the SELECT statement improves the statement's performance. This occurs because there are times when the query optimizer does not join tables in the most optimal order. As a result, more rows are examined than need to be examined in order to perform an effective join operation. By forcing the join order, you can sometimes see an improvement in performance because fewer rows are being searched. To force the order, you can add the STRAIGHT_JOIN option to your SELECT statement. (For more information about using the STRAIGHT_JOIN option, see Chapter 10.)

❑ **Try alternative forms of the query.** Sometimes you can improve performance simply by changing how you structure a SELECT statement. One example is turning subqueries into joins. Another example is changing the order of tables specified in a join condition. The more you use SQL, the more alternative methods that you'll find to perform the same operations. As a result, it is sometimes worth the effort to try different forms of a SELECT statement to produce the same results. You can then analyze each form to determine which version of the statement performs the best. If you decide to try out different versions of a SELECT statement, be certain to execute each one several times to ensure that one statement isn't simply reading from the disk cache for the previous statement.

Now that you have a good overview of how to optimize the performance of your SELECT statements, you can try out some of what you have learned. In the following exercise, you add two tables to the DVDRentals database. The tables match customers to the cities in which they live. After you create the tables, you execute a SELECT statement that retrieves data from the new tables as well as the Customers table. You then use EXPLAIN statements to determine what steps you can take to improve the performance of that SELECT statement.

Try It Out   Optimizing Performance of a SELECT Statement

The following steps describe how to optimize the performance of a SELECT statement:

1. Open the mysql client utility, type the following command, and press Enter:

```
use DVDRentals
```

You should receive a message indicating that you have been switched to the DVDRentals database.

2. First, create a table for the name of the cities. Execute the following SQL statement at the mysql command prompt:

```
CREATE TABLE Cities
(
    CityID SMALLINT NOT NULL PRIMARY KEY,
    CityName VARCHAR(20) NOT NULL
)
ENGINE=INNODB;
```

You should receive a message indicating that the table has been successfully created.

3. Now insert data in the table that you created in the previous step. Execute the following SQL statement at the mysql command prompt:

```
INSERT INTO Cities
VALUES (101, 'Seattle'), (102, 'Redmond'), (103, 'Bellevue'),
(104, 'Kent'), (105, 'Kirkland');
```

You should receive a messaging indicating that the statement successfully executed and that five rows were affected.

4. Next, create the second table. Execute the following SQL statement at the mysql command prompt:

```
CREATE TABLE CustCity
(
    CustID SMALLINT NOT NULL,
    CityID SMALLINT NOT NULL
)
ENGINE=INNODB;
```

You should receive a message indicating that the table has been successfully created.

5. Insert data in the table that you created in Step 4. Execute the following SQL statement at the mysql command prompt:

```
INSERT INTO CustCity
VALUES (1, 104), (2, 101), (3, 104),
(4, 103), (5, 102), (6, 105);
```

You should receive a messaging indicating that the statement successfully executed and that six rows were affected.

6. Before you perform any sort of analysis, you should create a SELECT statement that retrieves information from the Customers, CustCity, and Cities tables. Execute the following SQL statement at the mysql command prompt:

```
SELECT CustLN, CityName
FROM Customers AS cu, CustCity AS cc, Cities AS ci
WHERE cu.CustID=cc.CustID AND ci.CityID=cc.CityID;
```

You should receive results similar to the following:

```
+-----------+----------+
| CustLN    | CityName |
+-----------+----------+
| Weatherby | Seattle  |
| Taylor    | Redmond  |
| Cavenaugh | Bellevue |
| Johnson   | Kent     |
| Thomas    | Kent     |
| Delaney   | Kirkland |
+-----------+----------+
6 rows in set (0.00 sec)
```

7. Next, use an EXPLAIN statement to analyze the SELECT statement that you created in Step 6. Execute the following SQL statement at the mysql command prompt:

```
EXPLAIN SELECT CustLN, CityName
FROM Customers AS cu, CustCity AS cc, Cities AS ci
WHERE cu.CustID=cc.CustID AND ci.CityID=cc.CityID;
```

You should receive results similar to the following:

table	type	possible_keys	key	key_len	ref	rows
cc	ALL	NULL	NULL	NULL	NULL	6
cu	eq_ref	PRIMARY	PRIMARY	2	dvdrentals.cc.CustID	1
ci	ALL	PRIMARY	NULL	NULL	NULL	4

```
3 rows in set (0.00 sec)
```

The results shown here represent only a part of the results you will see. Your results should also include the id, select_type, and Extra columns. The id value for each row is 1, the select_type value for each row is SIMPLE, and the row for the ci (Cities) table should show an Extra value of Using where.

8. Use an ALTER TABLE statement to add the necessary indexes to the CustCity table. Execute the following SQL statement at the mysql command prompt:

```
ALTER TABLE CustCity ADD PRIMARY KEY (CustID, CityID),
ADD FOREIGN KEY (CustID) REFERENCES Customers (CustID),
ADD FOREIGN KEY (CityID) REFERENCES Cities (CityID);
```

You should receive a messaging indicating that the statement successfully executed and that six rows were affected.

9. Rerun the EXPLAIN statement that you executed in Step 6. You should receive results similar to the following:

```
------+--------+----------------+---------+---------+-----------------------+------+
table | type   | possible_keys  | key     | key_len | ref                   | rows |
------+--------+----------------+---------+---------+-----------------------+------+
ci    | ALL    | PRIMARY        | NULL    |    NULL | NULL                  |    5 |
cc    | ref    | PRIMARY,CityID | CityID  |       2 | dvdrentals.ci.CityID  |    3 |
cu    | eq_ref | PRIMARY        | PRIMARY |       2 | dvdrentals.cc.CustID  |    1 |
------+--------+----------------+---------+---------+-----------------------+------+
3 rows in set (0.01 sec)
```

Your results should also include the id, select_type, and Extra columns. The id value for each row is 1, the select_type value for each row is SIMPLE, and the row for the cc (CustCity) table should show an Extra value of Using index.

10. Use the OPTIMIZE TABLE statement to optimize the CustCity table. Execute the following SQL statement at the mysql command prompt:

```
OPTIMIZE TABLE CustCity;
```

You should receive results similar to the following:

```
+----------------------+----------+----------+----------+
| Table                | Op       | Msg_type | Msg_text |
+----------------------+----------+----------+----------+
| dvdrentals.custcity  | optimize | status   | OK       |
+----------------------+----------+----------+----------+
1 row in set (0.41 sec)
```

11. Rerun the EXPLAIN statement that you executed in Step 6. You should receive results similar to the following:

```
------+--------+----------------+---------+---------+-----------------------+------+
table | type   | possible_keys  | key     | key_len | ref                   | rows |
------+--------+----------------+---------+---------+-----------------------+------+
ci    | ALL    | PRIMARY        | NULL    |    NULL | NULL                  |    5 |
cc    | ref    | PRIARY,CityID  | CityID  |       2 | dvdrentals.ci.CityID  |    1 |
cu    | eq_ref | PRIMARY        | PRIMARY |       2 | dvdrentals.cc.CustID  |    1 |
------+--------+----------------+---------+---------+-----------------------+------+
3 rows in set (0.00 sec)
```

Your results should also include the id, select_type, and Extra columns. The id value for each row is 1, the select_type value for each row is SIMPLE, and the row for the cc (CustCity) table should show an Extra value of Using index.

12. Drop the CustCity and Cities tables from the DVDRentals database. Execute the following SQL statements at the mysql command prompt:

```
DROP TABLE CustCity;
DROP TABLE Cities;
```

You should receive messages indicating that the statements were executed successfully.

How It Works

In this exercise, you added the Cities table and the CustCity tables to the DVDRentals database, and then you populated the tables. You then created a SELECT statement that retrieved data from the two new tables as well as the Customers table. After you ran the SELECT statement, you created the following EXPLAIN statement to analyze the SELECT statement:

```
EXPLAIN SELECT CustLN, CityName
FROM Customers AS cu, CustCity AS cc, Cities AS ci
WHERE cu.CustID=cc.CustID AND ci.CityID=cc.CityID;
```

The EXPLAIN statement is made up of the EXPLAIN keyword followed by the SELECT statement that you want to analyze. In this case, the EXPLAIN statement indicates that 24 rows (6 x 1 x 4) will be examined to process the query. For the CustCity and Cities tables, MySQL will examine all rows in both tables to process the query. For the Customers table, the type is eq_ref, which indicates that MySQL will examine only one row in the Customers table for each combination of rows processed in the other tables. In general, this in itself is an efficient approach, as opposed to examining every row. The fact that every row must be examined in the other two tables is still a problem.

The EXPLAIN statement also shows that MySQL will use only the primary key index on the Customers table to process that query, and no indexes from any other table. In an effort to try to improve performance, you used the following ALTER TABLE statement to add foreign keys to the CustCity table to reference the Customers and Cities table:

```
ALTER TABLE CustCity ADD PRIMARY KEY (CustID, CityID),
ADD FOREIGN KEY (CustID) REFERENCES Customers (CustID),
ADD FOREIGN KEY (CityID) REFERENCES Cities (CityID);
```

After you modified the tables, you ran the EXPLAIN statement once again. This time your results showed that 15 rows would be examined to process the SELECT statement, which is an improvement over the 24 rows. In addition, MySQL will use the foreign key index on the CityID column of the CustCity table when processing the query, as well as the primary key index for the Customers table.

Because you altered the CustCity table, you used the following OPTIMIZE TABLE statement to ensure that the query optimizer uses the correct cardinality values:

```
OPTIMIZE TABLE CustCity;
```

After you ran this statement, you executed the EXPLAIN statement a third time. The results are the same as they were when you executed the statement previously, only this time the results showed that only five rows will be examined (5 x 1 x 1) when processing the query. In reality, at least six rows will be examined. (The SELECT statement returns six rows.) As stated earlier, the row values are only estimates of how many rows the optimizer believes will need to be examined. Regardless of the values, the goal is to reduce that number by as many rows as possible.

Optimizing Data Insertion

Because SELECT statements are the most common types of SQL statements executed against a MySQL database, optimization efforts tend to focus on improving performance when retrieving data. There might be times, though, when you want to improve the performance of your insert operations, especially when you want to add many rows of data to your database or must add data often. The following guidelines provide information about several steps that you can take to improve the performance of your insert operations:

❑ **Use a LOAD DATA statement rather than an INSERT statement.** Whenever possible, use a LOAD DATA statement to insert data from a text file, rather than use an INSERT statement. MySQL can add data in a database up to 20 times faster when using a LOAD DATA statement, as compared to using an INSERT statement. (For information about the LOAD DATA statement, see Chapter 11.)

❑ **Use INSERT statements with multiple VALUES clauses.** When using INSERT statements to add multiple rows in a table, you can use one of two methods to insert that data. The first is to create an INSERT statement for each row of data, and the second is to create one INSERT statement that contains multiple VALUES clauses. Using the second option is much faster because MySQL must process only one SQL statement rather than many statements, and any related indexes must be flushed only once, rather then one time for each INSERT statement. (Whenever you execute an INSERT statement that affects an indexed column, the related index must be updated and flushed. For information about the INSERT statement, see Chapter 6.)

❑ **When using multiple INSERT statements, group them together in a transaction.** There will be times when you must use multiple INSERT statements, such as when you're inserting data in multiple tables. In that case, you should isolate your INSERT statement in a transaction. This process reduces the number of times that the index must be flushed. (For information about the transactions, see Chapter 12.)

❑ **Let MySQL insert default values.** When using INSERT statements to add data to a table, you can often insert the data without having to specify default values. If this is an option, do not specify those values and instead allow MySQL to insert them. This method results in shorter SQL statements, which means that the server must do less processing on each statement.

❑ **When possible, use the DELAYED option in your INSERT statements.** When you specify the DELAYED option in an INSERT statement, the execution of that statement is delayed until no other client connections are accessing the same table that the INSERT statement is accessing. You can continue to take other actions while the INSERT statement is in queue. (For information about using the DELAYED option in an INSERT statement, see Chapter 6.)

When you're dealing with only small amounts of data, most of these steps are inconsequential. However, if you are inserting thousands of rows at a time, performance becomes an important issue. Of all these guidelines, the most important to remember is that bulk loading (by using a LOAD DATA statement) is almost always preferable to using INSERT statements to add large quantities of data. In addition to improving the performance of your insert operations, you might also find that you need to improve the performance of your data modification operations.

Optimizing Data Modification and Deletion

When considering the steps that you should take to optimize your data modification and deletion operations, take into account the WHERE clause in your UPDATE and DELETE statements. The WHERE clause is similar to the WHERE clause in the SELECT statement in the way in which it determines which rows are examined in each table. As a result, some of the methods that you would use to improve performance of a SELECT statement also apply to an UPDATE or DELETE statement. For example, do not use unnecessary wildcards in your LIKE clause, and try to isolate indexed columns used in a comparison expression.

Another consideration with your update and delete operations is how the table is indexed. When you execute an UPDATE or DELETE statement, MySQL optimizes that statement in the same way that it optimizes a SELECT statement, except that there is additional overhead from the actual data modification operations. If columns in your WHERE clause are indexed, those indexes are used to locate the target rows. Because indexes can affect the performance of an update or delete operation, the gains you make by using the index might be lost when modifying the data. Keep in mind, however, that indexes are used primarily to facilitate data retrieval, not data updates and deletions. You should not remove an index if it improves the performance of a few UPDATE or DELETE statements but hurts many SELECT statements. The best way to take indexes into account is to balance the needs of your data retrieval operations against your update and delete operations. In most cases, you want to optimize your system based on your data retrieval operations.

One way to get around this issue of improving data retrieval performance at the expense of data modification operations is to continue to assign indexes based on the performance of your SELECT statement operations, but try to delay updates or deletions until you can perform them at one time, preferably at time when your system's usage is usually low. In addition, enclose your UPDATE statements and DELETE statements in a transaction so that all your data modifications are treated as a unit, which minimizes system processing and index flushing.

One other strategy to consider when deleting data is to use a TRUNCATE statement rather than a DELETE statement when deleting all data from a table. When MySQL processes a TRUNCATE statement, it drops the table and then re-creates it. This process makes the operations extremely fast, much faster than simply trying to remove all the data with a DELETE statement.

For more information about UPDATE, DELETE, *and* TRUNCATE *statements, see Chapter 6.*

In addition to taking steps to improve the performance of your data retrieval and modification operations, you should also take performance into consideration when designing your tables. The choices you make in your table definitions can also affect how well your SQL data modification statements perform.

Optimizing MySQL Tables

When you set up a database, you should take into account your table designs when trying to optimize your system's performance. Of particular importance is how you set up your columns in each table. The following guidelines provide several suggestions for designing your columns:

- ❑ **Use identical column types for compared columns.** If you plan to compare columns in a query, as is the case when defining a join condition, use identical data types if possible. For example, if you are defining a foreign key on a table, the foreign key and the referenced column do not have to have identical data types, only compatible data types. This means that a CHAR(6) column can reference a CHAR(8) column. You can then use these two columns to join together the tables. MySQL, however, does not process this join condition as fast as it would if both columns are configured exactly the same, such as making them both CHAR(6). As a result, it is sometimes better to sacrifice a little storage in the interest of improving performance.

- ❑ **Specify data types that have the correct length.** When specifying column types, do not specify types with lengths greater than what you need. For example, if you are defining a numerical column, don't use an INT data type if a SMALLINT data type will do. The smaller the column, the quicker that MySQL can process values used in computations. In addition, the smaller the columns, the smaller the indexes and the more data that can be held in memory.

❑   **Define your columns as NOT NULL when appropriate.** Whenever you can define a column as NOT NULL, you should do so. Columns that permit NULL values take longer to process than those that do not. If you have a column in which values are often not known, you can still define the column as NOT NULL, but you can also define a default value for that column, such as Unknown.

❑   **Consider defining your columns with the ENUM data type.** An ENUM data type allows you to specify the values that are permitted in a string column. In some cases, you know exactly what values can be inserted in a column, there are relatively few of those values, and the values will seldom change, if ever. In cases such as this, you should use the ENUM data type. Because ENUM values are represented internally as numerical values, MySQL can process them much more quickly than a regular string value.

In addition to taking these steps to improve your table designs, you should also use the OPTIMIZE TABLE statement to defragment some of your tables once they are created. Earlier in the chapter, you were introduced to the OPTIMIZE TABLE statement. One of the functions that the statement performs is to defragment a table. For tables that are modified often or that contain a lot of variable length data (such as is found in VARCHAR columns), fragmentation of the table can affect performance. As a result, you should consider running the OPTIMIZE TABLE statement against tables of this sort as needed.

As you can see, you can take several steps at the table level to improve the performance of your SQL statements. You can also take steps at the server level to help improve performance, as the following section explains.

Optimizing Your System's Cache

As you learned in Chapter 13, MySQL includes a number of system variables that allow you to specify system variable settings for the MySQL server. Some of the most important of these settings, in terms of the performance of your SELECT statements, are those settings related to your query cache. A cache is a place in your system's memory that holds specific types of information. A query cache is a cache that is used specifically to hold the result sets returned by SELECT statements.

An application can access information held in memory much faster than information that is stored on a hard disk, particularly if you're accessing large amounts of data stored in a database. As a result, when optimizing performance in MySQL, you should give special consideration to your query cache and the system variables that are used to control that cache.

The query cache speeds up the processing of your SELECT statements by caching the result sets retrieved by different queries. When a SELECT statement is first executed, that result set is cached. Whenever the same SELECT statement is executed, MySQL merely retrieves the data from the cache, without reprocessing the query. If the underlying data is modified in any way, the query results are removed from the cache.

By default, the query cache is not enabled. You can set up query caching on your system by using the following three system variables:

❑ **query_cache_type:** Specifies the operating mode of the query cache. Three possible values can be assigned to this variable: 0, 1, and 2. A value of 0 (displayed as OFF) means do not cache queries. A value of 1 (displayed as ON) means cache queries unless the SQL_NO_CACHE option is specified in a SELECT statement. A value of 2 (displayed as DEMAND) means cache queries only if the SQL_CACHE option is specified in a SELECT statement. By default, this variable is set to 1 (ON).

❑ **query_cache_limit:** Specifies the maximum size that a result set can be in order to be cached. For example, if the limit is set to 2M, no result set larger than 2M will be cached. The default limit is 1M.

❑ **query_cache_size:** Specifies the amount of memory allocated for caching queries. By default, this variable is set to 0, which means that query caching is turned off. To implement query caching, you should specify a query_cache_size setting in the [mysqld] section of your option file. For example, the setting query_cache_size=10M enables query caching and allocates 10M of memory to the cache.

As you can see, the only action that you need to take to implement query caching is to set the query_cache_size variable, which is set to 0 by default. Of course, you can also change the query_cache_limit and query_cache_type system variables, but this is not necessary in order to implement query caching. You can set the query_cache_size variable at the command line or in an option file, but you cannot use a SET statement to specify the cache size. If you do specify a value for the query_cache_size variable in an option file, you need to shut down your server and then restart it.

The system variables related to your query cache are not the only variables that can affect performance. There are also system variables related to your table and index cache, as well as other components of MySQL. Refer to Chapter 13 and the MySQL product documentation for information about each system variable.

Now that you have an overview of the system variables related to the query cache, you can enable query caching on your system. The following exercise walks you through the process of viewing the settings for each of these variables and enabling the query cache.

Try It Out   **Setting Your System's Cache**

The following steps describe how to view query cache variables and set the query_cache_size system variable:

1.   Open the mysql client utility.

2.   View the current value set for the query_cache_type variable. Execute the following SQL statement at the mysql command prompt:

```
SHOW VARIABLES LIKE 'query_cache_type';
```

You should receive results similar to the following:

```
+------------------+-------+
| Variable_name    | Value |
+------------------+-------+
| query_cache_type | ON    |
+------------------+-------+
1 row in set (0.00 sec)
```

3. View the current value set for the `query_cache_limit` variable. Execute the following SQL statement at the mysql command prompt:

```
SHOW VARIABLES LIKE 'query_cache_limit';
```

You should receive results similar to the following:

```
+-------------------+---------+
| Variable_name     | Value   |
+-------------------+---------+
| query_cache_limit | 1048576 |
+-------------------+---------+
1 row in set (0.00 sec)
```

4. View the current value set for the `query_cache_size` variable. Execute the following SQL statement at the mysql command prompt:

```
SHOW VARIABLES LIKE 'query_cache_size';
```

You should receive results similar to the following:

```
+-------------------+-------+
| Variable_name     | Value |
+-------------------+-------+
| query_cache_size  | 0     |
+-------------------+-------+
1 row in set (0.00 sec)
```

5. Next, use a text editor such as Vim or Notepad to modify your option file to include a setting for the `query_cache_size` system variable. For Linux users, add a `query_cache_size` entry to the [mysqld] section of the .my.cnf file in the root directory. For Windows users, modify the existing setting in the [mysqld] section of the my.ini file in the `C:\WINDOWS` directory. Your option file should include the following command:

```
query_cache_size=10M
```

After you have modified or added the `query_cache_size` entry, save your option file.

6. Exit the mysql client utility.

7. For the changes in the option file to take effect, you must shut down the MySQL server. In Linux, execute the following command at your operating system's command prompt:

```
mysqladmin -u root -p shutdown
```

When prompted for a password, enter your password and press Enter. The service is stopped.

In Windows, execute the following command at your operating system's command prompt:

```
net stop mysql
```

You should receive a message indicating that the service has been stopped.

8. Now you must restart the MySQL server. In Linux, execute the following command at your operating system's command prompt:

```
mysqld_safe --user=mysql &
```

If, after you execute the `mysql_safe` command, you're not returned to the command prompt right away, you have to press Enter to display the prompt.

In Windows, execute the following command at your operating system's command prompt:

```
net start mysql
```

You should receive a message indicating that the service has been started.

9. Relaunch the mysql client utility.

10. Now view the settings for the `query_cache_size` system variable again. Execute the following SQL statement at the mysql command prompt:

```
SHOW VARIABLES LIKE 'query_cache_size';
```

You should receive results similar to the following:

```
+------------------+----------+
| Variable_name    | Value    |
+------------------+----------+
| query_cache_size | 10485760 |
+------------------+----------+
1 row in set (0.00 sec)
```

11. Close the mysql client utility.

How It Works

All the steps that you took in this exercise should be familiar to you from previous chapters. To begin, you used the SHOW VARIABLES statement to view the default settings for each system variable related to the query cache. For example, the following SHOW VARIABLES statement retrieved the current setting for the `query_cache_limit` system variable:

```
SHOW VARIABLES LIKE 'query_cache_type';
```

The results indicated that the query cache is on. When you viewed the setting for the `query_cache_limit` variable, you saw that each results set can be 1048576, or 1M. Next you viewed the `query_cache_size` variable, which was set to 0. This meant that no SELECT statement result sets were being cached.

Once you verified the settings for all three system variables, you added or updated the following setting in the [mysqld] section of your option file:

```
query_cache_size=10M
```

This entry sets the query cache size to 10M. You implemented the new setting by stopping the server and then restarting it. From there, you opened the MySQL client utility and used the SHOW VARIABLES statement once more to verify the `query_cache_size` system setting. The results indicated that the new setting had been implemented. Now your SELECT statements will be cached, which should improve the performance of your SELECT statements. You could have also specified different settings for the `query_cache_type` and `query_cache_limit` system variables in your option file, but it wasn't necessary. Because you didn't, the default values for both variables are used.

Summary

As you have learned in this chapter, there are many steps that you can take to try to improve how well your SQL statements perform. The most important step is to ensure that your tables have been properly indexed. You want to be sure that each table contains the indexes that it needs, while at the same time ensuring that the table is not over-indexed. When necessary, you should also analyze your SELECT statements to ensure that they are being executed as optimally as possible. You should also take the steps necessary to maximize the performance of your data modification statements. In addition, you should look at how your tables have been created, and you should consider enabling query caching. To help you optimize your system, this chapter covered the following topics:

- ❑ Setting up effective indexes
- ❑ Using the EXPLAIN statement to analyze SELECT statement performance
- ❑ Using the OPTIMIZE TABLE statement to optimize your table after changes have been made to that table
- ❑ Improving the performance of data retrieval and modification
- ❑ Enabling your system's query cache to improve query performance

The subject of optimization is a broad one that can cover many aspects of running MySQL. Although this chapter attempted to touch on many of the important issues concerning optimizing your system, it could not cover each subject as extensively as possible. In fact, the subject of optimization is a book in itself. In addition, this chapter does not cover hardware considerations in system optimization. Consequently, you're encouraged to refer to other resources for information about optimizing your system, particularly the MySQL product documentation and Web site (www.mysql.com). From this chapter, you should have been able to gain a solid foundation in understanding many of the steps that you can take to optimize your SQL statements. From here, you're ready to move on to the topics of replicating, backing up, and restoring your MySQL database, which are covered in Chapter 16.

Exercises

This chapter explains several of the steps that you can take to optimize your SQL statements. The following exercises help you build on your knowledge of optimization. To view the solutions to these exercises, see Appendix A.

1. You plan to execute the following SELECT statement for an application that you're developing:

```
SELECT PartID, PartName, ManfName
FROM Parts AS p, Manufacturers as m
WHERE p.ManfID = m.ManfID
ORDER BY PartName;
```

The PartID column of the Parts table is configured as the primary key, and the ManfID column of the Manufacturers table is configured as the primary key. You anticipate that the SELECT statement will be executed frequently. On which columns should you consider creating indexes?

2. You want to analyze the SELECT statement shown in Exercise 1 to determine how MySQL will process the statement. What statement should you use to analyze the SELECT statement?

3. You use an EXPLAIN statement to analyze a SELECT statement. The analysis shows that the statement is not using one of the indexes defined on the table. What can you do to force the SELECT statement to use that index?

4. You must insert a large amount of data in one of the tables in your database. What is the fastest way to insert that data?

5. You plan to delete all the data from the Parts table. You want the deletion to be executed as quickly as possible, and you don't need to know how many rows have been deleted. What SQL statement should you use to delete the data?

6. You are planning the table structure for a MySQL database. You want to ensure that your columns are defined to ensure the maximum performance. What guidelines should you follow when setting up your columns?

7. You want to implement query caching, and you want to ensure that the cache grows no larger than 10M. What should you do to implement query caching?

Managing Backup, Recovery, and Replication

Despite the steps you take to secure your databases or optimize the performance of SQL statements issued against those databases, disasters can occur that cause the loss or corruption of data. As a result, one of the most important steps that you can take to protect your data is to make certain that you maintain copies of your databases. One method that you can use to copy your databases is to create backup files that contain the database and table definitions necessary to re-create your database structure as well as the statements and data necessary to repopulate your tables after they've been created. Once you create backup files, you can immediately re-create your database environment if the need arises, returning your database to the state it was in at the time you performed the last backup. You can then use the binary log files to update your database to a current state.

In addition to performing regular backups of your databases, you can also replicate your databases so that you always have at least one up-to-date copy of each one. Replicating a database means that you maintain a copy of the database that is kept synchronized with the original database. If disaster should occur on the original database, you can then use the replicated database to provide services to applications and users. In addition, replication is also useful in facilitating the backup process and in load balancing queries. This chapter describes how to back up your databases, restore the databases from the backup, and replicate your databases to another server. Specifically, the chapter covers the following topics:

❑ Using the mysqldump client utility to back up tables in a single database and back up multiple databases

❑ Using the mysql client utility in batch mode and interactive mode to reload databases from backup files and then using binary log files to update the databases after they've been reloaded

❑ Setting up replication on master and slave servers and then managing the replication process

Backing Up Your Database

Ensuring that your MySQL databases are backed up regularly should be part of any maintenance routine. Despite your best efforts to protect your databases, events such as power failures, natural disasters, and equipment failure can lead to the corruption and loss of data. Consequently, you should ensure that your databases have been safely copied to safe and reliable systems.

The primary method that MySQL provides for backing up all types of tables in your database is the mysql-dump client utility. The utility allows you to back up individual databases, tables in those databases, or multiple databases. When you run mysqldump, the utility creates a text file that contains the SQL statements necessary to create your database and tables safely and add data to those tables. This file is referred to as a *backup file* or *dump file*.

The way in which you use the utility and the type of information contained in the file depends on the type of backup you're performing (whether you're backing up individual databases, individual tables, or multiple databases). This section describes how you use the mysqldump client utility to perform the various types of backups.

> *You can also back up your databases simply by copying the data directory to a backup location. This method has several limitations, though. For example, if data is being updated when you copy the tables, you might be copying tables that are in an inconsistent state. In addition, copying InnoDB tables can be more complicated than simply using the mysqldump utility. The utility also saves data to text files, which makes your backups more portable than copying the data directory.*

Backing Up a Single Database

MySQL allows you to back up all tables in a database or only specific tables in that database. In both cases, you use the mysqldump client utility and you specify the name of the database. When backing up only specific tables, you must specify those table names as well. In this section, you learn how to perform both types of backups.

Backing Up the Entire Database

The first form of the mysqldump command that you examine backs up all the tables in a database. The database is backed up to a backup file that includes the table definitions and the INSERT statements necessary to repopulate the tables. To use this form of the command, you must specify the name of the database and the path and filename of the backup file, as shown in the following syntax:

```
mysqldump <database> > <path and filename>
```

As you can see, your command includes the mysqldump utility name, followed by the database name. The path and filename are then introduced by a right arrow (>) that tells the mysqldump utility to send the backed-up definitions and data to the specified file. If you do not include the right arrow and path and filename, the backup output would merely be displayed in your command line.

As you have seen with other utilities in MySQL, you can specify additional options in your command line. For example, you can specify the -h, -u, and -p options to include a host, username, and password along with your command. In addition, mysqldump supports numerous options specific to the utility. As you work your way through this chapter, you are introduced to some of these options. For information about all the options available to the mysqldump client utility, see the MySQL product documentation.

So that you better understand how the mysqldump utility works, this chapter includes a number of examples. The examples are based on the following database and table definitions as well as the INSERT statements used to populate the tables in the database:

```
CREATE DATABASE BooksDB;
use BooksDB;

CREATE TABLE Books
(
    BookID SMALLINT NOT NULL PRIMARY KEY,
    BookTitle VARCHAR(60) NOT NULL,
    Copyright YEAR NOT NULL
)
ENGINE=INNODB;

INSERT INTO Books
VALUES (12786, 'Letters to a Young Poet', 1934),
(13331, 'Winesburg, Ohio', 1919),
(14356, 'Hell\'s Angels', 1966),
(15729, 'Black Elk Speaks', 1932),
(16284, 'Noncomformity', 1996),
(17695, 'A Confederacy of Dunces', 1980),
(19264, 'Postcards', 1992),
(19354, 'The Shipping News', 1993);

CREATE TABLE Authors
(
    AuthID SMALLINT NOT NULL PRIMARY KEY,
    AuthFN VARCHAR(20),
    AuthMN VARCHAR(20),
    AuthLN VARCHAR(20)
)
ENGINE=INNODB;

INSERT INTO Authors
VALUES (1006, 'Hunter', 'S.', 'Thompson'),
(1007, 'Joyce', 'Carol', 'Oates'),
(1008, 'Black', NULL, 'Elk'),
(1009, 'Rainer', 'Maria', 'Rilke'),
(1010, 'John', 'Kennedy', 'Toole'),
(1011, 'John', 'G.', 'Neihardt'),
(1012, 'Annie', NULL, 'Proulx'),
(1013, 'Alan', NULL, 'Watts'),
(1014, 'Nelson', NULL, 'Algren');

CREATE TABLE AuthorBook
(
    AuthID SMALLINT NOT NULL,
    BookID SMALLINT NOT NULL,
    PRIMARY KEY (AuthID, BookID),
    FOREIGN KEY (AuthID) REFERENCES Authors (AuthID),
    FOREIGN KEY (BookID) REFERENCES Books (BookID)
)
```

```
ENGINE=INNODB;

INSERT INTO AuthorBook
VALUES (1006, 14356), (1008, 15729), (1009, 12786), (1010, 17695),
(1011, 15729), (1012, 19264), (1012, 19354), (1014, 16284);
```

As you can see, the statements shown here create the BooksDB database and three tables: Books, Authors, and AuthorBook. The code also includes the INSERT statements necessary to add data to each table. Now suppose that, once the database has been set up, you want to back up the data to a file. To do so, you can issue a mysqldump command from your operating system's command prompt, as shown in the following example:

```
mysqldump BooksDB > c:\backup\booksdb_041031.sql
```

In this command, you specify the BooksDB database, which means that all tables in the database will be backed up. This includes both the CREATE TABLE and INSERT statements. The mysqldump command also includes the path and filename (c:\backup\booksdb_041031.sql) of the backup file. Notice that the filename includes 040131, which is the date that the file is created. It's a good idea to use some sort of consistent naming convention for your backup files so that you can easily distinguish one from another and find the most recent one when you need it.

Once the file has been created, you can view its contents by using a text editor such as Notepad or Vim. The contents of the booksdb_041031.sql file should be similar to the following:

```
-- MySQL dump 10.8
--
-- Host: localhost     Database: BooksDB
-- -------------------------------------------------------
-- Server version       4.1.6-gamma-nt-log

/*!40101 SET @OLD_CHARACTER_SET_CLIENT=@@CHARACTER_SET_CLIENT */;
/*!40101 SET @OLD_CHARACTER_SET_RESULTS=@@CHARACTER_SET_RESULTS */;
/*!40101 SET @OLD_COLLATION_CONNECTION=@@COLLATION_CONNECTION */;
/*!40101 SET NAMES utf8 */;
/*!40014 SET @OLD_UNIQUE_CHECKS=@@UNIQUE_CHECKS, UNIQUE_CHECKS=0 */;
/*!40014 SET @OLD_FOREIGN_KEY_CHECKS=@@FOREIGN_KEY_CHECKS, FOREIGN_KEY_CHECKS=0 */;
/*!40101 SET @OLD_SQL_MODE= L_MODE, SQL_MODE="NO_AUTO_VALUE_ON_ZERO" */;


--
-- Table structure for table 'authorbook'
--

DROP TABLE IF EXISTS 'authorbook';
CREATE TABLE 'authorbook' (
  'AuthID' smallint(6) NOT NULL default '0',
  'BookID' smallint(6) NOT NULL default '0',
  PRIMARY KEY  ('AuthID','BookID'),
  KEY 'BookID' ('BookID'),
  CONSTRAINT 'authorbook_ibfk_1' FOREIGN KEY ('AuthID') REFERENCES 'authors'
('AuthID'),
```

```
    CONSTRAINT 'authorbook_ibfk_2' FOREIGN KEY ('BookID') REFERENCES 'books'
('BookID')
)ENGINE=InnoDB DEFAULT CHARSET=latin1;


--
-- Dumping data for table 'authorbook'
--

/*!40000 ALTER TABLE 'authorbook' DISABLE KEYS */;
LOCK TABLES 'authorbook' WRITE;
INSERT INTO 'authorbook' VALUES
(1009,12786),(1006,14356),(1008,15729),(1011,15729),(1014,16284),(1010,17695),(1012,
19264),(1012,19354);
UNLOCK TABLES;
/*!40000 ALTER TABLE 'authorbook' ENABLE KEYS */;

<Authors table and Books table>

/*!40101 SET SQL_MODE=@OLD_SQL_MODE */;
/*!40014 SET FOREIGN_KEY_CHECKS=@OLD_FOREIGN_KEY_CHECKS */;
/*!40014 SET UNIQUE_CHECKS=@OLD_UNIQUE_CHECKS */;
/*!40101 SET CHARACTER_SET_CLIENT=@OLD_CHARACTER_SET_CLIENT */;
/*!40101 SET CHARACTER_SET_RESULTS=@OLD_CHARACTER_SET_RESULTS */;
/*!40101 SET COLLATION_CONNECTION=@OLD_COLLATION_CONNECTION */;
```

As you can see, the file includes a number of elements. It first begins with information that identifies the version of the mysqldump utility that you're using, the name of the host where the server resides, the name of the database, and the version of the MySQL server that is running. If the version is followed by -log, that indicates that logging was enabled at the time the backup file was created. Notice that each line of information is preceded by double dashes (--), which indicates that these are comments and that MySQL should ignore this information when executing the statements in the file.

The next part of the backup file is a series of SET statements that assign values to a number of user-defined variables. For example, the first of these statements defines a variable named @old_character_set_client:

```
/*!40101 SET @OLD_CHARACTER_SET_CLIENT=@@CHARACTER_SET_CLIENT */;
```

As discussed in Chapter 7, MySQL allows you to define a variable (either by using a SELECT statement or a SET statement) that stores a value in memory for the duration of a session. In this case, the SET statement assigns the current value associated with the character_set_client system variable to the @old_character_set_client user-defined variable. The following table describes the system variables that are used to assign values to user-defined variables in the backup file.

System variable	Description
character_set_client	The character set that MySQL uses to process SQL statements sent by a client application. By default, MySQL uses the latin1 character set.
character_set_results	The character set that MySQL uses to return query results to a client application. By default, MySQL uses the latin1 character set.

Table continued on following page

System variable	Description
collation_connection	The collation associated with the character set used for the connection. By default, MySQL uses the latin1_swedish_ci collation.
unique_checks	Specifies whether MySQL checks for uniqueness in a column configured with a unique index. By default, MySQL checks for uniqueness.
foreign_key_checks	Specifies whether MySQL checks foreign key constraints in a column configured as a foreign key. By default, MySQL checks foreign key constraints.
sql_mode	Specifies the SQL mode in which MySQL should operate. The mode determines what SQL syntax is supported and how data should be validated. By default, no mode is set.

MySQL assigns these values to the user-defined variables to ensure that the original system variable values can be reinstated should they be changed by any of the statements in the backup file. This guarantees that your environment is left in the same state after the execution of the statements as it was before the execution of the statements. At the end of the backup file, MySQL adds the necessary SET statements to set the system variables back to their original value. For example, the following SET statement uses the @old_character_set_client user-defined variable to assign the value to the actual character_set_client system variable, which is where that value originated:

```
/*!40101 SET CHARACTER_SET_CLIENT=@OLD_CHARACTER_SET_CLIENT */;
```

One thing to notice about the SET statements is that they begin with the /*! symbols and end with the */ symbols. The statements are enclosed in these symbols so that they are executed by MySQL but ignored if they are executed in another database management system. This allows your basic SQL statements in the backup file to be used by other systems, while ensuring that the statements unique to MySQL can be executed.

Also notice that the symbols at the beginning of the statements are followed by a number. This number represents a version of the MySQL server, and it tells MySQL to execute the statement only if that version or a later version is being used. For example, the 40101 in the preceding statement indicates that the statement should be executed only on MySQL version 4.01.01 or above.

Now take a look at one other SET statement that is included at the beginning of a backup file:

```
/*!40101 SET NAMES utf8 */;
```

The SET NAMES statement specifies the name of the character set that should be used during the execution of the statements in the backup file. The statement is specific to the connection, so once the connection is ended, the setting no longer applies. In this case, the SET NAMES statement specifies that the utf8 character set should be used, which is the character set used when the backup file was created.

The information in the backup file that you have looked at so far is typical of any backup file that you create when using the mysqldump client utility. The other information in the file is specific to the tables that you have backed up. For each table that is backed up, the file includes a table definition and an INSERT statement. The table definition is introduced by comments similar to the following:

```
--
-- Table structure for table 'authorbook'
--
```

In this case, the comments tell you that the information that follows applies to the AuthorBook table. The comments are then followed by a DROP TABLE statement to ensure that MySQL does not try to create a table that already exists, which would result in an error. The DROP TABLE statement ensures that the CREATE TABLE statement that follows can be successfully executed. The CREATE TABLE statement then defines the table as it existed when the file was created.

After the CREATE TABLE statement, the backup file then includes comments similar to the following:

```
--
-- Dumping data for table 'authorbook'
--
```

The comment indicates that the section that follows inserts data in the AuthorBook table. After the comment, you see the following set of statements:

```
/*!40000 ALTER TABLE 'authorbook' DISABLE KEYS */;
LOCK TABLES 'authorbook' WRITE;
INSERT INTO 'authorbook' VALUES
(1009,12786),(1006,14356),(1008,15729),(1011,15729),(1014,16284),(1010,17695),(1012,
19264),(1012,19354);
UNLOCK TABLES;
/*!40000 ALTER TABLE 'authorbook' ENABLE KEYS */;
```

An ALTER TABLE statement that tells MySQL to disable the indexes precedes each INSERT statement. The ALTER TABLE statement at the end of this group of statements then enables the indexes. MySQL does this to improve the performance of the insert operations so that the indexes are not created until the operation is complete. This process, however, works only for MyISAM table types and is ignored by other table types.

A LOCK TABLES statement also precedes the INSERT statement, placing a WRITE lock on the table so that no other values can be inserted in the table until after this INSERT statement has been executed. After the INSERT statement runs, the table is then unlocked. The INSERT statement itself is a straightforward statement that provides values for all columns in the table. One thing you might have noticed about both the INSERT statement and the CREATE TABLE statement that precedes it is that they create a table and insert data in a table that includes foreign key constraints. If you were to try to create the table manually, before creating the referenced tables, you would receive an error. MySQL, however, allows all tables to be created and values to be inserted when done through a backup file, regardless of the foreign key constraints. MySQL is indifferent to the order in which tables appear in the backup file.

One other aspect of the backup file to look at is the following component:

```
<Authors table and Books table>
```

This is actually only a placeholder for the Authors and Books tables. The statements that are used to create and populate the AuthorBook table are the same statements you would see for any table. As a result, a placeholder is used here merely to show that the other two tables would also appear in this file.

Now that you've seen the type of information that is included in a backup file, there's one other aspect of creating a dump file that you should consider using when running a mysqldump command. The option is the `--flush-logs` option, which flushes your log files. If you have binary logging enabled (which you should), a new binary log file is created. This is important when creating a backup because, as you see later in this section, binary log files allow you to restore your database fully. By flushing the logs, you're providing yourself with an exact starting point for using the binary logs when restoring your database. As a result, it is recommended that you use the `--flush-logs` option whenever you back up your data.

To flush the logs when creating a backup file, simply add the `--flush-logs` option to your mysqldump command, as shown in the following example:

```
mysqldump --flush-logs BooksDB > c:\backup\booksdb_041031.sql
```

Now when you go to restore the database, you will have a much easier time locating the proper log information.

As you have seen, the mysqldump utility allows you to back up all the tables in your database easily. There might be times when you want to back up only individual tables; in that case, you must include those table names in your mysqldump command.

Backing Up Individual Tables

To use the mysqldump client utility to back up individual tables in a database, your mysqldump command should be set up based on the following syntax:

```
mysqldump <database> [<table> [<table>...]] > <path and filename>
```

As you can see, the only difference between this command and the command that you use to back up all tables in a database is that now you must add the applicable table names after the database name. For example, the following mysqldump command backs up the Authors and Books table in the BooksDB database:

```
mysqldump --flush-logs BooksDB Authors Books > c:\backup\authbooks_041031.sql
```

The command creates a backup file named authbooks_041031.sql. The file contains the same SET commands that you find when you back up an entire database. The file now contains table definitions and INSERT statements only for those tables identified in the command.

Backing Up Multiple Databases

In addition to backing up the tables in a single database, you can also back up multiple databases. As with backing up a single database, you can use the mysqldump client utility; however, the command format is slightly different. In addition, the backup file includes not only table definitions and INSERT statements, but also the statements necessary to create the databases that are being backed up.

You can use two formats of the mysqldump utility to back up multiple databases. The first of these allows you to specify the databases that you want to back up, and the second format allows you to back up all databases that are currently stored on your MySQL server.

Backing Up Specific Databases

If you use the mysqldump utility to back up multiple databases, you must add the `--databases` option to your command, as shown in the following syntax:

```
mysqldump --databases <database> [<database>...] > <path and filename>
```

After you specify the `--databases` option, you must specify the name of at least one database. You can specify as many names as necessary, separating each name with a space. For example, the following mysqldump command backs up the BooksDB and BooksDB2 databases:

```
mysqldump --flush-logs --databases BooksDB BooksDB2 >
c:\backup\bookstore_041031.sql
```

Notice that the command includes the `--databases` option, followed by the name of the two databases. When you execute this command, the backed-up databases will be stored in a file named bookstore_041031.sql. The file will contain the same information that you've seen in previous backup files, with the addition of one element — the statements necessary to create the database. For example, the following data is added to the bookstore_041031.sql file:

```
--
-- Current Database: 'BooksDB'
--

CREATE DATABASE /*!32312 IF NOT EXISTS*/ 'BooksDB';

USE 'BooksDB';
```

The file first includes comments indicating that the statements that follow apply to the BooksDB database. After the comments, the file contains a CREATE DATABASE statement, which will add the BooksDB database to your system. Notice that the statement includes the clause `/*!32312 IF NOT EXISTS*/`. As you learned earlier, because the clause is enclosed in the `/*!` symbols and `*/` symbols, it is not executed unless the statement runs against a MySQL server, version 3.23.12 or later. The file then contains a use command, which instructs MySQL to make the BooksDB database the active database. This is done to ensure that the CREATE TABLE and INSERT statements that follow are correctly applied to the BooksDB database.

Using this form of the mysqldump command is also useful if you want to back up only one database but want to ensure that the backup file includes the necessary database definition. As you learn later in the chapter, if the backup file doesn't include the database definition, you must first manually create the database before you can restore the contents of that database. By including the database definition, restoring the database is an easier process.

Backing Up All Databases

If you plan to back up all the databases on your system, you can use the following form of the mysqldump client utility:

```
mysqldump --all-databases > <path and filename>
```

As the syntax shows, you need to specify the `--all-databases` option but not any database names. For example, the following statement backs up all your databases to a file named databackup_041031.sql:

```
mysqldump --flush-logs --all-databases > c:\backup\databackup_041031.sql
```

The backup file will contain all the necessary database and table definitions and `INSERT` statements for all the tables in all the databases. The file will also contain the necessary `SET` statements. As you can see, this form of the mysqldump utility is simpler than specifying the `--databases` option along with the name of every database that you want to back up. If you use this option, keep in mind that it will also back up the mysql administrative database, which could be a security risk if the backup file is not properly secured.

Now that you have an understanding of how to use the mysqldump client utility to back up your databases, you can try to back up a database for yourself. In the following exercise, you create a database named VideoRentals. The database includes a table named Videos, which is populated with information about several movies. After you create the database, you back up it up to your hard disk, where you can then view the contents of the file.

Try It Out   **Backing Up a Database to a Backup File**

The following steps describe how to create and then back up the VideoRentals database:

1. Open the mysql client utility.

2. First, create the VideoRentals database and the Videos table by executing the following SQL statements at the mysql command prompt:

```
CREATE DATABASE VideoRentals;
use VideoRentals;
CREATE TABLE Videos
(
    VideoID SMALLINT NOT NULL AUTO_INCREMENT PRIMARY KEY,
    VideoName VARCHAR(60) NOT NULL,
    Status ENUM('In', 'Out') NOT NULL
)
ENGINE=INNODB;
```

You should receive a message indicating that the statement executed successfully, affecting no rows.

3. Now insert data in the Videos table by executing the following SQL statement at the mysql command prompt:

```
INSERT INTO Videos (VideoName, Status)
VALUES ('Out of Africa', 'In'),
('The Maltese Falcon', 'In'),
('The Rocky Horror Picture Show', 'Out'),
('A Room with a View', 'In'),
('Mash', 'Out');
```

You should receive a message indicating that the statement executed successfully, affecting five rows.

4. Exit the mysql client utility. You should be returned to your operating system's command prompt.

5. Create a directory in which to store the backup file. For the purposes of this exercise, it is assumed that on Windows you will be using the `C:\backup` directory, and on Linux you will be using the `/backup` directory. If you use a directory other than these, replace them with your own directory name in any steps that require that you specify a directory.

6. If you're running MySQL on Windows, execute the following command at the Windows command prompt:

```
mysqldump --flush-logs --databases VideoRentals > c:\backup\videorentals001.sql
```

If you're running MySQL on Linux, execute the following command at the Linux command prompt:

```
mysqldump --flush-logs --databases VideoRentals > /backup/videorentals001.sql
```

After you execute the command, you're returned to your operating system's command prompt.

7. Use a text editor (such as Notepad or Vim) to open the videorentals001.sql file that you created in Step 6. The contents of the file should be similar to the following:

```
-- MySQL dump 10.8
--
-- Host: localhost    Database: VideoRentals
-- ------------------------------------------------------
-- Server version       4.1.6-gamma-nt-log

/*!40101 SET @OLD_CHARACTER_SET_CLIENT=@@CHARACTER_SET_CLIENT */;
/*!40101 SET @OLD_CHARACTER_SET_RESULTS=@@CHARACTER_SET_RESULTS */;
/*!40101 SET @OLD_COLLATION_CONNECTION=@@COLLATION_CONNECTION */;
/*!40101 SET NAMES utf8 */;
/*!40014 SET @OLD_UNIQUE_CHECKS=@@UNIQUE_CHECKS, UNIQUE_CHECKS=0 */;
/*!40014 SET @OLD_FOREIGN_KEY_CHECKS=@@FOREIGN_KEY_CHECKS, FOREIGN_KEY_CHECKS=0 */;
/*!40101 SET @OLD_SQL_MODE= L_MODE, SQL_MODE="NO_AUTO_VALUE_ON_ZERO" */;


--
-- Current Database: 'VideoRentals'
--

CREATE DATABASE /*!32312 IF NOT EXISTS*/ 'VideoRentals';

USE 'VideoRentals';


--
-- Table structure for table 'videos'
--

DROP TABLE IF EXISTS 'videos';
CREATE TABLE 'videos' (
  'VideoID' smallint(6) NOT NULL auto_increment,
  'VideoName' varchar(60) NOT NULL default '',
  'Status' enum('In','Out') NOT NULL default 'In',
  PRIMARY KEY  ('VideoID')
```

```
) ENGINE=InnoDB DEFAULT CHARSET=latin1;


--
-- Dumping data for table 'videos'
--

/*!40000 ALTER TABLE 'videos' DISABLE KEYS */;
LOCK TABLES 'videos' WRITE;
INSERT INTO 'videos' VALUES (1,'Out of Africa','In'),(2,'The Maltese
Falcon','In'),(3,'The Rocky Horror Picture Show','Out'),(4,'A Room with a
View','In'),(5,'Mash','Out');
UNLOCK TABLES;
/*!40000 ALTER TABLE 'videos' ENABLE KEYS */;

/*!40101 SET SQL_MODE=@OLD_SQL_MODE */;
/*!40014 SET FOREIGN_KEY_CHECKS=@OLD_FOREIGN_KEY_CHECKS */;
/*!40014 SET UNIQUE_CHECKS=@OLD_UNIQUE_CHECKS */;
/*!40101 SET CHARACTER_SET_CLIENT=@OLD_CHARACTER_SET_CLIENT */;
/*!40101 SET CHARACTER_SET_RESULTS=@OLD_CHARACTER_SET_RESULTS */;
/*!40101 SET COLLATION_CONNECTION=@OLD_COLLATION_CONNECTION */;
```

8. Close the videorentals001.sql file.

How It Works

In this exercise, you used the mysql client utility to create a database named VideoRentals, add a table named Videos to the database, and then insert data in the table. You then exited the mysql client utility and created a directory to store the backup file. From there, you executed a mysqldump command similar to the following:

```
mysqldump --flush-logs --databases VideoRentals > c:\backup\videorentals001.sql
```

The mysqldump command creates a backup file named videorentals001.sql in your backup directory. The `--flush-logs` command indicates that the logs should be flushed before creating the backup file. This ensures that any changes made to a table after the backup can be easily tracked in the binary log files. The `--databases` option indicates that you plan to back up one or more entire databases. In this case, you backed up only one database. As a result, you did not have to use the `--databases` option. By including the option, you're ensuring that the backup file contains the necessary CREATE DATABASE statement so that a database does not have to exist prior to restoring the database. If you had not included the `--databases` option, you would first have to create the database before you could restore the tables from the backup file. (You learn more about restoring a database later in the chapter.)

Once you created the backup file, you viewed the contents of the file. As you would expect, the file first lists general information about the backup and defines the necessary variables to hold values based on current system variables. For example, the following SET statement assigns a value to a user-defined variable named @old_character_set_results:

```
/*!40101 SET @OLD_CHARACTER_SET_RESULTS=@@CHARACTER_SET_RESULTS */;
```

The value assigned to the variable is based on the character_set_results system variable. You can retrieve that value currently assigned to the character_set_results system variable by using @@CHARACTER_SET_RESULTS. The @old_character_set_results variable holds the value until all statements in the backup file have been executed. The backup file then uses the variable to assign the stored value to the related system variable, as shown in the following statement:

```
/*!40101 SET CHARACTER_SET_RESULTS=@OLD_CHARACTER_SET_RESULTS */;
```

The backup file uses a SET statement to set the character_set_results system variable to the value that is stored in the @old_character_set_results user-defined variable. Because this value is the same value that was assigned to the character_set_results system variable before the backup file statements were executed, the character_set_results system variable is assigned its original value. This process ensures that the system variables are returned to the original state that they were in before the statements in the backup file were executed.

Each SET statement begins with /*! and ends with */, which means that the statement will be ignored by any database servers other than MySQL. Also, the opening symbols (/*!) are followed by version numbers, which means that MySQL will execute the statement only for that version of MySQL or later. For example, the number 40101 indicates that MySQL will execute the statement only if the server is version 4.1.1 or later.

In addition to the standard SET statements, the backup file also includes the SQL statements necessary to create the VideoRentals database and the Videos table. A DROP TABLE statement precedes the CREATE TABLE statement to ensure that the table doesn't exist before you try to create it. The CREATE TABLE statement is followed by the INSERT statement necessary to add the data to the Videos table. The INSERT statement is surrounded by two ALTER TABLE statements that specify that the indexes should be created after the data is inserted in the table. Because the table type is InnoDB, the ALTER TABLE statements do not apply and have no impact on your statements. The INSERT statement is also preceded by a LOCK TABLES statement that sets a WRITE lock on the table as data is being inserted, and then an UNLOCK TABLES statement that unlocks the table after the insertion has been completed.

The backup file that you created in this exercise contains only one database and one table. As a result, the file includes only one CREATE DATABASE statement, one CREATE TABLE statement, and one INSERT statement. You can, however, back up multiple databases that each contain multiple tables; in that case, the backup file will contain the SQL statements necessary for each database and table. Regardless of how many databases and tables are included in the file, once that file has been created, you can use it to restore your databases and tables in the event that your databases become corrupted or deleted.

Restoring Your Database

Despite your best efforts to protect your databases, disasters can occur, and you might find it necessary to restore one or more of your databases. If you have backed up your files regularly and enabled binary logging, restoring your database consists of only two steps:

1. Using the mysql client utility to reload your database into the MySQL server
2. Using the applicable binary logs to update the database

Together these two steps allow you to restore your database to the point where failure occurred, thus ensuring that no data is lost should you experience a disaster.

Reloading Your Database

In Chapter 3, you learned how to use the mysql client utility in batch mode and interactive mode to execute SQL statements and MySQL commands saved to a text file. You can also use the utility to execute the statements in the backup files that you created with the mysqldump utility. When using the mysql client utility in batch mode, you run the program from your operating system's command prompt. When using the mysql utility in interactive mode, you must first launch the utility and then execute the necessary commands at the mysql command prompt.

Using the mysql Client Utility in Batch Mode to Reload Your Database

To use the mysql client utility in batch mode to restore a database, you have to specify the mysql command (at your operating system's command prompt) along with the left arrow (<), path, and filename, as shown in the following syntax:

```
mysql [<database>] < <path and filename>
```

As you can see, you also have the option of specifying a database name. If you do specify a database name, the database must exist in the database, which means that you must create the database if it doesn't already exist. You would generally use this option if you are restoring data from a backup file that does not include a database definition. For example, suppose that you want to restore a database from the booksdb_041031.sql file, which does not include a database definition. You would use a statement similar to the following to restore the tables in the database:

```
mysql BooksDB < c:\backup\booksdb_041031.sql
```

As the command shows, you include BooksDB, which means that the database must already exist. If you are restoring a database from a backup file that includes the necessary database definition, you can use the following statement:

```
mysql < c:\backup\bookstore_041031.sql
```

In this case, the bookstore_041031.sql file includes the database definition, so the database does not have to exist and you do not have to specify it. You simply execute the statement as it is shown here, and the statements related to creating the database, creating the table, and inserting data are automatically executed.

Using the mysql Client Utility in Interactive Mode to Reload Your Database

You can also use the mysql client utility in interactive mode to restore a database. To do so, you merely specify the source command, along with a path and filename of the backup file, as shown in the following syntax:

```
source <path and filename>
```

Notice that specifying a database is not an option in this command. When you work with the mysql utility interactively, you must work in the context of a database to execute statements that create tables and insert data. As a result, if you are working with a backup file that does not include the necessary database definition, you must first create the database, switch to the new database, and then download the backup file. For example, suppose that you're restoring a database from the booksdb_041031.sql file, which doesn't include a table definition. Because of this, you would have to execute a series of statements:

```
CREATE DATABASE BooksDB;
use BooksDB;
source c:\backup\booksdb_041031.sql
```

The CREATE DATABASE statement creates the BooksDB database, the use command switches to the new database, and the source command retrieves the backup file. If your backup file includes the database definition, all you need to specify is the source command, the path, and the filename, as shown in the following example:

```
source c:\backup\bookstore_041031.sql
```

As you can see, creating a backup file that includes the necessary database definitions makes restoring your databases a simpler process. In addition, if you're restoring multiple databases from a single file, the file must contain the necessary database definitions. Regardless of which method you use to reload your database into your system, the database is only as current as your last backup, which is where binary logging comes in.

Updating the Restored Database from Binary Log Files

After you reload your database into your system, you will most likely want to apply any changes made to the database since it was backed up. Fortunately, binary logs track all data modifications that occur in your databases, so you can use binary logs to update your database to its more current state. MySQL provides two methods for applying updates from a binary log — restoring data directly from the binary log file or exporting binary log data to a text file and then restoring it from that file.

You must have binary logging enabled on your system to be able to use it to update a restored database. For more information about implementing binary logging, see Chapter 13.

Restoring Data Directly from a Binary Log

To apply updated data to the database that you've reloaded, you must know which log files apply. By comparing the log file timestamps to the backup file timestamp, you should be able to figure out easily which logs apply. In addition, if you used the --flush-logs option when you backed up the database, you know that you do not have to look for data starting in the middle of a log file. You can start right at the beginning of the file.

After you identify the log files that you should apply, you can use the mysqlbinlog client utility to execute the statements in the log file. For example, the following mysqlbinlog command executes the SQL statements in the server1-bin.000127 log file:

```
mysqlbinlog "c:\program files\mysql\mysql server 4.1\data\server1-bin.000127" |
mysql
```

As you can see, you must specify the mysqlbinlog command followed by the path of your data directory and the name of the file. In addition, you should specify that the command send the SQL statements to the mysql client utility to be executed as necessary. You do this by adding a vertical pipe (|) and the command mysql. If you plan to execute multiple log files, you should start with the oldest one first and work your way through to the most current file.

If you want to apply the change in the log files to only one database, you can specify the `--one-database` option after the mysql command, as shown in the following example:

```
mysqlbinlog "c:\program files\mysql\mysql server 4.1\data\server1-bin.000127" |
mysql --one-database BooksDB
```

Notice that you must include the name of the database after the `--one-database` option. When you do this, MySQL processes only those logged statements that apply to the specified database.

Using the mysqlbinlog utility to apply updates directly from the log file to the database can be a quick way to restore a database fully. But what if the log contains statements that you don't want executed? For example, the log file might contain DROP DATABASE statements or CREATE TABLE statements that you don't want executed. Unfortunately, you have little control of which statements are executed except for being able to specify that only statements related to a specific database be executed. You can get around this issue by exporting the contents of the binary log file to a text file.

Restoring Binary Log Data from a Text File

The mysqlbinlog client utility allows you to export data to a text file. From there, you can sort through the text file to remove any statements that you don't want to execute. Of course, the larger the log file, the more difficult this process can be, but there might be times when this is the only way you can ensure that your database is fully restored. After you're satisfied that the text file contains only the correct statements, you can use the mysql client utility to execute the statements.

The first step, then, is to export the data in the log file to the text file. For example, the following mysqlbinlog command exports the server1-bin.000127 log file to the binlog000127.txt file:

```
mysqlbinlog "c:\program files\mysql\mysql server 4.1\data\server1-bin.000127" >
c:\backup\binlog000127.txt
```

As you can see, you specify the path and filename of the log file, add a right arrow, and then specify the path and filename of the text file. You can then edit the text file as necessary. Once satisfied, you can execute the statements in the text file by using the following command:

```
mysql < c:\backup\binlog000127.txt
```

All SQL statements that are saved in the text file are executed. If you want to run only statements related to a specific database, you can use the `--one-database` option in the same way you saw earlier, as shown in the following example:

```
mysql --one-database BooksDB < c:\backup\binlog000127.txt
```

As the command shows, you specify the `--one-database` option and the name of the database, followed by the left arrow and the path and filename of the text file. Any updates that were recorded in the binary log file — and exported to the text file — are applied to the database.

Enabling and Disabling Binary Logging

When restoring databases and applying log file statements, you might find that you want to execute a statement that you don't want logged. For example, suppose that you want to drop a database before you restore it. If you run the DROP DATABASE statement, that statement is logged to the binary log file. You can manually turn off logging in a session by using a SET statement to set the sql_log_bin system variable, as shown in the following syntax:

```
SET SQL_LOG_BIN={0 | 1}
```

As you can see, the sql_log_bin system variable includes two options: 0 and 1. If set to 0, logging is disabled. If set to 1, logging is enabled. For example, if you want to execute a statement that should not be logged, you would first issue the following SET statement:

```
SET SQL_LOG_BIN=0;
```

The sql_log_bin variable will be turned off for the duration of the connection or until you explicitly turn it back on (by setting the variable to 1). This allows you to control which statements are logged, which can be critical to restoring your database effectively.

As this section demonstrates, restoring a database is as simple as retrieving a backup file from your hard disk and then applying the statements in the applicable binary logs. In the following exercise, you restore the database that was backed up in the previous Try It Out section. To restore the database, you first remove the original database from your system and then use the source command in the mysql client utility to execute the SQL statement in the backup file.

Try It Out Restoring a Database from a Backup File

The following steps describe how to restore the VideoRentals databases from the videorentals001.sql backup file:

1. Use the following command to open the mysql client utility and make the VideoRentals database active:

```
mysql VideoRentals
```

The mysql client utility is launched, and the VideoRentals database is active. The VideoRentals database is the one that you created in the previous Try It Out section.

2. Insert data in the Videos table in the VideoRentals database by executing the following SQL statement at the mysql command prompt:

```
INSERT INTO Videos (VideoName, Status)
VALUES ('Amadeus', 'Out');
```

You should receive a message indicating that the statement executed successfully, affecting one row.

3. Now turn off binary logging. Execute the following SQL statement at the mysql command prompt:

```
SET SQL_LOG_BIN=0;
```

You should receive a message indicating that the statement executed successfully.

4. Remove the original VideoRentals database so that you can test restoring the database. Execute the following SQL statement at the mysql command prompt:

```
DROP DATABASE VideoRentals;
```

You should receive a message indicating that the statement executed successfully, affecting one row.

5. Next, execute the contents of the videorentals001.sql backup file. If you're running MySQL on Windows, execute the following command at the mysql command prompt:

```
source c:\backup\videorentals001.sql
```

If you're running MySQL on Linux, execute the following command at the mysql command prompt:

```
source /backup/videorentals001.sql
```

You should receive the appropriate message for each SQL statement in the backup file that has been executed, indicating the successful execution of the statement and the number of rows affected. You should receive a warning that the DROP TABLE statement does not apply because no table exists. You should also receive warnings indicating that the ALTER TABLE statements do not apply because the ENABLE KEYS and DISABLE KEYS options apply only to MyISAM tables. (You had backed up an InnoDB table.)

6. Now re-enable binary logging. Execute the following SQL statement at the mysql command prompt:

```
SET SQL_LOG_BIN=1;
```

You should receive a message indicating that the statement executed successfully.

7. Next, view the contents of the Videos table. Execute the following SQL statement at the mysql command prompt:

```
SELECT * FROM Videos;
```

You should receive results similar to the following:

```
+---------+-------------------------------+--------+
| VideoID | VideoName                     | Status |
+---------+-------------------------------+--------+
|       1 | Out of Africa                 | In     |
|       2 | The Maltese Falcon            | In     |
|       3 | The Rocky Horror Picture Show | Out    |
|       4 | A Room with a View            | In     |
|       5 | Mash                          | Out    |
+---------+-------------------------------+--------+
5 rows in set (0.00 sec)
```

8. Exit the mysql client utility.

9. Now update the database with the statements in the last binary log file. Execute the following command at the operating system's command prompt:

```
mysqlbinlog "<path and filename>" | mysql
```

You need to enclose the data directory and filename in quotes only if the directory path or file-name contain a space. For the `<path and filename>` placeholder, insert the directory path for your MySQL data directory and the name of the most recent binary file in the data directory. Once you execute this command, you should be returned to your operating system's command prompt.

10. Use the following command to open the mysql client utility and make the VideoRentals database active.

```
mysql VideoRentals
```

The mysql client utility is launched.

11. Again view the contents of the Videos table. Execute the following SQL statement at the mysql command prompt:

```
SELECT * FROM Videos;
```

You should receive results similar to the following:

```
+---------+------------------------------+--------+
| VideoID | VideoName                    | Status |
+---------+------------------------------+--------+
|       1 | Out of Africa                | In     |
|       2 | The Maltese Falcon           | In     |
|       3 | The Rocky Horror Picture Show| Out    |
|       4 | A Room with a View           | In     |
|       5 | Mash                         | Out    |
|       6 | Amadeus                      | Out    |
+---------+------------------------------+--------+
6 rows in set (0.00 sec)
```

12. Because you do not need the VideoRentals database for additional exercises, you can remove it from your system. Execute the following command at your operating system's command prompt:

```
DROP DATABASE VideoRentals;
```

You should receive a message indicating that the statement executed successfully, affecting one row.

13. Exit the mysql client utility.

How It Works

In this exercise, you first inserted data in the Videos table. You did this in order to log an event to the new binary log that was created after you backed up the database. Next, you used the SET statement to turn off binary logging so that dropping and restoring the database were not logged. If they had been logged, it would have confused the restoration process. Once you turned off logging, you dropped the VideoRentals database so that you could test restoring the database. Next, you used a source command similar to the following to access the backup file that you created in the previous Try It Out section:

```
source c:\backup\videorentals001.sql
```

The `source` command includes only one argument: the path and filename of the backup file (`c:\backup\videorentals001.sql`). Because you used the `--database` option in the `mysqldump` command when you created the backup file, the file included the statement necessary to create the VideoRentals database as well as the Videos table.

Once the database and table were restored, you used another `SET` statement to re-enable binary logging. You then executed a `SELECT` statement that retrieved data from the Videos table, indicating that the table and database had been properly restored. The results show that the table did not contain the row that you inserted in Step 2. This occurs because you inserted the data after you created the backup file. The backup is current only until the time the file was created.

After you verified that the database had been reloaded, you exited the mysql client utility and then ran the following `mysqlbinlog` command:

```
mysqlbinlog "<path and filename>" | mysql
```

The mysqlbinlog utility allows you to read the contents of a binary log file. By adding the vertical pipe (|) and mysql to the command, you're telling the mysqlbinlog utility to use the mysql client utility to execute the SQL statements recorded in the binary log. Because this is the log that contains any statement executed since you created the backup, this process restores the database to its most current state.

After you executed the SQL statements in the binary log, you launched the mysql client utility and again viewed the contents of the Videos table, which showed that the insertion that had been logged now appears in the table, indicating that your database is now current. Once you verified the insertion, you dropped the VideoRentals database from your system and then exited the mysql client utility.

As this exercise demonstrates, the process of restoring a database is a straightforward one; however, it can be a very time-consuming process, which can mean substantial downtime for your database. Another alternative — in addition to performing regular backups — is to replicate your database to one or more servers, thus ensuring that you always have at least one additional copy of your database that is up to date.

Replicating Your Database

Replication refers to the process of maintaining a current copy of your database on a server separate from the server where the original database resides. Whenever the original database changes, those changes are automatically applied to the copy. As a result, you always have one or more up-to-date copies of your database that can be used in case of database or server failure. For example, if the original database becomes suddenly unavailable, you can switch to the copied database so that users and applications have immediate access to the same data, with a minimal amount of downtime.

Another advantage of replication is that it can be used to optimize performance. For example, you can make backups from the copied database rather than the production database, allowing you to create backup files without affecting the performance of the primary database. You can also use replication to split query loads. Queries that merely retrieve information are directed to the server that contains the replicated database, while queries that actually update data are sent to the original database. This way, only one database is being updated, but the load is shared between two servers.

In MySQL, replication is a one-way process. The primary MySQL server acts as the master server, and the servers that contain the copied databases are considered the slave servers. Data always moves from the master server to the slave server. As a result, only databases on the master server should be updated. The updates are then propagated to the slave servers.

MySQL replication is based on a number of principles:

❑   The master server must be configured with a user account that grants replication privileges to the slave server. The account allows the slave server to access the master server in order to receive updates.

❑   Binary logging must be enabled on the master server. The binary logs track all updates to a database, and the logged updates are then used to synchronize the database on the slave server.

❑   The slave server uses replication coordinates to track updates. The coordinates are based on the name of a binary log file on the master server and the position in that file. The file and position represent where MySQL left off when the last update was performed on the slave server. The coordinates — along with other logon information — are stored in the master.info file on the slave host.

❑   Each server that participates in the replication process must be assigned a unique numerical server ID. You assign the ID by specifying the `server-id` option in the `[mysqld]` section of the option file for each server.

❑   A master server can replicate data to one or more slave servers. A slave server can act as a master server to another slave server in order to create a replication chain. For example, ServerA can be configured as a master server that replicates data to ServerB, the slave server. ServerB can also be configured as a master server that replicates data to ServerC. As a result, ServerA is replicated to ServerB, and ServerB is replicated to ServerC. You can also replicate ServerA directly to ServerC so that ServerB and ServerC are slave servers to ServerA. (Note that a slave server can never have two master servers.)

❑   To set up replication, the master server and slave server must begin with databases in a synchronized state. In other words, the databases to be replicated must be identical when replication is initiated. Once initiated, updates on the master server are replicated to the slave server.

Although not always necessary, it is generally recommended that the master server and slave servers run the same version of MySQL.

When replication is implemented, the slave server maintains a set of files to support the replication. MySQL automatically creates the three types of files on the slave server:

❑   **<host>-relay-bin.<extension>:** Primary relay log files that contain the statements to be used to synchronize the replicated database with the database on the master server. The relay log files receive their data from the binary log files on the master server. The filename extension is a number, starting with 000001, that is incremented whenever a relay log file is added.

❑   **master.info:** Maintains connection information such as the master server hostname, the MySQL user account name, and the password for that account. Also maintains information about the last binary log file (on the master server) to be accessed and the position in that file.

❑   **relay-log.info:** Maintains information about the relay log files and tracks the last position in those files in which the replicated database was updated.

The replication log files are created automatically when you implement replication. MySQL deletes the relay log file (*<host>*-relay-bin.*<prefix number>*) after the statements in the file have been executed and the replicated database has been updated. The master.info and relay-log.info files are updated as needed to support the replication process and to keep the copied databases updated. If you back up a slave server, you should also back up the relay log files, the master.info file, and the relay-log.info file so that you can restore the slave server if necessary.

To give you a better overview of how replication is implemented in MySQL, take a look at Figure 16-1. As the illustration shows, updates to the databases on the master server are logged to the binary log files set up for that server. The applicable content in the binary log files is then copied to the relay log files, which reside on the slave server. The content of the relay log files is then used to update the replicated database on the slave server. This is a one-way process, which means that changes are always propagated from the master server to the slave server, but never the other way around.

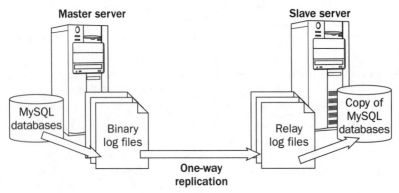

Figure 16-1

Support for replication is built into MySQL. There are no special add-ins or applications that you must install. Tou do have to configure your system to support replication, so the next section shows you how that is accomplished.

> *When working with replication, keep in mind that it's a relatively new MySQL technology, so it is still very much a work in progress and evolving continuously. For this reason, the way in which it is implemented in the version of MySQL that you're using might be a little different from the way it is described here. In addition, because it's still a relatively new technology, you might receive results different from what you expect when you try to implement and administer replication. If you plan to implement replication, be sure to refer to the most current product documentation.*

Implementing Replication

Before you setting up replication, binary logging should be enabled on the master server. From there, you can use the following steps to implement replication:

1. To allow a master server to replicate data to a slave server, you must set up a user account on the master server. The slave server then uses that account to establish a connection to the master server. To set up the account, launch the mysql client utility on the master server; then execute the following GRANT statement:

```
GRANT REPLICATION SLAVE ON *.*
TO '<slave account>'@'<slave host>'
IDENTIFIED BY '<password>';
```

The GRANT statement grants the REPLICATION SLAVE privilege at the global level, as specified by the ON clause. The privilege is specific to the process of replication and allows all changes to a database to be replicated to the copy of the database on the slave server. The TO clause defines the username on the account and host from which that account can connect. This is the host where the slave server resides. The IDENTIFIED BY clause then identifies the password that should be used when the slave server logs on to the master server. (For more information about the GRANT statement and setting up user accounts, see Chapter 14.)

2. Make a backup of the databases that you want to replicate. Use the --master-data option in the mysqldump command. The --master-data option adds a CHANGE MASTER statement similar to the following to your backup file:

```
CHANGE MASTER TO MASTER_LOG_FILE='master1-bin.000128', MASTER_LOG_POS=79 ;
```

The CHANGE MASTER statement identifies the binary log file and the position in that file at the time that the backup file is created. You use this information later when you set up replication on the slave server. This information allows you to synchronize the slave server with the master server. (The CHANGE MASTER statement is discussed in more detail later in this section. For information about backing up a database to a backup file, see the "Backing Up Your Database" section earlier in the chapter.)

3. Shut down the master server.

4. Next, you must modify the [mysqld] section of the option file on the master server. You must specify a server ID for the master server. The master server and any slave servers must each be assigned a unique numerical ID. In addition, if you don't want to replicate a specific database, such as the mysql or test databases, you can add a binlog-ignore-db option for each database to prevent changes to that database from being logged to the binary file. As a result, changes to those tables aren't replicated. When you're finished editing the option file, the [mysqld] section should include options similar to the following:

```
[mysqld]
log-bin
binlog-ignore-db=mysql
binlog-ignore-db=test
server-id=<master server id>
```

The log-bin option specifies that binary logging should be enabled. The two binlog-ignore-db options specify that changes to the mysql and test databases should not be logged to the binary files. The server-id option specifies the numbered ID for the master server.

If you use a predefined option file, a server-id *option might already exist. Be sure to check for other instances of* server-id. *If multiple options are specified and the numerical IDs are different, replication might not work.*

5. Restart the master server.

6. Shut down the slave server.

7. Modify the option file on the slave server so that the `[mysqld]` section includes the following settings:

```
server-id=<slave server id>
```

Make certain that this server ID is different from the master server ID and different from any other slave server IDs. Also be sure that this is the only `server-id` option defined on the slave server.

8. Restart the slave server.

9. Use the backup file that you created in Step 2 to load the databases into the slave server. (For information about loading a database from a backup file, see the "Reloading Your Database" section earlier in the chapter.)

10. Next, you must specify the settings that will be used for the slave server to connect to the master server and determine which binary log file to access. Launch the mysql client utility on the slave server, and then execute the following CHANGE MASTER statement:

```
CHANGE MASTER TO
    MASTER_HOST='<master host>',
    MASTER_USER='<user account>',
    MASTER_PASSWORD='<password>',
    MASTER_LOG_FILE='<log file>',
    MASTER_LOG_POS=<position>;
```

The CHANGE MASTER statement identifies the hostname of the master server, the username for the account that you created in Step 1, the password for that account, the binary log file on the master server, and the position in that file. The slave server adds this information to the master.info file, which is used when connecting to the master server. (The CHANGE MASTER statement is discussed in more detail later in this section.)

11. The final step that you must take is to start the replication process on the slave server. To do so, execute the following SQL statement on the slave server:

```
START SLAVE;
```

The statement initiates the threads that connect from the slave server to the master server. (The START SLAVE statement is discussed in more detail later in this section.)

Once you've set up replication, you should try it out. The easiest way to do this is to make a change to a table on the master server and then determine whether that change has been replicated to the slave server. If the change is reflected on the slave server, replication has been properly set up. Once replication is implemented, you might find that you need to view replication settings or make a change. Fortunately, MySQL allows you to administer the replication environment.

Managing Replication

To support administering replication, MySQL provides a number of SQL statements that allow you to view information about the replication environment or take a specific action. MySQL supports statements for both the master server and the slave server.

Managing the Master Server

As you have learned, the master server contains the original database. Changes made to databases on the master server are replicated to the slave servers. To allow you to manage replication on the master server, MySQL provides several statements.

Using the RESET MASTER Statement

When you're setting up replication, you might find that you first want to clean up the binary logs on your master server. Once you have backed up the log files and the index file, you can delete these files and start from scratch. The easiest way to do this is to issue the following statement:

```
RESET MASTER;
```

The RESET MASTER statement deletes all your binary log files, removes them from your binary index file, and starts logging with a new log file.

Using the SHOW MASTER STATUS Statement

Earlier in the chapter, you learned about the steps necessary to set up replication. One of the steps is to create a backup file of the databases that you want to replicate. Indeed, the step instructs you to use the `--master-data` option in your `mysqldump` command. The command adds a CHANGE MASTER statement to your backup file that contains the binary log filename and the position in the file that you should use as a starting point when implementing replication on a slave server.

Using the `--master-data` option in the `mysqldump` command is a handy way of preserving the filename and position when you go to implement replication on the server. You merely reference the backup file and retrieve that information from there. An alternative that you can use to determine the binary log filename and position is the following statement:

```
SHOW MASTER STATUS;
```

When you execute the statement, you should receive results similar to the following:

```
+--------------------+----------+--------------+------------------+
| File               | Position | Binlog_Do_DB | Binlog_Ignore_DB |
+--------------------+----------+--------------+------------------+
| master1-bin.000030 |      340 |              | mysql,test       |
+--------------------+----------+--------------+------------------+
1 row in set (0.00 sec)
```

As you can see, the results include a binary log filename (master1-bin.000030) and a position in the binary log (340). The Binlog_Do_DB column lists any databases that are specifically logged to the binary files. Currently, no databases are being explicitly logged. As a result, changes to all databases on the server are logged to the binary log file unless explicitly shown in the Binlog_Ignore_DB column. In this case, the mysql and test databases are shown, so changes to those two databases are not logged.

> You can log changes to a specific database by adding the `binlog-do-db` option to the `[mysqld]` section of your option file. You can prevent changes to a specific database from being logged by adding the `binlog-ignore-db` option to the `[mysqld]` section of your option file. If changes to a database are not logged to the binary log files, that database cannot be replicated.

The SHOW MASTER STATUS statement provides a quick method for discovering the current position in a log file. If you are using this information as part of setting up replication, you must be sure that it is applied exactly to when you backed up the databases. For example, suppose you create a backup file and then issue a SHOW MASTER STATUS statement. Now suppose that an update had been issued against the database in between when you created the backup file and when you checked the master status. The result would be that the master status information would no longer be accurate. As a result, if you cannot guarantee the accuracy of the master status information, you should simply add the --master-data option to your mysqldump command.

Using the SHOW SLAVE HOSTS Statement

You might find it useful at times to know exactly what slave servers are connected to your master server. This can be useful if you're troubleshooting your replication and you want to determine whether the slave server is connected to the master server. To verify the slave connections to your master that currently exist, execute the following statement:

```
SHOW SLAVE HOSTS;
```

The SHOW SLAVE HOSTS statement should return results similar to the following:

```
+-----------+-----------+------+--------------------+-----------+
| Server_id | Host      | Port | Rpl_recovery_rank  | Master_id |
+-----------+-----------+------+--------------------+-----------+
|         2 | server20  | 3306 |                  0 |         1 |
+-----------+-----------+------+--------------------+-----------+
1 row in set (0.00 sec)
```

The results should include a row for each slave that is connected to the master. In these results, only one slave is connected. As you can see, the row provides the server ID of the slave (2), the name of the slave host (server20), the port being used to connect to the master (3306), the replication recovery rank (0), and the server ID of the master server (1).

The replication recovery rank (the Rpl_recovery_rank column) refers to the rpl_recover_rank system variable, which has a default value of 0. Currently the system variable is not used by MySQL, so it has no meaning in this context. It appears that eventually it will be used to rank master servers so that, if a slave server has lost its master, it can select a new master based on the master ranks.

By default, a slave server is not listed in the results returned by the SHOW SLAVE HOSTS statement. To include a slave server in these results, you must add the --report-host=<host> option to the [mysqld] section of the option file on the slave server. When specifying this option, you should provide the name of the slave host, not the master host.

You can also use the SHOW PROCESSLIST statement to view a list of the threads that are currently running. This is useful if you want to see all your current connections, including the slave connections.

Managing the Slave Server

In addition to providing statements that allow you to manage replication on the master server, MySQL supports a number of statements that you can use to manage the replication environment on a slave server.

Using the *CHANGE MASTER* Statement

The CHANGE MASTER statement is probably the most important statement that you work with when managing replication. The statement provides the parameters that are used by the master.info file on the slave server. The following syntax shows how to define a CHANGE MASTER statement:

```
CHANGE MASTER TO <master option> [<master option>...]
```

As you can see, you must specify the CHANGE MASTER TO keywords along with one or more master options. The primary options that you'll be using are described in the following table.

Option syntax	Description
MASTER_HOST='<master host>'	The name of the master server
MASTER_USER='<user account>'	The name of the user account set up for the slave server
MASTER_PASSWORD='<password>'	The password for the user account set up for the slave server
MASTER_PORT=<port number>	The port number used to connect to the MySQL server on the master server
MASTER_CONNECT_RETRY=<count>	The number of times to try to reconnect to the master server if a connection cannot be established initially
MASTER_LOG_FILE='<log file>'	The name of the binary log file on the master server that the slave server should begin reading from when implementing replication on the slave server
MASTER_LOG_POS=<position>	The position in the binary log file that determines where to start searching the log files in order to synchronize the slave server with the master server
RELAY_LOG_FILE=<log file>	The name of the relay log file on the slave server that the slave server should begin reading from when implementing replication
RELAY_LOG_POS=<position>	The position in the relay log file that determines where to start searching the log files in order to implement replication

The CHANGE MASTER statement is most commonly used when first initiating replication on a slave server. The statement might also come in handy if connection information changes after replication has started. For example, you might have to change the password for the user account that connects to the master server. In that case, you simply specify the MASTER_PASSWORD='<password>' option as the statement's only option.

The MASTER_HOST='<master host>' option and the MASTER_PORT=<port number> option are a little different from the other options. If you specify either one, you must also specify the MASTER_LOG_FILE='<log file>' option and the MASTER_LOG_POS=<position> option. In addition, if you specify the MASTER_LOG_FILE='<log file>' or the MASTER_LOG_POS=<position> option, you cannot specify the RELAY_LOG_FILE=<log file> or RELAY_LOG_POS=<position> option. For example, the following CHANGE MASTER statement adheres to the statement rules:

```
CHANGE MASTER TO
    MASTER_HOST='server1',
    MASTER_USER='slave_acct',
    MASTER_PASSWORD='slave_pw',
    MASTER_LOG_FILE='server1-bin.001234',
    MASTER_LOG_POS=79;
```

In this statement, the master host is server1, the account used to log on to the host is slave_acct, and the password for that account is slave_pw. In addition, the master log binary file is server1-bin.001234, and the position in that log is 79. As you can see, a master host is specified, so a master log file and log position are included. In addition, the relay log file and relay position are not specified. When you execute this statement, the information is added to the master.info file.

Using the RESET SLAVE Statement

If you want to start over with setting up replication on the slave server, you can reset the slave by using the following statement:

```
RESET SLAVE;
```

The statement deletes all the relay log files as well as the master.info and relay-log.info files. The statement then re-creates all the necessary replication files, providing you with a clean start. As a result, the master.info file does not contain the values necessary to connect to the master server; in that case, you need to issue a CHANGE MASTER statement.

Using the SHOW SLAVE STATUS Statement

If you want to view information about a slave server, you receive the most complete information by using the following statement:

```
SHOW SLAVE STATUS;
```

The SHOW SLAVE STATUS statement provides status information about the connection to the master server, the binary log file and relay log file, and the positions in the log files. The following results show a part of what you receive when you execute this statement on a slave server:

```
+-----------------------------------+-------------+-------------+-------------+-----
| Slave_IO_State                    | Master_Host | Master_User | Master_Port | Conn
+-----------------------------------+-------------+-------------+-------------+-----
| Waiting for master to send event  | server1     | slave1      |        3306 |
+-----------------------------------+-------------+-------------+-------------+-----
1 row in set (0.00 sec)
```

The results shown here represent only a small part of the information you should receive when you run the SHOW SLAVE STATUS statement. The statement returns nearly any information you need about the slave server. For a complete list of the information returned by the statement, see the MySQL product documentation.

Using the START SLAVE Statement

If you have stopped the slave server for any reason or are implementing replication on a slave server for the first time, you can start the replication process on the slave server by using the following statement:

```
START SLAVE;
```

The statement starts the connections to the master server that are necessary for replication to work. Two connections are used by a slave server. The I/O connection accesses data in the binary log files on the master server and copies that data to the relay logs. The SQL connection reads the relay logs and executes the statements against the databases on the slave server.

Using the STOP SLAVE Statement

To stop replication on the slave server, you can issue the following statement on the slave server:

```
STOP SLAVE;
```

The statement stops both the I/O connection and the SQL connection, and changes to the databases are no longer replicated. The replication files, though, are preserved, so you can restart the replication process by issuing a START SLAVE statement.

Summary

As this chapter has demonstrated, MySQL supports several methods that you can use to protect your system from the loss of data. By backing up your system regularly, you're ensuring that you maintain an ongoing history of the changes made to your database. And should you need to restore your database, you can use the most recent backup file, along with the applicable binary log files, to restore your system to its original state. In addition to creating backup files, you can set up replication in order to maintain at least one synchronized copy of your database. Although replication doesn't provide the history that backup files provide, it does provide you with an up-to-date copy of your database. To provide you with the information necessary to back up and restore your databases, as well as set up replication, this chapter covered the following topics:

❑ Using the mysqldump client utility to back up tables in a single database

❑ Using the mysqldump client utility to back up multiple databases

❑ Using the mysql client utility in batch mode to restore databases

❑ Using the mysql client utility in interactive mode to restore databases

❑ Restoring data from your binary log files

❑ Replicating databases on a MySQL server

❑ Managing the master and slave servers used in replication

Although backing up your data and setting up replication are both effective methods that you can use to copy your data, these two methods are even more effective when used in conjunction with each other. In this case, you would set up a slave server that can be used to create backup files. This way, applications and users accessing the master server are not competing for resources also being used to back up the data. This approach can be particularly useful when developing Web-based applications that must be available around the clock and that can experience large numbers of concurrent users. As a result, an essential component of any administrative planning must include a strategy for ensuring that the data is properly backed up and replicated as is appropriate for your applications and users. Once you have that strategy in place, you're ready to begin developing applications that put to use the various components of MySQL that you've learned about in this book.

Exercises

The chapter explained how to back up your databases, restore databases from backup files, and implement replication. To help you build on your ability to carry out these tasks, the following exercises are provided. The exercises assume that you will create and access backup files in the mysqlbackup directory (C:\mysqlback on Windows and /mysqlbackup on Linux). To view solutions to these exercises, see Appendix A.

1. You are backing up all the tables in the ProduceDB database. The backup file should not include any database definition language. You plan to create a backup file named producedb001.sql. What command should you use to create the backup file?

2. You are backing up only the Produce table in the ProduceDB database. You plan to create a backup file named produce.sql. What command should you use to create the backup file?

3. You are backing up all the tables in the ProduceDB database. The backup file should include the necessary database definition language. You plan to create a backup file named producedb.sql. What command should you use to create the backup file?

4. You are restoring the ProduceDB database from the database file that you created in Exercise 3. You want to restore the database by using the mysql client utility in batch mode. What command should you use to restore the database?

5. You are preparing to replicate the databases on your MySQL server. To support that replication, you must set up a user account for the slave server. The username for the account is rep_user, and the name of the slave host is slave1. For the slave host to support replication, it must connect to the MySQL server on the master host by using the password rep_pw. What SQL statement should you use to grant replication privileges to the slave host?

6. You are setting up replication on a slave server named slave1. The name of the master host is master1, and replication has already been set up on that host. You plan to use the user account created in Exercise 5 to allow the slave host to connect to the master host. You shut down the MySQL server on slave host, add the server-id option to the option file, restart the server, and load the database from a backup file. The backup file indicates that the master log file is master1-bin.000127 and that the master log position is 79. You must now execute a CHANGE MASTER statement before starting the server as a slave. What CHANGE MASTER statement should you execute on slave1?

Connecting to MySQL from a PHP Application

Throughout the book, you have learned about many different aspects of MySQL, including how to install MySQL, create databases and tables, and retrieve and manipulate data in those tables. You have even learned how to perform administrative tasks such as granting privileges to user accounts and optimizing your queries. As you learned to perform these tasks, you often worked with MySQL inter-actively by issuing SQL statements and commands from within the mysql client utility. The majority of access to MySQL databases is through applications that use application programming interfaces (APIs) to connect to MySQL and issue SQL statements. As a result, the applications—along with the APIs—are the primary vehicles available to users to interact with MySQL data. At the very least, the applications allow users to view data that is retrieved from the database, but in many cases, they are also able to add to, update, or delete that data.

Because of the importance that applications play in accessing data in a MySQL database, the final three chapters of the book focus on connecting to a MySQL database from an application and then accessing data in that database. This chapter explains how to work with a MySQL database from a PHP application. Chapter 18 focuses on Java applications, and Chapter 19 focuses on ASP.NET applications. In each chapter, you learn how to create a database connection, retrieve data, and then modify the data, all in that particular application language. The book begins with PHP because it is one of the most common application languages used to connect to MySQL. The PHP/MySQL application has been implemented worldwide for systems that vary greatly in size and number of users. This chapter, then, provides you with the information you need to allow your PHP application to communicate with MySQL. Specifically, the chapter does the following:

❑   Introduces you to PHP and how it communicates with a MySQL server and its databases

❑   Explains how to build a PHP application that connects to a MySQL database, retrieves data from that database, inserts data in the database, modifies that data, and then deletes the data

Introduction to PHP

PHP is a server-side scripting language that is used in Web-based applications. PHP also refers to the preprocessor that is installed on your system when you install PHP. (PHP stands for PHP: Hypertext Preprocessor, which makes PHP a recursive acronym.) The PHP scripts are embedded in the Web pages, along with HTML, to create a robust Web application that can generate dynamic content that is displayed to the user. PHP is similar in some ways to other application languages. For example, PHP, Java, and C# (one of the languages used in ASP.NET applications) are all considered object-oriented procedural languages and are derived from a similar source — the C and C++ programming languages. PHP is used primarily for Web-based applications, whereas Java and C# are used not only to build Web-based applications but also to build larger PC-based and client/server applications that require a more rigid structure.

Although PHP is not as robust and as extensive as other languages, it does have its place, particularly for less complex Web-based applications. PHP is usually easier to use and implement, and the structure tends to be more flexible than those of some of the more complex languages. For example, you do not need to declare variables in PHP — you can simply start using them — and there is more flexibility in terms of the values that you can assign to them, compared to the other languages.

Another advantage to using PHP is that, like MySQL, it is an open-source technology. This means that you can download PHP for free and start experimenting with it immediately. By using Linux, MySQL, PHP, and Apache (an open-source Web server) in combination with one another, you can set up a completely open-source environment for your Web applications.

Like any regular HTML Web page, the pages in a PHP application are hosted by a Web server, one that supports PHP applications. Apache is such a Web server (and probably the most commonly used Web server for PHP applications). The PHP application connects with MySQL through the MySQL PHP API, which is included in PHP when you install it on your computer. As a result, in order to run a PHP Web-based application, you must have both PHP and a Web server installed. You can install MySQL on the same computer or on a different computer, depending on your environment and your security requirements and on how you will be using the PHP configuration. For example, if you are developing a PHP application, you might want to install everything on one computer; however, in a production environment, you may want to install MySQL on a back-end computer, perhaps separated from the front-end computer by a firewall.

When a Web browser on a client computer connects to a PHP page, the PHP script is executed and the results are returned to the browser, along with any HTML on that page. As you learn later in the chapter, the PHP script is separated from the HTML by special opening and closing tags that are specific to PHP. When the PHP preprocessor sees the opening tag, it switches from HTML mode to PHP mode. When it sees the closing tag, it switches back to HTML mode. Everything between the opening tag and closing tag is treated as PHP script.

The key, then, in connecting to a MySQL database and accessing data from a PHP application is to include in your application the PHP script necessary to communicate with the MySQL database. To this end, this chapter covers the information you need to connect to the database, retrieve data, and modify that data. Although the chapter does not provide an in-depth look at PHP, it does provide the basic details necessary to create a data-driven application. The chapter does assume, though, that you are already familiar with Web-based development, HTML, and, to some extent, PHP. From this foundation, you should be able to use the information in this chapter to build a PHP/MySQL data-driven application.

This chapter was written based on the following configuration: Apache 2.0.52, PHP 5.0.2.2, and MySQL 4.1.6 installed on a Windows XP computer. Details about the configuration of your operating system, Web server, and PHP are beyond the scope of the book. Be sure to view the necessary product documentation when setting up your application environment. For more information about Apache, go to www.apache.org. For more information about PHP, go to www.php.net.

Building a Data-Driven PHP Application

When you create a PHP application that accesses data in a MySQL database, you must first establish a connection to the database from that application. Once the connection has been established, you can then use PHP script elements, along with SQL statements, to retrieve or modify data. The remaining part of the chapter describes each aspect of database access. First you learn how to connect to a database from your PHP application, and then you learn how to retrieve data from the database. Next you learn how to insert data, modify data, and delete data.

The examples in these chapters focus on the PHP scripts used to create a basic Web-based application. The principles behind connecting to a database and accessing data, however, can apply to any Web or non-Web application written in other programming languages.

Connecting to a MySQL Database

The first step to working with a database in a PHP application is to create a database connection. Creating that connection consists of two components: connecting to the server and choosing a database. You connect to the server by using the mysql_connect() function. The function is a PHP function (specific to MySQL) that facilitates the process of authenticating the user and establishing a connection to the server. If the MySQL server authenticates the user, a link is established between the application and the MySQL server. This link is referred to as a resource link.

PHP supports numerous functions specific to MySQL. As you become more familiar with interacting with MySQL through your PHP applications, you'll discover that much of that interaction is through those functions. All PHP functions related specifically to MySQL begin with "mysql."

The mysql_connect() function takes three parameters: the hostname of the system where the MySQL server resides, the user account name that is authorized to connect to the MySQL server, and a password for that account. If no parameters are specified with the mysql_connect() function, PHP assumes that the hostname is localhost, the username is the user who owns the current server process, and the password is blank. In general, it's normally a good idea to specify all three parameters so that you always know exactly how the connection is being established.

Once that resource link has been defined, you should use the mysql_select_db() function to select the database that contains the data to be accessed. All queries to the MySQL server are then directed to that database, via the resource link. When using the mysql_select_db() function, you must specify the database name as the first parameter, and optionally you can specify a link identifier as a second parameter. A link identifier is a merely a way to reference the resource link, which is usually done through a variable that has been assigned a value based on the mysql_connect() function. If no link identifier is specified, PHP assumes that the last opened link should be used. If no link is open, PHP issues a mysql_connect() function that includes no parameters.

Generally, the easiest way to set up your MySQL connection is to define a variable that takes the `mysql_connect()` function as a value and then use that variable in your `mysql_select_db()` function. For example, suppose that you want to create a connection to the local computer for the cduser account. You could define a variable similar to the following:

```
$link = mysql_connect("localhost", "cduser", "pw")
    or die("Could not connect: " . mysql_error());
```

The name of the variable is `$link`. In PHP, all variable names begin with a dollar sign ($). To assign a value to a variable, you specify the variable name, followed by an equal sign, and then followed by the variable value. Variables are used to store various data including data retrieved from the database. Unlike some of the other programming languages, in PHP you do not have to declare the variable before assigning a value to it. By simply assigning a value to the variable, the variable is automatically available for use in your code.

In the preceding example, the variable is assigned a value based on the `mysql_connect()` function, which takes three parameters. The first parameter, `localhost`, refers to the computer where the MySQL server resides. The second parameter, `cduser`, is the name of the user account in MySQL that should be used by the application. Finally, the third parameter, `pw`, is the password that should be used for the user account. Notice that each string parameter is enclosed in double quotes and separated by a comma. You must separate parameters with a comma in a PHP function call.

The `mysql_connect()` function initializes the connection to the MySQL server and returns a link reference that is assigned to the `$link` variable. Because the link reference is assigned to the `$link` variable, you can reference the variable in your code whenever you want to invoke that particular link reference.

The second line of code in the previous example defines an `or die` statement that is executed if the `mysql_connect()` function fails (in other words, if a connection cannot be established). The `or die` condition uses the `or` operator and the `die()` function to specify the response that should be returned if a connection cannot be established. The `die()` function takes one parameter, which is the message to be returned. In this case, that message is made up of two parts: "Could not connect:" and the `mysql_error()` function, which returns the MySQL error that is received if the connection fails. Notice that the two parts are connected by a period, which indicates that they should be concatenated. In other words. "Could not connect:" should be followed by the error message — all in one response.

> *Notice that the entire two lines of code are terminated by a semi-colon (;). In PHP, each complete command ends with the semi-colon. If the code spans multiple lines, the semi-colon appears only at the end of the last line, just as it does when you're executing SQL statements in the mysql client utility.*

Once you have defined a variable to initialize a connection, you can use the variable as an argument in the `mysql_select_db()` function to connect to a specific server and database. For example, in the following line of code, the `mysql_select_db()` function takes two parameters: the name of the database and the `$link` variable:

```
mysql_select_db("CDDB", $link);
```

The `mysql_select_db()` function selects the database to be accessed by the application. The first parameter in the `mysql_select_db()` function is `CDDB`, which is the name of the database, and the second parameter is `$link`, which is the variable defined in the preceding example. Because the `$link` variable is assigned a link reference, that link reference is used to connect to the CDDB database. If the link reference is not included, the function uses the last operating resource link.

At the end of your PHP code, after you've processed all other statements related to the MySQL database, you should use the `mysql_close()` function to close your connection to the database. The function can take the resource link as a parameter so that you can close that connection. For example, the following code closes the connection established by the `$link` variable:

```
mysql_close($link);
```

If no parameter is specified, the function uses the last resource link that was established. Whether or not you specify an argument, you should always use the `mysql_close()` function when a database connection is no longer needed.

Retrieving Data from a MySQL Database

Once you have established your connection to the MySQL server and selected a database, you can retrieve data that can then be displayed by your PHP application. The primary mechanism that you use to retrieve data is the SELECT statement, written as it is written when you access data interactively. The SELECT statement alone, though, is not enough. You need additional mechanisms that pass that SELECT statement to the MySQL server and that then process the results returned by the statement.

When you're retrieving data from a MySQL database from your PHP application, you generally follow a specific set of steps:

1. Initialize a variable whose value is the SELECT statement.

2. Initialize a variable whose value is the result set returned by the SELECT statement. The variable uses the `mysql_query()` function to process the SELECT statement.

3. Use the second variable to process the results, normally in some sort of conditional structure.

Now take a look at this process step by step to get a better idea of how it works. For example, the first step is to define a variable to hold the SELECT statement. In the following code, a variable named `$selectSql` is defined:

```
$selectSql = "SELECT CDID, CDName, InStock, OnOrder, ".
             "Reserved, Department, Category from CDs";
```

Notice that the value assigned to the variable is a SELECT statement. If you want to split the statement into multiple lines, as has been done here, you enclose each portion of the statement line in double quotes. In addition, for each line other than the last line, you end the line with a period. This indicates that the two lines are to be concatenated when executed. Only the final line is terminated with a semi-colon.

> *Notice that a semi-colon follows the PHP statement, but not the SQL statement itself (inside the quotes). You do not include a semi-colon after the SELECT statement as you would when working with MySQL interactively in the mysql client utility.*

Putting the SELECT statement in a variable in this way makes it easier to work with the statement in other places in the code. For example, the next step in retrieving data is to create a variable that stores the results returned by the SELECT statement, as shown in the following example:

```
$result = mysql_query($selectSql, $link);
```

As you can see, the value of the $result variable is based on the mysql_query() function. The function sends the query to the active database for the specified link identifier. Whenever you use the mysql_query() function, the first parameter must be the SQL query, and the second parameter, which is optional, can be the resource link. If no resource link is specified, the most current link is used.

In the preceding example, variables are used for both parameters. The first variable, $selectSql, contains the SELECT statement that is to be sent to the database. The second variable, $link, contains the resource link that you saw defined in an earlier example. When the mysql_query() function processes the SELECT statement, the results are assigned to the $result variable, which can then be used in subsequent code to display results in the application.

After you've defined the $result variable, you can use an if statement to return an error message if the query results in an error, in which case the value of $result is set to false. In the following example, the if statement checks the value of $result, and then, if necessary, returns an error:

```
if (!$result)
   die("Invalid query: " . mysql_error(). "<br>".$selectSql);
```

The if statement first specifies the condition under which the die() function should be executed. The condition (which is based on the $result variable) is enclosed in parentheses. Notice that an exclamation point (!) precedes the variable name. The exclamation point means *not* and is used to indicate that, if the query (as represented by the variable) is not true, then the die() function should be executed. If the die() function is executed, it returns the message "Invalid query:" followed by the error returned by MySQL. The next part of the parameter —
 — indicates that a line break should be inserted and the rest of the message should start on a new line. The <br> symbol is HTML code. You can insert HTML in certain PHP command as long as you enclose the HTML in double quotes. Because of the <br> code, the original SELECT statement (as displayed by the $selectSql variable) is then displayed on a line beneath the first part of the message returned by the die() function.

A query that executes successfully but that returns no data is treated as a successfully executed statement and does not generate an error. This means that the $result variable still evaluates to true, but no results are displayed on the Web page.

Processing the Result Set

Once you have a result set to work with, you must process the rows so that they can be displayed in a usable format. In PHP, you must set up your code to be able to process one row at a time. You can do this by setting up a loop condition and by using a function that supports the row-by-row processing. For example, you can use the while command to set up the loop and the mysql_fetch_array() function to process the rows, as shown in the following example:

```
while($row = mysql_fetch_array($result))
{
   $cdId = $row["CDID"];
   $cdName = $row["CDName"];
   $inStock = $row["InStock"];
   $onOrder = $row["OnOrder"];
   $reserved = $row["Reserved"];
   $department = $row["Department"];
   $category = $row["Category"];
   printf("$cdId, $cdName, $inStock, $onOrder, $reserved, $department, $category");
}
```

The `while` command tells PHP to continue to execute the block of commands as long as the current condition is not false, meaning that `$row` has a value. The condition in this case is defined by `$row = mysql_fetch_array($result)`. The `mysql_fetch_array()` function returns the values from the query's result set one row at a time. Consequently, the `while` loop is executed for each row that is returned by the `mysql_fetch_array()` function. When the function no longer returns a row, it returns a value of false, and the `while` command stops executing. For example, if a query's result set contains 15 rows, the `while` command is executed 15 times.

The current row returned by the `mysql_fetch_array()` function is placed in the `$row` variable, which is an array of the columns. Each time the `while` command is executed, a new row is inserted in the variable. The variable can be used to return specific values as part of the loop construction. For example, as long as the `while` condition is not false, the array holds the current row. As a result, each column of the `SELECT` statement can be retrieved from `$row` by name. For instance, the `$cdId = $row["CDID"]` command retrieves the value that was returned from the CDID column and places it in the `$cdId` variable. Each time the `$row` variable is updated (when the `mysql_fetch_array()` function returns the next row), the `$cdId` variable is updated with the current CDID value.

To illustrate this, suppose that the first row returned by your query contains the following values:

- ❑ CDID = 101
- ❑ CDName = Bloodshot
- ❑ InStock = 10
- ❑ OnOrder = 5
- ❑ Reserved = 3
- ❑ Department = Popular
- ❑ Category = Rock

The `mysql_fetch_array()` function returns this row from the result set, which is available through the `$result` variable. Because the `$row` variable is defined to equal the `mysql_fetch_array()` function, the variable will contain the values included in that row. The `$row` variable and `mysql_fetch_array()` function are part of the `while` construction, however, so the value of the `$row` variable is used as part of the `while` loop. For instance, the current CDID value in the `$row` variable is 101. As a result, the `$cdId` variable is assigned a value of 101. For each column returned by the `mysql_fetch_array()` function, the current value is assigned to the applicable variable. The column-related variables can then be used to display the actual values returned by the `SELECT` statement.

The next step in the loop construction is to use the PHP `printf()` function to display the values saved to the column-related variables for that specific row. Each time the `while` command is executed, the values for a specific row (taken from the variables) are displayed on your Web page. By the time the `while` command has looped through the entire result set, all rows returned by the query are displayed. (Later, in the Try It Out sections, you see the results of using the `while` command to create a loop construction.)

Manipulating Data in PHP

When you retrieve data from a database, you might find that you want to manipulate or compare data in some way in order to display that data effectively. As a result, PHP includes several functions that support these types of operations. Two functions important to working with data are the `strlen()` function and the `strcmp()` function.

The `strlen()` function returns the length of a string. For example, if a string value is *book*, the `strlen()` function returns a value of 4.

The `strcmp()` function works differently from the `strlen()` function. Rather than checking the length of a string, it compares two strings to determine whether they have an equal value. The strings are compared based on a typical alphabetic sorting. For instance, banana is greater than orange. If the two strings are equal, the function returns a 0. If the first string is greater than the second string, the function returns a 1. If the first string is less than the second string, the function returns a -1. For example, if the first string is apple and the second string is strawberry, the function returns 1, but if the first string is apple and the second string is apple, the function returns 0.

Now take a look at how these two functions can be used in PHP script to manipulate data. Assume that your script includes a variable named `$department` and that a value has been assigned to that variable. You can use an `if` statement to specify conditions that use the two functions, as shown in the following example:

```
if((strlen($department) !=0) && (strcmp($department, "Classical")==0))
{
    printf("The $cdName CD is classified as $category.");
}
```

The `if` statement includes two conditions. The first condition uses the `strlen()` function to determine whether the length of the string stored in the `$department` variable is equal to an amount other than 0. The exclamation point/equal sign (`!=`) operator means *does not equal*. In other words, the function determines whether the variable is not empty. If it is not (it has a value that is not 0), then the condition evaluates to true.

The `strcmp()` function compares the value held in the `$department` variable to the string Classical. If `$department` equals Classical, then a 0 is returned. The `if` condition specifies that the two strings must be equal (must return a value of zero). The double equal signs (`==`) operator means *is equal* and is followed by a 0. In other words, the result returned by the `strcmp()` function must equal 0 in order for the condition to evaluate to true. The two conditions are then connected by the double ampersand (`&&`) operator, which means *and*. As a result, both conditions must evaluate to true for the `if` statement to be executed.

If both conditions evaluate to true, then the `printf()` function prints the message enclosed in the parentheses, replacing any variables with their actual value. For example, if the `$cdName` variable is currently set to Bloodshot, and the `$category` variable is currently set to Rock, the message is printed as "The Bloodshot CD is classified as Rock."

Another useful function when working with data is `substr()`, which extracts a specified number of characters from a string. The function takes three parameters. The first of these is the actual string from which you want to extract a value. The second parameter is the starting position from where you begin to extract characters. The function begins extracting values at the identified position. (The first position is 0.) The third argument specifies the number of characters to extract. For example, the function `substr("house", 2, 3)` returns the value *use*. If you want to extract a value starting with the first character, you should specify 0 as your starting position.

Now take a look at an example to better explain how the `substr()` function works. First, assume that the following three variables have been defined:

```
$firstName = "Johann";
$middleName = "Sebastian";
$lastName = "Bach";
```

The variables can then be used along with the `substr()` function to concatenate the composer's name, as shown in the following example:

```
$abbreviatedName = substr($firstName, 0, 1) . ". " .
                   substr($middleName, 0, 1) . ". " . $lastName;

printf($abbreviatedName);
```

In this example, a variable named `$abbreviatedName` is being defined. The variable concatenates the three variables by connecting them with periods, which indicates to PHP that these lines should be treated as a single unit. Note, however, that a period and space are enclosed in quotes. Because they're in quotes, they're treated as string values and so are part of the actual value.

Now take a look at the first instance of the `substr()` function. Notice that it takes the `$firstName` variable as the first argument. The second argument, which is 0, indicates that the substring should be created beginning with the first letter, and the third parameter, 1, indicates that only one character should be used. As a result, the first `substr()` function returns a value of *J*. The second instance of the `substr()` function works the same way and returns a value of *S*. When all the pieces are put together, the `$abbreviatedName` variable is set to the value *J. S. Bach*, which is then printed on the Web page through the use of the `printf()` function.

Converting Date Values

Often, when you're retrieving a date value from a MySQL database, you want to convert the value so that it can be displayed in a more readable format. PHP provides several date-related and time-related functions that allow you to work with date/time values. Two functions that are particularly useful are the `date()` and `strtotime()` functions. The `date()` function extracts part of a date from a value and puts it in a specified format. The `strtotime()` function converts a date that is retrieved as a string value (such as 2004-10-31) and converts it in a numerical format (as a timestamp) that can then be used by the `date()` function. For example, the following statement sets the `$saleDatePrint` variable to a date based on a value in the `$saleDate` variable:

```
$saleDatePrint = date("m-d-Y", strtotime($saleDate));
```

When a date is retrieved from MySQL, it is retrieved as a string value, displayed with the year first, then the month, and then the day. In this example, that value is stored in the `$saleDate` variable. The `strtotime()` function converts that value to a numerical timestamp value, which is then used by the `date()` function. The `date()` function takes two parameters. The first parameter defines the format that should be used. In this case, the format is m-d-Y, which translates to *<month>-<day>-<four-digit year>*. The second parameter is the actual date value. Because the `strtotime()` function is used, the `$saleDate` value is converted to the numerical timestamp. The `date()` function then extracts the month, day, and year from the timestamp and displays it in the desired format.

Working with HTML Forms

When working with Web-related applications, you often need to pass data from the client browser to the server. This is often done through the use of a *form*, which is an element on an HTML page that allows a user to submit data that can be passed to the server. For example, a form can be used to allow a user to log on to the application. The user can submit an account name and password, which the form then sends to a specified location.

An HTML form supports two types of posting methods: POST and GET. The POST method sends the data through an HTTP header. An HTTP header is a mechanism that allows commands and data to be sent to and from the browser and server. The GET method adds the data to a URL. Because the data is added to the URL, it is visible when the URL is displayed. For this reason, using the POST method is often preferable because the posted data is hidden.

> *A thorough discussion of HTML forms and HTTP headers is beyond the scope of this book; however, there are plenty of resources that describe forms, headers, and all other aspects of HTML and HTTP extensively. If you're not familiar with how to work with forms and headers, be sure to read the appropriate documentation.*

Once the data has been posted by the form, you can use elements in PHP to retrieve the data. To support form functionality, PHP provides the $_POST array and the $_GET array. An array is a set of data values that are stored as a unit but can be referenced as individual values. Data posted by a form is available in PHP through the array. The $_POST array provides the data submitted by a form if that form uses the POST method. The $_GET array provides the data submitted by a form if that form uses the GET method. Each value in the array is referenced by the name that is used on the form. For example, suppose that you create a form on your HTML page that includes the following <input> element:

```
<input type="text" name="department">
```

The input element determines the type of action that the user takes. In this case, the input type shown here is text, which means that a text box is displayed on the Web page and the user can enter a value in the text box. That value is then submitted to the target file either through the HTTP header or as an add-on to the URL. Your PHP script can then use that value by accessing the $_POST array and the $_GET array.

When you use one of the arrays to access a particular value, you must reference the name that is assigned to the input element. In the case of the previous example, the value that the user enters is referenced by using the name department, which is the name assigned to the input element. For example, suppose that the input element shown previously is part of a form that has been defined with the POST method. You can then use the $_POST array to retrieve this value that was entered by the user in the form, as shown in the following PHP script:

```
if(isset($_POST["department"]))
    $department = $_POST["department"];
```

The script is an if statement that uses both the $_POST array and the isset() function. The isset() function tests whether a variable has a value. The function can also be used to check if an array position holds a value, as in the preceding example. If the value has been assigned to the variable, the if condition evaluates to true, and the next line of code is executed. In this case, the isset() function is used to determine whether the $_POST array contains a value for the department input element. If a value exists, that value is assigned to the $department variable. As you can see, the $_POST array allows you to retrieve the data that was posted by the user and use that data in your PHP code.

Redirecting Browsers

Web application pages can sometimes decide that the user should be redirected to another page. This means that the current page stops processing and the server loads a new page and processes it. This process is usually part of a condition that specifies if a certain result is received; then an action must be taken based on that result. For example, suppose that you want to redirect a user if that user enters Classical in the department <input> element. You can set up your PHP code in a way similar to the following:

```
if(strcmp($_POST["department"], "Classical") == 0)
{
    header("Location: ClassicalSpecials.php");
    exit;
}
```

As you can see, a strcmp() function is used to compare the department value returned by the $_POST array to the string Classical. If the comparison evaluates to 0 (the values are equal), the header() function and the exit command are executed. The header() function redirects the client browser to the specified page (in this case, ClassicalSpecials.php). You must include the Location: prefix when specifying the new page. The exit command terminates the execution of the current page.

Technically, the HTTP 1.1 specification says that you should use an absolute URL when providing the filename for the Location argument. Many clients take relative URLs, which is what we used here. If your application will be accessed by different types of browsers, you would probably want to use a complete URL such http://localhost/cdsales/ClassicalSpecials.php.

Because you use the header() function and exit command in the context of an if statement, the user is redirected and the current page terminated only if the department value in the $_POST array equals Classical. Otherwise, the current page continues to be executed.

Working with Include Files

There might be times when you want to execute PHP script that is in a file separate from your current file. For example, suppose that your application includes PHP script that is repeated often. You can put that script in a file separate from your primary file and then call that file from the primary file. The second file is referred to as an include file, and you can simply reference it from your primary file to execute the script in the include file.

To reference an include file from your PHP script, you must use the include command, followed by the name of the include file. If the file is located someplace other than the local directory, you must also specify the path. For example, the following if statement uses the include command to execute the PHP script in the ClassicalSpecial.php file:

```
if (strcmp($_POST["department"], "Classical") == 0)
{
    include "ClassicalSpecials.php";
}
```

The if condition specifies that the department value in the $_POST array must equal Classical. If the condition is met, the include file is accessed and the script in the file is executed as though it were part of the current file. It would be the same as if the code in the include file actually existed in the primary file.

Now that you've been introduced to many of the basic PHP elements that you can use when retrieving and displaying data from a MySQL database, you're ready to build an application.

Creating a Basic PHP Application

In the Try It Out sections in this chapter, you build a simple Web application that allows you to view the transactions in the DVDRentals database. You are also able to add a transaction, edit that transaction, and then delete it from the database. As you'll recall when you designed the DVDRentals database, transactions are actually a subset of orders. Each order is made up of one or more transactions, and each transaction is associated with exactly one order. In addition, each transaction represents exactly one DVD rental. For example, if someone were to rent three DVDs at the same time, that rental would represent one order that includes three transactions. As a result, one row would be added to the Orders table to represent that order, and three rows would be added to the Transactions table to represent those orders. The rows in the Transactions table would then include a reference to the order ID.

The application that you build in this chapter is very basic and does not represent a complete application, in the sense that you would probably want your application to allow you to create new orders, add DVDs to the database, and add and edit other information. The purpose of this application is merely to demonstrate how you connect to a MySQL database from PHP, how you retrieve data, and how you manipulate data. The principles that you learn here can then be applied to any PHP application that must access data in a MySQL database.

When creating a Web application such as a PHP application, you usually find that you are actually programming in three or four different languages. For example, you might use PHP for the dynamic portions of your application, HTML for the static portions, SQL for data access and manipulation, and JavaScript to perform basic page-related functions. The application that you create in this chapter uses all four languages. At first this might seem somewhat confusing; however, the trick is to think about each piece separately. If you are new to these technologies, try doing each piece separately and then integrating the pieces. The application is fully integrated and can be run and examined to see how these technologies work. Keep in mind, however, that the focus of the Try It Out sections is to demonstrate PHP and SQL, so they do not contain detailed explanations about JavaScript and HTML. However, you cannot develop a PHP application without including some HTML, and JavaScript is commonly implemented in Web-based applications. As a result, in order to show you a realistic application, HTML and Java Script are included, but a discussion of these two technologies is well beyond the scope of this book. Fortunately, there are ample resources available for both of them, so be sure to consult the appropriate documentation if there is an HTML or JavaScript concept that you do not understand.

To support the application that you will create, you need two include files: one that contains HTML styles and one that contains the JavaScript necessary to support several page-related functions. You can download the files from www.wrox.com, or you can copy them from here. The first of these files is dvdstyle.css, which controls the HTML styles that define the look and feel of the application's Web pages. The styles control the formatting of various HTML attributes that can be applied to text and other objects. The following code shows the contents of the dvdstyle.css file.

```
table.title{background-color:#eeeeee}

td.title{background-color:#bed8e1;color:#1a056b;font-family:sans-serif;font-weight:
bold;font-size: 12pt}

td.heading{background-color:#486abc;color:#ffffff;font-family:sans-serif;font-
weight: bold;font-size: 9pt}

td.item{background-color:#99ff99;color:#486abc;font-family:sans-serif;font-weight:
normal;font-size: 8pt}

input.delete{background-color:#990000;color:#99ffff;font-family:sans-serif;font-
weight: normal;font-size: 8pt}

input.edit{background-color:#000099;color:#99ffff;font-family:sans-serif;font-
weight: normal;font-size: 8pt}

input.add{background-color:#000099;color:#99ffff;font-family:sans-serif;font-
weight: normal;font-size: 8pt}

td.error{background-color:#ff9999;color:#990000;font-family:sans-serif;font-weight:
bold;font-size: 9pt}
```

When you create an HTML element in your code, you can reference a particular style in the dvdstyle.css file, and then that style is applied. For example, the dvdstyle.css file includes the following style definition:

```
td.item{background-color:#99ff99;color:#486abc;font-family:sans-serif;font-weight:
normal;font-size: 8pt}
```

The `td.item` keywords identify the style definition. The td refers to the type of style definition, which in this case is a cell in a table, and item is the unique name given to this particular definition. The options defined in the paragraph are the various styles that apply to this definition. You can then reference this style definition in your HTML code. For example, if you are creating a table and you want a cell in that table to use this style, you would reference the *item* style name.

Whether you copy the file from the Web site or create the file yourself, you should save the file to the same directory where your PHP pages are stored. You can then modify the styles to meet your own needs.

The second file that you need to support the application is the dvdrentals.js file, which contains the JavaScript support functions for the Web form submission. These functions allow the program to manipulate the command values and the values of the form's action parameter. By using this technique, a user button click can redirect the form to a different page. The following code shows the contents of the dvdrentals.js file:

```
function doEdit(button, transactionId)
{
    button.form.transaction_id.value = transactionId;
    button.form.command.value = "edit";
    button.form.action = "edit.php";
```

```
      button.form.submit();
   }

   function doAdd(button)
   {
      button.form.transaction_id.value = -1;
      button.form.command.value = "add";
      button.form.action = "edit.php";
      button.form.submit();
   }

   function doDelete(button, transactionId)
   {
      var message = "Deleting this record will permanently remove it.\r\n" +
                    "Are you sure you want to proceed?";

      var proceed = confirm(message);

      if(proceed)
      {
         button.form.transaction_id.value = transactionId;
         button.form.command.value = "delete";
         button.form.submit();
      }
   }

   function doCancel(button)
   {
      button.form.command.value = "view";
      button.form.action = "index.php";
      button.form.submit();
   }

   function doSave(button, command)
   {
      button.form.command.value = command;
      button.form.submit();
   }
```

The dvdrentals.js includes numerous function definitions. For example, the following JavaScript statement defines the doEdit() function:

```
   function doEdit(button, transactionId)
   {
      button.form.transaction_id.value = transactionId;
      button.form.command.value = "edit";
      button.form.action = "edit.php";
      button.form.submit();
   }
```

The doEdit() function can be called from your HTML code, usually through an <input> element that uses a button click to initiate the function. The doEdit() function takes two parameters: button and transactionId. The button parameter is used to pass the HTML button object, which references the form element in the JavaScript function, and the transactionId parameter holds the transaction ID for the current record. The transactionId value, along with a command value of edit, is submitted to the form in the edit.php file when that file is launched. Again, whether you copy the file from the Web site or create the file yourself, you should save the dvdrentals.js file to the same directory where your PHP pages are stored in your Web server.

Once you've ensured that the dvdstyle.css and dvdrentals.js files have been created and added to the appropriate directory, you're ready to begin creating your application. The first file that you create— index.php—provides the basic structure for the application. The file contains the PHP script necessary to establish the connection to the DVDRentals database, retrieve data from the database, and then display that data. The page lists all the transactions that currently exist in the DVDRentals database. In addition, the index.php file provides the foundation on which additional application functionality is built in later Try It Out sections. You can download any of the files used for the DVDRentals application created in this chapter at the Wrox Web site at www.wrox.com.

Try It Out   Creating the index.php File

The following steps describe how to create the index.php file, which establishes a connection to the DVDRentals database and retrieves transaction-related data:

1. The first part of the index.php file sets up the basic HTML elements that provide the structure for the rest of the page. This includes the page header, links to the dvdstyle.css and dvdrentals.js files, and the initial table structure in which to display the data retrieved from the DVDRentals database. Open a text editor, and enter the following code:

```
<html>
<head>
   <title>DVD - Listing</title>
   <link rel="stylesheet" href="dvdstyle.css" type="text/css">
   <script language="JavaScript" src="dvdrentals.js"></script>
</head>

<body>
<p></p>

<table cellSpacing="0" cellPadding="0" width="619" border="0">
<tr>
   <td>
      <table height="20" cellSpacing="0" cellPadding="0" width="619"
bgcolor="#bed8e1" border="0">
      <tr align=left>
         <td valign="bottom" width="400" class="title">
            DVD Transaction Listing
         </td>
      </tr>
      </table>
      <br>
      <table cellSpacing="2" cellPadding="2" width="619" border="0">
      <tr>
         <td width="250" class="heading">Order Number</td>
         <td width="250" class="heading">Customer</td>
```

```
            <td width="250" class="heading">DVDName</td>
            <td width="185" class="heading">DateOut</td>
            <td width="185" class="heading">DateDue</td>
            <td width="185" class="heading">DateIn</td>
        </tr>
```

2. The next section of the file creates the connection to the MySQL server and then selects the DVDRentals database. Add the following code after the code you added in Step 1:

```
<?
// Connect to server or return an error
$link = mysql_connect("localhost", "mysqlapp", "pw1")
    or die("Could not connect: " . mysql_error());

// Select database or return an error
mysql_select_db("DVDRentals", $link)
    or die("Unable to select database: . mysql_error()");
```

The user account specified in this section of code — mysqlapp — is an account that you created in Chapter 14. The account is set up to allow you to connect from the local computer. If you did not set up this account or plan to connect to a host other than the local host, you must create the correct account now. If you want to connect to the MySQL server with a hostname or username other than the ones shown here, be sure to enter the correct details. (For information about creating user accounts, see Chapter 14.)

3. In the following section you create the query that retrieves data from the DVDRentals database and stores the results of that query in a variable. Add the following code to your file:

```
// Construct the SQL statement
$selectSql = "SELECT ".
            "Transactions.TransID, ".
            "Transactions.OrderID, ".
            "Transactions.DVDID, ".
            "Transactions.DateOut, ".
            "Transactions.DateDue, ".
            "Transactions.DateIn, ".
            "Customers.CustFN, ".
            "Customers.CustLN, ".
            "DVDs.DVDName ".
            "FROM Transactions, Orders, Customers, DVDs ".
            "WHERE Orders.OrderID = Transactions.OrderID ".
            "AND Customers.CustID = Orders.CustID ".
            "AND DVDs.DVDID = Transactions.DVDID ".
            "ORDER BY  Transactions.OrderID DESC, Customers.CustLN ASC, ".
            "Customers.CustFN ASC, ".
            "Transactions.DateDue DESC, DVDs.DVDName ASC;";

// Execute the SQL query
$result = mysql_query($selectSql, $link);

if(!$result)
    die("Invalid query: ".mysql_error()."<br>".$selectSql);
```

4. The next step in your application is to loop through the results returned by your query. Add the following code to your application file:

```
// Loop through the result set
while($row = mysql_fetch_array($result))
{
// Retrieve the columns from the result set into local variables
    $transId = $row["TransID"];
    $orderId = $row["OrderID"];
    $dvdId = $row["DVDID"];
    $dateOut = $row["DateOut"];
    $dateDue = $row["DateDue"];
    $dateIn = $row["DateIn"];
    $custFirstName = $row["CustFN"];
    $custLastName = $row["CustLN"];
    $dvdName = $row["DVDName"];
```

5. Now put the customer names and dates in a more readable format. Add the following code to your page:

```
// Convert nulls to empty strings and format the data
$customerName = "";
$dateOutPrint = "";
$dateDuePrint = "";
$dateInPrint = "";

if($custFirstName != null)
    $customerName .= $custFirstName." ";

if($custLastName != null)
    $customerName .= $custLastName;

if($dvdName == null)
    $dvdName = "";

$dateFormat = "m-d-Y";

if($dateOut != null)
    $dateOutPrint = date($dateFormat, strtotime($dateOut));

if($dateDue != null)
    $dateDuePrint = date($dateFormat, strtotime($dateDue));

if(strcmp($dateIn, "0000-00-00") != 0)
    $dateInPrint = date($dateFormat, strtotime($dateIn));
```

6. Next, insert the values retrieved from the database in an HTML table structure. Add the following code to the PHP file:

```
// Print each value in each row in the HTML table
?>
        <tr height="35" valign="top">
          <td class="item">
            <nobr>
              <?printf($orderId);?>
```

```
                   </nobr>
               </td>
               <td class="item">
                   <nobr>
                   <?printf($customerName);?>
                   </nobr>
               </td>
               <td class="item">
                   <nobr>
                   <?printf("$dvdName");?>
                   </nobr>
               </td>
               <td class="item">
                   <nobr>
                   <?printf($dateOutPrint);?>
                   </nobr>
               </td>
               <td class="item">
                   <nobr>
                   <?printf($dateDuePrint);?>
                   </nobr>
               </td>
               <td class="item">
                   <nobr>
                   <?printf($dateInPrint);?>
                   </nobr>
               </td>
           </tr>
    <?
    }
```

7. The final section of the file closes the connection and the PHP script. It also closes the `<table>`, `<body>`, and `<html>` elements on the Web page. Add the following code to the end of the PHP file:

```
// Close the database connection and the HTML elements

mysql_close($link);
?>
        </table>
    </td>
</tr>
</table>
</body>
</html>
```

8. Save the index.php file to the appropriate Web application directory.

9. Open your browser, and go to the address `http://localhost/index.php`. (If you saved the file to a different location, use that URL.) Your browser should display a page similar to the one shown in Figure 17-1.

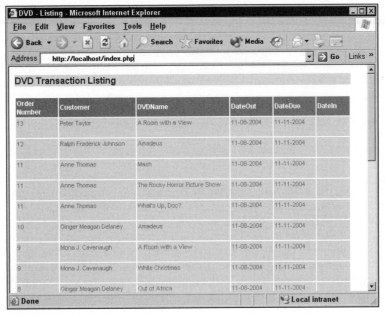

Figure 17-1

If you find that you cannot connect to the MySQL server when trying to open the PHP file, it might be because of the password encryption method used for the MySQL user account. Beginning with MySQL 4.1, a different method is used to encrypt passwords than was used in previous versions. Older versions of PHP (and other client applications) have not yet implemented this new encryption method. As a result, when you try to pass the password from the PHP application to MySQL, there is an encryption mismatch. You can test whether this is a problem by using the mysql client utility — logging in with the mysqlapp user account name and the pw1 password — to access the MySQL server. If you're able to log on to the server with mysql utility, then you know that the account is working fine; in that case, encryption mismatch is probably the problem. To remedy this, open the mysql client utility as the root user, and execute the following SQL statement:

```
SET PASSWORD FOR 'mysqlapp'@'localhost' = OLD_PASSWORD('pw1');
```

The OLD_PASSWORD() function saves that password using the old encryption method, which makes the password compatible with the version of PHP that you're using.

How It Works

In this exercise, the first step that you took was to set up the opening HTML section of your index.php file. The <head> section establishes the necessary links to the dvdstyle.css and dvdrentals.js files. You then added a <body> section that includes two HTML <table> elements. The first table provides a structure for the page title — DVD Transaction Listing — and the second table provides the structure for the data to be displayed on the page. The data includes the Order number, customer name, DVD name, and dates that the DVD was checked out, when it is due back, and, if applicable, when it was returned. As a result, the initial table structure created in this section sets up a row for the table headings and a cell for each heading.

For more information about HTML, file linking from HTML, style sheets, and JavaScript functions, refer to the appropriate documentation.

Once you set up your HTML structure on your Web page, you began the PHP section of the page, you established a connection to the MySQL server, and you selected a database, as shown in the following PHP script:

```
<?
$link = mysql_connect("localhost", "mysqlapp", "pw1")
    or die("Could not connect: " . mysql_error());
mysql_select_db("DVDRentals", $link)
    or die("Unable to select database: . mysql_error()");
```

First, you opened the PHP section by using the PHP opening tag (`<?`), which tells the PHP preprocessor that anything enclosed in the opening tag and the closing tag (`?>`) should be processed as PHP script. Next, you defined the `$link` variable based on the `mysql_connect()` function, which establishes a connection to the MySQL server on the local host, using the mysqlapp user account. In the statement that defines the connection, you included an or operator in case a connection cannot be established, in which case the `die()` function is executed. The `die()` function returns the "Could not connect:" message along with the actual MySQL error message. To retrieve the MySQL error message, you used the `mysql_error()` function.

Once you created the `$link` variable, you then used the `mysql_select_db()` function to select the DVDRentals database and again used the or operator to specify the `die()` function, in case the database cannot be selected.

After you established your connections, you then initialized the `$selectSql` variable to equal a SELECT statement, as shown in the following statement:

```
$selectSql = "SELECT ".
                "Transactions.TransID, ".
                "Transactions.OrderID, ".
                "Transactions.DVDID, ".
                "Transactions.DateOut, ".
                "Transactions.DateDue, ".
                "Transactions.DateIn, ".
                "Customers.CustFN, ".
                "Customers.CustLN, ".
                "DVDs.DVDName ".
                "FROM Transactions, Orders, Customers, DVDs ".
                "WHERE Orders.OrderID = Transactions.OrderID ".
                "AND Customers.CustID = Orders.CustID ".
                "AND DVDs.DVDID = Transactions.DVDID ".
                "ORDER BY  Transactions.OrderID DESC, Customers.CustLN ASC, ".
                "Customers.CustFN ASC, ".
                "Transactions.DateDue DESC, DVDs.DVDName ASC;";
```

As you can see, this is a basic SELECT statement that joins the Transactions, Orders, Customers, and DVDs tables in the DVDRentals database. You then used the `$selectSql` variable as a parameter in the `mysql_query()` function to submit the SELECT statement to the MySQL server:

```
$result = mysql_query($selectSql, $link);

if(!$result)
    die("Invalid query: ".mysql_error()."<br>".$selectSql);
```

You initialized the $result variable with the query results returned by the mysql_query() function (and subsequently the SELECT statement). As a precaution, you used the $result variable in an if statement to verify that a result set was actually returned. The if statement condition precedes the $result variable with an exclamation point (!), indicating that the condition evaluates to true if the variable contains no result set. As a result, if the result set is empty, the die() function is executed, and an error message is returned, along with the original SELECT statement (which is returned by the $selectSql variable).

Once you check for errors, you then use a while loop and the mysql_fetch_array() function to process the results returned by your query:

```
while($row = mysql_fetch_array($result))
{

    $transId = $row["TransID"];
    $orderId = $row["OrderID"];
    $dvdId = $row["DVDID"];
    $dateOut = $row["DateOut"];
    $dateDue = $row["DateDue"];
    $dateIn = $row["DateIn"];
    $custFirstName = $row["CustFN"];
    $custLastName = $row["CustLN"];
    $dvdName = $row["DVDName"];
```

The mysql_fetch_array() function allows you to process the result set by individual rows. The while loop executes the statements in the while construction for each row returned by the mysql_fetch_array() function. Each row returned by the function is placed in the $row variable, which is then used to assign values to individual variables. Each time a while loop executes, a variable is assigned a column value from the current row. The while loop continues to execute until no more rows are returned by the mysql_fetch_array() function.

After you assigned values to the variables, you formatted some of the variable values to make them easier to read. To support this process, you first initialized several new variables to prepare them to hold the formatted content. For example, you initialized the following $customerName variable as an empty string (indicated by the pair of double quotes):

```
$customerName = "";
```

The reason you did this is to ensure that if any part of a customer name is NULL, that NULL value is not displayed. That way, when you begin formatting the names, you can test for the existence of NULL values and assign names to the $customerName variable only if the values are not NULL. If they are NULL, then only a string is displayed or only one name, with no NULL values appended to the name. As a result, after you initiated the variables, you then began concatenating the names, starting with the first name, as shown in the following if statement:

```
if($custFirstName != null)
    $customerName .= $custFirstName." ";
```

The statement first checks whether the customer's first name is not NULL. If the condition evaluates to true, the value in the $custFirstName variable, plus a space (enclosed in the pair of double quotes), is added to the $customerName variable. Note that when a period precedes an equal sign, the existing variable value is added to the new values, rather than being replaced by those values. This is better illustrated by the next if statement, which then adds the last name to the first name:

```
if($custLastName != null)
    $customerName .= $custLastName;
```

In this case, unless the first name was NULL, the $customerName variable holds the first name value, along with a space, and that is added to the last name value. As a result, the $customerName variable now holds the customer's full name, displayed as first name, space, then last name.

You also used an if statement to ensure that the $dvdName variable contains a string, rather than a NULL value, if a NULL had been returned by the query, as shown in the following statement:

```
if($dvdName == null)
    $dvdName = "";
```

The reason for this is again to ensure that a NULL value is not displayed on the Web page, but rather a blank value if the DVD name is blank.

Next, you formatted the dates so that they're displayed in a more readable format. To support this format, you first initialized a variable with a defined format, and then you used that format to retrieve the data in the specified format. For example, the following statements take the $dateOut value and convert it in a more readable format:

```
$dateFormat = "m-d-Y";

if($dateOut != null)
    $dateOutPrint = date($dateFormat, strtotime($dateOut));
```

To display the date in the format that you want, you must use two PHP functions. The strtotime() functions converts the value stored in the $dateOut variable to a numerical format that can then be used by the date() function. The date() function then extracts the date from the strtotime() output and converts it to the format specified in the $dateFormat function. The output from the date() function is then held in the $dateOutPrint variable.

For one of the date values, you also used the strcmp() function as a condition in an if statement, as shown in the following code:

```
if(strcmp($dateIn, "0000-00-00") != 0)
    $dateInPrint = date($dateFormat, strtotime($dateIn));
```

Recalling the database design of the Transactions table, the DateIn column holds the date that the DVD is returned. That column, though, does not permit NULL values, so the default value is 0000-00-00, which is not a value you would want to display on your Web page. This is one reason why the $dateInPrint is initialized as an empty string. If 0000-00-00 is returned, it is converted to an empty string, and a blank value is displayed on the Web page. Because of the preceding if statement, the value is converted, using the date() and strtotime() functions, if anything other than 0000-00-00 is returned.

Once you have formatted the values in the way that you want, you can then display those values in an HTML table structure. This structure follows the same structure that is defined at the beginning of the file, thus providing the column heads for the rows that you now add. Keep in mind that you are still working in the `while` loop created earlier. Every step that you take at this point still applies to each row returned by the `mysql_fetch_array()` function.

To create the necessary row in the table, you used the PHP closing tag (`?>`) to get out of PHP mode and back into HTML mode. You then created a cell definition for each value that is returned by the result set (and subsequently held in variables). For example, you used the following definition for the first cell in the first row of the table (not counting the heading):

```
<tr height="35" valign="top">
   <td class="item">
      <nobr>
      <?printf($orderId);?>
      </nobr>
   </td>
```

You first used a `<tr>` element to start the row and then `<td>` and `</td>` elements to enclose the individual cell in the row. The `<nobr>` and `</nobr>` elements indicate that there should be no line break between the two tags. Notice that squeezed between all that is PHP script that is enclosed by opening and closing PHP tags. The script is the `printf()` function, which indicates that the value of the `$orderId` variable should be printed to the screen. As a result, the `$orderId` value is displayed in that cell.

This process is repeated for each value in the row, and it is repeated for each row until the `while` statement loops through all the rows in the result set. After the `while` loop, you closed your connection to the MySQL server:

```
mysql_close($link);
```

To close the connection, you used the `mysql_close()` function and specified the `$link` variable (which you initialized at the beginning of the file) to specify which connection to close.

As the insert.php file currently exists, your application does nothing but display a list of transactions in the DVDRentals database. In most cases, you want your applications to do more than that. For this reason, you now learn how to use PHP to insert data in your database.

Inserting and Updating Data in a MySQL Database

Many of the concepts that you learned when retrieving data from your database can be also be applied to inserting data. The main difference is that you do not have to process a result set; however, you must still set up your SQL statement and use the `mysql_query()` function to execute the statement.

For instance, suppose that you want your application to insert data in a table named CDs. You can start by defining a variable to hold the `INSERT` statement, as shown in the following example:

```
$insertSql = "INSERT INTO CDs (CDName, InStock, OnOrder, Category) VALUES
('Beethoven Symphony No. 6 Pastoral', 10, 10, 'classical')";
```

As you can see, this is a typical INSERT statement. Once it is assigned to the variable, you can use the mysql_query() function to execute that statement:

```
mysql_query($selectSql, $link);
    or die("Invalid query: " . mysql_error() . "<br>".$selectSql);
```

If the statement executes successfully, the data is inserted in the appropriate table. If the statement fails, the die() function executes, and an error message is returned.

Updating data in the database is very similar to inserting data. You must define your UPDATE statement and then execute it. For example, you can assign an UPDATE statement to the $updateSql variable, as shown in the following code:

```
$updateSql = "UPDATE CDs SET InStock=5 WHERE CDID = 10";
```

Once again, you can use your variable in the mysql_query() function to send the statement to the MySQL server:

```
mysql_query($updateSql, $link);
    or die("Invalid query: " . mysql_error() . "<br>".$updateSql);
```

As the statement shows, the data is either updated or an error is returned. You can use these data insert and update methods — along with a number of other methods that you've seen — to create an application far more robust than simply displaying data. Return now to your DVDRentals application.

Adding Insert and Update Functionality to Your Application

So far, your DVDRentals application displays only transaction-related information. In this section, you add to the application so that it also allows you to add a transaction to an existing order and to modify transactions. To support the added functionality, you must create three more files — edit.php, insert.php, and update.php — and you must modify the index.php file. Keep in mind that your index.php file acts as a foundation for the rest of the application. As a result, you should be able to add a transaction and edit a transaction by first opening the index.php file and then maneuvering to wherever you need to be in order to accomplish these tasks.

The first additional file that you create is the edit.php file. The file serves two roles: adding transactions to existing orders and editing existing transactions. These two operations share much of the same functionality, so combining them in one file saves duplicating code. If you're adding a new transaction, the Web page will include a drop-down list that displays each order number and the customer associated with that order, a drop-down list that displays DVD titles, a text box for the date the DVD is rented, and a text box for the date the DVD should be returned. The default value for the date rented text box is the current date. The default value for the date due text box is three days from the current date.

If you're editing a transaction, the Web page will display the current order number and customer, the rented DVD, the date the DVD was rented, the date it's due back, and, if applicable, the date that the DVD was returned.

The edit.php Web page will also contain two buttons: Save and Cancel. The Save button saves the new or updated record and returns the user to the index.php page. The Close button cancels the operation, without making any changes, and returns the user to the index.php page.

After you create the edit.php page, you then create the insert.php file and the update.php file in the Try It Out sections that follow this one. From there, you modify the index.php page to link together the different functionalities. Now take a look at how to create the edit.php file.

Try It Out   **Creating the edit.php File**

The following steps describe how to create the edit.php file, which supports adding new transactions to a record and editing existing transactions:

1. As you did with the index.php file, you must establish a connection to the MySQL server and select the database. Use a text editor to start a new file, and enter the following code:

```
<?
// Connect to server or return an error
$link = mysql_connect("localhost", "mysqlapp", "pw1")
or die("Could not connect: " . mysql_error());

// Select a database or return an error
mysql_select_db("DVDRentals", $link);
```

For security purposes and to streamline your code, you might want to store your connection information in a different file and then call that file from the PHP page. If you take an approach similar to this, you must still supply the necessary connection parameters.

2. To support error-checking operations, you need to initialize a variable and set its value to an empty string. Add the following statement your file:

```
// Initialize an error-related variable
$error = "";
```

3. Next, you want to put a mechanism in place that assigns posted values to the appropriate variables. Add the following code to the edit.php file:

```
// Initialize variables with parameters retrieved from the posted form
if(isset($_POST["command"]))
    $command = $_POST["command"];
if(isset($_POST["transaction_id"]))
    $transactionId = $_POST["transaction_id"];
if(isset($_POST["date_due"]))
    $dateDue = $_POST["date_due"];
if(isset($_POST["order_id"]))
    $orderId = $_POST["order_id"];
if(isset($_POST["dvd_id"]))
    $dvdId = $_POST["dvd_id"];
if(isset($_POST["date_out"]))
    $dateOut = $_POST["date_out"];
if(isset($_POST["date_in"]))
    $dateIn = $_POST["date_in"];
```

4. Next, the file should process the new or edited transaction when the user clicks the Save button. First, you must check to see whether the form is complete before you try to process the values. Enter the following error-related code:

```
// Process the save and savenew commands
if((strcmp("save", $command) == 0) || (strcmp("savenew", $command) == 0))
{
// Check for missing parameters
    if($orderId == -1)
        $error .= "Please select an \"Order\"<br>";

    if($dvdId == -1)
        $error .= "Please select a \"DVD\"<br>";

    if(($dateOut == null) || (strlen($dateOut) == 0))
        $error .= "Please enter a \"Date Out\" Value<br>";

    if(($dateDue == null) || (strlen($dateDue) == 0))
        $error .= "Please enter a \"Date Due\" Value<br>";
```

Note that the application does not check the format of the date submitted by users. Normally, an application would include some type of mechanism to ensure that submitted dates are in a usable format.

5. Next, you should format the date values to ensure that they can be inserted in the database. Then you can carry out the update or insert by calling the applicable include files. (These files are created in later Try It Out sections.) Enter the following code in your file:

```
    if(strlen($error) == 0)
    {

// Reformat dates so that they are compatible with the MySQL format
        if($dateOut != null)
            $dateOut = substr($dateOut, 6, 4)."-".substr($dateOut, 0, 2)."-
".substr($dateOut, 3, 2);

        if($dateDue != null)
            $dateDue = substr($dateDue, 6, 4)."-".substr($dateDue, 0, 2)."-
".substr($dateDue, 3, 2);

        if($dateIn != null)
            $dateIn = substr($dateIn, 6, 4)."-".substr($dateIn, 0, 2)."-
".substr($dateIn, 3, 2);
        else
            $dateIn ="0000-00-00";

        if(strcmp("save", $command) == 0)
        {
// Run the update in update.php
            include "update.php";
        }
        else
        {
// Run the insert in insert.php
```

```
        include "insert.php";
    }

// Redirect the application to the listing page
        header("Location: index.php");
        exit;
    }
}
```

6. The next step is to set up the file to support adding or updating a record when the user has been redirected to this page from the index.php page. This is done as part of the `else` statement in an `if...else` structure. This particular section sets up the default values for a new record. Add the following code to your file:

```
else
{
// If it is a new record, initialize the variables to default values
    if(strcmp("add", $command) == 0)
    {
        $transactionId = 0;
        $orderId = 0;
        $dvdId = 0;
        $dateOut = date("m-d-Y", time());
        $dateDue = date("m-d-Y", time() + 3*24*60*60);
        $dateIn = "";
    }
```

7. Next, you must set up the file with the values necessary to support editing a record. This involves retrieving records to set an initial value for a number of variables. Add the following code to your PHP file:

```
    else
    {
// If it is an existing record, read from database
        if($transactionId != null)
        {
// Build query from transactionId value passed down from form
        $selectSql = "SELECT ".
                     "OrderID, ".
                     "DVDID, ".
                     "DateOut, ".
                     "DateDue, ".
                     "DateIn ".
                     "FROM Transactions ".
                     "WHERE TransID = '$transactionId'";

// Execute query
        $result = mysql_query($selectSql, $link);

        if (!$result)
            die("Invalid query: " . mysql_error(). "<br>".$selectSql);

// Populate the variables for display into the form
```

643

```
            if($row = mysql_fetch_array($result))
            {
                $orderId = $row["OrderID"];
                $dvdId = $row["DVDID"];
                $dateOut = $row["DateOut"];
                $dateDue = $row["DateDue"];
                $dateIn = $row["DateIn"];

// Reformat the dates into a more readable form
                if($dateOut != null)
                    $dateOut = substr($dateOut, 5, 2)."-".substr($dateOut, 8, 2)."-
".substr($dateOut, 0, 4);
                else
                    $dateOut = "";

                if($dateDue != null)
                    $dateDue = substr($dateDue, 5, 2)."-".substr($dateDue, 8, 2)."-
".substr($dateDue, 0, 4);
                else
                    $dateDue = "";

                if($dateIn != "0000-00-00")
                    $dateIn = substr($dateIn, 5, 2)."-".substr($dateIn, 8, 2)."-
".substr($dateIn, 0, 4);
                else
                    $dateIn = "";
            }
        }
    }
}
?>
```

8. Now you must create the HTML section of your form to allow users to view and enter data. This section includes a form to pass data to PHP and the table structure to display the form. Add the following code to your PHP file:

```
<html>
<head>
    <title>DVD - Listing</title>
    <link rel="stylesheet" href="dvdstyle.css" type="text/css">
    <script language="JavaScript" src="dvdrentals.js"></script>
</head>

<body>
<form name="mainForm" method="post" action="edit.php">
<input type="hidden" name="command" value="view">
<input type="hidden" name="transaction_id" value="<?printf($transactionId);?>"
size="50">

<p></p>

<table cellspacing="0" cellPadding="0" width="619" border="0">
<tr>
```

```
<td>
<table height="20" cellspacing="0" cellPadding="0" width="619" bgcolor="#bed8e1"
border="0">
<tr align=left>
   <td valign="bottom" width="400" class="title">
      DVD Transaction
   </td>
   <td align="right" width="219" class="title"> </td>
</tr>
</table>
<br>
<?if(strlen($error) > 0){?>
<table cellspacing="2" cellPadding="2" width="619" border="0">
<tr>
   <td width="619" class="error">
      <?printf($error);?>
   </td>
</tr>
</table>
<?}?>
```

9. Now create the first row of your form, which allows users to view and select an order ID. Enter the following code in your file:

```
<table cellspacing="2" cellPadding="2" width="619" border="0">
<tr>
   <td width="250" class="heading">Order</td>
   <td class="item">
      <select name="order_id">
         <option value="-1">Select Order</option>
<?
// Retrieve data to populate drop-down list
   $selectSql = "SELECT ".
               "Orders.OrderID, ".
               "Orders.CustID, ".
               "Customers.CustFN, ".
               "Customers.CustLN ".
               "FROM Orders, Customers ".
               "WHERE ".
               "Customers.CustID = Orders.CustID ".
               "ORDER BY Orders.OrderID DESC, ".
               "Customers.CustLN ASC, Customers.CustFN ASC";

// Execute the query
$result = mysql_query($selectSql, $link);

if (!$result)
   die("Invalid query: " . mysql_error(). "<br>".$selectSql);

// Loop through the results
while($row = mysql_fetch_array($result))
{
// Assign returned values to the variables
```

```
    $orderId1 = $row["OrderID"];
    $custFirstName = $row["CustFN"];
    $custLastName = $row["CustLN"];

// Format the data for display
    $customerName = "";

    if($custFirstName != null)
        $customerName .= $custFirstName . " ";

    if($custLastName != null)
        $customerName .= $custLastName;

// If the order id matches the existing value, mark it as selected
    if($orderId1 != $orderId)
    {
?>
        <option value="<?printf($orderId1)?>"><?printf($orderId1);?> -
<?printf($customerName);?></option>
<?
    }
    else
    {
?>
        <option selected value="<?printf($orderId1);?>"><?printf($orderId1)?> -
<?printf($customerName);?></option>
<?
    }
}
?>
        </select>
    </td>
</tr>
```

10.   The second row of your form allows users to view and select a DVD to associate with your transaction. Add the following code to your edit.php file:

```
<tr>
    <td class="heading">DVD</td>
    <td class="item">
        <select name="dvd_id">
            <option value="-1">Select DVD</option>
<?
// Retrieve data to populate drop-down list
$selectSql = "SELECT DVDID, DVDName FROM DVDs ORDER BY DVDName";

$result = mysql_query($selectSql, $link);

if (!$result)
    die("Invalid query: " . mysql_error(). "<br>".$selectSql);

while($row = mysql_fetch_array($result))
{
```

```
    $dvdId1 = $row["DVDID"];
    $dvdName = $row["DVDName"];

    if($dvdName == null)
        $dvdName = "";

    if($dvdId1 != $dvdId)
    {
?>
        <option value="<?printf($dvdId1);?>"><?printf($dvdName);?></option>
<?
    }
    else
    {
?>
        <option selected
value="<?printf($dvdId1);?>"><?printf($dvdName);?></option>
<?
    }
}
?>
    </select>
    </td>
</tr>
```

11.   Next, create three more rows in your table, one for each date-related value. Enter the following code:

```
<tr>
    <td class="heading">Date Out</td>
    <td class="item">
        <input type="text" name="date_out" value="<?printf($dateOut);?>" size="50">
    </td>
</tr>
<tr>
    <td class="heading">Date Due</td>
    <td class="item">
        <input type="text" name="date_due" value="<?printf($dateDue);?>" size="50">
    </td>
</tr>
<?if((strcmp("add", $command) != 0) && (strcmp("savenew", $command) != 0)){?>
<tr>
    <td class="heading">Date In</td>
    <td class="item">
        <input type="text" name="date_in"  value="<?printf($dateIn);?>" size="50">
    </td>
</tr>
<?}?>
```

12.   Now add the Save and Cancel buttons to your form by appending the following code to your file:

```
<tr>
    <td colspan="2" class="item" align="center">
        <table cellspacing="2" cellPadding="2" width="619" border="0">
```

```
        <tr>
          <td align="center">
            <?if((strcmp("add", $command) == 0) || (strcmp("savenew", $command) ==
0)){?>
            <input type="button" value="Save" class="add" onclick="doSave(this,
'savenew')">
            <?}else{?>
            <input type="button" value="Save" class="add" onclick="doSave(this,
'save')">
            <?}?>
          </td>
          <td align="center">
            <input type="button" value="Cancel" class="add"
onclick="doCancel(this)">
          </td>
        </tr>
        </table>
      </td>
    </tr>
```

13. Close the various HTML elements, and close your connection to the MySQL server by entering the following code:

```
</table>
</form>
</body>
</html>


<?
// Close connection
mysql_close($link);
?>
```

14. Save the edit.php file to the appropriate Web application directory.

How It Works

In this exercise, you created the edit.php file, which supports the insert and update functionality in your DVDRentals application. The first code that you added to the file established the connection to the MySQL server and selected the DVDRentals database, just as it did in the index.php file. After you established your connection, you initiated the $error variable by setting its value to an empty string, as shown in the following statement:

```
$error = "";
```

The variable is used to display error messages if a user does not fill out the form properly. You set the value to an empty string so that you can use that to verify whether any error messages have been received, as you see later in the page. After you initiated the $error variable, you initiated a number of other variables based on values returned to the $_POST array. For example, the following if statement initiates the $command variable:

```
if(isset($_POST["command"]))
    $command = $_POST["command"];
```

The `if` statement first uses the `isset()` function to determine whether the `$_POST` array contains a command value. If it does, then that value is assigned to the variable. The `$_POST` array contains those values that are posted to the page when a form is submitted. For the command and transaction_id values in the `$_POST` array, the initial values are derived from a form on the index.php page. As you see later in the application development process, when you access the edit.php page from the index.php page (through the click of a button), the index.php form submits these values to the edit.php page.

After you assigned `$_POST` array values to your variables, you set up `if...else` statements that begin with the following if condition:

```
if((strcmp("save", $command) == 0) || (strcmp("savenew", $command) == 0))
```

The `if` statement specifies two conditions. The first condition uses the `strcmp()` function to compare the string save to the current value in the `$command` variable. If the values are equal (`== 0`), the condition evaluates to true. The second condition also uses the `strcmp()` function to compare the string savenew to `$command`. If the values are equal, the condition evaluates to true. Because the conditions are connected by the `or` (`||`) operator, either condition can be true in order for the if statement to be executed. If neither condition is true, the `else` statement is executed.

The save *and* savenew *command values are issued when you click the Save button. You learn more about that button shortly.*

The `if...else` statements contain a number of `if...else` statements embedded in them. Before getting deeper into the code that makes up all these statements, first take a look at a high overview of the logic behind these statements. It gives you a better sense of the bigger picture and should make understanding the individual components a little easier. The following pseudo-code provides an abbreviated statement structure starting with the outer `if` statement described previously:

```
if $command = save or savenew, continue (if !=, go to else)
{
    if incorrect form entry, return error and redisplay page (x 4)
    if no error, continue
    {
        if date != null, format date (x 2)
        if date != null, format date; else format date to 0000-00-00
        if $command = save, include update.php; else include insert.php
        redirect to index.php
        exit edit.php
    }
}
else (if $command != save or savenew)
{
    if $command = add, continue (if !=, go to else)
    {
        initialize variables (x 6)
    }
    else (if $command != add)
    {
        if $transactionId != null
        {
            process query
            if query results exist, fetch results
```

```
            {
                assign variables (x 5)
                if date != null, format date; else set date to empty string (x 2)
                if date != 0000-00-00, format date; else set date to empty string
            }
        }
    }
}
```

As you can see, the action taken depends on the values in the $command and $transactionId variables. The if statement basically determines what happens when you try to save a record, and the else statement determines what happens when you first link to the page from the index.php page. Embedded in the else statement is another set of if...else statements. The embedded if statement determines what happens if you want to add a transaction, and the embedded else statement determines what happens if you want to update a transaction.

To better understand all this, you now take a closer look at some of the statements in this if...else construction. You've already seen the opening if statement. Following this statement are four embedded if statements that handle errors if a user does not properly fill out the form on the page. For example, the first of these statements sets up a condition to return an error if it doesn't have a proper $orderId value:

```
if($orderId ==  -1)
    $error .= "Please select an \"Order\"<br>";
```

The if statement specifies that the condition is true of the $orderId value equals -1. If this occurs, the $error variable is appended. Notice that a period/equal sign (.=) follows the variable name, meaning that any message received is appended to whatever the current variable value is (rather than replacing that value). This allows multiple error messages to be returned, if more than one error occurs.

The four error-related if statements all work in a similar manner as the one shown previously. After you defined these statements, you added the following if statement, which is also related to errors:

```
if (strlen($error) == 0)
```

The if statement specifies that the current value for the $error variable must contain no characters in order for the condition to evaluate to true. In other words, if there is no error message, continue; otherwise, stop processing this part of the PHP script (which includes everything to the end of the if...else statements). Assuming that there are no errors, PHP continues processing the if statement by formatting the date values so that they are in a form compatible with MySQL. For example, the following if statement formats the value in the $dateOut variable:

```
if($dateOut != null)
    $dateOut = substr($dateOut, 6, 4)."-".substr($dateOut, 0, 2)."-
".substr($dateOut, 3, 2);
```

If the condition evaluates to true, the substr() function is used to extract specific characters from the $dateOut value. For example, the first substr() function extracts four characters starting with the sixth character. If the date in the application appears as 10-09-2004, the result will be 2004. This is then followed by a dash and two additional substr() functions. In the end, 10-09-2004 is converted to 2004-10-09 so that it can be inserted in the database.

Once the dates have been properly formatted, you then referenced the necessary include files that contain the update and insert code. (You create these files in later Try It Out sections.) You referenced the include files in the following `if...else` statements:

```
if(strcmp("save", $command) == 0)
{
    include "update.php";
}
else
{
    include "insert.php";
}
```

The `if` statement specifies that the `$command` variable must equal `save`. If this is the case, then the update.php file is called. Otherwise, the insert.php file is called, as indicated in the else statement. Once the statements in the include file are executed (and the database is updated), the `header()` function is executed, followed by the exit command:

```
header("Location: index.php");
exit;
```

The `header()` function redirects the user to the index.php page, and the `exit` command exits the current page. This completes the outer `if` statement that initiates this section of code. If the `if` statement is not applicable (`$command` does not equal `save` or `savenew`), PHP executes the `else` statement.

The `else` statement is made up of its own embedded `if...else` statements. The `if` statement applies if the `$command` variable currently holds the value `add`, as shown in the following code:

```
if(strcmp("add", $command) == 0)
{
    $transactionId = 0;
    $orderId = 0;
    $dvdId = 0;
    $dateOut = date("m-d-Y", time());
    $dateDue = date("m-d-Y", time() + 3*24*60*60);
    $dateIn = "";
```

If `$command` is set to `add`, this means that you are creating a new transaction. To prepare the Web page with the variables it needs to display the form properly when you open the page, you set a number of variables to specific values. For example, you set `$transactionId` to 0, which is an unused number so it does not match any current transaction IDs.

You also used the `date()` function to set default date values. For the `$dateOut` variable, you set a date that is based on `time()` function, which returns the current timestamp. The `date()` function extracts just the date part of the timestamp and puts it into the format defined by the first parameter (`m-d-Y`). The `$dateDue` variable is similar to the `$dateOut` variable except that it adds three days to the current timestamp (3 * 24 hours * 60 minutes * 60 seconds). The `$dateIn` variable is set to an empty string so that only a blank is displayed.

In the embedded `else` statement, you included an `if` statement that verifies that the `$transactionId` variable is not null, as shown in the following:

```
if($transactionId != null)
```

If the value is not null (a value does exist), the remaining part of the `if` statement is executed. This means that you are editing an existing transaction, in which case, the `$transactionId` variable identifies that transaction. You then added the code necessary to retrieve data from the database (based on the `$transactionId` value), which you then used to define the variables used to display the form. Because the user is editing an existing transaction at this point, the form should include the current order number, DVD ID, and dates. You then formatted the days so that they are properly displayed.

Once you set up the data to populate the form, you have completed the `if...else` block of code. If necessary, refer back to the summary code that is provided at the beginning of this description. This provides a handy overview of what is going on.

The next section of code that you created set up the HTML for the Web page. As with the index.php file, the HTML section includes header information that links to the dvdstyle.css file and the dvdrentals.js file. The section also includes a `<form>` element and two `<input>` elements:

```
<form name="mainForm" method="post" action="edit.php">
<input type="hidden" name="command" value="view">
<input type="hidden" name="transaction_id" value="<?printf($transactionId);?>"
size="50">
```

A form is an HTML structure that allows a user to enter or select data and then submit that data. That data can then be passed on to other Web pages or to PHP script. This particular form uses the `post` method to send data (`method="post"`) and sends that data to itself (`action="edit.php"`). Beneath the form, you added two `<input>` elements that create the initial values to be inserted in the `command` and `transaction_id` parameters. The `command` parameter is set to `view`, and the `transaction_id` parameter is set to the value contained in the `$transactionId` variable. To use the variable to set the `transaction_id` value, you must enclose the variable in the PHP opening and closing tags and then use the `printf()` function to print that value to HTML so that it can be used by the form. Also note that the input type for both `<input>` elements is hidden, which means that the user does not actually see these two elements. Instead, they serve only as a way to pass the `command` and `transaction_id` values, which is done in the background. The user does not enter these values.

Forms are a common method used in HTML to pass data between pages. They are also useful for passing values between HTML and PHP. For more information about forms, consult the applicable HTML documentation.

After you defined the form, you then set up the table to display the heading DVD Transaction at the top of the page. From there, you added another table whose purpose is to display error messages, as shown in the following code:

```
<?if(strlen($error) > 0){?>
<table cellspacing="2" cellPadding="2" width="619" border="0">
<tr>
   <td width="619" class="error">
      <?printf($error);?>
```

```
      </td>
    </tr>
  </table>
<?}?>
```

The HTML table structure is preceded by PHP opening and closing tags so that you can use an if statement to specify a condition in which the table is displayed. The if statement specifies that the $error variable must contain a string that is greater in length than 0. This is done by using the strlen() function to determine the length of the $error value and then comparing the length to 0. If the condition evaluates to true, the table is created and the error is printed. At the end of the table, you again used a pair of opening and closing tags to add the closing bracket of the if statement.

Once you have established a way for error messages to be displayed, you set up the table that is used to display the part of the form that the user sees. The first row of the form will contain a drop-down list of order IDs — along with the customer names associated with those orders — that the user is able to select from when adding a transaction. To populate this drop-down list, you retrieved data from the database, processed the data, and formatted the customer name. The methods used for retrieving and processing the data are the same methods that you've already used in the application. Once you retrieved the value, you added another form element to your Web page; only this form element is visible to the user:

```
    if($orderId1 != $orderId)
    {
?>
        <option value="<?printf($orderId1)?>"><?printf($orderId1);?> -
<?printf($customerName);?></option>
<?
    }
    else
    {
?>
        <option selected value="<?printf($orderId1);?>"><?printf($orderId1)?> -
<?printf($customerName);?></option>
<?
    }
```

The form element shown here is an <option> element. An <option> element allows a user to select from a list of options in order to submit data to the form. There are actually two <option> elements here, but only one is used because PHP if...else statements encloses the <option> elements. The if statement condition specifies that $orderId1 should not equal $orderId. If they are not equal, the if statement is executed and the first <option> element is used; otherwise, the second <option> element is used. The second element includes the selected option, which means that the current order ID is the selected option when the options are displayed.

The $orderId1 variable receives its value from the results returned by the SELECT statement used to populate the <option> element. The $orderId variable receives its value from the SELECT statement that is used to assign values to variables once it has been determined that the user is editing an existing transaction. (This occurs when the if...else statements earlier in the code are processed.) If the two values are equal, the second <option> element is used, which means that the current order ID is displayed when this page is loaded. If the two values are not equal, which is the condition specified in the if statement, no order ID is displayed, which you would expect when creating a new record.

The next row that you created for your form table allows users to select from a list of DVD names. The same logic is used to create the drop-down list available to the users. The only difference is that, because only DVD names are displayed, no special formatting or concatenation is required to display the values.

After you created your two rows that display the drop-down lists to the users, you created three date-related rows. Each row provides a text box in which users can enter the appropriate dates. For example, the first of these rows includes the following form element:

```
<input type="text" name="date_out" value="<?printf($dateOut);?>" size="50">
```

As you can see, this is an `<input>` element similar to the ones that you created when you first defined the form. Only the input type on this one is not hidden, but instead is text, which means that a text box will be displayed. The name of the text box is date_out. This is actually the name of the parameter that will hold the value that is submitted by the user. The initial value displayed in the text box depends on the value of the `$dateOut` variable. For new records, this value is the current date, and for existing records, this is the value as it currently exists in the database. (Both these values are determined in the earlier PHP script.)

Once you completed setting up the various form elements, you added two more elements: one for the Save button and one for the Cancel button. For example, your code for the Save button is as follows:

```
<td align="center">
    <?if((strcmp("add", $command) == 0) || (strcmp("savenew", $command) == 0)){?>
    <input type="button" value="Save" class="add" onclick="doSave(this, 'savenew')">
    <?}else{?>
    <input type="button" value="Save" class="add" onclick="doSave(this, 'save')">
    <?}?>
</td>
```

A button is also an `<input>` element on a form, but the type is specified as a button. The value for this element determines the name that appears on the button, which in this case is Save. The `class` option specifies the style that should be used in the button, as defined in the dvdstyle.css file, and the `onclick` option specifies the action to be taken. In this case, the action is to execute the `doSave()` function, which is defined in the dvdrentals.js file.

Notice that there are again two `<input>` elements, but only one is used. If the command value equals add or savenew, the first `<input>` element is used; otherwise, the second `<input>` element is used. When you click the Save button, the `doSave()` function is called. The function takes one argument, this, which is a self-referencing value that indicates that the action is related to the current HTML input button. When the function is executed, it submits the form to the edit.php page and sets the command parameter value to savenew or save, depending on which `<input>` option is used. Based on the command value, the PHP script is processed once again, only this time, the first `if` statement (in the large `if... else` construction) evaluates to true and that statement is executed. Assuming that there are no errors, the date values are reformatted for MySQL, the PHP script in the update.php or insert.php include file is executed, and the user is redirected to the index.php page.

As you can see, the edit.php page provides the main logic that is used to insert and update data. As the code in this page indicates, you must also create the include files necessary to support the actual insertion and deletion of data. In the next Try It Out section, you create the insert.php file. The file contains only that script that is necessary to insert a record, based on the value provided by the user in the edit.php form.

Creating the insert.php File

The following steps describe how to create the insert.php file:

1. In your text editor, create a new file, and enter the following code:

```
<?
// Build the INSERT statement
$sqlString = "INSERT INTO Transactions (OrderID, DVDID, DateOut, DateDue) VALUES
($orderId, $dvdId, '$dateOut', '$dateDue')";

// Execute the INSERT statement
mysql_query($sqlString)
    or die("Error in query $sqlString ".mysql_error());
?>
```

2. Save the insert.php file to the appropriate Web application directory.

How It Works

As you can see, this is a very simple file. You first initialized the $sqlString variable with the INSERT statement necessary to add the record:

```
$sqlString = "INSERT INTO Transactions (OrderID, DVDID, DateOut, DateDue) VALUES
($orderId, $dvdId, '$dateOut', '$dateDue')";
```

Notice that the INSERT statement includes the variables that have been assigned values through the process of the user filling out and submitting the form. The $sqlString variable is then used in the following mysql_query() function to execute the INSERT statement:

```
mysql_query($sqlString)
    or die("Error in query $sqlString ".mysql_error());
```

If the statement executes successfully, the rest of the applicable script in the edit.php file is executed and the user is returned to the index.php file. If the INSERT statement fails, the user receives an error.

In addition to creating the insert.php file, you must also create the update.php file. This file works just like the insert.php file in that it is included in the edit.php file. This is the same as including these statements directly in the edit.php file. In the following Try it Out section, you create the update.php file.

Creating the update.php File

The following steps describe how to create the update.php file:

1. Open a new file in your text editor, and enter the following code:

```
<?
// Build the UPDATE statement
$sqlString = "UPDATE Transactions SET OrderID = $orderId, DVDID = $dvdId, DateOut =
'$dateOut', DateDue = '$dateDue', DateIn = '$dateIn' WHERE TransID =
$transactionId";

// Execute the UPDATE statement
```

```
mysql_query($sqlString)
   or die("Error in query $sqlString " . mysql_error());
?>
```

2. Save the update.php file to the appropriate Web application directory.

How It Works

Once again, you initialized the $sqlString variable with an SQL statement. In this case, the statement is an UPDATE statement, as shown in the following code:

```
$sqlString = "UPDATE Transactions SET OrderID = $orderId, DVDID = $dvdId, DateOut =
'$dateOut', DateDue = '$dateDue', DateIn = '$dateIn' WHERE TransID =
$transactionId";
```

The UPDATE statement uses the variables that were set when the user submitted the form. Once the $sqlString variable is set with the UPDATE statement, you can use it in the mysql_query() function:

```
mysql_query($sqlString)
   or die("Error in query $sqlString " . mysql_error());
```

As you can see, this is the same process that you saw when executing the INSERT statement in the previous exercise. You set a variable with the SQL statement, and then you execute the statement by using the mysql_query() function. Now only one step remains to set up your application to insert and update data. You must modify the index.php file so that it includes the functionality necessary to link the user to the edit.php page. The following Try It Out section explains how to modify the index.php file. It then walks you through the process of inserting a transaction and then modifying that transaction.

<hr>

Try It Out   **Modifying the index.php File**

The following steps describe how to modify the index.php file to support the insert and update operations:

1. In your text editor, open the index.php file. Add a form, an <input> element, and a cell definition to your HTML code. Add the following code (shown with the gray screen background) to your file:

```
<html>
<head>
   <title>DVD - Listing</title>
   <link rel="stylesheet" href="dvdstyle.css" type="text/css">
   <script language="JavaScript" src="dvdrentals.js"></script>
</head>

<body>

<form name="mainForm" method="post" action="index.php">
<input type="hidden" name="command" value="view">
<input type="hidden" name="transaction_id" value="">

<p></p>

<table cellSpacing="0" cellPadding="0" width="619" border="0">
```

```
<tr>
    <td>
        <table height="20" cellSpacing="0" cellPadding="0" width="619"
bgcolor="#bed8e1" border="0">
        <tr align=left>
            <td valign="bottom" width="400" class="title">
                DVD Transaction Listing
            </td>
            <td align="right" width="219" class="title">
                <input type="button" value="New Transaction" class="add"
onclick="doAdd(this)">
            </td>
        </tr>
        </table>
        <br>
        <table cellSpacing="2" cellPadding="2" width="619" border="0">
        <tr>
            <td width="250" class="heading">Order Number</td>
            <td width="250" class="heading">Customer</td>
            <td width="250" class="heading">DVDName</td>
            <td width="185" class="heading">DateOut</td>
            <td width="185" class="heading">DateDue</td>
            <td width="185" class="heading">DateIn</td>
            <td width="99" class="heading"> </td>
        </tr>
```

When adding code to your file, be sure to add it in the position shown here.

2. Next, add an HTML table cell and an `<input>` element to the area of code that prints out the values returned by the database. Add the following code (shown with the gray screen background) to your file:

```
<td class="item">
    <nobr>
    <?printf($dateInPrint);?>
    </nobr>
</td>
<td class="item" valign="center" align="center">
    <input type="button" value="Edit" class="edit" onclick="doEdit(this,
<?printf($transId)?>)">
</td>
</tr>
```

3. Now you must close the form, which you do near the end of the file. To close the form, you must use a `</form>` element. Add the following code (shown with the gray screen background) to the end of the PHP file:

```
        </table>
    </td>
</tr>
</table>
</form>
</body>
</html>
```

4. Save the index.php file.

5. Open your browser, and go to the address `http://localhost/index.php`. Your browser should display a page similar to the one shown in Figure 17-2.

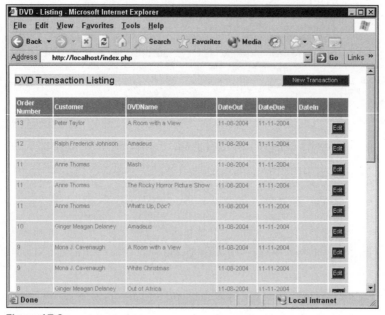

Figure 17-2

6. Click the New Transaction button at the top of the page. Your browser should display a page similar to the one shown in Figure 17-3.

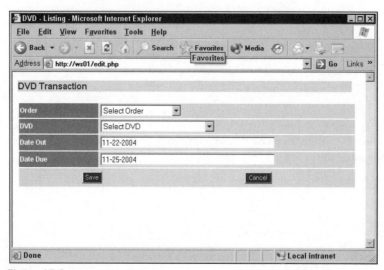

Figure 17-3

7. Now add a transaction to an existing order. In the Order drop-down list, select 13 - Peter Taylor. In the DVD drop-down list, select *Out of Africa*. Click Save. You're returned to the index.php page. The new transaction should now display at the top of the list.

8. Now edit the new transaction. In the row of the transaction that you just added, click the Edit button. Your browser should display a page similar to the one shown in Figure 17-4.

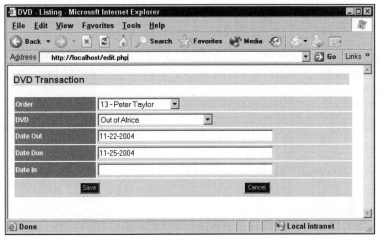

Figure 17-4

9. In the Date In text box, type the same date that is in the Date Due text box. Be certain to type the date in the same format that is used for the other date-related text boxes. Click the Save button. You should be returned to the index.php page.

How It Works

In this exercise, you added a form to your index.php file. This is similar to the form that you added to the edit.php file. The main difference between the two is that, in this form, the `transaction_id` value is set to an empty string. No ID is necessary initially, but you want the parameter to exist so that a vehicle has been provided to pass that ID through the form when you submit the form.

Once you created the form, you added the following HTML cell definition and `<input>` element at the top of the page:

```
<td align="right" width="219" class="title">
    <input type="button" value="New Transaction" class="add" onclick="doAdd(this)">
</td>
```

As you can see, the input type is button, and it calls the JavaScript `doAdd()` function. The function links the user to the edit.php page, allowing the user to create a new transaction. At the same time, the function passes a command value of `add` to the edit.php page. That way, the edit.php page knows that a new transaction is being created and responds accordingly. You next added the following code to the initial table structure that's created in the HTML code:

```
<td width="99" class="heading"> </td>
```

This creates an additional column head in the table to provide a column for the Edit button that is added to each row returned by your query results. Finally, you added the actual cell and button to your table definition, as shown in the following code:

```
<td class="item" valign="center" align="center">
    <input type="button" value="Edit" class="edit" onclick="doEdit(this,
<?printf($transId)?>)">
</td>
```

The Edit button calls the doEdit() function, which passes the transaction ID to the form and links the user to the edit.php page. At the same time, the function passes the command value of edit so that when the edit.php page opens, it has the information it needs to allow the user to edit a current record.

Once you modified and saved the file, you opened the index.php page, created a transaction, and then edited that transaction. The application, however, still does not allow you to delete a transaction. As a result, the next section describes how you can set up PHP statements to delete data.

Deleting Data from a MySQL Database

Deleting data from the database is very similar to inserting or updating data. You must create a DELETE statement again and then execute the mysql_error() function. For example, the following PHP statements delete data from the CDs table:

```
$deleteSql = "DELETE FROM CDs WHERE CDID = 10";

mysql_query($deleteSql, $link);
    or die("Invalid query: " . mysql_error(). "<br>".$deleteSql);
```

Once again, you create a variable that holds the SQL statement. You then use that variable in the mysql_error() function. If necessary, you can also include a connection-related parameter in the function to ensure that a specific connection is being used. In this case, the variable is $link, which is similar to what you've seen in previous examples throughout the chapter. As you have also seen throughout, you can include the or operator and die() function to specify that an error be returned if the statement does not execute properly.

Deleting data is no more difficult than updating or inserting data. The key to any of these types of statements is to make sure that you set up your variables in such a way that the correct information can be passed to the SQL statement when it is being executed. In the next Try It Out section, you see how you can delete a transaction from your database. To do so, you modify the index.php file and then create a delete.php include file.

Try It Out   **Modifying the index.php File and Creating the delete.php File**

The following steps describe how to set up delete capabilities in your DVDRentals application:

1. First, add a column head to your table so that you can include a Delete button for each row. The button is added next to the Edit button you added in the previous Try It Out section. Add the following code (shown with the gray screen background) to your file:

```
<tr>
    <td width="250" class="heading">Order Number</td>
    <td width="250" class="heading">Customer</td>
    <td width="250" class="heading">DVDName</td>
    <td width="185" class="heading">DateOut</td>
    <td width="185" class="heading">DateDue</td>
    <td width="185" class="heading">DateIn</td>
    <td width="99" class="heading"> </td>
    <td width="99" class="heading"> </td>
</tr>
```

2. Next, add the code necessary to initialize variables and call the delete.php include file. Add the following code (shown with the gray screen background) to your file:

```php
<?
// Connect to the server or return an error
$link = mysql_connect("localhost", "mysqlapp", "pw1")
    or die("Could not connect: " . mysql_error());

// Select the database or return an error
mysql_select_db("DVDRentals", $link)
    or die("Unable to select database: . mysql_error()");

// Initialize variables with parameters retrieved from the form
$command = null;
$transactionId = null;

if(isset($_POST["command"]))
    $command = $_POST["command"];

if(isset($_POST["transaction_id"]))
    $transactionId = $_POST["transaction_id"];

// Process the delete command
if($transactionId != null)
{
    if(strcmp("delete", $command) == 0)
    {
        include "delete.php";
    }
}
```

3. Now add the actual Delete button by adding the following code (shown with the gray screen background) to your file:

```php
<td class="item">
    <nobr>
    <?printf($dateInPrint);?>
    </nobr>
</td>
<td class="item" valign="center" align="center">
    <input type="button" value="Edit" class="edit" onclick="doEdit(this,
<?printf($transId)?>)">
</td>
```

```
            <td class="item" valign="center" align="center">
                <input type="button" value="Delete" class="delete"
onclick="doDelete(this, <?printf($transId)?>)">
            </td>
        </tr>
```

4. Save the index.php file.

5. Create a new file named delete.php in your text editor, and enter the following code:

```
<?
// Build the DELETE statement
$deleteSql = "DELETE FROM Transactions WHERE TransID = '$transactionId'";

// Execute the DELETE statement
mysql_query($deleteSql)
    or die("Error in query $deleteSql " . mysql_error());
?>
```

6. Save the delete.php file to the appropriate Web application directory.

7. Open your browser, and go to the address `http://localhost/index.php`. Your browser should display a page similar to the one shown in Figure 17-5.

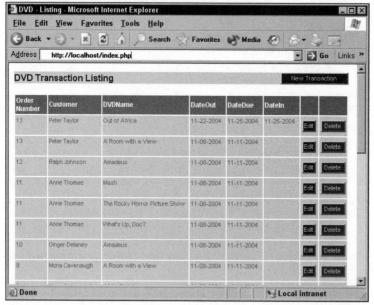

Figure 17-5

8. Click the Delete button in the row that contains the transaction that you created in a previous Try It Out section (Order number 13, DVD name *Out of Africa*). A message box similar to the one in Figure 17-6 appears, confirming whether you want to delete the record.

Figure 17-6

9. Click OK to delete the record. The index.php file should be redisplayed, with the deleted file no longer showing.

How It Works

In this exercise, you first created an additional column head for a column that holds the Delete button for each row. You then entered the following code:

```
$command = null;
$transactionId = null;

if(isset($_POST["command"]))
    $command = $_POST["command"];

if(isset($_POST["transaction_id"]))
    $transactionId = $_POST["transaction_id"];
```

First, you initialized the $command and $transactionId variables to null to ensure that they did not contain values from any previous transactions. You then used if statements and the $_POST array to assign the most current command and transaction_id variables to the variable. This process is necessary because, when you click the Delete button, you must have a mechanism in place to store the values that are submitted to the form when the button is clicked. The $_POST array contains the values that are submitted when the applicable JavaScript function submits the form to the index.php page.

Once you added the code necessary to initialize the variables, you added the following if statement to the file:

```
if($transactionId != null)
{
    if(strcmp("delete", $command) == 0)
    {
        include "delete.php";
    }
}
```

The if statement condition specifies that the $transactionId variable cannot be null, which it will not be if a form was submitted when the Delete button was clicked. If the condition evaluates to true, the PHP script in the delete.php include file is executed.

The last code that you added to the index.php file is the HTML cell definition and <input> element necessary to add the Delete button to each row displayed on the page:

```
<td class="item" valign="center" align="center">
    <input type="button" value="Delete" class="delete" onclick="doDelete(this,
<?printf($transId)?>)">
</td>
```

As you can see, the input type is button (type="button"), the button is named Delete (value="Delete"), the style is delete (class="delete"), and the doDelete() function is executed when the button is clicked. The doDelete() function takes two parameters. The this parameter merely indicates that it is the current button that is being referenced. The second parameter passes the value in the $transID variable to the transactionId parameter associated with the form. That way, PHP knows what record to delete when the DELETE statement is executed.

Once you set up your index.php file to support deletions, you created a delete.php file that contained the statements that actually deleted the transaction:

```
$deleteSql = "DELETE FROM Transactions WHERE TransID = '$transactionId'";
mysql_query($deleteSql)
    or die("Error in query $deleteSql " . mysql_error());
```

By now, you should be familiar with this process. The $deleteSql variable is set to the DELETE statement. The DELETE statement uses the $transactionId variable to determine which transaction to delete. The mysql_query() function sends the DELETE statement to the MySQL server. If the statement fails, the user receives an error. When the user clicks the Delete button, a pop-up message appears, verifying that the row should be deleted. If the user clicks OK, the row is deleted.

Now your application, at least this part of the application, should be complete. You can now view, insert, update, and delete transactions. In addition, you can build on this application if you want to extend your application's functionality. The code used to create this application is available at www.wrox.com, and you can use and modify that code as necessary. Keep in mind, however, that at the heart of your application is the MySQL database that manages the data that you need to run your application. The better you understand MySQL and data management, the more effective your applications can be.

Summary

In this chapter, you learned how you can build a PHP application that interacts with a MySQL database. The chapter first introduced you to PHP and then provided an overview of the PHP elements that you need to use to connect to your database and retrieve and manipulate data. The chapter also provided you with elements of PHP that demonstrate how PHP statements can be used to take different actions by first testing for specific conditions and then taking actions based on whether those conditions are true or false. Specifically, the chapter covered the following topics:

❑   Connecting to the MySQL server and selecting a database

❑   Using if statements to test conditions and take actions

❑   Retrieving data, formatting data, and then displaying data

❑   Inserting data in your database

❑   Updating existing data in your database

❑   Deleting data from your database

Much of this chapter was devoted to building an application that accessed the DVDRentals database. The application focused on retrieving and modifying data related to the transactions stored in the database. In the real world, this would no doubt represent only a part of a larger application that supports numerous other functions. The purpose of this application is merely to demonstrate the various aspects of PHP that allow you to interact with a MySQL database. The more you work with PHP and MySQL, the more you discover that the principles described in this chapter can be applied to additional functionality that allows you to build applications that are far more robust than the one shown here, while still using what you learned this chapter. Now that you have a sense of how PHP interacts with MySQL, you're ready to move on to Chapter 18, which describes how to create a Java Web-based application that uses a MySQL database.

Exercises

In this chapter, you learned how to connect to a MySQL database, retrieve data, and manipulate data from a PHP application. To assist you in better understanding how to perform these tasks, the chapter includes the following exercises. To view solutions to these exercises, see Appendix A.

1. You are establishing a connection to a MySQL server on a host named server1. To support your application, you have created a MySQL user account with the name app_user. The password for the account is app_pw. You want the connection parameters to be assigned to a variable named $myLink. What PHP statement should you use to establish the connection?

2. You are selecting the MySQL database for your PHP application. The name of the database is Sales_db, and your access to the database relies on the current server connection. What PHP statement should you use to select the database?

3. You plan to retrieve data from a MySQL database. You create a SELECT statement and assign it to the $myQuery variable. You want to assign the results returned by the SELECT statement to the $myResult variable. In addition, if no results are returned, you want to return an error message. The error message should begin with "Error in query:" and end with the actual error returned by MySQL. What PHP statement should you use?

4. You want to process the query results assigned to the $myResult variable. The query results include data from the CDName and InStock columns of the CDs table. The CDName values should be assigned to the $cdName variable, and the InStock values should be assigned to the $inStock variable. The variable values should then be printed out on your page. How should you set up your PHP code to display the returned values?

5. Your application will post data to a form that contains the user1 parameter. You want to retrieve the user1 value from within your PHP code and assign that value to the $user1 variable. You want to assign a value to the $user1 variable only if the user1 parameter contains a value. What PHP statement should you use?

6. You want users to be redirected to the index.php file at a certain point in your application. What PHP statement should you use to redirect users?

7. You must close the connection to the MySQL server that has been established earlier in your application. The connection parameters are stored in the $myLink variable. What PHP statement should you use to close the connection?

Connecting to MySQL from a Java/J2EE Application

Most users access data in a MySQL database by using an application that interfaces with that database. In many cases, the application is built with Web pages that reside on a application server or Web server such as Apache or Internet Information Services. Chapter 17 provides an example of a PHP application that access data in the DVDRentals database. However, Web-based applications are by no means limited to PHP. Another popular programming language that you can use to build Web-based applications is Java. Java supports the same functionality as PHP, and much more. In fact, Java can also be used to build client-server and multi-tiered systems that are not limited to Web-based applications — and all those systems can be built to access a MySQL database.

In this chapter, you learn how to build a Java Web-based application that accesses a MySQL database. The application is based on the Java 2 Enterprise Edition (J2EE) specification, which defines a collection of libraries that contain classes for server-side tasks, including support for the JavaServer Pages (JSP) technology. By using Java and JSP technology, you can create Web pages that deliver dynamic content to your users, similar to the way the PHP delivers content to users. In fact, if you're familiar with PHP, you'll find that creating JSP files is quite similar to creating PHP files. To demonstrate how to create a JSP application that connects to a MySQL database, this chapter covers the following topics:

❑   Introduces you to Java and how it communicates with a MySQL server and its databases

❑   Explains how to build a JSP application that connects to a MySQL database, retrieves data from that database, inserts data into the database, modifies the data, and then deletes the data

Introduction to Java/J2EE

Java is a robust application language based on the principles of object-oriented programming (OOP). As the name indicates, OOP refers to a programming model that is based on the concept of encapsulating code and the data that it manipulates into defined objects. Each object is based on an object class that specifies how that object can be built. An *object*, then, is an instance of the class from which it is derived.

A class is made up of fields and methods. The fields are variables that can contain data that describes the object, which is why the fields are sometimes referred to as data members. The variable values are what distinguish multiple object instances that are based on the same class. The methods defined on a class can perform some type of action on the data stored in the variables. A method is similar to a function in the way that it performs a predefined task. For example, suppose that you have a class named BookInventory. The class might include three fields, one to identify the book, one to identify the number in stock, and one to identify the number on order. The class also includes a method that calculates the total number of books that will be available by adding the values in the last two fields. As you can see, the three fields contain data about the book and the method performs an action on that data. Together, these elements make up the BookInventory class. You can then create an object based on the BookInventory class and assign unique values to the fields.

This example is, of course, an over-simplification of how objects work within Java, but it does help to distinguish between fields and methods. Although a thorough discussion of OOP is beyond the scope of this book, it's important that you recognize that Java is based on these concepts and that everything you do in Java is within the context of objects. For example, suppose that you retrieve data from a MySQL database and you now want to process that data so that you can display each row in your application. When you retrieve that data, it is stored in a ResultSet object. You can then use methods defined on that object to access the data in that result set.

In order for a Java application to access data in MySQL database, it must have some way to interface with that database. Two components are needed to provide that connectivity: JDBC and Connector/J. JDBC is a call-level API that allows a Java application to connect with a wide range of SQL databases. By using JDBC, a Java application can connect to the database, send SQL statements, and retrieve data. Because JDBC can communicate with different database products, Java applications are very portable, which means that you don't have to modify a lot of code if you were to switch the database product used to support the application. However, it does mean that you need a product-specific driver that completes the JDBC connection from the Java application to the database.

JDBC is sometimes said to mean Java Database Connectivity, but the makers of JDBC, Sun Microsystems, make no such claim. In fact, they list JDBC as a registered trademark, but not Java Database Connectivity.

To facilitate your ability to use JDBC to connect to a MySQL database, MySQL AB provides Connector/J, a JDBC-specific driver that implements most of the functionality supported by JDBC. The JDBC functionality that is not supported pertains to those functions that are not currently implemented in MySQL. However, for the most part, you will be able to perform nearly any SQL-related task from within a Java application that you would expect to perform from any application.

To implement a JSP-based application, you must run it under a Web server or application server that implements the J2EE Servlet container specification. For some application servers, such as JBoss, you must also create special build or configuration files that allow the JSP application to be implemented in that environment. However the JSP files themselves, which are the focus of this chapter, can be created with any text editor, as long as the files are saved with the .jsp extension. Now take a look at how you actually create those files.

This chapter was written based on the following configuration: the Java 2 SDK 1.4.2, MySQL 4.1.6, Connector/J 3.0.15, JBoss 4.0.0RC1 (an application server), and Apache Ant 1.6.2 (a Java-based build tool) installed on a Windows XP computer. Details about the configuration of your operating system, applications server, the Java SDK, and Apache Ant are beyond the scope of the book. Be sure to view the necessary product documentation when setting up your application environment. For more information about the Java 2 SDK, go to www.sun.com/j2se. *For information about Connector/J and MySQL, go to* www.mysql.com. *For information about JBoss, go to* www.jboss.org. *For information about Apache Ant, go to* http://ant.apache.org.

Building a Java/J2EE Web Application

When you create a JSP file, the first step that you must take is to tell the Java compiler where to find the language classes that will be referenced within the application. From there, you must establish your connection to the MySQL server and its database, and then you can select or retrieve data. Java supports numerous objects and statements that allow you to perform each of these tasks. In the remaining part of the chapter, you learn about each aspect of database access, from importing classes to closing connections. You also create a JSP application that accesses data in the DVDRentals database. If you created the PHP application shown in Chapter 17, you'll find that the application in this chapter achieves the same results.

The examples in this chapter focus on the JSP code used to create a basic Web-based application. However, the principles behind connecting to a database and accessing data can apply to any Web or non-Web application written in other programming languages.

Importing Java Classes

When creating a JSP file, you must specify the classes that will be used in your application. In Java, classes are organized into packages. In other words, a package is a collection of classes.) You can specify that all classes within a package be made available to the application, or you can specify individual classes. To specify the classes that your application will access, you should use a page directive that specifies the package or class name.

When specifying a directive in the JSP file, you must enclose the directive in an opening directive tag (<%@) and a closing directive tag (%>). For a page directive, include the `page` keyword. To specify a class or package, you must also use the `import` keyword. For example, the following statement imports the `java.lang` class package:

```
<%@ page import "java.lang.*" %>
```

As you can see, the statement is enclosed in the directive tags and includes the `page` and the `import` keywords, with the name of the package enclosed in double quotes. Notice that the package name ends with the asterisk (*) wildcard, which indicates that all classes within the package should be included in the directive. If you want to specify a specific class within that package, such as `Integer`, you would use the following statement:

```
<%@ page import "java.lang.Integer" %>
```

As you can see, the wildcard has been replaced with the class name, but everything else is the same as in the previous example. If you plan to use a lot of the classes within a package, you'll probably want to specify the entire package; otherwise, specify only those classes that you'll need so you minimize the impact on the Java compiler.

Declaring and Initializing Variables

Java is a strongly typed application language, which means that each variable must be explicitly declared and a data type must be assigned to that variable. In Java, a variable is either a primitive variable or an object variable. A *primitive* variable is a basic variable that is simply a specified placeholder that holds a value in memory, similar to the variables you see in MySQL. Primitive variables include such types as `boolean`, `int`, `char`, and `long`. They are unique within Java because, unlike other variables, they do not require that an object be created when you initialize them.

To declare a primary variable, you must specify the type and the variable name. For example, the following statement declares the `cdId` variable as an `int` type:

```
int cdId;
```

Once a variable is declared, you need to assign a value to it in order for that variable to be used within the code. The process of assigning a value is referred to as initializing the variable and you can do that simply by specifying a single equal sign (=) plus the value that should be assigned, as shown in the following example:

```
cdId = 42;
```

In this case, the value 42 is assigned to `cdId`. You can also declare and initialize a variable within one statement:

```
int cdId = 42;
```

This, of course, makes your code simpler; however, you might not always be able to initialize a variable at the time that you declare it, depending on the scope that you want the variable to have. Scope determines the lifetime of the variable, and scope is determined when the variable is declared. If you declare a variable within a block of code, the variable is available only to that block and to any blocks nested within the outer block. The outer block defines the scope of that variable. (A block of code is a set of Java statements that are enclosed in curly brackets.) As a result, if you want a variable to be available to all code, but you cannot assign a value to the variable until a specific operation within a block of code is completed, you should declare the variable outside any blocks of code and initialize the variable when the value is available. You see examples of this later in the chapter.

The second type of variable is the object variable. An *object* variable is always based on a class and is usually associated with an object that is based on the same class. In some cases, the object references a null value and is not associated with an object until initialized to an object. The variable references that object, which contains the value that is associated with the variable. For example, suppose that you want to create a variable that holds a string value. To do so, you must use the `String` class to declare the variable and initialize it, as shown in the following example:

```
String strName;
strName = new String("Strauss");
```

In the first statement, you have simply declared a variable named `strName` that is based on the `String` class. At this point, no object has been created. However, when you initialize the variable, a `String` object is created and configured with the value `Strauss`. The `strName` variable then references the new object. As a result, whenever you want to use `Strauss` in your code, you can use the `strName` variable, which in turn references the new `String` object, which contains the value `Strauss`.

Notice that the second statement includes the new keyword. Whenever you explicitly initialize a variable in this way, you must use the new keyword. This tells the Java compiler to create an object based on the specified class. The new keyword is followed by a constructor, which in this case is String(). A *constructor* is a special type of method defined within the class. A constructor always has the same name as the class and is used to create objects based on that class.

As with primary variables, you can also declare and initialize an object variable in one statement, as shown in the following statement:

```
String strName = new String("Strauss");
```

As you can see, all the same elements are there, only now condensed into one statement. You declare the variable and then initialize it by creating a String object that is assigned to the variable.

The String class allows you assign a string directly to a variable, and the object is created by the compiler and you are referencing it. In this way, a String variable appears similar to a primitive variable, which allows you to initialize a variable simple by assigning a value to that variable, as the following statement demonstrates:

```
String strName = "Strauss";
```

For some classes, you can create variables that use yet another approach to create the object that is assigned to the variable. In these cases, you use a method in one class to create an object in a different class. One example of this approach is when you establish a connection to a database, so next you review that process to see how it works.

Connecting to a MySQL Database

To establish a connection to a MySQL database, you must take two steps. The first is to dynamically load a Java class at runtime, specifically, the Driver class in the com.mysql.jdbc class package. This step is necessary to locate and instantiate the Connector/J driver. To load the Java class, you must use the forName() method in the Class object, and then you must use the newInstance() method to create a new class, as shown in the following statement:

```
Class.forName("com.mysql.jdbc.Driver").newInstance();
```

When the Driver class is located, the newInstance() method creates a new instance of the Driver class and names that instance DriverManager. The DriverManager class manages all currently installed JDBC drivers.

> To use the MySQL Connector/J driver, it must be properly installed on your system. For information about installing the driver, see the Connector/J documentation that comes with the installation files.

Once the DriverManager class has been created, you can use the getConnection() method in that class to create a Connection object. The getConnection() method takes three arguments, the connection URL, the user account name, and the password for that account. For example, the following statement uses the getConnection() method to connect to the MySQL server on the local computer:

```
conn = DriverManager.getConnection("jdbc:mysql://localhost/CDs", "cduser", "pw1");
```

671

The statement includes a number of components, so first take a look at the `getConnection()` method. The first argument includes the `jdbc` prefix, then `mysql`, and then a URL that specifies the location of the MySQL server and the name of the database. The location is localhost and the database is CDs. The second and third arguments specify the username and then the password.

Notice that the `DriverManager.getConnection()` structure is assigned to the `conn` variable. Normally this variable is declared prior to the running the statement above and is based on the `Connection` object, as shown in the following declaration:

```
Connection conn;
```

Once you declare this variable, you can initialize it with the `DriverManager.getConnection()` method, as demonstrated previously. In establishing a connection, the `getConnection()` method returns a `Connection` object, which is in turn assigned to the `conn` variable. The variable can then be used to reference the `Connection` object, which contains the connection to the database. As this demonstrates, you do not always have to initialize an object variable directly by using the `new` command and a `class` constructor, but you can instead use a method in another object, as has been done previously.

Retrieving Data from a MySQL Database

Once you have established your connection to the MySQL server database, you can retrieve data that can then be displayed by your Java application. The primary mechanism that you use to retrieve data is the `SELECT` statement, written as it is written when you access data interactively. However, the `SELECT` statement alone is not enough. You need additional mechanisms that pass that `SELECT` statement to the MySQL server and that then process the results returned by the statement.

When you're retrieving data from a MySQL database from within your JSP application, you generally follow a specific set of steps:

1. Declare and initialize a `String` variable that creates the `SELECT` statement.

2. Declare and initialize a `Statement` variable that creates a `Statement` object.

3. Declare and initialize a `ResultSet` variable that uses the `Statement` object to execute the query and to create a `ResultSet` object that contains the query results.

4. Use the `ResultSet` variable to process the results, normally within some sort of conditional structure.

Now take a closer look at each step. The first step creates a `SELECT` statement that is assigned to a `String` variable. For example, in the following statement, a variable named `selectSql` is defined:

```
String selectSql = "SELECT CDID, CDName, InStock, OnOrder, " +
                   "Reserved, Department, Category from CDs";
```

Notice that the value that is assigned to the variable is a `SELECT` statement. If you want to split the statement into multiple lines, as has been done here, you enclose each portion of the statement line in double quotes. In addition, for each line other than the last line, you end the line with a plus sign. This indicates that the two lines are to be concatenated when executed. Only the final line is terminated with a semi-colon.

Putting the `SELECT` statement in a variable in this way makes it easier to work with the statement in other places in the code. Once the variable has been declared and initialized, you should then create a

Statement object and assign that to a variable. The Statement object contains the methods that you need to execute your SELECT statement. The following variable is declared and then initialized by creating a Statement object:

```
Statement stmt = conn.createStatement();
```

The createStatement() method is part of the Connection class, as represented by the conn variable. You can access an object's method by calling it through the associated variable, as has been done here. The createStatement() method creates a Statement object, which is then associated with the stmt variable. Notice that the stmt variable has been declared and initialized within one statement.

Once you have created the Statement object and the variable that references that object, you can use the executeQuery() method in the Statement object to execute your SELECT statement, as shown in the following example:

```
ResultSet rs = stmt.executeQuery(selectSql);
```

In addition to executing the SELECT statement, the executeQuery() method also creates a ResultSet object that in turn is assigned to a ResultSet variable, which is named rs. You can now use the rs variable to call the methods in the ResultSet object to process your result set.

Processing the Result Set

Once you have a result set to work with, you must process the rows so that they can be displayed in a usable format. However, Java, like other procedural application languages, cannot easily process sets of data, so you must set up your code to be able to process one row at a time. You can do this by setting up a loop condition and by using a function that supports the row-by-row processing. For example, you can use the while command to set up the loop and the next() method of the ResultSet object to process the rows, as shown in the following example:

```
while(rs.next())
{
    int cdId = rs.getInt("CDID");
    String cdName = rs.getString("CDName");
    int inStock = rs.getInt("InStock");
    int onOrder = rs.getInt("OnOrder");
    int reserved = rs.getInt("Reserved");
    String department = rs.getString("Department");
    String category = rs.getString("Category");
    System.out.println("cdId=" + cdId + ", cdName=" + cdName + ", inStock=" +
                        inStock, " + "onOrder=" + onOrder + ", reserved=" +
                        reserved + ", " + "department=" + department +
                        ", category=" + category);
}
```

The while command tells Java to continue to execute the block of statements as long as the current condition equals true. The condition in this case is defined by rs.next(). The rs variable (which is associated with a ResultSet object) allows you to call the next() method. The method references each row in the results set, one row at a time, starting with the first row. Every time the while loop is executed, next() points to the next row.

Each value is retrieved from the ResultSet object by using the name of column, as it was returned by the SELECT statement. In this query, you retrieve MySQL integer and string values, so you use the getInt() and getString() methods of the ResultSet object to retrieve the applicable values. (The ResultSet object includes methods for other types of data as well.) The getInt() method returns an integer value, which is then assigned to the variable that is being declared for that particular column. The getString() method creates a String object to store the retrieved value and associates that object with the applicable variable.

To help illustrate this, suppose that the first row returned by your query contains the following values:

- ❑ CDID = 101
- ❑ CDName = Bloodshot
- ❑ InStock = 10
- ❑ OnOrder = 5
- ❑ Reserved = 3
- ❑ Department = Popular
- ❑ Category = Rock

When the while loop is executed the first time, the first call to the next() method points to the first row in the result set, which is stored in the ResultSet object that was created specifically to hold this result set. Because the rs variable is associated with that ResultSet object, you can use that variable to access the data stored in the object as well as the methods defined on that object (as inherited from the ResultSet class). You can then use the necessary method for each column within each row to return that particular value. For example, you can use the getInt() method to return the CDID value in the first row. As a result, the cdId variable is set to a value of 101. For each column returned by the next() method for a particular row, the column value is assigned to the applicable variable. The column-related variables can then be used to display the actual values returned by the SELECT statement.

The next step then is to use some sort of mechanism to print those values that have been returned. One such mechanism is to use the System.out.println() method to print the variable values. In addition, you can also print literal values by enclosing those values in double quotes, but you do not enclose the variable names in quotes, otherwise they will be treated as literal values, rather than printing the values that they represent.

Each time the while command is executed, the values for a specific row (taken from the variables) are displayed on your screen. By the time the while command has looped through the entire result set, all rows returned by the query are displayed. (Later, in the Try It Out sections, you'll see the results of using the while command to create a loop construction.)

Manipulating String Data

After you have retrieved string data from a database, you'll often find that you want to manipulate that data in some way. Because all string data is associated with String objects, you can use the methods defined in the String class to take some sort of action on that data. Two particularly useful methods are length() and equals(). To demonstrate how both these methods work, first take a look at the following statement:

```
String compName = "Strauss";
```

The statement declares a `String` variable named `compName`, whose purpose is to represent a composer's name. Initially, a `String` object that contains the value Strauss is assigned to the variable. Suppose now, that you want to determine the number of characters in the string value that the variable currently references. To do so, you can invoke the `length()` method to determine the number of characters, as shown in the following statement:

```
return compName.length();
```

The `return` command returns the value determined by `length()`. Because the `compName` variable is currently associated with the value Strauss, `length()` returns a value of 7.

The `equals()` method compares two strings and returns a value of true if the strings are equal and a value of false if they are not. To use this method, you must specify the first string, add the `equals()` method, and specify the second string as an argument in that method. For example, the following statement compares the Chopin string to the string in the `compName` variable:

```
return "Chopin".equals(compName);
```

The reason that the `equals()` method can be used with the string Chopin is because Java automatically treats a literal string value as an object, even when used as it is used in this example. As a result, you can call methods from the `String` class simply by specifying the string value, followed by a period, and then followed by the method. You can then pass the second string as an argument to the method. In this case, because the variable is currently associated with the value Strauss, the statement returns a value of false.

When working with string data, there might be times when you want to concatenate the string value in a variable with another string value. In that case, you would use the plus/equal signs (+=) to indicate that the value to the right of these signs should be concatenated to the value on the left. For example, the following statement adds Ricard to the value in the `compName` variable:

```
compName += ", Ricard";
```

This statement results in one value: Strauss, Ricard. If you were to use the equal sign without the plus sign, a new value would be assigned to the variable, resulting in the value Ricard (preceded by a comma) replacing the value Strauss.

Converting Values

In many cases when working with Java, you will find that you want to convert one type of value to another type. For example, when creating a Web application, numerical values are often passed as strings. However, you might find that you want to work with those values as integers, so you need to convert them. The way to do this is to use static methods in the `Integer` class to retrieve and convert the value to an integer. A *static* method is one that can be called directly from a class, without having to first create an object. The static methods that you use to convert numerical string values to integers are the `valueOf()` method and the `intValue()` method. The `valueOf()` method takes the numerical string as a parameter and returns it as an `Integer` object. The `inValue()` method then retrieves the value from the object and returns it as a primitive `int` type value. For example, the following statement returns the `int` type value of 100:

```
return Integer.valueOf("100").intValue();
```

As you can see, the string value is specified as an argument of the `valueOf()` method. From the `Integer` object created by this method, the `intValue()` method extracts the value and returns it as an `int` type.

In addition to converting numerical string values to integer values, you might find that you want to convert a string value to a date value and display that value in a specific format. This process often involves a couple of steps. The first step is to create a variable that is associated with a date-related object that allows you to convert and format a date value. For example, the following statement declares and initializes the `dateFormat` variable:

```
SimpleDateFormat dateFormat = new SimpleDateFormat("MM-dd-yyyy");
```

The `dateFormat` variable is based on the `SimpleDateFormat` class. To initialize the variable, you must create a `SimpleDateFormat` object by using the `new` keyword along with the `class` constructor. As an argument in the constructor, you should include the format of the date that you want to convert.

Once you've created the necessary variable, you can use the `parse()` method of the `SimpleDateFormat` object associated with the variable to convert the string value to a date value, as shown in the following statement:

```
Date newDate = dateFormat.parse("01-31-2000");
```

The `parse()` method converts the string value to a `Date` object, which is then assigned to the `newDate` variable. Now suppose that you want to convert the date value back to a string. You can use the `format()` method in the `SimpleDateFormat` object (associated with the `dateFormat` variable) to format the date as a string value, according to the format specified in the `SimpleDateFormat` object. For example, the following statement returns the value associated with the date variable as a string value:

```
return dateFormat.format(newDate);
```

When you want to insert a Java date value into a MySQL database, data conversion gets a little trickier. To convert date values, you must use two different objects: one is the `java.util.Date` class and other is `java.sql.Date` class. The `java.sql.Date` class is actually an extension of the `java.util.Date` class that allows you to enter date values into an SQL database from your Java application.

When you want to insert a date value in an SQL database, you should first create an object based on the `java.util.Date` class and assign it to a variable, as shown in the following statement:

```
java.util.Date utilDate = new java.util.Date();
```

You can now use the `utilDate` variable to access methods in the `java.util.Date` object. Specifically, you want to use the `getTime()` method to return the number of milliseconds that have passed since January 1, 1970. The value is then used by the `java.sql.Date` class to create an object to store the data value to be inserted into the SQL database, as shown in the following statement:

```
java.sql.Date sqlDate = new java.sql.Date(utilDate.getTime());
```

As the statement indicates, a new `java.sql.Date` object is created, based on the value returned by the `getTime()` method. The new object is then assigned to the `sqlDate` variable. By using this approach, you can convert two different date objects back and forth. In this example, the date value returned by the `getTime()` method is converted to a `java.sql.Date` value, which can then be used to insert the date value into the MySQL database.

As you can see in the last two examples, the Date *class name is fully qualified, which means that the entire package and class name are provided. If you import both classes into your JSP page and then simply call the* Date *class, Java does not know which class to use. In addition, if you import only one package and you use a* Date *object that has not been fully qualified, Java always uses the* Date *object from the imported class, even if you want to use a class that has not been imported. To use a class that has not been explicitly imported, you must fully qualify the class name.*

Working with HTML Forms

When working with Web-related applications, you often need to pass data from the client browser to the server. This is often done through the use of a *form*, which is an element on an HTML page that allows a user submit data that can be passed on to the server. For example, a form can be used to allow a user to log on to an application. The user can submit an account name and password, which the form then sends to a specified location.

An HTML form supports two types of posting methods: POST and GET. The POST method sends the data through an HTTP header. An HTTP header is a mechanism that allows commands and data to be sent to and from the browser and server. The GET method adds the data to a URL. Because the data is added to the URL, it is visible when the URL is displayed, which can create some security issues The POST method is often preferred because the POST data is hidden.

A thorough discussion about HTML forms and HTTP headers is beyond the scope of this book. However, there are plenty of resources that describe forms, headers, and all other aspects of HTML and HTTP extensively. If you're not familiar with how to work with forms and headers, be sure to read the appropriate documentation.

Like many other server-side programming languages, Java's JSP has built-in mechanisms that automatically process the data submitted by a form. In Java/J2EE, all JSP files are actually converted to Java classes and compiled. The classes that they are converted into are derived from a class called Servlet. This underlying process is fairly involved and beyond the scope of this book; however, the end result is that all pages have some pre-built classes available to them, including the HttpServletResponse and HttpServletRequest classes. From these classes, two objects are created: response and request. The request object abstracts the form parameters. Java then merges the GET and POST methods so that the server-side application can simply access the parameters via the getParameter() method of the request object. The getParameter() method takes as an argument the name of the parameter that was passed through the form, and then returns a string value or a null if no value is found.

To give you a better sense of how this works, the following example demonstrates this process. Suppose that your application includes an HTML form that contains an input element named department, as shown in the following code:

```
<input type="text" name="department">
```

Because the input element is a text type, the user enters a value into a text box and that value is assigned to the parameter named department. The response object abstracts this parameter, and Java makes it available to the application. You can then use the getParameter() method of the request object to retrieve that value, as the following statement demonstrates:

```
String strDept = request.getParameter("department");
```

The value entered into the form is returned as a string value that is assigned to a `String` variable named `strDept`. From there, you can use the `strDept` variable in other Java statements as you would any other string value.

Redirecting Browsers

Web application pages can sometimes decide that the user should be redirected to another page. This means that the current page stops processing and the server loads a new page and processes it. This process is usually part of a condition that specifies that, if a certain result is received, an action must be taken based on that result. For example, suppose that you want to redirect a user if that user enters Classical in the department `<input>` element (which is then assigned to the `strDept` variable). You can use the `sendRedirect()` method in the `response` object to redirect the user to another page, similar to the following statement:

```
if("Classical".equals(strDept))
{
    response.sendRedirect("ClassicalSpecials.jsp");
}
```

First, an `if` statement is created to compare the `strDept` value to Classical. If the two string values are equal, the condition evaluates to true and the `if` statement is executed. In this case, the `sendRedirect()` method in the response object is called and the user is redirected to the page specified as an argument to the method. As a result, the `ClassicalSpecials.jsp` page is displayed.

Including JSP Files

There might be times when you want to execute Java code that is in a file separate from your current file. For example, suppose that your application includes code that is repeated often. You can put that code in a file separate from your primary file and then call that file from the primary file. The second file is referred to as a include file, and you can simply reference it from your primary file to execute the code in the include file.

To reference an include file from within your current JSP file, you must use the `include` command, followed by the name of the include file. (If the file is located someplace other than the local directory, you must also specify the path.) The following if statement uses the `include` command to execute the Java code in the ClassicalSpecials.jsp file:

```
if("Classical".equals(strDept))
{
    %>
    <%@ include "ClassicalSpecials.jsp " %>
    <%
}
```

The first thing to notice is that the `include` command is enclosed in a opening (`<%@`) and closing (`%>`) directive tags. Most Java code in a JSP page is enclosed in opening (`<%`) and closing (`%>`) scriptlet tags. As a result, you must close a scriptlet before executing a directive, and then re-open the scriptlet, as necessary.

The example above also includes an `if` statement. The `if` condition specifies that the `strDept` value must equal Classical. If the condition is true, the include file is accessed and the script in the file is executed as though it were part of the current file. It would be the same as if the code in the include file actually existed within the primary file.

Managing Exceptions

To handle errors that occur when a statement is executed, Java uses a system based on the `Exception` class. When an error occurs, an exception is generated, which is a special class that can contain an error message. If your code includes ways to handle that exception, some sort of action is taken. For example, if an exception is generated, you might have it logged to a file or displayed to the user.

To work with exceptions, you must enclose your Java code in a try/catch block. The try part of this block includes all the primary application code, and the catch part of the block includes the code necessary to handle the exceptions. At its very basic, a try/catch block looks like the following:

```
try
{
    <Java application code>
}
catch(Exception ex)
{
    throw ex;
}
```

As you can see, two blocks have actually been created: the try block and the catch block. The try block includes all your basic program code, and the catch block processes the exception. The `catch()` method takes two arguments. The first is the name of the exception that is being caught, and the second is a variable that references the exception. The variable can then be used within the catch block.

In reality, you can include multiple catch blocks after the try block. In the example above, the `Exception` argument represents all exceptions. However, you can specify individual exceptions, rather than all exceptions. For example, you can specify the exception `ClassNotFoundException` if you want to catch the exception that is thrown if an object class cannot be found. In which case, your catch block would begin with the following:

```
catch(ClassNotFoundException ce)
```

If within the catch block you specify a throw statement, as shown in the preceding example, the applicable caller within the application server handles the exception. In some cases, the exception message is displayed to the user, depending on where the exception is occurs. If you want other action to be taken, you would create the necessary statements in the catch block.

Now that you've been introduced to many of the basic Java elements that you can use when retrieving and displaying data from a MySQL database, you're ready to build an application.

Creating a Basic Java/J2EE Web Application

In the Try It Out sections in this chapter, you build a simple Web application that allows you to view the transactions in the DVDRentals database. You will also be able to add a transaction, edit that transaction, and then delete it from the database. As you'll recall when you designed the DVDRentals database, transactions are actually a subset of orders. Each order is made up of one or more transaction, and each transaction is associated with exactly one order. In addition, each transaction represents exactly one DVD rental.

For example, if someone were to rent three DVDs at the same time, that rental would represent one order that includes three transactions.

The application that you build in this chapter is very basic and does not represent a complete application, in the sense that you would probably want your application to allow you to create new orders, add DVDs to the database, as well as add and edit other information. However, the purpose of this application is merely to demonstrate how you connect to a MySQL database from within Java, how you retrieve data, and how you manipulate data. The principles that you learn here can then be applied to any Java application that must access data in a MySQL database.

When creating a Web application such as a JSP application, you will usually find that you are actually programming in three or four different languages. For example, you might use Java for the dynamic portions of your application, HTML for the static portions, SQL for data access and manipulation, and JavaScript to perform basic page-related functions. The application that you create in this chapter uses all four languages. At first this might seem somewhat confusing; however, the trick is to think about each piece separately. If you are new to these technologies, try doing each piece separately and then integrating them. The application is fully integrated and can be run and examined to see how these technologies work. Keep in mind, however, that the focus of the Try It Out sections is to demonstrate Java and SQL, so you will not find detailed explanations about the JavaScript and HTML. However, you cannot develop a JSP application without including some HTML, and JavaScript is commonly implemented in Web-based applications. As a result, in order to show you a realistic application, HTML and Java Script are included, but a discussion of these two technologies is well beyond the scope of this book. Fortunately, there are ample resources available for both of them, so be sure to consult the appropriate documentation if there is an HTML or JavaScript concept that you do not understand.

To support the application that you will create, you need two include files, one that contains HTML styles and one that contains the Java script necessary to support several page-related functions. You can download the files from the Wrox Web site at www.wrox.com, or you can copy them from here. The first of these files is dvdstyle.css, which controls the HTML styles that define the look and feel of the application's Web pages. The styles control the formatting of various HTML attributes that can be applied to text and other objects. The following code shows the contents of the dvdstyle.css file.

```
table.title{background-color:#eeeeee}

td.title{background-color:#bed8e1;color:#1a056b;font-family:sans-serif;font-weight:
bold;font-size: 12pt}

td.heading{background-color:#486abc;color:#ffffff;font-family:sans-serif;font-
weight: bold;font-size: 9pt}

td.item{background-color:#99ff99;color:#486abc;font-family:sans-serif;font-weight:
normal;font-size: 8pt}

input.delete{background-color:#990000;color:#99ffff;font-family:sans-serif;font-
weight: normal;font-size: 8pt}

input.edit{background-color:#000099;color:#99ffff;font-family:sans-serif;font-
weight: normal;font-size: 8pt}

input.add{background-color:#000099;color:#99ffff;font-family:sans-serif;font-
weight: normal;font-size: 8pt}

td.error{background-color:#ff9999;color:#990000;font-family:sans-serif;font-weight:
bold;font-size: 9pt}
```

When you create an HTML element in your code, you can reference a particular style in the dvdstyle.css file, and then that style is applied. For example, the dvdstyle.css file includes the following style definition:

```
td.item{background-color:#99ff99;color:#486abc;font-family:sans-serif;font-weight:
normal;font-size: 8pt}
```

The `td.item` keywords identify the style definition. The `td` refers to the type of style definition, which in this case is a cell within a table, and item is the unique name given to this particular definition. The options defined within the paragraph are the various styles that apply to this definition. You can then reference this style definition in your HTML code. For example, if you are creating a table and you want a cell within that table to use this style, you would reference the item style name.

Whether you copy the file from the Web site or create the file yourself, you should save the file to the same directory where your JSP pages are stored. You can then modify the styles to meet your own needs.

The second file that you need to support the application is the dvdrentals.js file, which contains the JavaScript support functions for the web form submission. These functions allow the program to manipulate the command values and also the values of the form's action parameter. By using this technique, a user button-click can redirect the form to a different page. The following code shows the contents of the dvdrentals.js file:

```
function doEdit(button, transactionId)
{
    button.form.transaction_id.value = transactionId;
    button.form.command.value = "edit";
    button.form.action = "edit.jsp";
    button.form.submit();
}

function doAdd(button)
{
    button.form.transaction_id.value = -1;
    button.form.command.value = "add";
    button.form.action = "edit.jsp";
    button.form.submit();
}

function doDelete(button, transactionId)
{
    var message = "Deleting this record will permanently remove it.\r\n" +
                  "Are you sure you want to proceed?";

    var proceed = confirm(message);

    if(proceed)
    {
        button.form.transaction_id.value = transactionId;
        button.form.command.value = "delete";
        button.form.submit();
    }
}

function doCancel(button)
```

```
{
    button.form.command.value = "view";
    button.form.action = "index.jsp";
    button.form.submit();
}

function doSave(button, command)
{
    button.form.command.value = command;
    button.form.submit();
}
```

The dvdrentals.js file includes numerous function definitions. For example, the following JavaScript statement defines the doEdit() function:

```
function doEdit(button, transactionId)
{
    button.form.transaction_id.value = transactionId;
    button.form.command.value = "edit";
    button.form.action = "edit.jsp";
    button.form.submit();
}
```

The doEdit() function can be called from within your HTML code, usually through an <input> element that uses a button-click to initiate the function. The doEdit() function takes two parameters: button and transaction. The button parameter is used to pass the HTML button object that references the form element into the JavaScript function, and the transactionId parameter holds the transaction ID for the current record. The transactionId value, along with a command value of edit, is submitted to the form in the edit.jsp file when that file is launched. Again, whether you copy the file from the Web site or create the file yourself, you should save the dvdrentals.js file to the same directory where your JSP files are stored in your Web server.

Once you've ensured that the dvdstyle.css and dvdrentals.js file have been created and added to the appropriate directory, you're ready to begin creating your application. The first file that you create—index.jsp—provides the basic structure for the application. The file contains the Java statements necessary to establish the connection to the DVDRentals database, retrieve data from the database, and then display that data. The page lists all the transactions that currently exist in the DVDRentals database. In addition, the index.jsp file provides the foundation on which additional application functionality is built in later Try It Out sections. You can download any of the files used for the DVDRentals application created in this chapter at the Wrox Web site at www.wrox.com. The Web site also includes the build files used to implement the application on the JBoss application server.

Try It Out   Creating the index.jsp File

The following steps describe how to create the index.jsp file, which establishes a connection to the DVDRentals database and retrieves transaction-related data:

1.   The first part of the index.jsp file specifies the classes that will be used by the JSP page. Open a text editor and enter the following code:

```
<%@ page import="java.sql.*,
java.text.SimpleDateFormat,
java.lang.Integer" %>
```

2. After you specify the classes, set up the basic HTML elements that provide the structure for the rest of the page. This includes the page header, links to the dvdstyle.css and dvdrentals.js files, and the initial table structure in which to display the data retrieved from the DVDRentals database. Enter the following code:

```
<html>
<head>
    <title>DVD - Listing</title>
    <link rel="stylesheet" href="dvdstyle.css" type="text/css">
    <script language="JavaScript" src="dvdrentals.js"></script>
    </script>
</head>

<body>
<p></p>

<table cellSpacing=0 cellPadding=0 width=619 border=0>
<tr>
    <td>
        <table height=20 cellSpacing=0 cellPadding=0 width=619 bgcolor=#bed8e1
border=0>
        <tr align=left>
            <td valign="bottom" width="400" class="title">
                DVD Transaction Listing
            </td>
        </tr>
        </table>
        <br>
        <table cellSpacing="2" cellPadding="2" width="619" border="0">
        <tr>
            <td width="250" class="heading">Order Number</td>
            <td width="250" class="heading">Customer</td>
            <td width="250" class="heading">DVDName</td>
            <td width="185" class="heading">DateOut</td>
            <td width="185" class="heading">DateDue</td>
            <td width="185" class="heading">DateIn</td>
        </tr>
```

3. Next, you must declare two variables used to connect to the database and to retrieve data. Add the following statements to your file:

```
<%
// Variables for database operations
    Connection connection;
    Statement stmt;
```

4. The next section of the file first initiates a try/catch block to catch any exception that might have been thrown. From there, you can create the connection to the MySQL server and the DVDRentals database. Add the following code after the code you added in Step 2:

```
// Wrap database-related code in try/catch block to handle errors
   try
   {

// Create a DriverManager object to connect to the database
      Class.forName("com.mysql.jdbc.Driver").newInstance();

      connection = DriverManager.getConnection("jdbc:mysql://localhost/DVDRentals",
                                               "mysqlapp",
                                               "pw1");
```

The user account specified in this section of code — mysqlapp — is an account that you created in Chapter 14. The account is set up to allow you to connect from the local computer. If you did not set up this account or will be connecting to a host other than local host, you must create the correct account now. If you want to connect to the MySQL server with a hostname or username other than the ones shown here, be sure to enter the correct details. (For information about creating user accounts, see Chapter 14.)

You might decide that, for reasons of security, not to store the user account name and password in the JSP file, as is done here. Java provides other methods for accessing a MySQL database. For example, you can add the user account information to the application server's configuration file, and then use a DataSource object to reference the file.

5. In the following section you create the query that will retrieve data from the DVDRentals database and assign the results of that query to a variable. Add the following code to your file:

```
// Construct the SQL statement
      String selectSql = "SELECT " +
                          "Transactions.TransID, " +
                          "Transactions.OrderID, " +
                          "Transactions.DVDID, " +
                          "Transactions.DateOut, " +
                          "Transactions.DateDue, " +
                          "Transactions.DateIn, " +
                          "Customers.CustFN, " +
                          "Customers.CustLN, " +
                          "DVDs.DVDName " +
                          "FROM Transactions, Orders, Customers, DVDs " +
                          "WHERE Orders.OrderID = Transactions.OrderID " +
                          "AND Customers.CustID = Orders.CustID " +
                          "AND DVDs.DVDID = Transactions.DVDID " +
                          "ORDER BY Transactions.OrderID DESC, " +
                          "Customers.CustLN ASC, Customers.CustFN ASC, " +
                          "Transactions.DateDue DESC, DVDs.DVDName ASC";

// Create Statement object and execute the SQL Statement
      stmt = connection.createStatement();

      ResultSet rs = stmt.executeQuery(selectSql);
```

6. The next step is to loop through the results returned by your query. Add the following code to your application file:

```
// Loop through the result set
    while(rs.next())
    {
// Retrieve the columns from the result set into variables
        int transId = rs.getInt("TransID");
        int orderId = rs.getInt("OrderID");
        int dvdId = rs.getInt("DVDID");
        Date dateOut = rs.getDate("DateOut");
        Date dateDue = rs.getDate("DateDue");
        Date dateIn = rs.getDate("DateIn");
        String custFirstName = rs.getString("CustFN");
        String custLastName = rs.getString("CustLN");
        String dvdName = rs.getString("DVDName");
```

7. Now put the customer names and dates into a more readable format. Add the following code to your page:

```
// Format the result set data into a readable form and assign to variables
        SimpleDateFormat dateFormat = new SimpleDateFormat("MM-dd-yyyy");

        String customerName = "";
        String dateOutPrint = "";
        String dateDuePrint = "";
        String dateInPrint = "";

        if(custFirstName != null)
            customerName += custFirstName + " ";

        if(custLastName != null)
            customerName += custLastName;

        if(dvdName == null)
            dvdName = "";

        if(dateOut != null)
            dateOutPrint = dateFormat.format(dateOut);

        if(dateDue != null)
            dateDuePrint = dateFormat.format(dateDue);

        if(dateIn != null)
            dateInPrint = dateFormat.format(dateIn);
```

8. Next, insert the values retrieved from the database into an HTML table structure. Add the following code to the JSP file:

```
// Print each value in each row in the HTML table
%>
    <tr height="35" valign="top">
        <td class="item">
            <nobr>
            <%=orderId%>
            </nobr>
        </td>
```

```
            <td class="item">
                <nobr>
                <%=customerName%>
                </nobr>
            </td>
            <td class="item">
                <nobr>
                <%=dvdName%>
                </nobr>
            </td>
            <td class="item">
                <nobr>
                <%=dateOutPrint%>
                </nobr>
            </td>
            <td class="item">
                <nobr>
                <%=dateDuePrint%>
                </nobr>
            </td>
            <td class="item">
                <nobr>
                <%=dateInPrint%>
                </nobr>
            </td>
        </tr>
```

9. The final section of the file closes the connection and the Java code. It also closes the `<table>`, `<body>`, and `<html>` elements on the Web page. Add the following code to the end of the JSP file:

```
<%
        }
// Close the database objects and the HTML elements
        rs.close();
        stmt.close();
        connection.close();
    }
    catch(Exception exception)
    {
        throw exception;
    }
%>
        </table>
      </td>
</tr>
</table>
</body>
</html>
```

10. Save the index.jsp file to the appropriate Web application directory.

You might need to build your JSP application if you are using an application server. If you need to build the application in order to implement it, you should build it now and set up the application files according to the guidelines of the application server that you're using.

11. Open your browser and go to the address `http://localhost:8080/dvdapp`. The value `8080` represents the port number. If your application server or Web server use a different port number, use that one instead of `8080`. Your browser should display a page similar to the one shown in Figure 18-1.

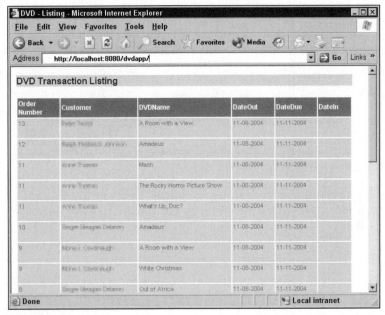

Figure 18-1

If you find that you cannot connect to the MySQL server when trying to open the JSP file, it might be because of the password encryption method used for the MySQL user account. Beginning with MySQL 4.1, a different method is used to encrypt passwords than was used in previous versions. However, some client applications have not yet implemented this new encryption method. As a result, when you try to pass the password from the Java application to MySQL, there is an encryption mismatch. You can test whether this is a problem by using the mysql client utility — logging in with the mysqlapp user account name and the pw1 password — to access the MySQL server. If you're able to log on to the server with mysql utility, then you know that the account is working fine; in which case, encryption mismatch is probably the problem. To remedy this, open the mysql client utility as the root user and execute the following SQL statement:

```
SET PASSWORD FOR 'mysqlapp'@'localhost' = OLD_PASSWORD('pw1');
```

The `OLD_PASSWORD()` function saves that password using the old encryption method, which makes the password compatible with the way your Java application has been implemented.

How It Works

The first step that you took in this exercise was to create a page directive that specified the classes that you will be using for the application, as shown in the following statement:

```
<%@ page import="java.sql.*,
java.text.SimpleDateFormat,
java.lang.Integer" %>
```

687

The page directive is enclosed in the opening and closing directive tags and includes the page keyword and the import command, which specifies the classes that you plan to use. In this case, you've specified that all classes in the java.sql package be used, plus the java.text.SimpleDateFormat and the java.lang.Integer classes. The java.sql package includes all the classes that you need to interact with a SQL database. The SimpleDateFormat class allows you to format date values, and the Integer class allows you to convert string values into primary int values.

After your page directive, you set up the opening HTML section of your index.jsp file. The <head> section establishes the necessary links to the dvdstyle.css and dvdrentals.js files. You then added a <body> section that includes two HTML <table> elements. The first table provides a structure for the page title — DVD Transaction Listing — and the second table provides the structure for the data displayed on the page. The data includes the order number, customer name, DVD name, and dates that the DVD was checked out, when it is due back, and, if applicable, when it was returned. As a result, the initial table structure that is created in this section sets up a row for the table headings and a cell for each heading.

For more information about HTML, file linking from within HTML, style sheets, and JavaScript functions, refer to the appropriate documentation.

Once you set up your HTML structure, you began the main Java section of the page, which you indicated by including an opening scriptlet tag. Following the tag, you declared two variables:

```
Connection connection;
Statement stmt;
```

The connection variable is based on the Connection class and will be used to establish a connection to the database. The stmt variable is based on the Statement class and will be used to access methods in that class. Once you declared the variables, you initiated a try/catch block by adding the following code:

```
try
{
```

The try/catch block is used to catch any exceptions that might be generated if a Java statement does not execute properly. After you set up the block, you created the statements necessary to establish a connection to the database:

```
Class.forName("com.mysql.jdbc.Driver").newInstance();

connection = DriverManager.getConnection("jdbc:mysql://localhost/DVDRentals",
                                         "mysqlapp",
                                         "pw1");
```

The first statement uses the forName() method of the class named Class to load the Driver class in the com.mysql.jdbc class package. This process locates and instantiates the Connector/J driver. The newInstance() method then creates a new class instance named DriverManager, which manages JDBC drivers.

In the next statement, you used the getConnection() method of the DriverManager class to connect to the MySQL computer on the local computer. The connection is specific to the DVDRentals database and the mysqlapp account in MySQL. The getConnection() method creates a Connection object, which is then assigned to the connection variable that you declared earlier in the code.

Once you established your connection, you declared a `String` variable named `selectSql` and assigned the necessary `SELECT` statement to that variable:

```
String selectSql = "SELECT " +
                    "Transactions.TransID, " +
                    "Transactions.OrderID, " +
                    "Transactions.DVDID, " +
                    "Transactions.DateOut, " +
                    "Transactions.DateDue, " +
                    "Transactions.DateIn, " +
                    "Customers.CustFN, " +
                    "Customers.CustLN, " +
                    "DVDs.DVDName " +
                    "FROM Transactions, Orders, Customers, DVDs " +
                    "WHERE Orders.OrderID = Transactions.OrderID " +
                    "AND Customers.CustID = Orders.CustID " +
                    "AND DVDs.DVDID = Transactions.DVDID " +
                    "ORDER BY  Transactions.OrderID DESC, Customers.CustLN ASC, " +
                    "Customers.CustFN ASC, Customers.CustMN ASC, " +
                    "Transactions.DateDue DESC, DVDs.DVDName ASC";
```

As you can see, this is a basic `SELECT` statement that joins the Transactions, Orders, Customers, and DVDs tables in the DVDRentals database. You then used the `createStatement()` method in the `Connection` object to create a `Statement` object, as shown in the following statement:

```
stmt = connection.createStatement();
```

The new `Connection` object is then assigned to the `stmt` variable, which you declared earlier in the code. You can now use the methods in the `Statement` object to execute the `SELECT` statement. To do so, you used the `executeQuery()` method and specified the `selectSql` variable as an argument to that method:

```
ResultSet rs = stmt.executeQuery(selectSql);
```

The `executeQuery()` method executes the `SELECT` statement and creates a `ResultSet` object that contains the query results returned by the statement. The `ResultSet` object is then assigned to the `rs` variable. From there, you created a while loop that uses `ResultSet` methods to process the query results:

```
while(rs.next())
{
```

The while loop begins with the `while` keyword and a condition in parentheses. Each time the condition evaluates to true, the while loop is executed. The condition uses the `next()` method of the `ResultSet` object to point to each row in the result set. Each time the while loop is executed, the `next()` method points to the next row. That row is then used by the statements within the while loop to retrieve values from the result set. For example, the first statement within the while loop retrieves a value from the TransID column and assigns that value to the `transId` variable:

```
int transId = rs.getInt("TransID");
```

To retrieve the value from the column, you used the `getInt()` method of the `ResultSet` object. The method returns a value that is a primary `int` type. That value is then assigned to the variable, which is the same type as the value. This process is repeated for each value in the row. The `ResultSet` method used depends on the type of data that is retrieved. The `getDate()` method is used for dates, and the `getString()` method is used for strings.

After you populate the variables for a particular row, you then started the process of formatting some of the values into a more readable form. The first step you took to prepare for this process was to declare a variable that creates a new `SimpleDateFormat` object:

```
SimpleDateFormat dateFormat = new SimpleDateFormat("MM-dd-yyyy");
```

The new object specifies that dates should be formatted as MM-dd-yyyy. For example, dates should have the format of 10-31-2004. The new `SimpleDateFormat` object is then assigned to the `dateFormat` variable, which is used in later code to format the dates that are retrieved from the database. Next, you declared several new variables that will be used to hold the reformatted values, at the same time, you initiated them as empty strings. For example, the following statement declares and initializes the `customerName` variable:

```
String customerName = "";
```

The `customerName` variable has been set as an empty string. The reason you did this is to ensure that if any part of a customer name is null, that null value is not displayed. That way, when you begin formatting the names, you can test for the existence of null values and assign names to the `customerName` variable only if the values are not null. If they are null, then only an empty string will be displayed or only one name, with no null values appended to the name. As a result, after you initiated the variables, you then began concatenating the names, starting with the first name, as shown in the following if statement:

```
if(custFirstName != null)
    customerName += custFirstName + " ";
```

The statement first checks whether the customer's first name is not null. If the condition evaluates to true, the value in the `custFirstName` variable, plus a space (enclosed in the pair of double quotes), is added to the `customerName` variable. Note that when a plus sign precedes an equal sign, the existing variable value is added to the new values, rather than being replaced by those values. This is better illustrated by the next if statement, which then adds the last name to the first name:

```
if(custLastName != null)
    customerName += custLastName;
```

In the case, unless the first name was null, the `customerName` variable currently holds the first name value, along with a space, which is then added to the last name value. As a result, the `customerName` variable now holds the customer's full name, displayed as first name, space, then last name.

You also used an `if` statement to ensure that the `dvdName` variable contains a string, rather than a null, as shown in the following statement:

```
if(dvdName == null)
    dvdName = "";
```

The reason for this is again to ensure that a null value is not displayed on the Web page, but rather a blank value if the DVD name is null.

Next, you formatted the dates so that they're displayed in a more readable format. To format the dates, you used the `format()` method of the `SimpleDateFormat` object assigned to the `dateFormat` variable. For example, the following statement takes the `dateOut` value and converts it into a more readable format:

```
if(dateOut != null)
    dateOutPrint = dateFormat.format(dateOut);
```

The `format()` method produces a formatted date string that is then assigned to the `dateOutPrint` variable, which, as you'll recall, is a `String` variable.

Once you have formatted the values in the way that you want, you can use the variables to display those values in an HTML table structure. This structure follows the same structure that is defined at the beginning of the file, thus providing the column heads for the rows that you now add. Keep in mind that you are still working within the while loop created earlier. So every step that you take at this point still applies to each individual row that is returned by the `next()` method.

To create the necessary row in the table, you used the scriptlet closing tag (`%>`) to get out of Java mode and back into HTML mode. You then created a cell definition for each value that is returned by the result set (and subsequently assigned to a variable). For example, you used the following definition in for first cell in the first row of the table (not counting the heading):

```
<td class="item">
    <nobr>
    <%=orderId%>
    </nobr>
</td>
```

You used the `<td>` and `</td>` elements to enclose the individual cell within the row. The `<nobr>` and `</nobr>` elements indicate that there should be no line break between the two tags. Notice that squeezed between all that is a Java variable that is enclosed by opening (`<%=`) and closing (`%>`) expression tags. As a result, the value of the `orderId` variable is displayed in that cell.

This process is repeated for each value in the row and repeated for each row until the `while` statement loops through all the rows in the result set. After the while loop, you closed the `ResultSet` object, the `Statement` object, and the `Connection` object:

```
rs.close();
stmt.close();
connection.close();
```

This process releases the application and database resources related to these objects. You should always close any objects that you no longer need. After you closed the objects, you closed the try block (by using a closing curly bracket), and then you created a catch block to catch all exceptions:

```
catch(Exception exception)
{
    throw exception;
}
```

Any exception thrown from within the try block will now be printed to a Web page. After you set up the catch block, you closed out the HTML elements and saved the file. You then opened the file in your browser and viewed the transactions in the DVDRentals database. As you discovered, you can view the transactions, but you cannot modify them. So now you can explore what steps you can take to allow your application to support data modification operations.

Inserting and Updating Data in a MySQL Database

Earlier in the chapter, you looked at how to retrieve data from a MySQL database. In this section, you look at how to insert and update data. The process you use for adding either insert or update functionality is nearly identical, except that, as you would expect, you use an INSERT statement to add data and an UPDATE statement to modify data.

Inserting and updating data is different from retrieving data in a couple ways. For one thing, when you execute a SELECT statement, you use the executeQuery() method of the Statement class to execute the query and create a ResultSet object. The data returned by the SELECT statement is contained in that new object. However, when you execute a data modification statement, you use a different approach, such as calling the executeUpdate() method of the PreparedStatement class, which executes the SQL statement and then returns an integer that represents the number of rows affected by the query. You can then use the value as necessary to display messages or take other actions.

To better understand how this works, take a look at this process one step at a time. First, as you did with the SELECT statement, you should declare a String variable and assign your SQL statement to that variable, as shown in the following example:

```
String insertSql = "INSERT INTO CDs (CDName, InStock, OnOrder, Category) VALUES
(?,?,?,?)";
```

What you probably notice immediately is that question marks are used in place of each value to be inserted. Later in the process, you will create statements that insert values in place of the question marks. However, you must first create a PreparedStatement object and assign it to a variable, as shown in the following statement:

```
PreparedStatement ps = conn.prepareStatement(insertSql);
```

As the statement shows, you create the PreparedStatement object by using the prepareStatement() method in a Connection object (which has been assigned to the conn variable). When calling the prepareStatement() method, you include the insertSql variable as an argument. The method then uses this INSERT statement to create a PreparedStatement object, which is then assigned to the ps variable. From there, you can use the variable to access methods in the PreparedStatement object that allow you to assign values to the question mark placeholders in the INSERT statement above. The following statements each assign a value to the placeholders:

```
ps.setString(1, "Beethoven Symphony No. 6 Pastoral");
ps.setInt(2, 10);
ps.setInt(3, 10);
ps.setString(4, "Classical");
```

The PreparedStatement class includes methods that are specific to the type of data that you're going to insert into the table. For example, the first statement uses the setString() method to insert a value in the CDName column of the CDs table. Notice that PreparedStatement method takes two arguments. The first argument is in integer that corresponds to the question mark placeholders in the INSERT statement. The numbers are assigned to placeholders in the order in which they appear in the SQL statement. In other words, 1 is associated with the first question mark, 2 is associated with the second question mark, and so on. The second argument in each method is the actual value to be inserted into the column. When the INSERT statement is executed, these values are used in place of the question marks.

Once you've assigned values to the placeholders, you can use the executeUpdate() method in the PreparedStatement object to execute the INSERT statement, as shown in the following statement:

```
int rowCount = ps.executeUpdate();
```

Because the INSERT statement is already associated with the PreparedStatement object (through the ps variable), you do not need to specify the query here. When the executeUpdate() method is called, the INSERT statement is executed and an integer is returned, indicating the number of rows that have been affected by the statement. This integer is then assigned to a primitive int variable. You can then use this variable to display the number of rows that have been returned or to notify users if the statement has affected no rows, depending on the needs of your users and the application that you're designing.

You could have just as easily executed an UPDATE statement in place of the INSERT statement, and the process would have been the same. It should also be noted that you can use a PreparedStatement object to execute a SELECT statement if you want to pass values into the statement as you did with the INSERT statement above. If you use this method, you must still use the executeQuery() method as you saw with other SELECT statements, and you can still process the result set. In the following Try It Out sections, you will see how all these processes work.

Adding Insert and Update Functionality to Your Application

So far, your DVDRentals application displays only transaction-related information. In this section, you add to the application so that it also allows you to add a transaction to an existing order and to modify transactions. To support the added functionality, you must create three more files — edit.jsp, insert.jsp, and update.jsp — and you must modify the index.jsp file. Keep in mind that your index.jsp file acts as a foundation for the rest of the application. You should be able to add a transaction and edit a transaction by first opening the index.jsp file and then maneuvering to wherever you need to in order to accomplish these tasks.

The first additional file that you create is the edit.jsp file. The file serves two roles: adding transactions to existing orders and editing existing transactions. These two operations share much of the same functionality, so combining them into one file saves duplicating code. If you're adding a new transaction, the Web page will include a drop-down list that displays each order number and the customer associated with that order, a drop-down list that displays DVD titles, a text box for the date the DVD is rented, and a text box for the date the DVD should be returned. The default value for the date rented text box is the current date. The default value for the date due text box is three days from the current date.

If you're editing a transaction, the Web page will display the current order number and customer, the rented DVD, the date the DVD was rented, the date it's due back, and, if applicable, the date that the DVD was returned.

The edit.jsp Web page will also contain two buttons: Save and Cancel. The Save button saves the new or updated record and returns the user to the index.jsp page. The Close button cancels the operation, without making any changes, and returns the user to the index.jsp page.

After you create the edit.jsp page, you then create the insert.jsp file and the update.jsp file in Try It Out sections that follow this one. From there, you modify the index.jsp page to link together the different functionality. Now take a look at how to create the edit.jsp file.

Creating the edit.jsp File

The following steps describe how to create the edit.jsp file, which supports adding new transactions to a record and editing existing transactions:

1. As with the insert.jsp file, you must import the necessary classes into your application. Use your text editor to start a new file, and enter the following code:

```
<%@ page import="java.sql.*,
java.text.SimpleDateFormat,
java.lang.Integer" %>
```

2. Next, you must declare and initialize a number of variables. Later in the code, you use these variables to perform different tasks, such as processing and verifying the data retrieved by a form. Add the following statements your file:

```
<%
// Initialize variables with parameters retrieved from the form
String command = request.getParameter("command");
String transactionIdString = request.getParameter("transaction_id");
String dateDueString = request.getParameter("date_due");
String orderIdString = request.getParameter("order_id");
String dvdIdString = request.getParameter("dvd_id");
String dateOutString = request.getParameter("date_out");
String dateInString = request.getParameter("date_in");

// Initialize variables with default values
java.util.Date dateDue = null;
int transId = -1;
int orderId = -1;
int dvdId = -1;
java.util.Date dateOut = null;
java.util.Date dateIn = null;

String error = "";

SimpleDateFormat dateFormat = new SimpleDateFormat("MM-dd-yyyy");

// Declare variables for database-related operations
Connection connection;
Statement statement;
```

3. As you did with the index.jsp file, you must establish a connection to the MySQL server and select the database. Add the following code to the edit.jsp file:

```
// Wrap database-access code in try/catch block to handle errors
try
{
// Create a DriverManager object to connect to the database
    Class.forName("com.mysql.jdbc.Driver").newInstance();
```

```
connection = DriverManager.getConnection("jdbc:mysql://localhost/DVDRentals",
                                          "mysqlapp",
                                          "pw1");
```

4. Next, the file should process the new or edited transactions when the user clicks the Save button. The first step in doing this is to check for missing parameters and reformat the date information. Enter the following Java code:

```
// Process the save and savenew commands
    if("save".equals(command) || "savenew".equals(command))
    {
// Check for missing parameters and reformat the dates for MySQL
        if(transactionIdString != null)
            transId = Integer.valueOf(transactionIdString).intValue();

        if(orderIdString != null)
            orderId = Integer.valueOf(orderIdString).intValue();

        if(orderId == -1)
            error += "Please select an \"Order\"<br>";

        if(dvdIdString != null)
            dvdId = Integer.valueOf(dvdIdString).intValue();

        if(dvdId == -1)
            error += "Please select a \"DVD\"<br>";

        if((dateDueString != null) && (dateDueString.length() > 0))
            dateDue = dateFormat.parse(dateDueString);
        else
            error += "Please enter a \"Date Due\"<br>";

        if((dateOutString != null) && (dateOutString.length() > 0))
            dateOut = dateFormat.parse(dateOutString);
        else
            error += "Please enter a \"Date Out\"<br>";

        if((dateInString != null) && (dateInString.length() > 0))
            dateIn = dateFormat.parse(dateInString);
```

Note that the application does not check the format of the date submitted by users. Normally, an application would include some type of mechanism to ensure that submitted dates are in a usable format.

5. Then you can carry out the update or insert by calling the applicable include files. (These files are created in later Try It Out sections.) Once the code in the applicable include file runs, you should redirect users back to the index.jsp page. Enter the following code in your file:

```
        if(error.length() == 0)
        {
            if("save".equals(command))
            {
// Run the update in update.jsp
```

```
%>
            <%@ include file="update.jsp" %>
<%
        }
        else
        {
// Run the insert in insert.jsp
%>
            <%@ include file="insert.jsp" %>
<%
        }

// Redirect the application to the listing page
        response.sendRedirect("index.jsp");
        }
    }
```

6. The next step is to set up the file to support adding or updating a record when the user has been redirected to this page from the index.jsp page. This is done as part of the else statement in an if...else structure. This particular section sets up the default values for a new record. Add the following code to your file:

```
else
    {
// If it is a new record, initialize the variables to default values
    if("add".equals(command))
    {
        transId = 0;
        orderId = 0;
        dvdId = 0;
        dateOutString = dateFormat.format(new java.util.Date());
        dateDueString = dateFormat.format(new Date((new
java.util.Date()).getTime() + 3L*24L*60L*60000L));
        dateInString = "";
    }
```

7. Next, you must set up the file with the values necessary to support editing a record. This involves retrieving records to set an initial value for a number of variables. Add the following code to your JSP file:

```
    else
    {
// If it is an existing record, read from database

        if(transactionIdString != null)
        {

// Build query from transactionId value passed down from form
        transId = Integer.valueOf(transactionIdString).intValue();

        String selectSql = "SELECT " +
                            "OrderID, " +
                            "DVDID, " +
                            "DateOut, " +
                            "DateDue, " +
```

```
                                "DateIn " +
                                "FROM Transactions " +
                                "WHERE TransID = ?";
// Execute query
            PreparedStatement preparedStatement =
connection.prepareStatement(selectSql);

            preparedStatement.setInt(1, transId);

            ResultSet rs = preparedStatement.executeQuery();

// Populate the variables for display into the form
            if(rs.next())
            {
                orderId = rs.getInt("OrderID");
                dvdId = rs.getInt("DVDID");
                dateOut = (java.util.Date) rs.getDate("DateOut");
                dateDue = (java.util.Date) rs.getDate("DateDue");
                dateIn = (java.util.Date) rs.getDate("DateIn");

// Reformat the dates into a more readable form
                if(dateOut != null)
                    dateOutString = dateFormat.format(dateOut);
                else
                    dateOutString = "";

                if(dateDue != null)
                    dateDueString = dateFormat.format(dateDue);
                else
                    dateDueString = "";

                if(dateIn != null)
                    dateInString = dateFormat.format(dateIn);
                else
                    dateInString = "";
            }

// Close the database objects
            rs.close();
            preparedStatement.close();
        }
    }
}
%>
```

8. Now you must create the HTML section of your form to allow users to view and enter data. This section includes a form to pass data to Java and the table structure to display the form. Add the following code to your JSP file:

```
<html>
<head>
    <title>DVD - Listing</title>
    <link rel="stylesheet" href="dvdstyle.css" type="text/css">
    <script language="JavaScript" src="dvdrentals.js"></script>
```

```
</head>

<body>

<form name="mainForm" method="post" action="edit.jsp">
<input type="hidden" name="command" value="view">
<input type="hidden" name="transaction_id" value="<%=transId%>">

<p></p>

<table cellspacing="0" cellPadding="0" width="619" border="0">
<tr>
   <td>
      <table height="20" cellspacing="0" cellPadding="0" width="619" border="0">
      <tr align=left>
         <td valign="bottom" width="400" class="title">
            DVD Transaction
         </td>
         <td align="right" width="219" class="title"> </td>
      </tr>
      </table>
      <br>
      <%if(error.length() > 0){%>
      <table cellspacing="2" cellPadding="2" width="619" border="0">
      <tr>
         <td width="619" class="error"><%=error%></td>
      </tr>
      </table>
      <%}%>
```

9. Now create the first row of your form, which allows users to view and select an order ID. Enter the following code in your file:

```
      <table cellspacing="2" cellPadding="2" width="619" border="0">
      <tr>
         <td width="250" class="heading">Order</td>
         <td class="item">
            <select name="order_id">
               <option value="-1">Select Order</option>
<%
// Retrieve data to populate drop-down list
   String selectSql = "SELECT " +
                      "Orders.OrderID, " +
                      "Orders.CustID, " +
                      "Customers.CustFN, " +
                      "Customers.CustLN " +
                      "FROM Orders, Customers " +
                      "WHERE " +
                      "Customers.CustID = Orders.CustID " +
                      "ORDER BY Orders.OrderID DESC, Customers.CustLN ASC, " +
                      "Customers.CustFN ASC";

// Execute the query
   statement = connection.createStatement();
   ResultSet rs = statement.executeQuery(selectSql);
```

```
   // Loop through the results
      while(rs.next())
      {
   // Assign returned values to the variables
         int orderId1 = rs.getInt("OrderID");
         String custFirstName = rs.getString("CustFN");
         String custLastName = rs.getString("CustLN");

   // Format the data for display
         String customerName = "";

         if(custFirstName != null)
            customerName += custFirstName + " ";

         if(custLastName != null)
            customerName += custLastName;

   // If the order ID matches the existing value, mark it as selected
         if(orderId1 != orderId)
         {
%>
                <option value="<%=orderId1%>"><%=orderId1%> -
<%=customerName%></option>
<%
         }
         else
         {
%>
                <option selected value="<%=orderId1%>"><%=orderId1%> -
<%=customerName%></option>
<%
         }
      }

   // Close database objects
      rs.close();
      statement.close();
%>
             </select>
           </td>
         </tr>
```

10. The second row of your form allows users to view and select a DVD to associate with your transaction. Add the following code to your edit.jsp file:

```
      <tr>
         <td class="heading">DVD</td>
         <td class="item">
            <select name="dvd_id">
               <option value="-1">Select DVD</option>
<%
   // Retrieve data to populate the drop-down list
      selectSql = "SELECT DVDID, DVDName FROM DVDs ORDER BY DVDName";

      statement = connection.createStatement();
```

```
        rs = statement.executeQuery(selectSql);

    while(rs.next())
    {
        int dvdId1 = rs.getInt("DVDID");
        String dvdName = rs.getString("DVDName");

        if(dvdName == null) dvdName = "";

        if(dvdId1 != dvdId)
        {
%>
                <option value="<%=dvdId1%>"><%=dvdName%></option>
<%
        }
        else
        {
%>
                <option selected value="<%=dvdId1%>"><%=dvdName%></option>
<%
        }
    }

// Close the database objects
    rs.close();
    statement.close();
%>
                </select>
            </td>
        </tr>
```

11. Next, create three more rows in your table, one for each date-related value. Enter the following code:

```
        <tr>
            <td class="heading">Date Out</td>
            <td class="item">
                <input type="text" name="date_out" value="<%=dateOutString%>"
size="50">
            </td>
        </tr>
        <tr>
            <td class="heading">Date Due</td>
            <td class="item">
                <input type="text" name="date_due" value="<%=dateDueString%>"
size="50">
            </td>
        </tr>
        <%if((!"add".equals(command)) && (!"savenew".equals(command))){%>
        <tr>
            <td class="heading">Date In</td>
            <td class="item">
                <input type="text" name="date_in" value="<%=dateInString%>" size="50">
            </td>
        </tr>
        <%}%>
```

12. Now add the Save and Cancel buttons to your form by appending the following code to your file:

```
        <tr>
            <td colspan="2" class="item" align="center">
                <table cellspacing="2" cellPadding="2" width="619" border="0">
                <tr>
                    <td align="center">
                        <%if(("add".equals(command)) || ("savenew".equals(command))){%>
                        <input type="button" value="Save" class="add"
onclick="doSave(this, 'savenew')">
                        <%}else{%>
                        <input type="button" value="Save" class="add"
onclick="doSave(this, 'save')">
                        <%}%>
                    </td>
                    <td align="center">
                        <input type="button" value="Cancel" class="add"
onclick="doCancel(this)">
                    </td>
                </tr>
                </table>
            </td>
        </tr>
        </table>
    </td>
</tr>
```

13. Close the various HTML elements and close your connection to the MySQL server by entering the following code:

```
</table>
</form>
</body>
</html>

<%
// Close connection and throw exceptions
    connection.close();
}
catch(Exception exception)
{
throw exception;
}
%>
```

14. Save the edit.jsp file to the appropriate Web application directory.

How It Works

In this exercise, you created the edit.jsp file, which supports the insert and update functionality in your DVDRentals application. The first step you took to set up the file was to add the page directive necessary to import the Java classes into your page. These are the same classes that you import for the index.jsp file. Once you set up the page directive, you declared and initialized a number of variables. The first set of variables is associated with values returned by the request object, which contains values submitted to the page by forms. For example, the following Java statement retrieves the command value returned by a form:

```
String command = request.getParameter("command");
```

The statement uses the getParameter() method of the request object to retrieve the command value. The value is returned as a string. As a result, a String object is automatically created. That object is then assigned to the command variable, which has been declared as a String type.

Once you assigned the form parameter values to the necessary variables, you then declared and initialized several variables used later in the code to display initial values in form. For example, the first variable that you declared was dateDue:

```
java.util.Date dateDue = null;
```

Notice that the dateDue variable is declared as a java.util.Date type. Because date values will need to be displayed, entered into a form, and subsequently added to a database, you need to create both java.util.Date objects and java.sql.Date objects. Keep in mind, however, that only the java.sql.Date class is actually imported into the page, not the java.util.Date class. So if you simply reference Date in your Java code, you're referring to the java.sql.Date class. However, whenever you're converting or manipulating date values in this page and using both types of Date objects, it's generally a good idea to use the fully qualified name in either case to ensure that you're referring to the correct Date class.

Also notice in the statement variable declaration above that an initial value of null is assigned to the dateDue variable. This is done to prepare the variable for processing later in the code, as you see in that section of the file.

The next variable that you declared and initialized was the transID variable, as shown in the following statement:

```
int transId = -1;
```

This is a straightforward primitive int type variable. You initialized the variable by assigning a -1 to the variable. The -1 value is used simply to ensure that no value is assigned that might conflict with a value retrieved by the database. As you see later in the code, the transId variable is associated with the transaction ID as it is stored in the Transactions table of the DVDRentals database. The IDs are stored in the TransID column, which is configured as a primary key. As a primary key, only positive integer values are stored in the column. As a result, by assigning an integer other than a positive integer, you're ensuring that the initial variable value will not conflict with an actual value.

Once you declared these variables, you then went on to declare the error variable and initiated it by setting its value to an empty string, as shown in the following statement:

```
String error = "";
```

The variable is used to display error messages if a user does not fill out the form properly. You set the value to an empty string so that you can use that to verify whether any error messages have been received, as you see in later in the page. After you initiated the error variable, you declared and initiated the following dateFormat variable:

```
SimpleDateFormat dateFormat = new SimpleDateFormat("MM-dd-yyyy");
```

In initiating the variable, you created a `SimpleDateFormat` object that specifies the format MM-dd-yyyy. As a result, you can use the variable to call methods in the `SimpleDateFormat` class. This variable is necessary to convert and format date values later in the page.

Next you set up a `Connection` variable and a `Statement` variable, as you did for the index.jsp file. You use these variables in the same way that you used the variables in index.jsp. After declaring the variables, you set up `if...else` statements that begin with the following if condition:

```
if("save".equals(command) || "savenew".equals(command))
```

The `if` statement specifies two conditions. The first condition uses the `equals()` method to compare the string `save` to the current value in the `command` variable. If the values are equal, the condition evaluates to true. The second condition also uses the `equals()` method to compare the string `savenew` to the `command` variable. If the values are equal, the condition evaluates to true. Because the conditions are connected by the `or (||)` operator, either condition can be true in order for the `if` statement to be executed. If neither condition is true, the `else` statement is executed.

> *The* save *and* savenew *command values are issued when you click the Save button. You learn more about that button shortly.*

The `if...else` statements contain a number of `if...else` statements embedded in them. Before getting deeper into the code that makes up all these statements, first take a look at a high overview of the logic behind these statements. It gives you a bigger picture of what's going on and should make understanding the individual components a little easier. The following pseudo-code provides an abbreviated statement structure starting with the outer `if` statement described previously:

```
if command = save or savenew, continue (if !=, go to else)
{
    if transactionIdString != null, assign to transID
    if OrderIdString != null, assign to orderId
    if OrderIdString = -1, return error message
    if dvdIdString != null, assign to dvdId
    if dvdIdString = -1, return error message
    if dateDueString != null and length > 0, assign to dateDue
        else return error message
    if dateOutString != null and length > 0, assign to dateOut
        else return error message
    if dateInString != null and length > 0, assign to dateIn
    if no error, continue
    {
        if command = save, include update.jsp
            else include insert.jsp
        redirect to index.jsp
    }
}
else (if command != save or savenew)
{
    if command = add, continue (if !=, go to else)
    {
        initialize variables (x 6)
    }
    else (if command != add)
```

```
{
    if transactionIdString != null
    {
        process query
        if query results exist, fetch results
        {
            assign variables (x 5)
            if date != null, format date and assign to String variable
                else set date to empty string (x 3)
        }
    }
}
}
```

As you can see, the action taken depends on the values in the `command` and `transactionIdString`
variables. The outer `if` statement basically determines what happens when you try to save a record, and
the outer `else` statement determines what happens when you first link to the page from the index.jsp
page. Embedded in the else statement is another set of `if...else` statements. The embedded `if` statement determines what happens if you want to add a transaction, and the embedded `else` statement
determines what happens if you want to update a transaction.

Now take a closer look at these statements. You've already seen the opening `if` statement. A number of
embedded `if` statements follow the outer `if` statement. For example, the following statements convert a
string value to an integer value and set up an error condition:

```
if(orderIdString != null)
    orderId = Integer.valueOf(orderIdString).intValue();

if(orderId == -1)
    error += "Please select an \"Order\"<br>";
```

The first `if` statement defines the condition that the `orderIdString` value should not be null. If the
condition evaluates to true, the `valueOf()` and `intValue()` methods of the `Integer` object are used to
assign a value to the `orderId` variable. The `valueOf()` method creates an `Integer` object based on the
string value assigned to the `orderIdString` variable. The `intValue()` method then returns that value
as an primitive `int` type, which is then assigned to the `orderId` variable.

The next `if` statement specifies the condition that `orderId` should equal a value of -1. If the condition
evaluates to true, an error message is returned, telling the user to select a value. (You assigned the value -1
to the variable earlier in the page, and the default value that you set up in the order ID and DVD drop-
down lists is -1.)

This section of code also includes embedded `if...else` statements. The `if` statement includes two conditions, as shown in the following code:

```
if((dateDueString != null) && (dateDueString.length() > 0))
    dateDue = dateFormat.parse(dateDueString);
else
    error += "Please enter a \"Date Due\"<br>";
```

The `if` condition specifies that the `dateDueString` value cannot be null *and* the value must have a
length greater than zero characters. If both these conditions are met, the `dateFormat` variable is used to
call the `parse()` method of the `SimpleDateFormat` class. The `parse()` method converts a string value

to a date value that is used to create a `Date` object. That object is then assigned to the `dateDue` variable. If either of the two if conditions evaluate to false, the `else` statement is executed and Java returns an error to the user.

The next step you took was to use the `length()` method to determine whether the error variable contained any characters. If the error variable is empty, the condition evaluates to true, which means that it contains no error messages and the rest of the code should be processed. This means that a file should be included in the page, as shown in the following code:

```
if(error.length() == 0)
{
    if("save".equals(command))
    {
%>
        <%@ include file="update.jsp" %>
<%
    }
    else
    {
%>
        <%@ include file="insert.jsp" %>
<%
    }
```

If no error messages are returned by the previous code, the embedded `if...else` statements are then applied. If the command value is `save`, the update.jsp file code is executed; otherwise, the insert.jsp file code is executed. (You create these files in later Try It Out sections.) Once the statements in the applicable include file are executed, the following statement is executed:

```
response.sendRedirect("index.jsp");
```

The statement uses the `sendRedirect()` method of the `response` object to redirect the user to index.jsp, which is specified as an argument in the method. This completes the outer `if` statement that initiates this section of code. However, if the `if` statement is not applicable (command does not equal save or savenew), Java executes the outer `else` statement.

The outer `else` statement is made up of its own embedded `if...else` statements. The `if` statement applies if the `command` variable currently holds the value add, as shown in the following code:

```
if("add".equals(command))
{
    transId = 0;
    orderId = 0;
    dvdId = 0;
    dateOutString = dateFormat.format(new java.util.Date());
    dateDueString = dateFormat.format(new Date((new java.util.Date()).getTime() +
3L*24L*60L*60000L));
    dateInString = "";
}
```

If `command` is set to add, this means that you are creating a new transaction. To prepare the Web page with the variables it needs to properly display the form when you open the page, you set a number of variables to specific values. For example, you set `transId` to 0, which is an unused number and so does not match any current transaction IDs.

Now take a look at the `dateOutString` variable. The goal here is to assign the current date to the variable and to assign that date as a string value. The first step is to create a new `java.util.Date` object based on the current date. This object serves as an argument to the `format()` method of the `SimpleDateFormat` class, which creates a new `String` object based on that date value. The `String` object is then assigned to the `dateOutString` variable, which can then be used to access the current date as a string value.

Next, take a look at the `dateDueString` variable. This is similar to the `dateOutString` variable except that it contains an additional element: it adds three days to the current date. It accomplishes this by using the `getTime()` method of the `Date` object to return the number of milliseconds that have passed since January 1, 1970. It then adds the equivalent of three days in milliseconds to that amount (3L days * 24L hours * 60L minutes * 60000L milliseconds). The L is included after the numbers to indicate that Java should use the long form of the `int` values to calculate the total milliseconds.

The new `java.util.Date()` object and its calculations are then passed as an argument to the `Date()` constructor in order to create a new `Date()` object. Because name of the `Date()` constructor is not fully qualified, the `java.sql.Date` class is assumed because that is the class that has been imported into the JSP page. As a result, a `Date` object is created that contains a date three days from the current date. Now you can use the `format()` method of the `SimpleDateFormat` class to convert the date value to a string, which is then assigned to the `dateDueString` variable.

After you set up the variables for the embedded `if` statement, you then added the necessary statements to the embedded `else` statement. You began the `else` block with another `if` statement that verifies that the `transactionIdString` variable is not null, as shown in the following code:

```
if(transactionIdString != null)
```

If the value is not null (a value does exist), the remaining part of the `if` statement is executed. This means that you are editing an existing transaction, in which case, the `transactionIdString` variable identifies that transaction. However, the value is returned as a string, but transaction IDs are stored in the database as integers. As a result, you used `Integer` class methods to convert the string value to an integer value. From there, you created a `SELECT` statement and assigned it to the `selectSql` variable:

```
String selectSql = "SELECT " +
                   "OrderID, " +
                   "DVDID, " +
                   "DateOut, " +
                   "DateDue, " +
                   "DateIn " +
                   "FROM Transactions " +
                   "WHERE TransID = ?";
```

As you can see, the `SELECT` statement includes a question mark placeholder. To assign a variable to the placeholder, you first created a `PreparedStatement` object, assigned a value to the placeholder, and executed the statement, as shown in the following code:

```
PreparedStatement preparedStatement = connection.prepareStatement(selectSql);
preparedStatement.setInt(1, transId);
ResultSet rs = preparedStatement.executeQuery();
```

The first statement uses the `prepareStatement()` method of the `Connection` class to create a `PreparedStatement` object based on the `SELECT` statement. The object is then assigned to the `preparedStatement` variable. You then used the `setInt()` method of the new `PreparedStatement` object to set the question mark placeholder to the value associated with the `transId` variable. Next, you used the `executeQuery()` method to execute the `SELECT` statement and create a `ResultSet` object, which is assigned to the `rs` variable. Once you set up the query, you used an `if` statement and `next()` method to process the result set. Because only one row is returned by the query, you do not need to use a while loop.

When you processed the result set, you used `ResultSet` methods to assign values to variables. This is the same method that you use in the index.jsp file to process query results. However, there is one element that you didn't see in the index.jsp file, as shown in the following statement:

```
dateOut = (java.util.Date) rs.getDate("DateOut");
```

Notice that, following the equal sign, the statement includes the `java.util.Date` class enclosed in parentheses. This is known as *casting* and is used to convert an object from a subclass to a parent class type. (The `java.sql.Date` class inherits from `java.util.Date` class.) The date value retrieved from the `DateOut` column is converted from a `java.sql.Date` value to a `java.util.Date` value when it is assigned to the `dateOut` variable, which is how it is retrieved from the database. You did this so that you can then convert the date values to strings, as shown in the following code:

```
if(dateOut != null)
    dateOutString = dateFormat.format(dateOut);
else
    dateOutString = "";
```

If the `dateOut` value is not null, the value is converted to a string and assigned to the `dateOutString` variable, otherwise the variable is set to an empty string. The first step (the `if` statement) is necessary to display the value on the form, and the second step (the `else` statement) is necessary to ensure that null is not displayed, should the value be null.

Once you set up the data to populate the form, you have completed the `if...else` block of code. If necessary, refer to the summary code provided at the beginning of this description. This provides a handy overview of what is going on.

The next section of code that you created set up the HTML for the Web page. As with the index.jsp file, the HTML section includes header information that links to the dvdstyle.css file and the dvdrentals.js file. The section also includes a `<form>` element and two `<input>` elements:

```
<form name="mainForm" method="post" action="edit.jsp">
<input type="hidden" name="command" value="view">
<input type="hidden" name="transaction_id" value="<%=transId%>">
```

A form is an HTML structure that allows a user to enter or select data and then submit that data. The data can then be passed on to other Web pages or to the Java code. This particular form uses the `post` method to send data (`method="post"`) and sends that data to the current page (`action="edit.jsp"`). Beneath the form, you added two `<input>` elements that create the initial values to be inserted into the `command` and `transaction_id` parameters. The `command` parameter is set to `view`, and the `transaction_id` parameter is set to the value contained in the `transId` variable. To use the variable to set the `transaction_id` value, you must enclose the variable in Java opening and closing expression tags so the value can be used by the form. Also note that the input type for both `<input>` elements is `hidden`, which means that the user does not actually see these two elements. Instead, they serve only as a way to pass the `command` and `transaction_id` values, which is done in the background. The user does not enter these values.

Forms are a common method used in HTML to pass data between pages. It is also useful for passing values between HTML and Java. For more information about forms, consult the applicable HTML documentation.

After you defined the form, you then set up the table to display the heading DVD Transaction at the top of the page. From there, you added another table whose purpose is to display error messages, as shown in the following code:

```
<%if(error.length() > 0){%>
<table cellspacing="2" cellPadding="2" width="619" border="0">
<tr>
    <td width="619" class="error"><%=error%></td>
</tr>
</table>
<%}%>
```

The HTML table structure is preceded by Java opening and closing scriptlet tags so that you can use an if statement to specify a condition in which the table will be displayed. The if statement specifies that the error variable must contain a string whose length is greater than zero characters. This is done by using the length() method to determine the length of the error value and then comparing the length to zero. If the condition evaluates to true, the table is created and the error is printed. At the end of the table, you again used a pair of opening and closing scriptlet tags to add the closing bracket of the if statement.

Once you have established a way for error messages to be displayed, you set up the table that will be used to display the part of the form that they user sees. The first row of the form will contain a drop-down list of order IDs — along with the customer names associated with those orders — that the user will be able to select from when adding a transaction. To populate this drop-down list, you retrieved data from the database, processed the data, and formatted the customer name. The methods used for retrieving and processing the data are the same methods that you've already used in the application. Once you retrieved the value, you added another form element to your Web page, only this form element is visible to the user:

```
        if(orderId1 != orderId)
        {
%>
                <option value="<%=orderId1%>"><%=orderId1%> -
<%=customerName%></option>
<%
        }
        else
        {
%>
                <option selected value="<%=orderId1%>"><%=orderId1%> -
<%=customerName%></option>
<%
        }
```

The form element shown here is an <option> element. An <option> element allows a user to select from a list of options in order to submit data to the form. There are actually two <option> elements here, but only one is used. This is because Java if...else statements enclose the <option> elements.

The `if` statement condition specifies that `orderId1` should not equal `orderId`. If they are not equal, the `if` statement is executed and the first `<option>` element is used, otherwise the second `<option>` element is used. The second element includes the selected option, which means that the current order ID is the selected option when the options are displayed.

The `orderId1` variable receives its value from the results returned by the `SELECT` statement used to populate the `<option>` element. The `orderId` variable receives its value from the `SELECT` statement that is used to assign values to variables once it has been determined that the user is editing an existing transaction. (This occurs when the `if...else` statements earlier in the code are processed.) If the two values are equal, the second `<option>` element is used, which means that the current order ID is displayed when this page is loaded. If the two values are not equal, which is the condition specified in the `if` statement, no order ID is displayed, which you would expect when creating a new record.

The next row that you created for your form table allows users to select from a list of DVD names. The same logic is used to create the drop-down list available to the users. The only difference is that, because only DVD names are displayed, no special formatting or concatenation is required to display the values.

After you created your two rows that display the drop-down lists to the users, you created three date-related rows. Each row provides a text box in which users can enter the appropriate dates. For example, the first of these rows includes the following form element:

```
<input type="text" name="date_out" value="<%=dateOutString%>" size="50">
```

As you can see, this is an `<input>` element, similar to the ones that you created when you first defined the form. Only the input type on this one is not hidden, but instead is text, which means that a text box will be displayed. The name of the text box is `date_out`. This is actually the name of the parameter that will hold the value that is submitted by the user. The initial value displayed in the text box depends on the value of the `dateOutString` variable. For new records, this value is the current date, and for existing records, this is the value as it currently exists in the database. (Both these values are determined in the earlier Java code.)

Once you completed setting up the various form elements, you added two more elements: one for the Save button and one for the Cancel button. For example, your code for the Save button is as follows:

```
<td align="center">
  <%if(("add".equals(command)) || ("savenew".equals(command))){%>
  <input type="button" value="Save" class="add" onclick="doSave(this, 'savenew')">
  <%}else{%>
  <input type="button" value="Save" class="add" onclick="doSave(this, 'save')">
  <%}%>
</td>
```

A button is also an `<input>` element on a form, but the type is specified as `button`. The value for this element determines the name that appears on the button, which in this case is Save. The `class` option specifies the style that should be used in the button, as defined in the dvdstyle.css file, and the `onclick` option specifies the action to be taken. In this case, the action is to execute the `doSave()` function, which is defined in the dvdrentals.js file.

Notice that there are again two `<input>` elements, but only one is used. If the command value equals add or savenew, the first `<input>` element is used, otherwise the second `<input>` element is used.

When you click the Save button, the `doSave()` function is called. The function takes one argument, `this`, which is a self-referencing value that indicates that the action is related to the current HTML input button. When the function is executed, it submits the form to the edit.jsp file and sets the `command` parameter value to `savenew` or `save`, depending on which `<input>` option is used. Based on the `command` value, the Java script is processed once again, only this time, the first `if` statement (in the large `if...else` construction) evaluates to true and that statement is executed. Assuming that there are no errors, the date values are reformatted for MySQL, the Java code in the update.jsp or insert.jsp include file is executed, and the user is redirected to the index.jsp page.

As you can see, the edit.jsp page provides the main logic that is used to insert and update data. However, as the code in this page indicates, you must also create the include files necessary to support the actual insertion and deletion of data. In the next Try It Out section, you create the insert.jsp file. The file contains only that script that is necessary to insert a record, based on the values provided by the user in the edit.jsp form.

Try It Out Creating the insert.jsp file

The following steps describe how to create the insert.jsp file:

1. In your text editor, create a new file and enter the following code:

```
<%
// Build the INSERT statement with parameter references
String insertSql = "INSERT INTO Transactions (OrderID, DVDID, DateOut, DateDue)
VALUES (?, ?, ?, ?)";

PreparedStatement preparedStatement = connection.prepareStatement(insertSql);

// Set the parameters
preparedStatement.setInt(1, orderId);
preparedStatement.setInt(2, dvdId);
preparedStatement.setDate(3, new java.sql.Date(dateOut.getTime()));
preparedStatement.setDate(4, new java.sql.Date(dateDue.getTime()));

// Execute the INSERT statement
int rowCount = preparedStatement.executeUpdate();

preparedStatement.close();
%>
```

2. Save the insert.jsp file to the appropriate Web application directory.

How It Works

In this exercise, you created the insert.jsp file, which is an include file for edit.jsp. The first step you took in creating the insert.jsp file was to assign an `INSERT` statement to the `insertSql` variable:

```
String insertSql = "INSERT INTO Transactions (OrderID, DVDID, DateOut, DateDue)
VALUES (?, ?, ?, ?)";
```

Instead of including the values to be inserted into the MySQL database, the statement includes four question mark placeholders. Values for the placeholders are defined later in the file.

After you created the INSERT statement, you assigned a PreparedStatement object to a variable:

```
PreparedStatement preparedStatement = connection.prepareStatement(insertSql);
```

First, you used the prepareStatement() method in the Connection class (accessed through the connection variable) to create a PreparedStatement object based on the INSERT statement. You then used methods in that object to assign values to the question mark placeholders. For example, the following statement uses the setInt() method to assign the value in the orderId variable to the first placeholder:

```
preparedStatement.setInt(1, orderId);
```

When you insert a date value in an SQL database, you must be certain that the value conforms to SQL standard. To do this, you must first use the setDate() method to specify the value to be inserted, as shown in the following statement:

```
preparedStatement.setDate(3, new java.sql.Date(dateOut.getTime()));
```

In this case, the setDate() method assigns the current date to the question mark placeholder. This is done by first using the getTime() method of the Date() object (accessed through the dateOut variable) to specify the date in the dateOut variable in milliseconds. Next, you created a java.sql.Date object based on dateOut.getTime(), which ensures that the date is passed to the in the format correct for SQL.

After you assigned values to the placeholders, you used the executeUpdate() method of the PreparedStatement class to execute the INSERT statement and to return the number of rows in the database that were affected by the statement. This number is a primitive int value and is assigned to the rowCount variable, as shown in the following statement.

```
int rowCount = preparedStatement.executeUpdate();
```

If you want, you can use this variable to take some sort of action, such as return a message to a user or log the results.

In addition to creating the insert.jsp file, you must also create the update.jsp file. This file works just like the insert.jsp file in that it is included in the edit.jsp file. This has the same effect as including the statements directly into the edit.jsp file. In the following Try it Out section, you create the update.jsp file.

Try It Out   Creating the update.jsp file

The following steps describe how to create the update.jsp file:

1.   Open a new file in your text editor, and enter the following code:

```
<%
// Build the UPDATE statement with parameters references
String updateSql = "UPDATE Transactions SET OrderID = ?, DVDID = ?, DateOut = ?,
DateDue = ?, DateIn = ? WHERE TransID = ?";

PreparedStatement preparedStatement = connection.prepareStatement(updateSql);

// Set the parameters
```

```
preparedStatement.setInt(1, orderId);
preparedStatement.setInt(2, dvdId);
preparedStatement.setDate(3, new java.sql.Date(dateOut.getTime()));
preparedStatement.setDate(4, new java.sql.Date(dateDue.getTime()));

// Provide a default value for the DateIn column if no value is provided
if(dateIn != null)
    preparedStatement.setDate(5, new java.sql.Date(dateIn.getTime()));
else
    preparedStatement.setString(5, "0000-00-00");

preparedStatement.setInt(6, transId);

// Execute the UPDATE statement
int rowCount = preparedStatement.executeUpdate();

preparedStatement.close();
%>
```

2. Save the update.jsp file to the appropriate Web application directory.

How It Works

In this exercise, you created the update.jsp file. The file uses the same types of objects and methods that you used in the insert.jsp file. First, you created an update statement that you assigned to the updateSql variable. Then you used the prepareStatement() method of the Connection class to create a PreparedStatement object and assign that object to the preparedStatement variable. From there, you used PreparedStatement methods to assign values to the placeholders. You then used the executeUpdate() method to execute the SQL statement and return an integer to the rowCount variable. The only new element added to the update.jsp file is the following statement:

```
if(dateIn != null)
    preparedStatement.setDate(5, new java.sql.Date(dateIn.getTime()));
else
    preparedStatement.setString(5, "0000-00-00");
```

This statement is a little different from what you've seen so far, although the elements that make up the statement should be familiar to you. First, you used the getTime() method retrieved through the dateIn variable to return that date in milliseconds. You passed this value as an argument in the java.sql.Date() constructor in order to create a new Date object based on that value. You then assigned that date value to the fifth question mark placeholder in your UPDATE statement.

The steps that you took to assign the value to the fifth placeholder apply only if the condition in the if statement evaluates to true, otherwise the else statement is executed. If that occurs, the value is set to 0000-00-00. This is done because the DateIn column in the Transaction table does not permit null values. As a result, if a value is not known, MySQL uses 0000-00-00 as the default.

Now that you have created the insert.jsp file and the update.jsp file, only one step remains to set up your application to insert and update data. You must modify the index.jsp file so that it includes the functionality necessary to link the user to the edit.jsp page. The following Try It Out section explains how to modify the index.jsp file. It then walks you through the process of inserting a transaction and then modifying that transaction.

Modifying the index.jsp File

The following steps describe how to modify the index.jsp file to support the insert and update operations:

1. In your text editor, open the index.jsp file. Add a form, an `<input>` element, and a cell definition to your HTML code. Add the following code (shown with the gray screen background) to your file:

```html
<html>
<head>
    <title>DVD - Listing</title>
    <link rel="stylesheet" href="dvdstyle.css" type="text/css">
    <script language="JavaScript" src="dvdrentals.js"></script>
    </script>
</head>

<body>

<form name="mainForm" method="post" action="index.jsp">
<input type="hidden" name="command" value="view">
<input type="hidden" name="transaction_id" value="">

<p></p>

<table cellSpacing=0 cellPadding=0 width=619 border=0>
<tr>
    <td>
        <table height=20 cellSpacing=0 cellPadding=0 width=619 bgcolor=#bed8e1
border=0><TBODY>
        <tr align=left>
            <td valign="bottom" width="400" class="title">
                DVD Transaction Listing
            </td>
            <td align="right" width="219" class="title">
                <input type="button" value="New Transaction" class="add"
onclick="doAdd(this)">
            </td>
        </tr>
        </table>
        <br>
        <table cellSpacing="2" cellPadding="2" width="619" border="0">
        <tr>
            <td width="250" class="heading">Order Number</td>
            <td width="250" class="heading">Customer</td>
            <td width="250" class="heading">DVDName</td>
            <td width="185" class="heading">DateOut</td>
            <td width="185" class="heading">DateDue</td>
            <td width="185" class="heading">DateIn</td>
            <td width="99" class="heading"> </td>
        </tr>
```

When adding code to you file, be sure to add it in the position shown here.

2. Next, add an HTML table cell and an `<input>` element to the area of code that prints out the values returned by the database. Add the following code (shown with the gray screen background) to your file:

```
<td class="item">
    <nobr>
    <%=dateInPrint%>
    </nobr>
</td>
    <td class="item" valign="center" align="center">
        <input type="button" value="Edit" class="edit" onclick="doEdit(this,
<%=transId%>)">
    </td>
</tr>
```

3. Now you must close the form, which you do near the end of the file. To close the form, you must use a `</form>` element. Add the following code (shown with the gray screen background) to the end of the JSP file:

```
    </table>
    </td>
</tr>
</table>
</form>
</body>
</html>
```

4. Save the index.jsp file.

5. Open your browser and go to the address `http://localhost:8080/dvdapp` (or to whichever address you're using for the application). The value `8080` represents the port number. If your application server or Web server use a different port number, use that one instead of `8080`. Your browser should display a page similar to the one shown in the Figure 18-2.

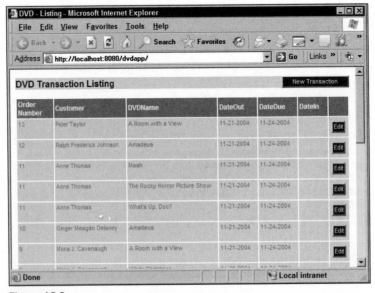

Figure 18-2

6. Click the New Transaction button at the top of the page. Your browser should display a page similar to the one shown in the Figure 18-3.

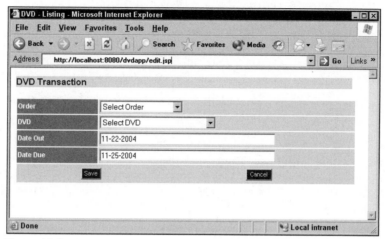

Figure 18-3

7. Now add a transaction to an existing order. In the Order drop-down list, select 13 - Peter Taylor. In the DVD drop-down list, select *Out of Africa*. Click Save. You're returned to the index.jsp page. The new transaction should now be displayed at the top of the list.

8. Now edit the new transaction. In the row of the transaction that you just added, click the Edit button. Your browser should display a page similar to the one shown in the Figure 18-4.

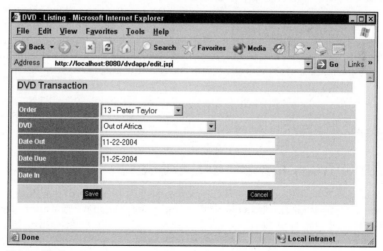

Figure 18-4

9. In the Date In text box, type the same date that is in the Date Due text box. Be certain to type the date in the same format that is used for the other date-related text boxes. Click the Save button. You should be returned to the index.jsp page.

How It Works

In this exercise, you added a form to your index.jsp file. This is similar to the form that you added to the edit.jsp file. The main difference between the two is that, in this form, the transaction_id value is set to an empty string. This is because no ID is necessary initially, but you want the parameter to exist so that a vehicle has been provided to pass that ID through the form when you submit the form.

Once you created the form, you added the following HTML cell definition and `<input>` element at the top of the page:

```
<td align="right" width="219" class="title">
   <input type="button" value="New Transaction" class="add" onclick="doAdd(this)">
</td>
```

As you can see, the input type is `button` and it calls the JavaScript `doAdd()` function. The function links the user to the edit.jsp page, allowing the user to create a new transaction. At the same time, the function passes a `command` value of `add` to the edit.jsp page. That way, the edit.jsp page knows that a new transaction is being created and responds accordingly. You next added the following code to the initial table structure that is created in the HTML code:

```
<td width="99" class="heading"> </td>
```

This creates an additional column head in the table to provide a column for the Edit button that will be added to each row returned by your query results. Finally, you added the actual cell and button to your table definition, as shown in the following code:

```
<td class="item" valign="center" align="center">
   <input type="button" value="Edit" class="edit" onclick="doEdit(this,
<%=transId%>)">
</td>
```

The Edit button calls the `doEdit()` function, which passes the transaction ID to the form and links the user to the edit.jsp page. At the same time, the function passes the `command` value of `edit` so that when the edit.jsp page opens, it has the information it needs to allow the user to edit a current record.

Once you modified and saved the file, you opened the index.jsp page, created a transaction, and then edited that transaction. However, the application still does not allow you to delete a transaction. As a result, the next section describes how you can set up Java statements to delete data.

Deleting Data from a MySQL Database

Deleting MySQL data from within your Java application is just like inserting and updating data. You must use the same Java statement elements. For example, suppose that you want to delete a CD listing from a table name CDs. The ID for the specific CD is store in the `cdId` variable. You can use the following statements to set up your application to delete the data:

```
String deleteSQL = "DELETE FROM CDs WHERE CDID = ?";
PreparedStatement preparedStatement = connection.prepareStatement(deleteSQL);
preparedStatement.setInt(1, cdId);
int rowCount = preparedStatement.executeUpdate();
```

As with inserting and updating data, you first assign the SQL statement to a variable (`deleteSql`). You then create a `PreparedStatement` object based on the `DELETE` statement and assign that object to a variable (`preparedStatement`). Finally you use a method in the `PreparedStatement` class to assign a value to the variable. In this case, you use the `setInt()` method to assign the value in the `cdId` variable to the placeholder in the `DELETE` statement. Finally, you use the `executeUpdate()` method in the `PreparedStatement` class to execute the `DELETE` statement and return a row count, which is assigned to the `rowCount` variable.

As you can see, deleting data is no more difficult than updating or inserting data. The key to any of these types of statements is to make sure that you set up your variables in such a way that the correct information can be passed to the SQL statement when it is being executed. In the next Try It Out section, you see how you can delete a transaction from your database. To do so, you modify the index.jsp file and then create a delete.jsp include file.

Try It Out   Modifying the index.jsp File and Creating the delete.jsp File

The following steps describe how to set up delete capabilities in your DVDRentals application:

1. First, add a column head to your table so that you can include a Delete button for each row. The button will be added next to the Edit button you added in the previous Try It Out section. Add the following code (shown with the gray screen background) to your file:

```
<tr>
    <td width="250" class="heading">Order Number</td>
    <td width="250" class="heading">Customer</td>
    <td width="250" class="heading">DVDName</td>
    <td width="185" class="heading">DateOut</td>
    <td width="185" class="heading">DateDue</td>
    <td width="185" class="heading">DateIn</td>
    <td width="99" class="heading"> </td>
    <td width="99" class="heading"> </td>
</tr>
```

2. Next, add the code necessary to initialize variables and call the delete.jsp include file. Add the following code (shown with the gray screen background) to your file:

```
<%
// Declare and initialize variables with parameters retrieved from the form

    String command = request.getParameter("command");
    String transactionIdString = request.getParameter("transaction_id");

// Declare and initialize variables for database operations

    Connection connection;
    Statement stmt;

// wrap the database code in a try catch block to handle any database related
// errors. the Catch statements are at the bottom.

    try
    {
// Create the connection
```

```
// Get the connection from DriverManager, this technique for getting the connection
// is generally not recommended for "real" applications because the password is in
the file.

        Class.forName("com.mysql.jdbc.Driver").newInstance();

        connection = DriverManager.getConnection("jdbc:mysql://localhost/DVDRentals",
                                                  "mysqlapp",
                                                  "pw1");
```

```
// Process the delete command

    if(transactionIdString != null)
    {
        int transactionId = Integer.valueOf(transactionIdString).intValue();

        if("delete".equals(command))
        {
// Include the delete.jsp file
%>
            <%@ include file="delete.jsp" %>
<%
        }
    }
```

3. Now add the actual Delete button by adding the following code (shown with the gray-screen background) to your file:

```
        <td class="item">
            <nobr>
            <%=dateInPrint%>
            </nobr>
        </td>
        <td class="item" valign="center" align="center">
            <input type="button" value="Edit" class="edit" onclick="doEdit(this,
<%=transId%>)">
        </td>
        <td class="item" valign="center" align="center">
            <input type="button" value="Delete" class="delete"
onclick="doDelete(this, <%=transId%>)">
        </td>
    </tr>
```

4. Save the index.jsp file.

5. Create a new file named delete.jsp in your text editor, and enter the following code:

```
<%
// Build the DELETE statement with a transactionId parameter reference
String deleteSQL = "DELETE FROM Transactions WHERE TransID = ?";

PreparedStatement preparedStatement = connection.prepareStatement(deleteSQL);

// Set the TransID parameter
preparedStatement.setInt(1, transactionId);

// Execute the DELETE statement
```

```
int rowCount = preparedStatement.executeUpdate();

preparedStatement.close();
%>
```

6. Save the delete.jsp file to the appropriate Web application directory.

7. Open your browser and go to the address `http://localhost:8080/dvdapp`. Your browser should display a page similar to the one shown in the Figure 18-5.

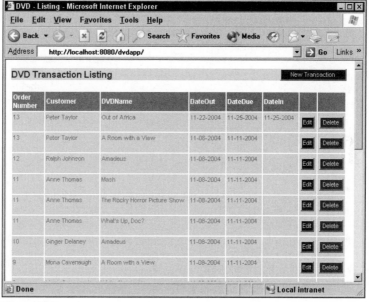

Figure 18-5

8. Click the Delete button in the row that contains the transaction that you created in a previous Try It Out section (Order number 13, DVD name *Out of Africa*). A message box similar to the one in Figure 18-6 appears, confirming whether you want to delete the record.

Figure 18-6

9. Click OK to delete the record. The index.jsp file should be redisplayed, with the deleted file no longer showing.

How It Works

In this exercise, you first created an additional column head for a column what will hold the Delete button for each row. You t.hen entered the following code:

```
String command = request.getParameter("command");
String transactionIdString = request.getParameter("transaction_id");
```

Both statements use the getParameter() method of the request object to retrieve parameter values from the form. The values are then assigned to the appropriate variables, which can then be used in your Java code just like any other variables. Next, you added the code necessary to include the delete.jsp file (which you create in a later step):

```
        if(transactionIdString != null)
        {
            int transactionId = Integer.valueOf(transactionIdString).intValue();

            if("delete".equals(command))
            {
%>
                <%@ include file="delete.jsp" %>
<%
            }
        }
```

The first if condition verifies that the transactionIdString variable contains a value. If the condition evaluates to true, the if block is executed. Next, you uses the valueOf() and intValue() methods of the Integer class to convert the transactionIdString value to an integer and assign it to the transactionId variable. The next if condition specifies that the command value must equal delete in order to proceed. If the condition evaluates to true, the delete.jsp file is included in the current file. This means that the Java statements in delete.jsp are executed as though they are actually part of the insert.jsp file.

The last code that you added to the index.jsp file is the HTML cell definition and <input> element necessary to add the Delete button to each row displayed on the page:

```
<td class="item" valign="center" align="center">
    <input type="button" value="Delete" class="delete" onclick="doDelete(this,
<%=transId%>)">
</td>
```

As you can see, the input type is button (type="button"), the button is named Delete (value="Delete"), the style is delete (class="delete"), and the doDelete() function is executed when the button is clicked. The doDelete() function takes two parameters. The this parameter merely indicates that it is the current button that is being referenced. The second parameter passes the value in the transId variable to the transactionId parameter associated with the form. That way, Java knows what record to delete when the DELETE statement is executed.

Now your application should be complete, at least this part of the application. You can view, insert, update, and delete transactions. In addition, you can build on this application if you want to extend your application's functionality. The code used to create this application is available online at www.wrox.com, and you can use and modify that code as necessary. Keep in mind, however, that at the heart of your application is the MySQL database that manages the data that you need to run your application. The better you understand MySQL and data management, the more effective your applications can be.

Summary

In this chapter, you learned how you can build a Java application that interacts with a MySQL database. The chapter included information about connecting to a MySQL server and database, retrieving data, and modifying data. Because Java is an object-oriented program, much of the discussion and examples in the chapter focused on how Java classes and their objects are used to interact with a MySQL database. You then used this information to create a JSP application that retrieved data from the DVDRentals database and modified that data. Specifically, the chapter covered the following topics:

- ❑ Specifying the Java classes to include in your application
- ❑ Connecting to the MySQL server and selecting a database
- ❑ Using if statements to test conditions and take actions
- ❑ Retrieving data, formatting data, and then displaying data
- ❑ Inserting data into your database
- ❑ Updating existing data in your database
- ❑ Deleting data from your database

The principles covered in this chapter can apply to any Java application that interacts with a MySQL database. The important point to remember with Java is that you are always working within the context of objects. These objects provide the structure for everything from establishing database connections to assigning string values to variables. Many of the concepts that you learned in this chapter can be applied to more extensive Java applications, including non-JSP applications. In all cases, the fundamentals of objects and connecting to a MySQL database are the same. And now that you have a foundation in how Java interacts with MySQL, you're ready to move on to the next chapter, which describes how to create a C# ASP.NET application that accesses a MySQL database.

Exercises

In this chapter, you learned how to connect to a MySQL database, retrieve data, and manipulate data from within a Java application. To assist you in better understanding how to perform these tasks, the chapter includes the following exercises. To view solutions to these exercises, see Appendix A.

1. You are creating a JSP file. You plan to use all classes in the java.sql package. What statement should you use to import those classes into your file?

2. You want to create a variable named strBook to hold a book title value. You plan to create a String object and assign it to the variable. The object will contain the string value *The Open Space of Democracy*, which is the title of the book. What statement should you use to declare and initialize the parameter?

3. You are establishing a connection to a MySQL database from with your JSP application. You plan to connect to the books database using the usr1 user account, which requires the pw1 password. The MySQL server resides on the same computer that the application will run. You have already declared the conn variable based on the Connection class. What Java statements should you use to establish the connection?

4. You are retrieving data from a MySQL database. You create a SELECT statement and assign it to the selectSql variable. You then create a Statement object and assign it to the stmt variable. You now want to execute the statement. You also want to assign the result set to a variable named rs. What statement should you use to execute the SELECT statement and initialize the rs variable?

5. Your application includes the Java code necessary to retrieve data from a MySQL database into a ResultSet object. You have assigned that object to a variable named rs. The result set includes data from the CDName column and the InStock column of the CDs table. You now want to display each row returned by the query. You plan to use the System.out.println() method to print out the values in the column. What java elements and statements should you to retrieve and display the data in the result set?

6. You want to convert a numerical string value to an integer and assign the value to a primitive int variable. The string value is 530, and the name of the variable is intValue. What Java statement should you use to convert the string value?

7. You are adding code to your Java application to insert data into a MySQL database. You create an INSERT statement and assign it to the insertSql variable. You also declare a variable named conn, which is based on the Connection class. You now want to create a PreparedStatement object based on the INSERT statement and then assign the new object to the ps variable. What Java statement should you use?

19

Connecting to MySQL from an ASP.NET/C# Application

MySQL allows users to access its databases from a variety of applications. If you reviewed chapters 17 or 18, you've seen how you can connect to MySQL from PHP and Java. In both cases, you can implement these types of applications from within any Web or application environment that supports the particular language. However, MySQL provides access from another type of application, the type that is implemented within the context of the Microsoft .NET Framework. The .NET Framework is an application development and implementation environment that supports a wide range of technologies. The framework is made up primarily of a library of code that can be utilized by a variety of application languages, such as C#, Visual Basic .NET, and JScript .NET. The .NET Framework also defines an extensive system of data types that facilitate the interoperability of languages that use the framework. The framework also provides the Common Language Runtime (CLR), which maintains the execution of applications developed through the .NET library.

An important component of the .NET Framework is ASP.NET, which allows you to create dynamic Web pages similar to what you'll find with Java and JSP. However, because ASP.NET is part of the .NET Framework, you can utilize the .NET library when developing Web-based applications. In addition, you can use any of the languages supported by .NET to create your application. In this chapter, you learn how to create an ASP.NET application based on C#. The reason that C# has been chosen is because it is the most powerful language supported by the .NET Framework and the only language that was developed with .NET in mind. (A language such as Visual Basic .NET was updated with .NET in mind, but not created for .NET.) By using C# and ASP.NET to develop your Web pages, you can create robust, powerful applications that can include a rich assortment of features and functionality. As a way to introduce you to ASP.NET and C#, and how you can access a MySQL database from within your application, this chapter covers the following topics:

❑ Introduces you to ASP.NET and C# and how they communicate with a MySQL server and its databases

❑ Explains how to build an ASP.NET/C# application that connects to a MySQL database, retrieves data from that database, inserts data into the database, modifies the data, and then deletes the data

Introduction to ASP.NET/C#

ASP.NET is a server-side technology that allows you to provide dynamic Web content to your users. Working in conjunction with the .NET Framework, ASP.NET is a component that is attached to your Web server, allowing you to display ASP.NET Web pages on any browser just like basic HTML pages. To build an ASP.NET application, you can use a full-fledged programming language such as C#. A programming language such as C# is far more powerful and extensive than a server-side scripting languages such as PHP and VBScript. As a result, you can build applications that extend far beyond the capabilities of those built with simple server-side scripting languages.

Just like Java, C# is an object-oriented programming (OOP) language. The C# language is based on the concept of encapsulating code and the data that it manipulates into defined objects. Each object is based on an object class that specifies how that object can be built. An object, then, is an instance of the class from which it is derived.

In C#, an object is made up of properties and methods. *Properties* represent data that describe the object. The property values are what distinguish multiple instances of an object class from one another. *Methods* perform some type of action on that data. A method is similar to a function in the way in which it performs a predefined task. For example, suppose that you have a class named CompactDisk. The class might include three properties, one to identify the CD, one to identify the number in stock, and one to identify the number on order. The class also includes a method that calculates the total number of CDs that will be available by adding the values in the last two properties. As you can see, the three properties contain data about the CD and the method performs an action on that data. Together, these elements make up the CompactDisk class. You can then create an object based on the new class and assign unique values to the properties.

Of course, the CompactDisk example is an over-simplification of how objects work within C#; however, it should provide you with at least an overview of how properties and methods work. Although a thorough discussion of OOP is beyond the scope of this book, it's important that you recognize that C# is based on these concepts and that everything you do in C# is within the context of objects. For example, suppose that you retrieve data from a MySQL database and you now want to process that data so that you can display each row in your application. When you retrieve that data, it is stored in an object. You can then use methods defined on that object to access the data in that result set.

In order for an ASP.NET application to access data in MySQL database, it must be able to interface with that database. One way you can establish this interface is through the use of Open Database Connectivity (ODBC) and Connector/ODBC. ODBC is a call-level API that allows an application to connect with a wide range of SQL databases. By using ODBC, an ASP.NET application can connect to the database, send SQL statements, and retrieve data. Because ODBC can communicate with different database products, ASP.NET applications are very portable, which means that you don't have to modify a lot of code if you were to switch the database product used to support the application. However, it does mean that you need a product-specific driver that completes the ODBC connection from the ASP.NET application to the database. As a result, MySQL AB provides Connector/ODBC, an ODBC-specific driver that implements the functionality supported by ODBC.

To implement an ASP.NET application, you must have ASP.NET installed on your system where your Web server resides, along with Connector/ODBC. You can create the files by using Visual Studio.NET or a text editor. For the purposes of the chapter, it is assumed that you are using a text editor and saving the files with an .aspx file extension. Although most ASP.NET applications often use other types of files, such as code-behind files, this chapter uses only the .aspx files to demonstrate how to connect to a MySQL database. Now take a look at how you actually create those files.

This chapter was written based on the following configuration: the MySQL ODBC 3.51 driver and Visual Studio.NET installed on a Windows XP computer, configured with Internet Information Systems (IIS). Details about the installation and configuration of your operating system, IIS, and Visual Stuio.NET are beyond the scope of the book. Be sure to view the necessary product documentation when setting up your application environment. For more information about the MySQL ODBC driver, go to www.mysql.com. For information about .NET, ASP.NET, and IIS, go to www.microsoft.com.

Building an ASP.NET/C# Application

When you create an ASP.NET data-driven application, you must take several steps to set up the application and access the database. The first step is to establish the page language and .NET namespaces to use. From there, you can create a connection to the database, issue an SQL statement, and, if appropriate, process the results returned by the statement. Those results can then be displayed on your Web page. ASP.NET and the .NET Framework support numerous classes and statements that allow you to perform each of these tasks. In the remaining part of the chapter, you learn about each aspect of database access, from importing classes to closing connections. You also create an ASP.NET application that accesses data in the DVDRentals database. If you created the PHP application in Chapter 17 or the JSP application in Chapter 18, you'll find that the application in this chapter achieves the same results.

The examples in this chapter focus on the C# code used to create a basic Web-based application. However, the principles behind connecting to a database and accessing data can apply to any Web or non-Web application written in other programming languages.

Setting up the ASP.NET Web Page

When you begin an ASP.NET page, you should include the necessary directives to specify the programming language and namespaces that will be used for the file. In both cases, you use statements that begin with an opening directive tag (<%@) and end with a closing directive tag (%>). To specify the language, you should use a Page directive similar to the one shown in the following statement:

```
<%@ Page language="c#" %>
```

The directive simply states that C# will be used for all the scripts on the page. From there, you can declare which namespaces will be used for the file. A *namespace* is a group of classes that share similar functionality. For example, the following statement imports the System.Data namespace into the page:

```
<%@ Import Namespace="System.Data" %>
```

By including this directive in your ASP.NET page, the System.Data namespace is made available to all the C# code on the page. However, the directive doesn't actually import all the classes in the namespace into the page, but instead creates a reference to the namespace so that classes can be used by the application. The directives tell the application where to look for those classes.

Declaring and Initializing Variables

C# is a strongly typed application language, which means that each variable must be explicitly declared and a data type must be assigned to that variable. By declaring a variable, you're specifying that a placeholder be created in memory that holds the value of that variable. To declare a variable, you must specify the type and the variable name. For example, the following statement declares the cdId variable as an int type:

```
int cdId;
```

Once a variable is declared, you need to assign a value to it for that variable to be used within the code. The process of assigning a value is referred to as initializing the variable. For most variables, you can initialize them by specifying a single equal sign (=) plus the value that should be assigned, as shown in the following example:

```
cdId = 42;
```

In this case, the value 42 is assigned to cdId. You can also declare and initialize a variable within one statement:

```
int cdId = 42;
```

This, of course, makes your code simpler; however, you might not always be able to initialize a variable at the time that you declare it, depending on the scope that you want the variable to have. Scope determines the lifetime of the variable and is determined when the variable is declared. If you declare a variable within a block of code, the variable is available only to that block and to any blocks nested within the outer block. The outer block defines the scope of that variable. (A block of code is a set of C# statements that are enclosed in curly brackets.) As a result, if you want a variable to be available to all code, but you cannot assign a value to the variable until a specific operation within a block of code is completed, you should declare the variable outside any blocks of code and initialize the variable when the value is available. You see examples of this later in the chapter.

You can also declare and initialize string variables in the same way that you initialize other variables, as shown in the following example:

```
string strName;
```

As you can see, the statement declares a variable named strName that is based on the String class. You can then initialize the variable by defining the string value that should be assigned to the variable, as the following statement demonstrates:

```
strName = "Strauss";
```

Notice that the string value is enclosed in double quotes. You must always use quotes when working with string values. As you saw with the int type variable, you can also declare and initialize a string variable in one statement:

```
string strName = "Strauss";
```

It should be noted that, when initializing a string variable, you're actually creating an object based on the String class. The new object contains the string value, which you then access through the variable. For this reason, you can also use the String type name (instead of string) when declaring a variable, as shown in the following statement:

```
String strName = "Strauss";
```

In C#, the keyword `string` is actually an alias for the `String` class, so you can use either `string` or `String` when specifying the variable type.

A `String` object is not the only type of object that can be associated with a variable. You can specify nearly any class name in your variable declaration. Most classes can act as types when declaring a variable. For example, suppose that you want to declare a variable based on the `Book` class. You can declare it by specifying the name of the class as the type, as shown in the following statement:

```
Book newBook;
```

The statement declares a variable named `newBook`, which is based on the `Book` class. When declaring a variable of this sort, you must often explicitly create the object that will be associated with the variable. Unlike `string` variables in which the `String` object is automatically created when you initialize the variable to a string, most objects require a more formal initialization. To associate the variable with an object, you must initialize the variable to the new object, as shown in the following statement:

```
newBook = new Book();
```

Notice that the statement includes the `new` keyword. Whenever you explicitly initialize a variable in this way, you must use the `new` keyword. This tells the compiler to create an object based on the specified class. The `new` keyword is followed by a constructor, which in this case is `Book()`. A constructor is a special type of method defined within the class. A constructor always has the same name as the class and is used to create objects based on that class.

As with other types of variables, you can also declare and initialize an object-related variable in one statement, as shown in the following statement:

```
Book newBook = new Book();
```

Once you declare and initialize an object-related variable, you can use that variable to access the methods and properties associated with the new object.

For some classes, you can initialize a variable that uses yet another approach to create the object that is associated with that variable. In these cases, you use a method in one class to create an object in a different class. One example of this approach is used is when you retrieve data from a database. Later in the chapter, you see examples of how this and other types of variables are initialized, but before you move on to that, you first learn how to establish a connection to a MySQL database.

Connecting to a MySQL Database

To establish a connection from within your ASP.NET application, you should take the following three steps:

1. Define the connection parameters.
2. Create the connection based on the connection parameters.
3. Open the connection.

In the first step, you simply define a string variable that contains the parameters necessary to connect to the MySQL database. For example, the following C# statement declares and initializes the string variable strConn:

```
string strConn = "driver={MySQL ODBC 3.51 Driver}; server=localhost;" +
    "database=BookDB; uid=bookapp; password=bookpw";
```

If you want to split the statement into multiple lines, as has been done here, you enclose each portion of the statement line in double quotes. In addition, for each line other than the last line, you end the line with a plus sign. This indicates that the two lines are to be concatenated when executed. Only the final line is terminated with a semi-colon.

The parameters assigned to the strConn variable include the name of the MySQL Connector/ODBC driver, the computer on which the MySQL server is running, the applicable database, the user account to use to access the database, and the password for that account.

Once you have declared and initialized the variable, you can use that variable to create a connection object and assign that object to a second variable, as shown in the following statement:

```
OdbcConnection conn = new OdbcConnection(strConnection);
```

This statement creates an object based on the OdbcConnection class, which includes the methods necessary to open and close the connection. The strConnection variable is passed as an argument in the OdbcConnection() class constructor. As a result, the new object will be created based on those connection parameters. This object is then assigned to the conn variable, which can then be used to access the methods available in the new OdbcConnection() object.

Once the object has been created and assigned to the variable, you can use the variable to open the connection:

```
conn.Open();
```

As you would expect, the Open() method opens the connection to the MySQL database, using the parameters assigned to the OdbcConnection object. Once you've established the connection, you can issue SQL statements against the database defined in the connection, which in this case is BookDB.

Retrieving Data from a MySQL Database

One of the most common SQL statements that you're likely to issue from within your ASP.NET application is the SELECT statement. By using this statement, you can retrieve data that can then be displayed on your Web pages. However, issuing a SELECT statement is not enough to display the data. You need additional mechanisms that pass that SELECT statement to the MySQL server and that then process the results returned by the statement.

When you're retrieving data from a MySQL database into your ASP.NET application, you generally follow a specific set of steps:

1. Declare and initialize a string variable that creates the SELECT statement.

2. Declare and initialize an OdbcCommand variable that is associated with a new OdbcCommand object. The new object should be based on the string variable associated with the SELECT statement and on the variable associated with the connection object.

3.   Use the `ExecuteReader()` method of the new `OdbcCommand` object to execute the `SELECT` statement and to create an `OdbcDataReader` object to store the result set. The object should then be assigned to a variable based on the `OdbcDataReader` class.

4.   Use methods within the `OdbcDataReader` variable to process the results, normally within some sort of conditional structure.

Now take a closer look at each step. The first step creates a `SELECT` statement that is assigned to a `String` variable. For example, in the following statement, a variable named `selectSql` is defined:

```
string selectSql = "SELECT CDID, CDName FROM CDs";
```

Putting the `SELECT` statement in a variable in this way makes it easier to work with the statement in other places in the code. Once the variable has been declared and initialized, you should then create an `OdbcCommand` object and assign that to a variable. The `OdbcCommand` object contains the methods that you will need to execute your `SELECT` statement. The following variable is declared and then initialized by creating an `OdbcCommand` object:

```
OdbcCommand comm = new OdbcCommand(selectSql, conn);
```

The `OdbcCommand()` constructor includes two arguments. The first is the `selectSql` variable, which contains the `SELECT` statement. The second argument is the `conn` variable, which you saw in an earlier example. The variable is associated with the `OdbcConnection` object that defines the parameters necessary to connect to the database. As a result, a new `OdbcCommand` object will be created that will include the `SELECT` statement and the connection parameters. This new object is then assigned to the `comm` variable. You can now use the `comm` variable to access methods in the new `OdbcCommand` object. For example, you can use the `ExecuteReader()` method to execute the `SELECT` statement and create an `OdbcDataReader` object that contains the result set, as shown in the following statement:

```
OdbcDataReader dataReader = comm.ExecuteReader();
```

The statement declares the `dataReader` variable, which is based on the `OdbcDataReader` class. The variable is associated with the new `OdbcDataReader` object created by the `ExecuteReader()` method. You can now use the `DataReader` variable to call the methods in the `OdbcDataReader` object to process your result set.

Processing the Result Set

Once you have a result set to work with, you must process the rows so that they can be displayed in a usable format. However, C#, like other procedural application languages, cannot easily process sets of data, so you must set up your code to be able to process one row at a time. You can do this by setting up a loop condition and by using an `OdbcDataReader` method that supports the row-by-row processing. For example, you can use the `while` command to set up the loop and the `Read()` method to process the rows, as shown in the following example:

```
while(dataReader.Read())
{
    int cdId = (int) dataReader["CDID"];
    string cdName = (string) dataReader["CDName"];
}
```

The `while` command tells C# to continue to execute the block of statements as long as the current condition evaluates to true. The condition in this case is defined by `dataReader.Read()`. The `dataReader` variable (which is associated with an `OdbcDataReader` object) allows you to call the `Read()` method. The method references each row in the results set, one row at a time, starting with the first row. Every time the while loop is executed, `Read()` points to the next row.

Each value is retrieved from the `OdbcDataReader` object by using the name of column, as it was returned by the SELECT statement. The value is then assigned to a related variable. To better understand how this works, you can look at each element of the statement in reverse order. For example, the first statement in the while loop assigns a value to the `cdId` variable. If you look at the end of the statement, notice that it retrieves its value from the CDID column. (The name of the column is enclosed in brackets.) The `dataReader` variable is used to call that value from the result set stored in the object associated with the variable. This is then preceded by `int`, which is enclosed in parentheses. This indicates that the value retrieved from the database should be converted to a value compatible with the C# `int` type. The value is then assigned to the `cdId` variable, which is declared as an `int` variable.

This process is used for each column returned by SELECT statement. In the case of the example above, only two columns are returned by the statement. This process is then repeated for each row in the result set. To help illustrate this, suppose that the first row returned by your query contains the following values: CDID = 101 and CDName = Bloodshot.

When the while loop is executed the first time, the first call to the `Read()` method points to the first row in the result set, which is stored in the `OdbcDataReader` object that was created specifically to hold this result set. Because the `dataReader` variable is associated with that `OdbcDataReader` object, you can use that variable to access the data stored in the object as well as the methods defined on that object (as inherited from the `OdbcDataReader` class). You can then retrieve the value from each column within each row. For example, you can retrieve the CDID value in the first row. As a result, the `cdId` variable is set to a value of `101`. For each column returned by the `Read()` method for a particular row, the column value is assigned to the applicable variable. The column-related variables can then be used to display the actual values returned by the SELECT statement.

Once you retrieve the values into the variables, you would normally include within your while loop the structure necessary to display those values. This is often done within the context of an HTML table that provides the necessary rows and columns for the returned data. In a Try It Out section later in this chapter, you see an example of how this is done.

Manipulating String Data

After you have retrieved string data from a database, you'll often find that you want to manipulate that data in some way. Because all string data is associated with `String` objects, you can use the methods and properties defined in the `String` class to take some sort of action on that data. Two class elements that are particularly useful are the `Length` property and the `Equals()` method. To demonstrate how both of these elements work, first take a look at the following statement:

```
string compName = "Strauss";
```

The statement declares a string variable named `compName`, whose purpose is to represent a composer's name. Initially, the value `Strauss` is assigned to the variable. Suppose now that you want to determine whether the current value assigned to the variable exceeds zero characters. To do so, you can invoke the Length property to determine the number of characters, as shown in the following statement:

```
if (compName.Length > 0)
{
    <take action if length is greater than zero>
}
```

The Length property is used as a condition in an if statement. If the variable contains more than zero characters, the condition evaluates to true and the statements within the if block are executed. The Length property is useful for testing whether a variable is currently an empty string or actually contains a value. Based on that information, you can then execute specific statements.

In addition to the Length property, the Equals() method can be very useful in setting up if conditions. The Equals() method compares two strings and returns a value of true if the strings are equal and a value of false if they are not. To use this method, you must specify the first string, then add the Equals() method, and then specify the second string as an argument in that method. For example, the following statement compares the Chopin string to the string in the compName variable:

```
if ("Chopin".Equals(compName))
{
    <take action if values are equal>
}
```

The reason that the Equals() method can be used with the string Chopin is because C# automatically treats a literal string value as an object, even when used as it is used in this example. As a result, you can call methods from the String class simply by specifying the string value, followed by a period, and then followed by the method. You can then pass the second string as an argument to the method. In this case, because the variable is currently associated with the value Strauss, the statement returns a value of false.

When working with string data, there might be times when you want to concatenate the string value in a variable with another string value. In that case, you would use the plus/equal signs (+=) to indicate that the value to the right of these signs should be concatenated to the value on the left. For example, the following statement adds Ricard to the value in the compName variable:

```
compName += ", Ricard";
```

This statement results in one value: Strauss, Ricard. If you were to use the equal sign without the plus sign, a new value would be assigned to the variable, resulting in the value Ricard (preceded by a comma) replacing the value Strauss.

Converting Values

When working with data in an ASP.NET application, particularly when retrieving data from a database or inserting data into a database, you will often find that you need to convert a value from one type to another. For values that are already of a similar type, you merely need to cast the value into the appropriate type. For example, if you retrieve string data from a MySQL database, you merely need to specify the string keyword (in parentheses) when assigning that value to a variable. You already saw an example of this earlier in the chapter when you retrieved integer and string data. The following statement uses an OdbcDataReader object (assigned to the dataReader variable) to retrieve the value from the FName column in a result set:

```
string fName = (string) dataReader["FName"];
```

For the purposes of this example, assume that values in the FName column are stored as strings. Because the data is in a similar format, you merely need to specify the `string` keyword (in parentheses) before the `dataReader` variable name. The column value is then cast into a C# string value that is assigned to the `fName` variable, which has also been declared as a string type variable.

When working with values of dissimilar types, you must specifically convert the value to the correct type. Normally you can do this by using a method from the class type on which the value is based. For example, suppose that you want to convert a date that is saved as a `String` value into a `DateTime` value. To do so, you can use the `Parse()` method of the `DateTime` class to convert that value, as shown in the following example:

```
DateTime dtBDay = DateTime.Parse(strBDay);
```

In this case, the `strBDay` variable holds a date value that is stored as a string. The `Parse()` method converts the string to a `DateTime` value, which is then assigned to a variable that is declared with the `DateTime` type.

Another method that is useful is the `ToString()` method, which converts a value to a string. For example, suppose that you want to convert a `DateTime` value to a string. You can use the `ToString()` method along with the `DateTime` variable, as shown in the following example:

```
string strBDay = dtBDay.ToString("MM-dd-yyyy");
```

Because the `dtBDay` variable is associated with the `DateTime` class, you can use the `ToString()` method from that class to convert the data. Notice that, as one of the arguments to the method, you specify the format in which you want the value converted. You can then assign the string value returned by the method to the `strBDay` variable.

In addition to the `String` and `DateTime` classes, the `ToString()` and `Parse()` methods are available to most type classes. In addition, other methods are available to each class for converting values from one type to another. Be sure to check the C# documentation if there is a conversion that you want to make that is not shown here.

Working with HTML Forms

When setting up your Web-based application, you often need to pass data from the client browser to the server. This is usually done through the use of a form, which is an element on an HTML page that allows a user submit data that can be passed on to the server. For example, a form can be used to allow a user to log on to an application. The user can submit an account name and password, which the form then sends to a specified location.

An HTML form supports two types of posting methods: POST and GET. The POST method sends the data through an HTTP header. An HTTP header is a mechanism that allows commands and data to be sent to and from the browser and server. The GET method adds the data to a URL. Because the data is added to the URL, it is visible when the URL is displayed, which can create some security issues The POST method is often preferred because the POST data is hidden.

A thorough discussion about HTML forms and HTTP headers is beyond the scope of this book. However, there are plenty of resources that describe forms, headers, and all other aspects of HTML and HTTP extensively. If you're not familiar with how to work with forms and headers, be sure to read the appropriate documentation.

Like many other server-side programming languages, ASP.NET and C# have built-in mechanisms that automatically process the data submitted by a form. As a result, you can access the values stored in form parameters by using the `Request` object from within your C# code. To give you a better sense of how this works, the following example demonstrates this process. Suppose that your application includes an HTML form that contains an input element named department, as shown in the following code:

```
<input type="text" name="department">
```

Because the `input` element is a `text` type, the user enters a value into a text box and that value is assigned to the parameter named `department` when the form is submitted. The parameter value is then made available to the ASP.NET application. You can then use the `Form` property of the `Request` object to retrieve that value, as the following statement demonstrates:

```
String strDept = Request.Form["department"];
```

The value entered into the form is returned as a string value that is assigned to a string variable named `strDept`. From there, you can use the `strDept` variable in other C# statements as you would any other string value.

Redirecting Browsers

Web application pages can sometimes decide that the user should be redirected to another page. This means that the current page stops processing and the server loads a new page and processes it. This process is usually part of a condition that specifies that, if a certain result is received, an action must be taken based on that result. For example, suppose that you want to redirect a user if that user enters Classical in the department `<input>` element (which is then assigned to the `strDept` variable). You can use the `Redirect()` method in the `Response` object to redirect the user to another page, as shown in the following statement:

```
if("Classical".equals(strDept))
{
    Response.Redirect("ClassicalSpecials.aspx");
}
```

First, an `if` statement is created to compare the `strDept` value to Classical. If the two string values are equal, the condition evaluates to true and the `if` statement is executed. In this case, the `Redirect()` method in the `Response` object is called and the user is redirected to the page specified as an argument to the method. As a result, the ClassicalSpecials.aspx page is displayed.

Including ASP.NET Files

There might be times when you want to execute C# code that is in a file separate from your current file. For example, suppose that your application includes code that is repeated often. You can put that code in a file separate from your primary file and then call that file from the primary file. The second file is referred to as a include file, and you can simply reference it from your primary file to execute the code in the include file.

To reference an include file from within your current .aspx file, you must use the `#Include` command, followed by the `File` setting, which specifies the name of the include file. (If the file is located someplace other than the local directory, you must also specify the path.) The following if statement uses the #Include command to execute the C# code in the ClassicalSpecials.aspx file:

```
if("Classical".equals(strDept))
{
    %>
    <!-- #Include File="ClassicalSpecials.aspx" -->
    <%
}
```

The first thing to notice is that the #Include command is enclosed in special opening (<!--) and closing (-->) tags. These tags are HTML comment tags that can be used to include a file. Most C# code in an ASP.NET page is enclosed in opening (<%) and closing (%>) scriptlet tags. As a result, you must close a scriptlet before including the file, and then re-open the scriptlet, as necessary.

The preceding example also includes an if statement. The if condition specifies that the strDept value must equal Classical. If the condition is true, the include file is accessed and the script in the file is executed as though it were part of the current file. It would be the same as if the code in the include file actually existed within the primary file.

Managing Exceptions

To handle errors that occur when a statement is executed, C# uses a system based on the Exception class. When an error occurs, an exception is generated, which is a special class that can contain an error message. If your code includes ways to handle that exception, some sort of action is taken. For example, if an exception is generated, you might have it logged to a file or displayed to the user.

To work with exceptions, you can enclose your C# code in try/catch blocks. The try block includes all the primary application code, and the catch block includes the code necessary to handle the exceptions. At its very basic, a try/catch block looks like the following:

```
try
{
    <C# application code>
}
catch(Exception ex)
{
    throw ex;
}
```

As you can see, two blocks have been created: the try block and the catch block. The try block includes all your basic program code, and the catch block processes the exception. The catch() method takes two arguments. The first is the name of the exception that is being caught, and the second is a variable that references the exception. The variable can then be used within the catch block.

In reality, you can include multiple catch blocks after the try block. In the example above, the Exception argument represents all .NET exceptions. However, you can specify individual exceptions, rather than all exceptions. For example, you can specify the SystemException class if you want to catch any exceptions thrown at runtime. In which case, your catch block would begin with the following:

```
catch(SystemException se)
```

If within the catch block you specify a `throw` statement, as shown in the preceding example, the applicable caller within the application server handles the exception. In some cases, the exception message is displayed to the user, depending on where the exception is occurs. If you want other action to be taken, you would create the necessary statements in the catch block.

Now that you've been introduced to many of the basic C# elements that you can use when retrieving and displaying data from a MySQL database, you're ready to build an application.

Creating a Basic ASP.NET/C# Application

In the Try It Out sections in this chapter, you build a simple Web application that allows you to view the transactions in the DVDRentals database. The application also allows you to add a transaction, edit that transaction, and then delete it from the database. As you'll recall when you designed the DVDRentals database, transactions are actually a subset of orders. Each order is made up of one or more transaction, and each transaction is associated with exactly one order. In addition, each transaction represents exactly one DVD rental. For example, if someone were to rent three DVDs at the same time, that rental would represent one order that includes three transactions.

The application that you build in this chapter is very basic and does not represent a complete application, in the sense that you would probably want your application to allow you to create new orders, add DVDs to the database, as well as add and edit other information. However, the purpose of this application is merely to demonstrate one way that you can connect to a MySQL database from within C# and ASP.NET, how you retrieve data, and how you manipulate data. The principles that you learn here can then be applied to any C# application that must access data in a MySQL database.

When creating a Web application such as an ASP.NET application, you will usually find that you are actually programming in three or four different languages. For example, you might use C# for the dynamic portions of your application, HTML for the static portions, SQL for data access and manipulation, and JavaScript to perform basic page-related functions. The application that you create in this chapter uses all four languages. At first this might seem somewhat confusing; however, the trick is to think about each piece separately. If you are new to these technologies, try doing each piece and then integrating them. The application is fully integrated and can be run and examined to see how these technologies work. Keep in mind, however, that the focus of the Try It Out sections is to demonstrate C# and SQL, so you will not find detailed explanations about the JavaScript and HTML. However, you cannot develop an ASP.NET application without including some HTML, and JavaScript is commonly implemented in Web-based applications. As a result, in order to show you a realistic application, HTML and JavaScript are included, but a discussion of these two technologies is well beyond the scope of this book. Fortunately, there are ample resources available for both of them, so be sure to consult the appropriate documentation if there is an HTML or JavaScript concept that you do not understand.

To support the application that you create in this chapter, you'll need two include files, one that contains HTML styles and one that contains the JavaScript necessary to support several page-related functions. You can download the files from the Wrox Web site at `www.wrox.com`, or you can copy them from here. The first of these files is dvdstyle.css, which controls the HTML styles that define the look and feel of the application's Web pages. The styles control the formatting of various HTML attributes that can be applied to text and other objects. The following code shows the contents of the dvdstyle.css file.

```
table.title{background-color:#eeeeee}

td.title{background-color:#bed8e1;color:#1a056b;font-family:sans-serif;font-weight:
bold;font-size: 12pt}

td.heading{background-color:#486abc;color:#ffffff;font-family:sans-serif;font-
weight: bold;font-size: 9pt}

td.item{background-color:#99ff99;color:#486abc;font-family:sans-serif;font-weight:
normal;font-size: 8pt}

input.delete{background-color:#990000;color:#99ffff;font-family:sans-serif;font-
weight: normal;font-size: 8pt}

input.edit{background-color:#000099;color:#99ffff;font-family:sans-serif;font-
weight: normal;font-size: 8pt}

input.add{background-color:#000099;color:#99ffff;font-family:sans-serif;font-
weight: normal;font-size: 8pt}

td.error{background-color:#ff9999;color:#990000;font-family:sans-serif;font-weight:
bold;font-size: 9pt}
```

When you create an HTML element in your code, you can reference a particular style in the dvdstyle.css file, and then that style is applied. For example, the dvdstyle.css file includes the following style definition:

```
td.item{background-color:#99ff99;color:#486abc;font-family:sans-serif;font-weight:
normal;font-size: 8pt}
```

The `td.item` keywords identify the style definition. The `td` refers to the type of style definition, which in this case is a cell within a table, and item is the unique name given to this particular definition. The options defined within the paragraph are the various styles that apply to this definition. You can then reference this style definition in your HTML code. For example, if you are creating a table and you want a cell within that table to use this style, you would reference the item style name.

Whether you copy the file from the Web site or create the file yourself, you should save the file to the same directory where your ASP.NET pages are stored. You can then modify the styles to meet your own needs.

The second file that you need to support the application is the dvdrentals.js file, which contains the JavaScript support functions for the web form submission. These functions allow the program to manipulate the command values and also the values of the form's action parameter. By using this technique, a user button-click can redirect the form to a different page. The following code shows the contents of the dvdrentals.js file:

```
function doEdit(button, transactionId)
{
    button.form.transaction_id.value = transactionId;
    button.form.command.value = "edit";
    button.form.action = "edit.aspx";
    button.form.submit();
}

function doAdd(button)
```

```
    {
        button.form.transaction_id.value = -1;
        button.form.command.value = "add";
        button.form.action = "edit.aspx";
        button.form.submit();
    }

    function doDelete(button, transactionId)
    {
        var message = "Deleting this record will permanently remove it.\r\n" +
                      "Are you sure you want to proceed?";

        var proceed = confirm(message);

        if(proceed)
        {
            button.form.transaction_id.value = transactionId;
            button.form.command.value = "delete";
            button.form.submit();
        }
    }

    function doCancel(button)
    {
        button.form.command.value = "view";
        button.form.action = "index.aspx";
        button.form.submit();
    }

    function doSave(button, command)
    {
        button.form.command.value = command;
        button.form.submit();
    }
```

The dvdrentals.js includes numerous function definitions. For example, the following JavaScript statement defines the doEdit() function:

```
    function doEdit(button, transactionId)
    {
        button.form.transaction_id.value = transactionId;
        button.form.command.value = "edit";
        button.form.action = "edit.aspx";
        button.form.submit();
    }
```

The doEdit() function can be called from within your HTML code, usually through an <input> element that uses a button click to initiate the function. The doEdit() function takes two parameters: button and transactionId. The button parameter is used to pass the HTML button object which references the form element into the JavaScript function, and the transactionId parameter holds the transaction ID for the current record. The transactionId value, along with a command value of edit, is submitted to the form in the edit.aspx file when that file is launched. Again, whether you copy the file from the Web site or create the file yourself, you should save the dvdrentals.js file to the same directory where your ASP.NET files are stored in your Web server.

Once you've ensured that the dvdstyle.css and dvdrentals.js file have been created and added to the appropriate directory, you're ready to begin creating your application. The first file that you create — index.aspx — provides the basic structure for the application. The file contains the C# statements necessary to establish the connection to the DVDRentals database, retrieve data from the database, and then display that data. The page will list all the transactions that currently exist in the DVDRentals database. In addition, the index.aspx file will provide the foundation on which additional application functionality will be built in later Try It Out sections. You can download any of the files used for the DVDRentals application created in this chapter at the Wrox Web site at www.wrox.com.

In the Try It Out sections that you use to create the DVDRentals application, it is assumed that you are using a text editor to create your .aspx files. However, if you're using the Visual Studio .NET development environment to create your application, the process for creating the files is slightly different, although the fundamental elements within the file are still the same. In most cases, an ASP.NET application will consist of multiple files, with the C# script placed in a code-behind file. This allows you to separate the presentation HTML from the actual C# code. However, the DVDRentals application uses only single .aspx files in order to clearly demonstrate each concept in as simple and straightforward way as possible. This approach also allows you to easily compare this application to the applications in chapters 17 and 18.

Try It Out   Creating the index.aspx File

The following steps describe how to create the index.aspx file, which establishes a connection to the DVDRentals database and retrieves transaction-related data:

1. The first part of the index.aspx file specifies the language and the classes that will be used by the ASP.NET page. Open a text editor and enter the following code:

```
<%@ Page language="c#" %>
<%@ Import Namespace="System" %>
<%@ Import Namespace="System.Web" %>
<%@ Import Namespace="System.IO" %>
<%@ Import Namespace="System.Collections" %>
<%@ Import Namespace="System.Data" %>
<%@ Import Namespace="System.Data.Odbc" %>
```

2. After you specify the classes, set up the basic HTML elements that provide the structure for the rest of the page. This includes the page header, links to the dvdstyle.css and dvdrentals.js files, and the initial table structure in which to display the data retrieved from the DVDRentals database. Enter the following code:

```
<html>
<head>
    <title>DVD - Listing</title>
    <link rel="stylesheet" href="dvdstyle.css" type="text/css">
    <script language="JavaScript" src="dvdrentals.js"></script>
    </script>
</head>

<body>

<p></p>

<table cellSpacing=0 cellPadding=0 width=619 border=0>
```

```
    }

    obj = odbcDataReader["DateDue"];

    if(!obj.GetType().Equals(typeof(DBNull)))
    {
        DateTime dateDue = (DateTime) obj;
        dateDuePrint = dateDue.ToString("MM-dd-yyyy");
    }

    obj = odbcDataReader["DateIn"];

    if(!obj.GetType().Equals(typeof(DBNull)))
    {
        DateTime dateIn = (DateTime) obj;
        dateInPrint = dateIn.ToString("MM-dd-yyyy");
    }

    String custFirstName = (String) odbcDataReader["CustFN"];
    String custLastName = (String) odbcDataReader["CustLN"];
    String dvdName = (String) odbcDataReader["DVDName"];
```

7. Now put the customer names into a more readable format and ensure that null values are not displayed as DVD names. Add the following code to your page:

```
// Format the result set into a readable form and assign variables
    String customerName = "";
    if(custFirstName != null)
        customerName += custFirstName + " ";

    if(custLastName != null)
        customerName += custLastName;

    if(dvdName == null)
        dvdName = "";
```

8. Next, insert the values that are retrieved from the database into an HTML table structure. Add the following code to the ASP.NET file:

```
// Print each value in each row in the HTML table
%>
    <tr height="35" valign="top">
        <td class="item">
            <nobr>
            <%=orderId%>
            </nobr>
        </td>
        <td class="item">
            <nobr>
            <%=customerName%>
            </nobr>
        </td>
        <td class="item">
            <nobr>
```

```
            <%=dvdName%>
            </nobr>
        </td>
        <td class="item">
            <nobr>
            <%=dateOutPrint%>
            </nobr>
        </td>
        <td class="item">
            <nobr>
            <%=dateDuePrint%>
            </nobr>
        </td>
        <td class="item">
            <nobr>
            <%=dateInPrint%>
            </nobr>
        </td>
    </tr>
```

9. The final section of the file closes the connection and the C# code. It also closes the `<table>`, `<body>`, and `<html>` elements on the Web page. Add the following code to the end of the ASP.NET file:

```
<%
    }

    odbcDataReader.Close();

    if(odbcCommand != null)
        odbcCommand.Dispose();

    if(odbcConnection != null)
        odbcConnection.Dispose();
    }
    catch(Exception ex)
    {
        throw ex;
    }
%>
    </table>
    </td>
    </tr>
    </table>
    </body>
    </html>
```

10. Save the index.aspx file to the DVDApp Web application directory.

11. Open your browser and go to the address `http://localhost/DVDApp/index.asp`. Your browser should display a page similar to the one shown in the Figure 19-1.

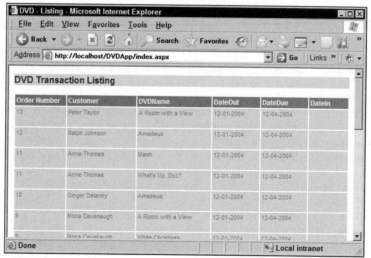

Figure 19-1

If you find that you cannot connect to the MySQL server when trying to open the ASP.NET file, it might be because of the password encryption method used for the MySQL user account. Beginning with MySQL 4.1, a different method is used to encrypt passwords than was used in previous versions. However, some client applications have not yet implemented this new encryption method. As a result, when you try to pass the password from the ASP.NET application to MySQL, there is an encryption mismatch. You can test whether this is a problem by using the mysql client utility — logging in with the mysqlapp user account name and the pw1 password — to access the MySQL server. If you're able to log on to the server with mysql utility, then you know that the account is working fine; in which case, encryption mismatch is probably the problem. To remedy this, open the mysql client utility as the root user and execute the following SQL statement:

```
SET PASSWORD FOR 'mysqlapp'@'localhost' = OLD_PASSWORD('pw1');
```

The OLD_PASSWORD() function saves that password using the old encryption method, which will make the password compatible with the way your ASP.NET application has been implemented.

How It Works

The first step that you took in this exercise was to create a page directive that specifies C# as the language to be used for the page:

```
<%@ Page language="c#" %>
```

To set up the directive, you enclosed it in opening and closing directive tags, added the Page keyword, followed by the language setting. The actual language — C# — follows the equal sign and is enclosed in double quotes. After the page directive, you set up several import directives such as the following:

```
<%@ Import Namespace="System" %>
```

In this case, you specified Import rather than Page and then defined the Namespace setting. The namespace represents the set of related classes that you plan to use within your ASP.NET page. You created an import directive for each namespace that you want to associate with the Web page.

After your page directive, you set up the opening HTML section of your index.aspx file. The <head> section establishes the necessary links to the dvdstyle.css and dvdrentals.js files. You then added a <body> section that includes two HTML <table> elements. The first table provides a structure for the page title — DVD Transaction Listing — and the second table provides the structure for the data that will be displayed on the page. The data includes the order number, customer name, DVD name, and dates that the DVD was checked out, when it is due back, and, if applicable, when it was returned. As a result, the initial table structure that is created in this section sets up a row for the table headings and a cell for each heading.

For more information about HTML, file linking from within HTML, style sheets, and JavaScript functions, refer to the appropriate documentation.

Once you set up your HTML structure, you began the main C# section of the page, which you indicating by including an opening scriptlet tag. Following the tag, you declared two variables:

```
OdbcConnection odbcConnection = null;
OdbcCommand odbcCommand = null;
```

The odbcConnection variable is based on the OdbcConnection class, and the odbcCommand variable is based on the OdbcCommand class. You use these variables later in your code to reference objects that allow you to create a connection and retrieve data from a MySQL database. Initially, you set the value of each variable to null. However, this only serves as a marker to indicate the current setting of the variable. Because both of the variables are object-related, until you assign an object to them, they cannot be used.

Once you declared the variables, you initiated the try/catch blocks by adding the following code:

```
try
{
```

The try/catch blocks are used to catch any exceptions that might be generated if a C# statement does not execute properly. After you set up the try block, you created the statements necessary to establish a connection to the database:

```
String strConnection = "driver={MySQL ODBC 3.51 Driver};" +
                       "server=localhost;" +
                       "database=DVDRentals;" +
                       "uid=mysqlapp;" +
                       "password=pw1";

odbcConnection = new OdbcConnection(strConnection);

odbcConnection.Open();
```

In the first statement, you declared a string variable and then assigned to that variable the parameters necessary to connect to the DVDRentals database. The driver setting refers to the Connector/ODBC driver that is available from MySQL AB. (Be sure to refer to the MySQL documentation for information on how to set up that driver.)

In the next statement, you assigned a new `OdbcConnection` object to the `odbcConnection` variable. You included as an argument in the `OdbcConnection()` constructor the `strConnection` variable. As a result, the connection information is added to the new `OdbcConnection` object. You then used the `odbcConnection` variable to call the `Open()` method in the `OdbcConnection` object. The method used the connection parameters assigned to the object to connect to the database.

Once you established your connection, you declared a string variable named `selectSql` and assigned the necessary SELECT statement to that variable:

```
String selectSql = "SELECT " +
                   "Transactions.TransID, " +
                   "Transactions.OrderID, " +
                   "Transactions.DVDID, " +
                   "Transactions.DateOut, " +
                   "Transactions.DateDue, " +
                   "Transactions.DateIn, " +
                   "Customers.CustFN, " +
                   "Customers.CustLN, " +
                   "DVDs.DVDName " +
                   "FROM Transactions, Orders, Customers, DVDs " +
                   "WHERE Orders.OrderID = Transactions.OrderID " +
                   "AND Customers.CustID = Orders.CustID " +
                   "AND DVDs.DVDID = Transactions.DVDID " +
                   "ORDER BY  Transactions.OrderID DESC, " +
                   "Customers.CustLN ASC, Customers.CustFN ASC, " +
                   "Transactions.DateDue DESC, DVDs.DVDName ASC";
```

As you can see, this is a basic SELECT statement that joins the Transactions, Orders, Customers, and DVDs tables in the DVDRentals database. You then created a new `OdbcCommand` object and assigned it to the `odbcCommand` variable, as shown in the following statement:

```
odbcCommand = new OdbcCommand(selectSql, odbcConnection);
```

The `OdbcCommand()` constructor includes two arguments: the `selectSql` variable and the `odbcConnection`. As a result, the data assigned to these variables is used by the constructor to create a new `OdbcCommand` object, which is then assigned to the `odbcCommand` variable. You can then use that variable to access the `ExecuteReader()` method of the `OdbcCommand` object, as you did in the following statement:

```
OdbcDataReader odbcDataReader = odbcCommand.ExecuteReader();
```

The `ExecuteReader()` method executes the SELECT statement and creates an `OdbcDataReader` object, which is then assigned to the `odbcDataReader` variable. The new object contains the result set returned by the SELECT statement, so you can use the `odbcDataReader` variable to access the result set, which you did in a while loop:

```
while(odbcDataReader.Read())
{
    int transId = (int) odbcDataReader["TransID"];
    int orderId = (int) odbcDataReader["OrderID"];
    int dvdId = (int) (short) odbcDataReader["DVDID"];
```

The while loop first uses the `odbcDataReader` variable to access the `Read()` method. If the method points to a row in the result set, the while condition evaluates to true. Each time a while loop is executed, the `Read()` method points to the next row in the result set. You then used the while loop to assign values from the result set to related variable. For many of these variables, you were able to cast the value returned from the database into the type used by the variable. For example, you cast the value returned by the `TransID` variable to an `int` type, and the value is then assigned to the `transId` variable.

Notice that the process for casting the `DVDID` value is a little different from the other variables. This is because the `DVDID` value is stored as a `SMALLINT` type. As a result, you must first cast it to a `short` type, and then cast it to an `int` type in order to assign the value to the `dvdId` variable, which is itself an `int` type.

For date-related values, you had to take a different approach, as shown in the following statements:

```
object obj;
String dateOutPrint = "";
String dateDuePrint = "";
String dateInPrint = "";

obj = odbcDataReader["DateOut"];

        if(!obj.GetType().Equals(typeof(DBNull)))
{
    DateTime dateOut = (DateTime) obj;
    dateOutPrint = dateOut.ToString("MM-dd-yyyy");
}
```

First, you declared the variables necessary to work with the date values. Basically, you want to convert the value from MySQL `DATE` values to C# `string` values. For each date value, you first assigned the value to the `obj` variable. Then you set up an `if` block that includes a condition that specifies that the `obj` variable should not be of the type `DBNull`. When ASP.NET extracts `DATE` values from a MySQL database, values of 0000-00-00 or null column values are converted to type `DBNull`. To check that this is not the case, you use the `GetType()` and `Equals()` methods of the `Object` class. As an argument to the `Equals()` method, you specified the `typeof()` function, which is used to identify that type, which in this case is `DBNull`. Also, because you preceded the condition with an exclamation point (!), the value returned from the database can *not* be of the type `DBNull`. In other words, it cannot have a value of 0000-00-00, which is the default value in a MySQL `DATE` column that is defined as `NOT NULL`.

If the `if` condition evaluates to true, the date value that has been assigned to the `obj` variable is then assigned to the `dateOut` variable as a `DateTime` value. However, ultimately, you want to work with this value as a string, so you took one more step, which was to convert the `dateOut` value to a string, which was then assigned to the `dateOutPrint` variable.

Next, you declared a new string variable to hold the entire customer name. At the same time, you initiated the variable as an empty string, as shown in the following statement:

```
String customerName = "";
```

The `customerName` variable has been set as an empty string to ensure that if any part of a customer name is null, that null value is not displayed. That way, when you begin formatting the names, you can test for the existence of null values and assign names to the `customerName` variable only if the values are not null. If they are null, then only an empty string will be displayed or only one name, with no null values appended to the name. As a result, after you initiated the variables, you then began concatenating the names, starting with the first name, as shown in the following if statement:

```
if(custFirstName != null)
    customerName += custFirstName + " ";
```

The statement first checks whether the customer's first name is not null. If the condition evaluates to true, the value in the custFirstName variable, plus a space (enclosed in the pair of double quotes), is added to the customerName variable. Note that when a plus sign precedes an equal sign, the existing variable value is added to the new values, rather than being replaced by those values. This is better illustrated by the next if statement, which then adds the last name to the first name:

```
if(custLastName != null)
    customerName += custLastName;
```

In this case, unless the first name is null, the customerName variable currently holds the first name value, along with a space, which is then added to the last name value. As a result, the customerName variable now holds the customer's full name, displayed as first name, space, then last name.

You also used an if statement to ensure that the dvdName variable contains a string, rather than a null, as shown in the following statement:

```
if(dvdName == null)
    dvdName = "";
```

The reason for this is again to ensure that a null value is not displayed on the Web page, but rather a blank value if the DVD name is null.

Once you have formatted the values in the way that you want, you can use the variables to display those values in an HTML table structure. This structure follows the same structure that is defined at the beginning of the file, thus providing the column heads for the rows that you now add. Keep in mind that you are still working within the while loop created earlier. So every step that you take at this point still applies to each individual row that is returned by the Read() method.

To create the necessary row in the table, you used the scriptlet closing tag (%>) to get out of C# mode and back into HTML mode. You then created a cell definition for each value that is returned by the result set (and subsequently assigned to a variable). For example, you used the following definition in for first cell in the first row of the table (not counting the heading):

```
<td class="item">
    <nobr>
    <%=orderId%>
    </nobr>
</td>
```

You used the <td> and </td> elements to enclose the individual cell within the row. The <nobr> and </nobr> elements indicate that there should be no line break between the two tags. Notice that squeezed between all that is a C# variable that is enclosed by opening (<%=) and closing (%>) expression tags. As a result, the value of the orderId variable will be displayed in that cell.

This process is repeated for each value in the row and repeated for each row until the while statement loops through all the rows in the result set. After the while loop, you closed or disposed of the necessary objects:

```
odbcDataReader.Close();

if(odbcCommand != null)
    odbcCommand.Dispose();

if(odbcConnection != null)
    odbcConnection.Dispose();
```

The Close() method closes the an object, whereas the Dispose() method closes the object and also releases any related resources. You should always close or dispose of any objects that you no longer need. After you closed the objects, you ended the try block (by using a closing curly bracket), and then you created a catch block to catch all exceptions:

```
catch(Exception ex)
{
    throw ex;
}
```

Any exception thrown from within the try block will now be printed to a Web page. After you set up the catch block, you closed out the HTML elements and saved the file. You then opened the file in your browser and viewed the transactions in the DVDRentals database. As you discovered, you can view the transactions, but you cannot modify them. So now you can explore what steps you can take to allow your application to support data modification operations.

Inserting and Updating Data in a MySQL Database

Earlier in the chapter, you looked at how to retrieve data from a MySQL database. In this section, you look at how to insert and update data. The process you use for adding either insert or update functionality is nearly identical, except that, as you would expect, you use an INSERT statement to add data and an UPDATE statement to modify data.

Inserting and updating data is different from retrieving data in a couple ways. For one thing, when you execute a SELECT statement, you use the ExecuteReader() method of the OdbcCommand class to execute the query. The data returned by the SELECT statement is then added to a new OdbcDataReader object. However, when you execute a data modification statement, you simply call the ExecuteNonQuery() method.

To better understand how the process works, take a look at it one step at a time. First, as you did with the SELECT statement, you should declare a string variable and assign your SQL statement to that variable, as shown in the following example:

```
String insertSql = "INSERT INTO CDs (CDName, InStock) VALUES (?,?)";
```

What you probably notice immediately is that question marks are used in place of each value to be inserted. Later in the process, you create statements that insert values in place of the question marks. However, you must first create an OdbcCommand object and assign it to a variable, as shown in the following statement:

```
OdbcCommand comm = new OdbcCommand(insertSql, conn);
```

The `OdbcCommand()` constructor takes two arguments: `insertSql` and `conn`. (Assume for this example that the `conn` variable references an `OdbcConnection` object that contains the necessary parameters.) Once you create the `OdbcCommand` object, you must create an `OdbcParameter` array that will be used to assign values to the question mark parameters in the `INSERT` statement:

```
OdbcParameter [] param = new OdbcParameter[2];
```

When you create an array, you're creating an object that can hold sets of values. In this case, the object is based on the `OdbcParameter` class. To create an array, you must add a set of square brackets when you declare the variable and when you call the constructor to create the new object. However, when calling the constructor, you must also specify the number of parameters. The example above specifies two parameters, which coincides with the number of question mark parameters in the `INSERT` statement.

After you assign the new `OdbcParameter` array to the `param` variable, you can use that variable to work with the individual parameters within the array. To work with individual parameters, you refer to them by number, in the order in which they are added to the `INSERT` statement. The number references start at 0 and go on up. For example, if your array includes two parameters, you reference the first parameter by using 0 and the second parameter by using 1.

For each parameter, you must create an `OdbcParameter` object and then assign a value to the object, as shown in the following statements:

```
param[0] = new OdbcParameter("", OdbcType.VarChar);
param[0].Value = cdName;
param[1] = new OdbcParameter("", OdbcType.Int);
param[1].Value = inStock;
```

The first statement assigns new object to the first parameter referenced by the `param` variable. Notice that 0 is used to reference that parameter. The `OdbcParameter` constructor takes two arguments. The first is an empty string to act as a placeholder for a value to be passed to it. The second argument defines the data type to be used for the parameter value. In the first statement, the type is `OdbcType.VarChar`.

Once you create a new `OdbcParameter` object for the parameter, you can use the `Value` property of the object to assign a value to the parameter. In the example above, a variable is assigned to the parameter. For the first parameter, the `cdName` variable is used to assign a value. For the second parameter, the `inStock` variable is used.

Once you have assigned values to your parameters, you must add them to your `OdbcCommand` object, which you access through the `comm` variable. To add the value to the object, you must use the `Parameters` property and the `Add()` method, as shown in the following statements:

```
comm.Parameters.Add(param[0]);
comm.Parameters.Add(param[1]);
```

As you can see, the `Add()` method take the `param` variable, along with the parameter number, as an argument. As a result, that parameter is added to the `OdbcCommand` object. From there, you can execute the `INSERT` statement. To do this, you use the `comm` variable to call the `ExecuteNonQuery()` method of the `OdbcCommand` object, as the following statement demonstrates:

```
comm.ExecuteNonQuery();
```

ASP.NET inserts the parameter values into the INSERT statement and sends it to the MySQL database. You could have just as easily executed an UPDATE statement in place of the INSERT statement, and the process would have been the same. It should also be noted that you can use this procedure to execute a SELECT statement if you want to pass values into the statement as you did with the INSERT statement above. If you use this method, you must still use the ExecuteReader() method as you saw with other SELECT statements, and you must process the result set. In the following Try It Out sections, you see how all these processes work.

Adding Insert and Update Functionality to Your Application

So far, your DVDRentals application displays only transaction-related information. In this section, you add to the application so that it also allows you to add a transaction to an existing order and to modify transactions. To support the added functionality, you must create three more files—edit.aspx, insert.aspx, and update.aspx—and you must modify the index.aspx file. Keep in mind that your index.aspx file acts as a foundation for the rest of the application. You should be able to add a transaction and edit a transaction by first opening the index.aspx file and then maneuvering to wherever you need to in order to accomplish these tasks.

The first additional file that you create is the edit.aspx file. The file serves two roles: adding transactions to existing orders and editing existing transactions. These two operations share much of the same functionality, so combining them into one file saves duplicating code. If you're adding a new transaction, the Web page will include a drop-down list that displays each order number and the customer associated with that order, a drop-down list that displays DVD titles, a text box for the date the DVD is rented, and a text box for the date the DVD should be returned. The default value for the date rented text box is the current date. The default value for the date due text box is three days from the current date.

If you're editing a transaction, the Web page will display the current order number and customer, the rented DVD, the date the DVD was rented, the date it's due back, and, if applicable, the date that the DVD was returned.

The edit.aspx Web page will also contain two buttons: Save and Cancel. The Save button saves the new or updated record and returns the user to the index.aspx page. The Close button cancels the operation, without making any changes, and returns the user to the index.aspx page.

After you create the edit.aspx page, you then create the insert.aspx file and the update.aspx file in Try It Out sections that follow this one. From there, you modify the index.aspx page to link together the different functionality. Not take a look at how to create the edit.aspx file.

Try It Out   Creating the edit.aspx File

The following steps describe how to create the edit.aspx file, which will support adding new transactions to a record and editing existing transactions:

1. As with the insert.aspx file, you must specify the language and import the necessary classes into your application. Use your text editor to start a new file, and enter the following code:

```
<%@ Page language="c#"%>
<%@ Import Namespace="System" %>
<%@ Import Namespace="System.Web" %>
```

```
<%@ Import Namespace="System.IO" %>
<%@ Import Namespace="System.Collections" %>
<%@ Import Namespace="System.Data" %>
<%@ Import Namespace="System.Data.Odbc" %>
```

2. Next, you must declare and initialize a number of variables. Later in the code, you use these variables to perform different tasks, such as processing and verifying the data retrieved by a form. Add the following statements to your file:

```
<%
// Initialize variables with parameters retrieved from the form
String command = Request.Form["command"];
String transactionIdString = Request.Form["transaction_id"];
String transIdString = Request.Form["TransID"];
String orderIdString = Request.Form["OrderID"];
String dvdIdString =   Request.Form["DVDID"];
String dateOutString = Request.Form["DateOut"];
String dateDueString = Request.Form["DateDue"];
String dateInString = Request.Form["DateIn"];

// Declare and initialize variables with default values
OdbcConnection odbcConnection = null;

DateTime dateDue = DateTime.MinValue;
DateTime dateOut = DateTime.MinValue;
DateTime dateIn = DateTime.MinValue;

int orderId = -1;
int dvdId = -1;
String error = "";
int transId = -1;

String selectSql;
OdbcCommand odbcCommand;
OdbcDataReader odbcDataReader;
```

3. As you did with the index.aspx file, you must establish a connection to the MySQL server and select the database. Add the following code to the edit.aspx file:

```
// Wrap database-access code in try/catch block to handle errors
try
{

// Create and open the connection
    String strConnection = "driver={MySQL ODBC 3.51 Driver};" +
                           "server=localhost;" +
                           "database=DVDRentals;" +
                           "uid=mysqlapp;" +
                           "password=pw1;";

    odbcConnection = new OdbcConnection(strConnection);

    odbcConnection.Open();
```

4. Next, the file should process the new or edited transactions when the user clicks the Save button. The first step in doing this is to check for missing parameters and reformat the date information. Enter the following C# code:

```
// Process the save and savenew commands
   if("save".Equals(command) || "savenew".Equals(command))
   {
// Check for missing parameters and reformat values for MySQL
      if(transIdString != null)
         transId = int.Parse(transIdString);

      if(orderIdString != null)
         orderId = int.Parse(orderIdString);
      if(orderId == -1)
         error += "Please select an \"Order\"<br>";

      if(dvdIdString != null)
         dvdId = int.Parse(dvdIdString);
      if(dvdId == -1)
         error += "Please select a \"DVD\"<br>";

      if((dateDueString != null) && (dateDueString.Length > 0))
         dateDue = DateTime.Parse(dateDueString);
      else
         error += "Please enter a \"Date Due\"<br>";

      if((dateOutString != null) && (dateOutString.Length > 0))
         dateOut = DateTime.Parse(dateOutString);
      else
         error += "Please enter a \"Date Out\"<br>";

      if((dateInString != null) && (dateInString.Length > 0))
         dateIn = DateTime.Parse(dateInString);
```

Note that the application does not check the format of the date submitted by users. Normally, an application would include some type of mechanism to ensure that submitted dates are in a usable format.

5. Then you can carry out the update or insert by calling the applicable include files. (These files are created in later Try It Out sections.) Once the code in the applicable include file runs, you should redirect users back to the index.aspx page. Enter the following code in your file:

```
      if(error.Length == 0)
      {
         if("save".Equals(command))
         {
// Run the update in update.aspx
%>
            <!-- #Include File="update.aspx" -->
<%
         }
         else
         {
// Run the insert in insert.aspx
%>
            <!-- #Include File="insert.aspx" -->
```

```
<%
        }

// Redirect the application to the listing page
        Response.Redirect("index.aspx");
    }
}
```

6. The next step is to set up the file to support adding or updating a record when the user has been redirected to this page from the index.aspx page. This is done as part of the `else` statement in an `if...else` structure. This particular section sets up the default values for a new record. Add the following code to your file:

```
    else
    {
// If it is a new record, initialize the variables to default values
        if("add".Equals(command))
        {
            transId = 0;
            orderId = 0;
            dvdId = 0;
            dateOutString = DateTime.Today.ToString("MM-dd-yyyy");
            dateDueString = DateTime.Today.AddDays(3).ToString("MM-dd-yyyy");
            dateInString = "";
        }
```

7. Next you must set up the file with the values necessary to support editing a record. This involves retrieving records to set an initial value for a number of variables. Add the following code to your ASP.NET file:

```
        else
        {
// If it is an existing record, read from database

            if(transactionIdString != null)
            {

// Build query from transactionId value passed down from form
                transId = int.Parse(transactionIdString);

                selectSql = "SELECT " +
                            "OrderID, " +
                            "DVDID, " +
                            "DateOut, " +
                            "DateDue, " +
                            "DateIn " +
                            "FROM Transactions " +
                            "WHERE TransID = ?";
// Execute query
                odbcCommand = new OdbcCommand(selectSql, odbcConnection);

                OdbcParameter odbcParameter = new OdbcParameter("", OdbcType.Int);
                odbcParameter.Value = transId;
                odbcCommand.Parameters.Add(odbcParameter);

// Populate the variables for display into the form
```

```
                    odbcDataReader = odbcCommand.ExecuteReader();

                    if(odbcDataReader.Read())
                    {
                        orderId = (int) odbcDataReader["OrderID"];
                        dvdId = (int) (short) odbcDataReader["DVDID"];

                        object obj = odbcDataReader["DateOut"];

                        if(!obj.GetType().Equals(typeof(DBNull)))
                        {
                            dateOut = (DateTime) obj;
                            dateOutString = dateOut.ToString("MM-dd-yyyy");
                        }
                        else
                            dateOutString = "";

                        obj = odbcDataReader["DateDue"];

                        if(!obj.GetType().Equals(typeof(DBNull)))
                        {
                            dateDue = (DateTime) obj;
                            dateDueString = dateDue.ToString("MM-dd-yyyy");
                        }
                        else
                            dateDueString = "";

                        obj = odbcDataReader["DateIn"];

                        if(!obj.GetType().Equals(typeof(DBNull)))
                        {
                            dateIn = (DateTime) obj;
                            dateInString = dateIn.ToString("MM-dd-yyyy");
                        }
                        else
                            dateInString = "";
                    }

// Close objects
                    odbcDataReader.Close();

                    if(odbcCommand != null)
                        odbcCommand.Dispose();
                }
            }
        }
%>
```

8. Now you must create the HTML section of your form to allow users to view and enter data. This section includes a form to pass data to C# and the table structure to display the form. Add the following code to your ASP.NET file:

```
<html>
<head>
    <title>DVD - Listing</title>
    <meta http-equiv="Content-Type" content="text/html; charset=windows-1252">
```

```
        <link rel="stylesheet" href="dvdstyle.css" type="text/css">
        <script language="JavaScript" src="dvdrentals.js"></script>
    </head>

    <body>

    <form name="mainForm" method="post" action="edit.aspx">
    <input type="hidden" name="command" value="view">
    <input type="hidden" name="TransID" value="<%=transId%>">

    <p></p>

    <table cellspacing="0" cellPadding="0" width="619" border="0">
    <tr>
        <td>
            <table height="20" cellspacing="0" cellPadding="0" width="619"
    bgcolor="#bed8e1" border="0">
            <tr align=left>
                <td valign="bottom" width="400" class="title">
                    DVD Transaction
                </td>
                <td align="right" width="219" class="title"> </td>
            </tr>
            </table>
            <br>
            <%if(error.Length > 0){%>
            <table cellspacing="2" cellPadding="2" width="619" border="0">
            <tr>
                <td width="619" class="error"><%=error%></td>
            </tr>
            </table>
            <%}%>
```

9. Now create the first row of your form, which allows users to view and select an order ID. Enter
the following code in your file:

```
        <table cellspacing="2" cellPadding="2" width="619" border="0">
        <tr>
            <td width="250" class="heading">Order</td>
            <td class="item">
                <select name="OrderID">
                    <option value="-1">Select Order</option>
<%
// Retrieve data to populate drop-down list
    selectSql = "SELECT Orders.OrderID, Orders.CustID, " +
                "Customers.CustFN, Customers.CustLN " +
                "FROM Orders, Customers " +
                "WHERE Customers.CustID = Orders.CustID " +
                "ORDER BY Orders.OrderID DESC";

// Execute the query
    odbcCommand = new OdbcCommand(selectSql, odbcConnection);

    odbcDataReader = odbcCommand.ExecuteReader();

// Loop through the results
```

```
        while(odbcDataReader.Read())
        {
// Assigned returned values to the variables
        int orderId1 = (int) odbcDataReader["OrderID"];;
        String custFirstName = (String) odbcDataReader["CustFN"];
        String custLastName = (String) odbcDataReader["CustLN"];

// Format the data for display
        String customerName = "";

        if(custFirstName != null)
            customerName += custFirstName + " ";

        if(custLastName != null)
            customerName += custLastName;

// If the order ID matches the existing value mark, it as selected

        if(orderId1 != orderId)
        {
%>
                <option value="<%=orderId1%>"><%=orderId1%> -
<%=customerName%></option>
<%
        }
        else
        {
%>
                <option selected value="<%=orderId1%>"><%=orderId1%> -
<%=customerName%></option>
<%
        }
    }

// Close objects
    odbcDataReader.Close();

    if(odbcCommand != null)
        odbcCommand.Dispose();
%>
            </select>
        </td>
    </tr>
```

10. The second row of your form allows users to view and select a DVD to associate with your transaction. Add the following code to your edit.aspx file.

```
    <tr>
        <td class="heading">DVD</td>
        <td class="item">
            <select name="DVDID">
                <option value="-1">Select DVD</option>
<%
// Retrieve data to populate drop-down list
```

```
        selectSql = "SELECT DVDID, DVDName FROM DVDs ORDER BY DVDName";

        odbcCommand = new OdbcCommand(selectSql, odbcConnection);

        odbcDataReader = odbcCommand.ExecuteReader();

// Loop through the result set
    while(odbcDataReader.Read())
    {
        int dvdId1 = (int) (short) odbcDataReader["DVDID"];
        String dvdName = (String) odbcDataReader["DVDName"];

        if(dvdName == null) dvdName = "";

        if(dvdId1 != dvdId)
        {
%>
                <option value="<%=dvdId1%>"><%=dvdName%></option>
<%
        }
        else
        {
%>
                <option selected value="<%=dvdId1%>"><%=dvdName%></option>
<%
        }
    }

// Close objects
    odbcDataReader.Close();

    if(odbcCommand != null)
        odbcCommand.Dispose();

    if(odbcConnection != null)
        odbcConnection.Dispose();

%>
            </select>
          </td>
        </tr>
```

11. Next, create three more rows in your table, one for each date-related value. Enter the following code:

```
        <tr>
          <td class="heading">Date Out</td>
          <td class="item">
            <input type="text" name="DateOut" value="<%=dateOutString%>" size="50">
          </td>
        </tr>
        <tr>
          <td class="heading">Date Due</td>
          <td class="item">
            <input type="text" name="DateDue" value="<%=dateDueString%>" size="50">
```

```
            </td>
        </tr>
        <%if((!"add".Equals(command)) && (!"savenew".Equals(command))){%>
        <tr>
            <td class="heading">Date In</td>
            <td class="item">
              <input type="text" name="DateIn"  value="<%=dateInString%>" size="50">
            </td>
        </tr>
        <%}%>
```

12. Now add the Save and Cancel buttons to your form by appending the following code to your file:

```
        <tr>
            <td colspan="2" class="item" align="center">
                <table cellspacing="2" cellPadding="2" width="619" border="0">
                <tr>
                    <td align="center">
                        <%if(("add".Equals(command)) || ("savenew".Equals(command))){%>
                        <input type="button" value="Save" class="add"
onclick="doSave(this, 'savenew')">
                        <%}else{%>
                        <input type="button" value="Save" class="add"
onclick="doSave(this, 'save')">
                        <%}%>
                    </td>
                    <td align="center">
                        <input type="button" value="Cancel" class="add"
onclick="doCancel(this)">
                    </td>
                </tr>
                </table>
            </td>
        </tr>
```

13. Close the various HTML elements and catch any exceptions by entering the following code:

```
        </table>
    </td>
</tr>
</table>
</form>
</body>
</html>
<%
}
catch(Exception ex)
{
    throw ex;
}
%>
```

14. Save the edit.aspx file to the appropriate Web application directory.

How It Works

In this exercise, you created the edit.aspx file, which supports the insert and update functionality in your DVDRentals application. The first step you took to set up the file was to add the page and import directives necessary to specify the language and .NET classes to be used on your page. These are the same classes that you import for the index.aspx file. Once you set up the page and import directives, you declared and initialized a number of variables. The first set of variables is associated with values returned by the HTML form. For example, the following C# statement retrieves the command value returned by a form:

```
String command = Request.Form["command"];
```

The statement uses the Form property of the Request object to retrieve the command value. The value is returned as a string and assigned to the command variable, which has been declared as a String type.

Once you assigned the form parameter values to the necessary variables, you then declared and initialized several variables used later in the code to display initial values in form. For example, one of the variables that you declared was dateDue:

```
DateTime dateDue = DateTime.MinValue;
```

The variable is declared as a DateTime type and is assigned a value from the DateTime class. The value is based on the MinValue property, which is the earliest date/time value (midnight on January 1, 0001) in the range of values supported by the DateTime class. The MinValue property is a fixed value and is used to provide an initial setting for the dateDue variable. This is done to prepare the variable for processing later in the code, as you'll see in that section of the file.

In the next set of variables that you declared, you initialized several of them with a value of -1, as shown in the following statement:

```
int orderId = -1;
```

The -1 value is used simply to ensure that no value is assigned that might conflict with a value retrieved by the database. As you'll see later in the code, the orderId variable is associated with the order ID as it is stored in the Transactions table and the Orders table of the DVDRentals database. Only positive integer values are used for order IDs. As a result, by assigning an integer other than a positive integer, you're ensuring that the initial variable value will not conflict with an actual value.

Once you declared and initialized the necessary variables, you set up and opened your connection, as you did in the index.aspx file. From there, you set up if...else statement blocks that begin with the following if condition:

```
if("save".Equals(command) || "savenew".Equals(command))
```

The if statement specifies two conditions. The first condition uses the Equals() method to compare the string saved to the current value in the command variable. If the values are equal, the condition evaluates to true. The second condition also uses the Equals() method to compare the string savenew to the command variable. If the values are equal, the condition evaluates to true. Because the conditions are connected by the or (||) operator, either condition can be true for the if statement to be executed. If neither condition is true, the else statement is executed.

The save and savenew command values are issued when you click the Save button. You learn more about that button shortly.

The `if...else` statements contain a number of `if...else` statements embedded in them. Before getting deeper into the code that makes up all these statements, first take a look at a high overview of the logic behind these statements. It will give you a bigger picture of what's going on and should make understanding the individual components a little easier. The following pseudo-code provides an abbreviated statement structure starting with the outer `if` statement described previously:

```
if command = save or savenew, continue (if !=, go to else)
{
    if transactionIdString != null, assign to transID
    if OrderIdString != null, assign to orderId
    if OrderIdString = -1, return error message
    if dvdIdString != null, assign to dvdId
    if dvdIdString = -1, return error message
    if dateDueString != null and length > 0, assign to dateDue
        else return error message
    if dateOutString != null and length > 0, assign to dateOut
        else return error message
    if dateInString != null and length > 0, assign to dateIn
    if no error, continue
    {
        if command = save, include update.aspx
            else include insert.aspx
        redirect to index.aspx
    }
}
else (if command != save or savenew)
{
    if command = add, continue (if !=, go to else)
    {
        initialize variables (x 6)
    }
    else (if command != add)
    {
        if transactionIdString != null
        {
            process query
            if query results exist, fetch results
            {
                assign variables (x 2)
                if date != null and != DBNull, assign to variable
                    else set date to empty string (x 3)
            }
        }
    }
}
```

As you can see, the action taken depends on the values in the `command` and `transactionIdString` variables. The outer `if` statement basically determines what happens when you try to save a record, and the outer `else` statement determines what happens when you first link to the page from the index.aspx page. Embedded in the else statement is another set of `if...else` statements. The embedded `if` statement determines what happens if you want to add a transaction, and the embedded else statement determines what happens if you want to update a transaction.

Now take a closer look at these statements. You've already seen the opening `if` statement. A number of embedded `if` statements follow the outer `if` statement. For example, the following statements convert a string value to an integer value and set up an error condition:

```
if(orderIdString != null)
    orderId = int.Parse(orderIdString);
if(orderId == -1)
    error += "Please select an \"Order\"<br>";
```

The first `if` statement defines the condition that the `orderIdString` value should not be null. If the condition evaluates to true, the `Parse()` method of the `int` class is used to assign a value to the `orderId` variable. The `Parse()` methods converts the string value to an integer value, which is then assigned to the `int` variable.

The next `if` statement specifies the condition that `orderId` should equal a value of -1. If the condition evaluates to true, an error message is returned, telling the user to select a value. (You assigned the value -1 to the variable earlier in the page, and the default value that you set up in the order ID and DVD drop-down lists is -1.)

This section of code also includes embedded `if...else` statements. The `if` statement includes two conditions, as shown in the following code:

```
if((dateDueString != null) && (dateDueString.Length > 0))
    dateDue = DateTime.Parse(dateDueString);
else
    error += "Please enter a \"Date Due\"<br>";
```

The `if` condition specifies that the `dateDueString` value cannot be null *and* the value must have a length greater than zero characters. If both these conditions are met, the `dateFormat` variable is used to call the `Parse()` method of the `DateTime` class. The converted value is then assigned to the `dateDue` variable. If either of the two `if` conditions evaluate to false, the `else` statement is executed and ASP.NET returns an error to the user.

The next step that you took was to use the `Length` property to determine whether the error variable contained any characters. If the error variable is empty, the condition evaluates to true, which means that it contains no error messages and the rest of the code should be processed. This means that a file should be included in the page, as shown in the following code:

```
if(error.Length == 0)
{
    if("save".Equals(command))
    {
%>
        <!-- #Include File="update.aspx" -->
<%
    }
    else
    {
%>
        <!-- #Include File="insert.aspx" -->
<%
    }
```

If there are no error messages returned by the previous code, the embedded if...else statements are then applied. If the command value is save, the update.aspx file code is executed; otherwise the insert.aspx file code is executed. (You create these files in later Try It Out sections.) Once the statements in the applicable include file are executed, the following statement is executed:

```
Response.Redirect("index.aspx");
```

The statement uses the Redirect() method of the Response object to redirect the user to index.aspx, which is specified as an argument in the method. This completes the outer if statement that initiates this section of code. However, if the if statement is not applicable (command does not equal save or savenew), ASP.NET executes the outer else statement.

The outer else statement is made up of its own embedded if...else statements. The if statement applies if the command variable currently holds the value add, as shown in the following code:

```
if("add".Equals(command))
{
    transId = 0;
    orderId = 0;
    dvdId = 0;
    dateOutString = DateTime.Today.ToString("MM-dd-yyyy");
    dateDueString = DateTime.Today.AddDays(3).ToString("MM-dd-yyyy");
    dateInString = "";
}
```

If command is set to add, this means that you are creating a new transaction. To prepare the Web page with the variables it needs to properly display the form when you open the page, you set a number of variables to specific values. For example, you set transId to 0, which is an unused number and so does not match any current transaction IDs.

Now take a look at the dateOutString variable. The goal here is to assign the current date to the variable and to assign that date as a string value. The first step is retrieve the current date by using the Today property of the DateTime object. You then use the ToString() method of the DateTime class to convert the value into a string in the format specified as an argument in the method. As a result, the current date, as a string value, is assigned to the dateOutString variable.

Next take a look at the dateDueString variable. This is similar to the dateOutString variable except that it contains an additional element: it adds three days to the current date. It accomplishes this by using the AddDays() method, which specifies that three days should be added to the current date. The date that is three days out from the current date is then converted to a string and assigned to the dateDueString variable.

After you set up the variables for the embedded if statement, you then added the necessary statements to the embedded else statement. You began the else block with another if statement that verifies that the transactionIdString variable is not null, as shown in the following code:

```
if(transactionIdString != null)
```

If the value is not null (a value does exist), the remaining part of the if statement is executed. This means that you are editing an existing transaction, in which case, the transactionIdString variable identifies that transaction. However, the value is returned as a string, but transaction IDs are stored in the database as integers. As a result, you used the `Parse()` method to convert the string to an integer value. From there, you created a SELECT statement and assigned it to the `selectSql` variable:

```
selectSql = "SELECT " +
            "OrderID, " +
            "DVDID, " +
            "DateOut, " +
            "DateDue, " +
            "DateIn " +
            "FROM Transactions " +
            "WHERE TransID = ?";
```

As you can see, the SELECT statement includes a question mark placeholder. To assign a variable to the parameter, you first created an `OdbcCommand` object and assigned it to the `odbcCommand` variable. From there you created an `OdbcParameter` object, assigned a value to the parameter, and added the parameter to the `OdbcCommand` object, as shown in the following code:

```
odbcCommand = new OdbcCommand(selectSql, odbcConnection);

OdbcParameter odbcParameter = new OdbcParameter("", OdbcType.Int);
odbcParameter.Value = transId;
odbcCommand.Parameters.Add(odbcParameter);

odbcDataReader = odbcCommand.ExecuteReader();
```

Because you are assigning only one parameter to the `OdbcCommand` object, you do not have to create an `OdbcParameter` array. Instead, you simply create the `OdbcParameter` object and use that object to add the parameter to the `OdbcCommand` object. From there, you were able to use the `ExecuteReader()` method to execute the SELECT statement and return a result set to the `odbcDataReader` variable.

Once you set up the SELECT statement and its parameters and then executed the statement, you processed the result set by using the `Read()` method of the `OdbcDataReader` object to assign values to the variables. This process included formatted date values to be used by the form. The methods that you used here to format the date values is similar to what you've used in other parts of the application. However, when processing the result set, you did not need to use a while loop because only one row is returned by the query. As a result, you can use a simple `if` statement to specify the `Read()` method.

After you set up the data to populate the form, you have completed the `if...else` block of code. If necessary, refer back to the summary code that is provided at the beginning of this description. This provides a handy overview of what is going on.

The next section of code that you created set up the HTML for the Web page. As with the index.aspx file, the HTML section includes header information that links to the dvdstyle.css file and the dvdrentals.js file. The section also includes a `<form>` element and two `<input>` elements:

```
<form name="mainForm" method="post" action="edit.aspx">
<input type="hidden" name="command" value="view">
<input type="hidden" name="TransID" value="<%=transId%>">
```

A form is an HTML structure that allows a user to enter or select data and then submit that data. The data can then be passed on to other Web pages or to the C# code. This particular form uses the post method to send data (`method="post"`) and sends that data to the current page (`action="edit.aspx"`).

Beneath the form, you added two `<input>` elements that create the initial values to be inserted into the command and `transaction_id` parameters. The command parameter is set to `view`, and the `transaction_id` parameter is set to the value contained in the `transId` variable. To use the variable to set the `transaction_id` value, you must enclose the variable in C# opening and closing expression tags so the value can be used by the form. Also note that the input type for both `<input>` elements is hidden, which means that the user does not actually see these two elements. Instead, they serve only as a way to pass the command and `transaction_id` values, which is done in the background. The user does not enter these values.

> *Forms are a common method used in HTML to pass data between pages. It is also useful for passing values between HTML and C#. For more information about forms, consult the applicable HTML documentation.*

After you defined the form, you then set up the table to display the heading DVD Transaction at the top of the page. From there, you added another table whose purpose is to display error messages, as shown in the following code:

```
<%if(error.Length > 0){%>
<table cellspacing="2" cellPadding="2" width="619" border="0">
<tr>
    <td width="619" class="error"><%=error%></td>
</tr>
</table>
<%}%>
```

The HTML table structure is preceded by C# opening and closing scriptlet tags so that you can use an `if` statement to specify a condition in which the table will be displayed. The `if` statement specifies that the error variable must contain a string whose length is greater than zero characters. This is done by using the `Length` property to determine the length of the error value and then comparing the length to zero. If the condition evaluates to true, the table is created and the error is printed. At the end of the table, you again used a pair of opening and closing scriptlet tags to add the closing bracket of the `if` statement.

Once you have established a way for error messages to be displayed, you set up the table that will be used to display the part of the form that they user sees. The first row of the form will contain a drop-down list of order IDs — along with the customer names associated with those orders — that the user will be able to select from when adding a transaction. To populate this drop-down list, you retrieved data from the database, processed the data, and formatted the customer name. The methods used for retrieving and processing the data are the same methods that you've already used in the application. Once you retrieved the value, you added another form element to you Web page, but this form element is visible to the user:

```
        if(orderId1 != orderId)
        {
%>
                <option value="<%=orderId1%>"><%=orderId1%> -
<%=customerName%></option>
<%
        }
        else
        {
%>
```

```
                        <option selected value="<%=orderId1%>"><%=orderId1%> -
<%=customerName%></option>
<%
```

The form element shown here is an `<option>` element. An `<option>` element allows a user to select from a list of options in order to submit data to the form. There are actually two `<option>` elements here, but only one is used. This is because C# `if...else` statements enclose the `<option>` elements. The `if` statement condition specifies that `orderId1` should not equal `orderId`. If they are not equal, the `if` statement is executed and the first `<option>` element is used, otherwise the second `<option>` element is used. The second element includes the selected option, which means that the current order ID is the selected option when the options are displayed.

The `orderId1` variable receives its value from the results returned by the SELECT statement used to populate the `<option>` element. The `orderId` variable receives its value from the SELECT statement that is used to assign values to variables once it has been determined that the user is editing an existing transaction. (This occurs when the `if...else` statements earlier in the code are processed.) If the two values are equal, the second `<option>` element is used, which means that the current order ID is displayed when this page is loaded. If the two values are not equal, which is the condition specified in the `if` statement, no order ID is displayed, which you would expect when creating a new record.

The next row that you created for your form table allows users to select from a list of DVD names. The same logic is used to create the drop-down list available to the users. The only difference is that, because only DVD names are displayed, no special formatting or concatenation is required to display the values.

After you created your two rows that display the drop-down lists to the users, you created three date-related rows. Each row provides a text box in which users can enter the appropriate dates. For example, the first of these rows includes the following form element:

```
<input type="text" name="DateOut" value="<%=dateOutString%>" size="50">
```

As you can see, this is an `<input>` element, similar to the ones that you created when you first defined the form. Only the input type on this one is not `hidden`, but instead is `text`, which means that a text box will be displayed. The name of the text box is DateOut. This is actually the name of the parameter that will hold the value that the user submits. The initial value displayed in the text box depends on the value of the `dateOutString` variable. For new records, this value is the current date, and for existing records, this is the value as it currently exists in the database. (Both these values are determined in the earlier C# code.)

Once you completed setting up the various form elements, you added two more elements: one for the Save button and one for the Cancel button. For example, your code for the Save button is as follows:

```
<td align="center">
    <%if(("add".Equals(command)) || ("savenew".Equals(command))){%>
    <input type="button" value="Save" class="add" onclick="doSave(this, 'savenew')">
    <%}else{%>
    <input type="button" value="Save" class="add" onclick="doSave(this, 'save')">
    <%}%>
</td>
```

A button is also an `<input>` element on a form, but the type is specified as button. The value for this element determines the name that appears on the button, which in this case is Save. The `class` option specifies the style that should be used in the button, as defined in the dvdstyle.css file, and the `onclick` option specifies the action to be taken. In this case, the action is to execute the `doSave()` function, which is defined in the dvdrentals.js file.

Notice that there are again two `<input>` elements, but only one is used. If the `command` value equals `add` or `savenew`, the first `<input>` element is used, otherwise the second `<input>` element is used. When you click the Save button, the `doSave()` function is called. The function takes one argument, this, which is a self-referencing value that indicates that the action is related to the current HTML input button. When the function is executed, it submits the form to the edit.aspx file and sets the `command` parameter value to `savenew` or `save`, depending on which `<input>` option is used. Based on the `command` value, the C# code is processed once again, only this time, the first `if` statement (in the large `if...else` construction) evaluates to true and that statement is executed. Assuming that there are no errors, the date values are reformatted for MySQL, the C# code in the update.aspx or insert.aspx include file is executed, and the user is redirected to the index.aspx page.

As you can see, the edit.aspx page provides the main logic that is used to insert and update data. However, as the code in this page indicates, you must also create the include files necessary to support the actual insertion and deletion of data. In the next Try It Out section, you create the insert.aspx file. The file contains only that script that is necessary to insert a record, based on the values provided by the user in the edit.aspx form.

Try It Out   Creating the insert.aspx file

The following steps describe how to create the insert.aspx file:

1. In your text editor, create a new file and enter the following code:

```
<%
// Build the INSERT statement with parameter references
String insertSql = "INSERT INTO Transactions (OrderID, DVDID, DateOut, DateDue)
VALUES (?, ?, ?, ?)";

odbcCommand = new OdbcCommand(insertSql, odbcConnection);

OdbcParameter [] odbcInsertParameters = new OdbcParameter[4];

// Set the parameters
odbcInsertParameters[0] = new OdbcParameter("", OdbcType.Int);
odbcInsertParameters[0].Value = orderId;
odbcInsertParameters[1] = new OdbcParameter("", OdbcType.Int);
odbcInsertParameters[1].Value = dvdId;
odbcInsertParameters[2] = new OdbcParameter("", OdbcType.Date);
odbcInsertParameters[2].Value = dateOut;
odbcInsertParameters[3] = new OdbcParameter("", OdbcType.Date);
odbcInsertParameters[3].Value = dateDue;

odbcCommand.Parameters.Add(odbcInsertParameters[0]);
odbcCommand.Parameters.Add(odbcInsertParameters[1]);
odbcCommand.Parameters.Add(odbcInsertParameters[2]);
odbcCommand.Parameters.Add(odbcInsertParameters[3]);

// Execute the INSERT statement
```

```
    odbcCommand.ExecuteNonQuery();

if(odbcCommand != null)
    odbcCommand.Dispose();

if(odbcConnection != null)
    odbcConnection.Dispose();
%>
```

2.   Save the insert.aspx file to the appropriate Web application directory.

How It Works

In this exercise, you created the insert.aspx file, which is an include file for edit.aspx. The first step you took in creating the insert.aspx file was to assign an INSERT statement to the insertSql variable:

```
String insertSql = "INSERT INTO Transactions (OrderID, DVDID, DateOut, DateDue)
VALUES (?, ?, ?, ?)";
```

Instead of including the values to be inserted into the MySQL database, the statement includes four question mark placeholders. Values for the placeholders are defined later in the file.

After you created the INSERT statement, you initialized the odbcCommand variable. You also declared and initiated an OdbcParameter array, as shown in the following statement:

```
odbcCommand = new OdbcCommand(insertSql, odbcConnection);

OdbcParameter [] odbcInsertParameters = new OdbcParameter[4];

odbcInsertParameters[0] = new OdbcParameter("", OdbcType.Int);
odbcInsertParameters[0].Value = orderId;
```

To set up the new OdbcCommand object, you used the values assigned to the insertSql variable and the odbcConnection variable. When you set up the OdbcParameter array, you specified that four parameters were to be included in the array. You then defined each of the parameters by first creating an OdbcParameter object and then assigning a value to the Value property associated with that object. For example, you assigned the orderId variable to the first parameter, which is referred by the 0 designator.

Your next step was to add each parameter to the OdbcCommand object. You did this by using the object's Parameters property and Add() method, as shown in the following statement:

```
odbcCommand.Parameters.Add(odbcInsertParameters[0]);
```

You repeated this step for each parameter, and then you used the following statement to execute the INSERT statement:

```
odbcCommand.ExecuteNonQuery();
```

The statement uses the ExecuteNonQuery() method to execute the INSERT statement. The method is associated with the OdbcCommand object assigned to the odbcCommand variable.

In addition to creating the insert.aspx file, you must also create the update.aspx file. This file will work just like the insert.aspx file in that it is included in the edit.aspx file. This has the same effect as including the statements directly into the edit.aspx file. In the following Try it Out section, you create the update.aspx file.

Try It Out — Creating the update.aspx file

The following steps describe how to create the update.aspx file:

1. Open a new file in your text editor, and enter the following code:

```
<%
// Build the UPDATE statement with parameters references
String updateSql = "UPDATE Transactions SET OrderID = ?, DVDID = ?, DateOut = ?,
DateDue = ?, DateIn = ? WHERE TransID = ?";

odbcCommand = new OdbcCommand(updateSql, odbcConnection);

OdbcParameter [] odbcUpdateParameters = new OdbcParameter[6];

// Set the parameters
odbcUpdateParameters[0] = new OdbcParameter("", OdbcType.Int);
odbcUpdateParameters[0].Value = orderId;
odbcUpdateParameters[1] = new OdbcParameter("", OdbcType.Int);
odbcUpdateParameters[1].Value = dvdId;
odbcUpdateParameters[2] = new OdbcParameter("", OdbcType.Date);
odbcUpdateParameters[2].Value = dateOut;
odbcUpdateParameters[3] = new OdbcParameter("", OdbcType.Date);
odbcUpdateParameters[3].Value = dateDue;

// Provide a default value for the DateIn column if no value is provided
if(!dateIn.Equals(DateTime.MinValue))
{
   odbcUpdateParameters[4] = new OdbcParameter("", OdbcType.Date);
   odbcUpdateParameters[4].Value = dateIn;
}
else
{
   odbcUpdateParameters[4] = new OdbcParameter("", OdbcType.VarChar);
   odbcUpdateParameters[4].Value = "0000-00-00";
}

odbcUpdateParameters[5] = new OdbcParameter("", OdbcType.Int);
odbcUpdateParameters[5].Value = transId;

odbcCommand.Parameters.Add(odbcUpdateParameters[0]);
odbcCommand.Parameters.Add(odbcUpdateParameters[1]);
odbcCommand.Parameters.Add(odbcUpdateParameters[2]);
odbcCommand.Parameters.Add(odbcUpdateParameters[3]);
odbcCommand.Parameters.Add(odbcUpdateParameters[4]);
odbcCommand.Parameters.Add(odbcUpdateParameters[5]);

// Execute the UPDATE statement
odbcCommand.ExecuteNonQuery();

if(odbcCommand != null)
```

```
    odbcCommand.Dispose();

if(odbcConnection != null)
    odbcConnection.Dispose();
%>
```

2. Save the update.aspx file to the appropriate Web application directory.

How It Works

In this exercise, you created the update.aspx file. The file uses the same types of objects and methods that you used in the insert.aspx file. First, you created an UPDATE statement that you assigned to the updateSql variable. Then you created an OdbcCommand object that you assigned to the odbcCommand variable. From there, you created an OdbcParameter array to hold the parameters to be used in the UPDATE statement. The process of assigning values to the parameters is similar to what you used when creating the insert.aspx file. However, there was one new element that you had not used:

```
if(!dateIn.Equals(DateTime.MinValue))
{
    odbcUpdateParameters[4] = new OdbcParameter("", OdbcType.Date);
    odbcUpdateParameters[4].Value = dateIn;
}
else
{
    odbcUpdateParameters[4] = new OdbcParameter("", OdbcType.VarChar);
    odbcUpdateParameters[4].Value = "0000-00-00";
}
```

First, you determined whether the value in the dateIn variable is equal to the value stored in the MinValue property of the DateTime class. If the dateIn value does not equal the MinValue date, then the if block is executed, otherwise the else block is executed. The if block specifies that the value in the dateIn variable should be assigned to the fifth parameter (number 4). This process is the same as you saw in for the other parameters. The else block specifies that the value used for the parameter should use the OdbcType.VarChar data type and should have the value of 0000-00-00, which is the default value of a MySQL DATE column that is configured as NOT NULL. This step is taken in case someone updates a transaction but does not include a DateIn value. This way, the default value is entered into the column.

Now that you have created the insert.aspx file and the update.aspx file, only one step remains to set up your application to insert and update data. You must modify the index.aspx file so that it includes the functionality necessary to link the user to the edit.aspx page. The following Try It Out section explains how to modify the index.aspx file. It then walks you through the process of inserting a transaction and then modifying that transaction.

Try It Out   **Modifying the index.aspx File**

The following steps describe how to modify the index.aspx file to support the insert and update operations:

1. In your text editor, open the index.aspx file. Add a form, an `<input>` element, and a cell definition to your HTML code. Add the following code (shown with the gray screen background) to your file:

```
<html>
<head>
    <title>DVD - Listing</title>
    <link rel="stylesheet" href="dvdstyle.css" type="text/css">
    <script language="JavaScript" src="dvdrentals.js"></script>
    </script>
</head>

<body>

<form name="mainForm" method="post" action="index.aspx">
<input type="hidden" name="command" value="view">
<input type="hidden" name="transaction_id" value="">

<p></p>

<table cellSpacing=0 cellPadding=0 width=619 border=0>
<tr>
    <td>
        <table height=20 cellSpacing=0 cellPadding=0 width=619 bgcolor=#bed8e1
border=0>
        <tr align=left>
            <td valign="bottom" width="400" class="title">
                DVD Transaction Listing
            </td>
            <td align="right" width="219" class="title">
                <input type="button" value="New Transaction" class="add"
onclick="doAdd(this)">
            </td>
        </tr>
        </table>
        <br>
        <table cellSpacing="2" cellPadding="2" width="619" border="0">
        <tr>
            <td width="250" class="heading">Order Number</td>
            <td width="250" class="heading">Customer</td>
            <td width="250" class="heading">DVDName</td>
            <td width="185" class="heading">DateOut</td>
            <td width="185" class="heading">DateDue</td>
            <td width="185" class="heading">DateIn</td>
            <td width="99" class="heading"> </td>
        </tr>
```

When adding code to you file, be sure to add it in the position shown here.

2. Next, add an HTML table cell and an <input> element to the area of code that prints out the values returned by the database. Add the following code (shown with the gray screen background) to your file:

```
<td class="item">
    <nobr>
```

```
            <%=dateInPrint%>
            </nobr>
        </td>
        <td class="item" valign="center" align="center">
            <input type="button" value="Edit" class="edit" onclick="doEdit(this,
<%=transId%>)">
        </td>
    </tr>
```

3. Now you must close the form, which you do near the end of the file. To close the form, you must use a `</form>` element. Add the following code (shown with the gray screen background) to the end of the ASP.NET file:

```
            </table>
        </td>
    </tr>
    </table>
    </form>
    </body>
    </html>
```

4. Save the index.aspx file.

5. Open your browser and go to the address `http://localhost/DVDApp/index.aspx`. Your browser should display a page similar to the one shown in the Figure 19-2.

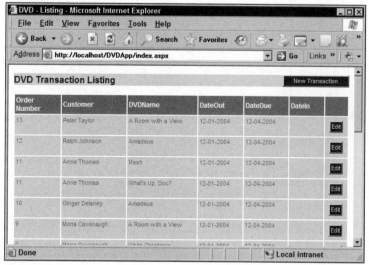

Figure 19-2

6. Click the New Transaction button at the top of the page. Your browser should display a page similar to the one shown in the Figure 19-3.

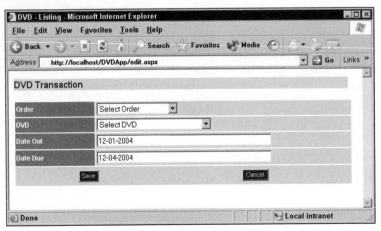

Figure 19-3

7. Now add a transaction to an existing order. In the Order drop-down list, select 13 - Peter Taylor. In the DVD drop-down list, select *Out of Africa*. Click Save. You're returned to the index.aspx page. The new transaction should now be displayed at the top of the list.

8. Next you can edit the new transaction. In the row of the transaction that you just added, click the Edit button. Your browser should display a page similar to the one shown in the Figure 19-4.

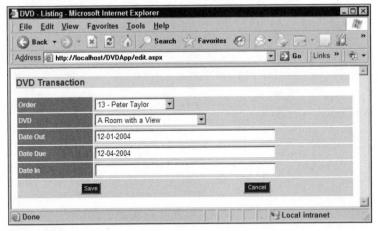

Figure 19-4

9. In the Date In text box, type the same date that is in the Date Due text box. Be certain to type the date in the same format that is used for the other date-related text boxes. Click the Save button. You should be returned to the index.aspx page.

How It Works

In this exercise, you added a form to your index.aspx file. This is similar to the form that you added to the edit.aspx file. The main difference between the two is that, in this form, the `transaction_id` value is set to an empty string. This is because no ID is necessary initially, but you want the parameter to exist so that a vehicle has been provided to pass that ID through the form when you submit the form.

Once you created the form, you added the following HTML cell definition and `<input>` element at the top of the page:

```
<td align="right" width="219" class="title">
   <input type="button" value="New Transaction" class="add" onclick="doAdd(this)">
</td>
```

As you can see, the input type is button and it calls the JavaScript `doAdd()` function. The function links the user to the edit.aspx page, allowing the user to create a new transaction. At the same time, the function passes a `command` value of add to the edit.aspx page. That way, the edit.aspx page knows that a new transaction is being created and responds accordingly. You next added the following code to the initial table structure created in the HTML code:

```
<td width="99" class="heading"> </td>
```

This creates an additional column head in the table to provide a column for the Edit button that will be added to each row returned by your query results. Finally, you added the actual cell and button to your table definition, as shown in the following code:

```
<td class="item" valign="center" align="center">
   <input type="button" value="Edit" class="edit" onclick="doEdit(this,
<%=transId%>)">
</td>
```

The Edit button calls the `doEdit()` function, which passes the transaction ID to the form and links the user to the edit.aspx page. At the same time, the function passes the `command` value of edit so that when the edit.aspx page opens, it has the information it needs to allow the user to edit a current record.

Once you modified and saved the file, you opened the index.aspx page, created a transaction, and then edited that transaction. However, the application still does not allow you to delete a transaction. As a result, the next section describes how you can set up C# statements to delete data.

Deleting Data from a MySQL Database

Deleting MySQL data from within your ASP.NET application is just like inserting and updating data. You must use the same C# statement elements. For example, suppose that you want to delete a CD listing from a table name CDs. The ID for the specific CD is stored in the cdId variable. You can use the following statements to set up your application to delete the data:

```
String deleteSQL = "DELETE FROM CDs WHERE CDID = ?";
OdbcCommand comm = new OdbcCommand(deleteSQL, conn);
OdbcParameter param = new OdbcParameter("", OdbcType.Int);
param.Value = cdId;
comm.Parameters.Add(param);
comm.ExecuteNonQuery();
```

As with inserting and updating data, you first assign the SQL statement to a variable (deleteSql). You then create an OdbcCommand object that is based on the deleteSql variable and a variable that is associated with the connection (conn). From there, you define your parameter and add it to the OdbcCommand object. Finally, you use the ExecuteNonQuery() method in the OdbcCommand class to execute the DELETE statement.

As you can see, deleting data is no more difficult than updating or inserting data. The key to any of these types of statements is to make sure that you set up your variables in such a way that the correct information can be passed to the SQL statement when it is being executed. In the next Try It Out section, you see how you can delete a transaction from your database. To do so, you modify the index.aspx file and then create a delete.aspx include file.

Try It Out   Modifying the index.aspx File and Creating the delete.aspx File

The following steps describe how to set up delete capabilities in your DVDRentals application:

1. First, add a column head to your table so that you can include a Delete button for each row. The button will be added next to the Edit button you added in the previous Try It Out section. Add the following code (shown with the gray screen background) to your file:

```
<tr>
    <td width="250" class="heading">Order Number</td>
    <td width="250" class="heading">Customer</td>
    <td width="250" class="heading">DVDName</td>
    <td width="185" class="heading">DateOut</td>
    <td width="185" class="heading">DateDue</td>
    <td width="185" class="heading">DateIn</td>
    <td width="99" class="heading"> </td>
    <td width="99" class="heading"> </td>
</tr>
```

2. Next, add the code necessary to initialize variables and call the delete.aspx include file. Add the following code (shown with the gray screen background) to your file:

```
<%
// Declare and initialize variables with parameters retrieved from the form
    String command = Request.Form["command"];
    String transactionIdString = Request.Form["transaction_id"];

// Declare and initialize variables for database operations
    OdbcConnection odbcConnection = null;
    OdbcCommand odbcCommand = null;

// Wrap database-related code in a try/catch block to handle errors
    try
    {
// Create and open the connection
        String strConnection = "driver={MySQL ODBC 3.51 Driver};" +
                               "server=localhost;" +
                               "database=DVDRentals;" +
                               "uid=mysqlapp;" +
                               "password=pw1";

        odbcConnection = new OdbcConnection(strConnection);

        odbcConnection.Open();
```

```
// Process the delete command
    if(transactionIdString != null)
    {
        int transactionId = int.Parse(transactionIdString);

        if("delete".Equals(command))
        {

// Include the delete.aspx file
%>

        <!-- #Include File="delete.aspx" -->
<%

        }
    }
```

3. Now add the actual Delete button by adding the following code (shown with the gray screen background) to your file:

```
        <td class="item">
            <nobr>
            <%=dateInPrint%>
            </nobr>
        </td>
        <td class="item" valign="center" align="center">
            <input type="button" value="Edit" class="edit" onclick="doEdit(this,
<%=transId%>)">
        </td>
        <td class="item" valign="center" align="center">
            <input type="button" value="Delete" class="delete"
onclick="doDelete(this, <%=transId%>)">
        </td>
    </tr>
```

4. Save the index.aspx file

5. Create a new file named delete.aspx in your text editor, and enter the following code:

```
<%
// Build the DELETE statement with a transactionId parameter reference
String deleteSQL = "DELETE FROM Transactions WHERE TransID = ?";

odbcCommand = new OdbcCommand(deleteSQL, odbcConnection);

// Set the TransID parameter
OdbcParameter odbcParameter = new OdbcParameter("", OdbcType.Int);
odbcParameter.Value = transactionId;
odbcCommand.Parameters.Add(odbcParameter);

// Execute the DELETE statement
odbcCommand.ExecuteNonQuery();

if(odbcCommand != null)
    odbcCommand.Dispose();
%>
```

6. Save the delete.aspx file to the appropriate Web application directory.

7. Open your browser and go to the address `http://localhost/DVDApp/index.aspx`. Your browser should display a page similar to the one shown in the Figure 19-5.

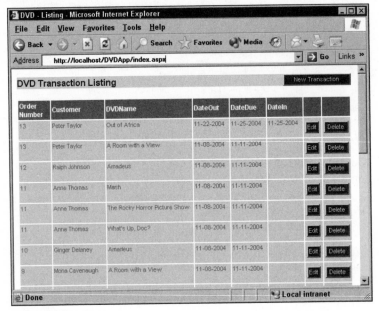

Figure 19-5

8. Click the Delete button in the row that contains the transaction that you created in a previous Try It Out section (Order number 13, DVD name *Out of Africa*). A message box similar to the one in Figure 19-6 appears, confirming whether you want to delete the record.

Figure 19-6

9. Click OK to delete the record. The index.aspx file should be redisplayed, with the deleted file no longer showing.

How It Works

In this exercise, you first created an additional column head for a column what will hold the Delete button for each row. You then entered the following code:

```
String command = Request.Form["command"];
String transactionIdString = Request.Form["transaction_id"];
```

Both statements use the `Form` property of the `Request` object to retrieve parameter values from the form. The values are then assigned to the appropriate variables, which can then be used in your C# code just like any other variables. Next, you added the code necessary to include the delete.aspx file (which you created in a later step):

```
if(transactionIdString != null)
{
    int transactionId = int.Parse(transactionIdString);

    if("delete".Equals(command))
    {
%>
        <!-- #Include File="delete.aspx" -->
<%
    }
}
```

The first if condition verifies that the `transactionIdString` variable contains a value. If the condition evaluates to true, the `if` block is executed. Next, you used the `Parse()` method of the `int` class to convert the `transactionIdString` value to an integer and assign it to the `transactionId` variable. The next `if` condition specifies that the `command` value must equal `delete` in order to proceed. If the condition evaluates to true, the delete.aspx file is included in the current file. This means that the C# statements in delete.aspx are executed as though they are actually part of the insert.aspx file.

The last code that you added to the index.aspx file is the HTML cell definition and `<input>` element necessary to add the Delete button to each row displayed on the page:

```
<td class="item" valign="center" align="center">
   <input type="button" value="Delete" class="delete" onclick="doDelete(this,
<%=transId%>)">
</td>
```

As you can see, the input type is button (`type="button"`), the button is named Delete (`value="Delete"`), the style is delete (`class="delete"`), and the `doDelete()` function is executed when the button is clicked. The `doDelete()` function takes two parameters. The `this` parameter merely indicates that it is the current button that is being referenced. The second parameter passes the value in the `transId` variable to the `transactionId` parameter associated with the form. That way, ASP.NET knows which record to delete when the `DELETE` statement is executed.

Now your application should be complete, at least this part of the application. You can view, insert, update, and delete transactions. In addition, you can build on this application if you want to extend your application's functionality. The code used to create this application is available online at www.wrox.com, and you can use and modify that code as necessary. Keep in mind, however, that at the heart of your application is the MySQL database that manages the data that you need to run your application. The better you understand MySQL and data management, the more effective your applications can be.

Summary

This chapter introduced you to ASP.NET, the .NET Framework, and the C# programming language and provided you with the details necessary to connect to a MySQL database, retrieve data from that database, and modify that data — all from within your ASP.NET application. You learned how to create a basic data-driven application that connected to a specific database on a MySQL server, executed SQL statements against that database, and displayed data on a Web page. Specifically, the chapter covered the following topics:

- ❑ Specifying the ASP.NET classes to include in your application
- ❑ Connecting to the MySQL server and selecting a database
- ❑ Using `if` statements to test conditions and take actions
- ❑ Retrieving data, formatting data, and then displaying data
- ❑ Inserting data into your database
- ❑ Updating existing data in your database
- ❑ Deleting data from your database

This chapter has attempted to provide you with an overview of how to connect to a MySQL database and access data from within an ASP.NET/C# application. Keep in mind, however, that C#, ASP.NET, and the .NET Framework provide an extensive development environment that supports a wide array of functionality and features. As a result, this chapter barely scratches the surface with regard to showing you the capabilities of an ASP.NET data-driven application. However, regardless of the type of ASP.NET/C# application you create, the fundamentals of object-oriented programming and database connectivity are the same. As a result, you are always working within the context of objects. These objects provide the structure for everything from establishing database connections to assigning string values to variables. So what you've learned in this chapter can be applied to any of your ASP.NET/C# applications.

Exercises

In this chapter, you learned how to connect to a MySQL database, retrieve data, and manipulate data from within an ASP.NET application. To assist you in better understanding how to perform these tasks, the chapter includes the following exercises. To view solutions to these exercises, see Appendix A.

1. You are setting up a new .aspx file. You add a page directive to your file to indicate that the code will be written in C#. You want the file to use classes from the `System.Data.Odbc` namespace. What statement should you use to import the namespace into your file?

2. You are setting up the database connection for your ASP.NET page. You declare a string variable named `strConn`. You then assign database connection parameters to the variable. The parameters include the ODBC driver name, the name of the MySQL server, the database, the user account name, and a password for that account. You now want to declare a variable named `odbcConn` and assign a new `OdbcConnection` object to that variable. The new object should be based on the `strConn` variable. What statement should you use to declare and initialize the `odbcConn` variable?

3. You want to open the connection that you created in Step 2. What statement should you use?

4. After you establish a connection to the database, you want to issue a `SELECT` statement against that database. You declare a string variable named `selectSql` and assign the `SELECT` statement to that variable. You now want to declare a variable named `odbcComm` and assign a new

OdbcCommand object to the variable. The new object should be based on the selectSql and odbcConn variables. What statement should you use to declare and initialize the odbcComm variable?

5. You now want to execute the SELECT statement and assign the result set to a variable named odbcReader, which is based on the OdbcDataReader class. What statement should you use?

6. You plan to include a file named change.aspx in your primary .aspx file. What directive should you add to your primary file to include change.aspx?

7. You plan to redirect users to a file named new.aspx. What statement should you use to redirect users?

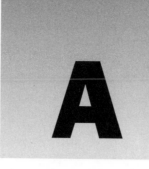

Exercise Answers

Chapter 1

Exercise 1 Solution

A hierarchical database is based on a parent-child configuration in which data is decomposed into logical categories and subcategories that use records to represent the logical units of data. The model is similar to an inverted tree, like the one you see in a file management system. A network database is built on the hierarchical model. It enhances that model by allowing records to participate in multiple parent-child relationships. Both hierarchical and network databases require developers to program record navigation in their application. As a result, any changes to the database or application can result in complicated updates. A relational database represents a departure from the strict structure of hierarchical and network databases. The relational database is based on tables that are made up of columns and rows, and it supports complex relationship between tables, without the restrictions of the earlier models.

Exercise 2 Solution

Use the following CREATE TABLE statement to create the table:

```
CREATE TABLE Employees
(
    EmpID INT NOT NULL,
    EmpName VARCHAR(40) NOT NULL,
    PRIMARY KEY (EmpID)
)
ENGINE=MYISAM;
```

Exercise 3 Solution

Use the following PHP code:

```
$connection=mysql_connect($host,$user,$pw) or die ("Connection failed!");
```

Chapter 2

Exercise 1 Solution

You should download the following file:

```
mysql-max-4.0.20-pc-linux-i686.tar.gz
```

Exercise 2 Solution

You should use the following command:

```
rpm -i mysql-server-5.0.0-0.i386.rpm
```

Exercise 3 Solution

You should use the following command:

```
/usr/local/mysql/bin/mysqld_safe --user=mysql &
```

Exercise 4 Solution

Run the MySQL Server Instance Configuration wizard after installing MySQL.

Chapter 3

Exercise 1 Solution

```
/usr/bin
```

Exercise 2 Solution

You should use the following command:

```
mysql -u myadmin -p
```

You can also use long option names rather than short option names in your command.

Exercise 3 Solution

You should add the following code to your configuration file:

```
[mysqladmin]
host=system3
user=mysqladmin
user=pw1
```

You do not have to include the [mysqladmin] heading if it already exists. Simply place the rest of the commands beneath that heading.

Exercise 4 Solution

You should use the following command:

```
mysql -t < c:\mysql_files\users.sql > c:\mysql_files\users.txt
```

Exercise 5 Solution

You should use the following SQL statement:

```
SET PASSWORD FOR 'myadmin'@'%' = PASSWORD('pw1');
```

Chapter 4

Exercise 1 Solution

Columns, rows, and a primary key.

Exercise 2 Solution

To be in compliance with the first normal form, a relation must meet the following requirements:

❑   Each column in a row must be atomic. In other words, the column can contain only one value for any given row.

❑   Each row in a relation must contain the same number of columns. Given that each column can contain only one value, this means that each row must contain the same number of values.

❑   All rows in a relation must be different. Although rows might include the same values, each row, when taken as a whole, must be unique in the relation.

Exercise 3 Solution

In a one-to-many relationship, a row in the first relation can be related to one or more rows in the second relation, but a row in the second relation can be related to only one row in the first relation. In a many-to-many relationship, a row in the first relation can be related to one or more rows in the second relation, and a row in the second relation can be related to one or more rows in the first relation.

Exercise 4 Solution

You should apply the rules of normalization to the data.

Exercise 5 Solution

Many-to-many relationships are implemented in MySQL by adding a junction table between the two tables and creating a one-to-many relationship between the junction table and the first original table as well as a one-to-many relationship between the junction table and the second original table.

Chapter 5

Exercise 1 Solution

You should use the following SQL statement:

```
CREATE DATABASE NewDB
COLLATE latin1_general_ci;
```

Exercise 2 Solution

You should use the following SQL statement:

```
CREATE TABLE Bikes
(
BikeID TINYINT UNSIGNED NOT NULL AUTO_INCREMENT PRIMARY KEY,
BikeName VARCHAR(40) NOT NULL
);
```

Exercise 3 Solution

You should use the following ALTER TABLE statement:

```
ALTER TABLE ModelTrains
ADD UNIQUE un_1 (ModelName);
```

Exercise 4 Solution

You should use the following ALTER TABLE statement:

```
ALTER TABLE ModelTrains
DROP INDEX un_1;
```

Exercise 5 Solution

You should use the following SQL statement:

```
SHOW TABLES;
```

Chapter 6

Exercise 1 Solution

You should use an SQL statement similar to the following:

```
INSERT INTO Books
VALUES (1001, 'One Hundred Years of Solitude');
```

You can also use the following SQL statement:

```
INSERT INTO Books (BookID, BookName)
VALUES (1001, 'One Hundred Years of Solitude');
```

Exercise 2 Solution

You should use an SQL statement similar to the following:

```
REPLACE INTO Books
SET BookID=1001, BookName='One Hundred Years of Solitude';
```

Exercise 3 Solution

You should use an SQL statement similar to the following:

```
UPDATE CDs
SET CDQuantity=CDQuantity+3;
```

Exercise 4 Solution

You should use an SQL statement similar to the following:

```
UPDATE CDs
SET CDQuantity=CDQuantity+3
WHERE CDName='Mule Variations';
```

Exercise 5 Solution

You should use an SQL statement similar to the following:

```
DELETE FROM CDs
WHERE CDID=1;
```

Chapter 7

Exercise 1 Solution

You should create the following SELECT statement to retrieve the information that you need:

```
SELECT CDName, InStock, OnOrder, Reserved
FROM CDs;
```

Exercise 2 Solution

You should create the following SELECT statement to retrieve the information that you need:

```
SELECT CDName, InStock, OnOrder, Reserved, InStock+OnOrder-Reserved AS Total
FROM CDs;
```

Exercise 3 Solution

You should create the following SELECT statement to retrieve the information that you need:

```
SELECT CDName, InStock, OnOrder, Reserved, InStock+OnOrder-Reserved AS Total
FROM CDs
WHERE Department='Classical' AND InStock<20;
```

Exercise 4 Solution

You should create the following SELECT statement to retrieve the information that you need:

```
SELECT Department, Category, COUNT(*) AS Total
FROM CDs
GROUP BY Department, Category WITH ROLLUP;
```

Exercise 5 Solution

You should create the following SELECT statement to retrieve the information that you need:

```
SELECT Department, Category, COUNT(*) AS Total
FROM CDs
GROUP BY Department, Category WITH ROLLUP
HAVING Total<3;
```

Exercise 6 Solution

You should create the following SELECT statement to retrieve the information that you need:

```
SELECT CDName
FROM CDs
ORDER BY CDName DESC;
```

Chapter 8

Exercise 1 Solution

You should create the following SELECT statement to retrieve the information that you need:

```
SELECT ProdName, InStock, OnOrder, InStock+OnOrder AS Total
FROM Produce
ORDER BY ProdName;
```

Exercise 2 Solution

You should create the following SELECT statement to retrieve the information that you need:

```
SELECT ProdName, Variety, InStock, OnOrder
FROM Produce
WHERE InStock+OnOrder>=5000
ORDER BY ProdName;
```

Exercise 3 Solution

You should create the following SELECT statement to retrieve the information that you need:

```
SELECT ProdName, Variety, InStock
FROM Produce
WHERE InStock>=1000 AND (ProdName='Apples' OR ProdName='Oranges')
ORDER BY ProdName;
```

Exercise 4 Solution

You should create the following UPDATE statement to retrieve the information that you need:

```
UPDATE Produce
SET SeasonAttr=SeasonAttr | 2
WHERE ProdName='grapes';
```

Exercise 5 Solution

You should create the following SELECT statement to retrieve the information that you need:

```
SELECT ProdName, Variety, InStock
FROM Produce
WHERE ProdName REGEXP BINARY 'Ch'
ORDER BY ProdName;
```

Chapter 9

Exercise 1 Solution

You should create a SELECT statement similar to the following:

```
SELECT ProdName, InStock,
    CASE ProdName
        WHEN 'Apples' THEN 'On Sale!'
        WHEN 'Oranges' THEN 'Just Arrived!'
        ELSE 'Fresh Crop!'
    END As Signage
FROM Produce
WHERE InStock>=1000
ORDER BY ProdName;
```

Exercise 2 Solution

You should create a SELECT statement similar to the following:

```
SELECT ProdName, Variety, CAST(InStock AS CHAR) AS InStock_CHAR
FROM Produce
WHERE InStock>=1000
ORDER BY ProdName;
```

Exercise 3 Solution

You should create a SELECT statement similar to the following:

```
SELECT CONCAT(ProdName, ' (', Variety, ')') AS ProduceVariety, InStock
FROM Produce
WHERE InStock>=1000 AND Variety IS NOT NULL
ORDER BY ProdName;
```

Exercise 4 Solution

You should create a SELECT statement similar to the following:

```
SELECT UPPER(CONCAT(ProdName, ' (', Variety, ')')) AS ProduceVariety, InStock
FROM Produce
WHERE InStock>=1000 AND Variety IS NOT NULL
ORDER BY ProdName;
```

Exercise 5 Solution

You should create a SELECT statement similar to the following:

```
SELECT Variety, OnOrder, DateOrdered, ADDDATE(DateOrdered, 4) AS DeliveryDate
FROM Produce
WHERE ProdName='Apples'
ORDER BY Variety;
```

Exercise 6 Solution

You should create a SELECT statement similar to the following:

```
SELECT ProdName, SUM(InStock) AS TotalInStock, SUM(OnOrder) AS TotalOrdered
FROM Produce
GROUP BY ProdName;
```

Chapter 10

Exercise 1 Solution

You should create a SELECT statement similar to the following:

```
SELECT BookTitle, CONCAT_WS(' ', AuthFN, AuthMN, AuthLN) As Author
FROM Books AS b, AuthorBook AS ab, Authors AS a
WHERE b.BookID=ab.BookID AND ab.AuthID=a.AuthID
ORDER BY BookTitle;
```

Exercise 2 Solution

You should create a SELECT statement similar to the following:

```
SELECT BookTitle, CONCAT_WS(' ', AuthFN, AuthMN, AuthLN) As Author
FROM Books AS b CROSS JOIN AuthorBook AS ab ON b.BookID=ab.BookID
    CROSS JOIN Authors AS a ON ab.AuthID=a.AuthID
WHERE AuthLN='Toole' OR AuthLN='Thompson'
ORDER BY BookTitle;
```

Exercise 3 Solution

You should create a SELECT statement similar to the following:

```
SELECT BookTitle, CONCAT_WS(' ', AuthFN, AuthMN, AuthLN) As Author
FROM Books AS b RIGHT JOIN AuthorBook AS ab ON b.BookID=ab.BookID
    RIGHT JOIN Authors AS a ON ab.AuthID=a.AuthID
ORDER BY BookTitle;
```

Exercise 4 Solution

You should create a SELECT statement similar to the following:

```
SELECT BookTitle, CONCAT_WS(' ', AuthFN, AuthMN, AuthLN) As Author
FROM Books AS b NATURAL RIGHT JOIN AuthorBook AS ab
    NATURAL RIGHT JOIN Authors AS a
ORDER BY BookTitle;
```

Exercise 5 Solution

You should create a SELECT statement similar to the following:

```
SELECT BookTitle
FROM Books
WHERE BookID IN
    (SELECT BookID FROM BookOrders WHERE Quantity>2)
ORDER BY BookTitle;
```

Exercise 6 Solution

You should create a SELECT statement similar to the following:

```
SELECT OrderID, BookID, Quantity
FROM BookOrders
WHERE BookID=
    (SELECT BookID FROM Books WHERE BookTitle='Letters to a Young Poet');
```

Exercise 7 Solution

You should create a SELECT statement similar to the following:

```
(SELECT AuthLN FROM Authors)
UNION
(SELECT AuthLN FROM Authors2)
ORDER BY AuthLN;
```

Chapter 11

Exercise 1 Solution

You should create a SELECT statement similar to the following:

```
SELECT ProdName, Variety, InStock
    INTO OUTFILE 'Apples.txt'
FROM Produce WHERE ProdName='Apples';
```

Exercise 2 Solution

You should create a SELECT statement similar to the following:

```
SELECT ProdName, Variety, InStock
    INTO OUTFILE 'Oranges.txt'
    FIELDS
        TERMINATED BY ','
        ENCLOSED BY '*'
FROM Produce WHERE ProdName='Oranges';
```

Exercise 3 Solution

You should create a CREATE TABLE statement similar to the following:

```
CREATE TABLE Produce2
(
    ProdName VARCHAR(40) NOT NULL,
    Variety VARCHAR(40) NULL,
    InStock SMALLINT UNSIGNED NOT NULL
)
SELECT ProdName, Variety, InStock
FROM Produce WHERE ProdName='Cherries';
```

Exercise 4 Solution

You should create an INSERT statement similar to the following:

```
INSERT INTO Produce2
SELECT ProdName, Variety, InStock
FROM Produce WHERE ProdName='Mushrooms';
```

Exercise 5 Solution

You should create a LOAD DATA statement similar to the following:

```
LOAD DATA INFILE 'Apples.txt'
INTO TABLE Produce2;
```

Exercise 6 Solution

You should create a LOAD DATA statement similar to the following:

```
LOAD DATA INFILE 'Oranges.txt'
INTO TABLE Produce2
FIELDS
    TERMINATED BY ','
    ENCLOSED BY '*';
```

Chapter 12

Exercise 1 Solution

You should use the following SQL statement to begin the transaction:

```
START TRANSACTION;
```

Exercise 2 Solution

You should use the following SQL statement to commit the transaction:

```
COMMIT;
```

Exercise 3 Solution

You should use the following SQL statement to roll back the transaction:

```
ROLLBACK;
```

Exercise 4 Solution

You should use the following SQL statement to create the savepoint:

```
SAVEPOINT save1;
```

Exercise 5 Solution

You should use the following SQL statement to roll back the transaction to the savepoint:

```
ROLLBACK TO SAVEPOINT save1;
```

Exercise 6 Solution

You should use the following SQL statement to turn the autocommit mode to off:

```
SET AUTOCOMMIT=0;
```

Exercise 7 Solution

You should use the following SQL statement to change the isolation level:

```
SET GLOBAL TRANSACTION ISOLATION LEVEL SERIALIZABLE;
```

Exercise 8 Solution

You should use the following SQL statement to lock the Produce and Orders tables:

```
LOCK TABLES Produce READ, Orders WRITE;
```

Chapter 13

Exercise 1 Solution

You should use the following command to retrieve the information that you need:

```
mysqladmin -u myadmin -p refresh status
```

Exercise 2 Solution

You should use the following SQL statement to retrieve the information that you need:

```
SHOW GLOBAL VARIABLES LIKE '%max%';
```

Exercise 3 Solution

You should use the following SQL statement to retrieve the information that you need:

```
SELECT @@query_cache_limit;
```

Exercise 4 Solution

You should use the following SQL statement to retrieve the information that you need:

```
SHOW STATUS LIKE '%cache%';
```

Exercise 5 Solution

You should use the following SQL statement to set the variable value:

```
SET MAX_TMP_TABLES=24;
```

Exercise 6 Solution

You should add the following command to the [mysqld] section of your option file:

```
log-bin
```

Exercise 7 Solution

You should use the following command to view the binary log file:

```
mysqlbinlog Server21-bin.000327
```

Chapter 14

Exercise 1 Solution

You should use the following SQL statement to create the user account and assign privileges:

```
GRANT SELECT, INSERT, UPDATE (PubName, City)
ON Books.Publishers
TO 'mgr1'@'localhost' IDENTIFIED BY 'mgr1pw';
```

Exercise 2 Solution

You should use the following SQL statement to change the password:

```
SET PASSWORD FOR 'mgr1'@'%' = PASSWORD('mgr2pw');
```

Exercise 3 Solution

You should use the following SQL statement to reload the privileges:

```
FLUSH PRIVILEGES;
```

Exercise 4 Solution

You should use the following SQL statement to display the privileges:

```
SHOW GRANTS FOR 'mgr1'@'%';
```

Exercise 5 Solution

You should use the following SQL statement to revoke the privileges:

```
REVOKE SELECT, INSERT, UPDATE (PubName, City)
ON Books.Publishers
FROM 'mgr1'@'%';
```

You can also use the following SQL statement to revoke the privileges:

```
REVOKE ALL PRIVILEGES, GRANT OPTION
FROM 'mgr1'@'%';
```

Exercise 6 Solution

You should add the following SQL statement to remove the user account:

```
DROP USER 'mgr1'@'%';
```

Chapter 15

Exercise 1 Solution

You should consider defining an index on the ManfID column of the Parts table.

Exercise 2 Solution

You should use the following SQL statement to analyze the SELECT statement:

```
EXPLAIN SELECT PartID, PartName, ManfName
FROM Parts AS p, Manufacturers as m
WHERE p.ManfID = m.ManfID
ORDER BY PartName;
```

Exercise 3 Solution

You should try to add a FORCE INDEX clause to your SELECT statement, then use an EXPLAIN statement against the updated SELECT statement to see whether the FORCE INDEX clause improves the performance of the statement.

Exercise 4 Solution

The fastest way to insert the data is to use a LOAD DATA statement to insert the data from a text file.

Exercise 5 Solution

You should use the following SQL statement to delete the data:

```
TRUNCATE Parts;
```

Exercise 6 Solution

When setting up your columns, you should take into account the following guidelines: Use identical column types for compared columns, specify data types that have the correct length, define your columns as NOT NULL when appropriate, and consider defining your columns with the ENUM data type.

Exercise 7 Solution

To implement query caching in Linux, add following entry to the [mysqld] section of your option file:

```
query_cache_size=10M
```

If you're implementing query caching in Windows, set the existing query_cache_size system variable to 10M.

Chapter 16

Exercise 1 Solution

On Windows, you should use the following command to create a backup file:

```
mysqldump --flush-logs ProduceDB > c:\mysqlbackup\producedb001.sql
```

On Linux, you should use the following command to create a backup file:

```
mysqldump --flush-logs ProduceDB > /mysqlbackup/producedb001.sql
```

Exercise 2 Solution

On Windows, you should use the following command to create a backup file:

```
mysqldump --flush-logs ProduceDB Produce > c:\mysqlbackup\produce.sql
```

On Linux, you should use the following command to create a backup file:

```
mysqldump --flush-logs ProduceDB Produce > /mysqlbackup/produce.sql
```

Exercise 3 Solution

On Windows, you should use the following command to create a backup file:

```
mysqldump --flush-logs --databases ProduceDB > c:\mysqlbackup\producedb.sql
```

On Linux, you should use the following command to create a backup file:

```
mysqldump --flush-logs --databases ProduceDB > /mysqlbackup/producedb.sql
```

Exercise 4 Solution

On Windows, you should use the following command to restore the database:

```
mysql < c:\mysqlbackup\producedb.sql
```

On Linux, you should use the following command to restore the database:

```
mysql < /mysqlbackup/producedb.sql
```

Exercise 5 Solution

You should use the following SQL statement to grant the necessary privileges to the slave server:

```
GRANT REPLICATION SLAVE ON *.*
TO 'rep_user'@'slave1'
IDENTIFIED BY 'rep_pw';
```

Exercise 6 Solution

You should execute the following CHANGE MASTER statement on the slave server:

```
CHANGE MASTER TO
    MASTER_HOST='master1',
    MASTER_USER='rep_user',
    MASTER_PASSWORD='rep_pw',
    MASTER_LOG_FILE='master1-bin.000127',
    MASTER_LOG_POS=79;
```

Chapter 17

Exercise 1 Solution

You should use a PHP statement similar to the following:

```
$myLink = mysql_connect("server1","app_user","app_pw");
```

Exercise 2 Solution

You should use a PHP statement similar to the following:

```
mysql_select_db("sales_db");
```

Exercise 3 Solution

You should use a PHP statement similar to the following:

```
$myResult = mysql_query($myQuery)
    or die("Error in query: " . mysql_error());
```

Exercise 4 Solution

You should use a PHP statement similar to the following:

```
while($row = mysql_fetch_array($myResult))
{
    $cdName = $row["CDName"];
    $inStock = $row["InStock"];
    printf($cdName, $InStock);
}
```

Exercise 5 Solution

You should use a PHP statement similar to the following:

```
if(isset($_POST["user1"]))
    $user1 = $_POST["user1"];
```

Exercise 6 Solution

You should use a PHP statement similar to the following:

```
header("Location: index.php");
```

Exercise 7 Solution

You should use a PHP statement similar to the following:

```
mysql_close($myLink);
```

Chapter 18

Exercise 1 Solution

You should use a Java statement similar to the following:

```
<%@ page import "java.sql.*" %>
```

Exercise 2 Solution

You should use a Java statement similar to the following:

```
String strBook = new String("The Open Space of Democracy");
```

You can also use a Java statement similar to the following:

```
String strBook = "The Open Space of Democracy";
```

Exercise 3 Solution

You should use a Java statement similar to the following:

```
Class.forName("com.mysql.jdbc.Driver").newInstance();
conn = DriverManager.getConnection("jdbc:mysql://localhost/books", "usr1", "pw1");
```

Exercise 4 Solution

You should use a Java statement similar to the following:

```
ResultSet rs = stmt.executeQuery(selectSql);
```

Exercise 5 Solution

You should use a Java statement similar to the following:

```
while(rs.next())
{
    String cdName = rs.getString("CDName");
    int inStock = rs.getInt("InStock");
    System.out.println(cdName + ", " + inStock);
}
```

Exercise 6 Solution

You should use a Java statement similar to the following:

```
int intValue = Integer.valueOf("530").intValue();
```

Exercise 7 Solution

You should use a Java statement similar to the following:

```
PreparedStatement ps = conn.prepareStatement(insertSql);
```

Chapter 19

Exercise 1 Solution

You should use a C# statement similar to the following:

```
<%@ Import Namespace="System.Data.Odbc" %>
```

Exercise 2 Solution

You should use C# statements similar to the following:

```
OdbcConnection odbcConn = new OdbcConnection(strConn);
```

Exercise 3 Solution

You should use C# statements similar to the following:

```
odbcConn.Open();
```

Exercise 4 Solution

You should use C# statements similar to the following:

```
OdbcCommand odbcComm = new OdbcCommand(selectSql, odbcConn);
```

Exercise 5 Solution

You should use C# statements similar to the following:

```
OdbcDataReader odbcReader = odbcComm.ExecuteReader();
```

Exercise 6 Solution

You should use a C# statement similar to the following:

```
<!-- #Include File="change.aspx" -->
```

Exercise 7 Solution

You should use a C# statement similar to the following:

```
Response.Redirect("new.aspx");
```

MySQL APIs

To facilitate your ability to connect to the MySQL server from various types of applications, MySQL supports a number of application programming interfaces (APIs) that allow client programs to connect to and interface with MySQL databases. As a result, you can create an application in any of the supported programming languages (as indicated by the list of APIs that follows) and use the applicable API to access a MySQL database from the application. The API acts as a bridge between the application language and the database, allowing you to establish a connection, execute SQL statements, and retrieve data that can then be displayed in your application.

If you created one of the applications in Chapter 17, 18, or 19, you already saw how an API is used to facilitate database connectivity. For example, the PHP application uses the PHP API that is included with the PHP preprocessor. On the other hand, the JSP/Java application uses Connector/J to connect to MySQL, and the ASP.NET/C# application uses Connector/ODBC, both of which are MySQL APIs that provide database connectivity. Currently, MySQL supports the following APIs:

❑ **MySQL C API:** The MySQL C API is the primary API to MySQL. The API is part of the mysqlclient library, which is written in the C programming language and is distributed with MySQL. The mysqlclient library—along with the C API—enables programs written in the C language to access the MySQL server and its databases. In fact, the client utilities distributed with MySQL, such as mysql and mysqladmin, use the C API to connect to MySQL. In addition, most of the other MySQL APIs (except Connector/J) are built on top of the C API. The C API includes routines that manage connections and construct queries as well as functions that support status and error reporting. For more information about the C API, go to www.mysql.com.

❑ **MySQL C++ API:** The MySQL C++ API, referred to as MySQL++, allows you to connect to MySQL from a C++ application. You can also use the C API to access a MySQL database from the C++ programming language; however, the MySQL++ API provides more extensive functionality, particularly when processing result sets. As a result, working with the MySQL++ API can sometimes be a more complicated process than working with the C API. If the C API provides the functionality that you need, you often do not need to add the extra layer of complexity of the MySQL++ API. For more information about the MySQL++ API or to download the API, go to www.mysql.com.

❑ **MySQL Connector/ODBC:** The MySQL Connector/ODBC API allows you to connect from any Open Database Connectivity (ODBC)-compliant application to MySQL. ODBC is a call-level API that allows an application to connect to a wide range of SQL databases. By using ODBC, an application can connect to the database, send SQL statements, and retrieve data. Because ODBC can communicate with different database products, you need a product-specific driver that completes the ODBC connection from the application to the database. For this reason, MySQL AB provides Connector/ODBC, an ODBC-specific driver that implements the functionality supported by ODBC. For more information about the Connector/ODBC or to download the API, go to www.mysql.com.

❑ **MySQL Connector/J:** The MySQL Connector/J API is used to provide connectivity from Java applications to MySQL. The Connector/J API is built to JDBC specifications. Like ODBC, JDBC is a call-level API that allows a Java application to connect to different types of SQL databases, which means that you need a product-specific driver that completes the JDBC connection from the Java application to the database. To facilitate your ability to use JDBC to connect to a MySQL database, MySQL AB provides Connector/J, a JDBC-specific driver that implements most of the functionality supported by JDBC. For more information about the Connector/J or to download the API, go to www.mysql.com.

❑ **MySQL Eiffel API:** The MySQL Eiffel API is an Eiffel wrapper that allows you to connect to a MySQL database from an Eiffel application. Eiffel is a programming language that is part of the Eiffel Development Framework, which provides a framework for beginning-to-end application development. For information about Eiffel, go to www.eiffel.com. To download the Eiffel wrapper, go to http://efsa.sourceforge.net/archive/ravits/mysql.htm.

❑ **MySQL Perl API:** The MySQL Perl API is a Perl Database Driver (DBD) interface to the Perl programming language. Perl is a scripting language that is commonly used for command-line scripts and utilities. The MySQL DBD is implemented as a Perl module named DBD::mysql that interfaces with the Perl Database Interface (DBI) module. DBI is a general abstraction layer that is not specific to any one type of database engine but can communicate with any database that supports an engine-specific DBD module. When the Perl script is processed, the Perl interpreter calls the DBI module, which then communicates with the DBD module that connects to the appropriate database. For a MySQL connection, DBI uses the DBD::mysql module. For more information about Perl and DBD::mysql, including how to install the module on your system, go to www.mysql.com.

❑ **MySQL PHP API:** The PHP API allows you to establish connections from your PHP applications to MySQL. PHP is a server-side scripting language that is used in Web-based applications. PHP also refers to the preprocessor that is installed on your system when you install PHP. The PHP application connects with MySQL through the MySQL PHP API, which is also part of the PHP installation. For more information about PHP and the PHP API or to download PHP, go to www.php.net.

❑ **MySQL Python API:** The MySQL Python API, referred to as MySQLdb, is a module that provides an interface between a Python application and MySQL. Python is an object-oriented programming language similar to Java that runs in a variety of platforms, including Unix and Windows. The MySQL module works in the object-oriented structure of the Python language to provide database connectivity. For information about the Python programming language, go to www.python.org. For information about the MySQLdb module or to download the module, go to http://sourceforge.net/projects/mysql-python.

❑ **MySQL Tcl API:** The MySQL Tcl API, referred to as MySQLTcl, is a simple interface for accessing a MySQL database from a Tcl application. Tcl, which comes from Tool Command Language (and is pronounced *tickle*), is a basic text language that is used basically to interact with programs such as shells and text editors. You can use the MySQLTcl API to issue Tcl commands that connect to a MySQL database, execute queries, and retrieve data. For information about Tcl, go to www.tcl.tk. For information about the MySQLTcl API or to download the API, go to www.xdobry.de/mysqltcl.

This list provides only an overview of each of the APIs supported by MySQL. If you plan to build an application that relies on one of these APIs, you should refer to the appropriate documentation for that API. A good place to start whenever creating an application that will connect to a MySQL database is the MySQL Web site at www.mysql.com. There you will find the most up-to-date information about database connectivity and MySQL APIs. The MySQL documentation also provides links to information specific to an API, including where you can acquire the API if it is not available from MySQL. For additional information specific to PHP, JSP/Java, and ASP.NET/C# application, be sure to refer to Chapters 17, 18, and 19, respectively.

MySQL 5

Throughout the book, you've seen examples and exercises that have all been based on MySQL version 4.1. For the most part, what you've seen is consistent with the 4.1.7 release of MySQL. If you visit the MySQL Web site (www.mysql.com), you'll find that MySQL AB is actively developing future versions of MySQL. What you'll discover is that plenty of new functionality is planned for version 5.0, 5.1, and beyond. In addition, existing functionality will be enhanced in various ways. (Each release of MySQL also includes numerous bug fixes.)

Although the MySQL functionality, as it has been presented in the examples and exercises, will be implemented in much the same way as it is described in this book, there will also be some changes. The following list highlights many of the new features that MySQL AB plans to add to its database management system:

❑ Extend the VARCHAR data type to support more than 255 characters.

❑ Add foreign key support for all table types, not just InnoDB tables.

❑ Extend replication to support online backups in order to add a new replication slave without shutting down the master server.

❑ Implement the RENAME DATABASE statement to allow authorized users to rename a database.

❑ Add the necessary data types so that MySQL supports all standard SQL and ODBC 3.0 types.

❑ Enhance the SHOW COLUMNS statement so that it is faster and requires less memory.

❑ Do not automatically add default values to columns that have not been explicitly defined with the DEFAULT option.

❑ Add a log file analyzer utility that can provide information such as which tables receive the most hits and how often joins are executed.

❑ Update the DATETIME data type so that it supports fractions of a second.

❑ Implement a date/time data type that support time zones in order to make working with dates in different time zones easier.

❑ Add functionality to support stored procedures, triggers, and views.

By no means does this information represent a complete list of all the new features that will be added to MySQL in future releases, but it does include some of the more important ones. Of these, the features listed in the last bullet (stored procedures, triggers, and views) are ones that you might find of particular interest because most database management systems already implement this functionality and they are part of the SQL standard. In addition, they can play a pivotal role in developing any data-driven application. The remaining part of the appendix looks at each one of these three features individually.

Stored Procedures

A stored procedure is a routine made up of a set of predefined SQL statements that take some sort of action on the data in your database. The SQL statements are bundled together in a named package that is stored on the MySQL server. Once the stored procedure has been created, you can invoke the SQL statements by calling the procedure name. MySQL then executes the statements as though you had issued them interactively or through an application (via an API).

By using stored procedures, client applications don't need to issue the same statements repeatedly. They can simply call the stored procedure. For example, suppose that you are creating an application that must issue the same SELECT statement numerous times in the course of a user session. If the statement is embedded in the application, it must be sent from the application to the database each time you need to retrieve data. If you create a stored procedure that contains the SELECT statement, however, you can simply call that procedure from your application.

To create a stored procedure, you must use the CREATE PROCEDURE statement, provide a name for the procedure, and add the necessary SQL statements. For example, the following SQL statement creates the BookAmount stored procedure:

```
CREATE PROCEDURE BookAmount (@bookId INT)
BEGIN
    SELECT BookName, Quantity FROM Books WHERE BookID=@bookId;
END
```

As you can see, you specify the CREATE PROCEDURE keywords, followed by a name for the procedure, and then followed by any necessary parameter definitions. In this case, there is one parameter definition: @bookId, which is defined as an INT type. If you do not need to include any parameter definitions, you must still include the parentheses. The actual SQL statement is enclosed in a BEGIN/END block. Notice that that SELECT statement is the only component of the stored procedure definition that ends with a semi-colon. You should terminate each SQL statement in the BEGIN/END block with a semi-colon.

There are other elements that you can add to a stored procedure definition, but this example provides you with the basic ones. All the elements shown in the example are required, except for the parameter definition. You do not have to define a parameter in a stored procedure, but you do have to include the BEGIN/END block and one or more SQL statements.

Once you've created your stored procedure, you can invoke it simply by using the CALL statement:

```
CALL BookAmount(101);
```

Notice that all you need to specify is the CALL keyword, then the name of the stored procedure, and then a parameter value, enclosed in parentheses. If no parameters are defined for the stored procedure, you must still include the parentheses, with no value enclosed in them.

Because stored procedures are still in development, the example SQL statements shown here might not accurately reflect how the statements will be implemented in the final release of a particular MySQL version. Be sure to consult the MySQL product documentation once the applicable version of MySQL has been released.

Despite the ease of creating and using stored procedures, they do have their down side. Because they're stored on the MySQL server, using them increases the load on your database system because more work has to be done on the server side and less on the presentation side. This can be an important consideration if numerous front-end servers are being supported by relatively few back-end database servers.

In some situations, stored procedures can be particularly helpful, especially when security is a critical concern (such as in banking applications). In this case, you can set up MySQL so that applications and users can only execute the stored procedures, but cannot access the database directly. In addition, each operation is properly logged, so you have a more complete record of everything that has transpired, should you need to track events.

As you can see, the decision to use a stored procedure depends on the needs of your application or how you want to distribute the workload across the server tiers. When you do decide to implement stored procedures, you'll find them to be a very useful tool in developing data-driven applications.

Triggers

Triggers are similar to stored procedures in that they are self-contained units of SQL code. You don't explicitly call a trigger, as you do with a stored procedure. Instead, MySQL invokes the trigger automatically when a predefined event occurs. For example, suppose that you're setting up a database to support a CD retail business. The database includes two tables: the CDs table, which includes a list of CDs currently sold by the business, and the CDsPast table, which includes those CDs that have been sold in the past but are no longer carried. You can create a trigger so that, whenever a CD is deleted from the CDs table, it is automatically added to the CDsPast table. When you create the trigger, you assign it to the CDs table. The trigger includes an INSERT statement that adds the deleted CD to the CDsPast table when a DELETE event occurs on the CDs table.

As of the writing of this book, the MySQL product documentation did not include any specifics about how triggers will be created and implemented in MySQL. Most RDBMSs generally support three types of triggers: insert, update, and delete. Regardless of the type of trigger, you define it on a specific table, and when a related event occurs, the trigger is fired. For example, if you define an insert trigger on a table, MySQL fires the trigger when data is inserted in the table. When the trigger is fired, MySQL executes the SQL statements that are defined in the trigger. In the same way, MySQL fires update triggers when the table is updated or delete triggers when data is deleted from the table.

Triggers have been available in most RDBMSs for many years, so if you've worked with one of those other products, you already know how valuable triggers can be. They help to ensure that different tables in a database stay in sync and ensure that the proper action is taken if a particular event occurs. Without triggers, you have to perform many operations manually through SQL or your application. As a result, when triggers become available to MySQL, you'll find them to be very useful to your database and application development, so be sure to check the MySQL product documentation when you're ready to implement a version of MySQL that support triggers.

Views

Views are yet another database feature that has been available to most RDBMSs for many years. A view is a virtual table whose definition is stored in the database but that does not actually contain any data. Instead, a view points to one or more tables and presents data from those tables in a structure similar to any other type of table. A view is basically a SELECT statement stored as a named object. You can then access a view as you would another table, and the result set is displayed as though you had invoked the SELECT statement directly.

Suppose that you are creating a database for a bookstore. The database includes three tables: Books, Authors, and AuthorBook, which matches books to their authors. If you want view the name of the books with a copyright date before 1980 and the books' authors, you can issues a SELECT statement similar to the following:

```
SELECT BookTitle, Copyright, CONCAT_WS(' ', AuthFN, AuthMN, AuthLN) AS Author
FROM Books AS b, AuthorBook AS ab, Authors AS a
WHERE b.BookID=ab.BookID AND ab.AuthID=a.AuthID AND Copyright<1980
ORDER BY BookTitle;
```

The SELECT statement retrieves the necessary information and displays it in a format similar to the following:

```
+-------------------------+-----------+--------------------+
| BookTitle               | Copyright | Author             |
+-------------------------+-----------+--------------------+
| Black Elk Speaks        |      1932 | Black Elk          |
| Black Elk Speaks        |      1932 | John G. Neihardt   |
| Hell's Angels           |      1966 | Hunter S. Thompson |
| Letters to a Young Poet |      1934 | Rainer Maria Rilke |
+-------------------------+-----------+--------------------+
4 rows in set (0.00 sec)
```

As you can see, the result set is typical of the numerous examples that you have seen throughout the book. The books, copyright dates, and authors are displayed as columns and rows, with the information sorted by the name of the book. Whenever you want to view this information, you must reissue the SELECT statement. Another alternative is to create a view that provides the same information, as shown in the following view definition:

```
CREATE VIEW BooksAuthors AS
    SELECT BookTitle, Copyright, CONCAT_WS(' ', AuthFN, AuthMN, AuthLN) AS Author
    FROM Books AS b, AuthorBook AS ab, Authors AS a
    WHERE b.BookID=ab.BookID AND ab.AuthID=a.AuthID AND Copyright<1980
    ORDER BY BookTitle;
```

As you can see, you begin the statement by using the CREATE VIEW keywords, followed by the name of the view (BooksAuthors), and then followed by the AS keyword. Next, you include the SELECT statement that returns the data that you want to display. You can then retrieve data from the view by issuing a SELECT statement as simple as the following:

```
SELECT * FROM BooksAuthors;
```

This statement will then return the same results as if you had issued the SELECT statement directly. As you can see, for a SELECT statement repeated often, a view can be a valuable tool in minimizing the size of a statement that must be sent to the MySQL server.

You might have noticed that a view is similar to a stored procedure in some respects. In fact, you could have created a procedure similar to the following:

```
CREATE PROCEDURE BooksAuthors ()
BEGIN
    SELECT BookTitle, Copyright, CONCAT_WS(' ', AuthFN, AuthMN, AuthLN) AS Author
    FROM Books AS b, AuthorBook AS ab, Authors AS a
    WHERE b.BookID=ab.BookID AND ab.AuthID=a.AuthID AND Copyright<1980
    ORDER BY BookTitle;
END
```

Now instead of using a SELECT statement to call the view, you would use the following CALL statement to call the procedure:

```
CALL BooksAuthors();
```

In this case, the view and the stored procedure achieve the same results. Stored procedures also support the use of parameters as well as other SQL statements, whereas views are limited to SELECT statements in which no parameters are passed. Still, if all you want to do is store this sort of SELECT statement, views are an easy alternative. They also allow you to be more selective in the values that are retrieved by the SELECT statement, as shown in the following query:

```
SELECT * FROM BooksAuthors WHERE Copyright<1960;
```

As you can see, you can refine the data returned by the view even more, which you can't do in a stored procedure unless a particular operation is supported through the use of parameters.

Because views and stored procedures are still in development — along with future releases of MySQL — the example SQL statements shown here are only an assumption of how these statements will be constructed in the final release. Be sure to consult the MySQL product documentation once the applicable version of MySQL has been released.

Views are a useful way to avoid repeating the same SELECT statements over and over again. Along with stored procedures and triggers, they will add valuable functionality to MySQL, functionality that has been used extensively in other RDBMS products. As a result, these new features are a welcome addition to MySQL, and you will no doubt find some or all of them beneficial to your database and application development.

Index

M